OCR

A2

PE

PHYSICAL EDUCATION

Dave Carnell • John Ireland • Ken Mackreth • Claire Miller • Sarah van Wely

www.heinemann.co.uk
✓ Free online support
✓ Useful weblinks
✓ 24 hour online ordering

01865 888118

Heinemann is an imprint of Pearson Education Limited, a company incorporated in England and Wales, having its registered office at Edinburgh Gate, Harlow, Essex, CM20 2JE. Registered company number: 872828

www.heinemann.co.uk

Heinemann is a registered trademark of Pearson Education Ltd

First published 2009

13 12 11 10 09
10 9 8 7 6 5 4 3 2 1

British Library Cataloguing in Publication Data is available from the British Library on request.

10-digit ISBN 0435 46685 2
13-digit ISBN 978 0 435 46685 5

Typeset by Tek-Art, Crawley Down, West Sussex
Illustrated by Tek-Art, Crawley Down, West Sussex
Cover design by Wooden Ark Studios
Picture research by Harriet Merry and Lindsay Lewis
Cover photo/illustration by Claus Andersen/Masterfile
Printed in Italy by Rotolito

Acknowledgements
The authors and publisher would like to thank the following individuals and organisations for permission to reproduce photographs:

The British Sporting Art Trust/The Bridgeman Art Library p3. The Art Archive/Eileen Tweedy p3. Mary Evans Picture Library p3. Mary Evans Picture Library p3. Topham p3. Topham/PA p3. Corbis p18. Topham p21. Corbis p22. Hulton Getty p.35. National Portrait Gallery p37. Getty Images/Christopher Furlong p42. Harrow School Archives/Hugh Marshall p54. Charterhouse School Archives p55. Bridgeman Art Library/DouglasMacpherson /Private Collection/ The Stapleton Collection p56. Alamy/Roy Lawe p58. Trustees of the British Museum p59. Getty Images/John Li p60. Alamy/Mary Evans Picture Library p61. Image courtesy of London Borough of Hackney Archives p61. Rugby School Archives p62. Shrewsbury School Archives p63. Mary Evans Picture Library p64. Hulton Getty p67. The Governing Body of Charterhouse p68. Topham/Fotomas p73. Mary Evans Picture Library p75. Popperfoto/Bob Thomas p75. Bridgeman Art Library/MCC London p76. Illustrated London News p76. Topham/Fotomas p78. Illustrated London News/Mary Evans Picture Library p80. Mary Evans Picture Library p92. Hulton Getty p93. Corbis/Hulton Deutsch p95. Topham p96. PA Photos/John Birdsall p97. Topham/Image Works p102. Corbis p103. TopFoto/John Topham p114. PA Photos/Neal Simpson p121. Getty Images/Jed Jacobsohn p121. NBAE/Getty Images p123. Corbis/Walter Bibikow p128. Topham/Image Works p129. Alamy/Image Source Black p136. Getty Images/Ronald Martinez p145. Popperfoto/Dave Joyner p162. Corbis/Reuters/Will Burgess p166. Winkipop Media p169. PA Photos/AP Photo/Marcio Jose Sanchez 179. Corbis/Sygma/John Van Hasselt p180. Empics p180. Getty Images/Adam Pretty 185. Getty Images/Paul Kane p188. Getty Images/Digital Vision p196. Corbis/Zainal Abd Halim/Reuters p197. PA Photos/AP/Anja Niedringhaus p199. PA Photos/John Birdsall p205. Imagesource p208. Getty Images/Cameron Spencer p210. Getty Images/AFP/ William West p213. ©PA Photos/Martin Rickett/PA Wire p214. Getty Images/Peter Schols p216. ©Rex Features/Sipa Press p217. PA Photos/AP/Greg Baker p227. Getty Images/Mike Hewitt p231. Getty Images/Taxi/Javier Pierini p232. Janine Wiedel Photo Library p237. Getty Images/Harry How p239. Ghislain & Marie David de Lossy/Getty Images p240. Rex Features/Marja Airio p246. Photodisc/Alamy p249. Getty Images/Michael Steele p252. PA Photos/Matthew Ashton p257. ©Corbis/Andreas Meier/Reuters p271. Getty Images/Phil Walter p272. ©Getty Images/Cameron Spencer p273. Getty Images/Brian Bahr p275. Getty Images/AFP/Lionel Bonaventure p277. Getty Images/Hamish Blair p278. ©Getty Images/Corey Davis p286. Corbis/Lucy Nicholson/Reuters p286. Motrax Motorcycle Accessories p296. PA Photos/AP/Joe Kaleita p302. Corbis/Kai Pfaffenbach/Reuters p302. Getty Images/ Julian Finney p303. Corbis/Tim De Waele p311. Getty Images/Sports Illustrated/Simon Bruty p311. PA Photos/Mike Egerton p321. KAZUHIRO NOGI/ AFP/Getty Images p327. Getty p340. Alamy p341. Shutterstock p349. PA photos p360. Getty p360. Alamy/Polka Dot/ Jupiter Images, p414. Tak/Assist Creative Resources Ltd p426. Tak/Assist Creative Resources Ltd p426. York Fitness p434. Photodisc/Lawrence M. Sawyer p446. Alamy/Ace Stock Ltd p446. Alamy/Interfoto Pressebildagentur p461. Getty Images/Koichi Kamoshida p461. Alamy/PHOTOTAKE Inc. p462. Geneva University Hospital/Professor C. Picard p462. Tanita UK Ltd p466. Food Standards Agency p474. PA Photos/AP Photo/Jason DeCrow p478. Corbis/Paul Kingstone/EPA p478. Getty Images/Digital Vision p479. Alamy/Bon Appetit p488. Reuters/Aly Song p490. PA Photos/ DPA/Gero Breloer p494. www.return2fitness.co.uk p495. Rex Features p496. www.vasatrainer.com p497. Alamy/Mira p497. Getty Images/Michael Turek p506. Alamy/Thinkstock/Jupiter Images p506. Alamy/Digital Vision p509. ©PA Photos/David Davies/PA Archive 513. ©PA Photos/Empics Sport/Tony Marshall p517. Corbis/Barbara Walton/EPA p522. Getty Images/Michael Steele p524.

We would like to thank the following people for permission to reproduce copyrighted material: Page 28, 29 Sport England's Active People Survey. Page 53 '*Sport in England: A History of Two Thousand Years of Games and Pastimes*', Harrap. Page 98 © Qualifications and Curriculum Authority. Reproduced under the terms of HMSO Guidance Note 10. Page 124 Federal Government, 2005. Page 369, 411 Reprinted, with permission, from J. Wilmore and D. Costill (1999) *Physiology of Sport and Exercise*, 2nd edn (Champaign, IL: Human Kinetics), p121.

Websites
The websites used in this material were correct and up-to-date at the time of publication. It is essential for tutors to preview each website before using it in class so as to ensure that the URL is still accurate, relevant and appropriate. We suggest that tutors bookmark useful websites and consider enabling students to access them through the school/ college intranet.

There are links to relevant websites in this book. The links are available on the Heinemann website at www.heinemann.co.uk/hotlinks. When you access the site, the express code is 6855P.

Table of contents

Introduction

This book is designed specifically for students following OCR's A2 Physical Education (PE) course. It will support and reinforce the teaching you receive in your centre following the principle of applying theory to practical performance and relating practical performance to theory. The OCR course also embraces the principles that:

- Practical performance is essential to the understanding of theory – students will be assessed in their practical activity with this mark contributing to their overall A2 grade.
- Students should develop their knowledge and understanding of factors that enable them to be physically active as part of a balanced, active and healthy lifestyle.

The content of the book covers the complete OCR specification. The information is presented in a practical context wherever possible as an aid to your understanding and to prepare you for your examination questions.

ORGANISATION OF THE BOOK

The book is divided into six sections that represent the areas which are examined. You will not study all of these areas.

1 Historical studies
2 Comparative studies
3 Sports psychology
4 Biomechanics
5 Exercise and sports physiology
6 The improvement of effective performance and the critical evaluation of practical activities in Physical Education

The sections are divided into chapters. Each chapter has an introduction which explains the content and how the theories relate to each other and to practical activities, participation and healthy lifestyles.

Wherever possible, theories will be applied to practical activities, participation and healthy lifestyles in order that you become accustomed to this approach. This is how you will be taught and examined.

FEATURES

Throughout each chapter you will find a series of tasks and features which are designed to help you understand, apply and remember the topics they relate to. This book contains the following features:

Exam tip – these feature throughout the book offering advice from the examiner. These are meant to give you guidance on how to improve your knowledge in order to get better grades in your A2 exams.

Key terms – an explanation of key words and concepts.

Tasks – motivating activities to help you practise while you learn.

Remember – short reminders of concepts you have covered previously (sometimes at AS).

Apply it! – this feature gives practical examples of activities to reinforce how the theory is used in real-life situations.

Stretch and challenge – more demanding activities to help facilitate your existing knowledge and to challenge you further.

EXAM CAFÉ

Exam Café is there to offer examiner advice and general study support. The Exam Café section appears at the end of each chapter and contains exam-style questions with model answers. These model answers also have examiner comments which help you to understand how to structure your answers to achieve the best marks.

FREE CD-ROM

You will also find a free CD-ROM in the back of the book. On the disk you will find an electronic version of the Student Book. In addition, you will find an interactive Exam Café with a wealth of exam preparation material including: multiple choice questions, audio tips and key concepts.

HOW YOU WILL BE EXAMINED

You have two units to complete, one of which has an examination paper (Unit 453) with the second being a coursework unit (Unit 454) for which your teachers will assess you. Unit 453 is examined in both January and the summer but Unit 454 can only be taken in the summer.

Unit 453
This unit is worth 70 per cent of your A2 marks. It consists of a 2½ hour examination paper in which you will answer three questions.

It will consist of two sections containing the following questions:

Section A
- An historical studies question
- A comparative studies question

Section B
- A sports psychology question
- A biomechanics question
- An exercise and sports physiology question

You will have to answer three questions: one question from Section A and one question from Section B, plus one other question.

Each question is worth a total of 35 marks but is broken down into smaller sections. Each of the smaller questions has the number of marks it is worth clearly indicated.

The last part of each question, which is worth 20 marks, will be where the examiners are stretching and challenging you as well as testing your synoptic skills. You will need to do a piece of extended writing in this part of the question. It is in the last part of each question where the quality of your written communication, including spelling, grammar, punctuation, sentence construction, technical language and the use of paragraphs, will be assessed.

Unit 454
This unit is worth 30 per cent of your A2 marks. This is the practical (coursework) unit and it is split into two parts.

a. Practical activities (20 per cent) – you are assessed in one practical activity. This assessment will be either:
   - performing one activity; or
   - coaching one activity; or
   - officiating one activity.
b. Evaluation, appreciation and the improvement of performance (10 per cent) – an oral evaluative response relating to a performance in the activity you have been assessed in.

Remember that this book will support the teaching you receive in your centre but it is not a substitute for it. This book will help you in your studies and give you ideas about where you can find additional information, which will enable you to expand your knowledge. Remember that there will be stretch and challenge aspects to the three questions you answer in your examination, where you will be rewarded for your depth and breadth of knowledge.

Good luck with your studies.
Ken Mackreth

Historical studies

CHAPTER 1:

Popular recreation in pre-industrial Britain

LEARNING OBJECTIVES

By the end of this chapter you should have knowledge and understanding of:

- how the past influences sport and PE today
- how to think like an historian and ask the right questions
- the importance of social class and gender on opportunities to participate over time
- the characteristics of popular recreation
- how social and cultural factors shaped popular recreation
- how popular recreation affected the physical competence and health of participants
- different opportunities for participation in pre-industrial Britain
- the impact of popular recreation on contemporary participation and performance
- the five case study activities as popular recreations (you will do this in more detail in Chapter 4).

INTRODUCTION

Our times and our thoughts, our games and our sports are shaped by the past. Your study of the history of sport and PE will help you to appreciate the contemporary scene. The 'Historical studies' specification is divided into four sections, which will be covered in the next five chapters as follows:

- *Chapter 1:* **Popular recreation** *in pre-industrial Britain*
  In this chapter you will focus on pre-industrial sports and pastimes, particularly of the lower class, and how these activities have impacted on contemporary participation and performance.

- *Chapter 2:* **Rational recreation** *in post-industrial Britain*
  This chapter is concerned with the emergence of comparatively sophisticated and civilised post-industrial rational recreations. The impact of the **industrial revolution** (which shaped late-nineteenth-century British sport), and the emergence of the middle class (for whom many of the rational sports and recreations were developed), will be key features. As with popular recreation, it is important that you know and understand the impact of post-industrial rationalised activities on participation and performance today.

- *Chapter 3:* ***Nineteenth-century public schools*** *and the development of athleticism*
  In this chapter you will focus on the English public schools such as Rugby, Eton and Charterhouse, which changed so dramatically during the nineteenth century. Initially they were riotous and **Spartan** institutions. However, by the 1870s they had become highly respected

places where most boys and many masters considered team games to be more important than academic work.

- *Chapter 4: Case studies*
  Here you will examine five case study activities through time. Your task is to:

  - analyse each activity as a **popular recreation**
  - assess the influence of nineteenth-century **public schools** on the development of each activity
  - analyse each activity as a **rational recreation**
  - consider participation and barriers to participation in each of the activities **today**, but only in so much as the present is a result of the past.

- *Chapter 5: Drill, physical training and Physical Education in state schools*
  This chapter reviews transitions in twentieth-century **state (primary) schools**. The objectives, content and ways of teaching military drill, therapeutic drill, physical training and more recently Physical Education (PE) will be studied along with reasons for the change from one approach to the next. Also, the effects of each change, both then and now, will be considered. Our historical story brings us up to the 1970s and 1980s, at which point your knowledge from AS socio-cultural studies links in.

EXAM TIP

As you develop knowledge and understanding of historical themes and ideas, start to get into the habit of considering how what you are learning has affected the situation today. Your exam questions will need knowledge of 'then' and 'now'. For example, an exam question might be: 'Describe factors that influenced participation in popular recreation in pre-industrial Britain. Which of these factors continue to affect participation in physical activity today?'

KEY TERMS

Popular recreation

Pre-industrial sports and pastimes mainly associated with the peasant/lower class. This term could also refer to the most popular pastimes at that time.

Rational recreation

Civilised and organised sports and pastimes of post-industrial Britain (i.e. after 1800).

Industrial revolution

The transformation of society from a rural agricultural system to an urban factory system.

Nineteenth-century public schools

Old, established, fee-paying schools dominated by upper- and upper-middle-class boys (and later girls).

Spartan

Poor or basic living standards. With regard to public schools, an environment where younger children were treated severely by masters and older boys.

State (primary) schools

Schools for junior-aged children funded by the government. State education began in Britain following the (Forster) Education Act of 1870.

FOUR ASPECTS OF SPORTS HISTORY

Fig 1.1 Fox hunting, a cock fight and a bare-fist fight – all pre-industrial sports and pastimes

Fig 1.2 Public school discipline at the beginning of the nineteenth century

Fig 1.3 Rational recreation – lawn tennis

Fig 1.4 Physical education in the 1950s

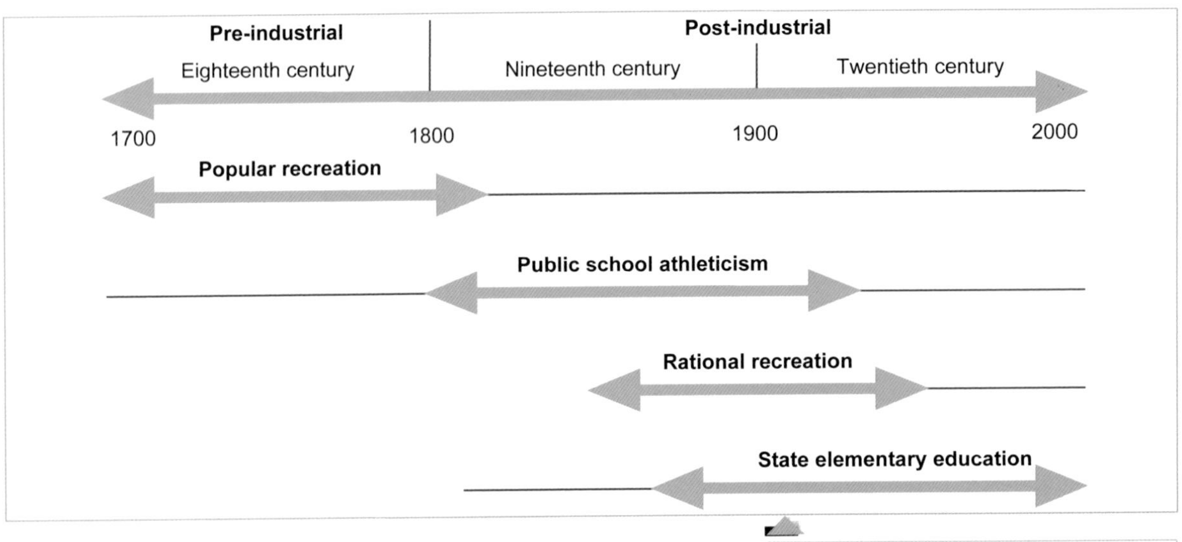

Fig 1.5 Four aspects of your historical studies

REMEMBER

Make sure you are clear about the dates of the eighteenth, nineteenth and twentieth centuries, and remember that anything before 1800 is considered to be pre-industrial.

We'll start our investigation with some background information. This will set the historical scene, put a few things in context, clarify what you need to do to start thinking like an historian and help you to begin asking the right questions.

BACKGROUND INFORMATION

Let's set the scene with some historical landmarks that had an impact on sport.

The general information in Table 1 below is to help you gain a general overview, to put your historical studies of sport and PE into context, and to start you thinking. (You do not have to learn and will not be examined on the information in the table.) Note the underlined words, which should help you to start thinking about opportunities (or lack of them) for participation.

Date	What happened?	Impact on sport?
1066	The Norman conquest by William the Conqueror	Introduction of the feudal system, whereby Norman Lords ruled over Anglo Saxon commoners (serfs). The 'Age of Chivalry' – tournaments and jousting (as in the 2001 Heath Ledger film *A Knight's Tale*).
1200–1485	Medieval England – The Middle Ages	Recreation for rural peasants (the majority) limited to annual festivals because of their hard and long working day; lack of time and lack of opportunity. Tournaments continued for the ruling class. Archery compulsory as military training. The Church opposed many popular sports and pastimes.
1485–1603	The Tudor era	Renaissance gentlemen needed to be both sporting (hunting, horsemanship, swordplay, jousting, real tennis, dancing) and cultural (art, poetry).

Date	What happened?	Impact on sport?
1509	Henry VIII	A keen sportsman – hunting, wrestling, real tennis – as well as feasting and partying. Play for the peasants centred on traditional local festivals and fairs, and Christmas.
1558	Elizabeth I	Mob games and animal baiting flourished during the Elizabethan period.
1603	James I – the Stewart Era	Seventeenth-century Puritans despised the spontaneity and freedom of traditional sports and pastimes, believing that only the sober, quiet and hard-working would be saved. They also opposed animal baiting and cruelty. However, James I's *Book of Sports* (1617) ensured the rights of the people to recreation as long as church attendance continued.
1649	Execution of Charles I; Oliver Cromwell becomes Protector of Britain	Following the English Civil War (1642–51), King Charles I was beheaded and England became a republic under the Parliamentarian Oliver Cromwell. Cromwell was a supporter of Puritanism, so this was a bleak time for sport.
1660	Charles II – the Restoration of the Monarchy	With the return of monarchy to England, some previously banned sports and pastimes, saints' days and parish feasts were restored.
1671	Game laws	These prevented ordinary people from hunting and shooting game.
1714–90	The Hanoverian era	The Church provided frequent feast days and a suitable space for gatherings. The period saw the early organisation of cricket (rules in 1727), horse racing (jockey club formed in 1752), prize fighting or bare-fist fighting (Broughton's rules in 1743) as spectator attractions and commercial enterprises.
1790–1830	The Regency period	A time of high fashion. Pedestrianism and prize fighting were at their peak of popularity. The Church continued to discourage popular recreations, considering them to be of the devil! There was pressure to stop Sunday play (the Church wanted no play on a Sunday – Sabbatarianism), traditional festivals, race meetings, prize fights and animal baiting.
1837–1901	The Victorian era	During the nineteenth century, society, education, sports and games changed dramatically. Christianity and the Protestant work ethic (the belief that working hard and making a profit were qualities of a good Christian) became established. Working hours and health provision improved for the working class in the latter part of the nineteenth century, while pay and provision of open spaces increased. A revolution in transport and communications had a massive impact on the development of sport.
1700–early 1900	The British Empire	Britain 'ruled the waves' in imperial dominance and spread its systems of government, education, sport, culture and religion abroad.

Table 1 An Overview – to put your historical studies in context.

KEY TERMS

English Civil War

War between the weakly-lead Royalists or Cavaliers, under King Charles I, who tended to be gentry, rural and High Church, and the Roundheads (supporters of Parliament), who were largely merchant class, urban and Low Church. The roundheads were strongly led by Oliver Cromwell. The climax of the English Civil War in 1649 was the trial and execution of Charles I. England was declared a republic and a Puritan lifestyle was imposed. This was a very bleak time for sports and games.

Restoration

In 1660 the army asked Charles I's son, Charles II, to take the throne, in this way restoring the monarchy to power. Puritanism was in decline and Church support for sports and recreations increased.

Game laws

These eighteenth- and nineteenth-century laws gave sole right to kill game to the upper class and caused deep and lasting hostility in many rural areas.

British Empire

The spread of British forms of government, religion and culture to nations considered to be less advanced or civilised. On the positive side this included the building of roads, schools and hospitals, but usually at a loss of inherent traditions and culture.

THINKING LIKE AN HISTORIAN

Part of your task is to imagine your way into the minds of the people who lived in earlier times and try to think about experiences as they did. Social history is about seeing what happened, working out why it happened, and putting both continuity and change into societal context.

You can find out what happened by looking at evidence. The most reliable evidence is from a primary source as it was observed and recorded first-hand by eyewitnesses. Primary sources include diaries, newspapers, magazines, pictures taken or painted at the time and authentic official documents. Libraries, public record offices and archives will help if you are keen and have time to do some primary research.

EXAM TIP

To be a really successful A2-level 'sports historian', you should combine chronology (the order of dates in which events took place) with causation (the relationship between cause and effect) and continuity with change.

Interviews are also a primary source, though clearly only the most recent aspects of our specification can still be researched in this way (such as the impact of industrial action on state school provision for PE and sport in the 1970s and 80s). Primary sources can make the past come alive. For example, we know from secondary evidence that many late nineteenth-century public school boys were obsessed with team games and other athletic pursuits, as this 1895 diary of a Charterhouse boy reveals. At the end of one particular day he wrote:

> *'I played five games of fives and then tried the high jump. Then we had a shootabout and a kind of runabout. Then we went down to the racquet courts and played racquets. Before tea we played in a football game on Big Ground. I put the weight and went again to shootabout ... I was awful tired at the end.'*
>
> Diary entry of a Carthusian, 1895

For your A2 historical studies you will mainly use secondary source material – books and articles that either interpret primary sources or re-tell a story originally told by someone else. These are obviously very valuable, but should be read with caution. Firstly, different historians interpret the same data in different ways, and secondly, a story that is retold is liable to change with each retelling!

ASKING THE RIGHT QUESTIONS

Essential information can be established by asking the right questions, the answers to which will provide plenty to think, talk and write about.

TASK 1

Look at the pictures in Figs 1.1–1.4. Attempt to get into the minds of the people illustrated and think about their experience as it is shown. Then consider the following questions.

1 What activity is being pursued? Is it an individual activity (for example, swimming or athletics) or a game (for example, cricket, tennis or football)? Also, what really happened? You need to distinguish romantic myth from historical reality. It might be fun to think that schoolboy William Webb Ellis simply picked up the football and ran with it while playing one day at Rugby School, thus creating a new game – but there is no evidence that he did this.
2 Who is taking part? In addition to satisfying curiosity, the 'who' questions can help you to think about power, responsibility and who was affected by those who dominated society. The focus here should be on class and gender. (You can read about varying opportunities for participation on page 10 of this chapter.)
3 When is the sport or pastime being pursued? The 'when' question highlights the fact that historians analyse continuity and change over time. Was the activity: pre-industrial (i.e. before 1800) or post-industrial; occasional or regular; at an informally organised time or a pre-set specific time?
4 Where is it taking place? In a rural or urban setting? In a simple, natural environment or a purpose-built facility?
5 Why are people taking part or spectating – is it purely for entertainment or perhaps as their profession? Are they betting on the outcome or is it a social occasion? The 'why' question highlights the importance of cause and effect, which is central to historical study.
6 How sophisticated is the activity? Is it being played in a civilised manner? Is it highly organised with rules, boundaries and a league system?
7 How is this activity linked with, similar to, or different from today?

EXAM TIP

Examiners like answers to the 'why' question and remember the importance of links with today.

The development of popular recreation in the United Kingdom

Pre-industrial popular recreation reflected the society, life and time in which it existed. The activities were often colourful and lively and were supported by a strict class system. Different classes sometimes shared activities (for example, cock fighting), sometimes took part in different activities (for example, mob football for the peasants and real tennis for the upper classes) and sometimes had different roles within the same activity (for example, the bare-fist fighter was lower class while his **patron**, or sponsor, was upper class).

KEY TERM

Patron

A member of the gentry who looked after a lower-class performer, such as runner (pedestrian) or (prize) fighter. He would arrange the contest, put up stake or wager money, and give board and lodging to the performer. He did it for prestige and because of the contemporary popularity of such contests. Today a patron is called an agent or sponsor.

The role and attitude of the Church in the development of sport is important, with popular recreations having been subject to periodic interference since medieval times. When Henry VIII broke with Rome in 1534, he had no desire to change fundamentally the religious, social or sporting habits of his subjects. Only later, as a result of the English **Reformation**, did attitudes change and the powerful force of **Puritanism** emerge. Puritans were fiercely opposed to the excess, unruliness, spontaneity, swearing and drinking associated with contemporary recreations.

KEY TERMS

The Reformation

A religious movement that started in sixteenth-century Germany which called for the reform of the Roman Catholic Church. The Reformation led to new types of Christian religion known as Protestantism and Puritanism, and an attack on the sports and pastimes of common people.

Puritanism

Puritans believed that idleness and playfulness were sinful and that salvation could only be earned through a life of prayer, self-discipline and moderation.

This was a bleak time for popular sports and pastimes. The Puritan ethic gave way to the work ethic and spreading of Protestantism, whereby leisure pursuits were acceptable only in that they restored people for work.

The life of the eighteenth-century peasant was tough, and sports and pastimes echoed this harshness. For example, baiting and blood sports, where trained dogs attacked tethered bears or bulls, attracted large crowds. In 'ratting' contests, dogs were released into an enclosed pit and had a set time to kill as many rats as possible. The rowdy crowd meanwhile bet on the outcome. In cock fighting, prize birds had sharp spurs attached to their claws to ensure maximum damage in a dramatic, brutal and comparatively well-organised activity, which would often take place in an inn's yard.

The eighteenth-century drinking house, or pub, was central to village life. Here was the place to socialise, do business, find work, receive wages and organise political activity. It was the stopping station for coaches, a place to change horses and a hotel for travellers. Most importantly for your study, it was the focus for leisure activities for the community. It hosted bear and badger baiting, dog fighting and prize fighting as well as less barbaric games such as billiards, quoits, bowls and skittles. Landlords often provided prizes for sporting matches and primitive equipment for ball games in order to stimulate interest and, perhaps more importantly, boost profit. The landlord promoted sports, arranged matches and provided prize money, as well as being the bookmaker. Many late-eighteenth- and early-nineteenth-century sports clubs used the public house as their base, most famously perhaps, the Hambledon Cricket Club at the Bat and Ball Inn, Hampshire, where the game of cricket was nurtured between 1750 and 1780. How does this compare to today?

Country pursuits (or field sports) such as hunting, **coursing** and shooting had functional origins. Hunting grew from the search for food and developed into a status symbol for wealthy landowners, whose Game Laws ensured that only the highest social groups had the right to hunt. If the lower class broke the Game Laws by poaching, they ran the risk of a six-month jail sentence and a public whipping.

REMEMBER

Game laws prevented ordinary people from hunting and shooting game.

KEY TERM

Coursing

The chasing of hares by trained dogs for a wager (bet).

Militaristic combat activities such as archery and fencing grew from the need to defend and attack. These skills developed into recreational, competitive sports when guns became available and they lost their original functional role. Today many of them are Olympic events.

Popular recreation – characteristics and cultural influences

The unsophisticated, even uncivilized, sports and pastimes of the common people were occasional rather than regular. The annual village fair, parish feast or Christmas celebration was an important time of universal merriment. Drinking and play have always been closely associated.

> *'In ... groups of villages in Wiltshire, the thirteenth-century practice was for the bachelors to have free ale as long as they could stand up, but once they sat down they had to pay!'*
>
> Dennis Brailsford
>
> *British Sports: A Social History* (1997)

On a smaller scale, the weekly market was social and sporting as well as an exchange of goods and services. Other than these occasional gatherings, the peasants had little free time for sports and pastimes.

In the eighteenth century, life was cheap, mortality rates were high and public hangings a spectator attraction, so displays of merciless cruelty in the name of entertainment and sport were common. Some sports developed from the occupation of participants, for example competitive rowing, which grew from the work of ferrymen taking passengers across the Thames. As the impact of the industrial revolution was not yet felt, life and sports were rurally-based using natural or easily accessible equipment and facilities. Organisation was basic, with rules being simple, unwritten and passed on by word of mouth. The National Governing Bodies such as the Football Association (FA) had not yet been formed (they grew rapidly in the 1860s and 70s), illiteracy was the norm, and primitive transport and communications caused sports to be local in nature. There was no need for

Fig 1.6 Characteristics of popular recreation and influential social and cultural factors

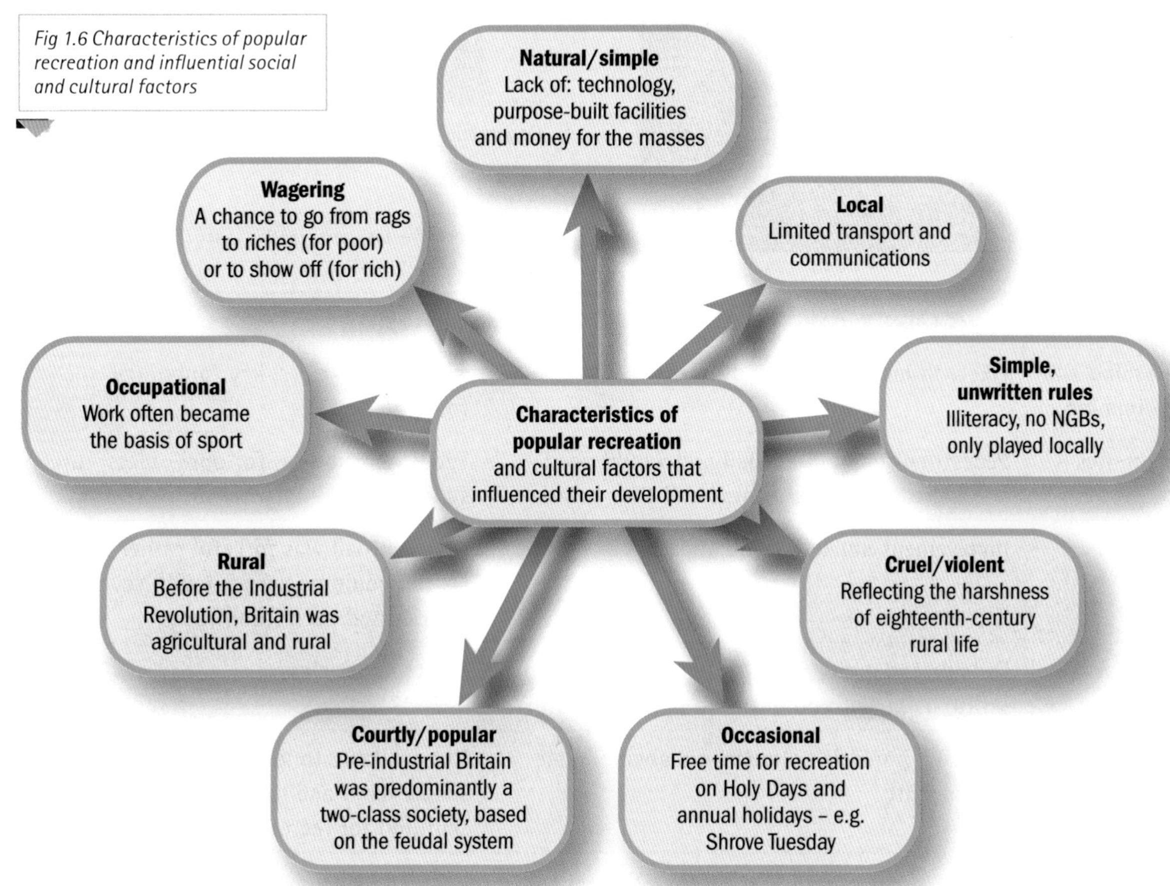

Characteristics of popular recreation and cultural factors that influenced their development
Natural/simple
Lack of: technology, purpose-built facilities and money for the masses
Local
Limited transport and communications
Simple, unwritten rules
Illiteracy, no NGBs, only played locally
Cruel/violent
Reflecting the harshness of eighteenth-century rural life
Occasional
Free time for recreation on Holy Days and annual holidays – e.g. Shrove Tuesday
Courtly/popular
Pre-industrial Britain was predominantly a two-class society, based on the feudal system
Rural
Before the Industrial Revolution, Britain was agricultural and rural
Occupational
Work often became the basis of sport
Wagering
A chance to go from rags to riches (for poor) or to show off (for rich)

widespread agreement about rules. Furthermore, it was not until the arrival of weekly papers such as the *Sporting Magazine* (from 1793), *Bell's Weekly Messenger* (from 1796) and the *Weekly Dispatch* (from 1801) that sport became widely advertised, discussed and promoted to a captive and increasingly literate audience.

A key feature of most popular recreations was wagering or betting on the outcome. From the poorest farm worker to the wealthiest aristocrat, wagering was an eighteenth- and nineteenth-century obsession. The poor focused on the slim chance of a big win, while betting by the wealthy was a social display of financial and social status. The story goes that at the Derby (horse race), two gentlemen witnessed a lady fainting; they did not help her, but rather bet on the length of time it would take her to come round!

REMEMBER

Make certain that you:

- know the characteristics of popular recreation
- understand the social reasons for the characteristics
- can discuss to what extent each of your case study activities 'fits' with the normally accepted characteristics.
- consider links to the next stage and alternatively to today.

Popular recreation – its effects on skill and health

There were several other activities such as rowing, bare-fist fighting and blood sports for the lower class, and hunting, shooting and fishing for the upper class. These varied in their likelihood of increasing physical competence and participation. (Specific knowledge of these is not required for your specification.)

Varying opportunities for participation

You will remember from your AS socio-cultural studies that opportunity, provision and esteem

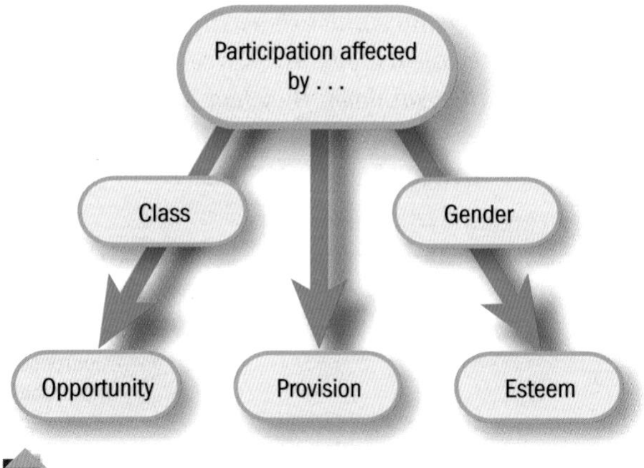

Fig 1.7 Factors affecting participation in sport

	Upper class	Lower class
Bathing and swimming	Likely to increase skill and health	As for upper class; key functional role for hygiene
Athletics	Pedestrianism required skill and would need and increase physical fitness and thus health	Pedestrianism – as for upper class; rural sports – predominantly for recreation
Football	Involvement unlikely so no impact	Mob football was forceful rather than skilful; could be harmful with severe injuries and even fatalities
Cricket	Outside and active during summer months, so a skilful game with potential to improve health	As for upper class
Real tennis	A skilful, potentially health-enhancing game for the elite	Not available to lower class, who played simple hand and ball games (perhaps skilfully) for recreation

Table 2 The impact of popular recreations on the physical competence and health of participants

greatly influence whether an individual takes part in physical activity in general or in a particular physical activity. For example, in Britain today only a minority of teenagers play polo. In pre-industrial Britain, just like today, class and gender were key factors affecting opportunities for participation.

GENDER

Freedom of opportunity has always been linked with class. In pre-industrial Britain, upper-class women were free to pursue certain elitist pastimes, such as hawking (the training of hawks to hunt smaller birds). Similarly, lower-class women were free to be physical, but in less sophisticated, more uncouth activities such as smock races (see fig 4.7 on page 59). The Victorian era brought new attitudes, especially for middle-class women for whom physical activity was thought to be unsuitable, undignified and even dangerous. Nineteenth-century women were later not only constrained by societal attitudes but also by lack of opportunity and provision.

CLASS

Pre-industrial Britain was predominantly a two-class society. There was also a merchant, trading or commercial class from whom the middle class later emerged. The upper class (also called the gentry or aristocracy) dominated the peasant (or lower) class. The upper class had opportunity, provision and esteem. That is: money (which bought facilities, equipment and transport); time which to some extent ensured their skilfulness; and societal status, which increased their self-worth or esteem.

'In their variety of sports and recreations no nation excels the English.

The nobility and gentry have their horse races, hunting, coursing, fishing, hawking, cock fighting, guns for birding, (real or royal) tennis, bowling, billiards, stage plays, dancing and all sorts of musical instruments.

The lower-class peasants have handball, football, skittles, stoolball, cudgels, bear baiting, bull baiting, bow and arrow, leaping, wrestling, pitching the barre and ringing the bells.'

TASK 2

1 Read the italicised quote above, and research each of the activities associated with the two classes in pre-industrial Britain (before 1800).
2 In pairs, think of reasons why the classes did different things. (Hint: consider opportunity, provision, esteem.)

Activities of the upper class were often...	Activities of the lower class were often...
sophisticated and expensive, for example real tennis	simple, accessible and inexpensive, for example mob football
rule-based with a dress code and etiquette	with simple unwritten rules and often violent and/or uncivilised
linked with patronage or acting as an 'agent', for example in pedestrianism	linked with occupation or doing it for a job, for example pedestrianism
distant due to opportunity to travel	local due to lack of opportunity to travel

Table 3 How the sporting activities of the gentry (upper class) compared with those of the peasants (lower class) in pre-industrial Britain

WHAT HAPPENED NEXT?

You will see in Chapter 2 that in post-industrial Britain the new middle class became a dominant social and sporting force. Meanwhile, the rural peasants who had migrated to towns to find factory work became known as the working class, and their opportunity and provision fell way below that of their social superiors.

LINKS TO TODAY

You need to consider the impact of popular recreation on participation and performance in physical activity today. In Chapter 2 you will consider the same for rational recreation and in Chapter 3 for public schools. The impact or link can be either direct or indirect (developmental). A direct link is something such as a pre-industrial festival that still occurs today, whereas an indirect or developmental link has come via a previous stage. Fig 1.8 illustrates this.

Your exam questions may focus on either direct or developmental links.

Arguably, popular recreations had some limited direct links to today but their impact is mainly indirect as they were the starting point of each activity on its developmental journey.

Direct links include illegally-staged bare-fist fights and blood sports such as badger baiting and dog fights. Both of these declined as law and order increased (in the nineteenth century), but they did not completely die out. Contemporary newspaper articles still occasionally report on bloody activities with betting as a central feature. Fox hunting continues among some groups amid ongoing debate.

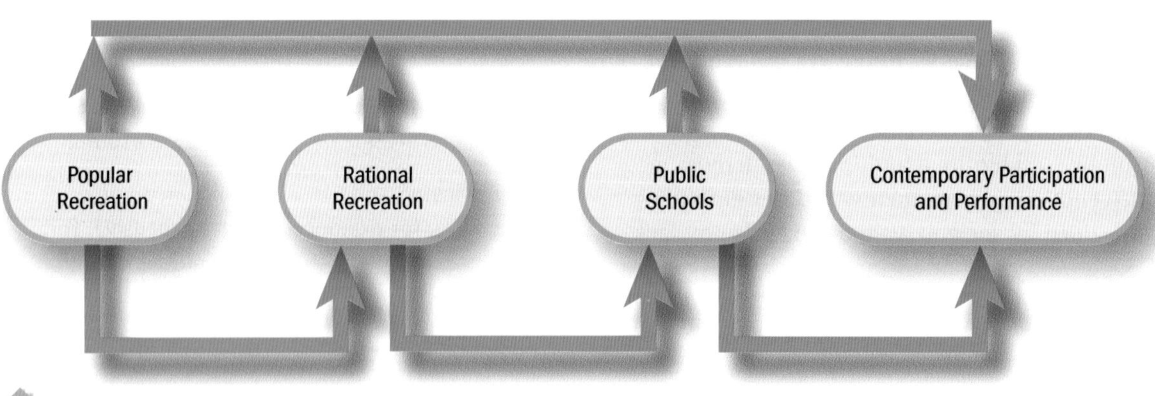

Fig 1.8 Direct and indirect (developmental) impacts of past to present

Sport	Examples of direct links
Swimming	There are links with lake-based swimming clubs or continued motives such as health, recreation and survival/safety.
Athletics	In April 2002 five British athletes (sponsored by Flora) repeated the unique feat of Captain Robert Barclay Allardice who ran 1000 miles in 1000 hours for a wager of over 1000 guineas at Newmarket Heath 200 years ago. That is, a mile an hour, every hour, every day and night for six weeks (see Chapter 4, page 61). Also, rural sports including races and tests of strength continue at some summer fetes and fairs; along with Traditional Olympics – Much Wenlock and Dover Games, for example.
Football	Surviving ethnic sports such as the Ashbourne football game. Occasional violent behaviour by players or spectators in the modern game is another unwelcome direct link.
Cricket	In pre-industrial times the game was for all classes – the English Cricket Board (ECB) stresses that this is the same today.
Tennis	In pre-industrial times the game of real tennis was exclusive and today it is largely the same.

Table 4 Examples of direct links from popular recreation/s to today

Case study activities

You need to look at five case study activities (bathing and swimming, athletics, football, cricket and tennis) through time. That is, as popular recreations, then in nineteenth-century public schools, as rational recreations and finally in modern-day Britain.

As popular recreations, we would expect each activity to be violent, simple, occasional, and so on. But this is not the case. A characteristic is a feature that is normally, but not necessarily, true. Real tennis in pre-industrial Britain, for example, was not violent, simple or occasional. It was sophisticated, complicated and played regularly by the upper-class males who had the time, the money and to some extent the manners to play it. (See Chapter 4 for a full analysis of the five case studies as popular recreations.)

Indirect (developmental) links from then to now (via the public schools and rational recreations) are probably stronger than direct links (see Chapter 4, page 50).

STRETCH AND CHALLENGE

Today news is available almost instantly, with reporters on the spot to give live updates as they happen. Email, satellite and telephone communications all play their part in bringing us up-to-the-minute sporting stories. This hasn't always been so.

Use the Internet or archives in your public library to research some sporting articles from the following nineteenth-century publications:

- *Sporting Magazine*
- *Bell's Weekly Messenger*
- *The Weekly Dispatch.*

What primary evidence can you find of sport being advertised, discussed and promoted? How does coverage compare with today?

Exam Café

Relax, refresh, result!

You should now have knowledge and understanding of:

- how the past influences sport and PE today
- how to start thinking like an historian and asking the right questions
- the importance of social class and gender on opportunities to participate over time
- the characteristics of popular recreation
- how social and cultural factors shaped popular recreation
- how popular recreation affected the physical competence and health of participants
- the different opportunities for participation in pre-industrial Britain
- the impact of popular recreation on contemporary participation and performance
- how to briefly consider the five case study activities as popular recreations (this will be covered in more detail in Chapter 4).

REVISE AS YOU GO!

1. What are the 'right questions' to ask when investigating like an historian?
2. What is meant by the term 'popular recreation'?
3. In pre-industrial Britain, name an activity that the two classes shared, one that was done mainly by the upper class and one that was done mainly by the lower class.
4. Describe the importance of the drinking house or pub in early village life.
5. State five different characteristics of popular recreation.
6. Explain how each of your chosen characteristics was influenced by social and cultural factors of the time.
7. State some factors that affected participation in popular recreations in pre-industrial Britain.

Try to answer these questions yourself. Ask your teacher if you need help.

Get the result !

Examination question

Explain how socio-cultural factors influenced the characteristics of mob football in pre-industrial Britain and how these factors continue to impact on participation in physical activity today. (6 marks)

Examiner's tips

Your A2 exam is 2½ hours long (150 minutes). You will have three structured questions to answer in that time – one for each of your three theory sections (for example, you may have done historical studies, exercise physiology and sports psychology in your A2 year). Each question is likely to have four parts: a–d. Parts a, b and c will be worth about 5 marks each – totalling 15 marks. Part d will be a 20-mark question.

- There are two parts to this 6-mark question.
- The first part asks for an explanation so make sure that you 'give reasons'.
- The second part asks you to consider today or the contemporary scene. We study sports history to have a better understanding of how and why things are as they are today – so be prepared to link forward to the present in all your historical studies questions.

xaminer says:

t's fine to plan your ınswer, but you must ılways answer in full entences. This plan is ine for the first part of he question on how ocio-cultural factors ıave influenced the haracteristics of mob ootball. You now ıeed to convert this ey information into a discursive explanation. he fact that you have not nentioned wagering or ower-class participation ıs characteristics is fine, ıs you do have plenty of asic information that you an develop here. Keep hose characteristics in nind, though. Your answer vill be greatly improved vith the inclusion of some elevant examples.

Plan for student answer

Mob football	Influential social and cultural factors	How these factors impact on football today
Violent	Reflection of violent society	No
Limited rules	Due to illiteracy among peasant class	No
Occasional	Limited to Saints' days and holy days	No
Rural	Occurred before industrial revolution	No
Local	Limited transport	Yes

Examiner says:

The second part of the question needs to be looked at again. Note that it is asking 'for factors that continue to impact on participation in physical activity today' – whereas your thoughts seem to have focused on football. This is one of those occasions when you will be heavily penalised for having done 'your version' of the question rather than the exact question that has been set.

Improved student answer

Socio-cultural factors had a massive impact on the characteristics of mob football and most other pre-industrial games.

Examiner says:

Clear, accurate, introductory sentence.

Mob football was a violent, occasional, pre-industrial game. It was predominantly rural and usually associated with wagering or gambling. It was locally significant and played mainly by the lower class with limited rules. Each of these characteristics or features was the result of social or cultural factors which include things such as transport, class and available time to take part.

Examiner says:

Good – you are getting into this question now and writing concisely with detail/development that can be given credit.

For example, the game was violent due to the times in which it existed, when life was cheap and times were hard. It was played occasionally, for example on Shrove Tuesday or Easter Monday, as time off was seasonal and often linked to Saints' Days or Holy Days. As the impact of the industrial revolution had not yet been felt, people were still mainly living rurally and so the game was rural in nature (though some town games did exist, for example in Kingston, Surrey). Wagering or gambling was associated with most popular recreations and mob football was no exception. The peasants dreamt of going from 'rags to riches' from a successful wager. The various games around the country were only locally significant due to limited transport and communications, which also influenced the rules which were simple, unwritten and passed on by word of mouth. Widespread illiteracy also meant that rules were not written down. The upper class had their own arguably more sophisticated sports, such as real tennis, so they left mob games to the lower class.

Examiner says:

This is an excellent paragraph with key points which you have developed as well as relevant, sound examples.

In contemporary Britain, many of these factors still have an impact on participation and they can usefully be examined under opportunity, provision and esteem. Opportunity includes factors such as available money and time, both of which affect whether someone can take part or not. Provision includes suitable equipment, facilities and coaching; all of which are key factors today. Esteem, linked to self-confidence, influences your likelihood of taking part as you might not feel you are good enough or that you fit in at a particular club.

Examiner says:

It is a good idea to clarify your thoughts and separate them into key headings like this; it keeps your mind focused and thought processes clear. You will need to do just that in the exam.

Examiner says:

A concluding sentence to wrap up your answer would have been great but you got away with it as overall this is a very high quality answer showing sound knowledge and understanding, detailed and accurate explanations and very good quality of language.

CHAPTER 2:

Rational recreation in post-industrial Britain

LEARNING OBJECTIVES

By the end of this chapter you should have knowledge and understanding of:

- the characteristics of rational recreation
- how to compare the characteristics of popular and rational recreation
- how the following social and cultural factors influenced the nature and development of rational recreations: the industrial revolution; the middle class; changing work conditions; free time and transport; the views of the Church; amateurism and professionalism; the status of women
- how to contrast pre- and post-industrial social and cultural factors relating to popular and rational recreation
- how rational recreation had an impact on the physical competence and health of participants
- the varying opportunities for participation during the nineteenth century
- the impact of rational recreation on participation and performance today, comparing participation rates then and now
- the five case study activities as rational recreations (you will do this in more detail in Chapter 4).

INTRODUCTION

By the mid-nineteenth century, Britain was a fully industrialised or mechanised society, railways were having a massive impact and ex-public schoolboys were promoting sport throughout the world. The contrast between the newly-emerging rational recreations and pre-industrial popular recreations such as mob football is striking.

Remember the 'W' and 'H' questions? Rational recreation differed from popular recreation in terms of *what* was played, *who* was playing, *where* they played, *when* they played, *why* they played and of course *how* their pastime was being played. These changes reflected societal change. And we, as social historians, are interested in societal change.

Fig 2.1 Lawn tennis is a perfect example of a rational recreation – a respectable, middle-class, rule-based game with purpose-built facilities and very little likelihood of wagering (gambling).

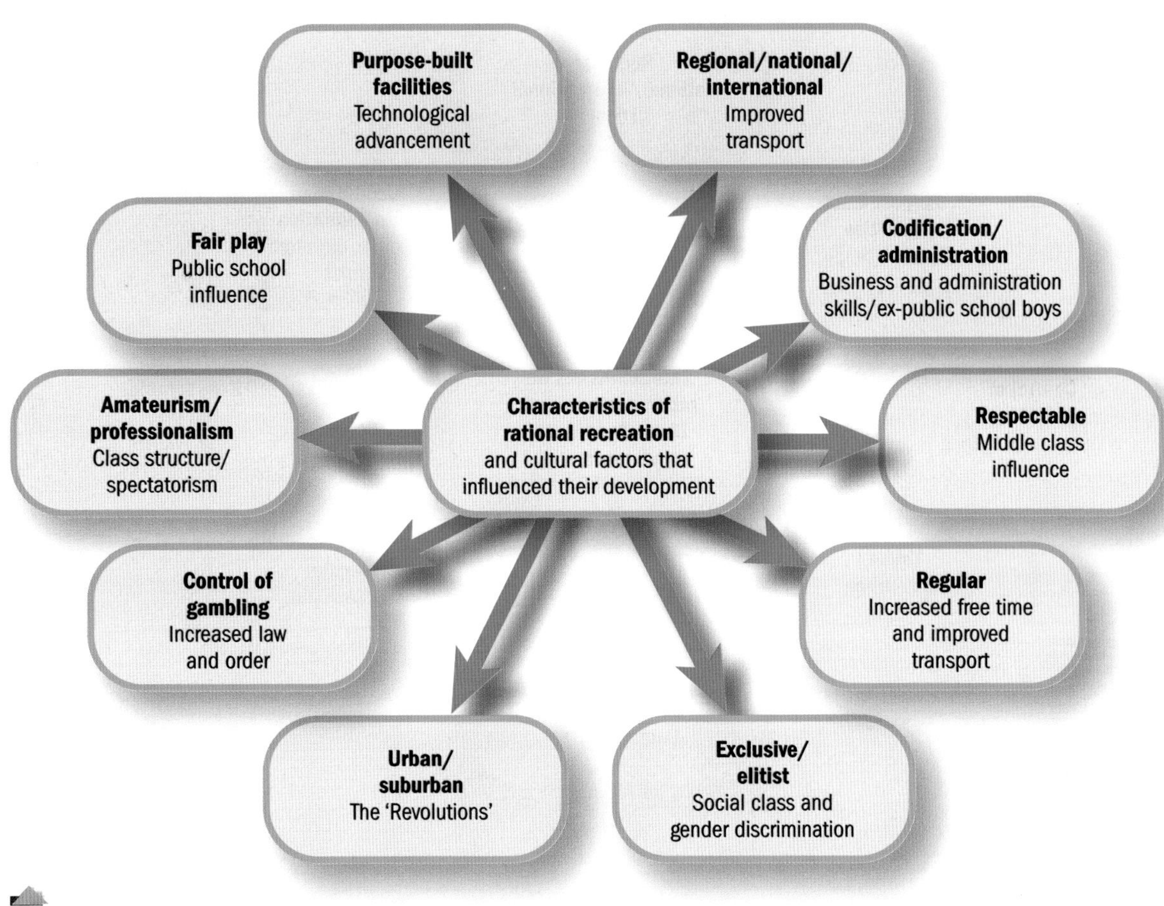

Fig 2.2 The characteristics of rational recreation and cultural factors that influenced them

EXAM TIP

It is essential that you know the characteristics of rational recreation and understand the social and cultural factors which influenced their nature and development.

You need to be able to contrast:

- the characteristics of popular and rational recreation
- pre- and post-industrial social and cultural factors relating to popular and rational recreation.

And, as with popular recreation, you will need to assess the extent to which your two individual case study activities (athletics and bathing/swimming) and three games (football, cricket and tennis) fit the norm. You will find this information in Chapter 4.

REMEMBER

A good way to remember some of the characteristics of rational recreation is to think of the letter 'R'. They were: rule-based, regular, regional, restrictive (class-wise), refined, respectable, and with clearly defined roles, such as centre forward in a hockey team.

TASK 1

With reference to Fig 2.1 on page 18 and Fig 4.15 on page 67, consider the 'W' and 'H' questions. Make direct comparisons and contrast the characteristics step-by-step, for example mob football was played occasionally whereas lawn tennis was played more regularly.

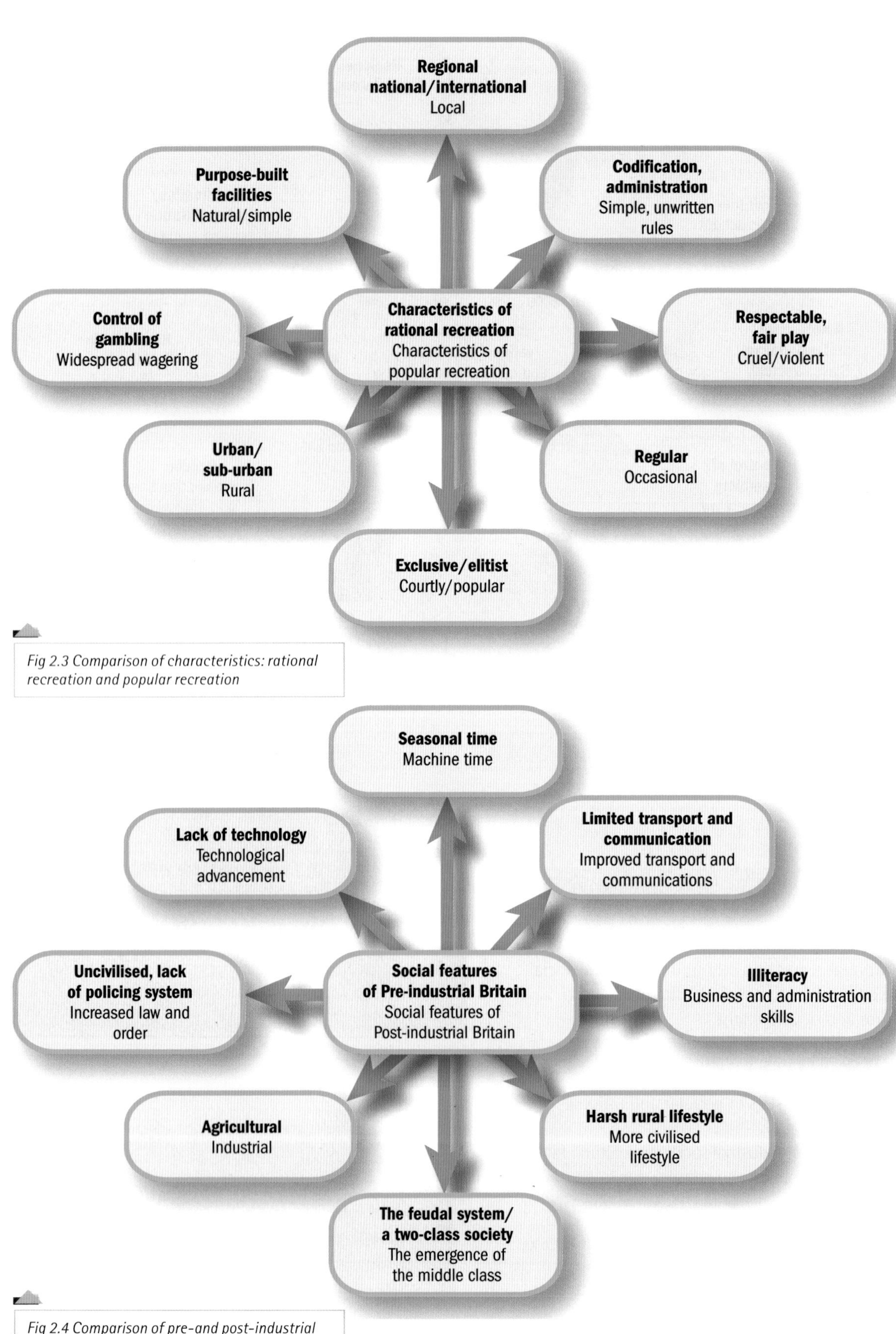

Fig 2.3 Comparison of characteristics: rational recreation and popular recreation

Fig 2.4 Comparison of pre-and post-industrial societal factors that influenced sport

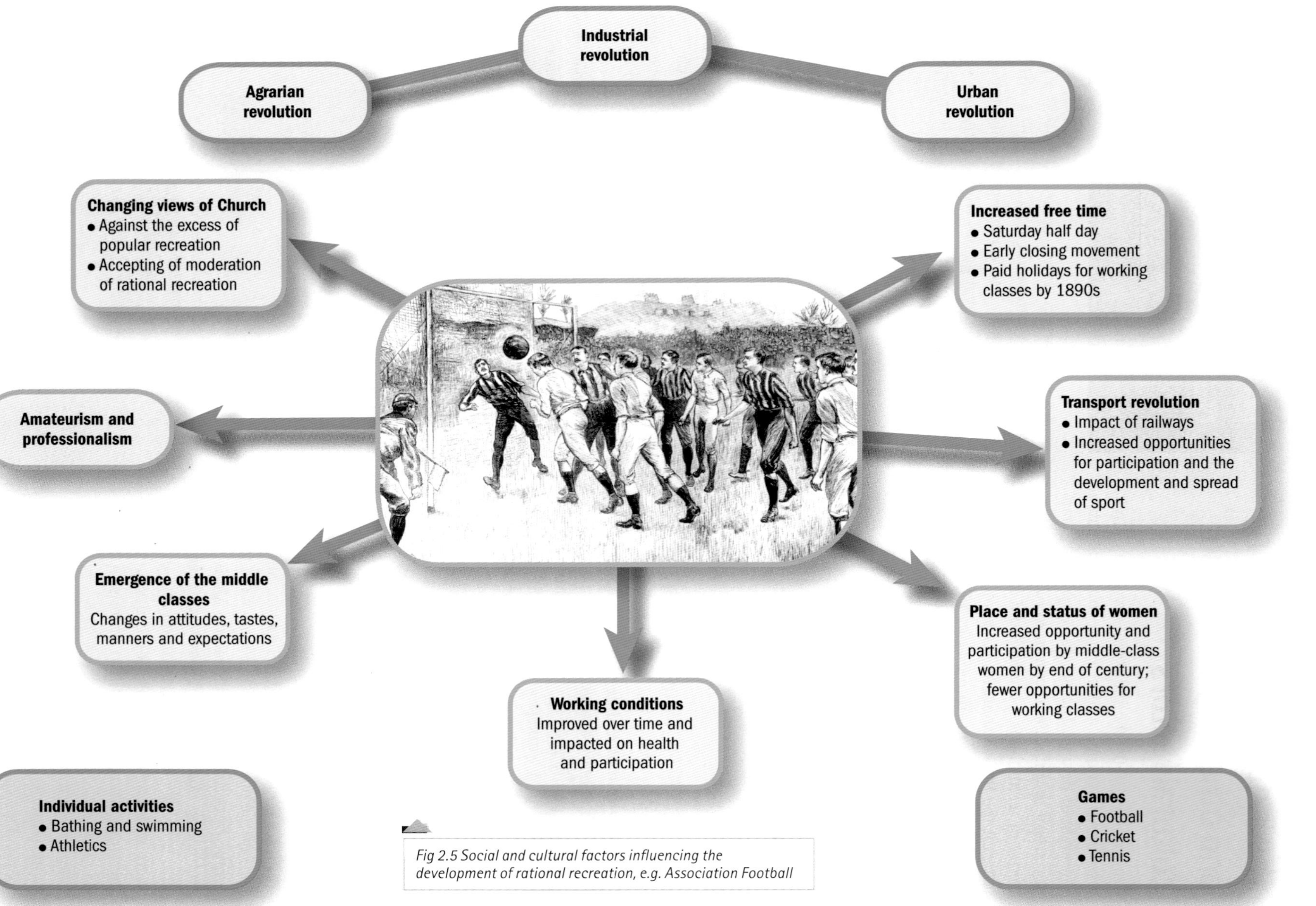

Fig 2.5 Social and cultural factors influencing the development of rational recreation, e.g. Association Football

The industrial revolution and other key social and cultural factors

During the 1800s, the industrial revolution and associated agrarian and urban revolutions spread throughout Britain. The process took more than a century to unfold and consisted of a complex series of technological and cultural changes. As a result the British sporting scene of 1900 was completely different from that in 1800 or 1850. And it's even more different today.

The industrial revolution, sometimes referred to as the 'machine age' due to the widespread use of steam-powered machines, went hand-in-hand with other massive changes such as new technology, farming and transport methods, urbanisation and a new class structure.

THE FIRST EFFECTS OF INDUSTRIALISATION

Industrialisation saw the emergence of a powerful, wealthy group of middle-class industrialists who needed to employ a large workforce to make the mills and foundries profitable. Thousands of agricultural workers and their families were eventually persuaded to migrate to cities, having been promised regular work and pay. Besides, farm workers' wages were comparatively low and rural jobs became harder to find as the use of new agricultural machinery became more extensive.

Cities were not ready for the great influx of people and soon filled to overflowing. Some sources report that in 1800 about one-fifth of Britain's population lived in London, and by 1851 half of the population did. Rooms were rented to whole or perhaps several families. Many stayed in lodging houses. Living space was cramped and unhygienic, and malnutrition and disease were widespread. Urbanisation caused a cholera epidemic which killed 31,000 Britons in 1832.

Soon, overcrowded living conditions, regular work patterns and excessive work hours took hold as people's space, energy and time were gradually eroded. Twelve-hour working days and 72-hour working weeks were common. This was a time of social decay and radical change, and a difficult time for sport. The violent, occasional pre-industrial festival games were clearly not suited to the new urban environment. If the recreations of the people were going to survive, they would have to conform to their new surroundings.

KEY TERM

Cholera

Water-borne disease which causes severe diarrhoea. Unless treatment is given, cholera can cause rapid dehydration and death.

In addition to the powerful twin forces of industrialisation and urbanisation, other factors were also bringing change. Social attitudes, tastes and expectations were shifting alongside a growing respectability within and civilising of society. The middle class were shaping how things should be done. Moreover, industrialists and the Church fought to change the behaviour, bad language and excesses of the old, traditional festivals and the people who had enjoyed them. As the new culture of respect and moderation began to take hold, new laws were passed. The RSPCA was in existence by 1824 and the Cruelty to Animals Act declared baiting sports illegal in 1835.

There were other changes too. The seasons became less meaningful and a daily cycle of fixed time

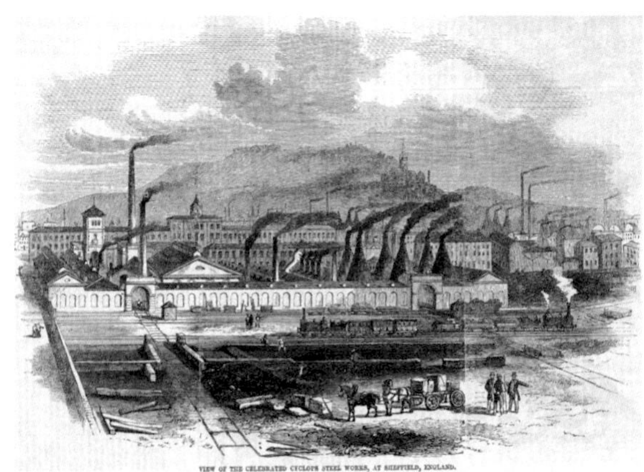

Fig 2.6 Industrial Britain – to what extent did rational recreations fit into this environment?

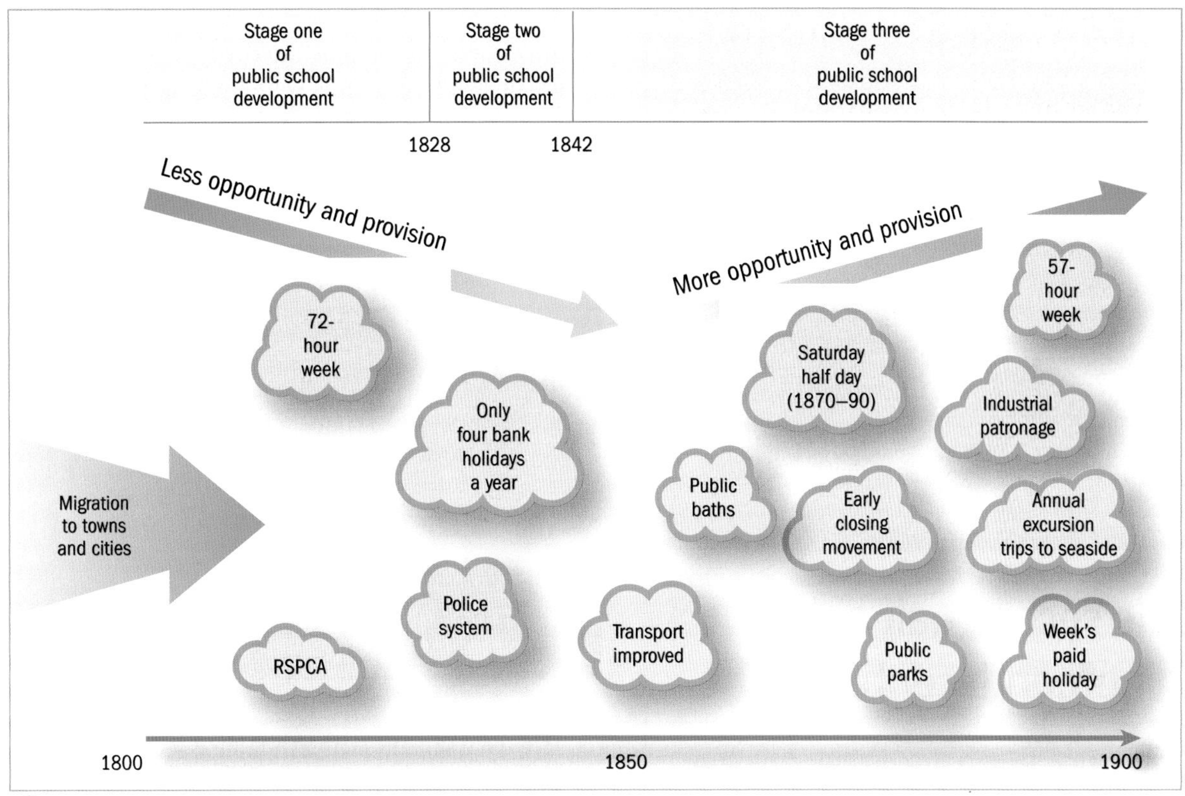

Fig 2.7 Changes in nineteenth-century working-class opportunity and provision as a parallel process to public school developments

became the norm. By 1834 the number of official holidays had been reduced from 47 in 1761 to just four, with obvious effects on sporting opportunity. By the early 1830s stage coaches were out of business and the opening of the Manchester to Liverpool Railway in 1830 marked the beginning of a dramatic new age for sport.

Fig 2.7 shows that when the rural peasants initially journeyed from countryside to towns, opportunities decreased. Life was bleak as they became slaves to the factory system, to machine time and to their employers. It was a time of decay, gloom and even hopeless poverty for those out of work who faced life on the streets. The formation and organisation of an effective workforce actually became a fierce struggle to lift the urban working classes from both oppression and depression. Clearly, the last thing on the minds of the industrial working class in the first half of the century was sport or recreation.

EXAM TIP

Mnemonics such as 'a shirt' can help you remember key facts relating to certain topics – in this case the impact of the industrial revolution on rural peasants. Rural peasants lost:

- **a**cceptance of their traditional activities (due to requirements of 'respectable' middle class)
- **s**pace to play (due to urbanisation/crowding)
- **h**ealth/energy (due to working long hours in the factories)
- **i**nfluence (due to being controlled by their social superiors)
- **r**ights (due to changes in criminal law and police enforcement, plus organisations such as the RSPCA)
- **t**ime (due to 72-hour working week and the reduction in the number of official holidays, or Holy Days).

REMEMBER

- Industrialisation was a multi-dimensional process which, though uneven in speed and geography, completely changed sport in England between 1800 and 1900.
- The first half of the nineteenth century was a period of decline and limited opportunity due to:
  - loss of space
  - the shift from seasonal to machine time
  - 12-hour days and no time to 'play'
  - poverty and low wages
  - loss of rural patronage
  - urbanisation, overcrowding and poor living conditions
  - poor working conditions.

The second half of the nineteenth century

IMPROVED LIVING CONDITIONS FOR THE WORKING CLASS

The emergence of sport for the masses (particularly spectator sport), excursion trips to the seaside and paid holidays were slow to come and hard won. However, reform, improvement and increased freedom for the working class shaped the second half of the century. Earnings improved, hours at work were reduced and **industrial patronage** became more widespread. Reform by groups of Evangelicals, Social Christians, temperance societies, trade unionists and humanitarians became both possible and desirable, with industrialists wanting a healthy and contented as well as a disciplined workforce. Some factory owners began to offer opportunities for social, recreational and sporting activity. Some had genuine paternalistic or Christian motives and were keen to improve the health and morale of the workforce; others simply wanted to win loyalty and increase work output. The annual excursion trip to the seaside was part of working-class culture by the end of the century.

The nature and scale of sport in Britain continued to evolve and change. Some rationalised that codified games such as rugby football came from **Oxbridge**, while others such as lawn tennis were invented by middle-class entrepreneurs. Municipal or public parks became features of enlightened towns and created much needed space, while urban swimming baths were built to wash manual workers. (For more on the development of swimming and lawn tennis as rational recreations, see Chapter 4 pages 53 and 78 respectively).

KEY TERMS

Industrial patronage

The provision of social, recreational and sporting opportunities by wealthy industrialists for their workers.

Oxbridge

The prestigious Oxford and Cambridge universities, where many ex-public school boys completed their Degree study.

THE TRANSPORT REVOLUTION

Improved transport and communications were almost certainly the greatest cause of change to sport, and the railways were the most significant mode of transport (road transport was still slow, canals were for goods and services, and air transport had not yet developed). The railways significantly increased the chance to both participate in and to watch sport. They were also the main factor that spread sport throughout Britain.

The railways:

- took people further in a shorter time
- enabled distant teams to play each other and take supporters
- caused a standardised set of rules to be needed
- speeded up the development of leagues, cups and competitions
- allowed people to get to the countryside – perhaps taking their (newly invented and acquired) bicycle with them to explore
- meant that kindly factory owners could lay on excursion trips to the seaside for their workers.

The train journey was also an enjoyable pastime in its own right. And, as horses no longer had to walk to their next race, the 'sport of kings' (horse racing) developed too!

THE CLASS SYSTEM

Fig 2.8 shows that a strict class system still underpinned and operated in British society. Class determined income, housing, lifestyle and sporting opportunities. It also determined your status as an amateur or professional, as will be clarified in your analysis of case study activities in Chapter 4.

FREE TIME: SATURDAY HALF-DAY AND THE EARLY CLOSING MOVEMENT

The early closing movement was a series of Bills through parliament that sought to reduce working hours, particularly in shops. Excessive working hours were increasingly thought to be damaging to the health and well-being of workers.

UPPER CLASS
Public school
Oxbridge
The army (possibly)
Country house for hunting season
London house for the ball season
Scottish house for shooting
Abroad for winter (The Grand Tour)
MIDDLE CLASS (subdivided: upper and lower middle class)
Public schools or proprietary colleges or grammar schools
University or business training
Work long hours in business and management
Large house in suburbs
Possibly with tennis court
Comfortable life
A holiday by the sea at home or abroad
WORKING CLASS
State elementary school
Work from early age
Long hours
Low wages
Cramped housing
Dread of unemployment, sickness and poverty
'The Peoples Game' Association Football as a spectator attraction

Fig 2.8 The class system in late nineteenth-century Britain – how it affected opportunity and provision for sport and leisure

Between 1870 and 1890, most workers had been granted their half-day of freedom on a Saturday afternoon, which created a nationwide time slot for watching or, for a few, even playing sport. By 1870 some workers had two to three days of paid holiday per year, and by the 1890s a week of paid holiday was common. Meanwhile, wages for the industrial worker had increased and more third-class rail fares had become available, allowing them more freedom to travel. Increases in free time were part of a process that started to give a healthier, more balanced and potentially more active lifestyle to the urban working class.

So, with reference to the game of football, in a period of fifty years, the pre-industrial mob game of the people had been taken into the gentry public schools, middle-class **proprietary colleges** and on to Oxbridge (as you will see in Chapter 3), had been codified and rationalised and now it was back with the people – but this time as a spectator sport.

In the space of 100 years, sport in England had changed from a free-ranging rural activity for participants to an enclosed, urban display for spectators.

TASK 2

1. Look at Fig 2.7 on page 23. In pairs, consider each of the identified features in the diagram that would have influenced the sporting opportunities and provision for the industrial working class. Discuss:
   a) the negative influences in the period 1800–50
   b) the positive influences in the period 1850–1900.
2. Compare the image of mob football in Fig 4.15 (page 67) with that of association football in Fig 2.5 (page 21). Ask the 'W' and 'H' questions (who, where, when, why, what and how).

KEY TERM

Proprietary college

Newly-established middle-class schools, such as Marlborough or Malvern, that modelled themselves on the traditional public schools such as Winchester or Rugby.

EXAM TIP

When an exam question asks you to compare two things (for example, mob football and association football), make sure that you make the comparison and don't just write about one or the other. It is best to make the comparisons as you go along, rather than to write all about one then all about the other. For example, 'mob football was occasional whereas association football was regular'.

CHANGING VIEWS OF THE CHURCH

The Church had different opinions about the status and value of sport throughout time (see also Table 1 on pages 4 and 5 of Chapter 1).

1 *The medieval period and Puritanism*
The Church opposed many popular sports at this time. The Puritans of the 1600s were against the spontaneity and freedom of traditional sports and pastimes, believing that only the prayerful, sober, quiet and hard working would be saved.

2 *From 1700 to 1850 and Protestantism*
By the 1700s the Church provided feast days and space for community gatherings. By 1800, however, they openly criticised the drunken excess, violence and mischief linked with traditional popular recreations and withdrew their support. This resulted in a decline in community participation. During the nineteenth century, Christianity and the Protestant work ethic became established.

3 *The 1850s, evangelism and social Christianity*
By the mid-nineteenth century, as **Muscular Christianity** and rational recreation came

together, the situation changed again. Newly-ordained ex-public school and university men started to promote sports and games in their parishes while the YMCA (an athletic and religious organisation) encouraged participation in rational sports by young clerks. This occurred against a backdrop of industrialisation which included provision for workers by social Christians, who thought it was their duty to provide for the less well-off.

KEY TERM

Muscular Christianity

The combination of godliness and manliness – the belief in having a strong and fit body to match a robust and healthy soul.

AMATEURISM AND PROFESSIONALISM

Amateurism and professionalism influenced the nature and development of rationalised sports and pastimes. Middle-class gentlemen amateurs took part for the love of the game and intrinsic rewards. Working-class men who could not afford to play games for enjoyment sometimes had a chance to play for money as a professional.

However, it was usually class that decided your status as an amateur or a professional. (See Chapter 4, page 71, for an analysis of amateurism and professionalism in the case study activities.)

WOMEN IN VICTORIAN BRITAIN

In early Victorian Britain it was thought inappropriate for a middle-class lady to exercise, sweat or display her body. This meant that physical activity was effectively outlawed. In addition, over-exertion was thought to be medically harmful for women. The invention of lawn tennis in the 1870s became a route to social and physical emancipation for women (see Chapter 4, page 82). This new game met women's needs and enthusiasm for a form of acceptable physical exercise. Those who continued to object on the grounds of immodesty and bad taste, increasingly had to counter the new argument of good health through exercise. Can you think of any links to today?

As physical exercise gradually became more acceptable for middle-class women, appropriate clothing was designed which encouraged freer movement and a gradual relaxation of traditional Victorian stuffiness. Of course, working-class women had a different set of rules to live by and they had neither the opportunity nor provision for leisure time physical activity.

Rational recreation: its effects on skill and health

	Upper and middle classes	Working class
Bathing and swimming	Increased skill and health for middle class as they took to and developed rational swimming in urban baths	Initially functional to combat urban disease – 'penny baths' provided in towns
Athletics	• Opportunities to increase skill and health for both classes as their respective governing bodies were formed • Note the ongoing existence of some early rural sports and the beginnings of urban athletics meetings for both classes, which would impact on health and skill	
Football	Amateur involvement, often in exclusive teams such as the Corinthian Casuals	• Mainly as spectators, so no physical health or skill development • Opportunities for a few very skilful players to become professional
Cricket	Skilful, with potential to increase health as a summer outdoor active game	
Lawn tennis	Skilful and potentially health-enhancing for middle class; new opportunities for women	Limited access for lower class until club and park provision developed

Table 1 The impact of rational recreations on the physical competence and health of participants

VARYING OPPORTUNITIES FOR PARTICIPATION

Class and gender continued to affect participation along with the three variables: opportunity, provision and esteem. The emergence of the middle class was particularly significant. Without access to horses they invented the bicycle and without access to real tennis they invented lawn tennis. The middle class drove the rationalisation and development of most sports, while the working class had to wait for opportunities to participate at a community level, perhaps via factory or local authority (municipal) public park provision.

Impact on and links to today

As you did for popular recreation, you need to consider the impact of rational recreation on participation and performance in physical activity today. You also need to compare participation then with now and think about reasons for differences.

Rational recreation had an impact on contemporary participation and performance. (See Chapter 4, page 50, for an analysis of each of the five case study activities as both rational recreations and today.) We still have a mainly decentralised, amateur and voluntary way of organising and administering sport in the UK, particularly at the lower levels. This is a direct result of the formation of most national governing bodies (NGBs) and many sports clubs by keen individuals over 100 years ago. Only quite recently have we started to move towards a more professional approach to sport at all levels, for example the focused and centralised formula adopted by the sport of cycling in the run up to the Beijing Olympics (2008) which resulted in phenomenal success. Ethics of sportsmanship are also linked to rational recreations.

EXAM TIP

Historical studies questions will always relate forward to the next stage, e.g. popular recreation to rational recreation, or to today, so it is important to consider the impact of the past on the present. For example consider working patterns, employment and unemployment, free time, transport and the place and status of women.

TASK 3

Research the date that local sports clubs in your town were founded. (Take particular note of the case study activities.) Now, consider if and how these clubs have impacted on contemporary participation and performance.

SPORT ENGLAND ACTIVE PEOPLE SURVEY, 2006

- 21 per cent of adults take part regularly in sport and active recreation with regular participation defined as at least three days a week at moderate intensity for at least 30 minutes.
- Participation ranged from 22.6 per cent in the South East to 19.3 per cent in the West Midlands.
- Walking is the most popular recreational activity in England, with over 20 per cent of adults aged 16 years and over walking recreationally for at least 30 minutes in the last four weeks.
- 13.8 per cent swim at least once a month and 10.5 per cent go to the gym.
- 25.1 per cent of the adult population are members of a club where they take part in sport.
- Regular participation in sport and active recreation varies across different groups – for example, male participation is 23.7 per cent and female participation is 18.5 per cent.

STRETCH AND CHALLENGE

Analyse participation in physical activity by women in Victorian society.

Answering this question requires investigation and consideration, so this is more of a thinking/ planning exercise than an exam-style question. Think about:

- class
- physical participation versus spectatorism
- at least two different sporting activities, such as lawn tennis and athletics.

EXAM TIP

You will not be expected to know specific data or figures relating to participation either then or now. Instead, you need an idea of how opportunity and provision have changed over time, especially as linked with class and gender.

TASK 4

Look at Table 2 and compare current participation rates in swimming, athletics, football, cricket and tennis. Try to compare likely participation rates then (i.e. the second-half of the nineteenth century) and now, remembering that a key difference today is the wide variety of different community activities on offer, including aqua aerobics, yoga, squash, weight training and martial arts.

Activity	Percent of the adult population (16 years plus) taking part at least once a month	Number of adults (16 years plus) taking part at least once a month
Recreational walking (moderate intensity for 30 plus minutes)	20.0	8,142,693
Swimming	**13.8**	**5,625,539**
Gym (including exercise bikes/ rowing machines)	11.6	4,722,762
Football	**7.1**	**2,910,684**
Running/jogging	4.6	1,872,819
Tennis	**2.1**	**874,040**
Cricket	**0.9**	**380,366**
Rugby Union	0.7	267,817
Athletics (track and field)	**0.6**	**244,281**
Netball	0.4	163,540
Hockey-field	0.3	141,351
Rugby League	0.3	110,553

Table 2 Sport England Active People Survey, 2006 (with your five case studies highlighted)

CASE STUDY ACTIVITIES

You need to consider bathing and swimming, athletics, football, cricket and tennis as rational recreations.

- We would expect the newly-rationalised case study activities to be sophisticated, rule-based and played regularly – was this always the case?
- How did they change/develop?
- Why did they change/develop?
- What was different in terms of participation and opportunities for participation?

Refer to Chapter 4, page 50, for a full analysis.

Exam**Café**

Relax, refresh, result!

Refresh your memory

You should now have knowledge and understanding of:

- the characteristics of rational recreation
- the comparisons between the characteristics of popular and rational recreation
- how the following social and cultural factors influenced the nature and development of rational recreations: the industrial revolution; the middle class; changing work conditions; free time and transport; the views of the Church; amateurism and professionalism; the status of women
- the contrasts between pre- and post-industrial social and cultural factors relating to popular and rational recreation
- how rational recreation had an impact on the physical competence and health of participants
- the varying opportunities for participation during the nineteenth century
- the impact of rational recreation on participation and performance today, comparing participation rates then and now
- the five case study activities as rational recreations (you will do this in more detail in Chapter 4).

REVISE AS YOU GO!

1. What is meant by the term 'industrialisation'?
2. Identify four characteristics of rational recreation that begin with the letter 'R'.
3. Compare the characteristics of rational recreation with those of popular recreation.
4. With reference to the mnemonic 'A SHIRT', identify what the lower class lost when they moved to towns and cities at the beginning of the nineteenth century.
5. How did the middle class differ from the working class?
6. How did working hours for the working class differ at the beginning and at the end of the nineteenth century?
7. How did improved transport, notably the railways, impact on the development of sport and recreation in the nineteenth century?
8. What is being described: 'newly-established middle-class schools such as Marlborough or Malvern that modelled themselves on the traditional public schools such as Winchester or Rugby.'
9. How did the views of the Church towards physical activity, sports and pastimes change over time?
10. List some key points relating to both amateurism and professionalism.

Try to answer these questions yourself. Ask your teacher if you need help.

Get the result!

Examination question

Analyse the impact of the railways on the development of football in the nineteenth century and comment on how transport and communications continue to impact on sport today. (6 marks)

Examiner's tips

Note the command word analyse. To analyse effectively you need to examine, consider and scrutinise the impact of the railways on rational recreation, not just give a list of facts. So be sure to include analytical and qualitative comments.

Student answer

The railways had a massive impact on participation in and the development of most sports in post-industrial Britain. Improved transport and communications – especially the railways – were probably the most significant factor in helping rational recreations for the masses to spread and grow. Increased free time for the industrial working class and the building of purpose-built facilities were other important factors.

xaminer says:

ffective opening ection to set the cene. You have clearly arted to answer the uestion in your first entence by telling me at the railways had a nassive impact'. This ualitative statement hows analysis.

Without the railways the game of football would not have become the national game. Until trains, football had rules as different as the public schools that played it. Now one set of rules was needed that worked throughout the country as games could be regional, national and even international. Teams and their supporters played further from home, taking their supporters with them. So spectatorism grew too, especially when special excursion trains were provided. This would not have happened without the railways. By 1890 most working-class men would be at the football game. Because teams could travel and fixtures became more regular leagues, cups and competitions were started, many of which still exist today. Manchester United was started by workers of the Lancashire and Yorkshire railway in 1878.

Examiner says:

You have developed/ analysed several different points so would score well on a 'levels of response' mark scheme. Your example of Manchester United as a railway workers' team is evidence of breadth of relevant knowledge and independent reading – well done.

Transport and communications continue to impact on all sport in Britain today from the bottom to the top of the sports development pyramid. Rail travel is less significant today as most families have a car and even flying from north to south is common. Communications also includes media, which has had as monumental an effect today as the railways had over 100 years ago.

xaminer says:

ithout this link to the resent day you could ot get the highest arks. Analysis of day will not need be as extensive s your historical nowledge and you ay not actually have overed everything your classroom in rms of today – this your opportunity show thinking and nking skills. To show at you are happy be stretched and hallenged!

is is an excellent nswer – well done!

CHAPTER 3:

Nineteenth-century public schools and their impact on the development of physical activities and young people

LEARNING OBJECTIVES

By the end of this chapter you should have knowledge and understanding of:

- the characteristics of nineteenth-century public schools
- the impact of the public schools on physical activities in general and on the five case study activities in particular (this will be covered in more detail in Chapter 4)
- the relevance of the Clarendon Report
- how nineteenth-century public schools went through three stages of development
- the development of sports and games in each stage
- the impact of the three stages on physical activities, on young people and on participation both in the nineteenth century and now
- the reasons for the slower development of athleticism in girls' public schools compared with boys' public schools.

INTRODUCTION

Certain schools were called public schools because they were not privately owned but were controlled by a group of **trustees** in charge of running each school. The riotous games and activities popular at these schools at the beginning of the nineteenth century were vastly different from those played there a century later, and even now.

KEY TERM

Trustees

Influential people responsible for managing and promoting an organisation or asset, such as a school.

Your task is to trace and explain this development from 'boy culture' (which had many of the characteristics of pre-industrial popular recreation) to regulated rationalised games. You also need to be clear about the changing nature and aims of public school sport throughout the nineteenth century. Remember, throughout your historical studies, you need to reflect forward to today. How did the past influence the present? For example, the **house system** which started in public boarding schools is central to the organisation of many schools today.

KEY TERM

House system

System whereby boys lived in individual houses while away at boarding school. For example, Charterhouse had four boarding houses when it was first founded in 1611 and has eleven boarding houses today. The house became the centre of social and sporting life.

EXAM TIP

Historical exam questions will not focus solely on the past; they will also reflect forward to the next stage or to today, either directly or indirectly.

The impact of the public schools on the five case study activities: bathing and swimming, athletics, football, cricket and tennis, will be dealt with in Chapter 4.

EXAM TIP

You will not be asked a simple, recall question such as 'Identify four characteristics of public schools.' Rather, your knowledge must be applied, so a more realistic question might be 'How did the characteristics of the public schools impact on the development of team games?'

Characteristics of public schools

The characteristics of public schools shaped the development of team games as shown in Figure 3.1.

Fig 3.1 Characteristics of nineteenth-century public schools and their impact on sports and games

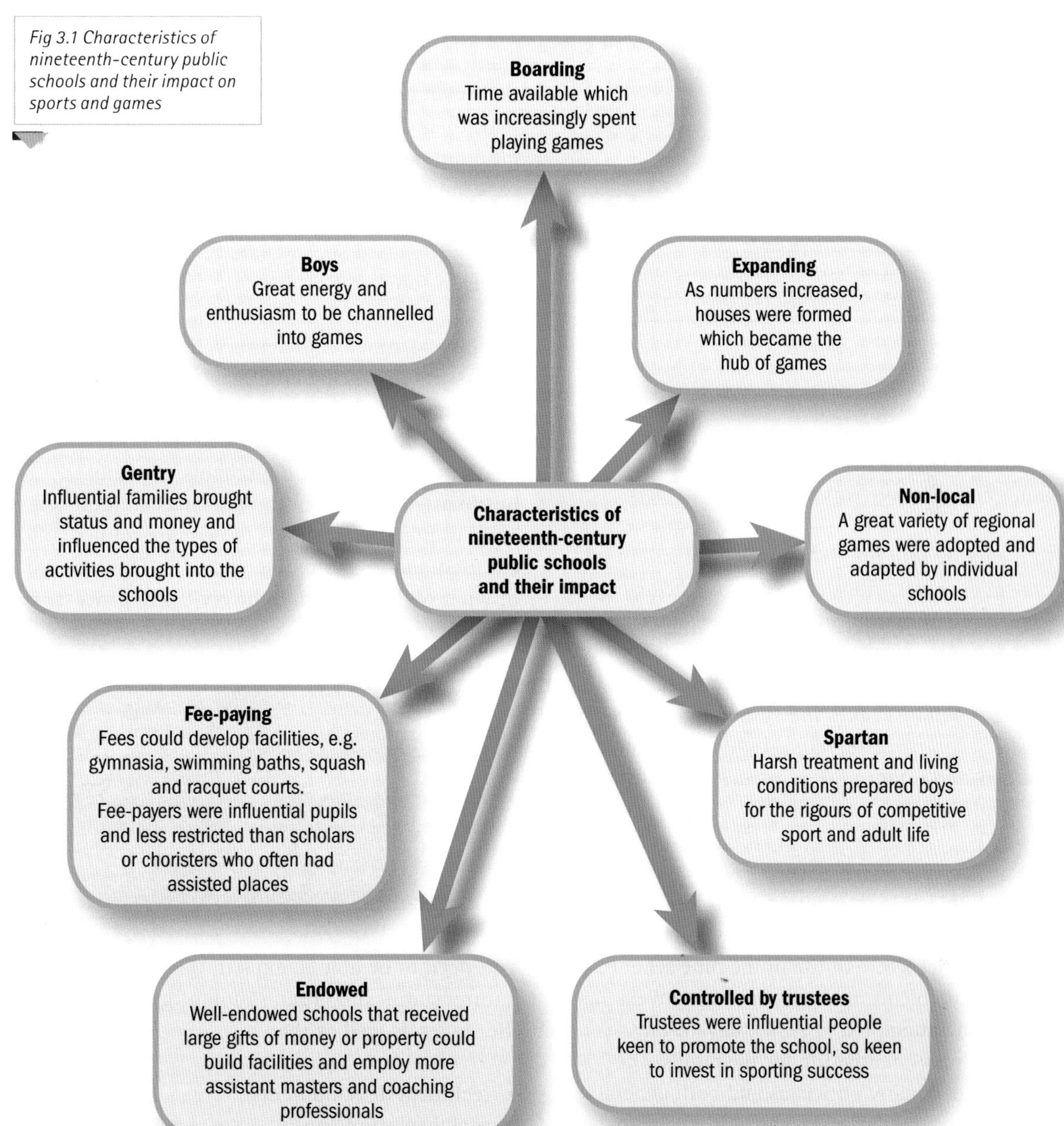
Characteristics of nineteenth-century public schools and their impact
Boarding
Time available which was increasingly spent playing games
Boys
Great energy and enthusiasm to be channelled into games
Expanding
As numbers increased, houses were formed which became the hub of games
Gentry
Influential families brought status and money and influenced the types of activities brought into the schools
Non-local
A great variety of regional games were adopted and adapted by individual schools
Fee-paying
Fees could develop facilities, e.g. gymnasia, swimming baths, squash and racquet courts.
Fee-payers were influential pupils and less restricted than scholars or choristers who often had assisted places
Spartan
Harsh treatment and living conditions prepared boys for the rigours of competitive sport and adult life
Endowed
Well-endowed schools that received large gifts of money or property could build facilities and employ more assistant masters and coaching professionals
Controlled by trustees
Trustees were influential people keen to promote the school, so keen to invest in sporting success

The Clarendon Report

Following complaints about the finances, buildings and management of Eton College, in 1861 Queen Victoria commissioned a group of officials to investigate the nine leading public schools of England. The nine schools are shown in Table 1.

Public school	Year founded
Winchester	1382
Eton	1440
St Paul's	1509
Shrewsbury	1552
Westminster	1560
Merchant Taylor's	1561
Rugby	1567
Harrow	1571
Charterhouse	1611

Table 1

The Earl of Clarendon headed the Clarendon Commission. His role was:

> '...*to enquire into the nature and application of the endowments, funds, and revenue belonging to or received by the colleges, schools and foundations... to enquire into the administration and management of the said colleges, schools and foundations... into the system and course of studies pursued therein... into the methods, systems and extent of the instructions given to the students.*'
>
> (Clarendon Report)

The thorough and high quality **Clarendon Report** was published in 1864, in two huge volumes. It gave a detailed picture of life in the nine schools, highlighted problems, recommended improvements, and generally attempted to enrich day-to-day academic and residential life for the pupils. The report included many criticisms and both general and specific advice for each school. It was arguably the prototype Ofsted inspection report!

KEY TERM

Clarendon Report

The account of public school life written by the Earl of Clarendon and his team of commissioners (officials) in 1864.

The three developmental stages of athleticism

The century-long process of change is usefully studied in stages. The schools were institutions in their own right, often out in the countryside and with their own rules, customs and even sometimes mini languages, yet the public schools did not exist in isolation. They reflected changes that were happening in society. It could also be argued that they caused social change – certainly in terms of sport and recreation.

By the mid-nineteenth century, the RSPCA was successfully reducing cruelty against animals while the police and changing tastes and manners were reducing the number of bare-fist fights. Similar changes were afoot in the schools, as many headmasters were keen to be seen as enlightened. They wanted their schools to be more refined and cultured and less primitive and wild. This was part of what sociologists call 'the **civilising process**.'

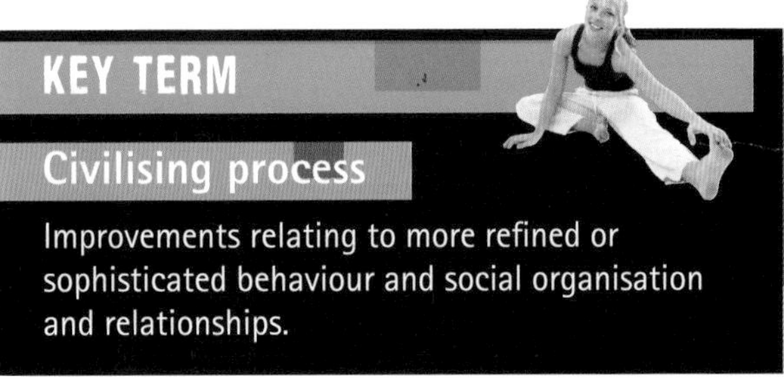

KEY TERM

Civilising process

Improvements relating to more refined or sophisticated behaviour and social organisation and relationships.

You need to be able to explain the evolving nature, status and organisation of games through the stages as well as the:

- **technical developments**
- **social relationships**
- **values** linked to sports and games in each stage.

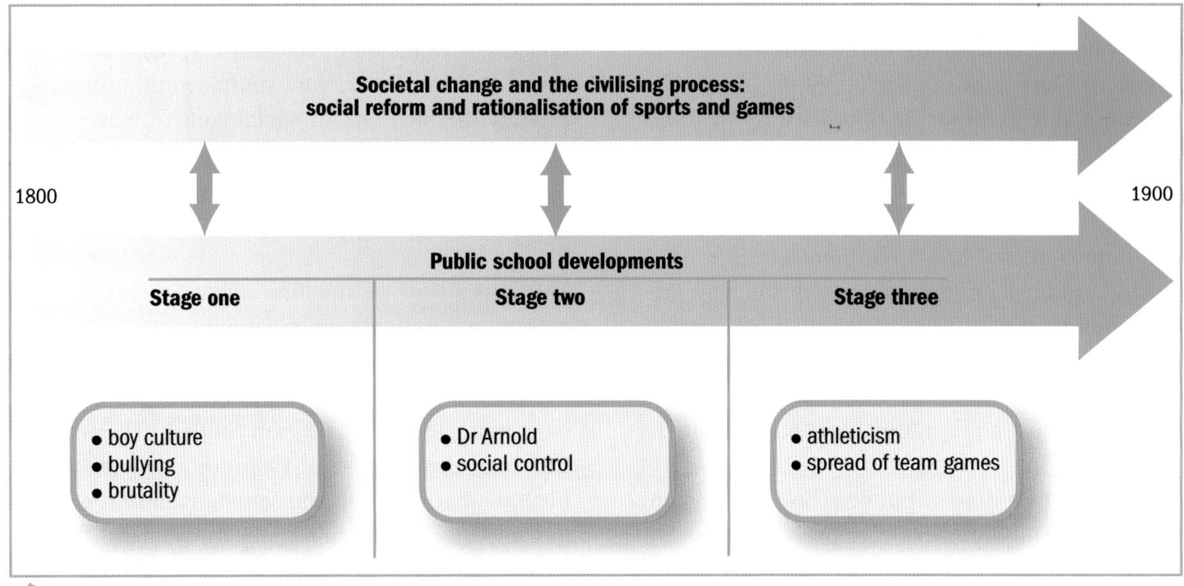

Fig 3.2 1800–1900: the stages of athleticism as a parallel process to societal change

You need to keep in mind the influence of each of the three stages on the development of physical activities and young people, both at that time and now. The development of physical activities links with **technical developments**. The development of young people links with both **social relationships** and values.

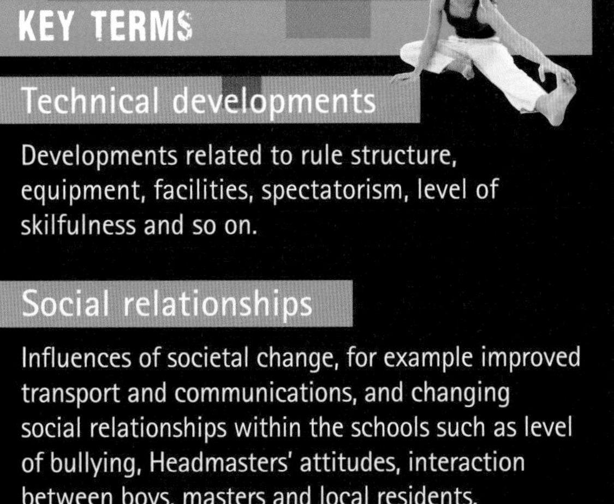

KEY TERMS

Technical developments

Developments related to rule structure, equipment, facilities, spectatorism, level of skilfulness and so on.

Social relationships

Influences of societal change, for example improved transport and communications, and changing social relationships within the schools such as level of bullying, Headmasters' attitudes, interaction between boys, masters and local residents.

Values

Benefits, ethics and morals that build character and become guidelines for living, such as teamwork, manliness, loyalty, honour and respect for opponents.

Stage one (c.1790–1824): Boy culture, bullying and brutality

At the end of the eighteenth century, English society consisted of contrasts between the high culture and fashion of the **Regency period** and the low culture and apparent brutality of blood sports and bare-fist fighting (see figures on page 3). Both ends of this social spectrum were mirrored in the public schools. This was a time of 'boy culture', when the confrontational behaviour of the French and American revolutions was

Fig 3.3 Cricket at Harrow School, 1802

copied by public schoolboys if things didn't go their way. The absence of a police force meant any unrest had to be controlled by the army. All recreational activities were organised by the boys for pure enjoyment and to relieve the boredom of academic work, which consisted solely of the classics (Latin and Greek). Masters 'ruled with the rod' in lessons, but had no influence or interest outside of the classroom. Perhaps this is why the boys took part in all sorts of mischief including trespass, truancy, poaching and fighting. In both society at large and in individual public schools, control was lost and tyranny and chaos resulted.

Stage one was a time of public school expansion when increasing numbers of upper-class boys were enrolling from a variety of different **preparatory schools** and bringing with them customs and recreations from all over the country. These customs were mixed and moulded, as in a **melting pot**, into schoolboy games and what were to become future traditions. Thus the sporting culture of each school began to be established along with a need for increased housing (expansion of the house system) and social control. Games and sports would ultimately provide the medium for **social control**, but meanwhile severe, imposed discipline by masters and resentful rebellion and hooligan behaviour by boys shaped the norm at this early stage.

This was a time of 'institutionalised popular recreation', with activities ranging from the childlike to the barbaric. Hoops, marbles and spinning tops were in the playground alongside bare-knuckle fights and mob football. The wall at Eton and the **cloisters** at Charterhouse were the birthplaces of unique and ferocious mob football games. Cricket, the rural game already **codified** and played by both classes, was immediately adopted by the schools, while fox hunting was adapted to **hare and hounds**. Boys would also hire boats from local boatyards, play **'fives'** and other ball games against suitable walls, swim in natural bathing places such as rivers and ponds and explore the countryside.

KEY TERMS

Regency Period

A time of high fashion during the late-eighteenth and early-nineteenth centuries, associated with the Prince Regent (the son of George III who ruled during his father's illness).

Preparatory or 'Prep' schools

Junior schools for younger boys, who would then advance to the public schools.

Melting pot

To combine different things to produce a new outcome; with respect to stage one, the mixing of games and traditions from a variety of areas or sources resulting in a standardised game or system of play.

Social control

The establishment of order, stability and good behaviour.

KEY TERMS

Cloisters

Covered walkways or corridors with a courtyard in the middle (see illustration of the cloisters at Charterhouse – fig 4.16 on page 68).

Codify

To collect together and organise rules and procedures.

Hare and hounds

An adaptation of fox hunting whereby one boy runs ahead of the pack dropping a trail of paper as 'scent', which is then followed by the chasing crowd.

Fives

A hand and ball or bat and ball game against a suitable wall or (later) in a purpose-built court. Similar to squash, the game was called fives because of the five digits on one hand. (See also the illustration on page 80 in Chapter 4.)

EXAM TIP

Whenever you come across a new historical concept or idea, think about 'then and now.' How did the past influence today? And was the influence direct or developmental?

Stage two (1828–42): Dr Thomas Arnold and social control

This was a time of change, both in society at large and in the English public schools. Parliament and criminal laws were changing (for example, laws banning cruelty to animals), transport and communications were dramatically improving (with the introduction of the **penny post** and the railways) and Queen Victoria was crowned in 1837. With life and society becoming more orderly, the freedom and wild escapades of stage one became more and more out of place.

KEY TERM

Penny post

New technology and printing machinery for producing postage stamps transformed the postal service in 1840. For the first time the person sending a letter paid the postage instead of the person receiving it! The new system was cheaper, faster and more reliable, and greatly improved communications throughout the country. Compare this to the speed and convenience of texting and emailing today.

Dr Thomas Arnold (1795–1842) is widely regarded as one of the key reformers of the English public school system at a time when it was out of control. He was Headmaster of Rugby School from 1828 until his death in 1842. He attended Winchester as a boy and showed no real interest in games but a great love of the countryside, which stayed with him throughout his life. Later, along with most public school headmasters at the time, he became an ordained clergyman and a doctor of divinity (meaning he had a PhD in theology). On joining Rugby he grew to be obsessed by what he saw as the immorality and sinfulness of boys and was determined to reform them, their attitudes and their school lives.

> *'Evil was something positive that Arnold could almost see and feel. When faced with it he would rise in anger, and indeed, on occasion, completely lose his self-control.'*
>
> T.W. Bamford, *Thomas Arnold on Education* (1970)

Arnold used games as a vehicle for establishing social control. He also made the Chapel the school's spiritual and symbolic centre, thereby establishing a new moral code, which was better suited to the increasingly civilised society to which the public schools now belonged. Arnold also established a more trusting and sympathetic relationship with the sixth form, while his masters gradually adopted roles of mentor and guide, rather than judge and 'executioner'. He then raised the status of the sixth form, gave them responsibility, increased their powers of discipline, and in return required them to be positive role models and his 'police force' around the school. The sixth formers became the link between masters and boys. Arnold's primary objective of delivering the Christian message could then be achieved. As a by-product, the status, regularity and organisation of games also increased.

Fig 3.4 Dr Thomas Arnold (1795–1842)

REMEMBER

Dr Arnold used games as a vehicle for achieving social control in Rugby School; he did not value games as an end in themselves.

As schools continued to expand, the house system also grew. Individual houses, run initially as commercial enterprises by a housemaster and his wife, became the focus of boys' personal, social, recreational and sporting existence. Games of inter-house cricket and football/rugby kept boys out of trouble in the daytime and ensured they went to bed exhausted. Thus the 'playground' became a central feature of public school life.

Arnold and other liberal headmasters of the time reformed the following aspects of public school life:

- the behaviour of boys
- the severity of punishments imposed by masters
- the role of the sixth form
- the academic curriculum.

MUSCULAR CHRISTIANITY

Arnold's main aim, though, was to produce Christian gentlemen and to preach good moral behaviour. This was all part of Muscular Christianity, or the belief in having a strong soul within a strong body. Sometimes the concept of Muscular Christianity is referred to as a combination of godliness and manliness. It was fine to play sport and to play hard, but always for the glory of God – not for its own sake or for any extrinsic values that could be achieved.

TASK 1

Try to think of contemporary sports performers who dedicate their performance in the same way that nineteenth-century Muscular Christians did.

Stage three (1842–1914): the 'cult' of athleticism

The conventional image of a late-nineteenth-century English public school is of mellow stone buildings, magnificent games fields, colours, caps and cricketers. These were all symbols of the **cult of athleticism**: the craze for team games and comparative disinterest in academic work.

Between 1850 and 1870, Britain and its Empire were 'ruling the waves' and military drill became part of public school life. The Football Association (FA) was founded and the effects of the publication of the *Clarendon Report* (1864) were felt. Meanwhile, games became compulsory at Harrow, cricket became compulsory at **Clifton**, and at **Uppingham** the gymnasium was built and the games committee was formed.

KEY TERMS

Cult

A craze or obsession.

Athleticism

The combination of physical endeavour (or trying hard) with moral integrity (a mix of honour, truthfulness and sportsmanship).

Clifton

Public school in Bristol, founded in 1862, built as a copy of Rugby.

Uppingham

Grammar School reformed under Edward Thring (1853–87), where games became central to school life. Thring played in the school teams.

Consider what some academics have said about the emergence of athleticism in this third stage.

- Money, in *Manly and Muscular Diversions* (2001), argues that by the 1850s headmasters had accepted team games as voluntary free-time activities, with cricket, football, rowing and various racquet games well established recreationally though not yet as part of the curriculum.

- Holt, in *Sport and the British* (1990), refers to the 1850s as 'the crucial decade in public school sport.'
- Mangan, in *Athleticism in the Victorian and Edwardian Public School* (2000), adds:

  '...from 1850 onwards, games were purposefully and deliberately assimilated into the formal curriculum of the public schools: suitable facilities were constructed, headmasters insisted on pupil involvement (and) staff participation was increasingly expected...'

- Newsome, in *Godliness and Good Learning* (1961), goes further, arguing that:

  'Between 1860 and 1880, games became compulsory, organised and eulogised at all the leading public schools.'

The ex-public school boy was expected to have a well-rounded character, impeccable manners and enviable personal qualities. Further, having led a team on the games field it was assumed that he could lead a regiment on the battlefield. According to one observer, public schools created men who would be 'acceptable at a dance and invaluable in a shipwreck!' So, in the space of 60 years, what had been an embarrassment to public school headmasters became their pride – games and athletic pursuits.

INFLUENCE OF EX-PUBLIC SCHOOL BOYS

Many public school boys went on to study at Oxford or Cambridge (Oxbridge). Here, sporting prowess was reflected in an Oxbridge 'blue', achieved when a student or graduate represented their university in a Varsity match against the opposing university. Old boys with a 'blue' became sought-after **assistant masters** in public schools. Arguably this is still the case today.

You will remember from your AS socio-cultural studies that on leaving university these young men would go into adult life taking the **games ethic** with them. For example, in 1938 in Kuala

Fig 3.5 The spread of team games throughout Europe and the British Empire

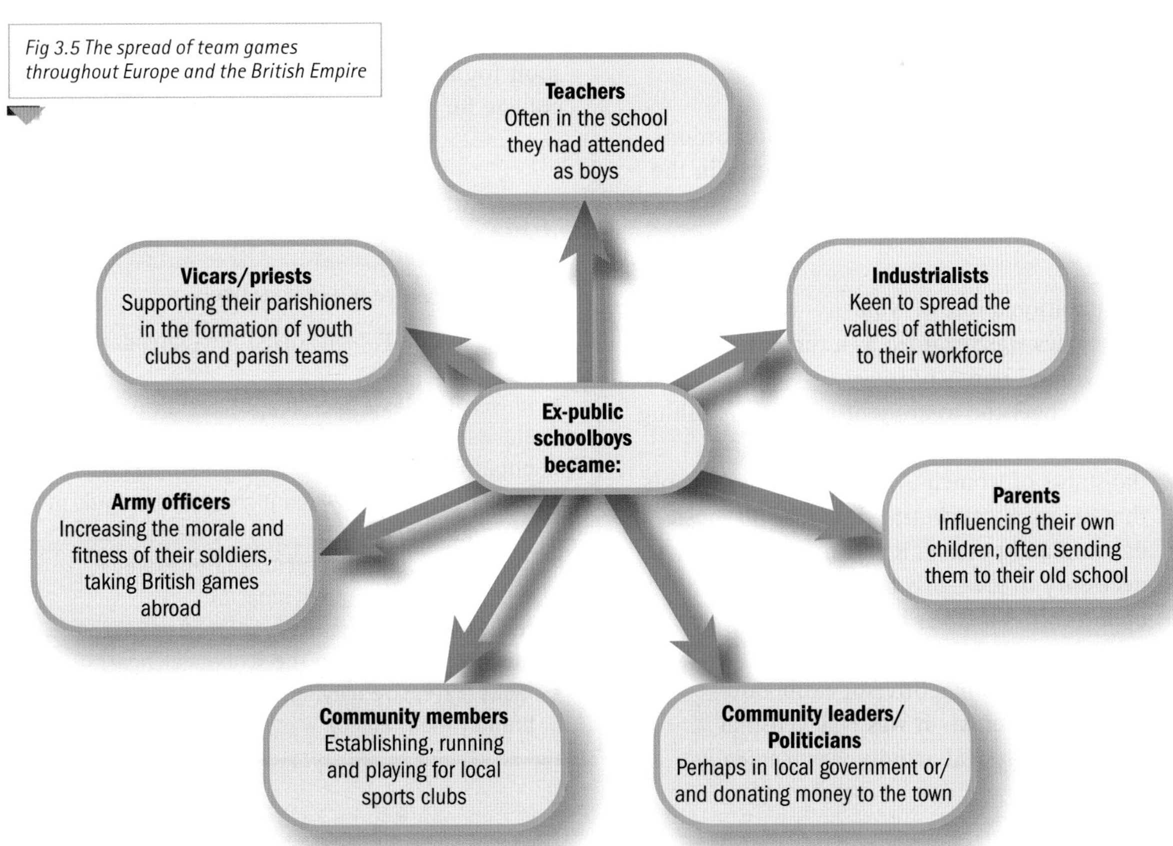
Ex-public schoolboys became:
Teachers
Often in the school they had attended as boys
Industrialists
Keen to spread the values of athleticism to their workforce
Parents
Influencing their own children, often sending them to their old school
Community leaders/ Politicians
Perhaps in local government or/ and donating money to the town
Community members
Establishing, running and playing for local sports clubs
Army officers
Increasing the morale and fitness of their soldiers, taking British games abroad
Vicars/priests
Supporting their parishioners in the formation of youth clubs and parish teams

Lumpur (now Malaysia), a group of expatriates associated with the rubber plantations started a modified paper chase in order to work up a thirst before retiring to the Selangor Club. There the restaurant was known locally as the 'Hash House', so the name was adopted by the harriers (runners) and is still used to this day.

KEY TERMS

Assistant master

Junior master without the responsibility of a house who taught an academic subject and was fully involved in the games programme.

Games ethic

A belief in the value of team games for the development of character. Clifton, Malvern and Cheltenham are examples of middle-class copies of Clarendon schools that took on the games ethic and had outstanding facilities.

ATHLETICISM IN GIRLS' PUBLIC AND PRIVATE SCHOOLS

While athleticism was reaching cult proportions in boys' public schools, there was a delay in the development of opportunities for upper- and middle-class girls. The reasons for this were:

- the traditional role of women – education of females was regarded as a threat to the behavioural norms of society
- anxiety over the wearing of revealing clothing for physical exercise
- the status of women in society – girls' schools that did exist concentrated mainly on music, dancing and posture; it was not considered necessary to give girls the same sporting opportunities as their brothers
- it was thought inappropriate (unladylike) for women to be competitive or exuberant
- medical concerns – it was believed that strenuous physical activity was medically dangerous and could complicate or even prevent child-bearing
- perceived physical inferiority – there were concerns that girls would not be able to cope with strenuous physical activity.

Also, there were fewer prominent personalities to match boys' school heads such as Arnold of Rugby or Thring of Uppingham. Three women who should be mentioned, however, are:

- Frances Mary Buss
- Dorothea Beale
- Madame Bergman Osterberg.

These women were all great pioneers of female physical education in the mid- to late-nineteenth century. They had to overcome prejudice and sometimes ridicule, but they successfully made a difference. In the 1860s, Frances Buss founded the North London Collegiate School and Camden School for Girls, while Beale transformed Cheltenham Ladies College into an esteemed school for upper- and middle-class girls. The Swedish Madame Bergman Osterberg became Lady Superintendent of Physical Education in London in 1881 and soon founded the first full-time specialist PE college for women – Dartford.

APPLY IT!

Note the influence of public schools on:

- other schools (which copied the Clarendon 'nine')
- universities (as a 'melting pot' for the standardisation of rules)
- organisations (formations of governing bodies)
- regularity of play (which increased standards of performance)
- building of specialist facilities (for example, swimming baths and gymnasia)
- festival days (for example, sports day which rivalled speech day in the school calendar)
- fields (extensive playing fields created and proudly maintained).

Impact of public schools

Impact of Stage 1 on:	Then	Now
Physical activity (technical development)	The impact was informal and unofficial rather than structured or planned. Many activities became institutionalised and took place both in school grounds and surrounding countryside, in free time outside of lesson time. Activities usually casual and/or spontaneous and both adopted (such as cricket, football and fighting) and adapted (such as hare and hounds and steeplechase). Also invented to suit natural facilities in schools.	Limited direct impact of Stage 1 today. Examples include maintenance of traditional football games such as the Wall Game at Eton College.
Young people (social relationships and values) (technical development)	On the positive side, young people had opportunities to develop independence and self-sufficiency. On the negative side there was institutionalised bullying linked with hooligan behaviour and the prefect/fagging system, poor relationships and severe punishments.	Limited direct impact – more indirect impact as a stage on route to athleticism.

Impact of Stage 2 on:	Then	Now
Physical activity (technical development)	As part of the process of social control, sports and pastimes became more controlled and less violent and/or spontaneous. Played more regularly and in school grounds with trespass reduced. A growing programme of games and individual activities played on an inter-house basis.	The house system still central to organisation in many schools today particularly independent boarding schools many of which are modelled on the nineteenth century format.
Young people (social relationships and values)	Games were used to establish social control in Rugby School. Dr Arnold required Christian attitudes and better behaviour especially from the sixth form to whom he gave responsibility. Arnold also keen to change the behaviour of the boys, the severity of punishments imposed by masters, the role of the sixth form, the academic curriculum, the relationships of boys and masters from mutual antagonism to mutual trust and respect.	Limited direct impact – more indirect impact as a stage on route to athleticism.

Impact of Stage 3 on:	Then	Now
Physical activities (technical development)	• Organisation – codification and regular fixtures including establishment of inter-school fixtures, leagues, cups and competitions such as public school championships. • Formation of NGBs by Old Boys. • Encouraged by headmaster. • Time, space and expertise available. • Impact of university melting pot on standardisation of rules.	• Some of the old established competitions still exist. • Participation in physical activities considered important for healthy balanced lifestyles.
Young people (social relationships and values)	Character development: • ***Physical*** – daily participation increased health and skill levels. • ***Intellectual*** – development of organisational, administrative and management skills. • ***Emotional*** – need for both independence and teamwork. • ***Social*** – loyalty to house, school and ultimately to country. Fixtures with local clubs and other schools giving opportunities for friendships. Also: • Fair play. • Appreciation of value of healthy exercise and fresh air. • Participation helped to develop 'all rounders' who were socially acceptable and respected. • The competitive experience useful in an increasingly competitive society. • Old Boys' societies established – financial generosity.	• PE in National Curriculum still focuses on development of whole child (see Chapter 5 – PE in state schools, page 98). • Life similarly competitive today as competitive sport making a come-back in state schools. • Old Boys' and Girls' societies still in existence.
Participation	• Massive impact – daily participation compulsory in many public schools. • Full staff involvement.	• Similar in some independent schools today. • KS3 focuses on participation and healthy balanced lifestyles.

Fig 3.6 Impact of the three stages of public school development on physical activity, young people and (stage three) participation. This is not an exhaustive list. You are probably able to think of more impacts

Fig 3.7 The Eton Wall game – an example of a stage one activity with direct links to today.

EXAM TIP

Exam questions could ask you to focus on one phase or to assess change over the three phases. Remember to read the question carefully to determine exactly what you need to do.

STRETCH AND CHALLENGE

Read and reflect on the following items written when athleticism was in full swing. What **values** are being promoted or encouraged?

'As on the one hand it should be remembered that we are boys, and boys at school... so on the other hand we must bear in mind that we form a complete social body... a society, in which... we must not only learn, but act and live, and act and live, not only as boys, but as boys who will be men.'
Rugby School Magazine

'For when the One Great Scorer comes
To write against your name
He marks – not that you won or lost –
But how you played the game.'
Alumnus Football, Grantland Rice (1880–1954)

There's a breathless hush in the Close to-night –
Ten to make and the match to win –
A bumping pitch and a blinding light,
An hour to play and the last man in.
And it's not for the sake of a ribboned coat,
Or the selfish hope of a season's fame,
But his Captain's hand on his shoulder smote
"Play up! play up! and play the game!"

The sand of the desert is sodden red,
Red with the wreck of a square that broke;
The Gatling's jammed and the colonel dead,
And the regiment blind with dust and smoke.
The river of death has brimmed his banks,
And England's far, and Honour a name,
But the voice of schoolboy rallies the ranks,
"Play up! play up! and play the game!"

This is the word that year by year
While in her place the School is set
Every one of her sons must hear,
And none that hears it dare forget.
This they all with a joyful mind
Bear through life like a torch in flame,
And falling fling to the host behind –
"Play up! play up! and play the game!"

Sir Henry Newbolt (1862–1938).

TASK 2

1 Try to think of 8–10 things that increased or decreased in the public schools from stage one to stage three, for example coaching increased and mob games decreased.
2 Create a mnemonic for the word 'ATHLETICISM' by thinking of a character-building value that was thought to be achievable through playing team games. For example 'H' for honour or 'M' for manliness. Learn this to use in your examination.
3 Why do you think that most sports organisations and national governing bodies (NGBs) were formed between 1863 and 1888? (Clue: think about the impact of public schools, the values associated with games, the impact of improved transport and communications and the needs of a modern industrial society.)

Newbolt was educated at Clifton School and Oxford University, after which he became a barrister. He was also a novelist, playwright, magazine editor and poet who supported the virtues of chivalry, loyalty, good manners and sportsmanship combined in the service of the British Empire.

CASE STUDY ACTIVITIES

Table 2 below gives a brief review of the technical development throughout the nineteenth century in public boarding schools. A more detailed analysis can be found in Chapter 4 (page 50).

	Stage one: Bullying and brutality	Stage two: Social control	Stage three: Athleticism
Bathing and swimming	Informal bathing in natural facilities during summer months (mainly for recreation)	More regular and regulated bathing (for hygiene, safety and recreation); increasingly thought to be beneficial as part of a healthy lifestyle	Increased technical development with changing huts, diving boards, purpose-built facilities and competitions; swimming masters (attendants) for teaching and to oversee safety
Athletics	Informal running and exploring the countryside; paper chase (hare and hounds) linked to trespass	Trespass restricted or banned (gave school bad name, irritated neighbouring landowners; against Christian ethics; need to keep boys on site). Hare and hounds and steeple chase continued in more formal style	Steeple chase and cross-country running; annual sports day as major sporting and social occasion
Football	Mob games and the first 'melting pot' of activities from 'home'	More formalised football rules for individual schools (see page 69). Inter-house competitions	Formal Football Association (FA) or Rugby Football Union (RFU) rules along with traditional games at individual schools. 'Colours', caps, inter-school fixtures
Cricket	Cricket – transferred directly into the public schools due to its non-violent nature, rule structure and upper-class involvement in society	Cricket encouraged with massive inter-house participation	Continued technical development such as professional coaching, 'colours,' caps and inter-school fixtures (for example, annually against MCC)
Tennis	Informal hand and ball games against suitable available walls and buildings were referred to as 'fives' or 'tennis' (note: lawn tennis had not yet been invented)	Some fives courts built though fives still an informal activity; game of racquets developing as more formal alternative; also squash racquets	Fives continued as recreational game; racquets a more formal game of higher status. Lawn tennis comparatively low status in boys' schools; very popular as summer game in girls' public schools

Table 2 Technical development of the five case studies

TASK 3

In which of the three stages of development would you place the following (some fit into more than one stage):

- melting pot
- inter-house
- Muscular Christianity
- hooligans
- values
- mob activities
- social control
- character development
- Dr Thomas Arnold
- recreation
- professional coaches.

EXAM TIP

The mnemonic PIES might help you when considering the development of young people or the benefits and values when participating in sports and team games.

Physical
Intellectual
Emotional
Social

STRETCH AND CHALLENGE

Read the following extracts about the development of athleticism at Charterhouse School. To what extent do you feel that Charterhouse mirrored the developmental stages outlined in this chapter?

THE DEVELOPMENT OF ATHLETICISM AT CHARTERHOUSE SCHOOL

BACKGROUND

Charterhouse was founded in 1611 as a combined almshouse for 80 paupers and a school for 40 clever but poor scholars. While Eton bordered the Thames and Windsor Castle, Winchester had its grassy hill and beautiful cathedral, Harrow had its picturesque hill and church, and Westminster had its grand old Abbey and was adjacent to the Houses of Parliament, Charterhouse was founded in the grim neighbourhood of a prison on the site of an old plague pit! Significantly, however, in 1872 after 258 years in London, Charterhouse moved to leafy Godalming in Surrey – and that's when athleticism took off!

STAGE ONE AT CHARTERHOUSE

Low-key activities ranged from playing with hoops, running races and skipping. Dice and card games were forbidden, however, for fear of boys gambling. In terms of facilities, the cloisters were central (see Fig 4.16 on page 68). The Charterhouse cloisters became the venue for a unique game of mob football and also for brutal fights which were officially discouraged but which happened anyway. They were good entertainment and, with few alternatives, were a symbol of courage and justice. There was very little space or grass, but cricket and 'open' football were attempted in spontaneous rather than pre-planned matches. Limited transport and problems of excessive drinking by boys meant that the Charterhouse Headmaster was against inter-school matches.

STAGE TWO AT CHARTERHOUSE

There was still evidence of informal popular reaction-style activities, for example the annual Shrove Tuesday Lemon Peel Fight, which was finally abolished in 1877 after boys were blinded and other severe injuries caused by lemons being loaded with stones. But cloister football was the most prestigious game. Twenty **'fags'** for each team had to guard their goal (a door at each end), while up to fifty other boys spread out waiting for the ball to be introduced halfway up on the open quadrangle side. Then massive scrums lasting up to 45 minutes would result in broken teeth, bloody noses, bruised shins and trampled fags!

Inter-house matches and games clubs had not yet been established at Charterhouse, so different teams such as 'A to K' versus 'Rest of alphabet' or 'Tall' versus 'Short' were concocted. The boys needed a channel for their energy and aggression, and with rebellion almost over and fighting on the wane, cloister football became the natural successor, with cricket as its nationally codified and socially acceptable summer alternative.

STAGE THREE AT CHARTERHOUSE

Athleticism grew out of all proportion in the 25 years after the move to Godalming. Both cloister and open football were played regularly, with cloister football gradually becoming less about brutality and more about character development. In terms of the open game, every public school had their own rules and refused to give them up or to join with others, so when matches were arranged against each other it was chaotic. So, with no hope of agreeing and writing a standardised set of rules directly through the schools, Old Boys were left to set up the Football Association (FA), which they did in 1863.

During the 1850s and 60s, cricket grew as a result of improved transport and communications. William Clarke's All England Cricket XI toured the country and the first England team visited Australia in 1861. There was a parallel development at Charterhouse, with more regular fixtures against schools, local clubs and, of course, the annual match against MCC. Still, it was the cricket captain rather than employed ground staff who organised groups of fags to prepare the pitches. Idiosyncratic school matches still took place occasionally, with 'the First XI with broomsticks' versus 'the Second XI with bats' being a favourite.

Although never officially compulsory at Charterhouse, everyone was expected to play some game every day or nearly every day. Each house interpreted this differently, with one house (Gownboys) requiring all boys in Lower School to score 18 points a week. If they didn't they were beaten with a toasting fork which was apparently worse than being beaten with a cane! A game of football or cricket counted for four points; fives counted as three points; squash racquets two and swimming one. Curiously, merely changing also earned one point, so it seems that merely getting changed 18 times a week avoided contact with the toasting fork. For many, however, such threats were unnecessary and games became their obsession; an obsession that was provided for, systematically administered and still, just about, in check.

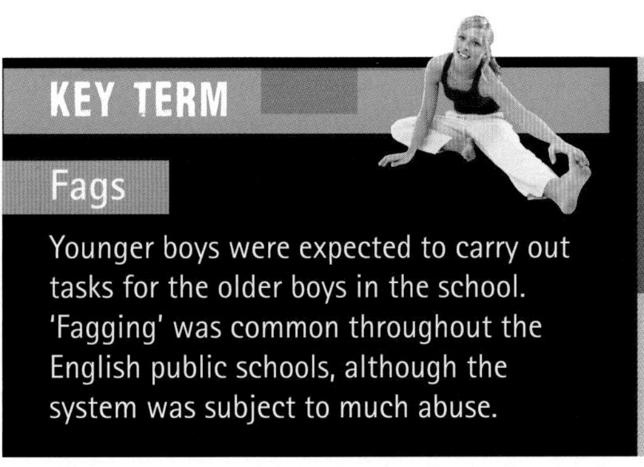

KEY TERM

Fags

Younger boys were expected to carry out tasks for the older boys in the school. 'Fagging' was common throughout the English public schools, although the system was subject to much abuse.

Exam**Café**

Relax, refresh, result!

Refresh your memory

You should now have knowledge and understanding of:

- the characteristics of nineteenth-century public schools
- the impact of the public schools on physical activities in general and on the five case study activities in particular (this will be covered in more detail in Chapter 4)
- the relevance of the Clarendon Report
- how nineteenth-century public schools went through three stages of development:
  - stage one was associated with bullying and brutality
  - stage two was a time when Dr Thomas Arnold established social control
  - stage three was the 'cult' of athleticism when team games were played obsessively by some and for the development of character
- the development of sports and games in each stage
- the impact of the three stages on physical activities, on young people and on participation both in the nineteenth century and now
- the reasons for the slower development of athleticism in girls' public schools compared with boys' public schools
- the meaning of the following terms: athleticism, Muscular Christianity, melting pot, Oxbridge.

REVISE AS YOU GO!

1. Identify four characteristics of early nineteenth-century public schools and explain how each characteristic influenced the development of team games.
2. What is meant by the following terms: melting pot; Muscular Christianity, athleticism, Oxbridge; cult?
3. Who was Dr Thomas Arnold and what did he want to reform?
4. Identify three key features of stage one of development.
5. Identify three key features of stage two of development.
6. What was the role of the sixth form during stage two of development when Dr Thomas Arnold was headmaster of Rugby School?
7. Identify three key features of stage three of development.
8. What is meant by the following terms: technical developments; social relationships; values?
9. How did ex-public school boys influence the spread of team games?
10. Give reasons for the slow development of athleticism and regular participation in sports and games in girls' public schools, as compared with boys' public schools.

Try to answer these questions yourself. Ask your teacher if you need help.

Get the result!

Examination question

Evaluate the impact of public school athleticism on participation in sports and games in the late-nineteenth century. Outline the extent to which the impact of athleticism is still felt in schools today. (6 marks)

Examiner's tips

First, as always, you need to check exactly what you are being asked to do. There are two commands here: *evaluate* and *outline the extent to which*. You must do both to score maximum marks. *Evaluate* is similar to 'weigh up' or 'calculate', so you will 'weigh up' the impact of public school athleticism on participation. As always in historical studies, you will then need to consider the past in the context of the present; here you are being asked to *outline* (summarise quite briefly) *the extent to which* (how great was) *the impact of athleticism is still felt in schools today* (the effect of the past on schools now).

- These commands require high-order thinking skills, so this would probably be a part C question. (Remember, your questions will progress in difficulty often from A, B and C up to 20-mark D.)
- Remember that athleticism was stage three – so don't waste time or effort going into details of stage one or two.
- How many marks are available? – 6.
- A brief plan to structure your thoughts should help you produce a high-quality answer.

Plan for student answer

Impact	Massive
At the time – in the schools	Athleticism involved or led to: • facilities • coaches – professional or assistant masters • inter-house and inter-school fixtures • compulsory/daily participation • Master involvement • but societal change too (e.g. railways).
After they left school – in society	TOP VICC
Impact on schools today	• House system • Sports day • Extra-curricular • Independent schools versus state schools • Coaches then versus SSCOs now

Examiner says:

Great plan – I like your mnemonic TOP VICC to help you remember that ex-university men went on to be **T**eachers, **O**fficers in the army, **P**arents/**P**oliticians, **V**icars, **I**ndustrialists, **C**ommunity members and Community leaders – and that in each of these roles they spread their passion for team games. This is only a 6-mark question, though – you won't need (or have time to) evaluate each one. Remember, it's fine to plan your answer, but you must always answer in full sentences.

The impact of late-nineteenth-century athleticism on participation in sports and games was phenomenal, both in the schools at the time and in society at large. The impact is still felt in schools today.

Examiner says:

Great introduction – you have basically answered the question in your opening paragraph – now you can pick it apart and do the evaluation.

Athleticism (linked to both physical endeavour and moral integrity) involved a passion for team sports by both boys and masters. By now, Headmasters believed participation in team games was crucial to the development of character. This adult support and involvement helped to drive the success of

Examiner says:

This is all true and provides useful context. However, it may be slightly away from the precise question set, so be careful to stay within your timings.

athleticism – especially after the boys left school and took their games to university.

These schools had great provision which helped participation. Because they had money (mirrored by most independent schools today), they had enough land for several pitches and could build specialist facilities such as swimming baths. Moreover, they could employ professional coaches in, for example, cricket, who would become role models and inspire both participation and high quality performance. Other coaching was done by young graduates from Oxbridge who had a teaching role but were fully involved in games (again, as in many independent schools today). Other graduates spread athleticism as vicars or wealthy generous industrialists who set up parish or works teams thereby increasing participation in the community.

In most schools participation was compulsory every day, which obviously had a positive impact on participation. All boys played for their house while the best played for their school. By now, improved transport and communications contributed too, which really helped athleticism to make its mark and for participation to grow.

Many schools today still have a house system, often have athletics sports days (as in the 1880s) and independent schools particularly have the provision for regular participation with high quality coaching and facilities. State schools may have less good provision but even they have school sports co-ordinators, who you could argue have a similar role to play to the visiting coaches in the late-nineteenth century.

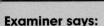

Examiner says:

It is interesting that your plan suggests that you expected to refer to today in a final paragraph tagged on to the end. To refer to today at relevant points throughout your answer like this is more effective – even though a bit harder. Well done.

Examiner says:

Your comment about the railways shows good contextual understanding and analysis, and again you have drawn your point back to participation.

Examiner says:

I'm glad you drew your key point back to the question set with the words 'so increasing participation'. Good.

Examiner says:

You have linked 'then' to 'now' very well.

- Your quality of written communication is very good.
- Your plan definitely helped bring structure and clarity to your answer.
- A short concluding sentence or two would have been great.
- Take care with your time keeping – remember, you have approximately 50 minutes for your historical studies question, which includes the long 20-mark part D.

Overall, this is an excellent answer – well done!

CHAPTER 4:

Case studies

LEARNING OBJECTIVES

By the end of this chapter you should have knowledge and understanding of:

- the five case study activities – bathing and swimming, athletics, football, cricket and tennis
- how these activities developed to the present day through the following stages: popular recreation, via the public schools and rational recreation
- how to analyse each activity as a pre-industrial popular recreation
- how to assess the influence of nineteenth-century public schools on each activity
- how to demonstrate knowledge and understanding of each activity as a rational recreation
- participation and barriers to participation in each activity today.

INTRODUCTION

Remember – you would expect the five case study activities to have at least some of the characteristics shown in Table 1.

As popular recreations:	As rational recreations:
• local	• regional, national or even international
• with simple unwritten rules	• with written (NGB) rules
• cruel and/or violent	• refined and respectable
• occasional	• regular
• divided by class (courtly and popular or high and low)	• divided by status (amateur and professional)
• rural	• urban or suburban
• occupational	• some (working-class) professionals
• wagering	• less wagering

Table 1 Characteristics of popular recreation and rational recreation

What about each of the five case study activities in the UK today?

- You need knowledge and understanding of both participation and barriers to participation in each activity today.
- You need to be aware of factors that have helped to develop each activity and contemporary participation and performance.

You will remember some general factors from your AS socio-cultural studies work. They relate to opportunity, provision and esteem, and are reviewed in Table 2 overleaf.

Fig 4.1 Access: three variables

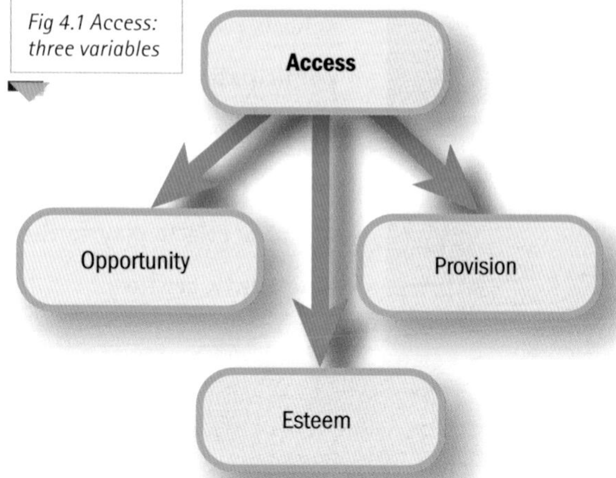

Factors relating to opportunity, provision and esteem that can influence mass participation and sporting excellence	
Mass participation	**Sporting excellence**
OPPORTUNITY – having the chance to take part and/or get to the top	
Disposable income	Funding and financial support, e.g. National Lottery or sponsorship money
Ability, skill, health or fitness or playing standard	Skill level and performance lifestyle
The amount of time available after work and other commitments	Chance to train full time
Do you actually want to take part? Are suitable and appealing activities available?	Whether individuals choose to make the sacrifices and give the all-round commitment needed to get to the top
PROVISION – having the conditions or physical tools to take part and/or get to the top	
The presence or absence of suitable equipment and/ or facilities	The availability of world-class facilities and equipment
Access – for example for wheelchairs if necessary	The availability of sport science and other 'high tech' support, e.g. modern technological products
Availability of suitable transport – privately owned or public transport	Distance from or access to high performance or National Institute centres, e.g. the National Tennis Centre in Roehampton, southwest London; warm weather or high altitude training venues for athletes
Suitable and available clubs, activities, leagues, competitions or courses nearby	Suitable and regular competitions with and against other high-level performers
The right coaching at the right level by suitably qualified staff	The right highly qualified and experienced coaches
Well-maintained and equipped, private and clean changing and social areas	Performance lifestyle advice and a holistic approach to excellence
ESTEEM – issues to do with respect, admiration, value and appreciation; the perception that society has of an individual or group affects their chances both of taking part and of achieving excellence	
Self-confidence and self-belief – which influences self perception	Self-confidence and self-belief, which impact on performance
Respect from others and social acceptance of everyone's 'right' to take part in any chosen activity	Respect from others – including team mates, opponents and the media
Positive or negative perceptions of certain physical activities	Recent results (good and/or bad) and national and international ranking
Status in society, for example whether from a disadvantaged group	Status in the sporting world

Table 2 Factors relating to opportunity, provision and esteem that can influence mass participation and sporting excellence

In addition to the contemporary factors shown in Table 2, the impact of the following factors on participation can be considered.

Children	• Mini versions of the activities • Children's holiday clubs and parties
Schools	• Positive or negative school experience • Whether the activity is compulsory on the National Curriculum • Strength/success of school club links and work of SSCOs • Passion and commitment of individual teachers • Impact of independent schools boosting local provision as part of their qualification for charitable status; for example, offering times when their tennis courts are available to local schools and clubs
Clubs	• Whether clubs get club mark status; for example, in cricket there are approximately ten focus clubs per county that are responsible for increasing participation locally • The quality of programmes/provision at local clubs or centres
Academies	• Whether the sport has an academy structure (for example, football, rugby, cricket) whereby talented youngsters sign up with clubs and receive the highest quality support • The down side is that the club might then pressure the young person not to play for their school or with their friends
Facilities and equipment	• Improved technology such as Astroturf, clothing or titanium • Cheaper versions of equipment available • The presence or absence of provision for disability sport
Organisation	• Private or NGB campaigns and initiatives • Local authority provision such as ladies-only or novice events • NGB coaching course opportunities and the change in Level One coaching courses, which makes it easier for non-specialists to become coaches. This should help to increase community participation • Provision of competitions, leagues and tournaments for young people
The golden triangle	• Media coverage, for example impact of having netball on Sky TV or the glamorisation of top-level sport particularly with HD televisions • Whether the sport is on Sky TV only, or available to all through the terrestrial channels • Impact of specialist magazines and press coverage • The presence or absence of role models and their success, such as Christine Ohuruogu, Rebecca Adlington and other Team GB athletes • Sponsorship • Lottery funding – both for community provision at the base of the sports development pyramid and for elite performers at the top, some of whom are able to train full-time without the need for a paid job
Additional factors	• Whether the activity is a lifetime sport, such as swimming or tennis, or a sport mainly limited to younger or middle-aged players such as football • Provision and organisation of development for young people such as whether the activity has academies throughout the country • There is a vast number of alternative choices for young people in contemporary Britain other than participation in sport/physical activity

Table 3 Participation and barriers to participation today

Bathing and swimming as a popular recreation

In the Middle Ages (c.1200–1500), towns were built at defensive sites and river crossing points. Bathing for pleasure was common, especially on hot summer days. As well as a natural playground, the river provided a ready supply of food, a means of transport and a place to wash. It was the commercial centre of the area. With work, play and the river so inter-related, learning to swim for safety also became a necessity. In the natural environment, it was as important to swim as to run!

'Take two strong men and in Temese cast them,
And both naked as a needle, their non sikerer than another;
The one hath cunnynge and can swymme and dyve,
The other is lewd of that laboure, lerned never to swym.
Which trowest of these two in Temese is most in dred,
He that never dived he nought can of swymmyng,
Or the swimmer that is safe if he himself lyke?'

A sixteenth-century writer, quoted by Joseph Strutt in *Sports and Pastimes of the People of England* (1830)

Just as the Roman nobility had done, the English aristocracy of the Middle Ages considered the ability to swim as part of their **chivalric code**.

TASK 1

In pairs, try to interpret the sixteenth-century English verse above in order to understand one person's view of swimming in the 1500s.

REMEMBER

Link bathing with recreation, survival and health. Also note the early development of competitive swimming at this time.

They would sometimes sponsor (or 'patronise') outstanding lower-class swimmers to represent them in wager races. They would also act as patrons to prize fighters, rowers and runners. These swimmers might become swimming 'masters', as described by Norman Wymer below. Charles II (1660–85) even established a series of fashionable swimming contests on the Thames and the first open-air swimming bath was built in London in 1784.

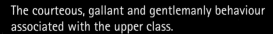

KEY TERM

Chivalric code

The courteous, gallant and gentlemanly behaviour associated with the upper class.

'All who dwelt by the river, or earned their living on it, now took out a form of insurance for their own safety, so that wherever there was a river or lake – or indeed, any suitable stretch of water – there would usually be found a band of swimming masters to teach the art to every local child, from the sons of the squire to the lowliest peasant. Many strokes were taught and if the child appeared particularly nervous or lacking in confidence they would fasten a bundle of bull rushes or a line of corks to his body to give him greater buoyancy.'

Extract from Norman Wymer, *Sport in England: A History of Two Thousand Years of Games and Pastimes* (1949)

ALSO NEAR THE RIVER

Throughout history, various other sports and pastimes have centred on the riverside, particularly in river loops and adjacent water meadows. These areas of common land had no trees or agriculture so provided a large flat space for casual, informal games, athletic sports, horse racing and shooting. They were liable to flooding, so in frozen conditions they also provided a shallow and relatively safe natural facility for sliding and skating. In 1896, *Cassell's Complete Book of Sports and Pastimes* included the advice that 'the boy who had never in his early days enjoyed a good slide is never very likely to enjoy any manly out-door exercise.' Occasionally, the river itself froze, providing a surface for multi-sports festivals called frost fairs or ice fairs. Pictures of Thames frost fairs in the 1600s show a variety of fairground stalls, bull baiting, prize fighting, sliding, football and feasting. When the Thames froze in 1813 a four-day frost fair was set up.

Fig 4.2 The Harrow Duck Puddle

TASK 2

To what extent did early swimming and bathing fit the normally accepted model of popular recreation? Work in pairs, and refer to Table 1 on page 50.

INFLUENCE OF THE PUBLIC SCHOOLS

At the beginning of the nineteenth century, bathing in public schools was spontaneous, unorganised and centred around natural facilities such as local rivers or ponds. Boys had swum in the open at home and brought this culture to school, bathing in their free time and with no master input or supervision. The river was a place to wash and have fun. As the century progressed and athleticism developed, swimming became more structured and regulated with natural facilities, such as the River Wey at Charterhouse or the Duck Puddle at Harrow, being transformed (often thanks to Old Boys' donations) into major bathing facilities with changing huts, diving boards, swimming instructors and competitions.

In terms of values and status, headmasters increasingly regarded swimming as a necessary athletic, as well as a safe and hygienic pursuit, and they followed contemporary fashion in believing water immersion to be therapeutic. No doubt the boys also enjoyed the excitement and relative freedom of swimming, especially once organised lessons and regular competitions were established.

> *'Ducker lies just across the road, and therein swimming, diving, and racing of all kinds is practised. Every boy, unless he holds a medical certificate, is compelled to learn to swim, though the distance which qualifies for a pass is not great. On a hot holiday afternoon, boys lounge there for hours, sometimes in the water and sometimes wrapped in their large ducker towels lying on the warm pavement, eating the "tuck" they are careful to provide for themselves.'*

From an article in the Harrow School magazine in the late 1800s

	Stage one: Bullying and brutality	Stage two: Social control	Stage three: Athleticism
Bathing and swimming	Informal bathing in natural facilities during summer months (mainly for recreation). In this way, very similar to popular recreation	More regular and regulated bathing (for hygiene, safety and recreation); increasingly thought to be beneficial as part of a healthy lifestyle	Increased technical development with changing huts, diving boards, purpose-built facilities and competitions. Swimming masters (attendants) for teaching and to oversee safety

Table 4 Bathing and swimming in the public schools – nineteenth-century developments

Fig 4.3 Bathing place at Charterhouse School

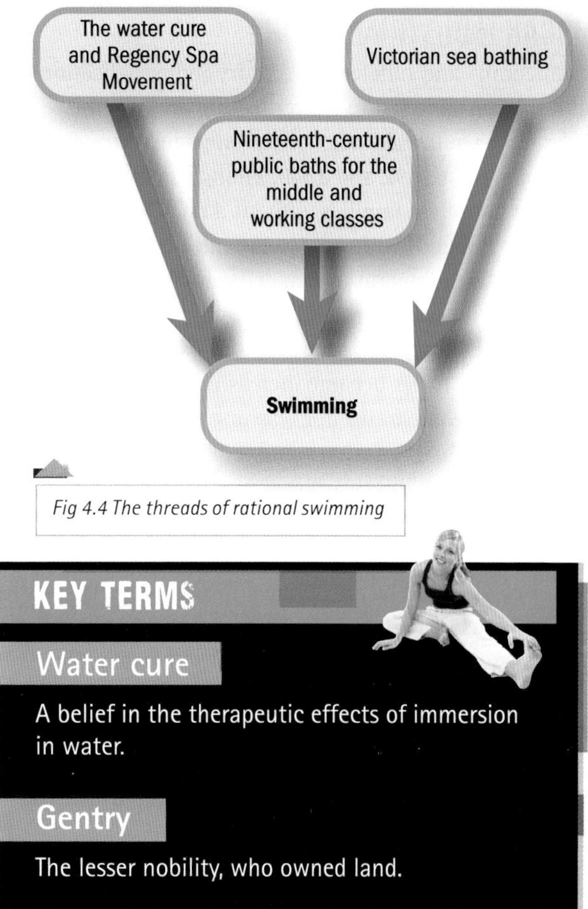

Fig 4.4 The threads of rational swimming

Safety was vital. A well-maintained and safe bathing place gave a good impression at a time of stiff competition between schools. Is this similar today? Even more impressive would have been purpose-built swimming baths, such as those built at Charterhouse in 1863. In comparison to major team games, however, the overall status of swimming and bathing was limited.

TASK 3

In pairs, discuss:

a) why swimming was considered valuable in late-nineteenth-century public schools
b) why swimming had less status than cricket, rugby or football.

KEY TERMS

Water cure

A belief in the therapeutic effects of immersion in water.

Gentry

The lesser nobility, who owned land.

Bathing and swimming as rational recreations

There are several roots to swimming as a rationalised activity. The **water cure** was popular in inland spas such as Bath and Cheltenham, which grew into large and prestigious resorts for the well-to-do. By the mid-nineteenth century the newly-emerged middle class started to take over these inland spas and chose them as sites for their new schools (for example, Clifton, Cheltenham and Malvern Colleges).

The **gentry**, meanwhile, had moved onto continental spas and to the English seaside, whose cold, salt-water, winter cure was now thought to have the most therapeutic effect. With the restrictive ethics of the Victorian era in full swing, beaches were designated as socially exclusive and single-sexed to ensure modesty and respectability. Bathing machines (wooden changing huts which were towed to the water) gave bathers some privacy, so mixed bathing was eventually allowed. By the 1870s the new rail network brought the working class to the seaside. They were keen to copy the activities of their social superiors, but also sought health and recreation.

Meanwhile, bathing facilities in river towns had started to become organised. Floating baths were built (two platforms at right angles to the bank with a chain across the open end) which increased respectability and safety. Swimming became fashionable for the middle class, and amateur swimming as an organised competitive event began with the formation of clubs and the re-establishment of some of the old swimming festivals.

URBAN INDUSTRIAL TOWNS

Eighteenth- and nineteenth-century industrialisation and urbanisation led to overcrowding and disease. Two major outbreaks of cholera rampaged through the country in 1832 and 1849, killing thousands and leaving countless families without a breadwinner. The first Public Health Act (1848) and the building of public baths sought to reduce such problems.

As only wealthy people could afford bathrooms at home and rivers became increasingly unsafe for poorer people to use for washing, central government had to take a stand. Politicians were keen to improve the cleanliness and health of the urban masses and so gave loans to town councils to build public baths on the understanding that the lower class would be encouraged to wash. The first public baths were opened in Liverpool in 1828 and the Baths and Wash-Houses Act of 1846 was really the start of bathing and swimming in industrial Britain. Public baths had first-class facilities for the fashionable middle class (whose plunge pools facilitated the development of indoor amateur swimming clubs and galas) and second-class facilities for the working class, who paid 1d (one penny) to hire a bathroom and to wash their clothes. Most of the loans were settled quickly and this attempt to encourage regular bathing, to prevent the spread of disease and to increase labour efficiency seemed to pay off as work efficiency increased and absenteeism from ill health decreased. An elaborate public baths would also increase the status of a town.

Fig 4.5 A late-nineteenth-century plunge bath

In 1869, various middle-class swimming clubs met to establish laws for amateur swimming, and in 1874 they were renamed the Swimming Association of Great Britain, which became the Amateur Swimming Association (ASA) in 1884. By 1902 over 500 clubs were members of the amateur association. While middle-class swimmers (like athletes and rowers) were initially determined to exclude the lower class, by the 1880s some of this exclusivity had diminished, and swimming and water polo clubs were becoming established for the working classes with the grudging support of the ASA. (See page 63 in this chapter for details of the exclusion clause linked with rational athletics.)

REMEMBER

- Towns grew and became overcrowded as a result of industrialisation.
- With industrialisation, many rivers and natural water supplies became polluted and unsuitable for washing.
- Public baths were built to improve public health.
- The Wash House Act of 1846 allowed local authorities to apply for grants to provide public washing facilities.
- Most major towns built a public bath which often included hot and cold water baths and/ or plunge baths as well as a public wash house with laundry and drying facilities.
- Baths had first- and second-class facilities which meant that the working class could afford the one-penny entrance fee ('penny baths').
- Plunge baths for swimming recreationally were added later.
- The Amateur Swimming Association (ASA) was formed in 1884.
- Public baths in urban industrial towns:
  - helped to stop the spread of disease
  - were eventually used for washing, recreation and sport.

EXAM TIP

Exam questions linked to bathing and swimming as a rational recreation will focus on developments in urban industrial towns. Candidates sometimes get muddled and incorrectly write about the water cure, the Regency Spa movement and Victorian sea bathing. This is background information that is not directly mentioned in your specification and so will not be directly examined.

Swimming today

Your specification says:	Factors that have helped develop bathing and swimming in the UK and the impact of these factors on contemporary participation and performance
General:	See pages 51 and 52 for features relating to opportunity, provision and esteem that might encourage or prevent participation in swimming today
Participation in swimming today:	Recommended and popular since easy on joints as a non-weight-bearing activity and a lifelong physical activity
Factors that have helped develop swimming and the impact of these factors on participation and performance:	• Pool technology including hoists for disabled people and modern teaching and learning aids – likely to increase participation • Improved material technology for clothing, which increases times, breaks records and increases interest in the sport • Leisure pools offering family entertainment with flumes, wave machines, 'splash time,' children's swim parties and so on – likely to increase participation • Blue Flag beaches indicating that water is safer/more pleasant for bathing – likely to increase participation • Continued awareness of safety – access to pools for families who holiday abroad • Antenatal and parent and baby/toddler classes, aqua aerobics and so on – likely to increase participation • Government targets for more pools, upgrade of existing pools and plans for more Olympic and 50m pools • Growth in number of health clubs and spas with swimming facilities and good changing provision – likely to increase participation • Government initiative for free entry to pools (initially for U16s and O60s) likely to increase participation • Success and inspiration of swimmers such as Michael Phelps (USA), and Rebecca Adlington (Team GB) in the Beijing Olympics 2008 and Eleanor Simmonds (Team GB) in the Beijing Paralympics • Increasing popularity and success of triathlon events (see athletics)
Specific factors that might be a barrier to participation in swimming today:	• Nature of activity (individual and in water) – some people may choose alternative activities that are arguably more sociable • Esteem – embarrassment or limited confidence due to poor body image • Limited media coverage, so impact of role models restricted to major world competitions • Cultural factors/ethnicity – e.g. reluctance to take part by some Asian females • Risk and pollution associated with seas and rivers

Table 5 Swimming and bathing today – factors affecting participation

EXAM TIP

Other relevant contemporary factors not identified in Table 5 can gain credit in your exam.

'Public swimming pools and lidos will be free for everyone by 2012 as part of a drive to get more people involved in sport.

The over-60s and children up to the age of 16 will be the first to enjoy free entry to council-run swimming pools, under Government plans to be announced. Local authorities are to be invited to apply to a £130 million fund over the next two years, to allow them to offer free swimming to older people in their area. Additional funds will be made available through a 'challenge fund' to extend the offer to under-16s as well. More funding will be available for councils to refurbish pools, many of which date back to the Victorian era. The announcement is being made as part of the Olympic Legacy Action Plan and which spells out the Government's plans to meet the target of getting two million more people involved in sport by the 2012 London games.

At present, 50 per cent of us take part in no sporting activity at all, and the Government believes that swimming is one of the most accessible ways for people, and particularly the elderly, to get fit.

A spokesman for the Department said: 'Swimming is a great sport because anyone can do it, even people with creaky bones. Free swimming will be particularly rejuvenating to older people, which is why they are being given access first. But the ambition is that as a long-term goal, but not later than 2012, public pools around the country will be free to all.'

Rosa Prince, 6 June 2008, www.telegraph.co.uk/news/uknews/2080781/Public-swimming-pools-to-be-free-of-charge.html

Fig 4.6 Contemporary leisure pool

Athletics as a popular recreation

FOLK SPORTS AND WAKES

A large range of popular games and contests were played in Britain before the advent of modern sports, many of which can be viewed as seeds from which rationalised athletics grew. Folk sports associated with annual parish feasts and fairs have already been mentioned (see Chapter 1, page 9). There were also hiring fairs and village wakes. Farm labourers and servants could be sacked at a moment's notice and if they had to find a new employer they could go to the nearest hiring or 'mop' fair. There they would stand in line, offering their services as maid, cook, shepherd or ploughman for example. Wakes originated from the time of **paganism**, when the fear of evil was great and superstitions were widespread. Wakes were annual religious celebrations, in thanksgiving for the harvest and for Christianity in the community. In harsh times, they were also an opportunity to pray for survival. Praise and worship were always followed by festivity and feasting.

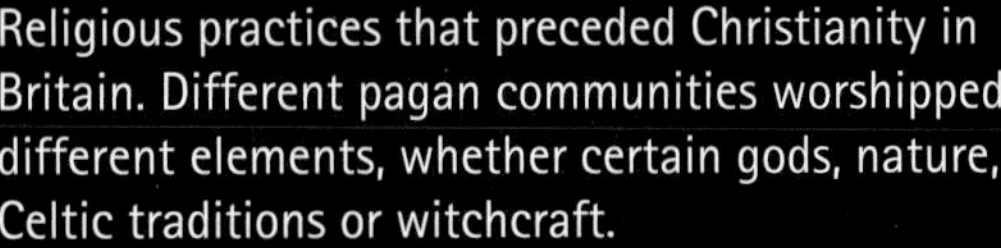

KEY TERM

Paganism

Religious practices that preceded Christianity in Britain. Different pagan communities worshipped different elements, whether certain gods, nature, Celtic traditions or witchcraft.

A traditional wake was a great social occasion, bringing all parts of the community together. These local events were associated with all kinds of excess such as drinking, blood sports and promiscuity. They were also opportunities for men to test their strength and prove their speed and virility in events such as stick fighting, wrestling and running. More playfully they would also try to catch pigs whose tails had been soaped and compete in whistling matches and grinning contests! Prizes were generally of practical use; shirts, smocks, hats, cheeses or joints of meat, for example. Free to be athletic and not yet restrained by nineteenth-century Victorian ethics, peasant women would also race.

> *'Nothing is more usual than for a nimble-footed wench to get a husband at the same time as she wins a smock.'*
>
> Peter Lovesey, *The Official Centenary History of the Amateur Athletic Association* (1979)

The Reformed Church frowned upon traditional wakes, and by the mid-nineteenth century fêtes and tea parties were organised as respectable alternatives that were much more suited to increasingly refined times. Many continue today.

The Cotswold Games, revived by Robert Dover in Gloucestershire in 1604, attracted huge crowds to watch contests of leaping, shin-kicking, wrestling, coursing and jousting. It attracted both upper- and lower-class participants. These 'Dover' games survived until the mid-nineteenth century, when rowdy Black Country families arrived by train, caused havoc and the event's suspension.

Fig 4.7 A smock race, early nineteenth century

You will remember from your AS socio-cultural studies that the Much Wenlock Olympian Games emerged from a rural sports festival, and when revived by Dr Penny Brookes in 1850 they became a highly respected rival to athletic developments at Oxford and Cambridge universities. Brookes was keen to add a pure form of athletics to traditional events, so along with twenty-a-side football matches, an old woman's race for a pound of tea, a blindfold wheelbarrow race and chasing a cornered pig, there were more refined running, jumping and throwing events.

REMEMBER

The Cotswold Games and Much Wenlock Olympian Games were relevant to your AS socio-cultural studies and link to the background to the Modern Olympic Games.

TASK 4

Read the description of the Hungerford Revels below. To what extent does this occasion 'fit' with the commonly accepted characteristics of popular recreation? (Consider the following: local; occasional; cruel, violent; wagering; rural; courtly/popular; with simple unwritten rules. and so on.)

THE HUNGERFORD REVELS

Wiltshire consists of beautiful and extensive downs, and rich meadow and pasture lands, which support some of the finest dairies and farms that can be met within the kingdom. The natives are a very strong and hardy set of men, and are particularly fond of robust sports; their chief and favourite amusement is back-swording, or singlestick, for which they are as greatly celebrated as the inhabitants of the adjoining counties, Somersetshire and Gloucestershire.

At this game there are several rules observed. They play with a large round stick, which must be three feet long, with a basket prefixed to one end as a guard for the hand. The combatants throw off their hats and upper garments, with the exception of the shirt, and have the left hand tied to the side, so that they cannot defend themselves with that hand. They brandish the stick over the head, guarding off the adversary's blows, and striking him whenever the opportunity occurs. Great skill is often used in the defence. I have seen two men play for upward of half an hour without once hitting each other. The blood must flow an inch from some part of the head, before either party is declared victor...

But Hungerford revel is not a scene of contention alone; it consists of all kinds of rustic sports, which afford capital fun to the spectators. They may be laid out thus:

First – Girls running for 'smocks', which is a well-knows amusement at country fairs.
Second – Climbing the greasy pole for a piece of bacon which is placed on the top. This affords very great amusement, as it is a difficult thing to be accomplished.
Third – Old women drinking hot tea for snuff. Whoever can drink it the quickest and hottest gains the prize.
Fourth – Griming through horse-collars. Several Hodges stand in a row, each holding a collar; whoever can make the ugliest face through it gains the prize. This feat is also performed by old women, and certainly the latter are the most amusing.
Fifth – Racing between twenty and thirty old women for a pound of tea. This occasions much merriment, and it is sometimes astonishing to see with what agility the old dames run in order to obtain the prize.
Sixth – Hunting a pig with a soaped tail. This amusement creates much mirth, and in my opinion is the most laughable.
Seventh – Jumping in sacks for cheese. Ten or eleven candidates are chosen; they are tied in sacks up to their necks, and have to jump about five hundred yards. It is truly laughable.
Eighth – Donkey racing. I will certainly defy anyone to witness these races, without being almost convulsed with laughter. Each candidate rides his neighbour's donkey, and he who arrives first at the appointed place claims the prize, which is generally a smock-frock, a waistcoat, a hat, etc.
Ninth – Duck hunting. This is very laughable, but certainly a very cruel amusement. They tie a poor unfortunate owl in an upright position, to the back of a still more unfortunate duck and then turn them loose. The owl presuming that his inconvenient captivity is the work of the duck, very unceremoniously commences an attack on the head of the latter, who naturally takes to its own means of defence. The poor animals generally destroy each other, unless some humane person rescues them.

A contemporary observer's description of the Hungerford Revels of 1826

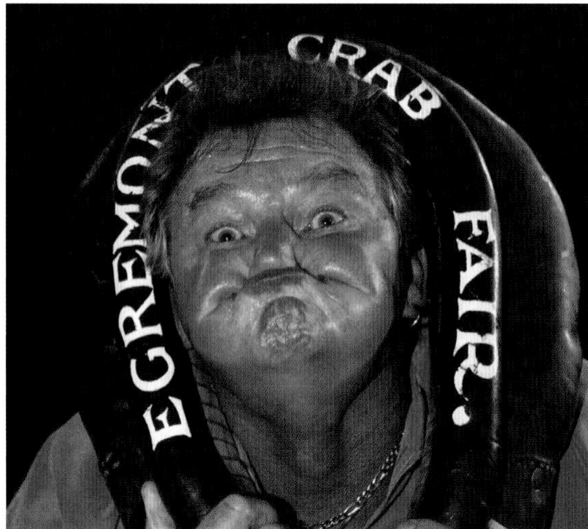

Fig 4.8 Gurning through a horse collar

TASK 5

Hold a whistling match and grinning contest in your class.

- In a whistling match, a number of contestants try to whistle to the end of a selected tune without interruption while a fun-loving 'merry Andrew' tries to make them laugh.
- In grinning or 'gurning' contests, contestants must pull the funniest or ugliest face they can. Instead of holding the customary horse collar try using hoops.

Judges award prizes to winners!

PEDESTRIANISM

Perhaps the most obvious ancestor to modern athletics is pedestrianism. From the late-seventeenth century the gentry employed footmen as messengers and competitive runners. Athletic success was seen as a way of enhancing a gentleman's social status. Pedestrian races attracted wagers of up to 1000 guineas (a guinea is worth just over £1), so a good living could be earned by a small number of professional athletes each being promoted by a gentry patron. As these events increased in popularity, large venues such as Newmarket Racecourse and the Agricultural Hall in Islington, London, were used. Men of all backgrounds competed. For example, Scottish landowner Robert Barclay Allardice attracted a crowd of over 10,000 in 1809 when he walked 1000 miles in 1000 hours (equivalent to about a month without a night's sleep!). Aided by supporters who slapped him round the face to keep him awake, and a pair of pistols to combat the gangs who attempted to stop him, Barclay managed to pull it off. For the next 40 years pedestrianism grew in popularity. Gambling was a key feature and for those accustomed to poverty and hardship, winning could mean the difference between starvation and survival.

The largest bets were for one-man challenges against the clock or calendar, though head-to-head matches were also popular. In addition to the more serious races, many novelty races were held, such as walking backwards, pushing wheelbarrows and gathering potatoes. For example, a 13-year-old named Mountjoy Jr. twice completed a 64-mile return trip between Swansea and Neath (south Wales) within the space of a few days in March 1844. During the challenge he managed one 45-minute period of running half-a-mile forwards, walking three-quarters of a mile backwards, running and hopping 100 yards each, picking up 100 eggs with his mouth, and finally clearing twenty hurdles.

Pedestrianism had its problems. Trickery was commonplace, with speedy amateurs entering races using false names, professionals impersonating unknown amateurs, and a lot of match-fixing, while riots amongst the crowds also brought the sport into disrepute.

Fig 4.9 Captain Robert Barclay Allardice (1779–1854) won £16,000 by walking 1000 miles in 1000 hours in 1809.

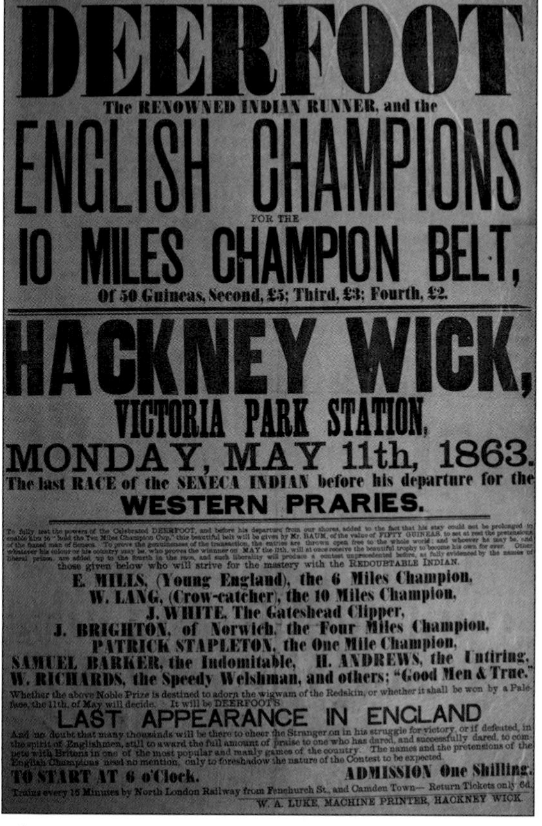

Fig 4.10 Bill poster for a head-to-head pedestrian contest, 1862

In the 1860s the great athlete Deerfoot visited England. This American Indian attracted huge crowds and along with other Victorian professionals he helped to inspire early amateur athletes.

REMEMBER

Early athletics involved community events, rural sporting festivals, commercial fairs and wakes as well as pedestrianism.

TASK 6

In pairs, consider what you think were the Church's views on activities such as rural sports, festivals and wakes which were linked with community events?

INFLUENCE OF THE PUBLIC SCHOOLS

Eighteenth-century public school boys took the sports of their local village wakes and fairs back to school after the holidays. They played them for fun and to relieve the boredom of early nineteenth-century school life. With no stabling or kennels at school, fox hunting could not be adopted. Instead it was adapted to 'hare and hounds', where the human 'hare' would run ahead and drop 'scent' (paper) for the 'hounds' (other schoolboys) to follow. Initially headmasters were against hare and hounds as it annoyed neighbouring farmers, led to truancy, gave the school a bad name and boys would often use their textbooks for the 'scent'!

Fig 4.11 The Rugby School paper chase champion of 1886 (stage three – athleticism)

'Long runs, steady exercise, careful diet, and especially early hours of bed-time are requisite to prepare for a severe Hare and Hound match... nothing but pluck and stamina combined brings the leaders to their places of honour at the finish.'

Advice from *Cassell's Sports and Pastimes* (1896)

	Stage one: Bullying and brutality	Stage two: Social control	Stage three: Athleticism
Athletics	Informal running and exploring the countryside; paper chase (hare and hounds) linked to trespass	Trespass restricted or banned. Hare and hounds and steeple chase continued more formally	Steeple chase and cross-country running; annual sports day as major sporting and social occasion

Table 6 The development of athletics in the public schools

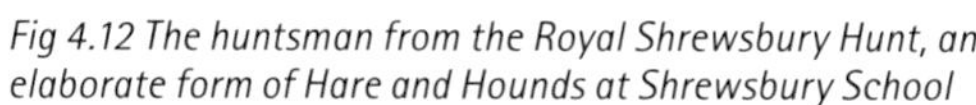

Fig 4.12 The huntsman from the Royal Shrewsbury Hunt, an elaborate form of Hare and Hounds at Shrewsbury School

EXETER COLLEGE, OXFORD

A more refined form of athletics came to public schools from Exeter College, Oxford, in 1850. A group of undergraduates, disappointed by their poor riding in the traditional steeplechase, ran in a 'foot grind' across country, and also staged an Autumn Meeting. The meeting followed the format of a Jockey Club meet, even to the weighing of top runners and the inclusion of a Consolation Stakes for beaten 'horses'. In spite of some concern by the school authorities that such events would lead to betting, the idea was soon copied, and by the 1870s athletic sports days had become both a major social occasion and a symbol of a more modern age. Unusually the impact here was from the universities back to the schools rather than the other way around (as it was for football and rugby, for example).

School sports days represented an era of technical advancement, more friendly social relationships between boys and masters, and a developing interest in skilfulness over brute force. They were also a useful day for the Headmaster to proudly display his school and to tout for financial support. Sports days were highly organised with elaborate ribboned programmes, press coverage, large numbers of spectators and often a military band.

REMEMBER

Athletics in public schools included hare and hounds, steeplechase and athletics sports days.

TASK 7

1 How were the character-building values of athleticism, so easily linked to football, rugby and cricket, achievable through athletics?
2 How did the status of athletics compare with:
   a) football and rugby
   b) cricket
   c) fives?

Athletics as a rational recreation

The steady urbanisation of England led first to the end of rural fairs and then to professional athletics becoming established in the big industrial cities. The lower class took to running as a source of income, even though the winnings were small by pre-Victorian standards (when pedestrianism was still thriving). Exploitation was rife, just as it was with pedestrianism. 'Roping' (holding back in order to lose), 'running to the book' (disguising one's form to keep a generous handicap) and 'ringing in' (where promoters conspired to size the handicapping unfairly) were widespread.

The first purpose-built tracks were built in the late 1830s, and by 1850 most major cities had a facility. Carefully-measured tracks led to more stringent timekeeping and the beginning of record keeping, so that by mid-century up to 25,000 would watch and wager on a single race.

EXCLUSION CLAUSE

Ex-university gentleman amateurs who wanted to compete against one another without having to mix with professionals formed the Amateur Athletics Club (AAC) in 1866. They were desperate to dissociate respectable modern athletics from the old corrupted professional form and so adopted the 'exclusion clause', which was already used by the Amateur Rowing Association (ARA). The exclusion clause was a device by upper-class administrators to exclude manual workers from sports associations. It was used particularly in athletics and rowing where amateurism was explained as follows:

> *'No person should be considered an amateur who had ever competed in an open competition for a stake, money or entrance fee, who had ever competed with or against a professional for any prize, who had ever taught, pursued or assisted in the practice of athletic exercises of any kind as a means of gaining a livelihood, been employed in or about boats for money or wages, or had been by trade or employment for wages, a mechanic, artisan or labourer.'*
>
> Exclusion clause adopted by the Amateur Athletics Club in 1866

TASK 8

With reference to Fig 4.14 above, try to explain the different motives for participation by both gentlemen amateur and professional athletes.

Fig 4.14 Six-day pedestrian race, the Royal Agricultural Hall, London, 1870 showing both gentlemen amateur and professional athletes.

In other words, the working classes could not join!

The Amateur Athletics Association (AAA) was established in 1880. This organisation was responsible for opening up the sport to all levels of society without compromising its upright image. So, the exclusion clause was withdrawn and a professional became someone who ran for money rather than someone from the lower classes.

Fig 4.13 The various aspects of athletics operating by the last quarter of the nineteenth century

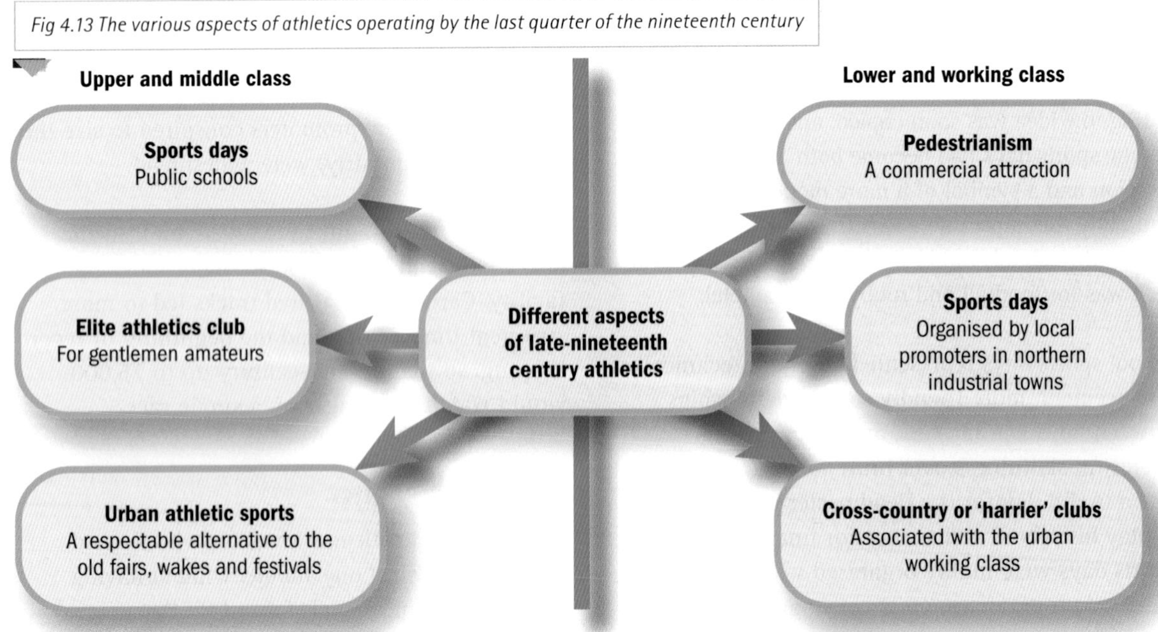

EXAM TIP

There is no great need to remember dates. It is much more important to understand and remember details of themes, such as the development of professionalism and detail of opportunities for working-class involvement in athletics in post-industrial Britain.

THE MODERN OLYMPIC GAMES

From your AS socio-cultural studies work, you will remember that the Modern Olympic Games was inspired by sport in the English public schools, and that Baron Pierre de Coubertin started the Modern Olympics in 1896 aiming to foster patriotism, athleticism and friendship between nations.

Unfortunately for de Coubertin, by the time the Games came to London in 1908 those ideals had largely been crushed, and international sport had become both an agent of international peace in a world moving towards war and a means of reviving national morale. This move was set against the public school ideal of playing sport honourably and for its own sake. Remember the gentleman amateur did not compete for extrinsic rewards, train seriously or aim to win at all costs.

This conflict was captured in the film *Chariots of Fire* (1981) that follows the preparations and Olympic fortunes of two British athletes in the Paris Games of 1924. Cambridge tutors criticise sprinter Harold Abrahams for being too single-minded in his desire to win. Lord Burghley, on the other hand, had the casual attitude of the gentleman amateur. The other main character is the Scot, Eric Liddell, whose need to win was based on a Calvinist belief that 'God made me fast,' which meant that he had a duty to use his talent to glorify God in the truest spirit of Muscular Christianity.

TASK 9

Try to get hold of a copy of the film *Chariots of Fire* and note:

- the place of university sport in the early twentieth century
- the contrast between amateurism and professionalism and attitudes towards both approaches to sport
- the level of organisation of Olympic teams and the Olympic Games in the early twentieth century.

REMEMBER

Amateurism and professionalism were linked to class and status before the titles were linked to whether a performer was paid or not.

Athletics today

EXAM TIP

Other relevant contemporary factors not identified in Table 7 overleaf can gain credit in your exam.

APPLY IT!

Hexham, Northumberland, had both a new eco-friendly swimming pool complex and re-surfaced athletics track in Autumn 2008. The swimming pool is used from 5am to 10pm daily whereas the new athletics track (the only one in Northumberland) is used for approximately four hours per week. Can you find any evidence of good use or under-use of facilities in your area?

Your specification says:	Factors that have helped develop athletics in the UK and the impact of these factors on contemporary participation and performance
General:	See pages 51 and 52 for features relating to opportunity, provision and esteem that might encourage or prevent participation in athletics today
Participation in athletics today:	• Jogging or running – in this cheap, simple and accessible activity, participation levels seem to be relatively high. It is a popular, fashionable, health-enhancing pastime, despite risks of potential injury from over-use. • In the much more specialist track and field athletics, participation rates are much lower • Note success of events such as the London Marathon, Great North Run, Race for Life, Hash House Harriers and so on • Increasing popularity of triathlon events
Factors that have helped develop athletics and the impact of these factors on participation and performance:	• Technological developments, for example tracks, clothing, titanium for javelins and so on • Sports hall athletics: indoor athletics for young people. Adapted events use scaled-down versions of mainstream athletics and modified equipment. The aim is for young people to enjoy and develop their athletic capabilities and possibly continue into life-long participation. • Playground athletics – similar to above with a teacher pack for schools showing how athletics can be done safely without specialist equipment • Adequate media coverage to promote role models and make a difference • Competition organisers and development officers who work for county councils and who in some areas run the sports hall athletics programmes • Passion of individual teachers and club members • In September 2008, former Olympic champion Sally Gunnell launched McCain 'Track and Field', a nationwide campaign aiming to make athletics more accessible • Sponsorship, such as from McCain, who in July 2008 announced a five-year £5-million sponsorship deal with UK Athletics • Lottery funding and prize money has meant that the elite can now be career athletes
Specific factors that might be a barrier to participation in athletics today:	• Many events are specialised and linked with risk, so there is a need for specialist coaches and strict, time-consuming health and safety procedures • Many young people get poached by team sports, which are arguably more sociable with less individual exposure; for example, running an 800m race you are fully exposed, whereas playing at a low-level within a hockey team it is easier to remain unnoticed • Teachers' lack of confidence or fear of legal action • Challenges for schools include: restricted time in summer term; impact of poor weather; expense of equipment; difficulty of getting equipment out (such as hurdles or high jump equipment); lack of throwing cages to reduce risk and increase safety, and so on • Lack of access to top-level clubs where access is determined by trials; such clubs are inaccessible to most young people who will not have seen the specialist equipment until Year 7 at earliest • Athletics is not generally considered to be a lifetime sport • Negative image due to drug scandals may deter young people or their parents • Negative image of some field events as not 'cool' or appealing compared to other events • Indoor facilities very selective and mainly restricted to use by high-performance athletes

Table 7 Athletics today – factors affecting participation

Football as a popular recreation – mob games

A variety of games involving kicking and throwing a ball were regular features of English pre-industrial society. They were sometimes bizarre, always lively and often tragic. As a rowdy, violent, locally-coded, occasional encounter between neighbouring villages, mob football is without doubt the best example of a popular recreation.

Early mob football games were played in restricted city streets as well as in the countryside. They were little more than massive brawls involving brute force between hordes of young men. They caused uproar, damage to property and a perfect setting for anyone attracted to violence. According to one early observer, mob football was:

> '*... abominable enough, and, in my judgement at least, more common, undignified, and worthless than any other kind of game, rarely ending but with some loss, accident or disadvantage to the players themselves*'.

In one game in 1772 it is recorded that:

> '*... the ball was drowned for a time in the Priory pond, then forced along Angle Street across the Market Place into the Artichoke beer-house, and finally goaled in the porch of St. Mary's Church.*'

Shrove Tuesday became a traditional day for mob games and an opportunity for fun and excitement before the seriousness of Lent. Some of the best known were in Ashbourne and Derby. In Derby the game between the parishes of St Peter and All Saints resulted in the term a local 'Derby', while in Ashbourne two teams consisting of anyone who lived in the town surged between 'goals' three miles apart. You will remember from your AS socio-cultural studies that many such games continue today.

Throughout history, kings, governments and local authorities have frowned on mob games because they caused:

Fig 4.15 A game of mob football, 1721, a perfect example of a popular recreation with lower-class males playing, often violently, in and around the local village

- damage to property
- injury to young men (often making them unfit for army training)
- disrespect for the Sabbath
- social unrest (which might lead to riot or even rebellion).

In spite of successive authorities declaring the game illegal, it still survived. Without an effective policing system laws were fairly easy to ignore.

REMEMBER

Some mob football games continue today, such as the Ashbourne Game, the Haxey Hood Game and Hallaton Bottle-Kicking and Hare Pie Scramble.

Mob games can be recognised by their lack of:

- set rules
- set positions
- set pitch
- referee or umpire
- specific boundaries
- skilfulness (they were forceful and violent)
- regularity (they were occasional festival games).

TASK 10

1 Research a surviving mob football game (for example, Ashbourne, Haxey Hood or Hallaton Bottle-Kicking) and try to find evidence of the characteristics of popular recreation such as local, occasional, wagering and so on.
2 To what extent did mob games fit the normally recognised characteristics of popular recreation?

INFLUENCE OF THE PUBLIC SCHOOLS

	Stage one: Bullying and brutality	Stage two: Social control	Stage three: Athleticism
Football and rugby	Mob games and the first melting pot of activities from home	More formalised football rules for individual schools; inter-house competitions	Full technical development: Football Association (FA) or Rugby Football Union (RFU) rules along with traditional games at individual schools; 'colours', caps, inter-school fixtures

Table 8 The development of football in the public schools

REMEMBER

The first melting pot occurred when boys brought their local games from home during stage one. The second melting pot involved the mixing of different schools' games at university.

From the earliest days of public school history, impromptu, natural forms of football were played. Boys brought games from home which developed into school games dependent on the natural facilities available.

During the second stage of public school development, with rebellion almost over and fighting on the wane, football became the place to settle disputes and to show courage and determination. Ironically, football thus helped the social class that had traditionally tried to kill it off and for the first time in English history it became respectable.

By the 1860s transport and communications had greatly improved. School football had also developed and a variety of internal and external contests were organised. Disagreement often occurred in inter-school matches, as each school

Fig 4.16 The cloisters at London Charterhouse, home to a unique game of mob football

had different rules, as shown in this letter to the *Times* from 5 October 1863. However, at first most schools were unwilling to give up their own codes or to join with others.

Dear Sir

I am myself an Etonian, and the game of football as played by us differs essentially in most respects from that played at Westminster, Rugby, Harrow, and most of the London clubs. Now, this difference prevents matches being made or played between either school or club; and, furthermore, prevents a player from gaining the credit of playing well anywhere but among his own associates... The Etonians have now for two years played against the Westminsters in Vincent Square; the game is a kind of compromise between the two, more closely resembling the Westminster game than ours; and display is therefore below mediocrity – neither of the sides can practice any of their favourite 'dodges' without infringing the rules of the other, and an advantage gained by one side is not lawful by the rules of the opposite party... Now Sir, all these annoyances might be prevented by the framing of set rules for the game of football to be played everywhere.

Letter to the *Times*, 5 October 1863

Public school	Football variations
Eton College	• The Wall Game. Played on 30 November. Teams: Collegers and Oppidans. 'Bosses' are scored by getting the ball to the opponent's 'calx' – marks on a door and a tree. • The Field Game. Played since 1847. Combinations of 'handling' and 'dribbling' rules. Score made by goals and 'rouges' – similar to rugby tries. Scrummage called a 'ram.'
Charterhouse	• The Cloister Game. Played in the old monastic cloisters until the school moved to Godalming in 1872. The cloisters had a smooth flagstone floor but sharp jagged flint walls making injuries frequent. The doorways at each end of the cloisters were used as goals and 20 fags would guard them against violent scrimmages that lasted up to an hour. Bloody noses and broken teeth were accepted as part of the experience. • The Association Game. Charterhouse was central to the formation of Association Football.
Harrow	Harrow Football. Mainly 'dribbling' rules but, if caught and a call of 'yards' was made, a free kick was awarded. Goals called 'bases.'
Rugby	Rugby Football. This is fundamentally the same game as played under Rugby Union (RFU) rules today.
Shrewsbury	Douling. Played up to around 1880. Similar to rugby. Line out called a 'squash'.
Winchester College	Winchester Football. 10ft-high nets, called 'canvases', run along the sides of the 80 x 25 yard field. Also ropes set alongside the 'canvases.' Ends of field marked with furrows, called 'worms.' Very complex rules.
Westminster	A game in which trees and rails formed 20-yard-wide goals. Between 12 and 15 'duffers' or small boys acted as goalkeepers.
Uppingham	As in most schools, up to the 1860s internal games were concocted within the school such as 'Tall versus Short', or 'Those with an R in Their Names' versus 'Those who have not'. There is a story of Headmaster Thring's anger when he discovered a proposed game between 'Those who have been Flogged by Mr Thring versus Those who have Not.' 'If that game goes ahead' he apparently said, 'all the players will be on the same side!'

Table 9 School football variations

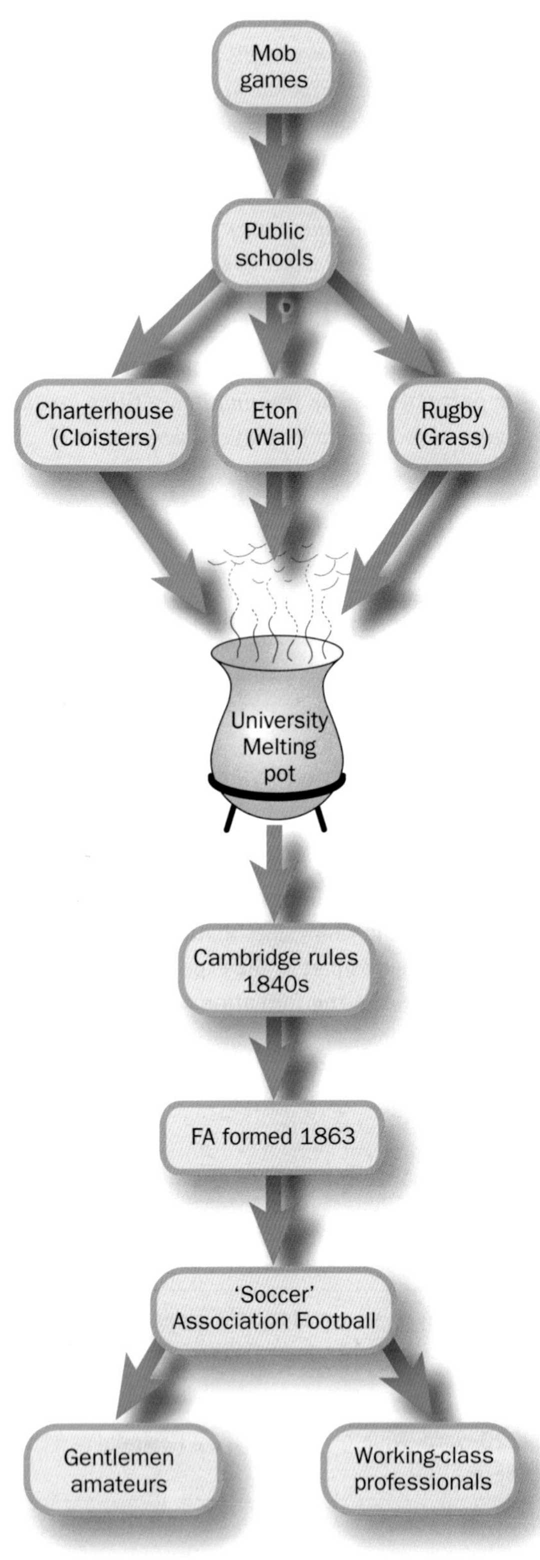

Fig 4.17 The emergence of Association Football from mob football

Popular recreation – mob games	• Mainly rural and played locally in and around villages • With simple unwritten local rules that were passed on by word of mouth from generation to generation • Violent with severe injuries and even deaths • Based on force not skill • Occasional, often annual events held on festivals or Holy days • By lower-class males to show virility and manliness • There were many attempts to stop mob games • Associated with wagering
Public school developments	• Football and/or rugby in public schools was usually compulsory • Inter-house and inter-school matches • Special games afternoons due to the time available • Part of the games cult and often played obsessively • Participation was thought to build character and promote values such as courage, leadership and loyalty • There was a mixing or 'melting pot' of ideas and later codification • Linked with technical developments such as improved facilities, equipment, kit, and so on
Rational recreation – Association Football	• Regional, national and finally international games • Governing body (FA) rules • Respectable and based on skill rather than force, with tactics and strategy and special positions within the team • Played regularly with a 'season' and leagues, cups and competitions • There were gentlemen amateur teams such as Corinthian Casuals, as well as teams for factory workers and opportunities for working-class professionals • Urban purpose-built stadia meant that workers could walk to the ground and spectatorism increased • Spectatorism rather than participation was the norm for the working-class man

Table 10 Summary of football through time

EXAM TIP

You will not be expected to know details of the different forms of football in different public schools.

TASK 11

Values and status: link the character-building values of athleticism (such as leadership, loyalty and so on) to participation in house of school football or rugby both then and now.

Football as a rational recreation

It was left to the ex-public schoolboys from the Universities of Oxford and Cambridge to form the Football Association (FA) in 1863. Prior to this, the dribbling game (soccer) and the handling game (rugby) co-existed. Now, the hackers and handlers moved away to form the Rugby Football Union (RFU), and 'soccer' (derived from the word 'association') became both an amateur game for gentlemen and a professional game for 'the people' – in other words the working classes. Now, however, in post-industrial Britain football was a regular spectator attraction rather than an annual festival occasion.

Why did football become so popular so quickly, especially in the northern industrial towns?

- It was simple.
- It fitted the limited space available.
- It fitted perfectly into the newly-free Saturday afternoon.
- It provided a focus for community, solidarity and comradeship.
- It was affordable.
- It was locally available.
- There was a dense working-class population on hand as spectators (who did not have a chance to participate other than in the street).
- Improved transport and communications made travel to away matches and the following of local teams in the press possible.
- Good-hearted factory owners often provided facilities.
- Many teams developed, almost spontaneously, from church and youth movements. Aston Villa, Birmingham, Everton, Fulham, Bolton and Barnsley, for example, were all originally church-based.
- For professionals, it offered an improved lifestyle and regular wages (but no security).
- It made them heroes among the working classes.

AMATEURISM AND PROFESSIONALISM

It soon became clear that the best players could not take unpaid time off work to play, and when the Football League was founded in 1888 the FA reluctantly accepted professionalism. The first international match between England and Scotland took place in 1870, and by 1885 all the home countries were playing each other. Quite quickly, the working-class dominance of soccer changed the nature of the game. Ex-public school boys fought back with amateur-only leagues, an amateur cup and amateur international fixtures. They criticised the fanaticism and exuberance of paying spectators, comparing them to pre-industrial mobs who chased pigs' bladders between villages. They also established a team of outstanding amateurs called 'the Corinthians' who successfully competed for many years, even against professional sides.

BROKEN TIME PAYMENTS AND THE SPLIT BETWEEN THE TWO CODES

In Rugby Football, meanwhile, there was an increasing need for professional players, particularly in the north of England. Again, players could not afford to take unpaid time from work or be out of action through injury. So, the game split and the Northern Football Union was formed in 1895, having failed to win **broken time payments** for players. Players could now be officially paid for loss of working time. Effectively, southern clubs excluded manual workers who needed to take time off to train and travel, thus cementing the tradition that their game was only for gentlemen amateurs – a belief that lasted for the next 100 years. With the spread of football across Europe and the Empire, the International Football Federation (FIFA) was formed in 1904, and by 1906 professional football had become the major form of male entertainment in Britain.

KEY TERM

Broken time payments

Payments made to working-class players to compensate for loss of earnings. It lead to professionalism and was looked down on by gentleman amateurs.

Football today

Your specification says:	Factors that have helped develop football in the UK and the impact of these factors on contemporary participation and performance
General:	See pages 51 and 52 for features relating to opportunity, provision and esteem that might encourage or prevent participation in football today
Participation in football today:	• Traditionally the national game with history of high participation • Community participation – 'lads and dads' • Boom sport for women and girls, for example at Cramlington Learning Village in Northumberland over 200 girls play football every Saturday morning • Simple, cheap and accessible game that can be modified and played anywhere • Played in majority of schools – curricular, extra-curricular and in playgrounds • Women's World Cup
Factors that have helped develop football and the impact of these factors on participation and performance:	• Spectator game has developed as family entertainment with family enclosures and payment incentives as well as safer, larger stadia; this will all increase spectatorism and arguably could impact on participation • Elite performers as 'rags to riches' icons • Technology and fashionable clothing – kit, boots, balls, turf, stadia (including new Wembley stadium) • Impact of sporting celebrities, for example David Beckham • Academies often provide community football camps • The international game with tournaments such as the African Nations Cup, which includes English and Scottish Premier League players and which thereby attracts interest in the UK • The FAs 'Respect' campaign to combat unacceptable behaviour at every level, both on the pitch and from the sidelines
Specific factors that might be a barrier to participation in football today:	• Less 'street football' due to more cars and/or parental concerns regarding safety • Smaller gardens – less suitable for playing games (decking, etc.) • Reputation of poor behaviour by minority • Selling off of school and municipal playing fields, for example for more profitable housing or supermarkets • Argument of decreasing parental involvement due to work commitments

Table 11 Football today – factors affecting participation

EXAM TIP

Other relevant contemporary factors not identified in Table 11 can gain credit in your exam.

KEY TERM

'Respect' campaign

The FA's initiative aimed at improving behaviour and stamping out dissent towards officials at all levels of the game but notably at grass roots level, where one match in three is currently played without a referee due to likely abuse. Go to www.heinemann.co.uk/hotlinks and enter the express code 6855P to watch a short film about the FA's 'Respect' campaign.

Cricket as a popular recreation

Village cricket was played from the early eighteenth century, especially in Kent, Sussex and Hampshire. From the start the social classes played together, reflecting the feudal or class structure of the village. Gentry patrons employed estate workers as gardeners and gamekeepers primarily for their cricketing talents. There were also some freelance professionals who played in a servant role to their current employer. Early clubs emerged from these rural village sides.

Fig 4.18 Cricket, 1743

TASK 12

Using Fig 4.18 to help you, describe the game of cricket as it existed in pre-industrial Britain. Consider equipment, boundaries, scoring, class, location, pitch, rules, wagering and violence.

Interest and patronage by the gentry led to the early standardisation of rules.

- 1727 – the first Articles of Agreement were written.
- 1744 – more extensive rules produced.
- 1774 – 'New Articles of the Game of Cricket' formalised the size of wicket, stumps and bat, added the third stump, made six balls an over and added the rule that it was illegal to charge fielders attempting to catch a ball.
- 1809 – 'The Laws of the Noble Game of Cricket' were set out by Marylebone Cricket Club (MCC).
- 1835 – round arm bowling was legalised (this style was originally adopted by ladies whose wide skirts prevented under arm bowling; it was soon adopted tactically by men who adapted it further to the over arm style used today).
- 1864 – over arm bowling legalised.

There are two or three key threads to the story of the early development of cricket.

1. THE BAT AND BALL INN

This pub in Hambledon, Hampshire, is nicknamed 'the cradle of cricket' as it was where the game was nurtured and developed from 1750. Outside the inn, on Broadhalfpenny Down, landlord Richard Nyren captained the side that dominated cricket for half a century. At its peak it could take on and beat the rest of England. Large crowds of up to 2000 spectators watched and wagered on the outcome of matches. Stakes of £5,000 (equivalent to about £500,000 in today's money) were paid to winning sides.

Cricket was a popular recreation because...	On the contrary...
• it attracted widespread **wagering** • it was played by both males and females (it took the restricting ethics of Victorianism later in the nineteenth century to restrict women's sporting pursuits) • it was predominantly **rural** • it was often associated with feasts and **festival days** • its rules could be locally **adapted.**	• it was predominantly **non-violent** • it had an early **rule structure** • it had national **touring sides** from the 1840s (see William Clarke XI in rational recreation section, page 75).

Table 12 Arguments for and against cricket being classed as a popular recreation

2. MARYLEBONE CRICKET CLUB

The gentlemen who developed the laws of cricket in 1774 formed the White Conduit Club which became the Marylebone Cricket Club (MCC) in 1788. The rise of MCC forced the decline of Hambledon. Why? Firstly, the gentry now supported the new London club, and also Hambledon players were now employed by MCC as coaches and players. MCC became the main club in England and took on the role of the governing body. It played at the first Lord's ground in 1787, moved to Lisson Grove 20 years later and finally to the present site in St John's Wood around 1811. MCC toured the country and had annual games against public schools.

REMEMBER

You need to be able to analyse the extent to which early cricket 'fits' the normally accepted model of popular recreation and identify similarities to or differences from today.

INFLUENCE OF THE PUBLIC SCHOOLS

Already a popular rural game by the mid-1700s, cricket was soon adopted by the public schools. Headmasters were happy to accept the game as its standardised rules, lack of violence and involvement by the gentry made it respectable. It also occupied boys and kept them out of mischief.

Changes that occurred during the three stages of development reflected changes in the game at large. During the 1850s and 60s, cricket grew: William Clarke's All England XI toured the country to entertain and inspire; the Lord's festival week was established as a social display of wealth for the Eton, Harrow and Winchester nobility; the first England team visited Australia in 1861.

As a reflection of these developments, cricket in public schools was now associated with:

- regularity as an inter-house and inter-school game

	Stage one: Bullying and brutality	Stage two: Social control	Stage three: Athleticism
Cricket	Transferred directly into the public schools due to its non-violent nature, rule structure and upper-class involvement in society	Cricket encouraged with massive inter-house participation	Continued technical development such as professional coaching, 'colours,' caps and inter-school fixtures (for example, annually against MCC)

Table 13 The development of cricket in the public schools

- compulsory participation
- investment in equipment and groundwork
- the employment of professional coaches
- more time spent in training
- the appointment of assistant teachers for their cricketing prowess (often Oxbridge blues)
- the hosting of matches as grand social occasions
- the belief that it instilled a range of character-building qualities, such as leadership and teamwork.

Fundamentally, though, this was the same game that rural peasants and gentry patrons had played over a century before.

VALUES AND STATUS OF CRICKET

The values thought to have been gained through participation in house and school cricket after 1870 included:

- physical endeavour, courage and commitment
- physical prowess
- moral integrity and linked qualities such as honesty, fair play and self-discipline
- teamwork, loyalty, leadership and loyal response to leadership
- decision making, problem solving and organisational skills
- healthy lifestyles and relief from academic work.

Fig 4.19 Eton v. Harrow at Lord's, 1864

Cricket as a rational recreation

THE WILLIAM CLARKE XI

William Clarke was an enterprising cricketer who took advantage of the changing economic and social conditions of the 1840s and helped change cricket from a fragmented localised sport to a national success. By the 1840s upper-class patronage of cricket had declined and professionals looked elsewhere for employment. Some went to the public schools and universities, while others joined professional touring sides such as the William Clarke XI (established 1847) or the breakaway United XI (formed by unhappy Clarke professionals who complained that they were not being paid enough). These sides toured England for many seasons, attracting huge crowds and taking on teams of up to 22 opponents.

Fig 4.20 William Clarke (1798–1856), who captained the All England XI in the 1840s

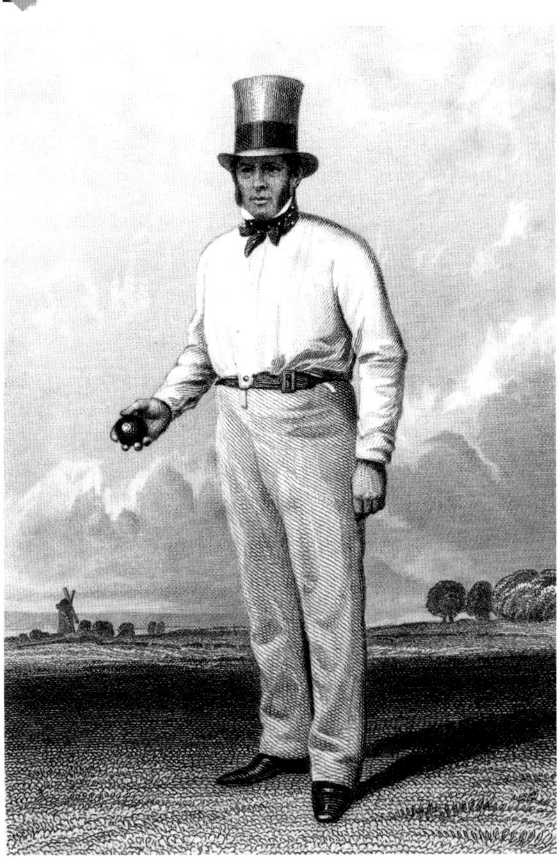

Fig 4.21 England versus Australia at Lord's, 1884

CLASS DIVISIONS

In the 1870s county cricket took over from the touring elevens as a spectator attraction. This rationalised form of the game had a strict class divide, and while the middle-class amateurs on the county committees needed and respected professionals, they kept them firmly in their social place:

- they had different names – professional versus amateur
- their names appeared differently in the programmes, for example *A. Mynn Esq.* for a gentleman and simply *Lillywhite* for a professional
- they had different eating arrangements
- they did not travel together or share a changing room
- they entered the field of play from a different door
- the captain and the opening batsman was always an amateur.

The university men (amateurs) looked after 'the lads' while 'the lads' (professionals) arguably respected the gentlemen for their leadership qualities and skills as thinkers and motivators. It was not until 1963 that the distinction between gentlemen and players was finally abolished in English cricket.

EXAM TIP

Remember that the different treatment of working-class players was associated with **rational recreation**. Candidates often incorrectly state this as being linked with pre-industrial popular recreation, when in fact the classes happily played cricket together and on a more equal footing.

TASK 13

Study the picture of England versus Australia at Lord's (Fig 4.21). How do you know that this is a rational game of cricket rather than a pre-industrial game?

W.G. GRACE

W.G. Grace (1849–1915) was a powerful all-round athlete, a dominant personality and the most famous cricketer of his time, who became bigger than the game itself. Once, after an early dismissal at the Oval, he complained to the umpire '*Nonsense, my man, they have come here to watch me play, not you umpire, play on*' – and they did! Grace was a doctor by profession and a gentleman amateur by status, yet he was paid £50 per game. Between 1870 and 1910 he earned £120,000 either directly or indirectly from cricket.

Fig 4.22 W.G. Grace, circa 1880

THE ASHES

In 1882 an Australian touring party beat England at the Oval. The *Sporting Times* published an obituary for English cricket, as follows:

> *In affectionate remembrance of English Cricket*
> *Which died at the oval on 19th August 1882*
> *Deeply lamented by a large circle of sorrowing friends and acquaintances.*
> *R.I.P.*
> *N.B. the body will be cremated and the ashes taken to Australia.*

The next winter, the English team in Australia won a three-match series. Some Australian women supporters burnt a bail, placed the ashes in a small sealed urn and presented them to the English captain. They are now in the Lord's cricket museum.

EXAM TIP

You will not get a direct question on W.G. Grace or on The Ashes.

Cricket today

Your specification says:	Factors that have helped develop cricket in the UK and the impact of these factors on contemporary participation and performance
General:	See pages 51 and 52 for features relating to opportunity, provision and esteem that might encourage or prevent participation in cricket today
Participation in cricket today:	• In its simplest form, a popular beach game • English Cricket Board (ECB) statistics show a 27 per cent increase in participation rates in the twelve months up to October 2008 and a 45 per cent increase in female participation over the same period • 8,000 cricket clubs in England of which 6,500 are affiliated to ECB and 3,700 have junior sections • Summer game in state schools but many constraints, such as need for time, adequate facilities and specialist coaching • Independent schools often able to provide more cricket opportunities than state schools
Factors that have helped develop cricket and the impact of these factors on participation and performance:	• A sophisticated and structured development programme by ECB with development targeted through clubs rather than through schools; programmes are designed and devised locally with regional support form ECB • Strategies and initiatives include adapted games for people with disabilities (blind, deaf, physically or mentally disabled) • The 'club mark' scheme whereby clubs gain a kite mark standard and accreditation as healthy safe places for young people • 'Chance to shine' • Technology for bats, bowling machines, protective clothing and so on • Twenty20, one-day matches • Media hype linked with test matches • Commercialisation of the game at top level – top teams visiting different towns to entertain and inspire (as they did in time of William Clarke) • Asian immigration since 1960s • The England women's victory in the Cricket World Cup in 2009
Specific factors that might be a barrier to participation in cricket today:	• Summer game – limited time available at school level • Kolpak ruling means that less money might be spent on coaching and developing young, home-grown players

Table 14 Cricket today – factors affecting participation

EXAM TIP

Other relevant contemporary factors not identified in Table 14 can gain credit in your exam.

KEY TERMS

Chance to shine

ECB campaign to regenerate competitive cricket in a third of state schools in England and Wales by 2015, providing high-quality, sustainable cricket programmes based upon continuous coaching, skills awards and competition. In addition, there will be coach and teacher training initiatives, the provision of facilities and equipment, as well as school holiday activities.

Kolpac ruling

A judgment in the European Court of Justice, May 2004. If a person has a valid UK work permit and is a national of a country which has a trade agreement with the European Union (South Africa, Zimbabwe and some West Indian Islands, for example) then, for the purpose of employment, they must be treated like a citizen of an EU country. This means that if a South African cricketer with a UK work permit is treated as if he were a British (or other European) citizen, he can therefore qualify as a domestic player for Competitive County Cricket.

Tennis as a popular recreation – real tennis

Real or royal tennis originated in France and became popular in Britain during the fourteenth century. It was an exclusive game for kings, nobles and merchants who played on purpose-built, highly-sophisticated courts which varied in size and shape. The one that became standard is shown in Fig 4.23, with a side passage for spectators.

Fig 4.23 Frontispiece of a book dated 1632, containing the first laws of real tennis known to exist. The court became a theatre, like most of the courts of the seventeenth century.

In keeping with the complicated court, real tennis had complex rules and required high levels of skill. Henry VIII (1491–1547) built the court at Hampton Court Palace which is still used today; it is reported on Henry VIII that he paid out considerable sums in lost wagers, so arguably he was not too skilled at the game. Most university colleges had a court and Charles I (1600–49) played at Oxford when the city was his stronghold during the Civil War.

REMEMBER

Real tennis was an exclusive, elitist, pre-industrial game.

EXAM TIP

You need to be able to compare real tennis with mob football. Compare step-by-step thinking about who played, where it was played, rule structure, numbers involved, dress, levels of skill or force, regularity of play and so on.

TASK 14

To what extent does real tennis 'fit' the normally accepted characteristics of popular recreation? This should be a straightforward analysis.

OTHER PRE-INDUSTRIAL VERSIONS OF TENNIS

A variety of hand or bat and ball games were all called tennis. Those not eligible to play real tennis would copy their social superiors and play their own versions against church or pub walls. Their games were variously called tennis, fives or racquets. The lower class also played field tennis or handball in the street and countryside.

RACQUETS

The story of racquets is one of rags to riches. It originated in Fleet prison, London, and ended up being played by upper-class public school and university men. These who played in Fleet prison were not hardened criminals, but debtors, and often gentlemen of high social standing, so they were allowed to exercise in the prison yard.

'The yard was just wide enough to make a good racquet court... one side, of course, (was formed) by the wall itself and the other by that portion of the prison which looked (or rather would have looked but for the wall) towards St Paul's Cathedral... sauntering or sitting about, in every possible attitude of listless idleness, were a great number of debtors... some were shabby, some were smart, many dirty... a few clean... lolling from the window which commanded a view of this promenade were a number of persons... looking on at the racquet players, or watching boys as they tried the game.'

Charles Dickens describes the game of racquets in his novel *Pickwick Papers* (1836–7)

Tennis and other striking games in the public schools

FIVES

The game of fives is ancient and informal in origin. The best-known structured version is Eton Fives, whose odd-shaped court is a modification of the space by the Eton Chapel steps (see Fig 4.24 and Fig 4.25). Fives was hugely popular in the public schools but failed to become a national game of any repute. This was because:

- it had a tradition of being played as a recreational game in free time
- there were different versions of the game (for example, Eton Fives and Winchester Fives)

	Stage one: Bullying and brutality	Stage two: Social control	Stage three: Athleticism
Tennis	Informal hand and ball games against suitable available walls and buildings. Referred to as fives or tennis (that is real tennis rather than lawn tennis which had not been invented yet)	Some fives courts built though fives still an informal activity. Game of racquets developing as more formal alternative; also squash racquets	Fives continued as recreational game. Racquets a more formal game of higher status. Lawn tennis comparatively low status in boys' schools; very popular as summer game in girls' public schools

Table 15 The development of tennis and other striking games in the public schools

Fig 4.24 The chapel steps at Eton

Fig 4.25 Eton Fives court

- it had limited scope for developing character
- the more sophisticated game of racquets was already established.

TASK 15

Try to find a suitable outside wall or corner in your school or college to develop a game of hand or glove fives. What rules will you use?

RACQUETS AND SQUASH

At first, racquets was played informally by schoolboys on naturally occurring 'courts'. By 1850 two standardised courts were built at Harrow at a cost of £850. By the time Old Boys took the game to university and to their private clubs, it had attained a high social status far beyond its beginnings in a debtors' prison. As the game became more sophisticated, the court was rationalised with four walls (instead of one) and a roof to guard against bad weather.

Many argue that racquets lead to the invention of the more compact and less expensive game of squash racquets. Boys at Harrow who were waiting to play racquets began knocking up outside. To avoid damage to windows they used

TASK 16

In pairs, discuss how the game of squash racquets could have developed the character of its public school enthusiasts. What physical qualities or aspects of character did it require?

a less hard, more 'squashy' ball than for racquets. By the 1860s, purpose-built squash courts were common and boys took the game on to university and often back to their country homes.

Lawn tennis

Lawn tennis was invented by, and for, the middle classes as a social experience. Importantly, it also became a vehicle for the **emancipation** of women. Little wonder, then, that it was not welcomed with open arms by the boys' public schools at a time when manliness and courage were all-important. Both its status and organisation in the public schools was limited and much less than for the major team games.

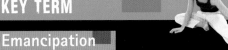

KEY TERM

Emancipation

Liberation linked with new found freedom. For women in late-nineteenth-century Britain, emancipation meant freedom from the restricting limitations society placed on them as women.

Why did the boys' public schools reject lawn tennis as anything other than an informal social event often on house courts, but seldom as an inter-school, serious event and never for the development of character?

- Lawn tennis courts took up a comparatively large space for the number of boys occupied.
- It did not require the courage or physicality of football or cricket.
- It could not rival the contemporary status of cricket or football.

REMEMBER

Lawn tennis was played occasionally in boys' public schools as a summer social game in the gardens of the houses, but it lacked the status of major team games. It was, however, adopted wholeheartedly by girls' public schools as their main summer game. (See Chapter 3, page 43.)

- It did not require the teamwork or co-operation of major games.
- It had a reputation of being 'pat ball' and suitable only for girls.
- As a new invention it was treated with some suspicion.

Tennis as a rational recreation

The game of lawn tennis was invented, **patented** and popularised by the middle-class army major Walter Clompton Wingfield in 1874. Wingfield sold the game in a painted box containing pole, pegs and netting for forming the court, four tennis bats, a supply of balls, a mallet and brush, and book of the game. Originally called 'Sphairistike' (derived from the Greek word for ball), it was played on an hourglass-shaped court (see Fig 1.3 on page 3), but within a few years the name was changed to lawn tennis and the court was modified to become rectangular. Lawn tennis was bought by the most fashionable upper-middle class families (see Fig 2.1 on page 18).

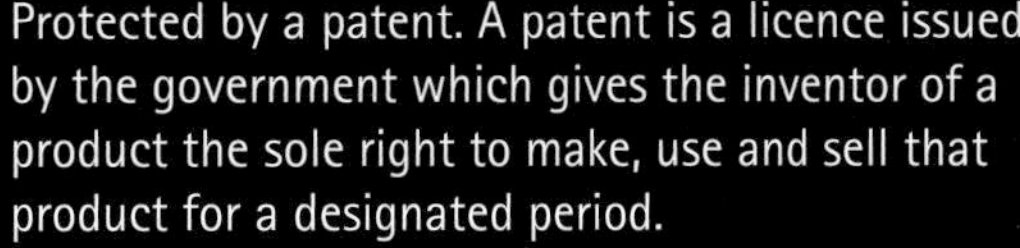

KEY TERM

Patented

Protected by a patent. A patent is a licence issued by the government which gives the inventor of a product the sole right to make, use and sell that product for a designated period.

In 1877 the All England Croquet Club introduced lawn tennis at Wimbledon. Twenty-two competitors took part and the finals attracted 200 spectators. By 1885, 3,500 spectators watched the men's final.

SUMMARY OF THE DEVELOPMENT OF LAWN TENNIS

- The middle classes were excluded from real tennis and invented their own alternative.
- The game was perfect for upper-middle class suburban gardens.
- It was an important social occasion.

- It was patented and became a fashionable status symbol.
- Tennis clubs were formed which allowed social gatherings of the same class of people.
- The lower-middle class, whose gardens were too small for courts, also frequented these private clubs.
- The working classes were excluded, and had to wait for public provision in parks, which delayed their participation.
- The development of tennis reflected the emergence of the urban middle class.

> *'... tennis filled a useful gap. Young ladies raised in the city could hardly get a husband at a hunt ball as earlier generations of marriageable 'gels' had done.'*
>
> Richard Holt, *Sport and the British* (1990)

LAWN TENNIS – WOMEN'S PARTICIPATION AND EMANCIPATION/LIBERATION

- The game helped to dispel some stereotypes of earlier Victorian times.
- As a social occasion it was part of family recreation.
- Women could participate but didn't have to exert themselves and weren't expected to excel in the sport.
- It did not require special dress.
- The true social importance of tennis was that it could be played by either sex or by both together.
- The privacy of the garden, with high hedges or walls, provided an opportunity to invite suitable members of the opposite sex for supervised sports.

Tennis today

Your specification says:	Factors that have helped develop tennis in the UK and the impact of these factors on contemporary participation and performance
General:	See pages 51 and 52 for features relating to opportunity, provision and esteem that might encourage or prevent participation in tennis today
Participation in tennis today:	• Focused on clubs with school links important • In spite of initiatives it could be argued that tennis is still predominantly a middle-class game
Factors that have helped develop tennis and the impact of these factors on participation and performance:	• Technology such as Astroturf, titanium racquets, low-compression balls, ball machines and other coaching aids • LTA and other schemes to increase participation in inner cities • Increasing number of indoor courts – David Lloyd and other tennis centres means more are able to play throughout year, as well as provision in public parks • Regionalisation of LTA • Media coverage – Wimbledon on terrestrial television available to all, so widespread exposure of role models including 2008 junior Wimbledon champion Laura Robson • Retractable roof on the centre court at Wimbledon 2009 • Free or heavily subsidised use of community courts in parks in some areas
Specific factors that might be a barrier to participation in tennis today:	• Public perception that tennis is a game for wealthy people (the cost of hiring a public tennis court can be as much as £9.00 per hour) • Quality of park/public provision – many community courts are neglected and in disrepair; others have been turned into skateboard parks or playgrounds • Summer game – limited time available at school level • Unpredictable British weather • Other challenges at school level, such as specialist coaches needed and 'expensive' space-wise (just as in the boys' public schools) • Courts converted to car parks at many schools/colleges • A comparatively difficult game • Computer alternatives to the 'real thing' such as Wii sports • Prevailing 'stuffy' attitudes at some private clubs (see over)

Table 16 Tennis today – factors affecting participation

'For all the good work that is done by the LTA looking for the stars of the future, no one has been radical enough to address the real problem – that tennis is seen by most of the population to be a stuffy game played by the middle classes.'

Quote from www.tennisforfree.com

EXAM TIP

Other relevant contemporary factors not identified in Table 16 can gain credit in your exam.

STRETCH AND CHALLENGE

Analyse the extent to which the public schools impacted on the development and emergence of each of the five case study activities. Do you think they would have emerged as rational recreations anyway? If so, why, and if not – why not?

ExamCafé

Relax, refresh, result!

Refresh your memory

You should now have knowledge and understanding of:

- the five case study activities – bathing and swimming, athletics, football, cricket and tennis
- how these activities developed to the present day through the following stages: popular recreation, via the public schools and rational recreation
- how to analyse each activity as a pre-industrial popular recreation
- how to assess the influence of nineteenth-century public schools on the development of each activity
- how to demonstrate knowledge and understanding of each activity as a rational recreation
- how to consider participation and barriers to participation in each activity today.

REVISE AS YOU GO!

Case studies as popular recreations:

1. What was the significance of bathing and swimming in pre-industrial river towns?
2. To what extent does football fit the normally accepted characteristics of popular recreation?
3. Describe pre-industrial cricket.

Case studies in the public schools:

4. With reference to athletics, outline the three stages of public school development.
5. In stage one, why did headmasters accept cricket but frown on hare and hounds (paper chase)?
6. Why did 'fives' fail to become a prominent national game?
7. Why was lawn tennis considered to be less valuable than cricket?

Case studies as rational recreations:

8. Explain the exclusion clause in athletics.
9. With reference to Association and Rugby Football explain the terms 'people's game' and 'broken time payments'.
10. Account for the growth of lawn tennis as a rational recreation.

Try to answer these questions yourself. Ask your teacher if you need help.

Get the result!

Examination question

Critically evaluate the development of cricket from its early pre-industrial roots to the present day. Your answer should include an analysis of the impact of class on participation at each stage of development and the comparative status of cricket in nineteenth-century public schools. (20 marks)

Examiner's tips

- There is likely to be a lot to think about in your 20-mark questions, and therefore a lot to write about.
- You will need to think clearly and logically – having already learned your work thoroughly.
- The 20-mark question should stretch and challenge the very best candidates.
- Top candidates will show that they can 'think outside of the box' and analyse and evaluate as well as show knowledge and understanding.
- The question will, however, allow all candidates to score some marks.
- Examiners are particularly looking for high levels of:
  - knowledge and understanding of the topic
  - critical analysis/evaluation
  - independent opinion and judgment supported by sound examples
  - high-quality written communication.
- This particular question on cricket has several aspects and needs careful thought and planning to ensure that each part is addressed. Ensure that you carefully divide the 2½ hours available. Many candidates make the mistake of over-writing on their first 20-mark question and leave too little time for the two remaining 20-mark questions later on.

Examiner says:

Very thorough plan. Good that you have not crossed it out – examiners will look at this if perhaps you have not transferred it all to your essay. Take care that you don't spend too much time planning. You'll have about 30 minutes for your 20-mark question. Remember, it's fine to plan your answer, but you must always answer in full sentences and cross out your planning.

Student answer

The development of cricket – Impact of class on participation	
Pre-industrial developments	• Emerged through village teams • Simple equipment, etc.; wagering • Early rules (1700s) • Bat and Ball / MCC • Class: both classes together reflecting class structure of village's gentry patrons employed estate workers; some lower-class profs

Developments in the public schools	• Stage 1 direct transfer – HM support (compare with other things) • Stage 2 inter-house • Stage 3 inter-school and full technical development (regular/compulsory/prof coaches/time/assistant teachers, etc.) • Character building – endeavour, prowess, integrity, teamwork, decision making, etc. • BUT? • Class: elite boarding schools then middle-class copies
Comparative status of game of cricket:	• High with other team games • Higher than individual activities • Some HMs joined in/MCC matches
Post industrial rational developments	• William Clarke (1850s) • County developments • AND – impact of transport, etc. • Class: working v middle/upper = professional v amateur; strict class divide – add examples
Current/present day developments	• ECB initiatives – Chance to Shine • 45% increase in women and girls • BUT – problems • Class: independent v state school opportunity and provision

A game of cricket in the 1700s wouldn't have looked that different from a game of cricket today. Everything would have been less sophisticated and 'modern', but the main idea of hitting a ball and scoring runs was the same.

Examiner says:

Nice little introduction to set the scene.

Early cricket was part of village life and took place on the village green outside the village pub – in the summer anyway. Many village pubs today take their name from the game, for example 'The Cricketers'. The most famous pub linked to cricket is probably the Bat and Ball Inn in Hampshire, where many major matches took place. Unlike many other games at the time, cricket had agreed rules (probably because the upper class were involved). These upper-class players set up the MCC which became the governing body. Most other sports didn't have their governing body until about a hundred years later, having gone through the public school system.

Examiner says:

I like the independent knowledge about pub names and also the contextualisation of cricket versus other games which didn't have early governing bodies – shows excellent knowledge and understanding.

Class had a main impact at this early stage. While both classes played together (the lower class were skilful and were needed to make up the numbers), it was the upper class who owned the equipment and made all the arrangements and often employed the lower class on their estates – just for their cricketing prowess.

Examiner says:

A good idea to have a separate paragraph for class. It would be easy to miss out this point of analysis and therefore lose credit. Because you had a clear plan it is much easier for you to structure your answer and include everything.

Cricket was of massive importance in nineteenth-century public schools. Throughout each of the three stages of development it had a major part to play.

Examiner says:

Again, a nice 'introduction' to this next part of your answer.

It was directly transferred into the schools in stage one with the support of the Headmaster, who could see its value as a non-violent, relatively structured, rule-based game which was played by the upper class. Mob football, on the other hand, was discouraged – it was always linked with trouble.

Examiner says:

Good – relevant link to class.

During stage two, when Dr Thomas Arnold was trying to establish social control through games, cricket really came into its own. The boys played obsessively each day on an

Examiner says:

Good – you have successfully linked the game to Arnold and social control.

inter-house basis and so learned important organisational skills and also went to bed exhausted. This reduced problems of riot and bad behaviour by boys (which had been widespread up until this time).

During stage three (when the game was also huge in society as a rational recreation), the game was a central feature of many schools. The cricket captain was a prestigious figure and the game was fully technically developed, with clearly marked-out pitches and professional coaches (who were working-class professional players who took positions in or visited the schools to make up their wages). This was the major stage. Cricket was the route to a wholesome young man with a rounded character. It was believed by many that the game directly developed characteristics such as loyalty, teamwork, endeavour and integrity – just the things needed by the ruling class.

Examiner says:

Good that you have linked stage three of public school developments with rationalised cricket in society – shows analysis. Also you have a thorough understanding of the role cricket had in developing the character of the boys.

The status of cricket in the public schools was exceptionally high. Not only was it an acceptable upper-class game when it was taken in to the schools, but it was non-violent and a perfect vehicle (better that individual activities) for the development of desirable values.

Examiner says:

I like the way you have spent a mini paragraph making sure that your analy of the status of crick is clearly covered.

In post-industrial times the game of cricket as a rational recreation grew. Two things were important here. Firstly, the William Clarke XI, and secondly, amateurism and professionalism. The William Clarke XI was a professional touring side that helped bring the game to national recognition – but only because of improved transport methods in the mid-nineteenth century. Amateurism and professionalism created a massive class divide in cricket. The middle- or upper-class gentleman amateur was always the captain and usually took the glory position of opening batsman, while the working-class professional was treated very differently in terms of travel and food and board and lodging.

Today cricket is developing due to initiatives by the governing body (ECB).

- Chance to Shine – clubs supporting state schools.
- Large increase in girls and women's participation.
- The Ashes win also helped boost participation in the game.

The NGB don't want class to be an issue any more – but it's hard to see how it isn't. Independent schools are likely to have better provision than state schools due to funding, time and expertise – just as they always have done.

Examiner says:

You are obviously running out of time here. Not surprising as the rest of your answer is so detailed. Under these circumstances, bullet pointing to show your knowledge and understanding is a good idea. While your analysis, independent opinion and quality of written communication is much weaker for this last part of the contemporary game, it is better to get your ideas down than to leave part of the answer undone.

Examiner says:

Let's look at the criteria on which your question is marked and compare them with how you did:

- Knowledge and understanding – yours was excellent at each stage of the question.
- Critical analysis/ evaluation – yours was very good throughout, for example your references to class and transport and Headmaster support.
- Independent opinion and judgment supported by sound examples – again, lots of relevant examples and independent thoughts, such as your reference to contemporary pub names and the ECB 'Chance to Shine' initiative.
- Written communication – on balance, very high quality even though you appeared to run out of time at the end and used bullet points.

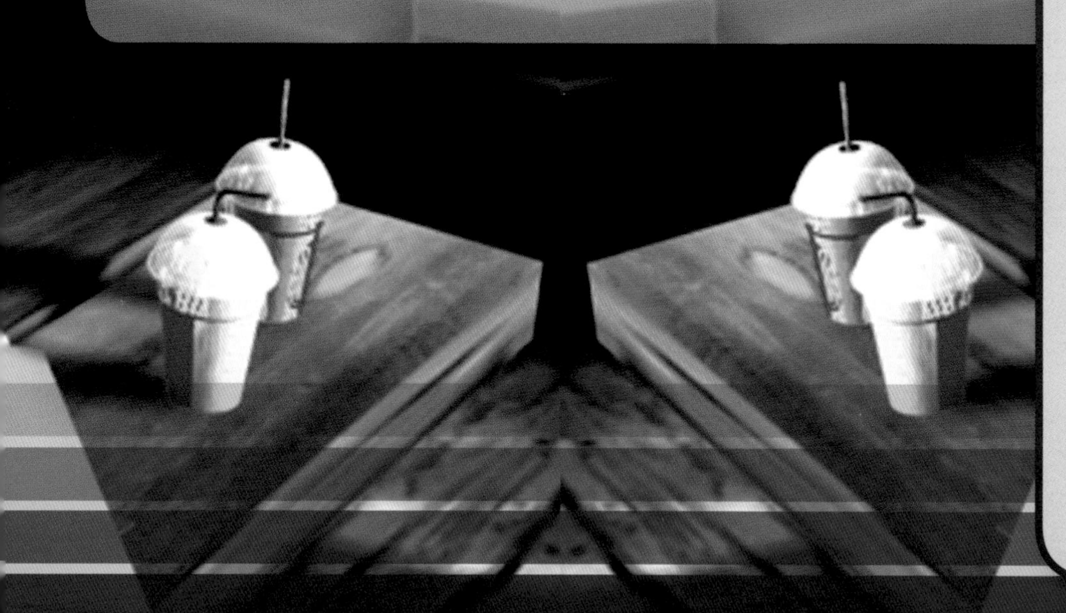

CHAPTER 5:

Drill, physical training and Physical Education in state schools

LEARNING OBJECTIVES

By the end of this chapter you should have knowledge and understanding of:

- how physical activity in state elementary schools progressed from military drill to physical training (PT) and then to Physical Education (PE) between 1900 and 1950
- the ways in which drill, PT and PE in state schools impacted on participation and the promotion of healthy lifestyles
- how to link what happened then to what is happening in schools today
- the objectives, content and teaching methodology of each approach
- how war affected the different approaches
- in what ways and why the 'sporting' experiences of working-class children in state schools differed from that of middle- and upper-class boys and girls in public schools
- the impact on participation of teachers' industrial action in the 1970s and 1980s
- the aims of the National Curriculum for PE and how to critically evaluate its impact.

INTRODUCTION

You need to know *how* and *why* the approach to and teaching of physical skills and activities changed throughout the twentieth century.

Answers to the 'W' and 'H' questions should help again. For each stage you need to identify:

- *What* was the main aim, for example drill, training or education?
- *Who* was doing the teaching and learning (with reference to class, gender and qualifications of teachers)?

Fig 5.1 Twentieth-century developments in state schools

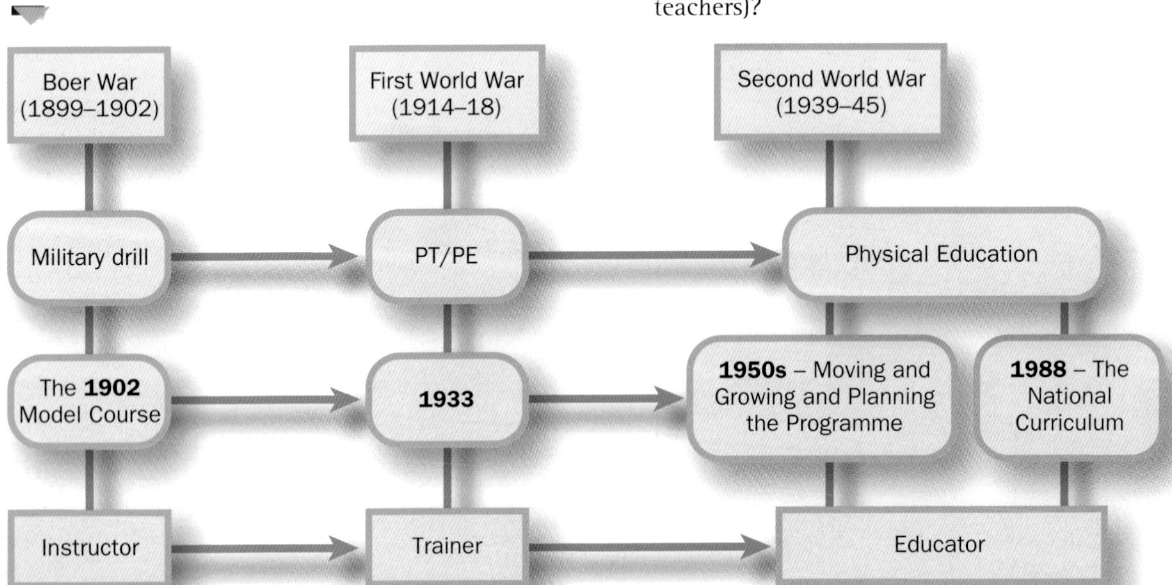

- *When* was it introduced (you will need to know dates here)?
- *Where* the activity took place, for example in the street, playground or purpose-built gymnasium?
- *Why* the system was introduced, for example due to the effects of war or as a result of particular individuals?
- *How* was it being 'taught'?

KEY TERMS

Objectives

Aims or intentions of a lesson or syllabus, for example physical or military fitness.

Content

The subject matter or activities taught in the lesson, for example weapons drill or games skills.

Methodology

The teaching style used for delivery, such as command or problem solving.

Board schools

State schools that opened as a result of the Education Act of 1870.

European gymnastic teachers

Swedish gymnastics was a system of freestanding exercise created by Ling in the late-nineteenth century that exercised the body systematically, sometimes called 'callisthenics.' In contrast, German gymnastics emphasised the use of apparatus for vaulting and strengthening, and was influenced by military and public school gymnastics.

Army non-commissioned officers (NCOs)

Low-ranking officers with little interest in, or knowledge of, child development and whose involvement in presenting the Model course lowered the status of the subject.

You need to understand and be able to explain reasons for change over time, which include:

- changes in educational philosophy from instructional (1902) to child-centred (1950s) and choice within a National Curriculum today
- changes from the idealism of the 1950s to increased accountability of teachers today
- changes in standard of living from early poverty to a welfare state system where the government is responsible for assuring basic health and education
- social change from a strict class system to emphasis on equality of opportunity for all
- changes in provision from a playground (at most) to purpose-built facilities and increased availability of equipment today
- changes in teacher training from general class teachers to a graduate PE profession today
- changes due to the effects of war
- reductions in class/group sizes over time
- changes in the needs of society from military readiness to health to combating obesity
- the impact of the National Curriculum and an awareness of initiatives for participation in schools, such as the impact of School Sports Co-ordinators (SSCOs).

KEY TERMS

Therapeutic

Beneficial or health-giving.

Boer War

War between the British Empire and the Boers of South Africa, 1899–1902. Britain lost prestige due to its poor performance in the war.

Colonel Fox

A long-serving army officer appointed in 1902 as a result of the Boer War to establish and ensure the adoption of the Model course.

Important points/background information

- In 1866, the army rejected 380 out of each 1000 recruits on physical grounds.
- **Board schools** (state schools) were established by the Forster Education Act 1870. Previously, the education of the poor had been a parish responsibility.
- School attendance became compulsory for children aged between five and ten years.
- By 1899, the school leaving age was raised to twelve years.
- By 1900, there had been great progress in terms of provision.
- There was restricted space for play and physical exercise.
- Many schools in industrial towns had no playing facilities.

Influences

- The work of European gymnastic teachers, including Guts Muths and Jahn (Germany) and Ling (Sweden), as well as the Briton A. Maclaren.

Elementary school drill
The end of the nineteenth century

Often built to look like churches, **board schools** had only small playgrounds and no playing fields.

Also note

- Lack of equipment other than staves (sticks) for dummy weapons drill.

Objectives

- Fitness for army recruits
- Discipline
- To do for working-class children what games was doing for public school boys

Content

- 1870 – military drill
- 1890s – Swedish drill
- 1900 – the Board of Education stated that games were a suitable alternative to Swedish drill

Methodology

- Authoritarian/Command-response
- Taught by **army non-commissioned officers** (NCOs) in 1870s
- Taught by qualified class teachers in 1890s

Fig 5.2 Setting the scene – state school drill at the end of the nineteenth century

Important points/background information

- Military needs became more powerful than educational theory.
- A backward step educationally with Swedish drill, innovation and a **therapeutic** approach abandoned.
- Condemned by progressives and supporters of the Swedish system.
- Girls and boys instructed together.
- Failed to cater for different ages and/or genders.
- Children treated as soldiers.
- Taught by army NCOs (or teachers who had been trained by them).
- Dull and repetitive – but cheap.
- Large numbers in small spaces.
- Set against backdrop of poor diets, bad housing and other forms of social deprivation.
- It lowered the status of the subject.

Influences

- Imposed as a result of Britain's poor performance in the **Boer War** (S. Africa).
- Produced and imposed by **Colonel Malcolm Fox** of the War Office (not Education Department).

The Model course
1902

Massed drill in the school yard around 1902

Also note

'It is important therefore that the short time claimed for physical training should be devoted wholly to useful exercises. No part of that time should be wasted on what is merely spectacular or entertaining, but every exercise should have its peculiar purpose and value in a complete system framed to develop all parts of the body.' (*Model Course of Physical Training, 1902*)

Objectives

- Fitness (for military service/war)
- Training in handling of weapons
- Discipline for the working class

Content

- Military drill/marching
- Static exercises, e.g. arm raises
- Weapon training
- Deep breathing

Methodology

- Command-response (for example, 'Attention', ' Stand at ease', 'Marching, about turn'.)
- Group response/no individuality
- In ranks

Fig 5.3 The Model Course, 1902

Reasons why the Model course of 1902 was quickly replaced:

- because it had been imposed by the War Office
- military drill, with its command style, was soon considered unsuitable for young children
- educationalists demanded a healthier approach linked to good posture and therapeutic exercises with children being allowed to play rather than being treated as little soldiers
- a medical doctor called Dr George Newman (see below) got involved
- teachers objected to army non-commissioned officers (NCOs) in schools and wanted **physical training** to be their responsibility.

Reasons why the 1933 syllabus was replaced:

- although this syllabus had (and still has) a great reputation it was replaced in the early 1950s
- times and thinking were changing and a more **holistic** approach to the physical education of young children was sought
- there was a desire to use fewer prescriptive 'tables' of exercises for teachers to go through and more creativity
- by the 1950s there were more female teachers who wanted a different movement style approach to physical activity
- post-war there were many new purpose-built gymnasia for gymnastic activity.

KEY TERM

Physical training

Term used between 1880 and 1950 to describe a form of physical exercise that consisted of Swedish gymnastics and drill.

DR GEORGE NEWMAN

Appointed as Chief Medical Officer within the Board of Education, Newman was interested in the health-giving/therapeutic effects of exercise. He was keen to fight off accusations that PT was to blame for the lack of fitness of the working class, and stressed recreational activities for the rehabilitation of injured soldiers.

> *'The purpose of physical training is not to produce gymnasts, but to promote and encourage the health and development of the body.'* Dr George Newman

KEY TERMS

Decentralised/Centralised

A decentralised lesson has the teacher as a guide and children can work at their own pace answering tasks in an individual way. It is in opposition to a centralised lesson, which involves the teacher using an instructive style and the children all answering the same task in unison.

Holistic

Considering the whole rather than the separate parts. The holistic approach to the physical education of young children would consider not only physical but also intellectual, emotional and social development of each individual child.

REMEMBER

You need to study the past and see how it links forward to the next stage in time or to today, so (among other things) consider:

- Improved or an increased variety or number of different facilities over time.
- Increasingly child-friendly or colourful or appropriate equipment today.
- A greater emphasis on accountability in schools today in comparison with, say the 1950s.
- Physical Education now as an all-graduate profession – compare with the NCOs of 1902!
- The impact of the National Curriculum on Physical Education.
- Initiatives in primary and secondary school to increase participation and to promote balanced, active and healthy lifestyle and lifelong participation.
- The balance between achieving balanced, active and healthy lifestyles with talent spotting the potential elite.
- The need to reduce discrimination and improve opportunities and provision for all.

Important points/background information
- The industrial depression of the 1930s left many of the working class unemployed (no state benefits were yet available).
- A watershed between the syllabuses of the past and the Physical Education of the future.
- This syllabus had one section for the under elevens and one for the over elevens.

Influences
- The Hadow Report of 1926 identified the need to differentiate between ages for physical training.
- Dr George Newman – this was the last syllabus to be published under his direction.

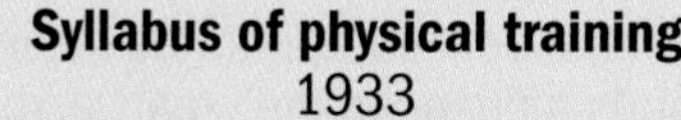

Syllabus of physical training
1933

Emphasis on skills and posture.

Also note
- A detailed, high quality and highly respected syllabus.
- Still set out in a series of 'tables' from which teachers planned their lessons.
- *'The ultimate test by which every system of physical training should be judged [is] to be found in the posture and general carriage of the children'* (1933 syllabus).
- Newman stated that good nourishment, effective medical inspection and treatment and hygienic surroundings were all necessary for good health as well as 'a comprehensive system of physical training ... for the normal healthy development of the body [and] for the correction of inherent or acquired defects.'

Objectives
- Physical fitness
- Therapeutic benefits
- Good physique
- Good posture
- Development of mind and body (holistic aims)

Content
- Athletics, gymnastic and games skills
- Group work

Methodology
- Still direct style for the majority of the lesson/centralised
- Some **decentralised** parts to the lesson
- Group work/tasks throughout
- Encouragement of special clothing/kit
- Five 20-minute lessons a week recommended
- Used many schools' newly built gymnasia
- Outdoor lessons recommended for health benefits
- Some specialist PE teachers

Fig 5.4 Syllabus of physical training, 1933

Important points/background information

- The (Butler) Education Act 1944 aimed to ensure equality of educational opportunity.
- It also required local authorities to provide playing fields for all schools.
- School leaving age was raised to fifteen years.
- These syllabuses should be viewed in the context of overall expansion of physical activities in schools.
- Intended to replace the under elevens section of the 1933 syllabus.

Influences

- The Second World War, which required 'thinking' soldiers, and the subsequent perceived need for increasingly 'thinking' children.
- Assault course obstacle equipment influenced apparatus design.
- Modern educational dance methods influenced the creative/movement approach.
- An experiment in Halifax, which rehabilitated children with disabilities by encouraging individual interpretation of **open tasks**, with no pre-set rhythm or timing. This influenced the problem-solving approach.

1) Moving and growing; 2) Planning the programme
(1952) (1954)

An apparatus lesson in the 1950s.

Also note

- The extensive post-war re-building programme lead to an expansion of facilities.

Objectives

- Physical, social and cognitive development
- Variety of experiences
- Enjoyment
- Personal satisfaction/sense of achievement
- Increased involvement for all

Content

- Agility exercises; gymnastics, dance and games skills
- Theme or sequence work
- Movement to music
- Apparatus work

Methodology

- Child-centred and enjoyment orientated
- Progressive
- More specialised PE teachers
- Teacher guidance rather than direction
- Problem-solving/creative/exploratory/discovery
- Individual interpretation of tasks/decentralised
- Using full apparatus (cave, ropes, bars, boxes, mats, and so on)

Fig 5.5 1) Moving and growing, 1952; 2) Planning the programme (1954)

KEY TERM

Open tasks

Problem-solving tasks that can be solved in many different ways.

1) Impact of industrial action by teachers in state schools (1970s and 1980s):

- reduced opportunity and provision
- extra-curricular activities severely restricted or stopped
- participation reduced in schools
- participation shifted to community clubs
- frustration/disappointment for both children and teachers
- negative press for teachers.

‘My first year of secondary school was great – but from my second year there were no lunchtime or after-school activities – it was really annoying. I just joined clubs outside of school.’
(PE Teacher who started secondary school just before the industrial action)

The 1970s and 1980s and the National Curriculum

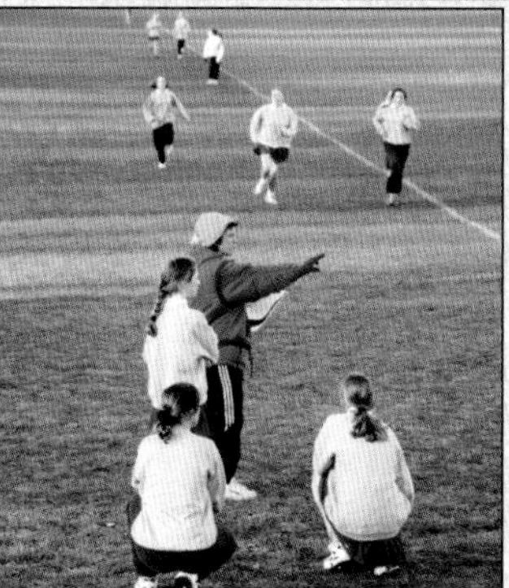

2) The National Curriculum of Physical Education:

- is one of five subjects which all pupils must pursue from age 5–16 years
- at each Key Stage (KS) children need to show knowledge, skills and understanding in a variety of practical areas.

Potential positive impacts of the National Curriculum include:

- higher standards
- clear national standards
- a broad and balanced PE experience for all
- consistent opportunity and content for all wherever they go to school
- easy transfer between schools
- learners gain the right to learn certain things
- increased likelihood of lifelong participation due to greater variety of activities experienced (especially at KS4)
- as a relatively open framework it can be adapted to the needs of learners
- provides some support, especially to non-specialist teachers of PE
- develops learning, thinking and analytical skills as well as creativity, innovation and enterprise
- develops social skills such as fair play
- helps pupils to manage risk and cope with difficulty
- can develop pupils' integrity and independence.

Potential negative impacts of the National Curriculum include:

- tracking and record keeping can involve large amounts of paperwork for teachers
- lack of assessment experience by some primary teachers can lead to confusion and skewed results at lower KS3
- may reduce creativity of certain teachers who feel constrained – though this may have been addressed with new KS3 curriculum
- can impose pressure on schools with facilities such as tennis courts
- schools are still able to offer an unbalanced programme, for example football and not rugby or avoidance of dance and/or gymnastics by teachers who prefer games
- demanding on teachers (especially at KS1) who may lack support. Partnerships and links between schools are addressing this issue.

Fig 5.6 1) 1970s and 1980s – the impact of industrial action on participation in state schools; 2) the impact of the National Curriculum on PE in state schools today

EXAM TIP

You will not need detailed knowledge of each key stage of the National Curriculum. Stick to being able to critically evaluate its impact on PE in state schools.

A high-quality PE curriculum enables all students to enjoy and succeed in many kinds of physical activity. They develop a wide range of skills and the ability to use tactics, strategies and compositional ideas to perform successfully. When they are performing, they think about what they are doing, analyse the situation and make decisions. They also reflect on their own and others' performances and find ways to improve them. As a result, they develop the confidence to take part in different physical activities and learn about the value of healthy, active lifestyles. Discovering what they like to do and what their aptitudes are at school, and how and where to get involved in physical activity, helps them make informed choices about lifelong physical activity.

PE helps students develop personally and socially. They work as individuals, in groups and in teams, developing concepts of fairness and of personal and social responsibility. They take on different roles and responsibilities, including leadership, coaching and officiating. Through the range of experiences that PE offers, they learn how to be effective in competitive, creative and challenging situations.

National Curriculum

TASK 1

Read this extract from the National Curriculum for PE and make a list of its key aims and outcomes.

EXAM TIP

It is important to be able to compare objectives, content and methodology over time because exam questions can ask for this information. You also need to compare then (historical) with now (contemporary).

REMEMBER

- The important role of Dr George Newman who oversaw the publication of three Board of Education syllabuses between 1909 and 1933. He was concerned with the health of young people.
- Also, lack of specialist teachers, facilities, equipment and playing fields meant that comparatively little improvement could be made in spite of broadening views between 1902 and 1933.

STRETCH AND CHALLENGE

Construct an argument in support of the 1902 Model Course that was unpopular and quickly replaced. Argue against the 1933 syllabus of physical training that was widely respected and lasted for many years.

TASK 2

Ask your teacher to take you through a five-minute practical role play of each of the approaches in this chapter. Or maybe you could be the teacher!

ExamCafé

Relax, refresh, result!

Refresh your memory

You should now have knowledge and understanding of:

- the progression from military drill to PT to PE and the National Curriculum in state schools today
- participation and healthy lifestyles both then and now
- the objectives, content and teaching methodology of each approach
- how war affected the different approaches
- how the physical activity experiences of working-class children in state schools differed from that of middle- and upper-class boys and girls in public schools
- why participation in schools reduced as a result of the industrial action by teachers in the 1970s and 80s
- the aims of the National Curriculum for PE and critically evaluate its impact today.

REVISE AS YOU GO!

1. What is meant by the following: objectives, content, methodology?
2. With which courses or syllabuses would you associate the following words or phrases?
   - Child-centred
   - Boer War
   - Dr George Newman
   - Army NCOs
   - Army assault apparatus
   - Colonel Fox
3. Compare the content of the 1902 Model course with that of Moving and Growing/Planning the Programme (early 1950s).
4. Who was Dr George Newman and why was he important?
5. Identify two things that influenced the development of Moving and Growing/Planning the Programme.
6. Identify reasons for changes to the physical training and/or education of children from 1900–2000.
7. How did industrial action of the 1970s and 1980s impact on provision for physical activity in schools?
8. What are the aims of the National Curriculum for PE?
9. Identify two potential advantages of the National Curriculum for PE.
10. Identify two potential disadvantages of the National Curriculum for PE.

Try to answer these questions yourself. Ask your teacher if you need help.

Get the result!

Examination question

Throughout history, Physical Education has impacted on young people's health and participation in physical activity, with the Model Course of 1902 being rapidly replaced.

Identify two main differences between the Model Course of 1902 and Physical Education in state schools today. (4 marks)

Examiner's tips

This looks like an opening part a) question with a straightforward command to *identify*, but with the additional requirement to point out clear *differences*.

- Take great care here that you really think before you start writing. Note that just two main differences have been asked for, so just your first two responses will be marked.
- Try to point out the differences as you go along, rather than writing a paragraph about 1902 and then a paragraph about today.

Examiner says

It's fine to plan your answer, but you must always answer in full sentences. Your knowledge is excellent and your comparisons correct, clear and logical.

- I'm glad that your first two responses were correct. Remember, points 3–8 would not be marked as just two responses were clearly asked for.
- Take great care to stick to the requirements of each question in the exam – you simply won't have time to include detail or evaluation of information that is either irrelevant or beyond what you have been asked to do.
- At A2, full prose is very strongly encouraged, especially in the longer question parts where credit is available for the quality of your written communication.

Plan for student answer

Model Course 1902	PE in state school today
Taught by army NCOs	Taught by specialist PE teachers
Centralised / in ranks / no individuality / command-response, e.g. 'attention'	Decentralised with variety of teaching styles
Command style	More student-centred
For discipline	For physical or personal or preparatory or qualitative benefits
Imposed by War Office	Imposed as National Curriculum by education department
Fitness for military service or war / training in handling weapons	For physical or personal or preparatory or qualitative benefits
Military drill / marching / weapons training /staves / deep breathing	There are different activity types that are part of the National Curriculum, such as gymnastics, games or dance

Comparative studies

CHAPTER 6:

Comparative study of the USA and the UK

LEARNING OBJECTIVES

By the end of this chapter you should have knowledge and understanding of:

- the cultural context of sport in the USA and the UK
- PE and school sport in the USA and the UK
- mass participation in sport in the USA and the UK
- sport and the pursuit of excellence in the USA and the UK
- how to critically evaluate the influence of the cultural context on all of the above.

INTRODUCTION

Physical Education in schools, and sport, both as a mass participation activity and as a pursuit through which the achievement of excellence is the aim, is given high priority in all three countries of study: the USA, Australia and the UK. The examination of the USA and Australia in comparison with the UK will reveal variations of approach, tradition and national rationale as each country seeks to promote the value, maximise the provision and endorse the benefits of active involvement in physical activities.

EXAM TIP

You will need to make comparisons relating to the systems, procedures, policies and practices in each of the USA and Australia as they compare to the UK.

In order to identify, explain and analyse the major points of comparison, it is necessary to view each country in a cultural context.

The USA: a cultural context

Prior to the first European **colonisation** of America (by Christopher Columbus in 1492), it is thought that a primitive form of lacrosse was played by Native American tribes. The first English settlers played a version of football at Jamestown (1607) in which play resembled the lawless 'mob games' of the lower classes in pre-industrial England.

KEY TERM

Colonisation

The process whereby a country is taken over by another more dominant country.

As colonisation increased, initially in the east of America, violent English sports like dog fighting were common among lower orders of society. Wrestling and bare-fist fighting attracted crowds and gave opportunities for gambling.

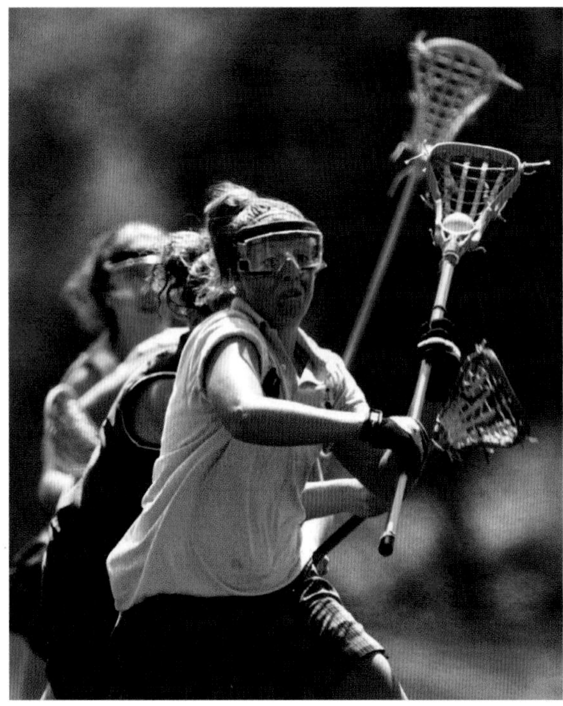

Fig 6.1 Lacrosse is not one of the 'big four sports', but it remains popular in the USA. Its origins are with the indigenous Native American tribes

TASK 1

The 'big four' sports in the USA are baseball, American gridiron football, basketball and ice hockey. Discuss the reasons why lacrosse is not promoted as one of the major 'big four' sports in the USA.

Sports of high culture belonging to the English aristocracy also found their way to eastern America. Horse racing was organised in New York as early as 1665, while provision for polo and hunting followed the rules and etiquette established in England. By the early 1800s cricket was also popular on the eastern seaboard and clubs were established in Boston, New York and Philadelphia, which by then were rapidly developing cities.

The recognition of the United States of America as a newly formed nation comprising the thirteen original States came about through the Declaration of Independence (1776). From this time, the USA adopted a **policy of isolation** to separate itself from the influence and traditions of the UK and Europe. Isolation is one of the major factors that shaped modern sport in the USA and made it different in terms of its nature, appearance and ethos to sports in the UK.

KEY TERM

Isolation policy

This policy fulfilled the desire of the USA for separation from the UK and Europe. The United States was determined to stand alone and sever connections with its colonial history.

TASK 2

Study an extract of play from a Rugby Union game of a high standard and a game of American gridiron football. Discuss the differences between the sports in terms of nature, appearance and ethos.

The number of America's 'states' increased westward until by the mid-nineteenth century it had a breadth of 3000 miles (4800 kilometres) and lateral boundaries determined by the Atlantic and Pacific oceans. The USA was now a nation of historical variation. To the east was the area in which colonisation had first taken place 200 years previously. The boundary marking the expansion of new settlements and a migrating population was at this time being constantly pushed westwards. The boundary of western expansion was given the name 'frontier'.

People who chose to live on the frontier endured hardship and difficult environmental conditions. They frequently experienced the danger of attack from Native Americans, who defended their traditional territories that were taken by the USA throughout this era of expansion. The fortitude demonstrated by the frontier settlers was termed '**frontierism**'. This 'frontier spirit' strongly impacted upon the early cultural development of the USA and was to help the shaping of the **American Dream.** It will later be seen that the legacy of the frontier spirit, by way of the tough and competitive ethic for which it stood, is a second factor that has influenced modern sport in the USA.

KEY TERMS

Frontierism

The frontier was the temporary boundary which marked the extent of Western expansion into country that was often hostile. Frontierism refers to the spirit of toughness, ruggedness and independence in the face of adversity.

American Dream

The belief that all people are equal in terms of opportunity and that regardless of background it is, through hard work, possible to succeed in the USA. It is the keystone of modern American culture.

APPLY IT!

The ultimate example of the American Dream is reflected in the achievement of Barack Obama, who in January 2009 became the first African American to become President of the USA.

As a result of massive immigration, essentially from the UK and Europe between the years 1840 and 1885, the population of the USA rose from 17 million to 55 million. Those seeking a new beginning believed that great wealth would reward their particular skills, and immigrants were prepared to work hard to achieve their ambitions. Such a positive work ethic when set alongside the spirit of frontierism formed the strong competitive ethos that is the hallmark of contemporary society and sport in the USA.

The '**New World**', like the UK, was becoming urban and increasingly industrialised and through necessity, the workforce became more concentrated. Thus the games and pastimes of the UK that were played during the colonial period gave way to the sports now associated with the USA. Society in the USA demanded its own brand of sport which was compatible with a competitive, diverse and dynamic culture associated with the 'New World'. For this reason, the sports developing in the UK such as Rugby Football, Association Football and cricket were considered unsuitable and were therefore **marginalised.**

KEY TERMS

New World

Term given to the United States of America in the period after the Declaration of Independence (1776). The term became associated with optimism and the notion of a land of opportunity.

Marginalised

Refers to a sport being put to one side and rejected by the mainstream culture.

APPLY IT!

Cricket was extremely popular in England and reflected the class system. The game was quickly rejected by the USA because it had little in common with the new 'American' culture.

Fig 6.2 The old sports of the UK were quickly marginalised to make way for sports of the New World, such as American Football. New 'American' sports reflected the frontier spirit and endorsed the policy of isolation from the UK.

TASK 3

By giving practical examples, identify the factors that caused the traditional sports from the UK to become marginalised.

Sports played in the USA can be placed into one of three categories, as shown in Table 1.

Table 1 Three categories of American sport

Category	Explanation
Adaptations	Adaptations are modifications that have been made to sports already in existence. For example, American Football (gridiron) is an adaptation of rugby. Baseball also developed from games played by children, for example goal ball and rounders.
Adoptions	Adoptions are games taken directly from other cultures or countries and placed directly into the USA context. For example, ice hockey has its origins in Canada.
Inventions	Sports like basketball were invented in the USA. Basketball is particularly well suited to the culture of the New World.

TASK 4

Watch the highlights of a basketball match. Discuss the reasons why basketball is suited to American culture.

During the twentieth century, baseball, American Football, basketball and lastly ice hockey were promoted as the 'big four sports'. For American society these became the major focus of attention. The 'big four' sports were promoted because:

- they were fast, intensive, entertaining and masculine
- they fulfilled the 'cult of manliness'
- the 'frontier spirit' was represented and could be reproduced through engagement in the 'win-at-all-cost' ethic
- the policy of isolation was indirectly endorsed by the promotion of America's own sports.
- these sports best facilitated commercial opportunity (as will be seen later, commercialism and sport link directly to the developing capitalist economy)
- by engaging as either a participant or spectator in the sports most popular in the New World, new settlers in the USA quickly became 'Americanised'.

KEY TERMS

Cult of manliness

Writers, educators and national leaders expressed concern that traditional, masculine 'frontier' characteristics would disappear in an increasingly urban society. Sport was the vehicle through which courage, ruggedness and hardiness could be endorsed.

Americanised

The process of becoming an American by accepting the culture and traditions of the USA. This is referred to later as assimilation.

The cultural context of the UK as a comparison with the USA

HISTORICAL DETERMINANTS AND THE IMPACT OF THE NINETEENTH-CENTURY PUBLIC SCHOOLS ON THE ORGANISATION OF SPORT IN THE UK

EXAM TIP

To gain maximum marks you must state a fact relating to the USA then make a comparison of that fact with the UK. By failing to compare, maximum marks cannot be achieved.

The sociological history of the UK extends much further than that of the USA. For example, the development of the English nation began a thousand years ago. The post-colonial history of the USA, by contrast, is little more than 200 years old and it is therefore considered to be a young culture.

As a small island, the UK did not have a 'frontier' to extend but followed a policy of aggressive expansion overseas, giving rise to an empire which came to include both America and Australia. Britain made its first overseas claim to territory in Newfoundland, Canada, as early as 1497. At its height, the British Empire was the largest in history, allowing the British to boast that it was an Empire upon which 'the sun never set'. The Empire finally came to an end with the formal handing over of Hong Kong to China in 1997.

The power and prestige emanating from imperial ownership influenced the traditions and class structure of UK society. Sport helped to establish UK traditions in the Empire, and in turn the Empire was to influence the development of sport both in the UK and across the world. By the same token, the isolation policy of the USA was endorsed by their Americanised sports.

EXAM TIP

It is essential that comparative statements are made in answer to all questions. Comparative statements can be similarities or contrasting facts.

APPLY IT!

Cricket was played across the entire British Empire. The values of the game reflected the British class system and English ideals.

British sports were played throughout the Empire, for example cricket and rugby were played in Australia. After the USA gained independence from Britain in 1776, sports from the UK became marginalised. Games in popular recreation, for example mob football, were played by the lower orders of British society and were initially replicated in the USA. These games descended into lawless brawls and were frowned upon by the ruling classes of both countries because they caused social unrest.

The UK also had games of sophistication. Real tennis was played as early as the fourteenth century but was exclusive to kings, nobles and merchants. Although this ancient titled hierarchy did not exist in the USA because it was a young and newly-founded society, sports exclusively for the higher orders such as polo and hunting did exist in the New World.

Organised cricket matches were played in southern England from the early-eighteenth century. The game developed roles both for the labourer and the aristocrat and appeared to suit the English class system. Cricket was initially played in the USA but the protocol and slow nature of the game was rejected by the young culture, once again endorsing the policy of isolation.

The greatest developmental influence on UK sport came from the reformed English public school system. It was largely through the impact of the public schools that in the period 1863 to 1888 most sports and national governing bodies were formed.

In the USA, by contrast, sports were adopted, adapted or invented either in the working-class environment, as was the case with baseball, or in the college (university) environment, for example gridiron football, basketball or ice hockey.

Sport developed in three stages in the UK public school system. This evolution took sport from engagement in brutal institutionalised popular recreation to a period of social control and reform when sport was used to educate boys as part of Muscular Christianity (see page 27). The final stage was that of the 'cult' of athleticism.

APPLY IT!

The Public School system instilled the notion of amateurism.

REMEMBER

Review the role of nineteenth-century public schools in promoting and organising sports and games. See pages 236–38 of *OCR AS PE* and pages 32–45 of this book.

CODIFICATION AND ATTITUDES TOWARDS SPORT

The combination of physical effort and moral integrity associated with good sportsmanship became the dominant ethos in the UK public schools. The public schools became instrumental in codifying major games such as Association Football and Rugby Football. Public schoolboys eventually took the games ethic into adult life and by so doing influenced culture. Their involvement stimulated the nineteenth-century notion of amateurism and the development of UK sports across the Empire.

APPLY IT!

Two of the major sports of the British Empire were cricket and rugby. Both reflected the traditions of hierarchical society and supported the notion of amateurism well into the twentieth century.

In the USA, by contrast, it was the traditional universities known as Ivy League colleges that had the greatest impact on sport in America. American Football (known as gridiron football) was adapted from UK rugby by the Ivy League colleges. Initially the game was uncompromisingly tough. In 1905, for example, the nature of this sport caused the death of 18 college players.

Unlike the ethos of the UK public schools, gridiron football in USA Ivy League colleges not only promoted a win ethic that was in line with the competitive American society, it also represented the 'cult of manliness' in keeping with the 'frontier spirit'. The American win-at-all-cost ethic, later to be called Lombardianism, is the third cultural factor that shapes American sport. By contrast, in the UK, in keeping with the legacy of the public schools, taking part was traditionally more important than winning.

Sports of the Ivy League also endorsed the policy of isolationism. By awarding scholarships, colleges outside the Ivy League tradition were later to become agencies through which athletes were prepared for professional sports careers.

KEY TERM

Lombardianism

A very important term describing a 'win-at-all-cost' ethic. See page 119.

APPLY IT!

To this day, Ivy League colleges compete at the highest level in collegiate sport. They do not, however, offer sports scholarships.

THE LATE-NINETEENTH-CENTURY NOTION OF AMATEURISM AND PROFESSIONALISM AND THE UK CLASS SYSTEM

In the late nineteenth century, a clearly defined class system based on hereditary privilege existed in Britain, the legacy of which continues today. Class determined income, lifestyle and, most significantly, sporting opportunities. The English 'gentleman' amateur belonged to the upper classes. Amateurs did not compete for extrinsic reward and believed that a 'win-at-all-cost' ethos was against the spirit of sportsmanship. Training was therefore rarely taken seriously.

As it was determined by a money meritocracy, the structure of the class system in the USA differed from that in the UK, but sporting involvement was remarkably similar. Wealthy Americans played exclusive sports like golf; they also sailed yachts and enjoyed dignified equestrian pursuits. In contrast with the UK, however, wealthy Americans employed private professional coaches to help them excel in their chosen activities.

The English amateur believed that sport was a vehicle through which desirable societal values could be developed. Similarly, a small group of American intellectuals, given the name **'Progressives'**, claimed that athleticism could help individuals meet the challenges of modern life in the New World. The American Progressives, like the English gentleman amateur, unsuccessfully tried to resist the professional movement in sport.

KEY TERM

Progressives

A group of American intellectuals who believed sport to be an ideal preparation for life in the 'New World'.

EXAM TIP

To achieve one mark, a point of comparison must be made. For example: wealthy American amateur sportsmen often employed private professional coaches; amateur sportsmen in the UK did not consider winning as important and so did not seek to be coached.

Organised professional sport, however, was emerging in both countries.

- The major professional sports in America during the late nineteenth century were baseball, boxing and horseracing. Horseracing was beset by gambling scandals while boxing and baseball suffered the stigma of being played by rowdy working-class ruffians.
- In the UK, Rugby Football remained a middle-class and strictly amateur game. The administrators of the amateur rugby union game were so protective of their values that players 'turning to' the professional game received a lifetime ban from all levels of the union code. 'Broken time' payments brought the advent of the Northern Union and with it professional rugby league, which was preferred by the working classes. Cricket also had clear class boundaries.
- The Football Association (FA), with its origins in the English public schools, was founded in 1863 as an amateur organisation. The FA reluctantly accepted professionalism in 1888 when the Football League was inaugurated. Association Football quickly became dominated by working-class professional players.

The rapid increase in the population of America, brought about by immigration, and the expansion of the working classes, who were now enjoying more leisure time, brought a change of sporting ethos to the USA. The latter factor was also true for the UK. Sport was no longer the preserve of the wealthy classes who played for intrinsic reasons only, but had become infiltrated by professionalism.

Improved transport brought about by the coming of the railways in the mid-to-late nineteenth century made fixture programmes possible, and the demands of the new industrial societies in both countries gave sport a new complexion. Professional games both in the USA and the UK, by way of necessity, were quickly developing into a spectacle for mass entertainment.

EXAM TIP

Credit will be given for comparative facts that indicate not only contrast but similarity. For example: the expansion of the working classes, who were enjoying more leisure time, brought a change of sporting ethos to both the USA and UK.

REMEMBER

In the UK, the traditional amateur approach changed to a more professional approach to sport; see page 239 in *OCR AS PE* and pages 27 and 71 in this book.

Geographic, demographic and socio-economic factors affecting sport in the USA and the UK

URBANISATION IN THE USA

The population of the USA is approaching 300 million with a population density of 30 people per square mile. Some areas of the USA are regarded as '**genuine wilderness**' and have no population. Conversely, New York and California are huge urban sprawls, which bring serious congestion and air pollution problems. Large unpopulated

USA: SIZE OF COUNTRY

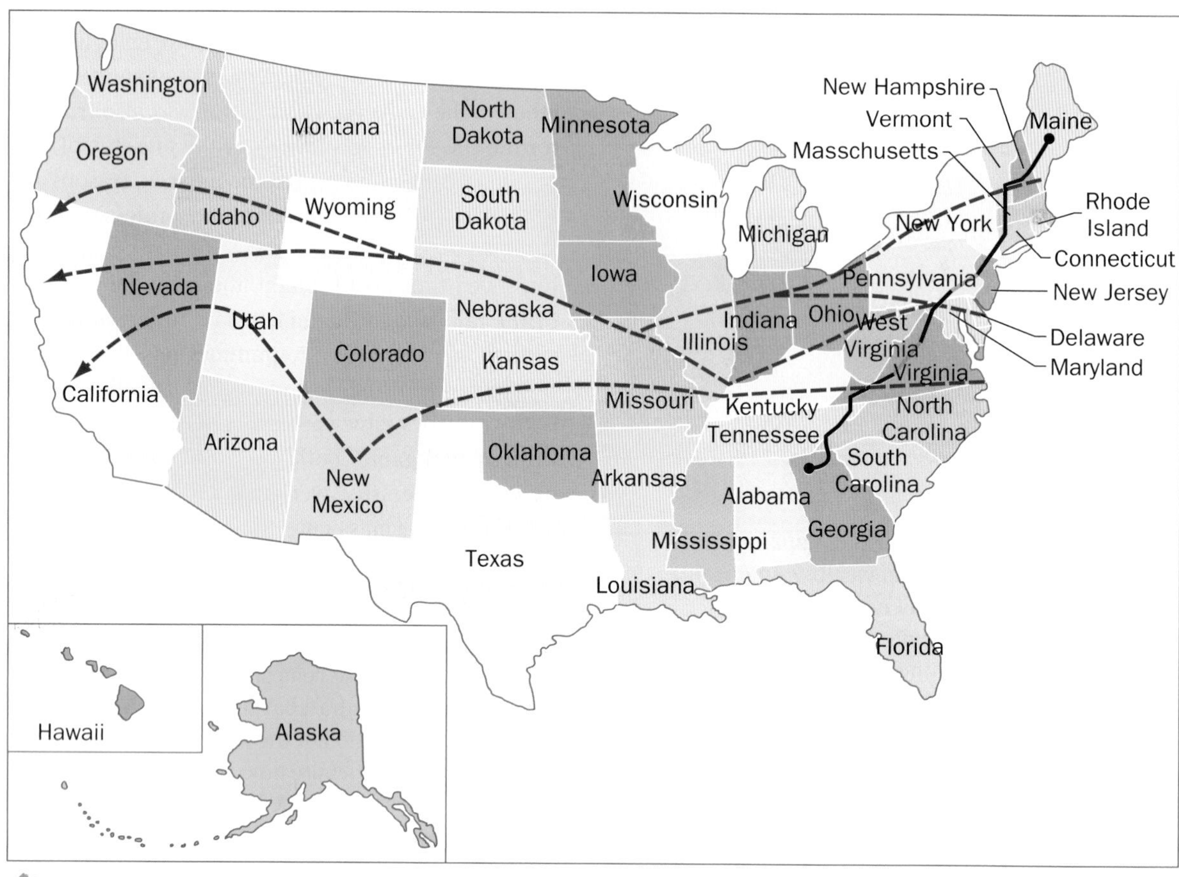

Fig 6.3 The vast size of the USA has influenced both the growth of sport and the development of Physical Education. Note that the UK is approximately two-thirds the size of California (Black line: Appalacian trail; Red arrows: Western Frontier movement)

areas of wilderness have helped to stimulate the US passion for the '**Great Outdoors**' and adventure challenges, while the densely populated settlements have been hotbeds in the development of the USA urban 'Big Four' sports.

KEY TERMS

Genuine wilderness

An uninhabited remote area, often with an inhospitable terrain and climate and occasionally frequented by savage animals.

Great Outdoors

The natural environment such as the mountains where outdoor adventure activities can be pursued.

POPULATION OF THE UK

The population of the UK is approaching 62 million. The UK has a relatively high population density at 200 people per square mile. There are, however, areas of relatively sparse population, for example in National Parks and in designated areas of outstanding natural beauty. Despite the remoteness of locations like the highland region of Scotland and areas of mid-Wales, there are, in contrast to the USA, no areas of genuine wilderness. This limits the scope for outdoor activities.

REMEMBER

Revisit your learning about outdoor education and outdoor recreation in the UK; see page 223 of *OCR AS PE*.

TRANSPORT IN THE USA

The overwhelming size of the USA influences the individual's perception of distance. A journey across a state may be considered as short to the American, while an equivalent excursion to a person in Britain would be considered a substantial distance to travel.

- In the USA there is an advanced network of urban and interstate highways to accommodate extensive car use.
- Inter-state air travel is essential in such a large country, and this mode of transport is easily accessible.
- Rail links are well established both as an intra- and inter-State service. Trans-American routes were laid down during the period of Western expansion during the 'frontier' years.

Transport and the capacity for good communications have impacted greatly on the development and subsequent growth of Physical Education and sport at all levels. For example, the early rise and success of professional 'major league' baseball in the 1890s as the national sport of the USA was dependent on an efficient railway system.

TRANSPORT IN THE UK

- Like the USA, the UK has an extensive motorway system linking all urban areas efficiently. Being a relatively small island with a high rate of car ownership has led to problems of overcrowding and pollution. Travel for sports fixtures although expensive is not inhibited by distance or accessibility.
- The advent of railways in the UK from the 1850s greatly facilitated the development of organised sport and recreational pursuits in the countryside.
- Air travel within the UK has well-developed network systems. Although this has contributed to increasing opportunities for accessibility to away venues, road and rail remain the major modes of transport.

CLIMATE AND TOPOGRAPHY IN THE USA

The North American continent has large ranges of latitude and altitude. As a result, the USA has a wide range of climatic zones. The terrain also varies markedly from wide plain to desert and high mountain ranges, such as the Western Cordilleras which accommodate the Rocky Mountains. These wilderness areas are termed 'frontier country' and they give wide opportunity for adventure.

REMEMBER

The 'frontier spirit' of the earlier pioneers – see page 103 and the map on page 108.

A wilderness adventure epitomising the frontier spirit in the Great Outdoors can be experienced by hiking on long distance routes such as the 2175-mile (3500-kilometre) Appalachian Trail. This long-distance footpath extends from Maine to Georgia through 14 eastern states and follows the route of the Appalachian mountain range (see map on page 108). Parts of the route are impassable during winter and very few people complete the full distance.

A combination of high mountain ranges and a suitable winter climate has enabled the USA to stage the Winter Olympic Games on two occasions.

CLIMATE AND TOPOGRAPHY IN THE UK

The UK has the climatic type termed Western Maritime. This climate tends to give warm summers and mild winters with persistent rainfall. Hostile extremes of weather are very rare, but rainfall is a factor that can adversely affect sport and recreation.

The UK does have stretches of unspoiled countryside, such as the Cotswolds, that facilitate outdoor recreation and education. Mountain upland areas such as Snowdonia and the Grampians provide challenge to climbers and mountain walkers, but a combination of low altitude and unsuitable climatic conditions severely restricts the possibilities for winter sports pursuits. For example, snow skiing has a limited and unpredictable season in northern Scotland.

The UK, like the USA, has designated long-distance footpaths. Possibly the most popular is the 256-mile (410-kilometre) Pennine Way that extends from the Peak District to southern Scotland. Large numbers of people complete this hike every year in all seasons.

APPLY IT!

A comparison made between the Appalachian Trail of the USA with the Pennine Way in the UK exemplifies the vast scale of America.

A combination of low altitude and unsuitable climatic conditions restricts the possibility of the Winter Olympic Games being held in the UK.

APPLY IT!

The size and natural potential of a country impact upon the opportunities for outdoor activity. For example, winter sports are big business ventures in the USA; in the UK winter sports are extremely limited.

US GOVERNMENT POLICY

The USA is a Republic with a strong democratic influence. The USA, unlike the UK, has never had a monarchy or hereditary class privilege that has had the power to determine or influence the opportunity of the people.

The USA government operates on three tiers:

1 Federal
2 State
3 Local.

The federal government, and ultimately the President, has overarching control and makes a broad impact on the domestic and foreign policies of the USA. The American constitution, however, ensures that the power of control is **decentralised** and granted to each state.

State government deals with policies relevant to that particular state and has its own constitution, government and code of laws. The State Governor presides over this tier.

Local government controls policies pertinent to a particular town or city. The position of Mayor is the highest office. There is a strong tradition of state autonomy made possible by the federal administration policy of **decentralisation.**

KEY TERM

Decentralisation

This means that the power base for government lies within the state and not with the central federal government. Power is therefore distributed equally throughout the USA.

State autonomy means that each state has self-rule or the power to control its own code of laws. The concept of decentralisation is very important in the USA; as will be seen later, it links to the economic system of capitalism and relates to the values of opportunity and freedom. Decentralisation applies not only to the governance of each state but also to the administration of business and other economic institutions. This includes education and sport.

EXAM TIP

To achieve the highest marks you are required to analyse and evaluate the points of comparison. Note the comparisons that are made between the USA and the UK, particularly those in the blue boxes.

Decentralisation impacts strongly on the organisation and delivery of Physical Education in the USA. There is no government-controlled national curriculum, as there is in the UK; neither is there a specific government agency in the USA with a role relating to policy or an agenda for sport. The President's Council on Physical Fitness and Sport, however, advises the President about sport, fitness and physical activity. They recommend initiatives to promote physical activity. Two examples of such initiatives are the President's Challenge and Healthy People 2010. Both initiatives aim to improve the health of all Americans.

The Olympic Games, when staged in the USA, are funded largely from multinational commercial businesses and not from central government. Businesses in turn benefit from their investment in elite sport.

KEY TERM

Public funding

Money from national and local government.

REMEMBER

Sport England is the government agency responsible for community sport in England. There are also sports councils in each of the Home Countries. See pages 268–69 of *OCR AS PE*.

TASK 5

Research fitness initiatives in the USA using the websites suggested at www.heinemann.co.uk/hotlinks; to access the sites, click on the relevant link and enter the express code 6855P.

However, in recent years, sport in the UK has also moved into the realm of global business and commerce. Success in, for example, the Olympic Games can bring great prestige and financial reward to a country. As a consequence, sport in the UK enjoys substantially increased government funding, and investment in sport is now considered by politicians to have considerable vote-catching potential. This is in direct contrast to the situation in the USA.

APPLY IT!

No specific American governmental agency oversees or funds America's international-level sports. Some funding has been supplied by the Federal Government for Olympic and World University Games.

GOVERNMENT POLICY IN THE UK

The UK, in contrast to the USA, has a constitutional monarchy. The monarch is Head of State and the prime minister is Head of Government. Overarching power is exercised by the UK government and the devolved governments of Scotland, Wales and Northern Ireland, which are autonomous bodies.

Local government has many tiers, ranging in status from regional government to parish council, and organisation of local government is complex. It is relevant, however, that metropolitan boroughs receive central funding and local taxation and have the power to authorise the building of sports facilities.

British politicians have traditionally looked on sport as a low-status activity and in consequence have provided meagre financial support in the form of **public funding**. This may possibly have been the legacy of the traditional amateur ethic in which taking part was more important than winning.

The UK government's investment of an additional £200 million for performance funding represents an effort to achieve fourth place in the 2012 Olympic medal table and first place in the Paralympics medal table.

The Department for Culture, Media and Sport (DCMS) is the government department responsible for sport. The USA does not allocate a position in federal government for the development of sport.

The DCMS provides grants of around £200 million annually. It decides how lottery grants are distributed through organisations such as UK Sport, the Olympic Lottery Distributor and the four home country sports councils. The investment is to promote sporting excellence and to encourage mass participation.

The UK has a decentralised system of sports administration which means that power is not centrally held, but shared by many sporting agencies that are largely self-governing. Central government contributes little in the way of sporting policies.

REMEMBER

Revisit your previous learning about sporting agencies in the UK; see page 268 of *OCR AS PE*.

The USA also has a decentralised system of administration, but their structure to encourage participation and promote excellence is different from the UK (see page 111). The USA federal government is not involved in sport and makes only indirect funding contributions.

REMEMBER

Public funding is funding from central government and local authorities. There is also private funding from businesses, and sponsorship and voluntary funding from donations or private clubs.

TASK 6

Identify the sporting agencies in the UK that receive public funding from the lottery. Discuss how these agencies use this money.

KEY TERMS

Capitalism

Economic system which allows an individual to accumulate great wealth through investment and ownership. The capitalist therefore controls the workforce and the capitalist view becomes the dominant one in society.

Commercialisation

The act of making something available to be bought or sold for a financial profit.

Commodity

A product that is demanded by the consumer.

STRETCH AND CHALLENGE

1 Explain why the economic system of capitalism depends upon decentralised administration.
2 Analyse the influence of capitalism and decentralised control on USA sport.

STRETCH AND CHALLENGE

Professional sport is inextricably linked to the media and sponsorship. This is a framework known as the 'Golden Triangle'. Each corner of the triangle represents a capitalist force. Discuss the extent to which sport has overall control of the triangle.

COMMERCIALISATION OF SPORT IN THE USA

Professional sport in the USA is seen as an entertainment commodity to be consumed by the American public. The key issue to understand about the social organisation of America is that it is driven by an economic system known as **capitalism** and this has led to the intensive **commercialisation** of sport. This means that sport is organised and presented in a way that likens it to a **commodity** to be sold to the consumer.

The concept of capitalism is important to understanding sport in America, not only because it is the economic system of the country but also because it controls social institutions. Capitalism therefore directly influences all that happens in professional sport, college sport and sport at high-school level. It will be seen later that capitalism also determines opportunities in physical and outdoor education.

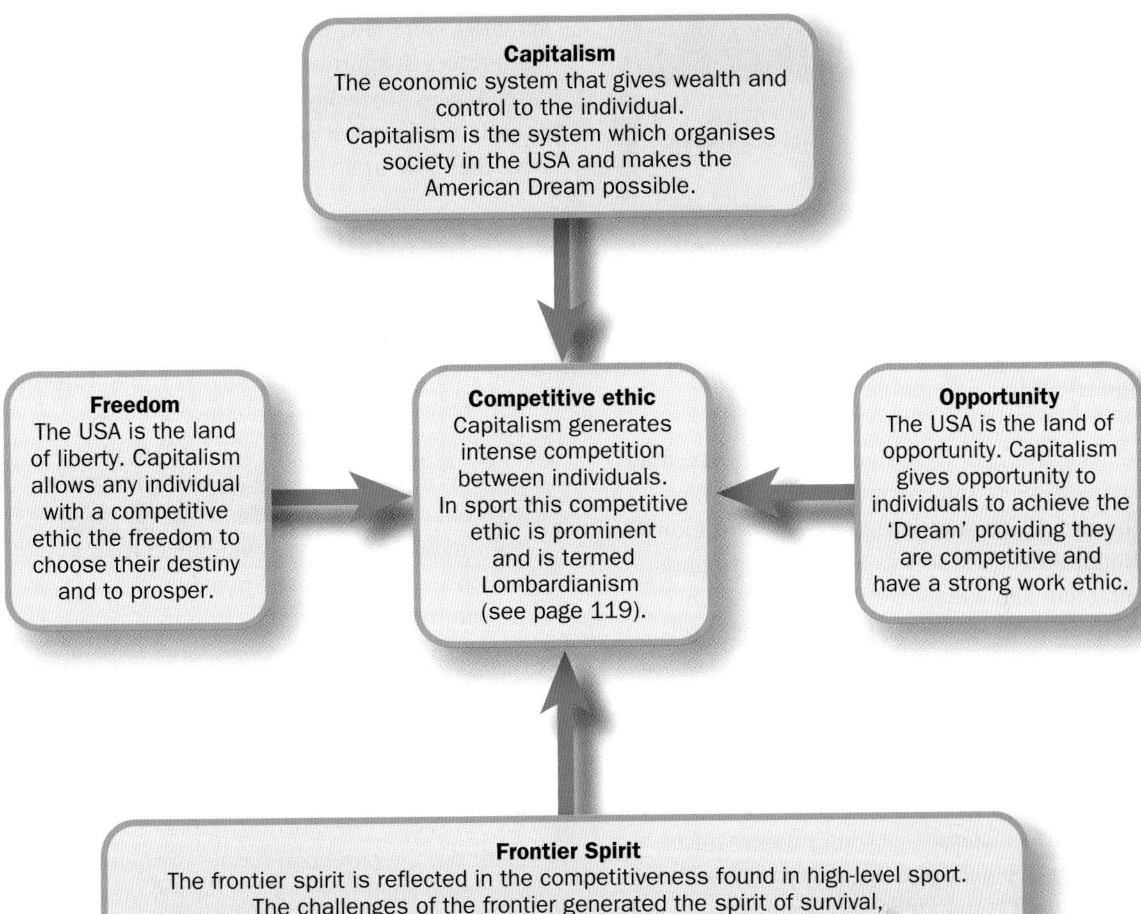

Capitalism
The economic system that gives wealth and control to the individual.
Capitalism is the system which organises society in the USA and makes the American Dream possible.
Freedom
The USA is the land of liberty. Capitalism allows any individual with a competitive ethic the freedom to choose their destiny and to prosper.
Competitive ethic
Capitalism generates intense competition between individuals.
In sport this competitive ethic is prominent and is termed Lombardianism (see page 119).
Opportunity
The USA is the land of opportunity. Capitalism gives opportunity to individuals to achieve the 'Dream' providing they are competitive and have a strong work ethic.
Frontier Spirit
The frontier spirit is reflected in the competitiveness found in high-level sport.
The challenges of the frontier generated the spirit of survival, toughness and individual enterprise that embraced the developing 'New World'.
The legacy of the frontier spirit has helped to instil love of liberty and opportunity.
The competitive ethic of the frontier spirit has influenced the promotion of capitalism.

Fig 6.4 Flow chart shows the link between the frontier spirit, the competitive ethic, the American Dream and capitalism

An overview of the cultural context of the USA, comprising national values and historical, geographical and social determinants, is presented above. The overview outlines the major cultural forces that control American society and provides the background information as to why sport is administered as a commercial business.

Commercialism has existed in American sports since the early twentieth century. It was only in the late twentieth century in the UK that the potential for commercialism in sport was exploited. Indeed, the 1920s are still regarded by some American writers as the golden era of sport. By that time the intrinsic values of the amateur player had disappeared and sport had moved toward a management-controlled organisation. From this point on, sport was in existence as a marketable **commodity**.

The amateur ethic and the idea that taking part was more important than winning delayed the onset of commercialism in UK sport.

Most Americans have contact with professional sport through the medium of television. The major television channels alone transmit 60 hours of sport per week and this figure rises significantly when the cable networks are included.

STRETCH AND CHALLENGE

With reference to specific sporting examples, explain how professional sport has been adapted to become a marketable commodity.

In the USA, the overriding focus of the media is on the 'Big Four' sports. The American Football Super Bowl event registers as the highest rated single television programme each year.

The media outlet of television became inextricably linked with sport and commercial sponsorship in the mid-1960s, largely through the operations of Roone Arledge, who was then Head of Sports Programming at a major American television network. By increasing the numbers of cameras at sporting events, deploying use of slow motion replays and introducing game analysis, Arledge revolutionised sports coverage. Sport was presented as entertainment and the game was portrayed as only one part of the overall sporting experience. This emphasis increased viewing ratings which in turn meant higher rates for advertising and therefore rapid corporate growth resulted.

From this time, the economic foundations of sport had changed. The innovations of presentation developed in the USA were eventually to have global influence.

COMMERCIALISM OF SPORT: A COMPARISON WITH THE UK

Television, initially a luxury for the wealthy, became available both in the UK and the USA during the early 1950s. At this time Britain was enduring a period of **post-war austerity**. People had little disposable income and leisure time activities were few, while admission to stand on the terraces at sporting venues was inexpensive. Attendances at weekly sporting events, such as Association Football and Rugby League matches, were therefore at a record high.

- In contrast to the terraced accommodation on UK sports grounds, venues for professional sports in America tended to be seated stadiums. This, unlike in the UK, is because matches in the USA incorporated sideshow entertainment and were therefore of extended duration.
- Seated stadiums in America were more conducive to family attendance whereas the terraces in the UK perpetuated an all-male culture that may have stimulated crowd violence during football matches. People were herded like cattle onto open terraces; this was uncomfortable and promoted a social environment that was less than dignified. Crowd violence in the USA was not a significant occurrence.
- As only short distances need to be travelled in the UK, access to sporting venues was easy. In addition, the parochial nature of society that was associated particularly with football and rugby negated the need for television. Indeed, one prominent Rugby League club refused the offer to televise a game because the gate attendance was thought to be threatened.
- In the USA the 'Big Three' sports had emerged (ice hockey was to come later) and spectator interest, as with Association Football in the UK, was high.
- Distance between venues in the USA was greater than in the UK, and American consumers, who were possibly more affluent than their UK counterparts, more readily embraced the idea of televised sport.
- Television had made an appearance in both countries by the mid-1950s. Therefore it was necessary to consider the management of televised sports coverage.
- The UK government and the only available television channels at the time, namely the BBC and ITV, agreed that ten sporting events could be shown by either company. Exclusive coverage was to be avoided. This agreement was in direct contrast to the 'revolution' in sports coverage that was about to take place in the USA.

KEY TERM

Post-war austerity

Period of financial hardship that applied to Britain in the late-1940s and 1950s.

APPLY IT!

There was no sponsorship in UK sport at this time. Gate receipts were the major source of income for professional clubs.

STRETCH AND CHALLENGE

Analyse the factors that have:

1 stimulated crowd violence in some sports in the UK
2 prevented crowd violence in USA sports.

REMEMBER

Easy access to sporting fixtures was possible because the UK is a relatively small landmass and rail links at the time were the best in the world.

REMEMBER

Review the 'Golden Triangle' relationship between sport, sponsorship and the media; see pages 303–06 in *OCR AS PE*.

British Satellite Broadcasting began in 1988 using sport to attract a mass audience. The presentation of sport as entertainment in the USA was by now well advanced and many techniques were replicated by the British company. This is an example of **cultural borrowing.**

KEY TERM

Cultural borrowing

This occurs when an idea which has appeal in one country is copied and embedded into the culture of the adopting country.

In the UK, the Broadcasting Act of 1990 declared that all rights to broadcast sport could be sold to the highest bidder. This declaration coincided with a merger between British Satellite Broadcasting and Sky to create BSkyB. BSkyB paid over £3 million to Division One football clubs for the exclusive rights to televise matches. Division One football clubs then broke away from the Football League to form the Premiership. Association Football has now entered the realm of 'big business' and remains the only UK sporting activity that can match the commercial status of the USA 'Big Four'.

Fig 6.5 Large numbers of UK fans tolerated the discomfort of the terraces up to the 1990s to watch sport. Most sports can now be enjoyed as a commercial product from the comfort of a stand seat

The Bosman Ruling in 1997 stated that professional football players could command their own fees for transfer and were free agents at the end of their contractual period. This is very important in terms of commercialism. The constraints for players were dropped and therefore they became individual entertainers rather than being bound by a club. The **Golden Triangle** is never more clearly evident than in the football entertainment industry.

KEY TERM

Golden Triangle

Defines the inextricable link between sport, the media and sponsorship.

- Media finance can be precarious and companies have been known to collapse, for example in 2002 ITV Digital was declared bankrupt while owing £200 million to football clubs. Financial risk, often called 'boom or bust' in the UK, is the underpinning factor of American capitalism.
- The withdrawal of media finance can also occur in the UK because of the traditional system of promotion and relegation.
- Relegation is now a serious business, involving the loss of media revenue and a reduced demand for merchandising.
- By contrast, in the USA, as will be seen later, relegation is not a part of the professional sports scene.
- At the commencement of the 2009 season, the UK-based rugby league adopted the American model and abolished the policy of relegation for an experimental period.

TASK 7

Discuss the advantages and the disadvantages of abolishing the traditional UK method of promotion and relegation.

STRETCH AND CHALLENGE

Explain how the teams finishing at the bottom of the table in USA sport manage to remain solvent and inevitably recover to become a major force.

In the UK, exclusivity of viewing has extended to other sports; for example, Channel 4 paid £50 million for the rights to televise cricket Test Matches from 1999 to 2002. More recently, cricket has taken on a new guise in the form of the Twenty20 version of the game. This faster, shorter and more intensive form of the sport has immediate entertainment appeal; coloured uniforms add to the spectacle. A winning team is certain to emerge in Twenty20 cricket matches often staged in the evening under floodlights for the convenience of the consumer.

TASK 8

Using examples from a range of sports, discuss the changes that have been made to these sports by the governing bodies in order that the sports become commercially viable.

STRETCH AND CHALLENGE

With reference to American culture and the nature of Twenty20 cricket, discuss the prospect of cricket becoming a marketable product in America.

In the UK, the Rugby Football Union (RFU) withstood commercial pressure and remained strictly compliant to the ideals of amateurism until the 1990s. After the success of the first World Cup in 1988, however, and as a consequence of increased global television interest, rugby union agreed, in what became known as the Paris Declaration, to break with tradition and adopt professionalism. This announcement was greeted with astonishment in England where amateurism had remained firmly ingrained and there was no dependence on commercialism. The English RFU was forced to commit to commercialism.

EXAM TIP

The comparison between the UK and the USA sports scene is a popular examination topic.

Social determinants affecting sport in the USA and the UK

SOCIAL DETERMINANTS IN THE USA

While promoting itself as the 'land of opportunity' and the 'land of the free', the USA, like other countries, has been socially discriminatory in matters involving sport. Ethnic minority groups have traditionally lacked the opportunity to play a full part in all sports, but have a history of producing champions in gladiatorial contests and the explosive events in athletics. For example, African Americans and Puerto Rican Americans have excelled in boxing, sprinting and long jump.

Often the provision of facilities for ethnic groups has not been of the same standard as that enjoyed by members of the mainstream culture. As a consequence, the esteem and belief among minority cultures that success across all sports is possible has been less than positive.

In the last fifty years this situation has changed. Role models from ethnic communities have emerged in sports that were traditionally the preserve of wealthy, white and mainstream people. Even today, however, in sports like baseball and American gridiron football, the legacy of discrimination is evident. It will later be seen that the allocation of field positions in these sports may reflect racial discrimination.

This topic is covered in greater depth on pages 139–141.

SOCIAL DETERMINANTS IN THE UK: A COMPARISON WITH THE USA

Discrimination against minority groups is also evident in the UK. A significant majority of UK citizens is denied access to sport participation and the chance to excel at an elite level; indeed, it is true to say that sport for all is not, as yet, a reality.

As in America, access to sport in the UK is determined by three factors:

- *Opportunity* – that is, having the chance to take part or to achieve the highest levels in sport; chance may be determined by time and money.
- *Provision* – having the conditions, equipment and facilities to participate or reach the top in sport.
- *Esteem* – this indicates that confidence is a determining factor in the decision to participate and to strive for the top levels in sport.

REMEMBER

The three factors of opportunity, provision and esteem influence mass participation and sporting excellence; see pages 280–81 *OCR AS PE*.

Social factors relate to how society is organised. The boundaries that indicated social class in the UK gradually became less distinct in the second part of the twentieth century. Society in the UK, however, continues to be stratified. The dominant group in the UK, as in the USA, remains white, middle-class and male. This group has the greatest opportunity in sport. Conversely, other groups that are lower in the hierarchy, for example Asian women, have considerably less opportunity.

In the USA, hierarchical organisation of society also exists and this correlates positively with opportunity. It will be seen, however, that the dominance of the white male is challenged in the USA as the cultural esteem of ethnic minorities increases.

Cultural factors relate to traditions, customs and even sports that are considered important to a race or group of people. Often the culture of a minority group may cause separation from the **mainstream culture**. This detachment may be chosen or it may come about through **segregation**. The latter implies unfair treatment and is a key factor of **discrimination**. Although the Americans claim to have a culture of **pluralism**, the hard fact is that discrimination exists on both sides of the Atlantic.

The groups that are most likely to suffer from discrimination or social exclusion from sport in the UK are shown in the spider diagram in Fig 6.6.

Sport England, the government agency responsible for community sport in England, is an example of a UK organisation that is addressing the problems of these excluded groups of people. Such groups are termed 'target' or 'priority' groups.

The USA also has strategies to promote community sport but the equivalent of the Sport England organisation does not exist.

KEY TERMS

Segregation

The policy or practice of keeping people of different ethnic and cultural backgrounds separate.

Mainstream culture

The established, dominant culture.

Discrimination

To treat people less favourably than others as a result of their race, nationality, or cultural or ethnic background.

Pluralism

Culture in which peoples of all ethnic or cultural backgrounds are tolerated and welcomed.

SOCIAL VALUES IN THE USA

The economic system of capitalism is a determinant that has directly influenced and shaped the values held by American society. These values are outlined below.

1 *The American Dream*

The American Dream relates to equality of opportunity and the belief that happiness is secured through the generation of wealth. The 'Dream', although available to all, can be achieved only through hard work. American society, however, is also uncompromisingly competitive. Failure in the workplace will result in dismissal. This is directly reflected in sport through the 'hire and fire' contract often given to coaches and players.

2 *The Land of Opportunity*

This value is closely linked to the 'Dream' and is often interpreted as 'Rags to Riches'. The inference

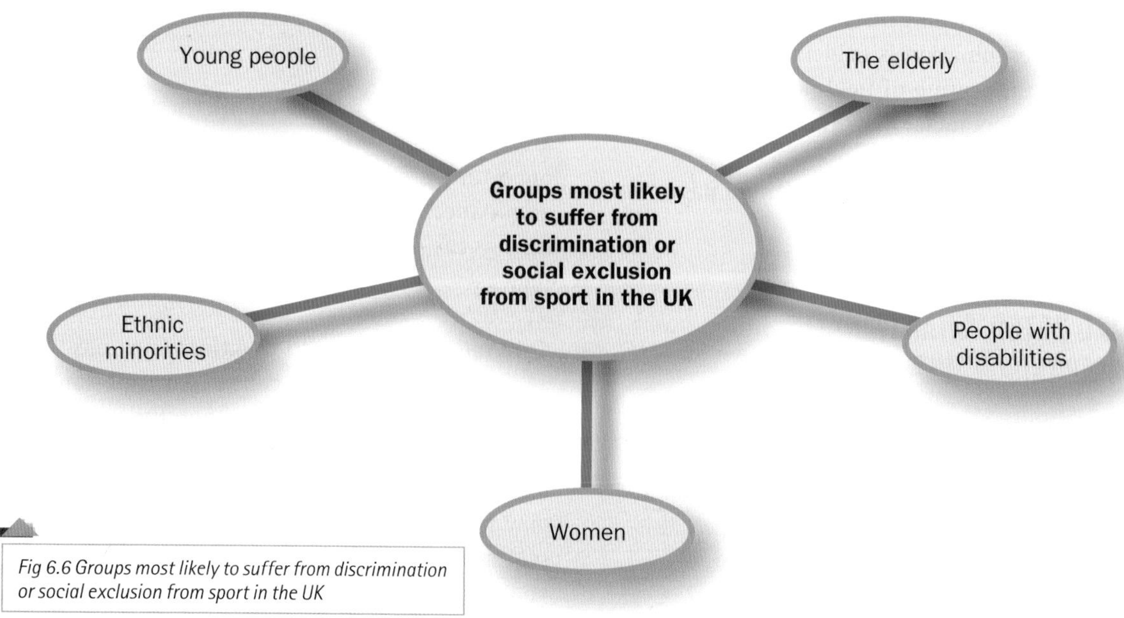

Fig 6.6 Groups most likely to suffer from discrimination or social exclusion from sport in the UK

is that all citizens have the opportunity and the freedom to rise from a lowly beginning to achieve success. To reach the 'Dream' is the ideal of every American and this ambition drives the machine of capitalism.

3 *Lombardianism*

The mainstream competitive culture has acquired the name Lombardianism after the football coach Vince Lombardi coined the phrase, 'Winning isn't everything – it is the only thing'. This win-at-all-costs ethic fits with capitalism, freedom and opportunity. It is instilled by the frontier legacy.

REMEMBER

The ethic of Lombardianism and the development of capitalism as an economic system have been influenced by the legacy of frontierism, as depicted by Fig 6.4 on page 113.

REMEMBER

The 'New World' of the USA was attractive to the European immigrants of the mid-nineteenth century because it was known to be 'the land of opportunity'.

The possibility of achieving success in a land boasting freedom, liberty and equal opportunity must have been an inspiration to immigrants who in Europe had experienced oppression. Many, by electing to adopt the culture, customs and sports of their new country, welcomed **assimilation** into American society. However, not all sectors of society were able to assimilate successfully and it could be argued that American society gave equal opportunity to some but not to all.

KEY TERM

Assimilation

The process of identifying oneself with and being accepted into a new culture. In the USA, this process has previously been referred to as Americanisation.

To understand the reason for exclusion from opportunity, it is necessary to be aware that American society is organised not only by wealth but also on the basis of race. Being the first to become established in the New World, the White Anglo Saxon Protestants (WASPs) assumed and have retained domination. Ethnic minority groups have a place on the hierarchy and this is depicted in Fig 6.7. This model can be described in the context of centrality and stacking.

Fig 6.7 Hierarchy of ethnic groups in the USA

1. WASP
2. Ethnic Europeans
3. African Americans
4. Mexicans & Puerto Ricans
5. Vietnamese
6. Native American Indians

The WASP mainstream culture is the central controlling dominant culture, while the ethnic minority groups are stacked in order of status and power. It will later be seen that the terms 'stacking' and 'centrality' are also applied to the correlation between racial background and the positions of players in prominent American team sports (see page 140).

The USA has always comprised many races and ethnic groups, and this accounts for the hierarchical organisation of their society and the dominant WASP culture. Britain, by contrast, has experienced mass immigration only since the 1950s, and this has stimulated problems relating to the inequality of opportunity.

There is another less overt discriminatory process in American society involving two ideas: **hegemony** and pluralism. This can be explained clearly if it is imagined that two groups operate as follows:

KEY TERM

Hegemony

Culture in which one social group dominates or has leadership over another.

1 *The Hegemonic Group*:
This group has the power to influence and dominate USA society. It comprises a small minority of the wealthiest people. People in this group are extreme capitalists who tend to be the managers of large businesses, of which sport is one.

2 *The Pluralistic Group:*
This group comprises the vast majority of Americans who believe that liberty and justice are equally available to all Americans. They are the people who believe the American Dream is available to all who adopt a positive work ethic. People in this group could well be players in professional sport.

Discrimination occurs because the exclusive hegemonic group, for its own gain, manipulates the pluralistic group. Increasingly the hegemonic group allows players from ethnic minorities into decision-making roles because they may improve the quality of the game. For example, in gridiron football, more African American players are being selected into the role of the quarterback decision maker.

American mainstream culture is centred on competitiveness and the importance of winning. This is evident in the workplace and is reflected in sport where the 'win-at-all-costs' ethic is paramount. However, there are also alternative ethics. It is important to be aware that three ethics are applied to physical recreation and sport in the USA, as shown in Table 2.

REMEMBER

The frontier spirit of the USA centred on the need for the individual to be strong and competitive.

SOCIAL VALUES: A COMPARISON WITH THE UK

- Society both in the UK and the USA is organised on the basis of a democracy.
- British citizens, like their American counterparts, enjoy voting rights and freedom of speech.
- The constraints of the class system may have determined opportunities and lifestyle in the UK, but the changing nature of employment, the economy and greater access to higher education are eliminating traditional class boundaries.
- Working as part of a team has been a traditional British value since possibly the struggle for Empire and the incorporation of team games in the public schools. The USA, by contrast, encourages the individual to be self-sufficient.
- Working as a team and learning to interact with others certainly remains a prominent value in UK schools in the twenty-first century.
- A sense of fair play is central to the British sporting ethos. The participation ethic continues to override the 'win-at-all-cost' ethic that is the mainstream prevalence in the USA.
- Both the USA and the UK are striving to overcome discrimination.

Table 2 Three ethics applied to physical recreation and sport in the USA

Lombardian ethic	Radical ethic	Counter culture
Winning means everything and is the prime motive for participation. This ethic prevails in inter-scholastic, inter-collegiate and professional sport. It is often linked with profit-making commercialism.	A winning outcome is important, as this is a mark of achievement. The process of arriving at achievement is, however, most important. This ethic prevails in intra-mural college games and is associated with Lifetime Sport, which is the equivalent of lifelong activity and lifetime sport in the UK.	This approach has an anti-competitive focus and emphasises the intrinsic benefits which can be derived from participation. An extreme example is eco culture, which involves fun and health promotion in the outdoor environment.

TASK 9

Identify the measures that are now in place in the UK which are helping to prevent discrimination in sport. (You may wish to refer to page 285 of *OCR AS PE*.)

Fig 6.8 A traditional English cricket match

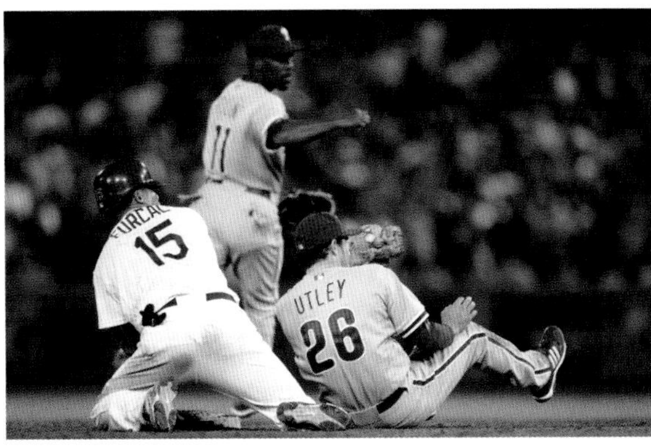

Fig 6.9 A typical scene from an American baseball game

TASK 10

1 Compare the variations between the UK's traditional game of cricket and the American national sport of baseball. Use only the evidence in the photographs shown in Figs 6.8 and 6.9 to make your comparisons.
2 Compare the cultural determinants that have caused the UK to adopt cricket as a major sport while the USA has elected baseball as the national sport.

REMEMBER

In the exam, one mark is given when a fact relating to the UK is compared with a fact relating to the other country in question.

EXAM TIP

In the exam, the 20-mark Stretch and Challenge question is likely to ask you to relate differences in sport between the USA and the UK to cultural determinants.

Physical education and school sport in the USA and the UK

Health, fitness and obesity levels in developed countries are the cause of growing concern. These concerns are global, but it would appear that America is experiencing major problems.

- According to one study (Zametkin, 2006), 15 per cent of American children aged between 6 and 19 years are regarded as clinically obese.
- In the United States, over 40 million people are considered obese.
- In the total population, 75 per cent of Americans are not reaching basic activity recommendations and 25 per cent of people in this category are completely sedentary (Wellness International Network Statistics).

There are similarities between the health patterns in the UK and USA. It is alleged that in the UK fitness levels have reached an all-time low.

- Of all adults in the UK, 38 per cent are considered overweight while almost 25 per cent have been diagnosed as obese.
- Statistics also indicate that almost 20 per cent of children under 16 years old in the UK are obese (Department of Health). It would appear that the sedentary lifestyle adopted by the urban population in America during the 1950s is now evident in the UK.

TASK 11

Review the factors contributing to a sedentary lifestyle in the UK. Discuss the UK recommendations for an active, balanced and healthy lifestyle (see page 214 of *OCR AS PE*).

It is recommended in a report issued by the Chief Medical Officer for the UK that young people should undertake one hour of moderate physical activity every day. This activity need not be continuous but can be an intermittent commitment. It would appear that although greater numbers of young people are taking up an activity, obesity continues to increase.

TASK 12

Conduct research into the strategies that are being implemented to improve health and fitness while reducing obesity levels among young people in the UK.

PHYSICAL EDUCATION IN THE USA

Physical Education is facing a crisis in USA. Up to the mid-1970s, daily Physical Education lessons were compulsory for all ages. However, this is not the case in the twenty-first century.

After the Nixon administration abolished military conscription in 1970, all states became less vigorous in enforcing compulsory Physical Education. In 2000, Illinois (see map on page 108)remained the only state to enforce the subject, but since that time it has also withdrawn the policy of compulsory PE. Chicago officials estimated that they would save $16 million a year by making PE optional in grades 11 and 12. This is in contrast to the UK, where a National Curriculum ensures compulsory PE is in place for all children up to the age of 16 years.

APPLY IT!

Schools in the USA are decentralised autonomous bodies and are run as businesses.

Participation in PE for all American students was approximately 70 per cent in the 1980s but fell below 60 per cent by the end of the twentieth century. The greatest decline comes after primary school. The warning given by the National Association for Sport and Physical Education (NASPE) is that the subject is costly to run and is now becoming an expensive luxury. **School boards** are therefore eliminating PE from the timetable, not only because it is uneconomic but also because it is unpopular with students and is taking up time that could be spent on academic subjects.

KEY TERM

School board

In the USA, the authority that controls the school.

APPLY IT!

The daily PE programme in the USA comprised direct skill learning and fitness. It involved a great deal of practical testing which was unpopular with many students.

It is alleged that the 'No Child Left Behind' Act of 2001 implemented by the federal government may be a major culprit in the diminishing of the PE curriculum. This Act was designed to raise academic standards across all ability ranges and to make schools accountable for the quality of academic standards. Subjects perceived as non-academic like PE began to be withdrawn from the curriculum from this point onwards.

REMEMBER

PE in the UK has distinctive characteristics and clear benefits for young people; see page 220 of *OCR AS PE*.

STRETCH AND CHALLENGE

How does the term 'accountability' relate to the major American values? Explain the factors that have increased the accountability of professional sports in the UK and USA.

As will later be seen, the status of PE in the USA is lower than that of High School sport.

REMEMBER

Education in the USA is decentralised; each school has autonomy. This means there is no National Curriculum, as there is in the UK.

Erosion of physical activities during curriculum time has accelerated existing health problems. The Californian Department of Education reported recently that 80 per cent of the one million students in Grades 5, 7 and 9 (the 10–14 age group) failed to achieve minimum standards in the '**fitnessgram**' assessment. There are plenty of links to fitnessgrams on Internet search engines. Try one out and see how well you do.

KEY TERM

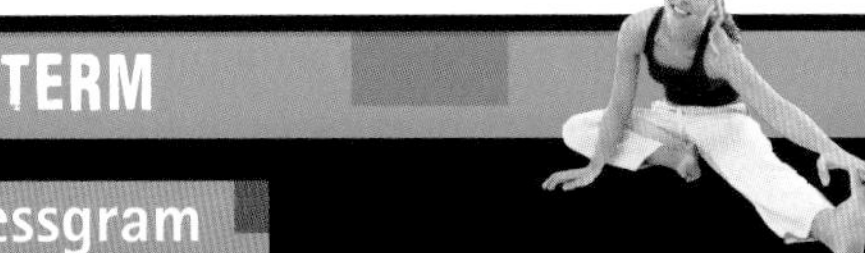

Fitnessgram

A simple test of physical fitness used worldwide.

STRATEGIES TO PROMOTE PE IN THE USA

Strategies are being put into place to reverse this declining trend and to improve the quality of timetabled PE experiences which the National Association for Sport and Physical Education (NASPE) believe to be the cornerstone of healthy active lifestyles. To this end, $60 million has been invested into a programme entitled Physical Education for Progress (PEP).

The PEP programme aims to improve the quality and quantity of PE from kindergarten through to grade 12 (equivalent to Year 13 in the UK). Local school districts and community organisations can access grant funds to promote activities, develop the curriculum, purchase equipment and train teachers.

Further strategies to promote PE will be considered at the end of this section.

REMEMBER

PE in the UK has high status and facilitates many benefits. It is also a core curriculum subject and is part of the National Curriculum. (See pages 220–22 of *OCR AS PE*.)

EXAM TIP

You could be asked to compare PE in the USA with PE in the UK in the exam. Take care to review UK PE in the socio-cultural section of the AS textbook: Chapter 11.

LEGISLATION IN THE USA: TITLE IX

Title IX was passed as law in 1972 and is an example of central federal legislation. It addressed the issue of gender inequality in all areas of education and stated: 'No person in the United States shall on the basis of gender be excluded from participation in any education programme or activity receiving federal assistance.' Schools can lose federal funding if they are not compliant with the legislation.

In terms of sport, the law was not primarily concerned with opening the traditional physical contact activities like wrestling or gridiron football for female participation. Nor did it state that the exact amount of money granted to men should also be invested into women's sports.

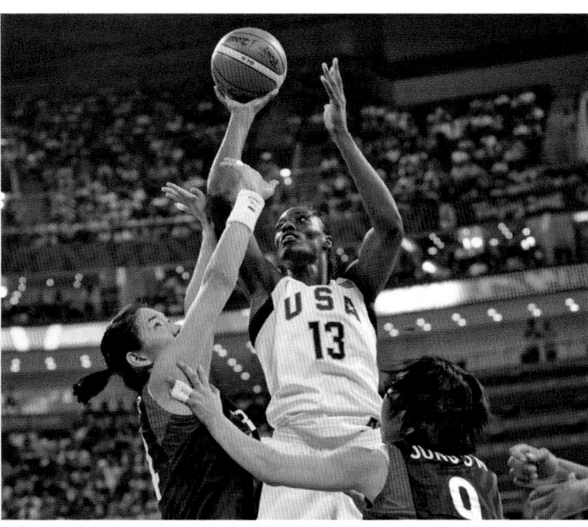

Fig 6.10 Title IX has greatly increased the sporting opportunities for women in the USA

The focus of Title IX was for women to have equal opportunities.

Title IX has critics who claim there are disadvantages with the legislation. It is believed that money to support women has been taken directly from men and that minority sports like wrestling are being withdrawn from High School and College for political and financial reasons.

Title IX is not, however, intended to have a **zero-sum** outcome. Some schools may have chosen to withdraw male sports programmes in an effort to comply with the law and to meet budget constraints. It is a federal claim that parity has now been created both for men and women in athletic opportunity and quality of experience.

> *'There's been real growth in the number of women who participate in sports, receive scholarships and benefit from increased budgets. There are more opportunities to compete at elite levels through competitions like the Olympics, World Championships and professional leagues.'*
> (Federal Government Report, 2005)

KEY TERM

Zero-sum

This means the winner takes all. It is an American term that relates to the mainstream competitive ethos.

EXAM TIP

Use technical language in your answers when appropriate. Zero-sum is an example of technical language.

APPLY IT!

Before the implementation of Title IX, only 1 in 27 girls participated in High School sport. Participation rates are now claimed to be 1 in 2.5.

ADAPTED PHYSICAL EDUCATION PROGRAMMES

The USA has a very active policy of sports provision, particularly in education for disabled people. Federal law states that PE must be provided for students with special needs and disabilities. The provision made for these children is through the Adapted Physical Education Programme. This programme involves activities that have been modified to enable full participation. In order to raise the quality of experience and increase awareness of disability, students with special needs are integrated into the mainstream high school curriculum.

STRATEGIES TO PROMOTE PE AND SCHOOL SPORT IN THE UK

The Physical Education School Sport and Club Links strategy (PESSCLS) was a government strategy to promote Physical Education and school sport in the UK and was launched in 2002. In 2008, PESSCLS was renamed the PE, School Sport and Young People (PESSYP*)* strategy. The Prime Minister pledged to invest an extra £100 million in 2007.

There are nine interlinked work strands of the PESSYP (formerly called PESSCLS) and these are displayed in Table 3 opposite. Each strand represents a strategy to promote PE and sport in the UK.

TASK 13

Find out more about the nine strands of the PE, School Sport and Young People (PESSYP) strategy by going to www.heinemann.co.uk/hotlinks, entering the express code 6855P and clicking on the relevant link.

The American Physical Education for Progress (PEP) scheme is not a direct equivalent of PESSYP but it is driven by the federal government and receives state funding.

Table 3 The PE, School Sport and Young People (PESSYP) strategy

Strand	The strategy promoted by the strand
Sports colleges	Sports colleges receive additional government funding to increase the opportunities for young people to become involved in sport. Sports colleges link with other local schools to form School Sports Partnerships.
School Sports Partnerships (SSPs)	The School Sports Partnerships strategy brings together individual Sports Colleges with groups or 'clusters' of schools. The principle aims of SSPs are to increase participation, promote excellence and develop sporting links in the wider community.
Professional development	The professional development of teachers and coaches involves providing teachers with training to improve the quality of their lesson delivery.
Step into sport	This strategy provides a clear framework to enable young people aged 14–19 years to be involved with sports leadership.
Club links	Club links aim to strengthen the associations between schools and sports clubs.
Gifted and talented	This strategy is designed to help young people with identified ability develop core skills that are the basis of all sports.
Sporting playgrounds	This strategy involves the development of primary school playgrounds to promote play and physical activity.
Swimming	Via this strategy, the teaching of swimming is being increasingly promoted in primary schools, not only as a healthy activity but as part of a healthy lifestyle.
High quality Physical Education and School Sport (PESS)	PESS involves guidance as to how a school can improve the quality of Physical Education.

REMEMBER

The aims and the network links of sports colleges promote sporting opportunities for young people and the wider community. (See pages 272–73 of *OCR AS PE*.)

In addition to the PESSYP strategy, Kitemarking is a strategy that is designed to promote participation in sporting activities in UK schools. Kitemarking for School Physical Education involves a scheme to reward schools who are delivering the PESSYP strategy to a particularly high standard. There are three Kitemark awards:

1 Activemark – an award for Primary Schools
2 Sportsmark – an award for Secondary Schools
3 Sports Partnershipmark – an award for achievement across the School Sport Partnership.

REMEMBER

Special Kitemarks are awarded to schools within the School Sport Partnership; see page 275 of *OCR AS PE*.

In the USA, increased opportunities are provided for children with special needs to engage in physical activity through the Adaptive PE Programmes. Similarly, in the UK the skills of children with special needs are rewarded in Healthy Living schemes that include opportunities in sports.

OUTDOOR EDUCATION IN THE USA

The size, beauty and geographical diversity of North America coupled with the colonial and frontier legacy have placed the love of the 'outdoors' deep in the traditional values of the nation. An association with the natural environment has become part of the American Dream.

REMEMBER

To remind yourself of the diverse climate and topography of the USA, refer to page 109 of this chapter.

The term 'outdoor education' implies a formal process of conveying educational values. This takes the form of teaching physical skills and facilitating personal and social development in the outdoor natural environment. Appreciation of the natural environment is a highly regarded educational experience in the USA.

REMEMBER

Consider the concept of outdoor education in the UK and the necessity of 'perceived risk' as opposed to 'real risk' during activities.

Since the mid-twentieth century, Summer Camps (sometimes called Camp Schools) for young people have increased significantly. Summer Camps take place in the summer vacation for durations of a few days or up to eight weeks. There are three classifications of camps:

1. state-sponsored camps
2. camps sponsored by business, ethnic and religious groups
3. commercial camps.

State-sponsored camps enable less wealthy children to have a basic outdoor experience, while commercial camps can be very lavish and extremely expensive, being available only to rich families.

APPLY IT!

The range of Summer Camps available to the individual extends with increasing wealth. This reflects, once again, the discriminatory nature of a capitalist economy.

It is estimated that there are 12,000 camps in America: 8000 are residential while 4000 are day camps. There are many different types of camps. Some examples are given below:

- academic camps for gifted children
- self-improvement camps offering courses in modelling, weight loss and etiquette
- special needs camps for children with learning difficulties and sensory impairment.

A camp is chosen on the basis of the experience required by the child. The most popular specialist activity camps include outdoor adventure and sports.

Most camps have a mission to perpetuate a patriotic culture. For example, the bugle sounds the morning reveille and the Stars and Stripes flag is ceremonially unfurled and displayed. In the evening, the 'camp fire' rituals are a highlight and enjoyed by all children. These features reflect a military ethos and the spirit of frontierism, both of which underpin national pride.

There are many values and benefits to be offered by Summer Camps. The major physical benefits promote activity and healthy, balanced and active lifestyles. Other benefits are listed in the spider diagram in Fig 6.11.

REMEMBER

There are constraints on widespread participation in outdoor education for children in the UK – see page 224 of *OCR AS PE*.

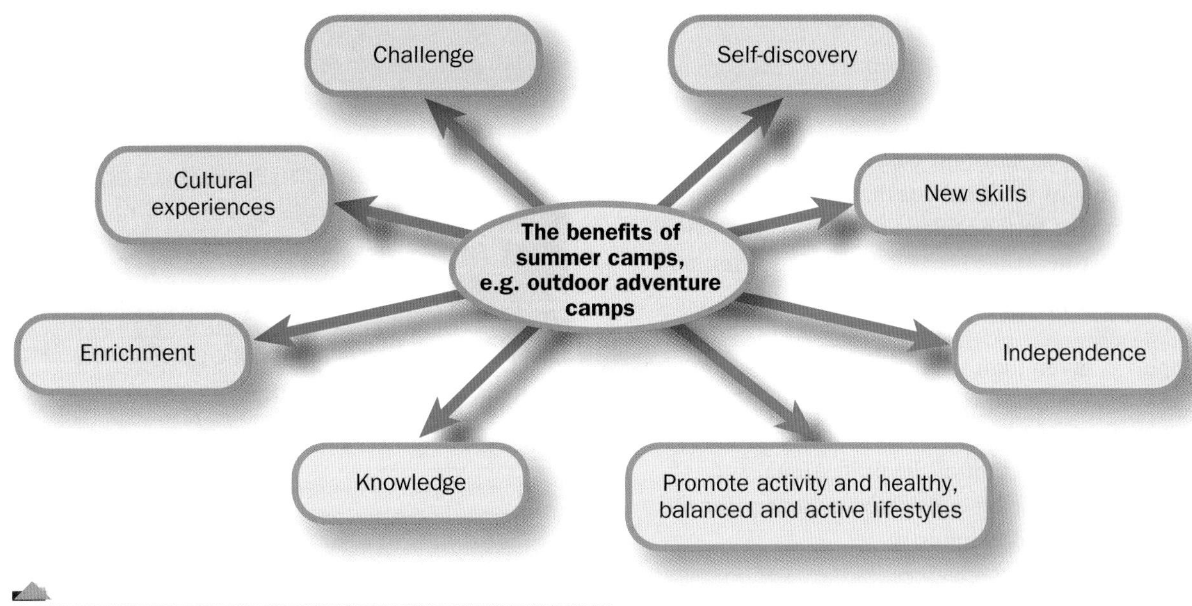

Fig 6.11 The benefits of summer camps, e.g. outdoor adventure camps

EXAM TIP

A popular exam question is to compare outdoor education in the UK and the USA in terms of its constraints and benefits. Refer to page 224 of the *OCR AS PE* book.

HIGH SCHOOL INTER-MURAL SPORT

If a crisis exists in the provision of daily Physical Education in the USA, it must be said that inter-mural or inter-school sport is strong and, for several reasons, this fact is important. Although generalisation is inevitable in such a large country like the USA, most major sports are represented in high schools for the purpose of inter-school competition.

As they are three of the 'Big Four' national sports, there is an emphasis on American gridiron football, basketball and baseball.

Despite Title IX legislation, girls tend not to participate in American Football but engage in track and field athletics, volleyball, gymnastics and increasingly soccer. In more affluent 'districts' opportunities arise to participate in sports requiring large expenditure. Minneapolis High in Minnesota (see map on page 108), for example, has an ice rink, which as a facility is used intensively by students and the community for ice hockey and figure skating.

Inter-mural or inter-school sport is well organised in the USA. The State High School Athletic Association (SHSAA), which is a national advisory body, has branches in each state and controls inter-scholastic athletic competition.

An example of a state branch department is the Arizona Interscholastic Association (AIA). Like all branch associations, the AIA receives no federal funding, as individual schools finance their own athletic programmes. It promotes the mission that inter-school sport competition is beneficial to the total education process.

REMEMBER

Each school funds its own athletic programme; no federal funding is forthcoming. This is in contrast to the UK where central funding is in place.

For the purposes of competition, schools throughout America are classified into five 'conferences' based on the number of enrolled students. A school classified as 'one A' would comprise up to 200 students, while a school with an excess of 1,900 students would constitute an 'AAAAA' conference.

Specialist coaches are in charge of the USA school teams. Assistant coaches work under the leadership of the head coach, who in turn is accountable to the athletic director of the school. The latter manages both Physical Education and inter-scholastic sport.

Sport is given high status in American schools and has a higher priority than Physical Education. The motive behind this is that inter-school sport is a direct reflection of the professional sports scene and could be considered a nursery for the commercial sports industry.

APPLY IT!

Mission High in the state of Texas is a 5A conference school with a strong tradition of gridiron football. Fixtures are played on Friday nights in autumn. Accommodated in the school stadium is a crowd of around 15,000 people. Schools at this standard are perceived as centres of sports excellence and operate as the first progression in the production of elite professional performers.

Fig 6.11 The American High School sports scene reflects the commercial professional scene

Matches are played in the school stadium in an atmosphere often enhanced by marching bands and cheerleaders. There is a strong commitment to Lombardianism, not only because the community is a critical presence but also because the competence of the coach is judged on the team's result. The coach can be dismissed if the team is unsuccessful. The players also have a powerful incentive to 'win at all costs' as College Athletic Scholarships are on offer to the best players.

Inter-mural sport is expensive and the individual school, through gate receipts, sponsorship, media payment and **alumni** donations, generates the

Fig 6.12 The status of inter-mural school sport in the USA

Inter-mural school sport has high status in America because...
The High School is the centre of junior sporting excellence
There is the incentive of the College scholarship for the best players
The Lombardian ethos is instilled and skill is at a high level
The sporting venue is a stadium at the school
Large crowds are present
School sport reflects the professional sports scene
The coach is responsible and requires success because employment is on the basis of a 'hire and fire' contract
Sport is a commercial business for the school, attracting sponsorship and the media

Fig 6.13 The High School coach who is employed on the basis of a 'hire and fire' contract is required to instil the 'win-at-all-costs' ethos of Lombardianism

necessary finance. These sources of revenue are precarious and dependent on the team providing the public with entertainment through attractive play and successful results.

KEY TERM

Alumni

Former students or friends of the institution who donate money.

There is evidence that American culture is reflected in inter-mural school sports. Opportunity is available for all to play and with it the chance to excel. Only the elite performers of Lombardian disposition, however, achieve the college scholarship that brings professional status and the ultimate 'American Dream' one step closer.

TASK 14

Compare the American High School sport scene with your own experience of inter-school sport in the UK.

EXAM TIP

A popular exam question is to compare American High School sport with secondary school sport in the UK. Be prepared to compare the role of the American High School coach with that of the UK Physical Education teacher.

INTRA-MURAL SPORTS IN THE USA

Intra-mural sports are recreational sports that take place within the High School. At this level activities may involve leagues and are open to all students who form their own teams. The fact that all students are encouraged promotes participation in physical activities. The nature of the games is intended to be informal, but in reality competition can be intensive.

APPLY IT!

The radical ethic as opposed to the Lombardian ethic is associated with intra-mural sports; see page 131 of this chapter.

Intra-mural sports start in the elementary schools (equivalent to primary schools in the UK) and develop through high school into college (university) education. Popular recreational sports include flag football (which is non-contact American gridiron football), lacrosse, field hockey, soccer and volleyball.

REMEMBER

Recreational sport is important in UK schools; see page 217 of *OCR AS PE*.

CONTEMPORARY INITIATIVES TO PROMOTE PE AND SCHOOL SPORT IN THE USA

The major strategies to promote Physical Education, school sport and physical activity in the USA have for the most part already been discussed in this chapter; Fig 6.14 below provides a summary.

REMEMBER

Adaptive Physical Education Programmes promote opportunities for students with special needs.

In addition, many different programmes can be found on the Internet that are designed to promote health and participation in physical activity. Examples of these are Hip Hop to Health and the Child and Adolescent Trial for Cardiovascular Heath (CATCH programme). While these programmes are important, they may be short-lived.

TASK 15

Carry out a search on the Internet to find sites for American programmes to promote health and participation in physical activity. Discuss the potential effectiveness of the new programmes that you find.

INTRA-SCHOOL SPORT IN THE UK

Intra-school sport in the UK is organised on similar lines to USA intra-mural sports. Intra-school sport is most prominent in secondary schools and operates both in the private and state-funded sectors of education. As with intra-mural sports in the USA, intra-school sport tends to be recreational but has the scope to be very competitive.

An example of competitive intra-school sport in the UK is the traditional athletics sports day held both in primary and secondary schools. Competitions are usually arranged between school 'Houses', and although traditional sports like football and netball continue to be dominant, most schools offer a wide range of activities.

Fig 6.14 Initiatives to promote PE, school sport and physical activity

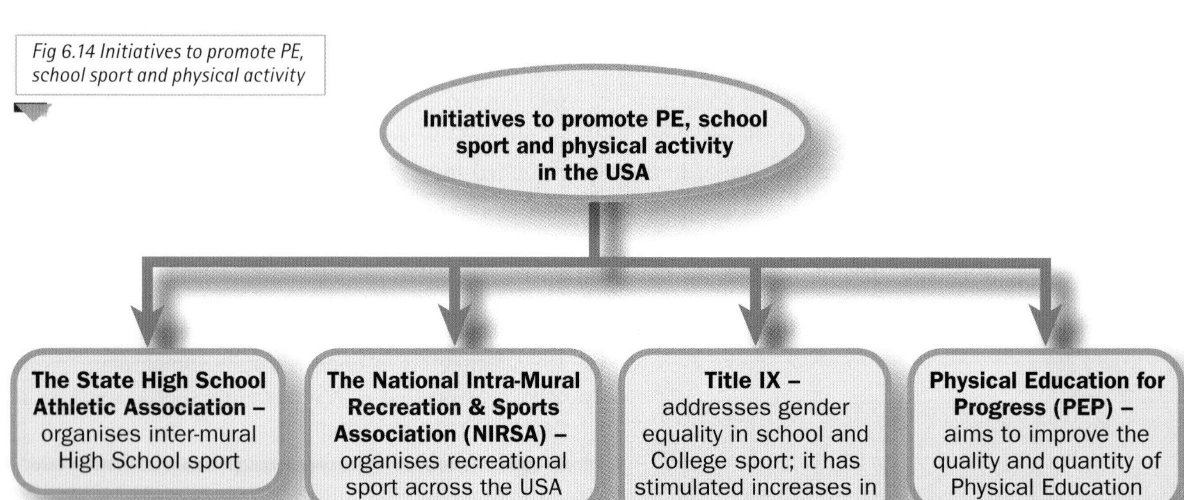
Initiatives to promote PE, school sport and physical activity in the USA
The State High School Athletic Association – organises inter-mural High School sport
The National Intra-Mural Recreation & Sports Association (NIRSA) – organises recreational sport across the USA
Title IX – addresses gender equality in school and College sport; it has stimulated increases in female participation
Physical Education for Progress (PEP) – aims to improve the quality and quantity of Physical Education

In the UK, intra-school sport is associated with a participation ethic. Intra-mural sports in the USA have a similar philosophy which is termed the radical ethic.

In keeping with the organisation in the USA, intra-school/college sports leagues in the UK may be organised by teachers or students. Teams are formed on the basis of friendship groups. Matches are often arranged during timetabled PE and sports lessons, but also take place during lunch periods and after school.

For students aged 16–18 in further education, intra-school sports may be the basis of an Enrichment Programme.

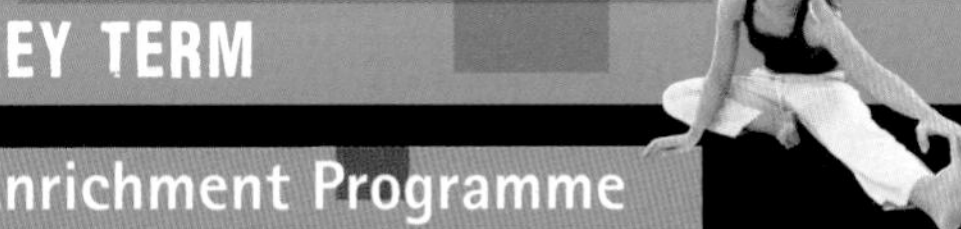

KEY TERM

Enrichment Programme

A voluntary commitment made to an activity, club or project that lies outside of the student's timetabled course.

School sport in the UK endured a difficult period during the latter part of the twentieth century, but more recently participation rates have increased. This improvement has taken place because of government support and an awareness of the importance of promoting a balanced, active lifestyle in schools.

INTER-SCHOOL SPORT IN THE UK

Inter-school sport in the UK involves sports matches and competitions with other schools and colleges. In the USA the term given for sports fixtures with other high schools is inter-mural sports. According to government statistics, involvement in competitive games on this basis is increasing; it is estimated that 400,000 students engaged in inter-school sport during the academic year 2007–08. Andrew Burnham, the Culture Secretary, commented: 'School sport is stronger in 2008 than it has been for the last thirty years.' The government plan to invest £2.4 billion in school sport up to 2011.

REMEMBER

Government health statistics indicate that fitness levels in the UK are at an all-time low; see page 121.

School sport is important in the UK, but in direct contrast with the USA it is Physical Education which has the higher status. The school sports scene in the UK, as will be seen below, differs markedly from that in the United States. In the UK, matches, competitions and leagues are administered by several agencies and organised as **extra-curricular** activities. This is in contrast with America, where the School Athletic Associations have responsibility for fixture organisation on a national scale.

KEY TERM

Extra-curricular

Outside of timetabled lessons.

In the UK, individual teachers organise friendly fixtures and some administer leagues comprising local schools and colleges. The School Sport Coordinator (SSCO) will have a specific responsibility to promote competitive sporting opportunities in and around their sports college. The Further Education Sports Co-ordinator (FESCO) will have the responsibility to extend and enhance physical activity provision in and around their sports college.

Sporting governing bodies tend to organise competitions culminating in national finals after progress has been achieved at local and regional level. The British Colleges Sport arranges national sporting competitions in a broad range of activities for Further Education (FE) colleges.

APPLY IT!

In the UK, *The Daily Mail* organises a national rugby union competition. Over 400 schools and colleges are entered.

Despite the title of 'sports college', secondary schools and FE colleges in the UK tend not to be centres of sporting excellence as they are in the USA. Kelly College in Devon and Millfield School, Somerset, have outstanding traditions in sport, but this does not equate to the USA model. Some schools and colleges have developed academies of sport, but these tend to be associated with professional sports clubs. Sports scholarships are offered to promising students by some private schools; the scholarship will include tuition and boarding fees.

In contrast with the USA, the sporting governing bodies in UK select county, regional and national teams; for example: Lancashire netball U16; North West hockey U18; Wales U18 rugby union.

Despite high standards at representative level, a participation ethic prevails in the UK. This is in direct contrast to the United States where Lombardianism is prevalent.

Sponsorship does exist on a small scale in the UK, but school fixtures tend not to attract great crowds of spectators. There may be local newspaper reports, but the media do not have a presence in UK school sport. By comparison, in the USA the media will focus on High School sport. In the UK, as a consequence of limited sponsorship and media coverage, extra-curricular sport, unlike in the USA, is not organised as a commercial business. Indeed, a lack of financial support continues to impede the development of UK school sport.

In the UK, the PE teacher tends to organise and coach school teams, whereas in America the specialist sports coach, usually under the management of the athletic director, has control. The USA specialist coach is employed on a 'hire and fire' basis, in contrast with the UK PE teacher who, in most cases, has a permanent contract.

Sport in UK schools does not attempt to replicate the professional sports scene. Indeed, it is regretted that the gamesmanship and dysfunctional behaviour sometimes witnessed in professional sport are occasionally displayed in school games. In contrast with the UK, inter-mural sport in the USA is a direct replication of professional sport.

REMEMBER

In the exam, one fact from the UK and one fact indicating a comparison from the USA will earn one mark.

Participation rates in sport in the USA and the UK

MASS PARTICIPATION IN THE USA

Mass participation in sports-related physical activity is not high in the USA. It is estimated by the Federal Department of Health and Human Services that about 19 per cent of people above the age of 16 years engage in a high level of physical activity.

In general, men are more likely than women to engage in high-level physical activity such as the level required in competitive sport, and this rate declines with age. It is also evident that activities undertaken on an individual basis are more popular than team games. The degree of affluence also significantly affects the opportunity to participate in physical activity. Statistics from Brown University School of Medicine indicate that about 60 per cent of USA adults are thought to be under active and that a significant minority of these people experience no activity.

The Sports Goods Manufacturers Association (SGMA) undertook research to find out the most popular sports and activities in the USA. Table 4 indicates the top ten sports, games or physical activities.

A gym and jogging culture has been evident in the USA since the 1950s and statistics indicate that engagement in fitness activities is increasing. In addition, over 40 million Americans are members of health clubs and the greatest increase

Table 4 The top ten sports, games or physical activities in the USA, 2007 (adapted from Sporting Goods Manufacturers Association (SGMA, 2008))

Activity/sport ranking	2007 participation figure	Level of frequency (days per year)
1 Walking	76,837,000	50+
2 Treadmill	29,182,000	50+
3 Stretching	28,318,000	50+
4 Weight training	28,186,000	50+
5 Running/jogging	24,240,000	50+
6 Fishing	23,714,000	8+
7 Cycling	21,151,000	25+
8 Basketball	18,005,000	13+
9 Bowling	15,422 000	13+
10 Low-impact aerobics	13,056,000	50+

in popularity for an activity is Pilates training. This type of fitness training engaged over 9 million people in 2007 and its growth rate since 2000 is approximately 500 per cent.

NATIONAL FITNESS LEVELS IN THE USA

The topic of fitness levels for the USA was covered earlier in this chapter, in the section dealing with Physical Education (see page 121). It is important, however, to emphasise that while trends in the fitness industry are positive, the majority of Americans need to be more active. Obesity is a major concern. Government statistics indicate that in the period 1985–2007 there has been a dramatic increase in obesity in the USA:

- in 2007 Colorado (see map on page 108) was the only state to have an obesity prevalence of less than 20 per cent
- thirty states were found to have 25 per cent or more of their population diagnosed as obese.

MASS PARTICIPATION RATES IN THE UK

The results of Sport England's Active People's Survey 2007 shows that sports participation in the UK has risen by almost 400,000 and that 75 per cent of people engage in physical activity (this includes walking). Mass participation rates in the UK are, in relative terms, higher than those in the USA.

Research was undertaken in 2007 by the General Household Survey (GHS) to find out about trends in sport participation in the UK; Fig 6.15 overleaf indicates the top sports, games or physical activities in the UK in terms of popularity. Although excluded from this list, walking for pleasure and fitness is as popular in UK as it is in America.

It appears that on both sides of the Atlantic, activities undertaken on an individual basis, such as swimming, keep fit, yoga, cycling and weight training, show higher participation rates than team games.

- On the whole, more men participate in sport in the UK than women, and this mirrors the trend in the USA. It is significant to indicate that swimming and fitness activities tend to be more popular with women.
- As in the USA, it was found that younger people in the UK are more likely to participate in activities and that involvement decreases with age. Participation is significantly reduced after the age of 45 years.

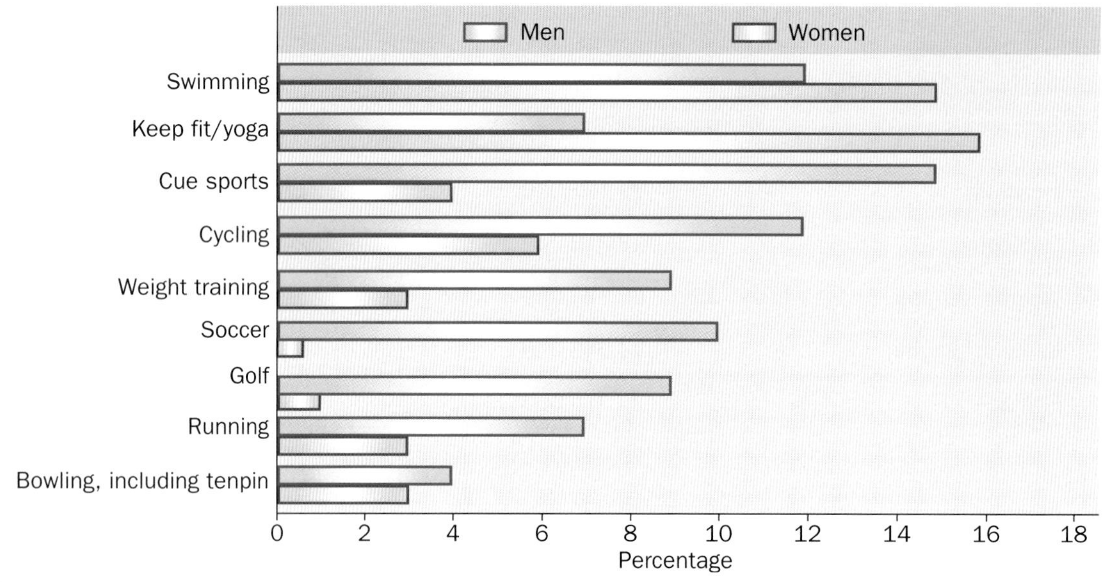

Fig 6.15 The top sports, games or physical activities in the UK in terms of popularity, 2007 (Source: Sport England Active People Survey)

- As in the USA, wealth is an important determinant in sports participation in the UK.
- In 1980 there were fewer than 200 gyms in the UK. In 2008 there were almost 6000. The USA 'gym culture' has influenced this trend.

It is significant that the only major game to feature in the top ten sports in the UK was soccer. There are parallels here with USA because basketball was the only major game to be represented there. (For information on national fitness levels in the UK, refer to page 121 of this chapter.)

STRETCH AND CHALLENGE

Analyse the statistics on sports participation in the USA and in the UK. Consider any comparisons that can be made about participation rates and trends. Discuss any cultural factors that may have influenced these trends.

STRATEGIES TO PROMOTE PARTICIPATION AND ENSURE LIFELONG INVOLVEMENT AND HEALTHY LIFESTYLES IN THE UK

- Organisations like Sport England, along with other home country sports councils such as the Sports Council for Wales, promote mass participation.
- Sport England funds the Sportsmatch project, which supports the development of grassroots sport in England. This scheme involves club or community facility organisations providing initial investment. The sum raised is then doubled by a Sportsmatch grant.
- Special interest groups, or groups that tend not to participate in sport, are targeted by Sport England. For example, Sport England has invested to improve participation by women and people with disabilities.
- National governing bodies receive central funding to encourage young people to take up sport. The Rugby Football Union, for example, employs local and regional development officers to promote participation.
- Local initiatives are also important community sport providers. For example, in the Greater Manchester area, 'Sport for all' centres organise basketball, netball, badminton and 5-a-side football for all abilities and age groups.

- Participation and healthy lifestyles are promoted as part of the national curriculum for PE in schools.

EXAM TIP

Credit will be given in the examination for reference to other national or local campaigns, regardless of whether they are current or past initiatives.

TASK 16

Undertake a mini case study of your own sports club or a sports club in your area. Here are some questions that could help to define the club.

1. Is the club sport-specific or does it offer multi-sport provision?
2. When was the club founded?
3. How is the club funded?
4. How many teams does the club organise in a specific sport?
5. How are teams determined; for example by gender, ability or age?
6. Does the club own facilities or does it hire from the local sports or leisure centre provider?
7. Who organises the fixtures for the club?

AMATEUR SPORTS CLUBS

In the UK, an amateur club may enjoy a long tradition, have its own facilities and organise several teams on the basis of age, ability and gender. The club will be dominant in one sport but may also organise other sports as sections of the club. For example, some cricket clubs organise tennis or crown green bowling teams as subsidiary activities.

UK clubs often exist through voluntary funding from members' subscriptions, which are often relatively inexpensive. There may, however, be some private funding in the form of sponsorship and public funding from local authorities and the National Lottery via Sport England.

In the USA, private clubs enable some participants to enjoy recreational sports provision. This tends to be exclusive provision because sport in America operates from the investment of private sponsorship as opposed to public funding. Private sports clubs, therefore, tend to be very expensive to join and are usually sport-specific, such as golf, tennis and sailing clubs.

It must also be emphasised that the fitness industry had its origins in the USA, and today the gym culture is popular.

The tradition of the amateur club as it is understood in the UK does not exist in the USA. In the UK a person may elect to join an institutionalised sports club, whereas in the USA the emphasis appears to be placed on the individual or groups of friends to form teams. These friendship groups can choose to compete in competitions and leagues; this will be seen in operation in the Midnight Basketball League structure described overleaf.

The Amateur Athletic Union (AAU) is a national organisation in the USA which coordinates social groups into competitive sports leagues and promotes the development of amateur sport. As the coordinator of over thirty different sports for all age groups, the AAU claims to be one of the largest non-profit-making volunteer organisations in the USA. Men's fast-pitch softball, women's baseball, soccer and baton twirling are among the many sports coordinated in the USA by the AAU.

The AAU is an event-driven organisation and is not involved with selection, coaching, athletic sponsorship or club administration. As an additional commitment, the AAU administers the National Youth Fitness Programme as part of the President's Challenge. Each year, this scheme registers over 4 million young people between the ages of 6 and 17 years, who are required to demonstrate exceptional physical achievement in five activities.

COMMUNITY PROVISION IN THE USA: MIDNIGHT BASKETBALL LEAGUES

Midnight basketball leagues (MBL) were established in 1986 in an attempt to control the behaviour of inner city, ethnic youths who were at risk of being involved in crime. MBL adheres to the rules of the National Basketball Association but is played between 10:00 pm and 2:00 am on outdoor asphalt playground areas funded by local government. Players are taken from the street and must attend a one-hour workshop which focuses on personal skills and awareness of drug and alcohol abuse. A strict code of conduct is applied to all participants, who are predominantly males belonging to the 17–25 age group. Standards of play are high and fifty 'chapters' engage in regular competition. The Association of MBL estimates that 200,000 spectators attend matches each night and television viewing has reached 3.5 million.

REMEMBER

Midnight League Basketball is now being played in the UK. Remember a direct copy from another country is called 'cultural borrowing'.

Fig 6.16 Midnight basketball is played to a high standard and has a television audience. It also serves to prevent crime in inner city areas

CASE STUDY OF MBL PLAYER

Anthony Carter, a 22-year-old African American, is a star player in the University of Hawaii (see map on page 108) Basketball team. He has already received lucrative offers from prestigious clubs in the National Basketball Association (NBA) league. Not long ago, Carter was one of many poor young males looking for opportunities in Atlanta's south suburb, which is well known for high crime rates. His life took a different turn after joining the local Midnight Basketball League, where he spent three years. As a result Carter now has a basketball scholarship at the University of Hawaii and is likely to accept a professional contract at the end of his study period.

LITTLE LEAGUES AND PARTICIPATION IN COMPETITIVE SPORT FOR YOUNG PEOPLE IN THE USA

For children and young people in the USA, there exist well organised opportunities to become involved in sport. In addition to high status intra-mural sport throughout the education system, 'Little League' sports involvement is very popular. Little League sports cater for children aged 7–16 years. Teams are coached and managed by volunteers who in the main tend to be parents. Examples of Little League sports include:

- Pop Warner Little League for American gridiron football
- Biddy Basketball organises Little League basketball
- Pee Wee baseball administers Little League baseball.

Glen 'Pop' Warner, who is remembered in Little League football, was a prominent college coach in the late-nineteenth and early-twentieth century.

REMEMBER

Junior and mini teams in the UK also tend to be organised by volunteers.

There is a strong moral philosophy within Little League sport and a great emphasis on safety. The win ethic is, however, strongly evident, even in the youngest age groups. This is partly because the parents involved often come from a competitive sports background and are frequently considered to be living out their own sporting ambitions through their children. The teams play in structured competitions and the format reflects the professional game. Mini 'Superbowl' finals inspire competition and Little League matches attract both commercial and media attention.

The saying 'Little League to Superbowl' highlights the importance of junior sport as a preparation for professionalism. However, the slogan was updated in the era of the Bush administration (2003) to 'Little League to White House', when the President revealed that his leadership skills had their foundation in Pee-wee baseball. If Little Leagues are criticised for the promotion of the win ethic, the counter argument is that this prepares children for the competitive nature of American life.

STRETCH AND CHALLENGE

Analyse the differences between the Little League sports scene in the USA and the junior and mini sports scene in the UK.

CONTEMPORARY INITIATIVES TO DEVELOP MASS PARTICIPATION IN THE USA

You have already covered some of the major initiatives to develop participation. These initiatives are highlighted in Fig 6.17 below.

There are countless small initiatives that are intended to increase participation. Some are private enterprises that are organised as profit-making schemes and may have a very short lifespan.

Fig 6.17 Contemporary initiatives to develop mass participation in the USA

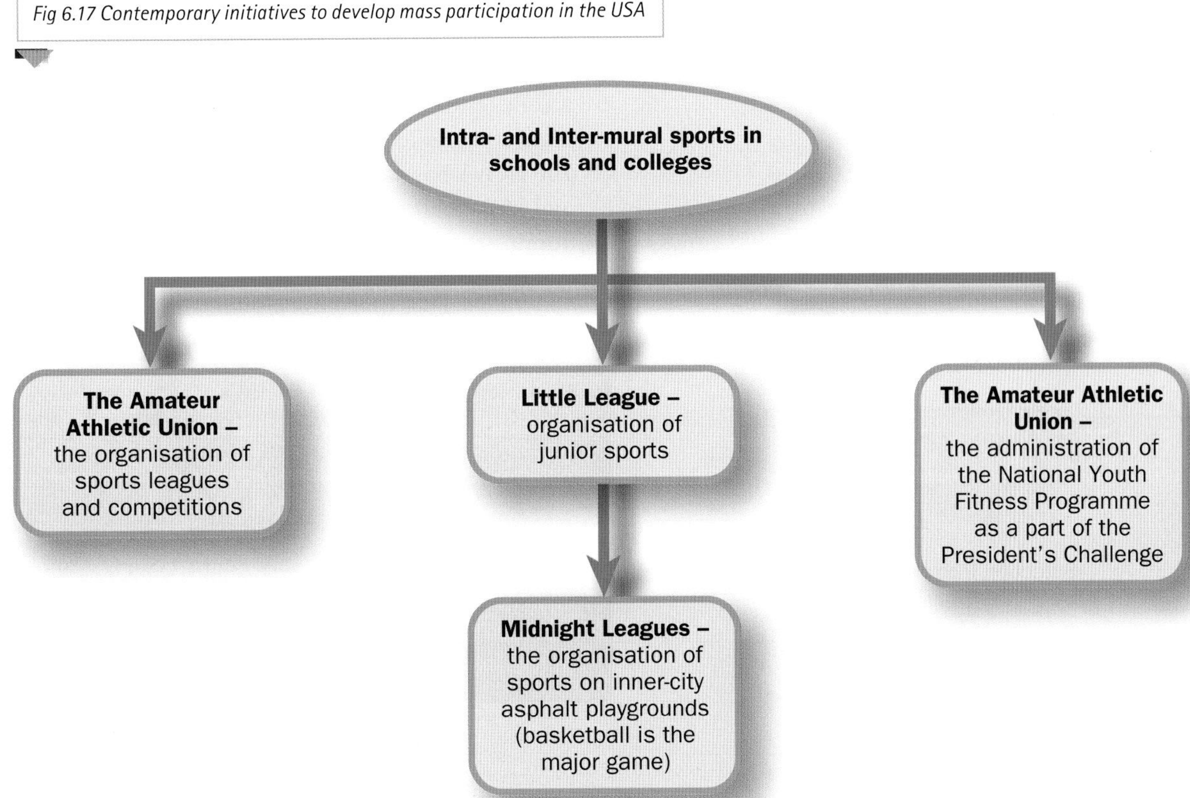

Examples of minor initiatives include Time Out for Better Sports for Kids and Hook a Kid on Golf. More information about these schemes can be found on the Internet.

TASK 17

Carry out research on the Internet to find out about five minor initiatives that promote sports participation in the USA.

PATHWAYS TO PROFESSIONAL SPORT IN THE USA

The conventional pathway into professional sport in the USA is through the education system; see Fig 6.18.

The High School performer is given a scholarship grant from the college (university). Scholarships are available in most major sports and under Title IX legislation women are funded equally to men. College sport provides the progressive step into professional and international sport. The 'Big Four' American sports are also successful commercial businesses at collegiate level and make vast profits from sponsors and media interest. Talented and well trained players, often fresh from High School, provide a high standard of sports entertainment to spectators who pay high admission prices.

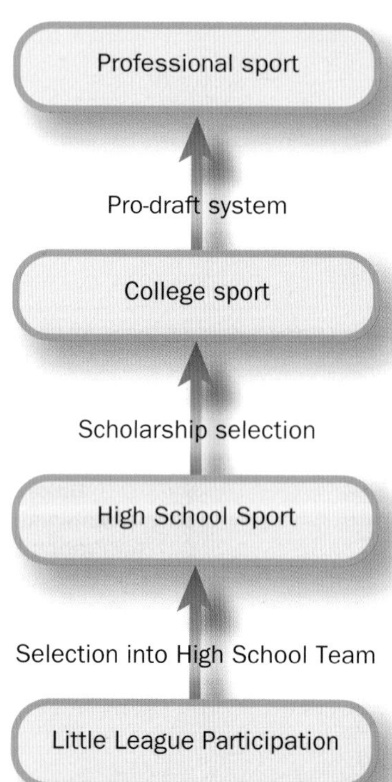

Fig 6.18 Pathways to professional sport in the USA

APPLY IT!

A family of four can pay $200 to attend a Collegiate American gridiron football match.

Three major athletic associations administer collegiate sport. The largest and oldest of these is the National Collegiate Athletic Association (NCAA).

Controversy has always been associated with the sports scholarship system. It has been apparent over the years that college administrators have enrolled students who are excellent sports performers but academically under-qualified for degree courses. Leniency in recruitment enables a college to compete in sport and remain at the highest levels to sustain commercial viability. The NCAA has stated that 20 per cent of football and basketball players enter university on **special admit programmes**.

KEY TERM

Special admit programmes

Some student athletes do not achieve the necessary grades from High School to follow conventional degree courses, but because the student has been accepted on a sport scholarship, an academic programme (degree) is found that matches their academic ability. These are known as special admit programmes.

Problems in college (varsity) sport arise when coaches and directors, in their bid for success, exert excessive control over students. When this 'win-at-all-cost' ethos arises, sport loses its educational value. It has also been an issue that when media rights are in question, the academic progress of the student athlete is considered secondary to financial profit.

Athletic directors, coaches, trainers, publicity directors and support staff make a good living from collegiate sport. Some athletic directors and coaches earn in excess of $500,000 per year, and this salary can be further enhanced through sponsorship and TV contracts. The student athlete does not get paid; in fact, it is a contravention of association rules that a player receives any financial benefits.

A sports scholarship may be worth about $10,000 a year, and this relatively meagre sum is granted by the college to pay for meals, accommodation and tuition fees. The questionable impression given by the university is that a student has been granted a 'free ride' through to a degree in higher education. However, far from being a 'free ride', a scholarship is in reality a binding contract to play sport for the college teams. Athletes might be seen as little more than labourers: they devote in the region of 50 hours per week to their sport and in so doing generate income for thousands of employers who are directly involved with the collegiate sports industry, the mass media and the corporations that advertise through college sport.

Despite hardship, lack of pay and circumstances verging on exploitation, college athletes do not protest against the collegiate sport system and continue to strive and compete for scholarships. Students remain compliant with this system for the following reasons:

- the opportunity to play big time college sports is a dream come true
- it is exciting to play in the top flight in front of large crowds; for example, the College Rose Bowl attracts 90,000 spectators
- there is kudos and social status for the athlete at a major university
- most athletes have been conditioned from early High School through the domination of sports leadership, so they willingly accept the tough-minded disciplined approach and are dependent on the ethos of team conformity
- the self-esteem of the athlete grows in direct proportion to athletic prowess
- college athletes become single-minded in their ambition to be successful; this conforming approach is termed 'pragmatic role acceptance'
- student athletes may become professional players if selected through the **Pro Draft system**, which focuses on selecting the best college players.

KEY TERM

Pro draft system

Professional clubs select the best college players when they become available after graduation. The team finishing at the bottom of the National Football League can have the first pick of the college players. This keeps the bottom clubs competitive and financially viable, since they remain attractive to the media and sponsors.

TASK 18

Conduct a case study of a college and sport of your choice in the USA. Find out the conditions of the scholarship they are offering. Consider the advantages and disadvantages of accepting a sports scholarship.

STRETCH AND CHALLENGE

The collegiate scholarship can be viewed as a provider of opportunity or a system of exploitation. Discuss.

EQUALITY AND DISCRIMINATION IN THE USA

Discrimination against minority groups has been an issue in American sport since the nineteenth century. For example, John L. Sullivan, the first American heavyweight boxing champion, would accept challenges from white men only. Black players were also excluded from Major League Baseball until 1947, but after this time a gradual integration began to take place. After African American players had broken into white professional sport in the 1950s, a period of **tokenism** followed. This meant that only a limited number of sporting positions were filled by African American players.

KEY TERM

Tokenism

The practice of hiring only a small group of people from a minority ethnic group in order to give the appearance of a non-discriminatory equal opportunities policy. For example, many sports clubs felt obliged to include one ethnic member in the team just to keep the media happy.

Stacking

In relation to sport this refers to the practice of putting players belonging to ethnic minority groups in peripheral positions. These positions often require considerable athleticism but minimal strategic influence.

As more black players entered professional sport, they tended to be **stacked** into positions which required physical athleticism rather than decision-making skills. For example, in baseball most African American players were stacked at outfield cover positions for the purposes of running and catching. Similarly, in gridiron football the running back, wide receiver and defensive back positions, i.e. those requiring physical prowess rather than strategic organisational skills, were constantly allocated to black players. In contrast, white Anglo-American players tended to occupy decision-making roles in the centre of play. The term given to this core focus is **centrality** and its occurrence endorsed the racial hierarchy in American society.

Further integration and a more even positional distribution have taken place in the twenty-first century. Major League baseball now has a 20 per cent black playing staff while 68 per cent of players in the National Football League are African American. Basketball has the greatest number of African American players, who now dominate the game on court; only 20 per cent of players registered with the NBA are white and this represents an exit of Anglo Americans from the game. This exit of white players from basketball is termed **white flight**.

KEY TERM

Centrality

This refers to sporting positions with decision-making responsibilities, such as the pitcher in baseball and quarter back in gridiron football

White flight

White players have withdrawn from basketball. The game is increasingly perceived as belonging to African Americans.

The success of ethnic minority groups in American sports can be explained through the understanding and application of three key terms:

- *Opportunity* – ethnic minority groups have been given the chance to take part in sport and to excel without prejudice in their chosen areas. Opportunity is an important American value but did not apply to all American citizens until after the midpoint of the twentieth century.
- *Provision* – ethnic minority groups now share the same quality of facilities and conditions that were formerly exclusive to the white mainstream culture.
- *Esteem* – this relates to the respect, admiration, value and appreciation that society chooses to bestow on an individual or group. The cultural esteem of ethnic groups has deservedly risen because of success. Esteem refers to confidence and the belief that achievement is possible.

Success in sport has become significant to ethnic minorities. The ability and potential of the minority group is endorsed through achievement and consequently the expectation of future success is increased.

There have been outstanding role models, particularly from the African American ethnic communities – world renowned athletes such as Jesse Owens and Mohammed Ali. Particular recognition may be given to Althea Gibson who overcame racial prejudice and broke through the '**glass ceiling**' by becoming the first black person to win the Wimbledon Ladies tennis championship in 1957.

KEY TERM

Glass ceiling

This term indicates a division between two layers of society. The people beneath the glass can see their ambition and the position which they wish to occupy. The glass symbolises a barrier which cannot be broken.

TASK 19

Research the career of Althea Gibson. Consider her achievements in the light of great bigotry and racial prejudice.

Contemporary ethnic sports stars as role models include the Williams family in tennis and Tiger Woods in golf. All have emerged during the early years of the twenty-first century. Their achievements and dignity in their respective sports have increased the belief and esteem of minority races that now have the confidence and motivation to strive for recognition in sports which traditionally were the preserve of the dominant WASP culture group. Success has brought identity and in turn unity to the ethnic groups. With it has come the chance to dominate and even take over in sports which were formerly inaccessible, for example basketball, track athletics, golf and tennis. When Venus Williams won the 2000 Wimbledon Championship, *The Times* headlined 'Golden crown for the girl from the ghetto.'

Commitment to multiculturalism has not been easily achieved in the USA. Commercial opportunities, however, now exist for ethnic minorities in sport in the form of endorsements and sponsorship. Furthermore, on retirement, successful performers from ethnic minorities are beginning to be engaged as coaches and opportunities are emerging for ownership of commercial enterprises.

SPORT AND THE PURSUIT OF EXCELLENCE IN THE UK

In the UK, like America, entry or 'access' into sports participation is not the same for everyone. If a person is denied access into sport, talent of international standard may remain undiscovered. As with the USA, opportunity, provision and esteem are the major factors that prevent equal access for all. In the UK, sport for all is not yet a reality.

REMEMBER

The factors that prevent access to participation and excellence in the UK are explained on page 281 of *OCR AS PE*.

UK SPORT

UK Sport is the organisation with the overall responsibility for producing sporting excellence in the UK. The ambition of UK Sport to achieve fourth place in the 2012 Olympic Games medal table indicates a clear philosophy that Olympic and Paralympic sport can no longer be trusted to enthusiastic and talented amateurs. Athletic performance, coaching and organisation structure must have a professional focus. After the bid to stage the 2012 Olympic Games was won in 2005, UK Sport produced a submission to the government for extra funding. A performance funding package of £300 million was requested.

REMEMBER

In addition to distributing funds to help the production of sporting excellence, UK Sport has ten functions. These are explained on page 265 of *OCR AS PE*.

TASK 20

There is not an American equivalent of UK Sport. Undertake a case study to focus on the methods used in the USA to produce sports excellence. Address how the USA provides funding to Olympic athletes.

STRETCH AND CHALLENGE

The American view is that second place is first loser yet UK Sport set a target for Team UK to achieve fourth place in the 2012 Olympic Games. Critically evaluate this aim.

SPORTS INSTITUTES IN THE UK

Sports Institutes in the UK are a network of centres that are dedicated to providing support to elite athletes. The four devolved Home County Sports Institutes are shown in the spider diagram in Fig 6.19.

The Sport Institutes have underpinned the successes of Team UK in Olympic and Paralympic competition, but not all sports find it necessary to take advantage of the institutes. For example, non-Olympic sports like cricket have their own governing body pathways leading towards professional status.

The UK government, like the US federal government, is not involved with sporting policies. It does, however, fund sport through the National

REMEMBER

America does not have an equivalent of an institute of sport but it has clear ways of producing excellence. The pathway to professional sport in the USA lies in the education system; high schools and colleges tend to be centres of sports excellence.

Fig 6.19 The four devolved Home County Sports Institutes

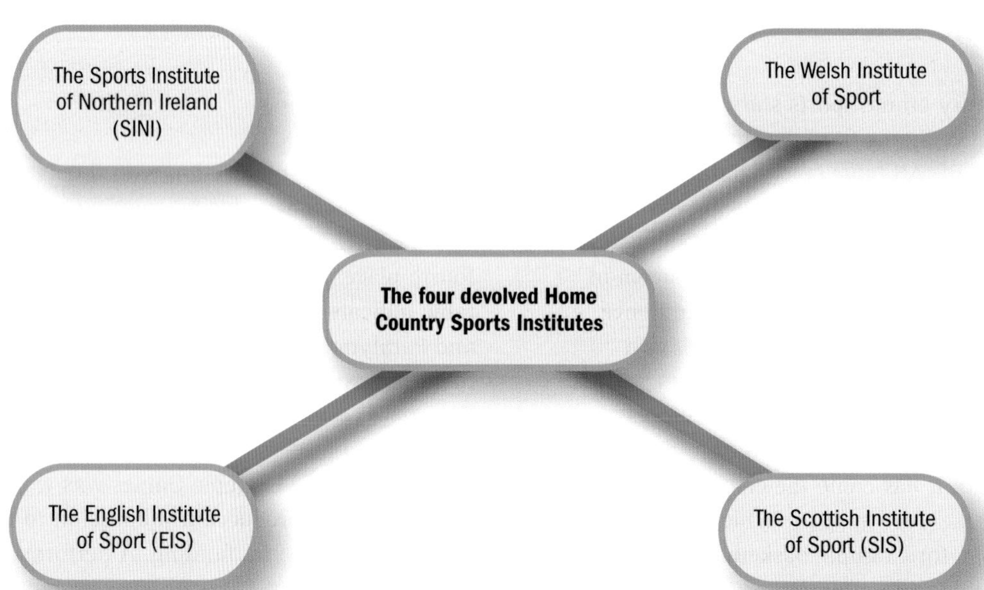

Lottery and Sport England. In contrast, in the USA very little federal money is invested in sport.

UK Sport is responsible for the strategic direction of the institute network with a mission to support elite athletes. The supportive services provided by the institutes are:

- sport-specific coaching programmes
- physical conditioning programmes
- sport science and sports medicine
- physiotherapy
- nutrition advice
- performance analysis and planning
- vocational, educational and lifestyle advice.

There is no equivalent agency with over-arching control of elite performance development in the USA, though a similar support system exits for student athletes who are following a sports scholarship programme at college. It should be remembered, however, that the sporting ethos of the UK institutes and the American colleges will differ; sport in American colleges is organised as a commercial business and directly reflects the professional scene; the UK Sport institutes do not aim to promote sport as an entertainment commodity.

During the 20th century, scholarship provision gave the American Olympic athletes a great advantage over British athletes: the American team could benefit from full-time training and scientific support. In the UK, by contrast, performers at Olympic level were talented amateurs who at this time worked in employment by day and trained whenever possible. Through sponsorship, UK athletes in the twenty-first century can now engage in full-time training on a professional basis.

EXAM TIP

You should be aware that methods used to produce sporting excellence in the UK and the USA are popular exam topics. You will need to relate your answer on this topic to the cultural determinants of both countries.

Case study of the 'Big Four' American sports

The 'Big Four' sports in America are baseball, gridiron football, basketball and ice hockey. Association Football (soccer) is striving to become the fifth 'Big' sport in the USA. This ambition, despite increases in attendance, lucrative sponsorship deals and media attention, has yet to be fulfilled. One reason that is given for the rejection of soccer as one of the premier American games is the concept of 'sport space'. Sport space is the view that more prominent games will restrict the development of the less dominant game. In this case the dominance of the 'Big Four' has limited the opportunity or closed the space for soccer.

REMEMBER

All professional sports, particularly the 'Big Four', operate as business enterprises and fit with the capitalist model of the USA. Professional sports exist solely to make profit and are inextricably linked with sponsorship and the media to form the Golden Triangle.

APPLY IT!

Sports corporations like the New York Yankees (baseball) and Dallas Cowboys (American Football) are comparable as businesses in organisation and financial turnover to the car manufacturers General Motors or film producers Warner Brothers.

BASEBALL

Baseball has been known as the national pastime for over a hundred years and is by far the most popular game in the United States. Boys played early forms of baseball, known as goal ball or rounders, regularly during the colonial period. However, this was to become the national game by the mid-nineteenth century. It became the game of the city in the nineteenth century and was played predominantly by the youth of the working classes. Very few schools and colleges elected to play baseball as adults tended to disapprove of the game.

Baseball became an obsession, being the expression of defiant youth and a game of impact comprising hard striking and lots of energetic fielding. This resulted in endless bursts of action and limitless quick sprinting. There was as a result very little dead time in the game. Baseball was preferred to cricket, which by contrast lacked the required sensationalism to satisfy the increasing pace of American life.

Baseball spread quickly to all states and to all classes. Rapid growth was aided by the coming of the railway system, which enabled long distance fixtures to be played. As professionalism became widespread, the gentlemanly etiquette of the founder clubs on the peripheries of the cities was lost and players contrived to win at all costs.

REMEMBER

Lombardianism is the win-at-all-costs ethic.

The National Association of Baseball Players assembled in 1858 to organise leagues and clarify rules. It placed a ban on African American players, which prevailed until 1947. In 1903 play was intensified and spectator interest further stimulated when the first World Series was inaugurated. In 1920, match fixing brought disgrace to the sport when the Chicago White Sox contrived to lose games in return for considerable sums of money. Thereafter, baseball was reorganised and a commissioner was appointed to ensure the integrity of the game.

APPLY IT!

The term World Series is misleading because the only contestants are North American teams. Here is an example of a huge country aiming high; see the cultural determinants relating to geography on pages 101–108.

Baseball is played in American colleges on an inter-mural basis and the NCAA set up a national championship tournament in baseball in 1947.

The scale of Major League Baseball (MLB) as a twenty-first century business is immense. In 2007, 80 million people attended World Series matches – an average of 32,000 people per game. The commercial status of the game is reflected in the team value of the New York Yankees baseball squad (see Fig 6.20). The business was bought in 1973 for $10 million.

AMERICAN GRIDIRON FOOTBALL

Variants of football were played throughout the colonial period and up to the time of the American Civil War (1861–65). It was after the civil war that the development of this particular sport was stimulated.

American gridiron football was adapted from English Rugby Football, which toward the end of the nineteenth century had a structured club system having been founded in the UK public schools. The origin of American Football lies in the Ivy League colleges, notably Princeton, Colombia, Harvard and Yale.

Through the nature of the rules drawn up at the colleges, the game was initially extremely physical. The teams were compelled to conform to 'down and distance' rules which caused head-on confrontation and collision at each restart in play. Other rules that promoted aggressive play were 'blocking' and 'slugging'. The violence of such play led to the deaths of eighteen players in 1905, prompting intervention from the President of the USA.

Fig 6.21 The NFL Superbowl championship is a playoff between the best team in the American Football Conference (AFC) and the Nation Football Conference (NFC). It is a prime example of the presentation of sport as a commercial commodity

TASK 21

Use the model that outlines the cultural background of the USA on pages 101–104 to analyse why American gridiron football suited the new culture of the United States.

The popularity of collegiate football accelerated in the first part of the twentieth century, when innovations in play came from the coaches who were prominent in college football at that time. The forward pass had by now been legitimised, giving American Football an identity that was clearly separate from Rugby Football.

REMEMBER

The isolation policy of the USA was reflected in the games preferred by Americans; see page 102.

The showpiece event of American Football in the twenty-first century is the Superbowl, which is the championship game of the National Football League (NFL). With viewing figures of 130 million in 2007, the event commands the highest television audience in America. In addition to the spectacle of play, popular singers and musicians perform during pre-game and half-time ceremonies. Television commercial breaks are numerous and thirty seconds of advertising time costs $2.5 million.

The Dallas Cowboys is a prominent football team. In 1989 it was bought for $150 million; by 2007 the team was worth $1.1 billion.

BASKETBALL

In contrast with gridiron football, baseball and ice hockey, basketball did not evolve through adaptation. Basketball was invented in 1891 by James Naismith at the private Springfield YMCA Training School and was instantly successful in high schools and colleges. Basketball was rooted in white educational institutions, and although a few professional teams played early attempts to cash in on the game were unsuccessful.

A century later, this profile had changed drastically. Basketball teams make up 13 per cent of franchised sport in America. The combined revenue of the thirty National Basketball Association (NBA) teams is approximately $3.5 billion and rising quickly. The average attendance of three prominent NBA teams in 2007 is shown in Table 5.

Table 5 Average attendance of three prominent NBA teams in 2007

Team	Average attendance
Chicago Bulls	22,103
Detroit Pistons	22,076
Cleveland Cavaliers	20,500

An African American player, Michael Jordan, while playing for the Chicago Bulls in the 1990s, became the highest paid sports person in the world, earning $33 million per year. The Chicago Bulls business was bought in 1985 for $16 million but now has a team value of $500 million, with annual revenue of approximately $140 million. The game is prominent in the sports entertainment industry because it is fast, high-scoring and commercial advertising fits naturally into the many breaks in play.

Basketball is now a game of the inner city because urban playgrounds provide inexpensive sport for large numbers of poor and at-risk American youths. Two female professional basketball leagues began in 1997.

REMEMBER

Midnight Leagues also have television audiences; see page 136.

ICE HOCKEY

Ice hockey is not as popular as the 'Big Three', but its commercial operation is organised on similar lines. The first indoor match was recorded in Montreal, Canada, in 1875, where the game remains the national sport.

Like American Football, the game in the USA has roots in the collegiate system, and the NCAA inaugurated an ice hockey national tournament for universities in 1948. The first professional ice hockey league was formed in 1904 with the initial National Hockey League (NHL) franchises in eastern Canada. In 1924 Boston was granted a franchise followed quickly by other USA cities including New York, Chicago and Detroit.

The gold medal achievement in the 1980 Olympic Games gave a boost to the popularity of ice hockey in the USA, particularly as ten of the squad were signed by NHL teams. Out of 26 NHL teams that exist today, twenty are located in the USA while only six have venues in Canada. Canadian players in the NHL, however, outnumber American players.

The Stanley Cup is the showpiece trophy of the NHL and is the oldest professional sports trophy in America. The Carolina Hurricanes are the 2008 holders of the Stanley cup. This club was bought in 1994 for $48 million and has a team value of $144 million. The total attendance for all NHL matches in 2008 was 20 million people.

REMEMBER

The sports business industry as it exists in America (and as it is developing in the UK) cannot operate without the links between sport, sponsorship and the media. This three-cornered link is referred to as the 'golden triangle'.

The increasing commercialism of sport in the UK

Sport was originally played in the UK for the intrinsic benefit of the participants; it was never intended that sport would develop into a commercial entertainment industry. Spectators have always been drawn to sport for the purpose of entertainment, but the commercial possibilities were being utilised in the United States on a large scale long before they were taken up in the UK. The UK is still some way behind the USA in terms of the overall financial value of sport. Only Association Football can match the 'Big Four' American sports in terms of monetary value.

REMEMBER

The coverage of sport was revolutionised in the USA during the 1960s, and this process further stimulated the move toward commercial sport (see page 114).

The lead that has been made by the USA in sport commercialism is not only copied by the UK but is being followed globally. For example, China is developing football and India has installed the India Professional League (IPL) in limited-over cricket.

REMEMBER

Copying an idea from another country is termed cultural borrowing.

On both sides of the Atlantic, money is made from ticket sales, merchandise, media rights, satellite and cable television deals. In America, commercial breaks happen every ten minutes and last up to five minutes. In the UK, breaks from advertising are an important source of revenue but are limited to three breaks per hour for a duration of three minutes per interlude.

The American **franchise system**, which has been in operation since the early twentieth century, is now evident in the UK and Europe. A sport which has the franchise system in the UK is Rugby League. The top teams have formed into a 'Super League' and this traditional parochial game from northern England now has sponsored teams in London and southern France.

KEY TERM

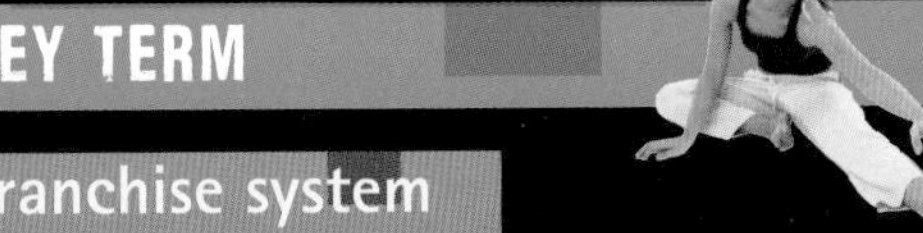

Franchise system

This allows a team to be moved from its home base to a different part of the country, for profit-making reasons.

For the 2009 season, the Rugby League Super League competition experimented with the American sports league system, which has abolished promotion and relegation. The Welsh Rugby Union clubs also restructured to make their league more commercially viable.

The American Lombardian ethic is becoming increasingly widespread in UK sport as the financial stakes increase, for example relegation in Association Football from the Premiership would represent commercial failure. Players in the UK and the USA are now experiencing shorter playing careers as the frequency and intensity of play increases to fulfil the criteria of entertainment.

Increased commercialism has caused the traditional format of sport in the UK to change. Some examples of the changes in format are outlined below.

- The introduction of Twenty20 cricket as a shortened version of the game is more lucrative than traditional county cricket because it is more attractive to the casual spectator.
- Sporting events are now arranged not only on Saturday, as was the tradition, but take place throughout the week to align with television timings.
- Super League rugby has elected to become a summer game to increase its commercial potential.
- Professional sport in the UK is beginning to adopt the American approach of introducing side attractions to sporting events, such as pre-match entertainment, cheerleaders and music, to add drama and excitement to play. These are all direct copies of the American commercialised professional sports scene.

EXAM TIP

You should be prepared to discuss the extent to which the UK is adopting the approach of the USA in commercial sport.

Exam Café

Relax, refresh, result!

Refresh your memory

You should now have knowledge and understanding of:

- the cultural context of sport in the USA and the UK
- PE and school sport in the USA and the UK
- mass participation in sport in the USA and the UK
- sport and the pursuit of excellence in the USA and the UK
- how to critically evaluate the influence of the cultural context on all of the above.

REVISE AS YOU GO!

1 Describe the policy of isolationism in the USA and the policy of Empire building in the UK.
2 Define the term frontierism in the USA and describe the term hierarchical society in the UK.
3 What is meant by the term commercialisation of sport as it is applied in both countries?
4 Outline the attitudes towards Physical Education in the UK and USA.
5 Outline three differences between USA inter-mural sport and UK inter-school sport.
6 Outline the major trends in sports participation both in the USA and the UK.
7 Explain why the traditional amateur sports club does not exist in the USA but is a key feature of sporting mass participation in the UK.
8 Outline the pathways to professional sport that exist in the UK and the USA.
9 Describe the factors opportunity, provision and esteem as they relate to inequality and discrimination in sports participation in the USA and in the UK.
10 List five reasons why the 'Big Four' sports were promoted in the USA while the four sports named in the UK case study were marginalised.

Try to answer these questions yourself. Ask your teacher if you need help.

Get the result!

Examination question

Explain how the experience of playing inter-school sport in the UK would differ from the experience of playing inter-mural sport in the USA. (6 marks)

Examiner's tips

Try to begin your response with a statement that both sets the scene and embraces the major points of your answer. You are trying to impress the examiner from the beginning, so do not begin by explaining a minor point. The initial statement displays the whole picture. Remember that to score one mark, one fact is given from the UK and then a point of comparison is made from the USA. Vary the words that join points of comparison together, for example use words such as 'whereas', 'conversely' and 'however'.

Student answer

In the USA, the high school is the centre of junior sporting excellence. When it is played inter-mural sport looks like professional games. Matches are often played in the school stadium in front of large crowds, for example Mission Eagles High School in Texas play American football in front of 15,000 people. There is a coach who runs the team and he can be sacked if they loose. Matches attract media attention and sponsorship. A Lombardian attitude can be seen in the players.

In the UK, PE is more important than sport. You do not play in front of large crowds and you do not play in a stadium. The teacher organises the fixtures and coaches the team and does other things. The televisions never come to our games and once a garage gave us kit with their names on it. When we play we like to win but it doesn't matter if we loose because the teacher says it doesn't matter.

Examiner says:

The content of this response is good but it is badly organised and presented. Organise your points of comparison in one sentence or adjacent sentences. Do not write a paragraph on the UK and a separate paragraph on the USA.

Examiner says:

The sentence about the coach is expressed badly and the incorrect spelling of lose (as loose) is a common student mistake. Correct spelling is important.

Examiner says:

Avoid the word 'you' and the word 'thing'. These words are indicators of a poor style of writing, limited knowledge and a lack of planning.

Examiner says:

An introduction is lacking and sentences tend to recall information and read more like a list than continuous prose writing.

Examiner says:

A very good example is given and factual information is accurate.

Examiner says:

The reference to the first person 'we' must be avoided.

Improved student answer

The experience of playing inter-school sport in the UK and inter-mural sport in the USA differs because of variations in the organisation, status and ethos of sport at this level.

Examiner says:

This is a good introduction that sets the scene and directly reflects the wording of the syllabus.

Inter-mural sport in the USA is organised by the State High School Athletic Association (SHSAA), which is a national advisory body. In the UK, by contrast, inter-school fixtures tend to be organised by a number of agencies including teachers, sport colleges and national governing bodies.

Examiner says:

The content of knowledge demonstrated here is advanced. This student has read th text carefully and revised thoroughly. The marker is aware that a high quality response is likely to follow.

The USA high school aspires to be a centre of sporting excellence whereas schools and sports colleges in the UK promote a participation ethic as a priority over excellence. For the school athlete in the USA there is a powerful incentive to earn a sport scholarship from a college. While sports scholarships exist in the UK universities, both the scale and motives for the award differ from those in the United States.

Examiner says:

Points of comparison are located in adjacent sentences. The response has obviously been well planned and it is easy to mark.

A strong Lombardian win ethic is instilled into the players involved in USA inter-mural sport. In the UK, by contrast, although sport is competitive it is the participation in sport that is the overriding motive during play. This difference in ethos is a direct reflection of the variation in the cultural background of both countries.

Examiner says:

A good reference is made to the cultural backgroun of both countries. Although marks are not given in this response for cultura background, it links to every topic on th syllabus. Relevant inclusion indicates that a student has acquired a deep understanding of Comparative Studie

The coach has responsibility for American schools teams and is employed on a temporary contract that is renewed if success is achieved. This arrangement is known as a 'hire and fire' contract. In the UK, on the other hand, the teacher of Physical Education has responsibility for organising and coaching school teams. The contract of the latter is usually of a permanent nature, as the teaching priority is with

Examiner says:

The major issues of comparison which include organisation, status and ethos have now been addressed.

Physical Education and not sport. In the USA, the status of school sports is higher than Physical Education.

Large crowds are attracted to USA inter-mural sports events because, among many reasons, play is of exceptionally high standard and reflective of the professional sports scene. For example, the Mission Eagle High School in Texas play to a crowd of 15,000 in a floodlit school stadium. Few spectators tend to be present during inter-school games in the UK. Fixtures are normally played on school fields. The organisation and the motives for play tend to reflect the culture of English amateur participation and fair play rather than mirror the professionalism evident in inter-mural sports, etc.

Examiner says:

[T]here are many reasons [f]or large crowds. Two [a]re given here. These [r]easons are relevant [t]o the answer and [l]ead into the next [p]oint. The other reason [i]s that the nearest [p]rofessional team [m]ay have a home [v]enue at a distance [t]hat is inaccessible [f]or the spectator. Do [n]ot be drawn into [d]escribing factors that [a]re irrelevant. Avoid the [t]erm 'etc'.

USA high school sport attracts media attention and therefore sponsorship is also drawn to the inter-mural scene. Together with large crowd attendances, school sport in the USA is organised as a business and on a minor scale has a commercial reliance on the 'golden triangle'. In the UK, although some minor sponsor arrangements are sometimes made, funding for sport is usually managed through school with no direct commercial reliance.

Examiner says:

Remember that maximum marks can only be achieved if points of comparison are made. Clear points of comparison have been made throughout this response.

CHAPTER 7:

Comparative study of Australia and the UK

LEARNING OBJECTIVES

By the end of this chapter you should have knowledge and understanding of:

- the cultural context of sport in Australia and the UK
- PE and school sport in Australia and the UK
- mass participation in sport in Australia and the UK
- sport and the pursuit of excellence in Australia and the UK
- how to critically evaluate the influence of the cultural context on all of the above.

The cultural context of Australia

Australia is believed to have a 'sporting obsession'. Whether the relationship with sport is stronger in Australia than in other countries is debatable, but it is beyond doubt that in Australia physical activity is a major priority. The high status given to sport is reflected in the schools' Physical Education programmes, the commitment to mass participation and the pursuit of excellence.

To understand such prolific involvement in sport it is necessary to consider Australia in a cultural context and compare this with the UK.

Historical determinants of Australia and how they compare with the UK

Modern Australia began as a penal colony when in 1788 around 1000 men and women from the UK were transported as convicted criminals to Port Jackson, the present site of Sydney. Life was brutally hard for these people. Even after their release from the convict settlements, they continued to be treated with disdain by military personnel and by **free settlers**. A return to the UK was, in most cases, impossible.

KEY TERM

Free settlers

These people had chosen to emigrate from the UK to Australia. In the nineteenth century, their numbers were low.

APPLY IT!

The term Prisoners of Her Majesty was given to the convict population. This was abbreviated to POM and is a term used to this day to identify Britons.

Despite considerable disadvantages, the children of the convict settlers proudly claimed to be the first generation of native born Australians. Most importantly, they confidently asserted their right to live on equal terms with the free settlers.

The name 'currency' was given to the children of the convicts. This was a disparaging term which reflected the crude system of payment given to their parents on release from the penal settlement. As recognition of their wealth, the free settlers who were born in the '**Mother country**' were named 'sterling'. These people of English origin were considered superior in breeding to the native-born 'currency' Australians and assumed, therefore, a higher place on the social scale. However, on account of the favourable climate, outdoor physical labour and a basic but nutritious diet, the currency 'lads' grew to be tall, strong and physically fit. They were generally healthier than the smaller, pale and often weaker sterling group. The taller currency lads were later referred to as 'cornstalks' and had physiques that best suited physical pursuits.

KEY TERM

Mother country

The terms 'Mother country' and 'Motherland' were used to refer to England.

From the outset, sports associated with the UK were readily adopted by the first generation of native-born Australians. For example, cricket, the first team sport played in Australia, was a direct copy of the English game. The 'currency' lads frequently arranged sports contests both against the sterling sector and the British military. Heavy betting was common when these matches took place. Victory, which the 'currency' achieved regularly, was perceived as success against the British Empire and therefore celebrated publicly.

Pride in successful sporting performance against the British settlers was the forerunner of modern-day Australian patriotism. To the 'currency', sport was associated with the promotion of social status and the claim of national identity. Winning was therefore far more important than merely taking part.

APPLY IT!

The 'currency' lads became the first Australian sportsmen to play cricket and compete in athletics, rowing, sailing, boxing and horse racing.

From the mid-nineteenth century, sport in Australia followed closely behind developments in England and, as with the ethos of the UK public schools, it was thought to build character, develop manliness and endorse social values.

Rivalry between the UK and Australia in sport was intense from the outset and replicated both the spirit and the motives of the 'currency' social group. Victory over the Motherland came initially in the world sculling championships of 1876, but subsequently and more notably in cricket and rugby in 1882 and 1899 respectively. Success against the Motherland, even at the end of the twentieth century, was seen by Australians as a benchmark against which general national progress could be judged.

REMEMBER

From the beginning, Australia regarded the UK as the Motherland and copied the UK sports. By contrast, the USA isolated itself and adapted UK sports to suit their rapidly changing culture.

More recently, however, global achievements have become the focus of Australian ambition. The outstanding success of the 2000 Sydney Olympic Games was a national triumph and the winning of the World Cup in Association Football in 2018 is considered a realistic possibility. Australia is a progressive nation with an energetic young culture. Sport is a reflection of this spirit and continues to be an expression of national pride.

TASK 1

1. List the sports in which Australia has won Olympic medals since 2000. Compare this list with Great Britain's record.
2. Discuss the extent to which global sports success may influence an individual to adopt an active lifestyle.

EXAM TIP

The factors of comparison given throughout this section will score marks in the exam. The list, however, is not definitive.

COMPARISON WITH THE HISTORICAL DETERMINANTS OF THE UK

The sociological history of the UK extends much further than Australia and this difference has strongly influenced the ambitions, values and structure of the respective societies.

The British Empire, which was the largest known to the world before its final demise in 1997, included Australia. (Australia was granted independence from the British Empire in 1901.) As an older culture, the UK used imperial policy to endorse its status. The young Australian culture, by contrast, has always used sport as a benchmark to measure progress and as an expression of national pride. As a long-established culture, the UK had a social class system that was strictly hierarchical, whereas Australia as a new culture did not have a rigid class system.

Games in popular recreation, for example fist fighting and mob football, were played by the lower orders of British society, and these were replicated by the convict settlers who initially colonised Australia.

The greatest developmental influence on UK sport came from the English public school system. It is largely through the impact of the public schools in the mid-nineteenth century that in the period 1863 to 1888 most sports and national governing bodies were formed. Australia looked to the UK as the Motherland and copied the sports of the home country. Alongside the spirited approach instilled by the 'currency' lads, Australian sport tended to follow the developments of the English public schools.

REMEMBER

The public schools impacted on the organisation, codification and attitudes toward sport; see pages 32–40 of this book and page 237 of *OCR AS PE*.

EXAM TIP

An exam question could ask for a comparison of the social and historical influences that limit or encourage involvement in physical activity both in the UK and Australia.

Geographical determinants of Australia and how they compare with the UK

THE SIZE OF AUSTRALIA

It is important to understand the size of Australia: the country is 32 times larger than the UK. Fig 7.1 opposite gives an accurate indication of its scale when compared to Europe.

Great distances separate the major cities in Australia. This has impacted significantly on the development of sport, even in the latter part of the nineteenth century. For example, the first

Fig 7.1 Australia is a huge landmass compared to the size of Europe. A flight from Brisbane to Perth takes more than five hours.

Australasian athletics match staged in Melbourne (1897) brought together competitors from Victoria, New South Wales and New Zealand. It was easier to travel from New Zealand than it was from the western Australian states.

Look at the map of Australia. Note the distance, for example between Perth and Melbourne. Travel between these cities would have been difficult in the nineteenth century. This inaccessibility was referred to as the 'tyranny of distance'.

Similarly, when the Australian Institute of Sport was opened as a centre to develop sports excellence, in Canberra in 1981, it could not effectively develop sporting excellence for the whole of Australia. The government therefore invested money to build an institute in each state in order to reduce the distances that athletes had to travel.

REMEMBER

The UK is a relatively small island. Travel for sports fixtures from the advent of the railways in the mid-nineteenth century promoted the development of sport; see page 24.

TOPOGRAPHY OF AUSTRALIA

Australia divides into four areas of distinctive terrain.

1 The low sandy eastern coastal plains of Australia are the most habitable areas. The concentration of population in these areas stimulated the early development and later commercialisation of sport.
2 The Eastern Highlands is a mountainous region with Mount Kosciusko being the highest point at over 7000 feet (2200 metres). The Kosciusko National Park is renowned for winter sports and has reliable snow conditions. It was, however, only in the 1970s that skiing resorts opened on a commercial basis.
3 The Central Plains are flat scrublands. Although for the most part environmentally inhospitable, these wilderness areas are popular for bushwalking and trekking.
4 The Western Plateau comprises desert areas, large sand ridges and rocky wastes. Almost 40 per cent of the Australian landmass is considered desert.

EXAM TIP

Be aware that consumer-focused commercial sport is a factor that can both limit or encourage involvement in physical activity in the UK, Australia and America.

COMPARISON WITH THE TOPOGRAPHY OF THE UK

The UK does have stretches of unspoiled countryside, such as the Cotswolds, that facilitate outdoor recreation and education, but unlike Australia, the UK does not have areas of genuine wilderness. Mountain upland areas such as Snowdonia and the Grampians provide challenge to climbers and mountain walkers, but a combination of low altitude and unsuitable climatic conditions severely restricts the possibilities for winter sports pursuits. Snow skiing, for example, has a limited and unpredictable season in northern Scotland.

APPLY IT!

In Australia, the winter sports industry is smaller than in the USA. However, it is larger and far more viable than in the UK.

CLIMATE OF AUSTRALIA

Australia is a country of considerable climatic diversity. The eastern seaboard enjoys warm summers and mild winters and this favourable climate has contributed significantly to the high level of sports participation and the achievement of sporting excellence. Tropical conditions prevail in northern Queensland and survival activities are promoted in the forests of this area. Furthermore, arid desert conditions prevail over a significant area and it has been proposed to establish a Desert Institute of Sport in the centre of the country as an alternative training resource.

COMPARISON WITH THE CLIMATE OF THE UK

The UK has one climatic type termed Western Maritime. This climatic type tends to give warm summers and mild winters with recurrent rainfall. The climate of the UK, when compared to the climate of the populated areas of Australia, is less favourable to outdoor participation.

The favourability of Australia's climate is a considerable advantage in developing physical activities in schools, mass participation in sport, sporting excellence and commercialised sport.

REMEMBER

The climate of the UK cannot reliably support winter sports activities.

THE URBANISATION AND POPULATION DENSITY OF AUSTRALIA

Australia has a population of around 22 million. Of this total, nearly 18 million (approximately 80 per cent) live on the eastern seaboard, which is known for its warm and sunny climatic conditions. These conditions have stimulated Australia's famous beach culture and an association with an outdoor healthy lifestyle. These trends were started by the colonial settlers but certainly appealed to the thousands of UK immigrants who were tempted by government subsidies in the period 1945–65 to 'enjoy a better lifestyle' **down under**.

KEY TERM

Down under

This phrase refers to the geographical position which appears to be underneath the globe.

The population density of Australia, although only seven people for every square mile, gives a misleading impression. Australia has a concentrated urban population because habitable land is relatively scarce; consequently some parts are overcrowded and congested. South Sydney, for example, has a population density of nearly 10,000 people per square mile.

Despite its considerable size and areas of extensive wilderness, Australia is considered to be an urban environment. This concentrated population has impacted on the development of physical activities and in particular the commercialisation of sport in the late twentieth and early twenty-first centuries, as will be seen on page 159.

APPLY IT!

Commercial sport needs a large urban population in order to develop.

COMPARISON WITH URBANISATION AND POPULATION DENSITY OF THE UK

- The population of the UK is approaching 62 million people.
- The UK has a relatively high population density of 200 people per square mile.
- As in Australia, National Parks and Areas of Outstanding Natural Beauty exist in the UK.
- The UK is highly urbanised.

REMEMBER

The UK has sufficient scope and natural resources to develop outdoor education and outdoor recreation, but the potential for these activities is limited compared to larger countries such as Australia and the United States (see pages 108 and 154).

TRANSPORT IN AUSTRALIA

The immense scale of Australia gave rise to the term 'tyranny of distance', which up to the early twentieth century impeded the development of sport. As major cities had coastal locations, travel was undertaken by sea voyage or river steam boat. Railway construction began in the mid-nineteenth century. Journeys were long and time-consuming and impacted on sport. For example, cricket matches between settlements in the outback often took two Saturdays to complete.

From the mid-twentieth century, Australia has developed a sophisticated transport system. A highly efficient road system incorporating state and urban highways connects all major centres. Airports for internal air travel are accessible and railways link suburbs to the cities.

It is possible to travel across Australia via the transcontinental railway routes, but this tends to be the preserve of the luxury tourist industry, being uneconomical in terms of time and expenditure for travelling sports teams.

COMPARISON WITH TRANSPORT IN THE UK

In the UK, distance did not present a problem to the development of sport. Easy access to away fixtures through the expanded railway links in the nineteenth century and the sophisticated road network system from the mid-twentieth century have helped to promote sport in the UK.

Government policy and the agendas for sport both in Australia and the UK

While Australia was granted independence from the British Empire in 1901, and has a federal parliament based in the capital city of Canberra, the nation has remained part of the Commonwealth and retains the monarch of England as Chief of State. An elected prime minister heads the Parliament and selects a ministerial Cabinet.

There are three levels of government in Australia, as shown in Fig 7.2:

- the central government operating at a federal level
- state and territory government
- local government.

The constitution of Australia places local government outside federal jurisdiction. A decentralised system of control is therefore in place giving autonomy to each state. Consequently, the systems operated by local government differ significantly between the states and territories.

It is important to be aware of the influence of decentralisation. Education in Australian schools is the responsibility of the state and is not controlled by the federal government. It is for this reason that, unlike in the UK, a National Curriculum does not exist in Australia.

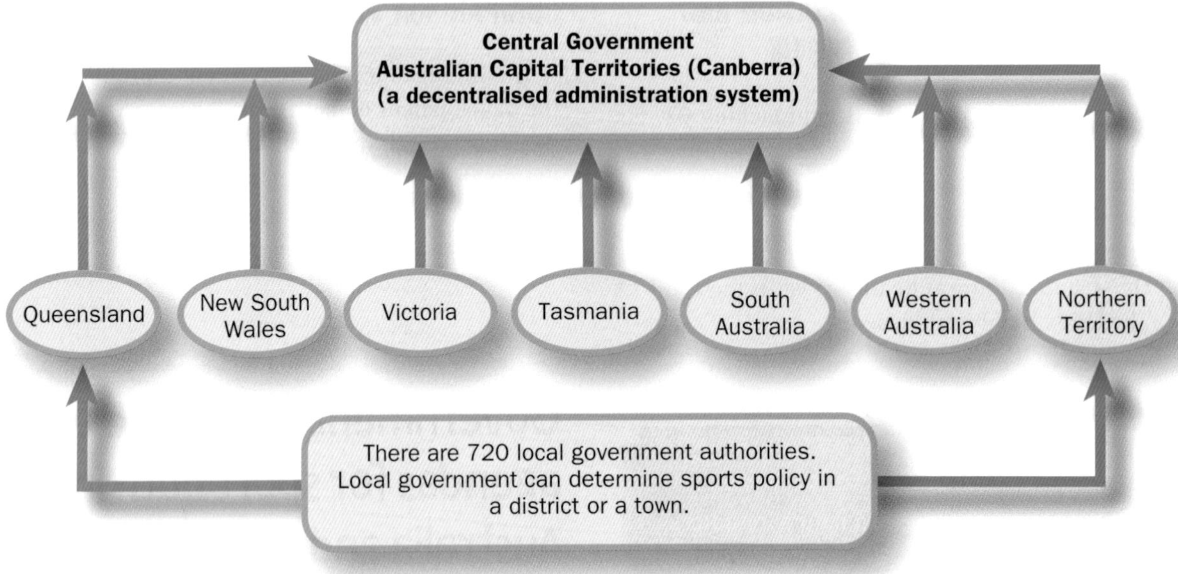

Fig 7.2 The constitution of Australia: levels of government

In 1992, however, the federal government held an inquiry into the perceived falling standards in sport and Physical Education in Australia's schools on a national scale. The resulting action promoted the subject and significantly changed the delivery of physical activity in schools. These changes will be seen in the case study of Physical Education and school sport in the State of Victoria on page 166.

The federal government through the administration of the **Australian Sports Commission (ASC)** takes an active role in policy-making both in mass participation and in the pursuit of excellence in sport.

KEY TERM

Australian Sports Commission (ASC)

Government department in charge of sport. (See also page 173.)

COMPARISON WITH GOVERNMENT POLICY IN THE UK

- The UK also operates through decentralised government. Like Australia, the organisation of local government is complex.
- In the UK, Metropolitan Boroughs receive government funding for sports facilities. In Australia, by contrast, finance and policy are directed by the Australian Sports Commission.
- British politicians have traditionally looked on sport as a low-status activity and in consequence have provided meagre financial support in the form of public funding. The Australian government, however, recognised the need to invest in sport after a poor team performance in the 1976 Olympic Games. The UK government now acknowledges that success in the Olympic Games, for example, can bring great political prestige and financial reward to the country. As a consequence, sport in the UK enjoys substantially increased government funding. Also following the trend in Australia, investment in sport is now considered by UK politicians to have considerable vote-catching potential.
- While the British government provides funding for sport it has no involvement in policy making. This contrasts directly with the function of the ASC.

The commercialisation of sport in Australia and in the UK

The major professional sports of Australia are, in common with those in the UK and the USA, highly commercialised.

From its nineteenth century beginnings up to the 1970s, professional sport in Australia derived revenue mostly from gate receipts and club membership fees. During the 1970s, major sports such as Australian Football, Rugby League and cricket supplemented their income with the fees from television broadcasting. Commercial changes occurred in the 1980s when the television fee became the major source of revenue for professional sport in Australia.

The irreversible move to commercialisation of sport in Australia began in 1977 when Kerry Packer rivalled the International Cricket Conference by signing the best players in the world to play World Series Cricket exclusively on his own television network channel. The game differed greatly from conventional cricket and rapidly became a commodity of the entertainment business. (The impact of World Series Cricket is described further on page 181.)

APPLY IT!

To become commercially viable, professional sport in Australia needed to adapt to have a broader consumer focus.

Although Kerry Packer's World Series Cricket competition undoubtedly influenced sport in the UK, it could be argued that the Broadcasting Act of 1990 triggered the commercialisation of sport in the United Kingdom.

REMEMBER

Turn to page 114 to revisit the development of commercialised sport in the UK.

APPLY IT!

The onset of commercialism is exemplified by the New South Wales Rugby League (NSWRL), which in 1976 was paid $15,000 by national television for the right to broadcast the Grand Final. In 1990, Channel Ten paid $45 million to televise rugby for three seasons.

As with the UK and the USA, the link in Australia between professional sport, the media and sponsorship is inextricable. The media became a powerful force in sport in Australia in 1995 with the introduction of pay television. This increased the value of sport as a **corporate commodity** because it introduced a new form of media outlet which fundamentally altered the way of life in Australia. It was now possible, through subscription, to select a sport with high entertainment appeal and watch it at home. However, the relationship between pay television as a media outlet and sport was not free from problems.

KEY TERM

Corporate commodity

A product that can be bought by a consumer.

The most striking example of discord between the media and sport was in Rugby League. During the late 1990s, the transition this sport was making to full-time professionalism can be traced through the corporate forces that were attempting to restructure Rugby League in Australia.

The rights to televise the sport were owned by the aforementioned Kerry Packer, but Rupert Murdoch was about to launch a new pay television network and required a new 'product' to attract subscribers. As a rival to the existing Australian Rugby League (ARL), Murdoch developed a new form of the game and gave to it the brand name 'Super League'. Unprecedented sums of money bought leading names from both union and league codes into Super League. Australia did not, however, have a large enough population to support two elite Rugby League competitions, and the unpopular Super League was disbanded after a year.

KEY TERM

Multinational company

A company with outlets in many countries.

APPLY IT!

Restarting a televised Australian Football game is still the responsibility of the referee. A light on the scoreboard, however, indicates to the official when the commercial break has ended, so that action can recommence.

REMEMBER

The concept of 'sport space' manifests itself when the population is not large enough to support an emerging sport; see Chapter 6, page 143.

Multinational companies are attracted by prolific media involvement to sponsor sport in Australia. In 2008 cricket was benefiting from lucrative sponsorship from an American food chain. The limited-over version of the game carrying the brand name 'Twenty20 Bash' was to be promoted by the same sponsor. This association caused controversy. It was alleged by health experts that the unhealthy nature of the food sold by the sponsor was causing a rise in rates of obesity.

Currently, the popularity of Association Football in Australia is dramatically increasing, to the extent that the Football Federation of Australia (FFA) plans to host the 2018 World Cup competition. This proactive governing body has secured sponsorship deals from several multinational companies, the most notable of which is a Japanese car manufacturer. The renaming of the Telstra Dome in Melbourne to the Etihad Stadium involved a naming rights deal with the national airline of the United Arab Emirates.

The processes that bring about the commercialisation of sport are stimulated by historical, geographical and socio-economic determinants. These determinants shape national culture and the consequent status of sport in society. They must be in place, therefore, before a country can promote sport as a part of its commercial entertainment industry.

The determinants essential to the commercialisation of sport in Australia are outlined in Fig 7.3. Although differing in size and magnitude, they are the same ones which prevailed in the USA and the UK.

STRETCH AND CHALLENGE

Study Fig 7.3. Discuss the extent to which this model could explain the growth of commercialism in sport in the UK.

EXAM TIP

Marks are awarded when comparative facts about two countries have been stated. Remember that a comparison can be made in two ways:

- when points of similarity are drawn together
- when a contrast is made between two points.

Historical
There is a long tradition of sport.
Sport is an indicator of progress and an expression of national pride; for example, the 'currency' sports contests and the Sydney Olympic Games of 2000.

Geographical
The society is urban.
There are densely populated cities that can supply a large spectator base.

Geographical
Transport systems are diverse, efficient and sophisticated. The tyranny of distance no longer prevails.

Socio-economic
A capitalist market economy prevails. Material reward has high status in society.

Socio-economic
Australia is an affluent country. Society has access to a variety of media outlets, for example satellite and digital television.

Socio-economic
Large amounts of capital are available to build and maintain stadiums. Naming rights are important, e.g. Telstra dome.

Fig 7.3 Determinants essential to the commercialisation of sport in Australia. The same determinants also underpin the development of commercialised sport in the UK

EXAM TIP

The determinants that frame a country in a cultural context are likely to emerge in the Stretch and Challenge question worth 20 marks. Be prepared to compare the cultural background of the UK with that of Australia or the USA, as cultural determinants influence physical activity in school, mass participation in sport and the pursuit of excellence.

Social determinants and equality in Australia and how these compare with the UK

In Australia, as with the UK, it would appear that certain social groups find it more difficult to participate in sport because of discrimination. In order to ensure anti-discrimination both countries are addressing the issues of opportunity, provision and esteem as factors to increase participation.

- The Australian Sports Commission (ASC) is dedicated to the development of sport for all people in Australia. They manage programmes for ethnic minorities, disabled people and women of all ages.
- Sport England supports groups that are under-represented in sport participation (see page 262 of *OCR AS PE*).

REMEMBER

Opportunity, provision and esteem are discriminatory factors that make it difficult for people to participate in sport; see pages 51 and 52.

The Aborigines are the **indigenous** people of Australia and Tasmania. The Aboriginal population prior to the UK settlement in the late-eighteenth century is thought to have been about 350,000. They lived in separate tribes and the rich Aboriginal culture is displayed through art, ritual and sport. The Aborigines did not display hostility to the UK intruders, but the white settlers persecuted the native population and took possession of their territories. The policies of

'White Australia' established by government were highly discriminatory and designed to control the composition of Australian society. This policy was withdrawn in 1971 when Australia committed to **multiculturalism**. In 2007 the Prime Minister of Australia made a public apology to the Aboriginal people for crimes committed against them by the UK settlers.

KEY TERMS

Indigenous

People belonging to a particular ethnic group who were the original inhabitants of an area, i.e. who have the earliest known historical connection to that area.

Multiculturalism

Government policy that recognises the equality of all peoples, regardless of ethnicity, race or cultural background.

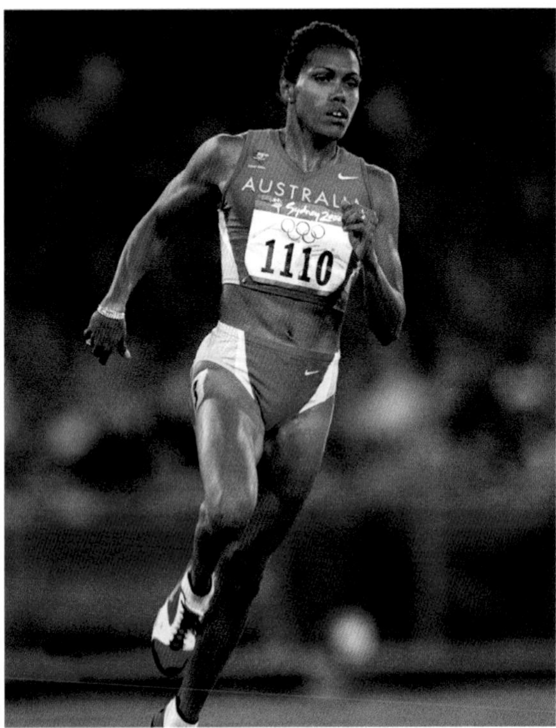

Fig 7.4 Cathy Freeman was a gold medallist and a central figure in the 2000 Olympic Games in Sydney. Being of Aboriginal origin, she has done much to create harmony between Aborigines and the mainstream culture of Australia

Aborigines make up less than 2 per cent of the total population of Australia. They have been under-represented in sports like tennis and cricket. In other sports, namely boxing, Rugby League and Australian Football, however, Aborigines have a high proportional representation and are held in high regard as performers.

The life expectancy and the general standard of living enjoyed by the Aborigines is below that of mainstream Australian society.

INDIGENOUS SPORT PROGRAMME

The Australian Sports Commission (ASC) is addressing the problem of Aboriginal under-representation in sport with the introduction of the Indigenous Sport Programme. This was developed to encourage indigenous people to be more active and to play sport at all levels. The programme also works to increase the opportunities for indigenous people to learn the skills needed to organise, deliver and manage community-based sport. At an elite level, the aim is to ensure that talented indigenous sportsmen and women are able to access the support they need to reach their competitive goals.

DISABILITY SPORT PROGRAMME

Priority has been given by the ASC to improving the participation opportunities for people with disabilities. In a programme called Disability Sport, coaches, teachers and organisers of sports can access resources to enhance practical teaching. Information is also given on the initiatives that sporting organisations are implementing, and issues such as the classification of disabilities are addressed.

At an elite level, the ASC strives to increase opportunity and improve the standards of disabled athletes. The product of this work is evident in Australia's Paralympic achievement. Australia has been represented at every Paralympic Games since their inauguration in Rome in 1960. Significantly, in 2008 Australia selected its largest ever Paralympic team for the Beijing Games. The team hoped to take Australia's collective medal tally for

Paralympic competition over 48 years to 1000 – an aim which they achieved.

GENDER

The 'frontier' attitude of early colonialism established male domination and led to serious discrimination against women in general and particularly in sport. The image of femininity was thought to be threatened by participation in all but the most genteel of pastimes.

Media comment relating to female success in sport during the 1950s and early 1960s was erratic and often negatively misleading. For example, gold medallists Betty Cuthbertson and Marjorie Jackson were accepted by the public because the press portrayed them as feminine. Sprinter Shirley Strickland was criticised for being competitive. Since that time, the negative male view has been challenged and women have begun to adopt male styles and strategies. Female representation has been conceded in horseracing, distance running, bodybuilding and triathlon.

More recently, in response to an increased need to address the issue of gender equality in Physical Education, mass participation and the pursuit of sports excellence, a medical paper has advised women to train and 'work out' like males to achieve fitness. In schools, Sport Education and Physical Education Programme (SEPEP) classes are mixed whenever possible. Female role models, often from the Australian Institute of Sport, are used frequently in Sports Person in Schools Projects to inspire teenage female participation. (SEPEP and Sports Person in Schools Project are part of the High School PE programme; see page 167.)

The ASC has now assigned a department – the Women and Sport Unit – specifically to gender and sport. The department is in charge of research and programme policy, and in 2008 it awarded sports leadership grants to women.

Despite these policies and the fundamental change of attitude in society, female sports representation is still disproportionately low in a country where women are in the majority.

A COMPARISON OF SOCIAL DETERMINANTS AND EQUALITY IN THE UK

- Discrimination against minority groups is also evident in the UK.
- A significant majority of UK citizens is denied access to sport participation and the chance to excel at an elite level.

As in Australia, access is determined by the three factors: opportunity, provision and esteem (see Chapter 6, page 140).

The boundaries that indicated social class in the UK gradually became less distinct in the second part of the twentieth century. Australia, by contrast, has never experienced the restrictions of a social class hierarchy.

Today, society in the UK continues to be stratified. The dominant group in the UK, as in Australia, remains white, middle-class and male. This group has the greatest opportunity in sport. Conversely, other groups that are lower in the hierarchy, for example Asian women, have considerably less opportunity. The groups that are most likely to suffer from discrimination or social exclusion from sport in the UK are shown in Fig 6.6 on page 118. These group categories are similar to the groups who are under-represented in sport participation in Australia.

REMEMBER

Opportunity, provision and esteem influence mass participation and sporting excellence; see pages 280–81 in *OCR AS PE*.

REMEMBER

The Australian Sports Commission (ASC) addresses the issues relating to under-representation in Australia, whereas in the UK home country organisations like Sport England have the aim to increase participation. Sport England is the government agency responsible for community sport in England; it is funded by the government and National Lottery.

The social values of Australia and the UK

The original convicts, first generation Australians and free settlers from the UK all experienced hardship in the difficult conditions that existed in the new colony. Often survival was the priority for individuals and their families. This struggle helped to promote equality and a sense of community as all people depended on the mutual help of others.

The discovery of gold prompted the gold rushes of the nineteenth century that attracted thousands of fortune hunters to the extensive resources of the Victorian fields. This second migration meant that people, many from overseas, were required not only to work together in the attempt to prosper but also to endure uncompromising difficulties. A strong sense of loyalty and social cohesion developed as both the size of population and economic prosperity of the colony increased. Australia had become a '**social melting pot**' into which all backgrounds and classes were blended.

KEY TERMS

Social melting pot

This describes a situation in which people from different cultures blend together to form a unified culture comprising many different strands.

Egalitarian

The belief that all people are, in principle, equal and should enjoy the same rights and opportunities.

Later in the nineteenth century, the integrated society that emerged from the melting pot had acquired a strong **egalitarian** ethos in which deference and social class privilege had been eliminated. The spirit of this emerging social harmony was endorsed by church minister and politician John Dunmore Lang (1799–1878), who claimed that Australia 'offers a fair field for all and no favour'. From this point Australia portrayed itself as 'the land of the fair go'. Despite this claim, a century was to pass before the Australian government committed to the policy of multiculturalism and officially recognised that all social groups in society would have equal status.

Throughout the period of colonisation, adversity was overcome through a common display of determination and tenacity. These characteristics were reflected in the 'bush culture' image that epitomised the hard-edged belief that the new Australian society had in controlling its own destiny.

KEY TERM

Bush culture

This describes the positive approach with which the settlers faced up to hardship in Australia. Bush culture is similar to the frontier spirit displayed in the USA (see page 103).

In contemporary society, the legacy of bush culture is still evident in the Australian's passionate approach to competitive sport. Australia in the twenty-first century has evolved, however, into a sophisticated, cosmopolitan and technically advanced nation comprising 200 different races. This diversity has promoted national expression not only in sport but in literature, theatre and more recently fine art. The image of the bush culture has therefore been consigned to the past.

REMEMBER

Australian society is egalitarian largely because of the social melting pot effect during the colonial era.

A COMPARISON WITH THE SOCIAL VALUES IN THE UK

- British citizens, like Australians, enjoy voting rights and freedom of speech.
- The constraints of the class system may have determined opportunities and lifestyle in the UK, but the changing nature of employment, the economy and greater access to higher education are eliminating the traditional class boundaries.
- Working as part of a team has been a traditional British value since possibly the struggle for Empire and the incorporation of team games in the public schools system. Team work and learning to interact with others certainly remains a prominent value in UK schools in the twenty-first century.
- Both the UK and Australia are multicultural societies striving to overcome discrimination.
- A sense of fair play is central to the British sporting ethos as it is in Australia. While the participation ethic continues to override the 'win-at-all-cost' ethic in both countries, it would appear that Australia has a greater motivation for achievement in sport.

TASK 2

Discuss the reasons why Australia may have a greater motivation for achievement in sport when compared with the UK.

The model below (Fig 7.5) summarises the cultural forces that stimulate the Australian focus for quality in Physical Education and school sport, the demand for mass participation, and the obsession with sport and the pursuit of excellence.

Fig 7.5 The cultural background of Australia and its influence on the pursuit of physical activity

The cultural background of Australia influences the pursuit of physical activity as part of a balanced active lifestyle

1) Political
Government has close involvement in sports policy and funding. In no other nation does sport have such vote-catching potential.

2) Ideological
Sport is a benchmark against which the progress of the nation can be measured. Sport is an expression of national pride. Global and Olympic achievement is desired.

3) Geographical
The climate has a favourable impact on sport. Urbanisation has also had a positive influence.

4) Social
Australia has an egalitarian society formed from the social melting pot of colonialism and the Gold Rush era. Sport expresses equality and reflects multiculturalism.

5) Economic
Australia's economic system is based on a capitalist model. The country is affluent and material reward has high status in society. This promotes sport as a marketable commodity.

6) Commercialism
Australia is an advanced and sophisticated consumer society that has readily embraced commercial sport.

7) Tradition
The sports tradition can be traced to the early days of colonialism and first generation Australians when Currency challenged Sterling. The legacy of the Bush Culture is expressed through sport.

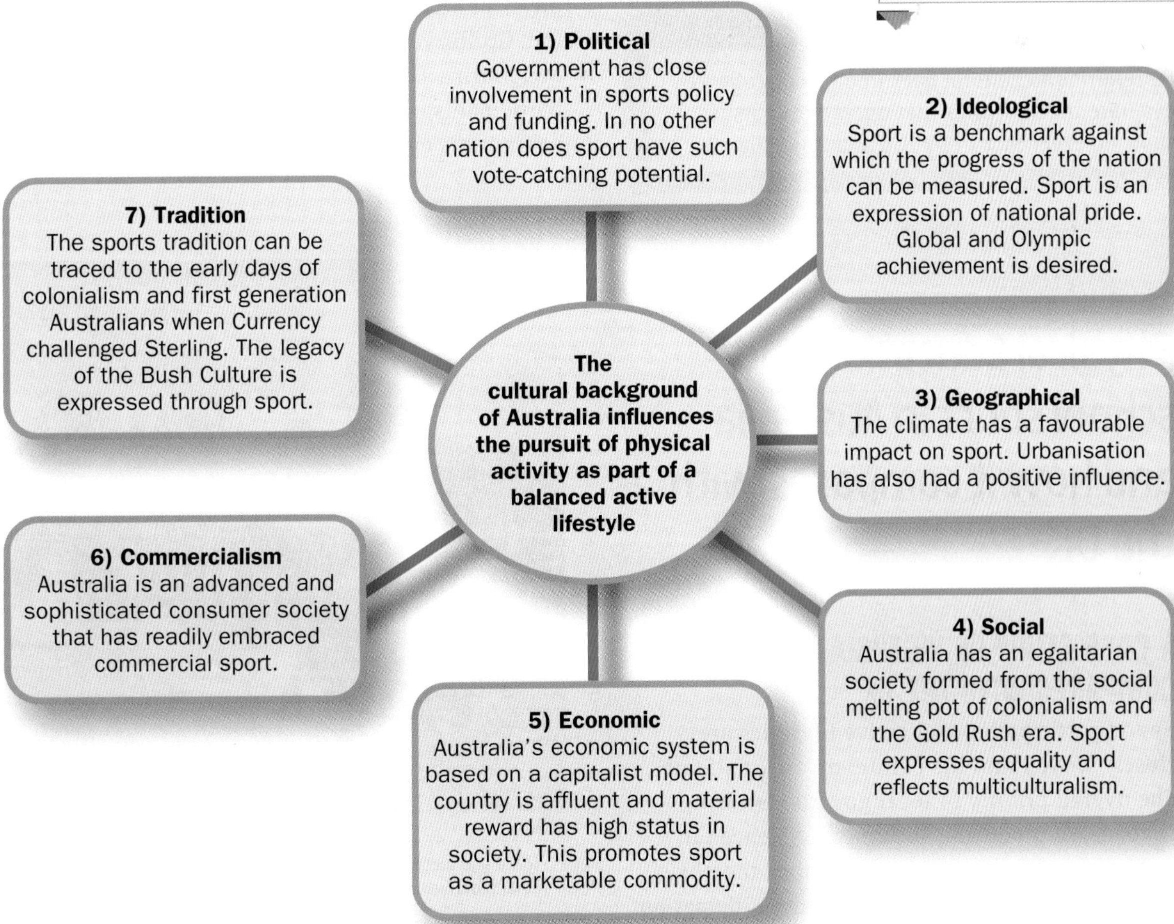

TASK 3

It is important to draw together the cultural determinants of both the UK and Australia. Using the same headings as depicted in the model on the previous page, outline the cultural determinants of the UK. Make comparisons between the models by identifying similarities and differences.

EXAM TIP

The cultural context of each country is important. It could be linked to any other topic in a comparative question and may therefore feature in a 20-mark question. An example of such a question is given below.

STRETCH AND CHALLENGE

By referring to cultural background, critically evaluate the strategies that operate to pursue sporting excellence in the UK and Australia.

Physical Education and school sport in Australia and how it compares with the UK

A CASE STUDY OF VICTORIA AND HOW IT COMPARES WITH THE UK

Sports participation and active lifestyles are closely woven into the culture of Victoria State. The overall priority of local government is not to focus on producing sporting excellence but to improve the skills of young people, thereby increasing the possibility of lifelong participation.

While Physical Education and sport are compulsory up to the age of 16 years, it is estimated that 65 per cent of school-age young people participate in sport outside of school hours. This figure indicates that Victoria is second only to Western Australia in participation rates for young people.

Government statistics indicate that the most popular activity for boys is outdoor Association Football, while netball is most favoured by girls. When both genders are considered together, swimming is most popular, with 17 per cent of total participants regularly engaging in this activity. Australian Rules Football is enjoyed by 14 per cent of total male participants while only 9 per cent engage in cricket. Nearly half of the participants train in their activities more than once a week.

The government of Victoria is particularly innovative in the promotion of active lifestyles. For example, the 'Go for your life' scheme is a government initiative which sets out to encourage healthy eating and to increase the levels of physical activity in young people. In 2008, the 'Go for your life' games were staged near Melbourne. This multi-sport event involved 6000 participants of all ages and abilities. The motive behind this event was to encourage participation.

Fig 7.6 The Victoria State government regard participation and lifelong active lifestyles as a priority policy

The Victoria government has also been proactive both in primary and secondary schools to develop participation and lifelong involvement in physical activity. The government of Victoria has developed ten strategies which promote the delivery of sport and Physical Education in Victoria's schools.

SPORT EDUCATION AND PHYSICAL EDUCATION PROGRAMME (SEPEP)

The Sport Education and Physical Education Programme (SEPEP) was made compulsory for pupils up to Year 10 in the State of Victoria after the Monigetti report of 1992. SEPEP was also included in the Curriculum Standards Framework (CSF), which comprises eight compulsory core learning areas that are delivered to pupils up to Year 10.

- The Sport Education programme focuses on teaching game strategies and incorporates both intra- and inter-school games. Although inter-school competitions are very well organised, enabling a school team to progress through local, regional and on to national standards of competition, considerable emphasis is also placed on inclusivity and participation.
- The Physical Education programme is concerned with teaching basic motor skills. The aim is to ensure skills are well learned in order to increase the likelihood of lifelong participation.

APPLY IT!

Sport Education and Physical Education are really two programmes under one heading!

Each component programme of SEPEP requires sessions of 100 minutes per week, and pupil engagement is a government requirement. The Australian Sports Commission funded the initial research relating to the SEPEP programme.

Although SEPEP provides a framework and is available to all throughout the Australian Physical Education system, it forms but a small part of curriculum delivery. Teachers are free to adapt and create their own programmes to accommodate the variations in ability of their pupils, the teaching environment and their department expertise. The overriding emphasis in Australian schools is on enjoyment and maximum participation. This ethos is at the grass roots of '**Active Australia**' and the mission is to promote fitness, skill and participation.

KEY TERM

Active Australia

The slogan for Australia's sport-for-all policy. This policy has recently been updated and is now termed More Active Australia.

PHYSICAL AND SPORT EDUCATION (PASE)

The Victoria government also commits to the training of non-specialist teachers who may become involved in teaching physical activities of a sports nature. Primary teachers tend to take courses in Physical Education while secondary deliverers focus on Sport Education.

Courses for teachers are intensive and come under the all-embracing title of Physical and Sport Education (PASE). PASE is a professional development programme. It is financed by the government and delivered by the Australian Council for Health Physical Education and Recreation (ACHPER). High quality online teaching resources are available, and teachers are given support to deliver a programme that will encourage lifelong participation in sports activities.

EXEMPLARY SCHOOLS

Exemplary Schools are those with outstanding sports and Physical Education departments. Teachers from Exemplary Schools are selected to deliver professional development and share good practice with neighbouring institutions, called cluster schools. Exemplary Schools are required to be exceptional and make significant contributions to improving the quality of sport delivery in their 'cluster' schools. Government grants are given to cover the cost of teacher release and considerable prestige is associated with the 'exemplary' title. Forty high schools in Victoria have earned this status. The Exemplary Schools system is an aspect of the PASE initiative.

APPLY IT!

Examples of Exemplary Schools are Northcote High in Melbourne and Frankston School, also in Victoria. Both schools have developed special fitness programmes and are model deliverers of sport education.

FUNDAMENTAL SKILLS PROGRAMME (FSP)

The Fundamental Skills Programme is a compulsory Physical Education programme for primary school children. The focus of FSP is to increase competence in eleven fundamental motor skills and not to be overly concerned with teaching games strategies. The logic of this approach is that if skill levels of children are high they will enjoy participation and be less likely to withdraw from sport in later years.

SPORTS LEADER PROGRAMMES

A Sports Leader is usually a senior pupil who can elect to become involved in administration, refereeing and coaching. In this capacity they may help a senior coach to deliver a sport education lesson, enabling the teacher to take up a coordinator's role. The leader is facilitating sporting opportunities for others, and this may later develop into a career in sports development. A Sport Leader Programme is a timetabled course and considered to be part of a senior pupil's SEPEP commitment.

STATE AWARD SCHEMES

The government of Victoria offers two types of award for achievement in school sport.

- A 'State Blue' is awarded for attainment and fair play while engaged in school sport. The latter recognises not only the achievements of pupils but also those of outstanding staff and schools.
- The De Coubertin awards are presented to students who have made outstanding contributions to administration, coaching and other important non-playing roles. The award reflects the original spirit of the modern Olympics that taking part is more important than victory.

SPORT LINKAGE SCHEME.

The Sport Linkage Scheme involves an alliance between schools and sports clubs, sharing facilities on a dual-use basis. In some cases teachers and coaches will interchange. While stressing the non-elitist approach to sport education in Victoria, the Sports Linkage Scheme directs talented pupils toward club participation. This strategy is intended to encourage young people to continue participation in sport beyond school and into adulthood.

SPORT PERSON IN SCHOOLS PROJECT

This project involves engaging a sport performer from the Victoria Institute of Sport (VIS) as a teaching assistant in schools. The VIS athlete may be an international performer who will be given a specification to coach and advise all children and to raise the profile of sport. (The VIS is a centre of sports excellence which sponsors promising athletes.)

Sports professionals must plan lessons and workshops, as these engagements are part of the Athletes Career Education (ACE). For this reason, the government through the VIS pays the athletes for their commitment. The role of the athlete is to supplement curriculum delivery. To be eligible for visits, schools must state how the contribution will integrate with their SEPEP programme.

SPORTS SEARCH

Sports Search is a computer programme into which students can enter their sporting interests and any relevant statistical information. The programme will then advise students regarding the sports to which they would best be suited.

TEACHER GAMES

The Teacher Games are residential competitive sport experiences for Victoria teachers. By electing to take part in the games, teachers have an opportunity to raise their own profiles as role models and are then better placed to encourage young people to become active. This event provides network opportunities and endorses the participation ethic, which is the prime mover in Australian Physical and Sport Education.

PACIFIC SCHOOL GAMES

A further incentive for promising school performers is the possibility of selection for the Pacific School Games (PSG). These games are held every four years and the Victoria Department of Education hosts the event in Melbourne. The games involve in excess of 3000 able-bodied and disabled primary and secondary school pupils, representing all states and territories. Competitors are also drawn from Pacific Island countries. The Pacific Games is a multi-sport event and has been describe as a mini Olympic Games.

Fig 7.7 The opening ceremony of the Pacific School Games

OUTDOOR EDUCATION

The term outdoor education has the same meaning in Australia as in the USA and the UK. This curriculum area relates to the provision of educational experiences in the natural environment.

REMEMBER

Outdoor education in the UK is described on page 223 of *OCR AS PE*.

Outdoor education is heavily promoted in Victoria, essentially because the state has the advantages of wonderful natural resources. Beyond the urban population concentrated in Melbourne, there are wild outback territories, forested areas, upland ranges comprising the Australian Alps and extensive coastal stretches.

Outdoor education is promoted in Victoria for the following reasons:

- The climate is favourable for an outdoor lifestyle.
- It is associated with a balanced, active and healthy lifestyle – nearly one million Australians engage in bushwalking.
- The bush or frontier culture can be experienced.
- It is perceived as an important area of education and is an examined subject.
- The environment has outstanding natural resources and aesthetic appeal.
- Nationalism and pride in the country are promoted through outdoor education.
- Survival and safety skills are necessary in a state that has populated coastal stretches and inland areas of hostile environment.
- The early colonial influence encouraged outdoor activities.

Primary schools offer outdoor adventure activities as part of a balanced Physical Education programme to promote participation and active lifestyles. From Year 4 onwards (7 years old) there is a tradition of the 'school camp', which is strictly supervised.

Each state in Australia offers a Youth Development Programme (YDP) and in Victoria this is entitled the VYDP. From Year 9 (14 years old), the subject is a voluntary elective (subject option) and out of necessity it is linked to a community service. The community services comprise:

- army cadets
- ambulance
- fire service
- surf life saving.

The Duke of Edinburgh Award (D of E) scheme operates throughout Australia, as it does in the UK. The D of E scheme in Australia includes **outward bound** challenges as part of its award and can be offered in schools as an extra-curricular subject. As will be seen in the case study below, the D of E award can be incorporated into the VYDP.

KEY TERM

Outward bound

Relates to outdoor adventure activities.

A CASE STUDY OF A VICTORIA YOUTH DEVELOPMENT PROGRAMME AT FRANKSTON HIGH SCHOOL

Frankston High School has a coastal location. For its VYDP it has a community services link with Mount Elisa Life Saving Club. Specialists from this service help to deliver the course. The programme has four components.

- surf lifesaving techniques
- cardio pulmonary resuscitation (CPR) qualification
- first aid qualification
- Duke of Edinburgh expedition.

In the case of Frankston High, the Duke of Edinburgh expedition is organised from the Life Saving Club. The course is government-funded and all participants are given appropriate kit and uniforms.

Skiing is a sport not often associated with Australia, but for the past forty years Camp Big Foot on Mount Buller has been the venue for the Victoria Interschools SnowSports Championships.

During years 9-10, Outdoor Education can be taken as High School Certificate (HSC) course (equivalent to an A-level). The subject has a large theoretical input but involves practical assessment in a number of options. It is a popular examination elective and the subject is given high status.

The character-building concept relating to the outdoors, pioneered by British public schools, has continued in Victorian independent schools. Timbertop is an upland forested Adventure Centre belonging to Geelong Grammar School for the purpose of residential outdoor education experiences.

The Alpine School is the Victoria state schools equivalent of Timbertop. At this venue courses in Outdoor Leadership and Skills are delivered. The centre has a transient Year 9 population, as students are resident for ten weeks or one term duration.

A COMPARISON WITH PHYSICAL EDUCATION AND SCHOOL SPORT IN THE UK

- Unlike in the UK, there is no National Curriculum or schools inspection service in Australia. Sport Education and Physical Education Programme (SEPEP) is the equivalent to the national curriculum which operates in the UK.
- The Physical Education School Sport and Club Links strategy (PESSCLS) was a government strategy to promote Physical Education and school sport in the UK and was launched in 2002. In 2008, PESSCLS was renamed the PE, School Sport and Young People (PESSYP) strategy. There are nine strands to this strategy; see Chapter 6, page 125.
- In addition to the PESSCLS strategy, Kitemarking is a scheme that is designed to promote participation in sporting activities in the UK schools (see Chapter 6, page 125). There is no Kitemark scheme in Australia, but to receive the title Exemplary School, with its government recognition and funding, is considered an award of high status.

- In the UK, the home country organisation, for example Sport England, administers PESSCL, whereas the ASC in Australia and state government are in charge of school policy.
- In common with the UK, the Australian government implemented strategies to improve the quantity and quality of the provision for physical activities in schools.

STRETCH AND CHALLENGE

Compare the strategies that are implemented by the UK and Australia to encourage young people to adopt a balanced, active and healthy lifestyle.

REMEMBER

Ten strategies have been implemented by the Australian government to improve the delivery of physical activity in schools; see page 167.

- Sports colleges in the UK promote sporting opportunities for young people and the wider community. The equivalent in Australia is the Exemplary Schools programme.
- In the UK, intra-school sport is played in recreation time or as organised house matches. Intra-school sport in Australia is an integral part of SEPEP.
- Inter-school sport is considered important, is organised by a number of agencies in the UK and tends to be extra-curricular. In Australia the inter-school sports programme is organised through SEPEP and overseen by the national school sport governing body, namely School Sport Australia (SSA).
- The teacher in the UK is in charge of Physical Education and sport, and although there may be some input from coaches on the Sports Linkage Programme, the situation is the same in Australia.
- Both countries are committed to a participation ethic and to the development of fair play. The win ethic is not instilled, nor is there an overt attempt to replicate the professional sports scene in either country.
- Both countries have national schools teams in a variety of sports and have national sports competitions. In the UK, although there is a national schools athletics championship, there is not an Australian Schools Pacific Games equivalent.

Mass participation in sport and physical activity in Australia and how it compares with the UK

PARTICIPATION RATES IN THE OVER-18 AGE GROUP CATEGORY

- According to 2007 government statistics, nearly two-thirds (62 per cent or 9 million) of Australians over the age of 18 years claim to participate in sport or physical activity.
- At 65 per cent and 60 per cent respectively, slightly more males than females appear to be actively engaged.
- Almost one-third (32 per cent) of the over-18 category are registered as club participants.
- Of the 38 per cent who did not undertake sufficient physical activity to obtain a health benefit, 15 per cent were classed as sedentary.

The growth and decline of Australia's top ten sports since 2001 are shown in Table 1 overleaf.

TASK 4

1 Explain the growth in fitness and aerobics gym activities both in Australia and the UK.
2 Explain why both in Australia and the UK, participation in Association Football is popular while participation in Rugby League is relatively low.

Table 1 Participation in Australia's top ten sports, 2001–07

Activity	2001	2004	2007
Total participation rate as a percentage			
Walking	28.8	39.0	33.0
Aerobics/fitness	13.0	17.1	20.2
Swimming	16.0	16.5	12.0
Cycling	9.5	10.5	9.7
Running	7.2	8.3	7.6
Tennis	9.2	8.4	5.8
Walking (bush)	5.3	5.2	5.7
Golf	8.2	7.9	5.6
Football (Association)	3.7	4.2	4.2
Netball	4.1	3.6	3.2

NATIONAL FITNESS LEVELS IN THE OVER-18 AGE GROUP CATEGORY IN AUSTRALIA AND THE UK

In common with the UK and USA, Australia is experiencing health-related problems associated with lifestyle. In 2007, 60 per cent of Australian adults were considered overweight and 21 per cent of this number was diagnosed as obese.

In 2007, 67 per cent of men and 56 per cent of women were considered to be overweight in the UK. Most significantly, it is estimated that 25 per cent of adults are obese.

MASS PARTICIPATION IN SPORT AND PHYSICAL ACTIVITY FOR THE 5–17 AGE GROUP CATEGORY IN AUSTRALIA

Statistics from the Australian National Children's Nutrition and Physical Activity survey of 2007 indicate the following:

- Approximately 70 per cent of boys and girls complete at least 60 minutes of moderate to vigorous physical activity on most days.
- On average, boys devote 2.5 hours to exercise while girls average almost 2 hours of moderate to vigorous physical activity per day.
- The time spent doing moderate to vigorous activity decreases with age.

Table 2 Prevalence of overweight and obesity in Australian children and adolescents aged 5–17 expressed as a percentage

Gender	Percentage overweight but not obese	Percentage obese	Total percent of overweight and obese
Boys			
1995	9.3	1.4	10.7
2005	15.3	4.7	20.0
Girls			
1995	10.6	1.2	11.8
2005	16.0	5.5	21.5

Table 2 indicates that along with the UK and USA, Australia is experiencing increases in childhood obesity.

A COMPARISON OF NATIONAL FITNESS LEVELS IN THE 5–17 AGE GROUP CATEGORY WITH THE UK

UK government statistics for 2005 revealed that nearly 30 per cent of young people in this category were overweight. Furthermore, 17 per cent of boys and 14 per cent of girls were considered to be obese.

PROMOTION BY THE GOVERNMENT OF REGULAR PARTICIPATION IN PHYSICAL ACTIVITY IN AUSTRALIA

The need for federal involvement in sport was emphasised by the failure of the Australian team in the 1976 Montreal Olympic Games. A master plan for sport led to the establishment of the Australian Sports Commission.

The role of the Australia Sports Commission (ASC) is to promote excellence and to increase mass participation. In doing so, the ASC determines policy and funds sport on a national basis.

In fulfilling these roles the ASC seeks to:

- enhance Australia's leadership in the international sports community
- manage the internationally acclaimed Australian Institute of Sport (AIS), maintaining it as a world centre of excellence for the development of elite performers
- develop growth in sport participation at the grassroots level, particularly by young people, women, indigenous Australians and people with disabilities
- increase the adoption of the values of fair play, self-improvement and achievement.

ASC funding is carefully structured and applied to develop sport from grassroots to the elite level.

Following the ASC review entitled 'Backing Australia's Sporting Ability' in the early twenty-first century, the More Active Australia policy was introduced with the aim of increasing sports participation. It is the Australian government's sport-for-all policy. More Active Australia is funded by the ASC and its main focus is to increase the active membership of sports clubs across the country through national and state sporting associations.

ADAPTED GAMES FOR YOUNG PEOPLE

In 1986, the government invested in a junior sports programme called Aussie Sport. The Aussie Sport initiative set out to modify the rules, reduce the dimensions of the playing environment and introduce child-friendly equipment. The new simplified games engaged over 2 million children and by 1995 Aussie Sport was implemented by many clubs and 100 per cent of primary schools. Aussie Sport Resource Kits introducing 30 modified sports and including guidelines for sporting conduct were made available to teachers and coaches. Coaching courses and an awards system were established by the ASC and Aussie Sport Coordinators were established in all states and territories.

Australia has become the world leader in adapting sport to suit young people. Programmes which are modelled on the Aussie Sport system now operate in 16 different countries.

The term Aussie Sport was changed in 2000 and the initiative is now called The Junior Sport Programme.

Table 3 Examples of strategies designed to promote sports participation in Australia

Strategy	How it promotes participation in sport
1. Primary and high schools	Ten strategies to ensure that sport and PE are taught to the highest quality in primary and high schools are explained on pages 167–169. School Sport Australia (SSA) coordinates national inter-school competition.
2. School Sport Network	The Network is a support agency for all teachers who are involved in sports activity. It recognises the importance of schools in encouraging and preparing young people for an active life. Help is given to schools by the Network to extend opportunities for sport and physical activities; this includes advising schools on addressing the barriers that prevent participation.
3. Junior Sport Programmes	These involve the promotion of adapted or modified games for the 5–17 age group. The programmes provide resource materials for teachers and coaches. Coaching and the organisation of sports competitions is part of the programme.
4. Active After School Communities Programme (AASC)	The AASC provides primary-school-aged children with access to free, structured physical activity programmes after the school day has finished. The programme aims specifically at traditionally non-active children. The intention is to encourage youngsters to join sports clubs.
5. Local Sporting Champions Programme	Through this programme, the ASC provides financial support to individual youngsters or youth teams. Grants cover equipment, uniforms and travel expenses for young people in the 12–18 age group. In 2008, nearly 2000 individual youngsters received grants of $500 while 200 teams were granted $3000.
6. Bluearth Programme	This is a health and movement education initiative which is available to schools. Specialists in health and movement education work alongside teachers to improve fitness and motor skills. Its mission is to encourage an active lifetime involvement in sport and exercise.

STRATEGIES TO PROMOTE PARTICIPATION IN SPORT

Some of the major strategies that promote sports participation in Australia, particularly among young people, are outlined in Table 3. All the initiatives described below can relate to physical activity programmes in primary schools or SEPEP in high schools.

TASK 5

With reference to Chapter 5 page 91 and Chapter 6 pages 134 and 135, discuss the strategies that operate to promote mass participation both in the UK and Australia.

Sport and the pursuit of excellence in Australia and how this compares with the UK

AUSTRALIAN INSTITUTE OF SPORT (AIS)

While there is a strong commitment to increasing mass participation, there is an equally strong and dedicated ambition in Australia to achieving global sporting excellence.

REMEMBER

Sporting success was measured during the twentieth century by winning against the 'Motherland'. In the twenty-first century, Australia seeks global recognition and benchmarks achievement against success in events like the Olympic Games and the World Cup in Association Football.

There are clear networks established to develop sports talent up to international standard. The most important of these networks is the Australian Institute of Sport (AIS).

The concept of a sports institute gained momentum in 1976 when Australia failed to win a gold medal at the Olympic Games in Montreal. An equally poor performance followed two years later at the Commonwealth Games in Edmonton. Public opinion demanded that the government should intervene to provide a solution.

EXAM TIP

A comparison of the strategies to pursue sporting excellence in the UK and in Australia is a popular exam question.

STRUCTURE OF THE AUSTRALIAN INSTITUTE OF SPORT

Based in Canberra, the AIS opened in 1981. It was funded by the federal government through a department named the Australian Sports Commission (ASC). Elite athletes were selected from all states to live and train together. To improve the effectiveness of the development of elite athletes, the ASC elected to provide funds to establish an Institute of Sport in each Australian state.

The AIS continues to be funded by both the federal government and the state governments. This central funding is now supplemented by private sponsorships. For example, the Victoria Institute of Sport (VIS) has received support from over fifty private sponsors.

Fig 7.9 on the next page shows the location of the nine state institutes, the name of each institute and the official opening date.

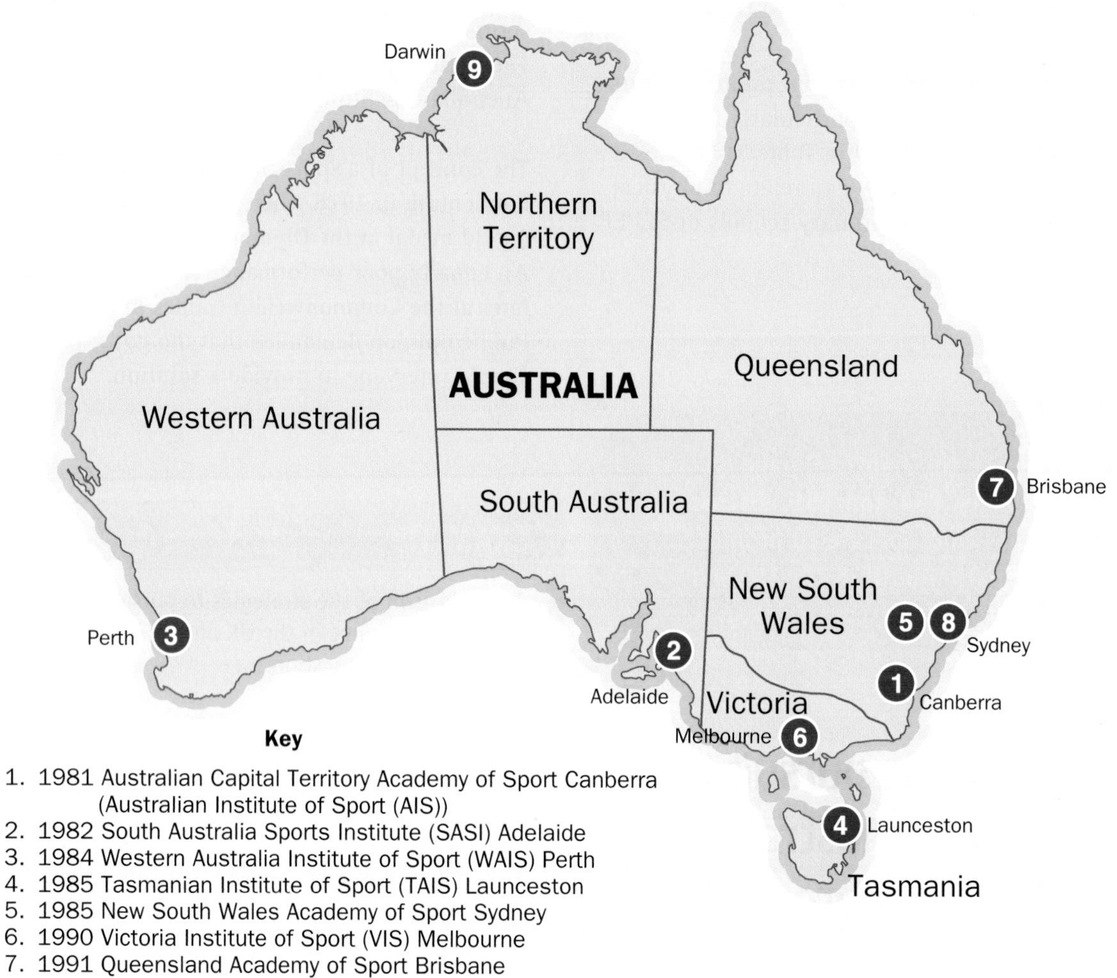

Fig 7.8 Australia's nine institutes of sport

The Australian Institutes of Sport operate in parallel; there is no hierarchy or specialisation. The whole network is designed to enable athletes to train in their own locality and to prevent the need for great distances to be travelled.

Not all institutes have onsite facilities. For example, the VIS operates as a resource from an office premises and not from a facility centre. It is a non-residential institute from which the facilities of Melbourne can be utilised. Elite athletes are coached online and through digital imagery.

APPLY IT!

Sports facilities in Melbourne are of world-class standard. Melbourne claims to be the sports capital of the world.

Although each institute has a high degree of autonomy and the whole network is decentralised, the AIS system is closely monitored by the National Elite Sports Council.

FUNCTION OF THE AUSTRALIAN INSTITUTES OF SPORT

The major function of the AIS is to sponsor and support young athletes with outstanding potential to become world class performers. The major route for potential Olympic performers is by way of the AIS and the institute provides support to 26 different sports. Players are selected from clubs or are nominated by a sporting governing body to receive an AIS scholarship. Training is organised by the institute and the programme for the given sport is supervised by the head coach. Fig 7.10 below outlines the major functions of the Australian Institute of Sport.

REMEMBER

The Athletic Career Education (ACE) programme is utilised by Australian high schools; see page 168. ACE also links to the Sports Person in Schools Project (see page 168).

The following example from Australian Rules Football illustrates how the AIS operate with individual sports and sporting governing bodies in order to develop young talent.

The AIS Australian Football programme was set up in 1997 to provide high-quality training and education to footballers at the elite junior level. Through a partnership with the Australian Football League (AFL), scholarship holders become part of AIS and the AFL Academy. Athletes, while remaining in their own state or territory, undertake intensive training that is overseen by the AIS High Performance Coach, who also links with the AFL. The programme aims to prepare scholarship holders for professional status in Australian Football through the drafting process which leads to the senior AFL clubs.

ALTERNATIVE PATHWAYS INTO PROFESSIONAL SPORT

The Australian Institutes of Sport are perceived as 'finishing schools in sport'. They do not, however, guarantee progress to higher levels, and some athletes achieve international standard without

Fig 7.9 The major functions of the Australian Institute of Sport

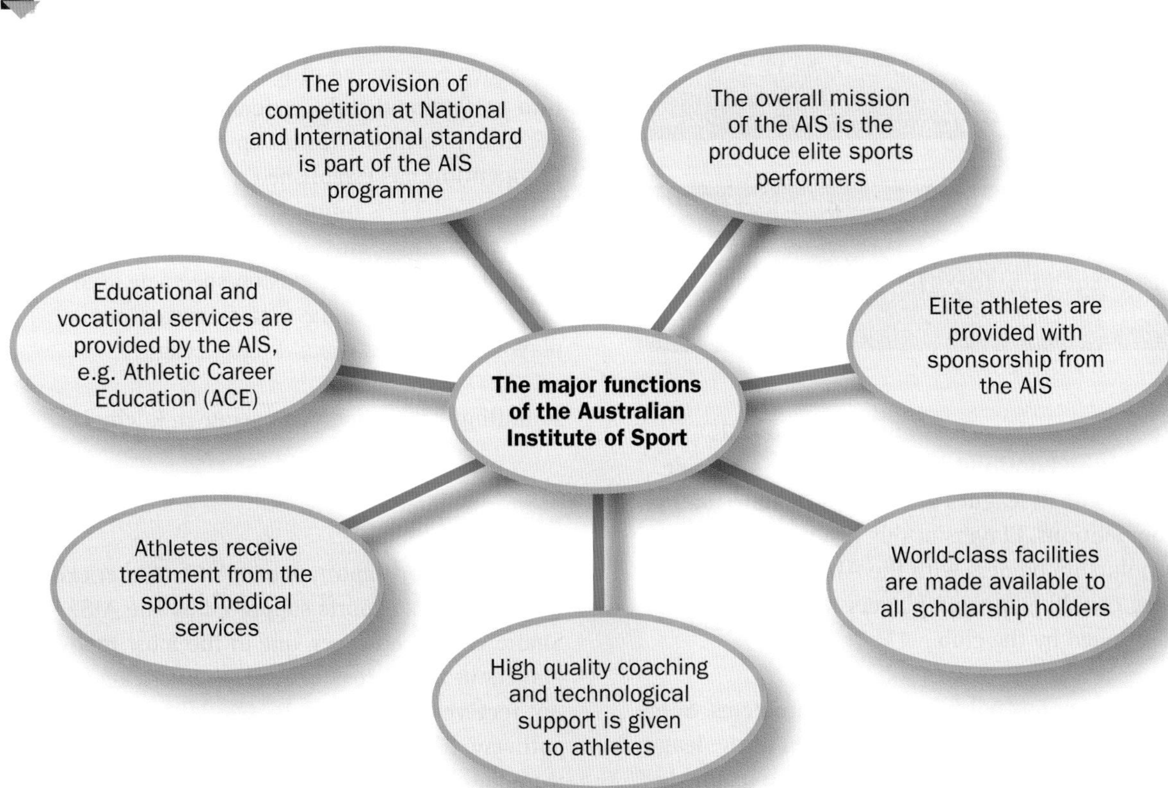

The major functions of the Australian Institute of Sport
The provision of competition at National and International standard is part of the AIS programme
The overall mission of the AIS is the produce elite sports performers
Educational and vocational services are provided by the AIS, e.g. Athletic Career Education (ACE)
Elite athletes are provided with sponsorship from the AIS
Athletes receive treatment from the sports medical services
World-class facilities are made available to all scholarship holders
High quality coaching and technological support is given to athletes

AIS support. A scholarship from the AIS may be an advantage to some players, but it is not essential to undergo training at an institute in order to become a sports professional. There are alternative pathways available to allow access into professional sport.

THE DRAFT SYSTEM IN AUSTRALIAN RULES FOOTBALL

The governing body for Australian Rules Football is the Australian Football League (AFL). The AFL operates a **draft system** in order to recruit players into professional teams. The AFL Draft is designed to give clubs that finish the season low down in the league table the first opportunities to select the best players who are not under contract with other clubs. For example, the bottom club will have the first pick in the Draft. This model follows the American system of the Pro Draft. The draft system is an attempt to intensify league competition.

KEY TERM

Draft system

The AFL draft is the process which involves the selection of young and new players into the senior professional clubs.

REMEMBER

The Pro Draft in the USA is taken from college sport; see page 139.

Each club in the AFL is allowed to have 35 players and drafting takes place from open age state football leagues and under-18 state football competitions. Players at this level may well be scholarship holders with the AIS. Alternatively, they could be talented players who have been developed by the club.

The system has not been without problems. Some teams which are close to the bottom of the league towards the end of the season may be tempted to field under-strength teams and accept defeat in order to have the first Draft. This negative strategy is termed 'tanking'.

RUGBY LEAGUE

Rugby League has a very well-structured and diverse plan to facilitate progress up to professional levels of the game. A promising young Rugby League player may well be a scholarship holder with the AIS. As an alternative, however, a talented performer could be nurtured through the **club academy** after selection from school or junior club. AIS support is therefore unnecessary.

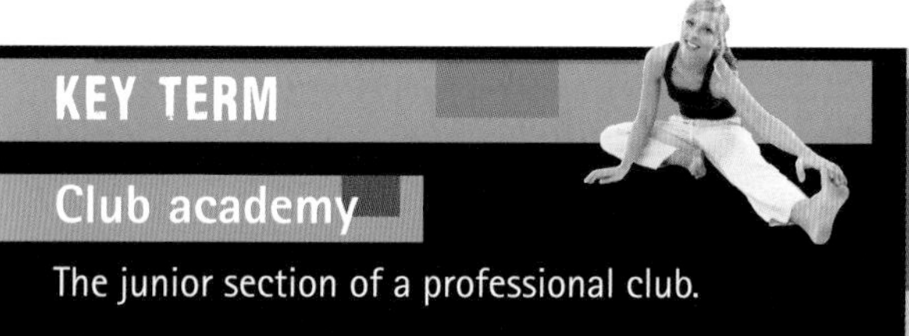

KEY TERM
Club academy
The junior section of a professional club.

The Kids to Kangaroos scheme is a new national development plan in Australian Rugby League that brings together all states at all levels of the game. Outstanding junior talent from clubs and a well-organised schools system participate in the scheme, enabling gifted players to progress into professional club academies. In addition, the newly formed Toyota Cup National Youth Competition has established a development pathway which is unique in the organisation of Australian sport. This under-18 competition has been promoted as a television spectacle, and this exposure appears to have 'fast-tracked' some players into professional Rugby League.

A drafting system does not operate in Rugby League.

CRICKET

Being of major importance in Australia, cricket is one of the 26 sports supported by the AIS. Shane Warne, however, one of the most renowned players in the history of Australian cricket, did not receive AIS support. By way of an alternative pathway, he was promoted to professional status through club and representative selection.

Fig 7.10 Shane Warne had an outstanding career in cricket for Australia but did not follow the conventional pathway into professional sport. He bypassed the AIS and graduated to the international scene via club and direct selection to state cricket

A COMPARISON WITH SPORT AND THE PURSUIT OF EXCELLENCE IN THE UK

- UK Sport is the organisation with the overall responsibility for producing sporting excellence in the UK. The ambition of UK Sport is to achieve fourth place in the 2012 Olympic Games medal table. Australia also is looking for global success through prestigious international events.

EXAM TIP

Marks in the exam are scored by making comparisons between the UK and Australia or the UK and the USA. The lists of comparisons given throughout these sections are not definitive.

- After the bid to stage the 2012 Olympic Games was won in 2005, UK Sport produced a submission to the government for extra funding. A performance funding package of £300 million was requested. UK Sport has a clear philosophy that Olympic and Paralympic sport can no longer be trusted to enthusiastic and talented amateurs and this view has partly been triggered by Australia's sporting success.
- UK Sport ensures that athletic performance, coaching and organisation structure in the UK have a professional focus.
- UK Sport has ten functions; these are explained on page 265 of *OCR AS PE*.

SPORTS INSTITUTES IN THE UK

- The Sports Institutes of the UK are direct copies of the Australian Institute of Sport (AIS). Sports Institutes in the UK and Australia are centres that are dedicated to providing support to elite athletes. The Institutes in both countries operate on a decentralised basis.
- There are four devolved Home Country Sports Institutes in the UK:
  1. The English Institute of Sport (EIS)
  2. The Sports Institute of Northern Ireland (SINI)
  3. The Scottish Institute of Sport (SIS)
  4. The Welsh Institute of Sport.

  In Australia there is at least one institute in each state or territory.
- The Home Country Sports Institutes have promoted the successes of Team GB in the Olympic and Paralympic competitions. The AIS has also promoted Olympic success.
- In the UK, not all sports find it necessary to take advantage of the institutes. As in Australia, the UK also has alternative pathways which access professional sport. For example, non-Olympic sports like cricket have their own governing body pathways leading towards professional status.
- The whole network of the UK Sports Institute is funded from the National Lottery and government contribution. In Australia, funding is supplied by the government and business sponsorship.
- The UK government is not involved with sporting policies, whereas the ASC are directly involved in policy decisions.

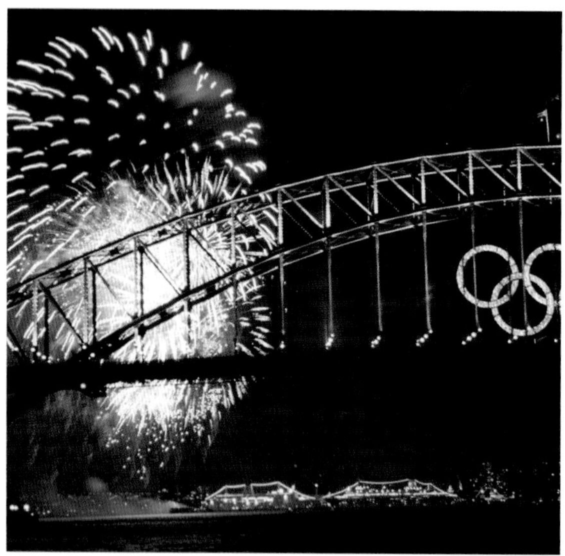

Fig 7.11 The Sydney Olympic Games of 2000 were a global success and a national triumph. As the host nation, Australia created a standard to which other countries must aspire

- UK Sport is responsible for the strategic direction of the Home Country Sports Institutes. Similarly, the Australian Institutes are closely monitored by the National Elite Sports Council.

CASE STUDY OF CRICKET IN AUSTRALIA

Cricket is a little different in Australia compared to the version seen in the UK. The light is brighter and the pitches harder with more bounce to encourage attack. There are variations in terminology. In Australia 'extras' are 'sundries' and the 'googly' is the 'wrong un'.

Great rivalry has always existed between England and Australia in cricket. Cricket was seen by the Australians as a way of establishing national unity and victory over the 'Motherland', and was the benchmark against which the general progress of the young nation could be measured.

The phrase 'test match' was originally coined during the first English tour to Australia in 1861. The matches played on this tour resembled exhibition games, with Australia often fielding more than eleven players. It was not until the fourth expedition to the colony in 1876 that a combined team from Melbourne and Sydney played England in what is accepted as the first official test match.

In 1882, the 'Ashes' mythology came into being as a result of the first Australian victory, in England, over a full strength England cricket team. The *Sporting Times* carried a mock obituary notice stating that the body of English cricket would be cremated and the Ashes taken to Australia. Since that time an Ashes series has stimulated arguably the greatest interest in the world of cricket, and in the twenty-first century the event has become a major focus of media and commercial interest. Ticket sales for the 2009 Ashes series in England had reached a record high almost a year before the first test matches.

The development of Australian cricket has not been without controversies. During the infamous 'bodyline' tour of 1932, England's tactics were deemed unfair and both sporting and diplomatic relations between the countries became strained.

Fig 7.12 Sir Donald Bradman remains Australia's greatest sporting icon. If, when batting, Bradman had been struck by the English 'bodyline' bowlers in 1932, diplomatic relations between the two countries would have been compromised

KEY TERM

Bodyline

This describes the tactic of bowling at the batter's body. It must be remembered that helmets and body protection were not worn in those days.

In 1977 Australian television magnate Kerry Packer introduced 'World Series' cricket, which took power away from the traditional International Cricket Board. This had a direct impact on the development of the modern game. World Series cricket offered lucrative financial contracts to the world's best players to form what was described as a 'cricket circus'. Players who signed up to the circus were subsequently banned from playing for their countries.

Australia hosted the World Series, which for the first time involved floodlit cricket, imported pitches and modifications to dress and rules. A limit on overs ensured that a game could be finished in one day and a result was guaranteed. The spectacle became popular, and irrevocably changed the image of cricket. For the first time, television royalties brought wealth to prominent players. In effect, World Series cricket had intensified the professional approach to the game.

REMEMBER

The 1977 'cricket circus' impacted on the UK and also stimulated the development of commercialised sport in Australia; see page 159.

More recently the Australian team of 2007 won the World Cup in the limited-overs version of the game, completing a sequence of 29 consecutive wins. This achievement confirms Australian supremacy in all types of cricket. The 50 overs World Cup format has generated $550 million in television royalties during the 2003 and 2007 competitions. Hosted in 2007 by the West Indies, who invested $81 million in ground improvements, matches were televised in 200 countries.

In 2008 the Australian authorities were planning to establish a Twenty20 cricket competition. The model for the competition would reflect the Indian Professional League (IPL), which proved to be appealing as mass entertainment and therefore very lucrative. This endorses the strong 'golden triangle' association that has developed between cricket, sponsorship and the media.

A CASE STUDY OF CRICKET IN THE UK AS A COMPARISON TO AUSTRALIA

Cricket originated in England and is closely associated with English tradition and values. The first recorded adult game was in 1611. It was some time later that club cricket became established, with Hambledon, a village in Hampshire, becoming in 1756 the first to acquire a reputation for success. The Marylebone Cricket Club (MCC) soon became the force of English and later international cricket. The MCC ground at Lords remains the most prestigious in the world. Australia have replicated the status and tradition of the Lords ground at the Melbourne Cricket Club (MCC).

Cricket in Australia was a direct copy of the English game. The rules were identical and the format was the same. Differences were evident, however, in approach, terminology and attitudes relating to social class. As in the UK, the first competitive matches in Australia were played as hastily arranged challenges between the 'currency lads' and the English military and free settlers. These matches often involved heavy betting. County cricket in the UK began in 1839, and with the expansion of the railway network most venues became accessible, so the game spread rapidly. In Australia, however, travel was more difficult. The tyranny of distance impeded the development of state cricket and the Sheffield Shield, an inter-state professional cricket competition, was established in 1892.

In the UK, cricket strongly reflected the values of the British Empire. For example, while every man had a separate role to play, teamwork was the key element. While the game was considered to be manly, a strict code of behaviour prevailed emphasising dignity, a reserved attitude and sporting honesty associated with the English ruling classes. Cricket thrived in the UK public schools where it was believed to develop character and leadership skills. The match between the public schools of Eton and Harrow was considered one of the most important annual fixtures to be staged at the Lords ground.

During representative matches, the classes often mixed. The amateur players were referred to as gentlemen and often occupied batting positions which reflected their position as the privileged class. The professionals, however, belonging to the lower orders, adopted the role of labouring bowlers. Gentleman amateurs and professional players changed in separate rooms, entered the field of play through different gates and travelled in carriages that were commensurate with their class. The captain of England up to the mid-twentieth century was required to be amateur. With its discriminatory involvement of working-class players, display of imperial values and the association with public schools, cricket became an accurate reflection of the English class system.

Australian sportsmen, in contrast, were openly critical of the class divisions that were obvious in English teams. Australia was the 'land of the fair go' with no concept of class privilege or deference. Cricket in Australia reflected the egalitarian ethos of its 'melting pot' society and had no room for the snobbishness of English cricket.

Victory for Australia in England in 1882 was significant as it was seen as a benchmark against which national progress could be measured. At the time, winning in sport was more important to Australia as success was helping to forge a nation. England, on the other hand, still looked towards dominance over the old Empire for national prestige. Allegations that tactics adopted by England's amateur captain on the 1932 'bodyline tour' to Australia were unfair almost caused a diplomatic incident between the countries. To be accused of cheating was considered by the privileged classes to be the greatest insult.

Limited-over cricket was initiated in England in 1963 as a novelty competition at the end of season. The first time the shortened version of the game was promoted at international level was in 1971 in Australia.

In the UK, Twenty20 cricket was introduced in the early twenty-first century to boost the commercial potential of cricket. Australia is now following this lead with the same version of the game, to which they have given the commercial brand name of Twenty20 bash.

A CASE STUDY OF RUGBY LEAGUE IN AUSTRALIA

Rugby League in Australia tends to be more popular than Rugby Union. Rugby League in Australia has an east–west divide with the strongest states being New South Wales and Queensland. Melbourne Storm is a professional Rugby League team located in Victoria. This is an example of the expansion of the game to states which previously had no tradition of Rugby League.

In 1907 Australian professionalism followed the northern England 'breakaway' movement whereby players could be paid for time spent away from work on playing duties. In general terms, Rugby League offers social acceptance and integration for players and supporters of non-British heritage, however, the League code still displays evidence of its working-class origins.

The 1950s was a progressive period for the code in both countries. During the 1970s, however, Rugby League attendances declined necessitating major modifications. A five-team semi-final series, changes in scoring and the six-tackle rule were implemented to increase spectator appeal. Rugby League needed to be a superior spectacle, as gate receipts from the paying public paid the player's wages. Eastern Suburbs became the first team to display sponsorship on club jerseys and the inaugural State of Origin match – a series of three interstate games between New South Wales and Queensland – was played in 1980. The State of Origin series is a level higher than club rugby and is a considerable commercial success. The intensity and high standard of play help to prepare talented players for the international arena.

The contemporary professional game has salary capped all players and looks increasingly to commercial methods in a competitive market. Although a draft system does not operate, each professional 'club' has an 'academy' team which has a mission to nurture young local talent. It is significant that the British Rugby League is following the Australian lead.

A CASE STUDY OF RUGBY LEAGUE IN THE UK AS A COMPARISON TO AUSTRALIA

Rugby League in the UK is traditionally associated with the former industrial areas of Lancashire, Yorkshire and Cumberland. The game in Australia is also associated with specific areas. Unlike in Australia, Rugby League in the UK tends to be less popular than Rugby Union.

Rugby League originates from the UK and was brought into being as the result of a dispute over 'broken time' payments between the English Rugby Union governing body and a number of northern clubs. Many players from the north worked on Saturday in traditional industrial occupations. Northern clubs wanted to pay compensation for loss of earnings, but the southern-based Rugby Union claimed this to be a breach of the amateur ethic. The professional Northern Union was formed in 1895. Spectator attendance was initially low so the organisers of the breakaway movement changed the rules to attract larger crowds; Rugby League had taken its first step towards commercialism.

Similar to the game in Australia, Rugby League in the UK has always been considered as a working-class sport.

Rugby League in Australia was copied directly from the 'Motherland' and adopted in 1907.

The first international matches between Great Britain and Australia took place in England during the 1908 season. As a direct imitation of cricket, test matches played between these countries are known as 'Ashes Tests'.

In recent years, the UK attempted to copy the State of Origin competition in a series named 'Battle of the Roses'. This tournament matched Lancashire with Yorkshire, but unfortunately the venture was less successful than the State of Origin because it had less commercial appeal.

In the twenty-first century, strenuous efforts have been made to develop the game at a professional level in London and in Wales. There remains, however, a clear north–south divide regarding preference of code.

As in Australia, interest in the UK Rugby League began to diminish in the late 1960s. Measures were implemented to revive the code with the inauguration of Sunday rugby in 1967, and in 1971 the first sponsors invested capital into the game. After failing in Australia (see page 160), Rupert Murdoch successfully launched 'Super League' in the UK as a product of BSkyB television. The code changed from its traditional winter season to become a summer game in 1996. Like their Australian counterparts, Super League players became full-time professionals for the first time and the game attracted immediate media appeal. Rugby League changed its image to promote itself as a commercial product. Team names changed to Bulls, Rhinos and Warriors while traditional grounds took on the names of sponsors. Rules were modified and tactical substituting helped to sustain a high level of physical intensity. For the 2009 season, Super League planned to adopt the approach taken to commercial sport in the USA by abolishing relegation and introducing a franchise system to expand its operations to include teams from London, Wales and France.

APPLY IT!

Super League in the UK is a direct replication of the Australian Rugby League and an American influence is evident in the game in both countries.

Strategies are also in place in Australia to expand Rugby League. The sport has recently been promoted in Victoria, which formerly had no tradition of Rugby League.

The UK Grand Final is a copy of the Australian model and is now the showcase commercial event at the end of the UK season. The champion clubs from the UK and Australia are matched together in March in an event that opens the season in both hemispheres.

CASE STUDY OF RUGBY UNION IN AUSTRALIA

Informal games of Rugby Union were played at Sydney University from 1863 onwards, and the club is recognised as the first official rugby club in Australia. In these early days, Rugby Union was an upper-class game having been influenced by the colonial tradition and played by boys in private schools, university students and later by graduates.

By the late nineteenth century, New South Wales, Queensland and an Australian XV had played fixtures with New Zealand and England. As an indication of the strength of the game 'down under', Australia won the Rugby Union gold medal at the London Olympic Games in 1908.

The Olympic Games was at that time a strictly amateur affair and Australia had in 1907 lost some of its better players to the newly formed professional code of Rugby League. The temptation offered by professionalism in Australia mirrored the situation in the UK when in 1895 the Northern Union, which was the forerunner of Rugby League, was formed.

In contrast with the UK, Rugby Union in Australia is less popular than Rugby League. A major boost for Rugby Union, however, proved to be the inaugural World Cup in 1987. Success in this competition increased sponsorship and attracted greater television coverage on a commercial network. Eventually professionalism was accepted by Rugby Union with the signing of the Paris Declaration in 1995.

APPLY IT!

Despite losing to England in the 2003 World Cup, the drama of the final and traditional rivalry further stimulated the commercial interest in Australian Rugby Union.

As with Rugby League, growing commercialism has prompted rule changes and professionalism has brought advances in athleticism and skilfulness. International competition throughout the southern hemisphere has become increasingly intense and greater rivalry with the European rugby nations has been generated, attracting a wider audience. High quality club competitions, such as the prestigious 'Super 12s', have raised both the profile of the game and television revenue in Australia and New Zealand.

A CASE STUDY OF RUGBY UNION IN THE UK AS A COMPARISON WITH AUSTRALIA

A code of rules for what eventually became Rugby Union was established in 1845, but the governing body was formed in 1871. The origins of Rugby Union are rooted firmly in the public schools and universities of the UK. There is also a strong tradition of the game in twentieth-century grammar schools. The influence of the schools impacted on the senior game as many clubs were formed as **'Old Boys' associations**. In the industrial areas of Lancashire and Yorkshire, **secondary modern schools** played Rugby League as it was the game of the working classes.

KEY TERMS

Old Boys' associations

Clubs run by the former pupils of the public or grammar schools.

Secondary modern schools

Schools attended by those pupils who did not pass the grammar school entrance examination at 11 years. This divide was often the result of social class advantage.

Similarly in Australia, the elite and exclusively private schools of Queensland and New South Wales play Rugby Union, while Catholic schools which cater for students from a different level of society predominantly play Rugby League.

In the UK, as in Australia, Rugby Union is strongly permeated by the middle-class amateur ethos. Although a 'League' competition structure existed in Wales, Rugby Union fixtures were for the most part organised on a 'friendly' basis up until the 1990s. Matches were very competitive but a fixture could be 'dropped' if it was considered unsuitable. This system of organisation reflects once again an affiliation with middle-class amateurism.

Both the Australian and the home countries Rugby Football Unions withstood commercial pressure and remained strictly compliant to the ideals of amateurism until the 1990s.

After the success of the second World Cup, won by the Australians in 1991, and as a consequence of increased global television interest, Rugby Union agreed, in what became known as the Paris Declaration of 1995, to break with tradition and adopt professionalism.

This announcement was greeted with astonishment in England, where amateurism had remained firmly ingrained and there was no dependence on commercialism. The English RFU was forced to commit to commercialism. A league competition structure was put in place, and a sponsored European cup was assigned to increase the commercial potential of the game. Players became full-time professionals. In a similar way, Australian players became professional and the southern hemisphere introduced a 'Super 12' competition.

The laws of the game have been modified since 1995 in an attempt to make the game more attractive and easier to understand for the casual spectator. Like all major professional games in the UK, Rugby Union has evolved into a highly commercialised sport reliant on media revenue and corporate sponsorship. The advent of professionalism stopped good Rugby Union players from signing up to the Rugby League code. Indeed, the trend of a hundred years appears to have been reversed, in that League players are now moving to the more lucrative union clubs.

APPLY IT!

Although at the time an amateur competition, the organisers made a profit from the 1991 World Cup of $85 million.

APPLY IT!

Prior to 1995, once a player had signed for a League club – indeed, if he had merely played as an amateur in the breakaway code – he would receive a lifetime ban from Rugby Union.

Unlike in the UK, the administration and structure of the game in Australia has not kept pace with professionalism. Although in Australia the flow of junior players from Rugby Union to Rugby League has slowed, the defection remains significant. Australia has failed, furthermore, to successfully promote a club or franchise a league below elite level. As a result, Rugby League in Australia remains the dominant code.

Fig 7.13 England's victory over Australia in the 2003 World Cup competition greatly increased both the popularity and the marketing potential of the game in the country of its origin

A CASE STUDY OF ASSOCIATION FOOTBALL IN AUSTRALIA

Association Football, unlike other colonial games, did not transfer well to Australia. In the colonial period it was played only by the UK immigrants and was known dismissively as the 'Pommie game'. Play tended to be very physical and was, when compared to the standard of the UK play, unsophisticated. Association Football was the least popular of four different versions of the game, but it was feared by the mainstream culture to have the potential to become the dominant code. This threat caused further rejection of Association Football on the grounds that there was not a sufficient number of players to play all forms of the game. Sport space was a convenient excuse to reject Association Football in Australia.

REMEMBER

The concept of 'sport space' implies that there is no place for a given sport in society on the grounds that there will be too few to play it (see also page 143).

After the Second World War (1939–45), European immigrants were allowed to settle in Australia and they introduced a style of football that was in keeping with their 'continental' culture and tradition. Play became fluent, skilful and less abrasive. The new style, however, also appeared to condone shirt pulling, dissent towards officials and the feigning of injury. These tactics brought negative media publicity and contempt from the majority of the Australian sporting public. Standards of play were not high; an England XI defeated the Australian national team 17–0 in 1951.

Football remained the natural first-choice sport of the working-class European immigrants. These people chose to live in their ethnic communities and settled in particular areas of cities forming 'ghetto cultures'. Each community celebrated its country of origin in the name of the football team. Team names like Melbourne Croatia and St. George Budapest stimulated racial rivalry and consequent crowd violence. Mainstream Australians could not tolerate the football ethos and effectively marginalised the sport labelling football as the 'foreign game'. The rejection of Association Football therefore appears to contradict the claim that Australia is the 'land of the fair go'.

THE INCREASING POPULARITY OF ASSOCIATION FOOTBALL IN AUSTRALIA

Association Football has undergone a great change in the twenty-first century and the popularity of the game has risen significantly. It is now one of the major Australian games. Ten factors have contributed to the increasing status of Association Football; these are identified and explained in Table 4 below.

Table 4 Factors contributing to the increasing status of Association Football in Australia

Factor	Explanation
Government	The Australian government at the turn of the twentieth century initiated an inquiry into the governance and management of football and this effectively changed the face of football.
Governing body	The Football Federation of Australia (FFA) was established as the new governing body with a mission to promote the status of Association Football as a major Australian game.
Structure	In 2002 a new National League was established by the FFA.
Ethnicity	The FFA defused racial problems by enforcing the withdrawal of ethnic team names. For example, Sydney Hellas, a team with a Greek origin, became Sydney Knights.

Media	The National League competition increased spectator interest and stimulated positive media interest.
Sponsorship	Increased public and media interest attracted lucrative sponsorship deals to the National League competition.
Success	Victory against England in 2003, progress in the 2006 World Cup and successful affiliation to the Asian Football Confederation have stimulated excellence and increased popularity.
Excellence	Excellence has developed further with the creation of a new Youth League, a national competition for women and the inclusion of football as one of the 26 sports supported by the AIS.
Participation	It is estimated that there are one million players in Australia and football is the fastest-growing 'elective' in high schools.
Ambition	The FFA is bidding to host the 2018 World Cup. There is great confidence within the FFA that Australia can win the World Cup competition as the host nation.

A CASE STUDY OF ASSOCIATION FOOTBALL IN THE UK AS A COMPARISON TO AUSTRALIA

> *'One of the greatest achievements of the British Empire was to spread Association football around the world.'*
>
> (Philip Mosely, Bill Murray, *et al.*, *Sport in Australia: A social history*, 2008)

However, despite Mosely's assertion, it is significant that football has not enjoyed great popularity in the English-speaking members of the former Empire, such as Australia.

The Football Association (FA) was founded in the UK in 1863 as an amateur organisation. At this time, the amateur ethic was strong as football had its origins in the English public schools. The organisation was identical in Australia as the sport was directed by English public school graduates.

The FA reluctantly accepted professionalism in 1888, with the formation of the Football League. Association Football in the UK quickly became dominated by working-class professional players. In Australia, by comparison, professionalism was difficult to sustain and football found it hard to survive even in working-class areas. Indeed, working-class status damaged the reputation of the sport in Australia and the game was marginalised.

In the UK, easy access to away venues was facilitated by the expanded railway network that now existed in the UK, making national league and home country international competition possible. By contrast, travel in Australia was more difficult and international fixtures in the nineteenth century were not possible because of the isolated geographical position of the country.

During the early twentieth century, professional footballers in the UK earned a relatively good wage. For example, by 1939 the average weekly footballer's wage was £8 while an industrial worker earned £4 per week. By 1960 this gap had narrowed significantly, with a professional player earning £20 while an industrial employee's wage had risen to £15. The threat of strike action in January 1961 prompted the Football League to abolish the maximum wage. This changed the culture of football as the professional could earn significantly more than a working man. In 1961 the captain of England, J. Haynes, became the first footballer to be paid £100 per week. Manchester United set a wage cap of £50 per week but later changed this ruling to remain competitive. Football in the UK now had to adapt to become a commercial business. In Australian professional football, this wage bill could not be supported.

As sports like Rugby League and cricket in the 1960s were losing spectators, English football was enjoying considerable success. Victory as the host nation in the 1966 World Cup tournament boosted public and media interest, but the difference in affluence between clubs was beginning to emerge.

Association Football in Australia was by now also experiencing growth, but it was held back and in some cases banned by people of influence in mainstream culture.

In 1988 British Satellite Broadcasting began using sport to attract a mass audience and this was to impact powerfully on UK professional football. The Broadcasting Act of 1990 declared that all rights to broadcast sport could be sold to the highest bidder. This declaration coincided with a merger between British satellite Broadcasting and Sky to create BSkyB.

BSkyB paid over £3 million to Division One football clubs for the exclusive rights to televise matches. Division One football clubs then broke away from the Football League to form the Premiership. Association Football had now entered the realm of 'big business'; it remains well ahead of all other major UK sports in terms of commercial potential. The Golden Triangle – the inextricable link between sport, the media and sponsorship – is never more clearly evident than in the football entertainment industry.

The Bosman Ruling of 1997 stated that professional football players could command their own fees for transfer and were free agents at the end of their contractual period. The average weekly pay received by a premiership player in 2008 is £13,000 per week (£676,000 per annum).

A CASE STUDY OF AUSTRALIAN RULES FOOTBALL

Known correctly in the twenty-first century as Australian Football, this is not a game of international renown. It has, however, grown beyond its Melbourne origins and Victoria State development to become the national sport of Australia.

There is strong evidence to suggest that the game is of genuine Australian origin. Allegedly, Tom Wills witnessed Aborigines in Queensland playing a leaping game. He combined this ethnic activity with the basic principles of the form of football he had experienced in the English public schools, and as a result codified the sport of Melbourne Rules in 1858.

Australian Football carries a Latin motto – *Populo Ludus Populi* – which means 'the game of the people for the people'. This description is significant as the game is associated with cultural and ethnic diversity. The reasons for this wide range of appeal are outlined in Table 5 opposite.

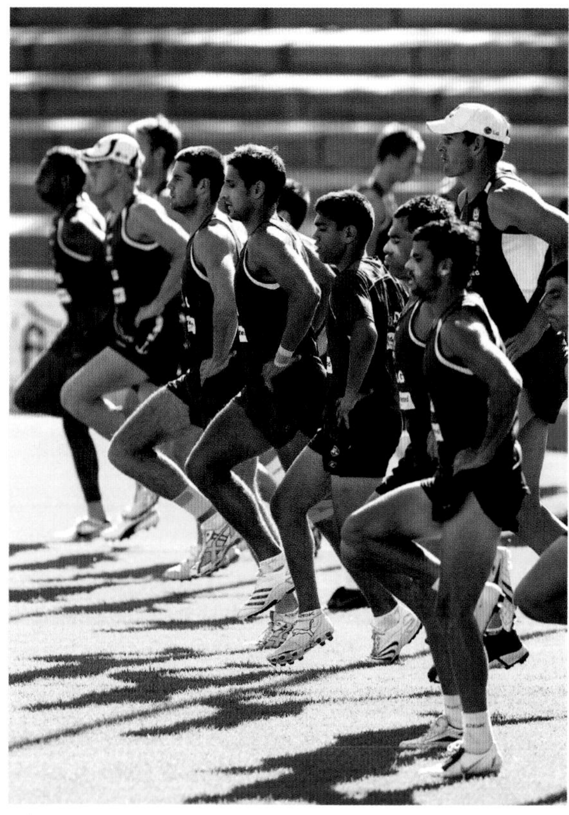

Fig 7.14 Australian Football openly publicises ethnic diversity whereas Association Football in Australia plays down ethnic links

Table 5 The wide appeal of Australian Football

Origin	The game has been described as Australia's own. It is thought to have roots in an Aboriginal ethnic game and in the version of football played in the nineteenth century in the UK public schools. The game was designed to be manly but not overly aggressive, as its original purpose was to keep cricketers fit in winter.
Ethnicity	Australian Football has always been accessible to all ethnic groups. The 'cornstalks' brought the aspiring new manly image of young Australia to the sport (see page 153), while the Irish immigrants exemplified strength and ruggedness. Ethnic Europeans were prominent from the 1950s and were the group who probably most reflected the growing cultural and ethnic diversity of Australia. From the 1960s, the Aborigines demonstrated their great athleticism and are well represented in the game.
Class	For those both in the role of player and the capacity of spectator, the game appeals to all classes. Australian Football reflects and contributes to the egalitarian nature of Australian society. The game has given skilled players from the working classes a chance to be respected in society. In turn, their supporters, taking vicarious pleasure from this, have viewed Australian Football as a positive expression of working-class life. This endorsed the view that Australia is 'the land of the fair go'.
Gender	Various governing bodies, such as the Victoria Women's Football League, promote female participation, although women have not taken up the game in significant numbers. Even though women have acquired positions as umpires at senior level and some hold salaried promotional positions on club staff, it is accepted that play is dominated by men. There are, however, 10,000 registered female Australian Football players; male participants number 300,000.

In a country where space is boundless, Australian football, commonly referred to as 'footy', is played on huge cricket ovals with dimensions far in excess of the largest fields in rugby or Association Football. Teams comprise eighteen players with half-forwards running an estimated 20 kilometres (12.4 miles) during a match. There is rarely a pause in play and the game requires a skilful as opposed to an aggressive approach. Six officials are required to control a professional game as one referee could not cover the field.

Australian Football approaches the level of commercialism found in professional football in the UK. As in the UK and the USA, the game is dependent on the links between the media and sponsorship.

REMEMBER

For more on Australian Football, revisit page 250 in *OCR AS PE*.

'Footy' has evolved rules, skills and tactics of its own and is the game of the cosmopolitan Australian nation. It has been moulded by the cultural, social and economic environment of the nation. Despite the physical and manly disposition of the sport, fair play is a high priority. The Brownlow medal is presented to the best and fairest player in the Australian Football League (AFL) at the end of each season.

STRETCH AND CHALLENGE

NETBALL IN AUSTRALIA

Netball in Australia is a predominantly female participation sport.

Netball is a major sport in Australia and has one of the largest sports associations with 350,000 members. There is a Junior Sports Programme for netball and the modified game associated with this programme is called netta. The game is played by children from the age of 7 years.

The women's national netball teams have won Olympic and Commonwealth gold medals in recent years and have never been beaten by England. As a tribute to its status in Australia, netball was one of the eight inaugural sports to be included in the excellence development scheme when the AIS opened in Canberra in 1981. The game facilitates high mass participation and mixed competitions are growing in popularity.

Research netball as it is played in Australia. Compare how netball is approached and developed in the UK and Australia in the following areas:

- Physical Education and school sport
- mass participation (particularly among young people)
- sport and the pursuit of excellence for commercial motives.

Exam Café

Relax, refresh, result!

Refresh your memory

You should now have knowledge and understanding of:

- the cultural context of sport in Australia and the UK
- PE and school sport in Australia and the UK
- mass participation in sport in Australia and the UK
- sport and the pursuit of excellence in Australia and the UK
- how to critically evaluate the influence of the cultural context on all of the above.

REVISE AS YOU GO!

1. Explain why Australian bush culture contrasts with the traditions of the hierarchical society that exists in the UK.
2. Describe how the sports of the 'currency' lads and the impact of the English public schools influenced the development of Australian sports.
3. List the groups of people who are most likely to suffer discrimination in sport both in Australia and the UK.
4. How does SEPEP, which is delivered in Australian high schools, differ from the National Curriculum for PE in the UK?
5. Explain how associations are formed in Australia and in the UK between sports clubs and schools.
6. What are adapted games (Junior Sports Programme) in Australia? Identify the UK equivalent.
7. List the strategies that are implemented both in Australia and in the UK to promote participation and ensure lifelong involvement in sporting activities.
8. Outline alternative pathways into professional sport that are available to performers in Australia and the UK.
9. Identify reasons why Rugby League tends to be more popular in Australia than Rugby Union. Why is the situation reversed in the UK?
10. Explain why Australian Rules Football openly publicises ethnic diversity whereas Association Football in Australia plays down ethnic links.

Try to answer these questions yourself. Ask your teacher if you need help.

Get the result!

Examination question

Explain the factors that have stimulated the growth of commercialised sport in the UK and in Australia. (6 marks)

Examiner's tips

Remember that a point of comparison can indicate a similarity as well as a contrast. Reference must be made to both countries before a mark can be given. If reference is made to one country, some marks will be given but the higher scores will be inaccessible. Try to begin your answer by making an overarching point by way of an introduction. See the improved student answer opposite for an example of this.

Examiner says:

There are a number of correct facts in this response but the student does not quite fully understand. Poor expression has also held back the conveyance of knowledge.

Examiner says:

Sport has been important in both countries from the mid-nineteenth century. This statement in the student answer contains no specialist knowledge.

Student answer

Sport has always been important in Australia and the UK but now there is more money in it. The population of Australia is about 19 million whereas the UK has a population of 62 million. Both countries have good transport systems, for example London and Sydney. Australia and the UK are rich countries and therefore there is money to spend on stadiums and other things. Everyone has a television in the UK and Australia so everyone can see big sporting events like Premiership football in the UK and the Melbourne Cup in horse racing in Australia. There are big stadiums in the UK

Examiner says:

The statement on population is corre[ct] but the knowledge displayed does no[t] relate to the questi[on].

Examiner says:

This point scores a mark. Both countrie[s] are affluent. Money can therefore be sp[ent] on stadiums which promote commerci[al] sport. Never use the word 'things'.

Examiner says:

This is a generalisati[on] as not everyone ha[s] access to television. [...] done on the examp[le]. This point may earn a mark under what [is] termed by the exam[iners] 'benefit of doubt'.

and America which cost a great deal of money but help sport to become commercialised.

Examiner says:

This reflects a point made earlier. It is obvious what the student wants to say, but poor expression makes the point vague. No mark can be awarded. Note that America has been the point of reference; the question asks about Australia. This error is common and occurs when students rush, lose concentration or plan badly.

Improved student answer

The growth of commercialised sport both in the UK and Australia has been stimulated by historical, geographical and socio-economic factors.

Examiner says:

This is a good introduction that sets the scene and directly reflects the contents of the specification relating to the cultural context of Australia and the UK.

Since the days of the Empire and the impact made by the public schools, sport has influenced the cultural values of the UK. In Australia sport has always been a vehicle through which national pride is expressed and remains as a benchmark to measure national progress. Furthermore, although sport in Australia has a longer tradition with politics than the UK, the governments of both countries contribute to the growth of participation and the pursuit of sporting excellence. In both countries, therefore, historical and political roots have given high status to sport which has helped to facilitate the growth of commercialism.

Examiner says:

Comparisons can be contrasts or similarities. There are many parallels to be made in response to this question.

Despite the difference in the size of population, both Australia and the UK have areas of dense urban population. The latter makes possible a large spectator base that is required to promote sport as a commercial business.

Examiner says:

A detailed understanding has been conveyed from the outset. The student is aware of the cultural determinants as they relate to sport in Australia and the UK.

In addition, both countries have sophisticated transport systems to allow easy access for travel to sporting events and this has helped the growth of commercialism. Melbourne and Sydney are well served by air, road and rail links for domestic and international sporting events. Examples of these events include rugby union, Australian football and the Commonwealth and Olympic Games. Similar transport networks serve important UK venues and London has been chosen as the venue for the 2012 Olympic Games partly because of accessibility.

Examiner says:

Review the diagram indicating cultural determinants on page 161. They have been applied to this question.

The capitalist market economy which has encouraged societies to place high status on material reward has helped to promote sport as a consumer product. For example, the UK Grand Final in rugby league is a copy of the Australian model, and like its counterpart is the showcase commercial event that is sold as a consumer product at the season's end.

Examiner says:

Good use is made of applied examples, some of which have been taken directly from the sporting case studies relating to Australia and the UK.

The affluence of both countries has stimulated commercialised sport as disposable income is increasingly directed toward sport. In addition, sport requires diverse media outlets in order to exist in the entertainment industry. Both Australia and the UK can support the necessary media outlets, such as Sky and digital television.

The economies of both countries have the potential to supply the financial capital to build multi-purpose stadiums in which top sporting events can be staged for the commercial market. For example, Stadium Australia was the venue of the 2000 Olympic Games and the Millennium Stadium is the national sports stadium for Wales.

Examiner says:

The response continues to be factually accurate by conveying comparisons and supporting them by providing applied examples.

iner says:

ponse is clearly and well sed. Marks for of comparison arded in each aph.

Finally, stadiums both in the UK and Australia are sponsored by way of businesses owning and naming sports stadiums. The so-called 'naming rights', although often controversial, provide a further source of finance that has influenced the growth of sport as a commercial product; for example, the Telstra Dome in Australia and the United Emirates Stadium in London.

Sports psychology

CHAPTER 8:

Individual aspects of performance that influence young people's participation and aspirations

LEARNING OBJECTIVES

By the end of this chapter you should have knowledge and understanding of:

- personality and its importance in producing effective performance and in following a balanced, active and healthy lifestyle
- attitudes and their influence on performance and lifestyle
- achievement motivation and its effect on performance and on following an active and healthy lifestyle
- attribution theory and the impact of attribution on performance and sustaining a balanced, active and healthy lifestyle
- aggression and its impact upon performance and behaviour.

INTRODUCTION

The 'Sports psychology' section is a continuation of the AS section 'Acquiring movement skills'. The focus at AS was upon how skills are learned and controlled. By way of extension, 'Sports psychology' addresses the important mental processes that work together to facilitate effective performance in sport.

In their separate ways, both 'Acquiring movement skills' and 'Sports psychology' demonstrate how sporting competence and participation can be increased. Through this, a common theme emerges, as both areas set out to encourage and sustain a balanced, active and healthy lifestyle.

In this chapter you will be focusing on personality and its influence on a healthy, balanced lifestyle.

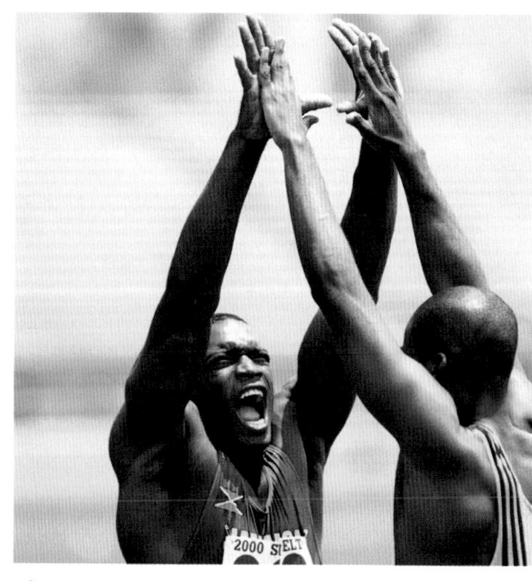

Fig 8.1 All areas of the sport psychology syllabus combine to facilitate effective performance while encouraging the pursuit of a balanced, active and healthy lifestyle

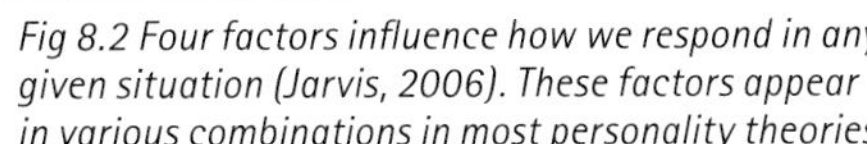
Fig 8.2 Four factors influence how we respond in any given situation (Jarvis, 2006). These factors appear in various combinations in most personality theories

Personality

Athletes display their own unique patterns of behaviour whilst engaged in sports performance. Some psychologists believe that quality of performance and participation in sport are determined by personality.

It is unlikely that a definition of personality will be examined directly. To clarify the term is, however, important.

The term personality is derived from the word 'persona', which was a mask in Greek drama. This implies that a person may give the appearance of being unlike their true self, which makes the assessment of personality difficult. A psychologist named Allport defined personality simply as, 'What a man really is!'; to which Whiting later added, 'Not what he appears to be.'

Among the more recent definitions, two are important to us:

> *'Personality is the sum total of an individual's characteristics which make a human unique.'* (Hollander)

> *'Personality represents those characteristics of the person that account for consistent patterns of behaviour.'* (Pervin, 1993)

In your exam, you will need to demonstrate knowledge of personality theories. These theories are based on three very different views or perspectives. Each perspective must be clearly understood.

The three views on personality development are known as:

1 trait perspective
2 social learning perspective
3 interactionist approach.

EXAM TIP

Exam questions often ask for explanations of the three personality perspectives. You need to be aware of the drawbacks found in trait and social learning perspectives and the advantages of the interactionist approach.

Trait perspective

The **trait theory** of personality formation suggests that personality is made up of a range of different secondary **traits** inherited from parental **genes**. The trait view, therefore, maintains that all behaviour is innate and genetically programmed. For example, a person may have a natural inclination towards ambition, competition or **aggression**. Traits are thought to be stable, enduring and consistent in all situations.

Trait theory is depicted as:

Behaviour = Function of Personality (B = F(P)).

KEY TERMS

Trait theory

People are born with established personality characteristics.

Trait

A single characteristic of personality that is believed to be a natural force or instinct causing an individual to behave in a predicted way.

Genes

Biological units of inheritance found in each individual cell in the body. A person's genes determine their physical and psychological characteristics.

Aggression

An action intended to bring about harm or injury. Aggressive behaviour is undesirable and dysfunctional in the context of sport.

The drawback with the trait approach is that, in reality, behaviour is not always predictable. It does not account for the fact that people adapt their behaviour in response to a particular environmental situation. Similarly, the influence that the environment and other people have on the shaping of personality is not considered.

There are two specific theories that belong to the trait perspective of personality that you need to understand. They are:

- personality types (Eysenck and Cattell)
- Narrow Band Theory Type A and Type B (Girdano).

PERSONALITY TYPES

Eysenck identified four primary personality traits or types. These personality types are arranged in Fig 8.3 on a two-dimensional model.

EXAM TIP

The relationship between personality and **arousal** often features in questions on social facilitation and inhibition.

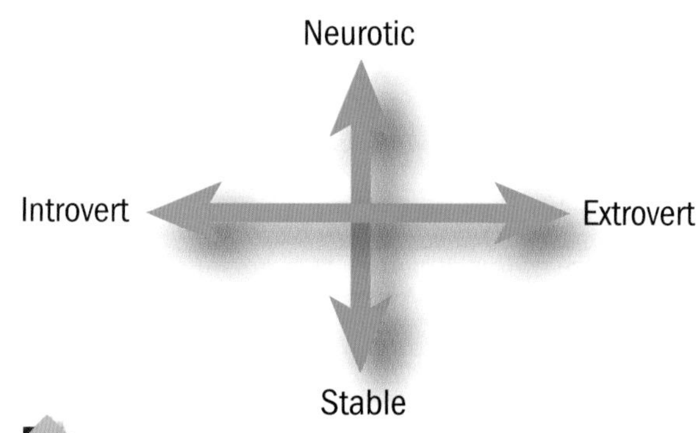

Fig 8.3 Personality traits of introvert/extrovert and neurotic/stable

KEY TERMS

Reticular activating system (RAS)

Introverts are more easily aroused than extroverts because of the sensitivity of an area of the brain called the reticular activating system. There is a greater likelihood that with increased stimulation the introvert will become over-aroused.

Arousal

A physical and mental state of preparedness.

Personality type or primary trait	Description of personality type
Extrovert	• Affiliate well to other people • Outgoing, gregarious and sociable • Become aroused more slowly than introverts • There is low sensitivity of the reticular activating system (RAS)
Introvert	• Tend to be shy and reserved • Prefer isolation from others • Become aroused more quickly than extroverts • There is high sensitivity of the reticular activating system (RAS)
Neurotic	• Display extreme and unpredictable emotions in the form of mood swings • Their moods are unreliable • They experience high degrees of stress • Their recovery from stress is slow
Stable	• Display predictable emotions in appropriate situations • Their moods are predictable • They tend not to experience intense stress • Their recovery from stress is rapid

Table 1 Eysenck's four primary personality types

Fig 8.4 Extroverted people perform best in conditions that stimulate high arousal. Introverts tend to be more aroused by events than do extroverts. This is due to differences in the individual's reticular activation system (RAS)

Eysenck proposed the existence of four personality types and that one type belonged in each quadrant.

1 Extrovert and Stable
2 Extrovert and Neurotic
3 Introvert and Stable
4 Introvert and Neurotic.

Later, Eysenck (1975) added a third scale to his personality model which he termed psychoticism. Psychoticism is a measure of how tender or **tough-minded** people are. Eysenck used this third scale in a test to determine an individual's **personality profile**. The test was called Eysenck's Personality Questionnaire (EPQ).

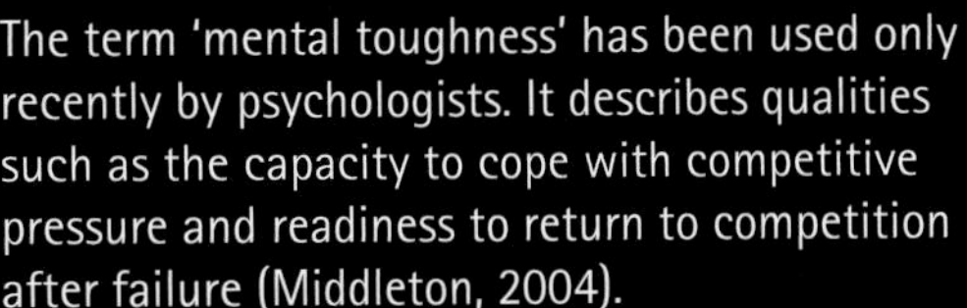

KEY TERMS

Tough-minded

The term 'mental toughness' has been used only recently by psychologists. It describes qualities such as the capacity to cope with competitive pressure and readiness to return to competition after failure (Middleton, 2004).

Personality profile

An overall assessment of an individual's personality.

Cattell was also a believer in trait theory. Cattell, however, questioned whether personality could be understood by examining just three dimensions. Instead, he proposed that it was necessary to consider a much larger number of traits before a complete picture of personality could be revealed. Cattell examined 16 personality factors in a questionnaire called Cattell's 16PF test.

TASK 1

1. To carry out a Cattell 16 PF test, go to www.heinemann.co.uk/hotlinks, enter the express code 6855P and click on the relevant link.
   Consider whether there are links between the sport that you most enjoy and your personality profile.
2. Discuss the value of personality profiling as a way of selecting a team or when advising a person as to which sport to take up.

NARROW BAND THEORY

Girdano was another trait theorist. He proposed that there are two distinct personality types – Type A and Type B.

Type A characteristics	Type B characteristics
Highly competitive	Non-competitive
Works fast	Works more slowly
Strong desire to succeed	Lacking in desire to succeed
Likes control	Does not enjoy control
Prone to suffer stress	Less prone to stress

Table 2 Girdano's Type A and Type B characteristics

You will see links between the trait approach (including Narrow Band Theory) and the adoption of a balanced, active and healthy lifestyle when personality profiling is explained later in the section (see page 202–203).

Social learning perspective

Social learning theory, in direct contrast to trait theory, proposes that all behaviour is learned. Learning occurs by way of environmental experiences and through the influence of other people. Personality is, therefore, not genetically programmed.

Social learning theory is depicted as:

Behaviour = Function of Environment (B = F(E))

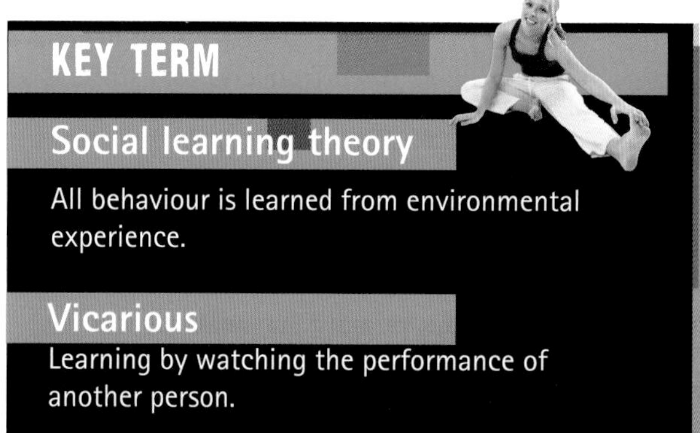

KEY TERM

Social learning theory
All behaviour is learned from environmental experience.

Vicarious
Learning by watching the performance of another person.

The social learning approach was presented by the psychologist Bandura. He believed learning was stimulated by environmental experiences. Two processes are involved in social learning:

- the behaviour of others being imitated through observation
- new behaviour being acquired after observation, but only when it is endorsed through social reinforcement.

For example, a sports performer who is inexperienced may be inspired by the positive attitude and commitment displayed in training by an experienced player. The novice elects to copy the desirable approach of the role model and receives positive reinforcement from both coach and peers. The process of reinforcement has facilitated learning.

Social learning is often termed **vicarious** learning and is most likely to take place in the following conditions shown in Fig 8.5.

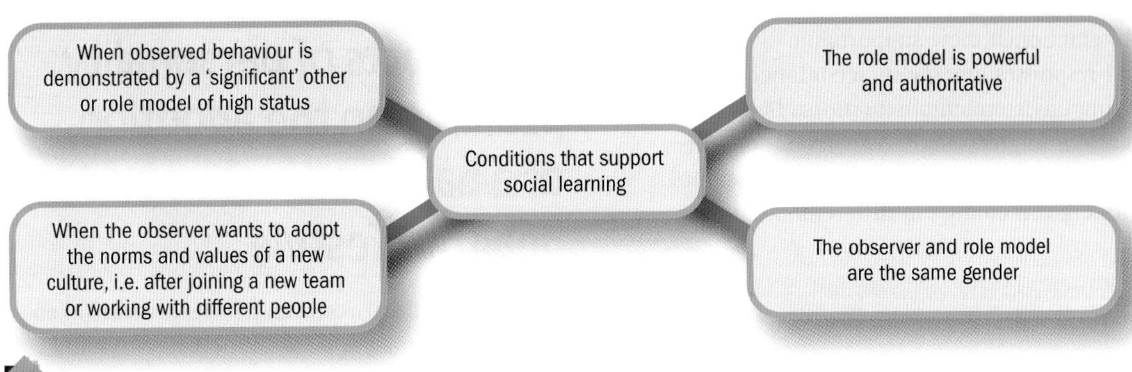
When observed behaviour is demonstrated by a 'significant' other or role model of high status
When the observer wants to adopt the norms and values of a new culture, i.e. after joining a new team or working with different people
Conditions that support social learning
The role model is powerful and authoritative
The observer and role model are the same gender

Fig 8.5 Conditions that support social learning

REMEMBER

Bandura's model of observational learning was covered in *OCR AS PE SB*, Chapter 8.2, pages 197–8.

A drawback with the social learning perspective is that it does not take into account genetically-inherited factors.

Social learning theory provides one explanation as to why there are individual differences in the attitude, aggression and motivation of sports performers, and you will be looking at this area later in the chapter (page 204). Social learning theory may also offer insight into why young people develop an interest in sport and as a consequence elect to follow a lifestyle which is healthy, active and balanced.

Interactionist approach

Modern thinking on personality has moved away from the more extreme trait theories and toward social learning theories. According to Gill (2000), however, most personality psychologists prefer the **interactionist theory** as an explanation of behaviour.

The interactionist approach is based on the work of Hollander (1967). Hollander proposed that personality has three levels that interact to form personality.

KEY TERMS

Interactionist theory

Behaviour occurs from the influence of inherited traits and learned experiences.

1 *Psychological core*
This is the most internal of the personality levels and is thought to be the true self. Inaccessibility makes it the most difficult level to research but it is known to be stable and remains relatively constant over time.

2 *Typical responses*
Typical responses are changeable and are learned behaviours. They become modified as the person responds to environmental situations. They often reflect the makeup of the personality core.

3 *Role-related behaviour*
This is the most external of the personality levels. It is therefore the level that is dynamic and changeable. An individual may have to adjust in order to fulfil many different roles in one day, for example the role of student, coach or friend. Role-related behaviour is a direct consequence of the immediate environment.

While the core of personality, according to Hollander, provides the structure of true self, the changing and dynamic levels of personality allow learning to take place.

Interactionist theory is depicted as:

Behaviour = Function of Personality x Environment (B = F (P x E))

The interactionist view combines the trait and social learning perspectives. It proposes that personality is modified and behaviour is formed when genetically-inherited traits are triggered by an environmental circumstance.

The interactionist view supports the claim that typical responses emerge in accordance with changing environmental situations. Behaviour is therefore unpredictable. This approach offers an explanation why the personalities of sports performers can change in different situations.

EXAM TIP

Although Hollander is not included on the specification, you should be aware of Hollander's contribution to the interactionist approach to personality.

The interactionist approach is not simple. Any behaviour or response in sport can be the outcome of unlimited combinations of personality and environmental factors. For example, a player may respond positively to the autocratic leadership of a captain for most of the time, but this leadership style may trigger an aggressive response on one occasion. This unpredictable response from the team player may have been the result of frustration, a build-up of anxiety or even a lack of sleep prior to the game.

Despite these complexities, Bowers (1977) stated that the interactionist view alone explains twice as much as trait and social learning perspectives.

STRETCH AND CHALLENGE

Discuss the implications of Hollander's interactionist approach for the physical educator who wishes to improve the performance of an established athlete or as a base from which an individual may be encouraged to pursue a balanced, active and healthy lifestyle.

To get the most out of 'Stretch and Challenge' questions you must read ahead and look at other recommended texts. While you must address the question directly, it will become apparent that many other topics will relate and link to the task that has been set. If you are able to make and understand these connections, a deep and versatile understanding of A-level Sport Psychology will develop.

The effects of personality profiling on the adoption of a balanced, active and healthy lifestyle

A large volume of research has been undertaken into the relationship between personality and sporting behaviour. Differences between the personalities of athletes and non-athletes have been explored together with comparisons between successful and less successful performers. Of most interest to you is the research into whether personality factors are associated with:

- participation in general
- the choice of sport and physical exercise.

While social learning theory provides a strong explanation as to why vicarious processes draw young people to games and athletic activities, Eysenck *et al.* (1982), using the Eysenck Personality Questionnaire, proposed that people who were attracted to sport scored highly on the scales of extroversion and psychoticism.

Schurr (1977), using Cattell's 16PF test, found athletes to be more independent and less anxious than non-athletes, but differences between the two groups were not significant. Using the same test, Francis *et al.* (1998) agreed with Eysenck in that he found hockey players to be higher in extroversion and psychoticism than non-hockey players.

In contrast, McKelvie (2003) found no differences in extroversion between athletes and non-athletes. In this study, however, athletes emerged as being more stable. Furthermore, performers in high-risk sports like surfing and mountaineering scored highly in extroversion while being low on the scale of neuroticism (Diehm and Armatas, 2004).

Research in this area is detailed but confusingly inconclusive. By way of a definitive statement on the subject, Weinberg and Gould (2007) propose:

> *'No specific personality profile has been found that consistently distinguishes athletes from non-athletes.'*
>
> (Weinberg and Gould, 2007)

Personality profiling may not be helpful as a predictor of those who are likely to participate or excel in sport or physical activity.

While the inclination to participate in sport cannot be predicted by personality profiling, it may be that the identification of traits can be used by a psychologist to recommend participation in sport. Through this intervention, personality profiling may therefore help a person and lead them toward an active, healthy and balanced lifestyle.

Two examples are given below.

1 The competitive nature of Type A behaviour (see page 200) has been linked to anger and increased incidence of cardiovascular disease. Blumenthal (1988) proposed that aerobic exercise significantly reduced unhealthy cardiovascular reactions to mental stress. Thus Type A patterns of behaviour can be altered through exercise.
2 Exercise and increased levels of fitness appear to increase the self-esteem of those individuals who register initially as having low self-esteem (Biddle *et al.*, 1995).

Although personality profiling may help a coach to get to know people and provide the motivation for the individual to change behaviour and lifestyle, it must be understood that sport and exercise can not fundamentally change overall personality (Gill, 2000).

EXAM TIP

You need to know that personality profiling helps when observing and questioning an individual. Getting to know the individual may help to formulate intervention strategies. Personality profiling has, however, only limited value.

EVALUATE CRITICALLY PERSONALITY PROFILING IN SPORT

Whether it is through displays of dysfunctional aggression, variations in cognitive processes or debilitating levels of stress and anxiety, all individuals differ in their response to sporting situations. These differences have preoccupied psychologists to the extent that countless studies have been undertaken to find a definitive link between personality and sport. Despite this, there remain serious limitations to personality profiling in sport. These limitations are listed below.

Key word to identify limitation	Explanation of limitation
Proof	A link between personality types and sport performance cannot be proved. A psychologist named Martens believes that the relationship between sport participation and personality are doubtful.
Evidence	There is no evidence that an ideal sports personality exist, e.g. the most stable and extroverted squad member may not be the best player in the team, or the most appropriate to create team cohesion.
Subjectivity	Profiling results are often subjective. This means that conclusions may be influenced by personal opinions and are not totally supported by scientific evidence.
Invalidity	Profiling results are often inaccurate and invalid. Invalid means that tests do not measure that which they intend to measure.
Modification	The performer may unconsciously modify their behaviour to match up to the profile ascribed to them.
Reliability	Many profiles are calculated by using self-report questionnaire studies. The results of these studies are not always reliable as performers may not answer all questions accurately.
Stereotyping	There is a danger that profiling will stereotype a person.

Table 3 Limits of personality profiling

KEY TERM

Team cohesion

This term describes team work. It will be covered in Chapter 9 on page 230.

EXAM TIP

Explanations of the three personality approaches and the drawbacks of personality profiling in sport are popular examination questions.

Attitudes and their influence on performance and lifestyles

An **attitude** is a mode of behaviour that is thought to be the typical response of an individual. Attitudes are invariably associated with personality and are believed to influence a response or behaviour in a given situation. Moody (1980), a leading sports psychologist, defines attitude as:

> '*A mental state of readiness organised through experiences that influences the response of an individual towards any object or situation with which it is related.*'
>
> (Moody, 1980)

An attitude is an emotional response that can be enduring; meaning that it can last throughout life. Attitudes are also unstable, however, and can be changed.

KEY TERM

Attitude

A learned behavioural predisposition.

TASK 2

Choose five different sports or physical activities, for example rugby, netball, boxing, dance and cricket.

1. Discuss with the group your attitude toward each of these activities.
2. What factors have helped you to form these attitudes?
3. Do you believe that you may have developed a prejudice? Explain your answer.

An attitude is directed toward an **attitude object.** The object of an attitude could be a place, a situation or the behaviour of others. For example, an attitude object of a team player may be the issue of fitness training for which they have developed a dislike. A negative attitude toward fitness training may develop and this would strongly influence the behaviour of the individual.

Long-standing and well-entrenched attitudes may adversely influence behaviour causing an individual to be inconsistent in judgment. Inconsistencies in behaviour may be revealed in the form of **prejudice.** Prejudice is a pre-judgement arising from an evaluation based on unfounded beliefs or opinions.

KEY TERMS

Attitude object

The people, subject or situation towards which an attitude is directed.

Prejudice

A predetermined view or opinion which may be unfairly biased.

Attitude prejudice could seriously reduce the possibility of a young person participating in sport. This could occur in two ways. Firstly, prejudice could be directed toward sport in general; secondly, the young person may be discouraged by being the victim of prejudice. With prejudice in mind, another definition of attitude is:

> '*An attitude is a predisposition to act in a certain way towards some aspects of the person's environment including other people.*'
>
> (Mednick)

For example, the coach may regard a talented sports player as lazy and disinterested because the player chooses to opt out of additional practice sessions. It may be that the player has good reason to withdraw from practice. In this situation, an unjustified negative prejudice could be displayed by the coach toward the player.

Undesirable prejudice is evident in gender issues. For example, negative feelings about their participation and performance has caused women to be an under-represented group in sport. Also, racism and ageism arise from negative prejudice.

Research tends to focus on negative prejudice, although positive prejudices do also exist. For example, the coach may favour a particular player; this is recognised as favouritism.

ORIGIN OF ATTITUDES

Attitudes are formed mainly through experiences. A pleasant experience in Physical Education, brought about when positive reinforcement follows success, is likely to promote a positive attitude towards sport and motivate the individual to engage in lifelong participation. Conversely, an unpleasant experience at school, such as failure, criticism or injury, would bring about a negative attitude. Sport then becomes the 'object' to be avoided in the future.

Socialisation is another key element in the formation of an attitude. In early childhood, parents play the most significant role by encouraging positive attitudes toward sport. In teenage years, the **peer group** has the most powerful influence. If a group of friends participates enthusiastically at the tennis club, it is likely that, in an effort to conform and gain acceptance, the reluctant individual may join in. The influence of the media is also an important factor in the process of socialisation and in itself can stimulate the formation of an attitude.

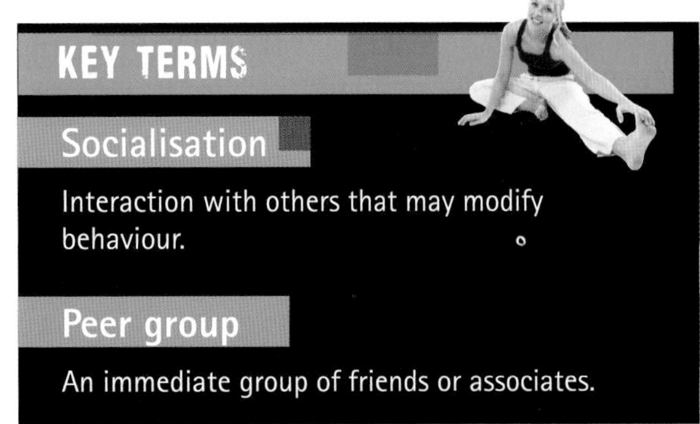
KEY TERMS

Socialisation

Interaction with others that may modify behaviour.

Peer group

An immediate group of friends or associates.

Fig 8.6 When the outcome is positively reinforced, pleasant, worthwhile experiences can encourage favourable attitudes toward physical activity

The origin of an attitude could also stem from culture. Culture is a very complicated issue and can be determined by religion, race and peer groups. Social class is also linked to culture and in turn impacts upon attitudes in sport. For example, even in contemporary society, Rugby League is strongly associated with working-class origins, while membership at the private golf club continues to be dominated by a middle-class population.

The components of attitude

THE TRIADIC MODEL OF ATTITUDE

According to this model, an attitude comprises three components:

1. *Cognitive component*
   This component reflects beliefs and knowledge that an individual holds about the attitude object. For example, a person may know that jogging three times a week is psychologically beneficial. This component is also known as the information component.
2. *Affective component*
   This consists of feelings or an emotional response toward an attitude object and is therefore known as the emotional component. It is here that an evaluation of an attitude object is made. For example, jogging is a pleasurable activity.
3. *Behavioural component*
   This concerns how a person intends to behave or respond towards an attitude object. For example, the individual will continue to jog three times in the week.

CHANGING ATTITUDES

We need to explain two psychological theories that set out to change an attitude; these theories are:

1. Cognitive dissonance theory
2. Persuasive communication theory.

COGNITIVE DISSONANCE THEORY

This theory was described by a psychologist named Festinger and states that if two attitude components can be made to oppose or come into conflict with each other, then the individual experiences emotional discomfort. This emotional discomfort is called **dissonance**.

KEY TERM

Dissonance

An emotional conflict.

For example, an overweight person needs to improve their appearance and feel better about their image and physical condition. Through previously bad experiences they have learned, however, to dislike exercise and find it hard work. They therefore avoid exercise. In this case, all three attitude components are negative. After consultation, a personal trainer may indicate that a specific fitness programme at the gym would help weight loss and improve lifestyle. The subject has now been given the knowledge of the benefits of exercise and realises that participation is essential. Dissonance is now experienced because the cognitive knowledge component is in conflict with evaluation, which is the affective component. Once this happens the unfit person is more likely to follow an exercise programme.

If one attitude component can be changed to bring about cognitive dissonance there is then an increased possibility of changing the whole attitude. This change need not be restricted to the cognitive component. Both the evaluative and behavioural components can also be modified to bring about dissonance.

By providing a person with new and positive experiences, the affective component can be modified. For example, a student who has a negative experience through excessive physical contact in rugby may enjoy the indoor 'tag' version of the game and therefore change their attitude towards participation in that sport.

If a skill is simplified or if some form of guidance is used to make execution easier, the behavioural component of the attitude can be changed. For example, fitting the novice skier with short skis would give more control and reduce apprehension.

PERSUASIVE COMMUNICATION THEORY

Persuasive communication could be applied within cognitive dissonance as an additional technique in changing attitude. It is highlighted here as a separate theory. There are four elements to Persuasive Communication Theory.

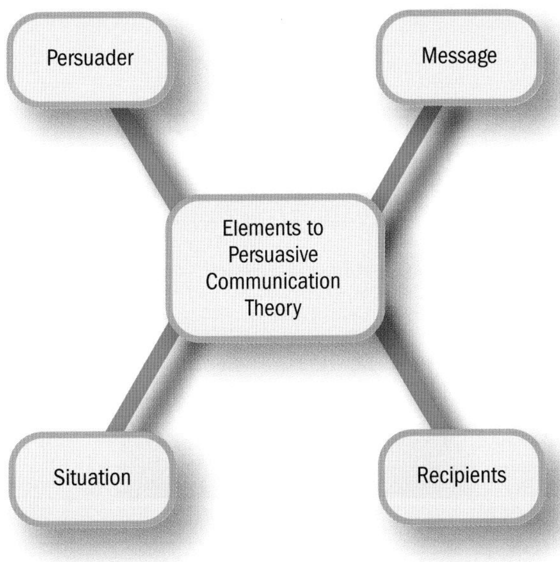

Fig 8.7 The four elements to Persuasive Communication Theory

1. *Persuader*
   This person needs to be one who is perceived to be significant and to have high status, for example the swimming instructor.
2. *Message*
   The message needs to be presented in a way that makes the recipient want to change an attitude, for example learning to swim will enhance the possibility of a balanced, active and healthy lifestyle.
3. *Recipients*
   The attitude is more easily changed if the recipient really wishes to be changed, for example the student understands the task and realises the benefits of learning to swim.
4. *Situation*
   Attitudes are easier to change if there are other persuaders present, for example other students help the persuasion by emphasising the social and physical benefits of swimming.

A CRITICAL EVALUATION OF ATTITUDES

Although it is assumed that attitudes direct an individual to behave positively or negatively toward an attitude object, attitudes in general are poor predictors of behaviour and may not necessarily indicate the likelihood of a desirable lifestyle choice. For example, a person may have a very positive attitude toward physical fitness but this alone will not guarantee that they will attend circuit-training sessions three times per week.

A psychologist named Dishman (1986) said that an individual's positive attitudes and beliefs relating to the health benefits of exercise do not guarantee that they will commit to an exercise programme. Both social and situational factors can intervene to significantly influence actual behaviour, even when an attitude is well established.

Fishbein (1974) said that when attitudes become more specific, they are more likely to predict behaviour. For example, the student who is positive about fitness activities but specifically enjoys circuit training is more likely to attend a session. The most accurate predictor of behaviour according to Fishbein occurs, however, when a person makes a clear commitment of intent. For example, the student making the statement that they will definitely attend the extra football session arranged for after school.

This clear declaration is called behavioural intention and it arises when a positive attitude is reinforced by significant others. This emphasises the fact that social processes impact strongly on the origins of attitude formation and this has implications when making lifestyle choices.

> '*Behavioural intention is determined by attitudes toward the behaviour and the social norms that relate to the behaviour.*'
>
> (Gill, 2000)

REMEMBER

Social learning perspective and vicarious learning were looked at during the study of personality (see page 200).

Fig 8.8 Attitudes are in themselves poor predictors of behaviour; specific attitudes and behavioural intention predict behaviour more reliably

APPLY IT!

1 Organise a fitness activity group that will run during lunchtimes at your school. (You may already be assistant fitness instructors but teacher supervision will still be required).

2 Engage in market research by interviewing a sample of students (between 50 and 100) to find out their attitude toward fitness training and to enquire as to whether they would be interested in participating in a lunchtime fitness club.

3 Administer and evaluate the success of the fitness club.

4 Draw conclusions about the reliability of attitude as a predictor of behaviour.

5 How would you try to change a negative attitude that a person may have toward fitness training?

Achievement motivation

Achievement motivation links personality with the degree of **competitiveness** shown by an individual. Its main focus is the extent to which an individual is motivated to attain success.

Some psychologists believe that a competitive inclination is a product of **nature**. Murray (1938) indicated that it was natural for one individual to strive to surpass another. Conversely, Bandura (1977) believed that a competitive drive was a product of learning. The theory most relevant to this section is an interactionist view proposed by Atkinson and McClelland (1976). It predicts that achievement motivation is generated through a combination of personality and situational factors.

KEY TERMS

Competitiveness

The degree to which a person has the motivation to approach and achieve success in sport.

Nature

A product of the genes of our parents; a genetically-inherited predisposition.

REMEMBER

The interactionist approach was looked at during the study of personality (see page 201).

Atkinson and McClelland (1976) view achievement motivation as a personality trait which is activated by a situation. The situation comprises the probability of success and the **incentive value** of success.

- *Probability of success* – the extent to which success is likely; for example, success is more likely if the task is found by the individual to be easy.
- *Incentive value of success* – the intrinsic value experienced by the individual after success has been achieved; for example, the harder the task the greater will be the incentive value because the probability of success is reduced.

KEY TERM

Incentive value

Relates to the degree of pleasure experienced when success is achieved.

Fig. 8.9 identifies two personality traits that determine achievement motivation:

1 *High need to achieve (high Nach)*
This is also associated with low need to avoid failure (low Naf). With these characteristics, the desire to succeed far outweighs the fear of failure. These performers are high in achievement motivation and are referred to as high achievers.

2 *Low need to achieve (low Nach)*
This is also associated with a high need to avoid failure (high Naf). With these characteristics the fear of failure far outweighs the desire for success. These performers are low in achievement motivation and are referred to as low achievers.

The achievement motivation personality traits are shown in Fig 8.9 and Table 4 opposite.

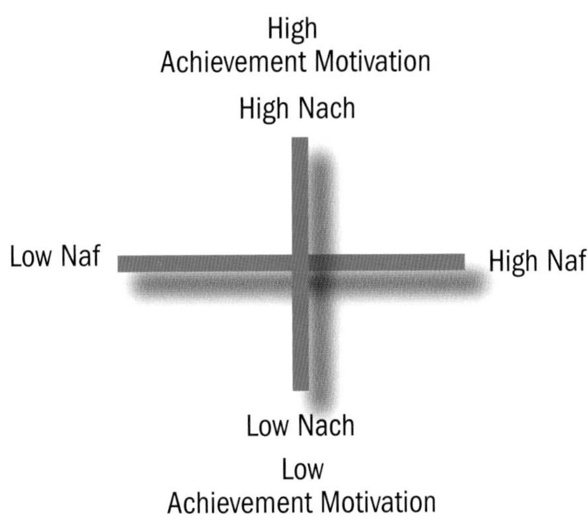

Fig 8.9 Achievement motivation personality traits

The characteristics of high and low achievement motivation personality traits	
High Nach personality characteristics	**Low Nach personality characteristics**
High need to achieve	Low need to achieve
Low need to avoid failure	High need to avoid failure
Approach behaviour is adopted	Avoidance behaviour is adopted
Challenge is accepted	Challenge is rejected
Risks are undertaken	Risks are declined
Shows persistence and perseverance when task is difficult	Curtails effort when task is difficult
Success tends to be attributed to internal factors	Success tends to be attributed to external factors
Failure tends to be attributed to external factors	Failure tends to be attributed to internal factors
Failure is seen as a route to success	Failure is seen as the route to further failure
Aspire to mastery orientation	Adopt learned helplessness

Table 4 Achievement motivation and high Nach and low Nach characteristics

KEY TERMS

Approach behaviour

Describes behaviour that accepts a challenge.

Avoidance behaviour

Describes behaviour that rejects a challenge.

Attribution

The process that predicts reasons for success or failure.

Mastery orientation

The strong motive to succeed found in the high achiever. This type of person will expect to succeed but will persist when failure is experienced.

Learned helplessness

The belief that failure is inevitable and that the individual has no control over the factors that cause failure.

EXAM TIP

You need to be aware of a strong link between achievement motivation and attribution. Attribution will be studied later in this chapter (see page 211).

TASK 3

Identify two situations that you have experienced in sport. Describe one which would have resulted in a high incentive value and one in which the outcome would have given a low incentive value. Give reasons to suggest why these values are different.

The Atkinson and McClelland theory of achievement motivation is best at predicting behavioural responses in situations where there is a 50/50 chance of success. Such a situation is most likely to trigger the motivation to achieve in those performers with high achievement traits; they are likely to display approach behaviour and mastery orientation characteristics in these circumstances. The incentive value will be high when the chance of success is evenly balanced.

By contrast, performers showing personality traits that are associated with low achievement motivation would experience greatest anxiety in situations with a 50/50 chance of success. In the latter situation, low achievers are most likely to adopt avoidance behaviour and experience learned helplessness.

Approach or avoidance behaviours are most likely to arise when a person is in an evaluative situation. This is a situation in which an individual believes they are being assessed.

APPLY IT!

Performers who have high achievement characteristics should be given challenges or goals that give a 50 per cent chance of success.

Fig 8.10 If the probability of success is low, the incentive value will be high

EXAM TIP

It is important to understand that there is no correlation between achievement motivation and extroverted and introvert personality types (Eysenck), nor is there a link with Type A and Type B personality characteristics (Girdano).

EXAM TIP

There is an important link between sport-specific achievement motivation and Vealey's work on sports confidence. An explanation of Vealey's model of sports confidence can be found in Chapter 10, pages 251–253.

A drawback with achievement motivation theory is that achievement or success can be interpreted in many ways. Some performers regard success as victory over other people, for example a long jump athlete winning an event. These people are said to have **ego goal orientation.** Those with ego orientation believe that ability and comparison against others are the criteria for success. Ego goal orientation is also a 'product' goal (see Chapter 10, page 247).

Other performers judge on the basis of personal improvement in a given task, for example a second long jump athlete may view success as the achievement of an improved performance. These people are said to have **task orientation.** Those with task orientation value internal goals and believe that effort and comparison with self are the criteria for success. Task orientation can be achieved through 'performance' or 'process' goals (see Chapter 10, page 247).

The term achievement motivation is a general term and is used to cover achievement in all areas. This has led sport psychologists to focus onto sport-specific achievement motivation, which implies an inclination towards competitiveness.

SPORT-SPECIFIC ACHIEVEMENT MOTIVATION (COMPETITIVENESS)

Competitiveness in this context means the motivation to achieve in sport. Gill and Deeter (1988), using their own test called the Sport Orientation Questionnaire (SOQ), confirmed that the athletes were far more competitive than non-athletes. As a statement, this would appear to be obvious.

What is of greater significance is that the athletes favoured performance goals (task orientation) while non-athletes emphasised the importance of winning (ego orientation).

The type of goal set by the teacher as the measure of success in sport-related activities has, therefore, a significant influence upon the decision to adopt and sustain an active and healthy lifestyle.

The important association between sport-specific motivation (competitiveness), confidence and goal setting will be looked at in Chapter 10.

TASK 4

1. Divide into groups, preferably of no less than ten.
2. Look at the methods of fitness testing that are identified and explained in the Exercise and Sports Physiology section on page 411.
3. Select an agreed number of fitness tests and work through them several times during lessons over a number of weeks.
4. Log your individual results carefully after each session.
5. After compiling results over a number of weeks, put them into a group table or plot them on a graph.

Attribution theory

Attribution theory looks at the reasons given by coaches and players themselves to account for successes and failures in sport. The study of **attribution** has been shown by Weiner (1971) to have powerful implications for achievement-related behaviour. There are strong links between attribution and achievement motivation.

Weiner's model of attribution will be the focus of this section. This model is structured on two dimensions:

1 locus of causality
2 stability.

The **locus of causality** dimension indicates whether the attribution relates to factors that are either internal or external to the performer. Effort and ability represent internal factors while task difficulty and luck are external and are known as environmental variables.

Stability indicates whether attributions are stable or unstable. Stability refers to the degree of permanence associated with an attribution factor. A stable factor is considered permanent and unchangeable, for example ability. An unstable factor, by contrast, is temporary and can be changed. Luck is an example of an unstable factor.

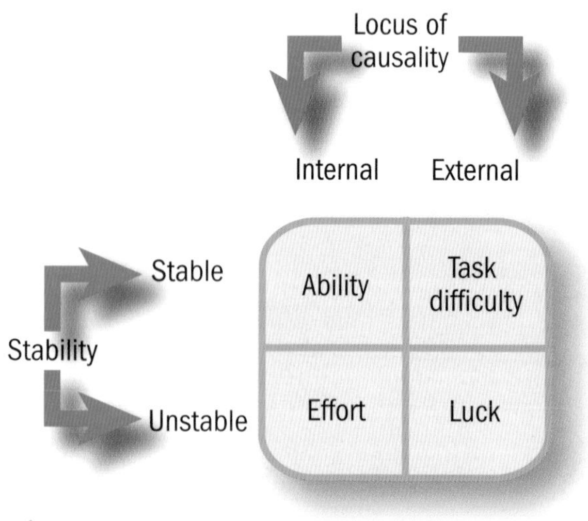

Fig 8.11 Weiner's attribution model

KEY TERMS

Attribution

Attribution theory identifies the reasons (attributions) given by performers to explain success and failure.

Locus of causality

Identifies the perceived cause of success or failure, i.e. an external cause is outside of the performer's control while an internal cause is within their control.

TASK 5

1 Draw and label Weiner's model of attribution.
2 Enter the specific attributions in each of the four 'boxes'.
3 Explain the reason for the location of each attribution. For example: task difficulty is stable because it cannot be changed; opponents being determined by an organised fixture list is external because opposition is an environmental variable.
4 Discuss the attribution which you as a coach would give to a player who has failed, after a final trial match, to be selected for a representative team, such as a county hockey team.

Control, which will be considered later, is a third dimension of the attribution model. It is not referred to directly in the specification but is a key factor in the important process of attribution retraining (see page 214).

REASONS FOR SUCCESS AND FAILURE

In general, the coach should attribute failure to external causes in order to sustain confidence and to give reassurance that achievement is a realistic expectation in the future. External factors take away the responsibility of the loss from the players. This would help to maintain self-esteem, sustain motivation, and restore pride and confidence. An example of external attributions would be to suggest the opposition were lucky. Luck is a changeable environmental factor.

Internal attributions should be used to reinforce success, for example achievement is the result of ability. Internal attributions for success would elevate confidence and endorse future expectation of high achievement.

High achievers, or people who adopt approach behaviour, tend to attribute their success to internal factors, for example high ability level. This will result in greater effort. Failure, on the other hand, is put down to external variables such as bad luck. Failure, therefore, is seen as a temporary setback. This is known as **attribution bias** or self-serving bias. As a consequence, high achievers tend to remain persistent in the face of failure. This is a positive application of attribution. Consistent achievement and positive application of attribution would encourage mastery orientation. This is likely to encourage a physically active lifestyle.

KEY TERM

Attribution bias

Attribution bias, or self-serving bias, refers to the performer's belief that the separate attributions given for success and failure never change. For example, the performer may feel that failure is always due to poor ability or success occurs because of good luck. These factors may have become for the performer a state of mind and may not be the true reasons for the outcome.

Low achievers or people who adopt avoidance behaviour tend to attribute a lack of success to internal factors, such as a lack of ability. Low achievers also tend to attribute success to external factors; for example, achievement was the outcome of luck. This type of attribution would

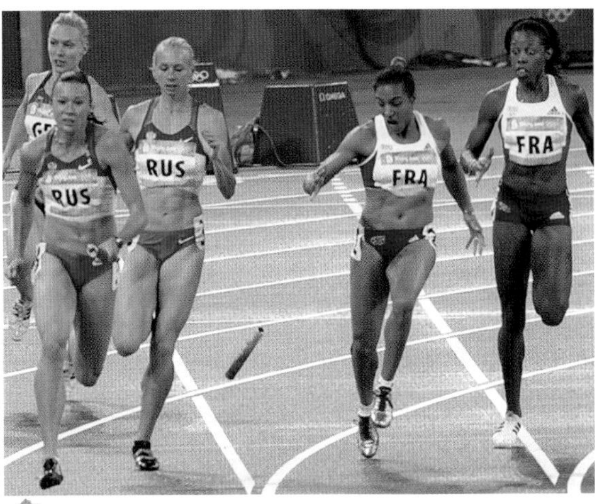

Fig 8.12 Performers tend to be biased and inaccurate when making attributions about their own performance. This self-serving bias is a way to protect self-esteem

take away confidence and reduce expectation of future achievement. This is negative application of attribution. Repeated failure and negative application of attribution would cause the athlete to experience learned helplessness. This condition may cause an individual to avoid an activity and drop out of participation altogether.

REMEMBER

Mastery orientation involves a focus on learning and developing new skills, for example competency in the task. Learned helplessness is the belief that failure is inevitable and that the individual has no control over the factors that cause failure.

ATTRIBUTION RETRAINING

It is unlikely that external attributions alone can change consistent failure into success, nor will they convert learned helplessness into mastery orientation.

Attribution retraining involves changing the performer's perception of the causes of failure. The belief that poor ability is the cause of failure is changed to a belief that a lack of effort was the most important attributional factor in failure.

As an internal and stable attribution, ability is a direct reflection of personal competence and, significantly, the individual has no way of changing it. The application of effort is changeable, however, because effort is unstable. Effort attributions are also internal so that the individual can experience pride in any positive changes. Effort is a particularly valuable attribution as it can be controlled by the performer. It is a fear of having no control over failure that underpins learned helplessness.

Attribution retraining, therefore, involves focusing the reason for failure onto internal, unstable and controllable factors.

TASK 6

1. Identify other attributions that are internal, unstable and controllable.
2. Discuss why the attributions you have identified could help to promote mastery orientation and help a person to avoid learned helplessness.
3. Consider why mastery orientation is likely to encourage lifelong participation in physical activity.

The process of attribution retraining can be justified because it can help to raise confidence, convert avoidance behaviour into approach behaviour, and encourage mastery orientation within an individual. This will promote the likelihood of lifelong sport participation.

APPLY IT!

If you are a coach, incorporate positive attribution and attribution retraining into your coaching session. Consider the effect of these processes on the motivation, confidence and commitment of your group.

If you are not a coach but you are a participant, assess how your coach makes use of positive attribution and attribution retraining. Consider the effect of these processes on the motivation, confidence and commitment of your group.

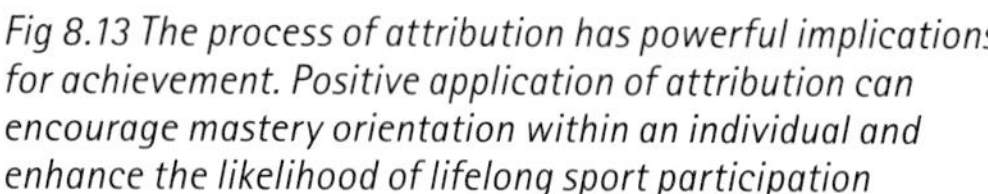

Fig 8.13 The process of attribution has powerful implications for achievement. Positive application of attribution can encourage mastery orientation within an individual and enhance the likelihood of lifelong sport participation

STRATEGIES FOR THE PROMOTION OF MASTERY ORIENTATION AND AVOIDANCE OF LEARNED HELPLESSNESS

Mastery orientation is associated with having the self-belief and the desire to achieve performance competence. This inclination is based on the individual's level of confidence. Specific strategies relating to confidence and goal setting will be addressed later (page 245). You will see that these later strategies can be applied to the promotion of mastery orientation and the avoidance of learned helplessness.

We saw earlier that an appropriately designed exercise programme can improve the personality trait of self-esteem and can modify the negative characteristics of Type A behaviour. Furthermore, attitudes toward physical activity can be changed by giving positive experiences in Physical Education and rewarding achievement with

REMEMBER

Changing attitudes from negative to positive promotes participation in physical activity and enhances the possibility of adopting a balanced, active and healthy lifestyle.

positive reinforcement. Negative attitudes can also be reversed by applying verbal persuasion and the psychological theory of cognitive dissonance.

Attribution retraining can also have a positive influence on sports performance and promote mastery orientation by improving the confidence of the individual. This gives the performer an element of control over the outcome, thus eliminating the onset of learned helplessness. In addition, controllable effort attributions will change ego orientation (success judged on the goal of being better than others) into task orientation (success judged on improving personal performance).

STRETCH AND CHALLENGE

Discuss the strategies that will help to promote mastery orientation while at the same time serving to eliminate learned helplessness.

EVALUATE CRITICALLY THE EFFECTS OF ATTRIBUTION ON PERFORMANCE AND ON SUSTAINING A BALANCED, ACTIVE AND HEALTHY LIFESTYLE

Although it will be of greater significance in the next section, there is a link between aggression and goal orientation. Kavussanu (1997) proposed that ego-orientated athletes in competitive situations were more likely to display aggressive behaviour with the intent to injure an opponent, than were task-orientated athletes.

In conclusion, it could be said that the processes of attribution and attribution retraining influence the development of self-esteem and task orientation. In turn, according to Roberts *et al.* (1997), task goals facilitate a lifestyle that is both active and physical.

Aggression and its impact upon performance and behaviour

The term **aggression** is used to describe forceful behaviour in sport. The smash in badminton, fast bowling in cricket or a punch thrown in anger are some examples of ballistic actions that have been

	Positive applications of attribution that will facilitate performance and help to sustain a balanced active and healthy lifestyle	Negative applications of attribution that will inhibit performance and reduce the drive to sustain a balanced active and healthy lifestyle
Success	Internal attributions given for success help to: • endorse mastery orientation • elevate confidence or self-esteem • develop pride • increase the expectation of success in the future.	External attributions given for success take away: • the pride normally associated with success • the incentive value derived from mastery orientation.
Failure	External attributions given for failure help to: • encourage the pursuit of mastery orientation • sustain confidence or self-esteem • eliminate shame • improve the expectation of success in the future.	Internal attributions given for failure take away: • confidence by highlighting ability incompetence • mastery orientation by leading to learned helplessness.

Table 5 Positive and negative applications of attribution

classified by the media recently as aggressive acts. Not all of these examples, however, can strictly be defined as aggression.

Two definitions of aggression given by Baron and Bull are:

> 'Aggression is any behaviour that is intended to harm another individual by physical or verbal means.'
>
> (Bull, 1990)

> 'Aggression is any form of behaviour directed toward the goal of harming or injuring another living being who is motivated to avoid such treatment.'
>
> (Baron)

The smash in badminton is not intended to injure nor is it directed to the goal of inflicting harm. The term aggression therefore needs to be clearly defined.

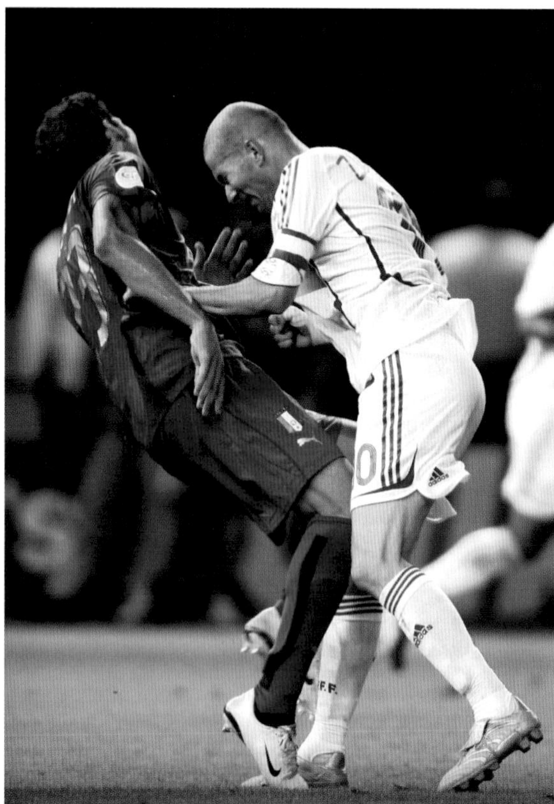

Fig 8.14 The primary aim of hostile aggression is to harm or injure another person. It is detrimental to performance

To understand the term it is necessary to divide aggression into two categories:

- **hostile aggression**
- assertive behaviour (often referred to as **channelled aggression**).

AGGRESSION

The prime motive of hostile aggression is to harm an opponent and the chief aim of the aggressor is to inflict injury. Aggressive actions violate the rules of any game and such indiscretions are dysfunctional in the context of sport. Often an aggressive player will disrupt the team's performance and spoil the cohesion of the group. Aggression has been described as hostile destructiveness (Parens, 1988). Aggression needs, therefore, to be eliminated from sport.

ASSERTION

Assertive behaviour does not attempt to harm and is strictly within the rules and spirit of the game. Assertion often involves forceful, robust but functional play, primarily focused upon completing the skill successfully. The major aim of assertion is the successful completion of the task. For example, to drive forcefully through a group of players to score in basketball is assertive and not aggressive. Assertion was described by Parens (1987) as non-hostile self-protective mastery behaviour. Assertion is also known as channelled aggression.

KEY TERMS

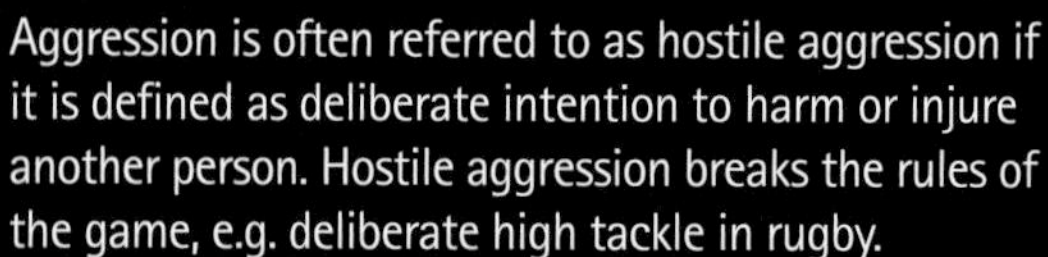

Hostile aggression

Aggression is often referred to as hostile aggression if it is defined as deliberate intention to harm or injure another person. Hostile aggression breaks the rules of the game, e.g. deliberate high tackle in rugby.

Channelled aggression

Channelled aggression is often referred to as assertion and involves robust play which is directed towards completing the skill successfully and is not primarily involved with inflicting injury e.g. a legitimate tackle in rugby.

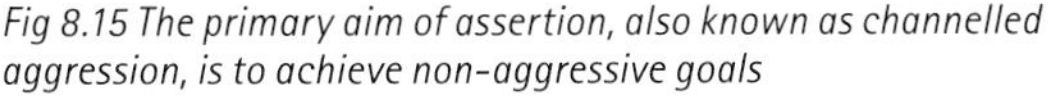

Fig 8.15 The primary aim of assertion, also known as channelled aggression, is to achieve non-aggressive goals

THE CAUSES OR ANTECEDENTS OF AGGRESSIVE BEHAVIOUR

There are thought to be many causes or **antecedents** of aggressive behaviour in sport. Some of these are given in Fig 8.16 below.

KEY TERM

Antecedent

A prior event which can lead to aggression. Note that an antecedent is a cause and not a theory of aggression.

Fig 8.16 Causes of aggression in sport

Major causes of aggression in sport

- Actual or perceived unfairness during play
- Frustration at poor performance or losing a game
- Displaced aggression or an influence outside sport
- Excessive pressure to win
- Playing in a game where there had been previous ill-feeling
- Retaliation to an incident
- Being on losing team when there is a wide score margin
- Reaction to hostile situation, e.g. crowd chants
- Nature of the game, e.g. ice hockey is a fast, collision-style game
- Copying the behaviour of other players

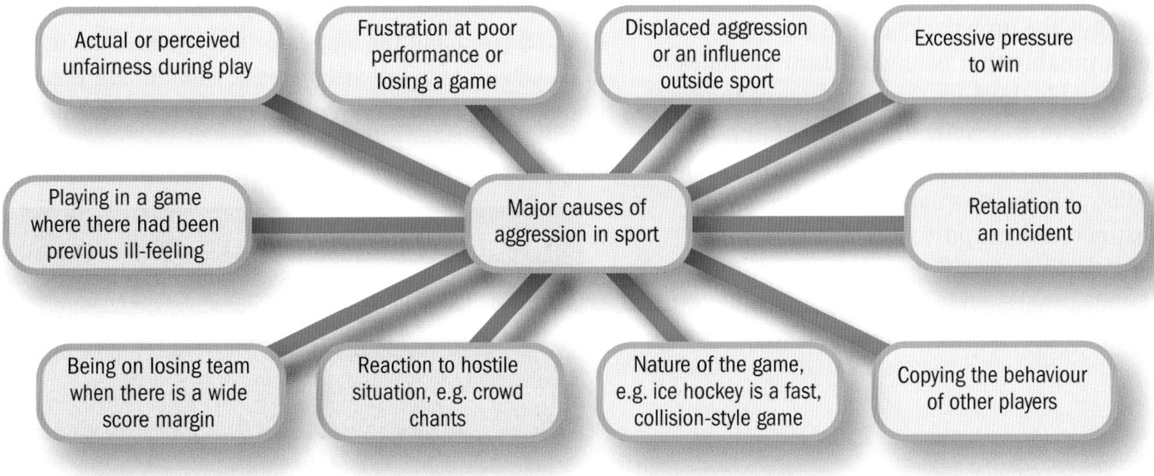

KEY TERM

Displaced aggression

To change the direction of aggression, e.g. play harder

TASK 7

For a short period, watch a number of sports which involve physical contact. Identify and count the number of acts of assertion and the number of acts of aggression in the allocated period. Discuss the following:

- What is the proportion of assertion to aggression in each activity?
- Does aggression follow any particular antecedent?
- Is it the home or away team that is most aggressive?

Theories of aggression

INSTINCT THEORY

Freud (1920) initially proposed instinct theory but Lorenz later extended his work in 1966. This is a trait view of behaviour and therefore displays the drawbacks of this perspective, most notably that behaviour is at all times predictable. Instinct theory proposes that aggression is genetically inherited and that a trait of violence lies within everyone. Freud called this innate characteristic the 'death instinct', the purpose of which is to seek aggressive destruction. Lorenz put forward the idea that aggressive energy is constantly building up and needs to be released.

SOCIAL LEARNING THEORY

Bandura presented social learning theory in 1966. This theory associates with the view that all behaviour is learned. Aggression is not a genetically-based innate characteristic but is **nurtured** through environmental forces. Aggression can, therefore, be learned by watching and copying from role models and becomes an accepted mode of behaviour if it is reinforced. Aggression is likely to occur if it is part of the social and cultural norm of a group.

KEY TERM

Nurture

A learned pattern of behaviour acquired through reinforcement, imitation of the behaviour of others and general environmental influences.

FRUSTRATION AGGRESSION HYPOTHESIS

This is an interactionist theory which was proposed by Dollard (1939).

Frustration develops when goal-directed behaviour or a need to achieve is blocked. The tendency toward frustration is increased when the pursued goal reflects ego or outcome orientation. Frustration could occur through environmental situations such as defeat, good opposition and poor officiating. This is considered to be an interactionist theory because frustration generated by the environment triggers the aggressive gene. If the aggressive act is successful, frustration is released and the aggressor feels good. This is known as a cathartic release. Should aggression fail and result in punishment, further frustration is generated.

REMEMBER

Trait perspective, social learning perspective and interactionist approach as they related to the formation of personality are described on pages 197–202.

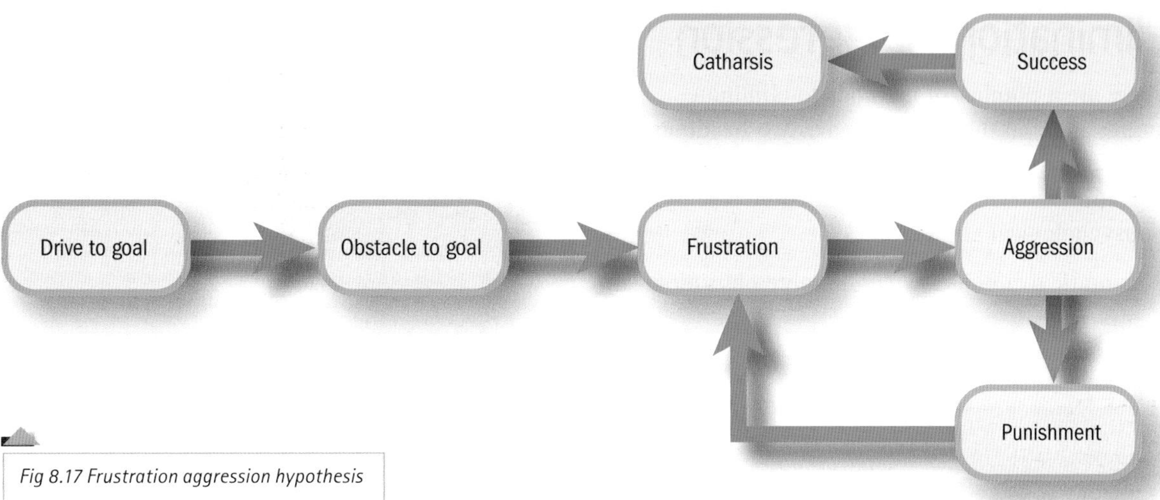

Fig 8.17 Frustration aggression hypothesis

AGGRESSION CUE HYPOTHESIS

This theory presents a second interactionist perspective and builds upon Dollard's work. Berkowitz (1969) believes that frustration leads to an increase in arousal. However, he disagrees that frustration alone will always trigger aggression. He proposes that frustration creates a 'readiness' for aggression which is triggered only when a provocative environmental cue is present.

Aggressive cues such as perceived unfairness, the opposition shirt or the nature of the game will trigger aggression in sport if arousal among participants is high. However, better players have the capacity to control frustration and arousal.

Controlling and eliminating aggression is a major factor in optimising performance. Aggressive behaviour inhibits concentration and team cohesion. Gill (2000) confirms that there is no evidence that aggressive behaviour improves sport performance.

REMEMBER

- Of the trait perspective, social learning theory and interactionist approach to personality formation, the interactionist approach appears to be the one most favoured by psychologists. (See Chapter 9, page 235.)
- Aggression has been associated with ego goal orientation. Together, it would appear they could have a negative effect on the likelihood of lifelong participation in sport.

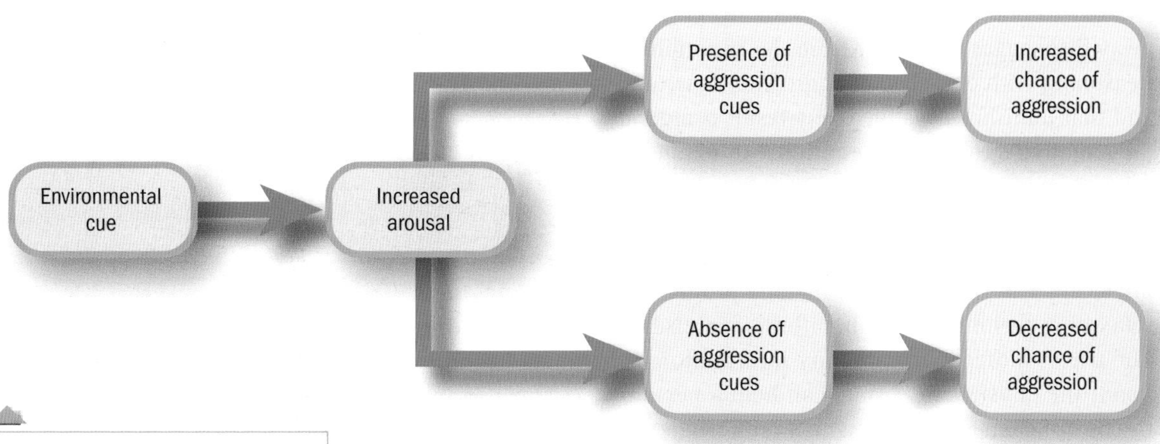

Fig 8.18 Aggression cue hypothesis

Elimination of aggression

There are a number of methods to eliminate aggression and these come under two headings:

1 **cognitive** techniques which involve psychological strategies

2 **somatic** techniques which involve physiological strategies.

KEY TERM

Biofeedback

A stress management technique that uses electronic instruments to measure physiological reactions to stress, such as increased heart rate. By observing traces that indicate increasing heart rate it may be possible to control this changing state.

KEY TERMS

Cognitive

Relating to mental or psychological processes.

Somatic

Relating to physical processes such as increases in breathing rate, heart rate and sweating.

Cognitive strategies are to do with thought processes and are designed to lower psychological/cognitive arousal. They include imagery which focuses on achieving a calm state of mind while forming a mental image of quiet places, and mental rehearsal (imagining one's own movements during performance). Positive self-talk and concentrating on repeated words or phrases can also lower an inclination to be aggressive. Counting up to ten will give the opportunity to regain composure. Forgetting or distancing oneself from aggressive cues is a good strategy to prevent aggression, while walking away disengages the player from the situation. Reasoning with oneself that aggression is wrong and that punishment is the likely result is a good preventative measure, while rational thinking in general would be advised.

Somatic methods to eliminate aggression mean physical strategies and these include progressive relaxation techniques and breathing exercises. The use of **biofeedback** and any information about the physiological state can help a person to control somatic arousal which may trigger aggression.

In addition, the aggressive person could be given a role of responsibility or dysfunctional behaviour could be punished. Furthermore, emphasis on non-aggressive role models will help to eliminate aggressive behaviour. Non-aggressive behaviour should be positively reinforced to ensure that a desirable S–R learning bond is strengthened between successful performance and non-aggressive play.

REMEMBER

An S–R learning bond is the connection or link that is made between a stimulus and the response made to that stimulus (see page 189 in *OCR AS PE SB*).

Aggression can also be controlled through the process of attribution. Success should be attributed to ability and the effort applied during performance. The reason for success should not be attributed to tactics that intimidate opponents.

REMEMBER

A link between aggression and goal orientation was made by Kavussanu (1997); see page 215.

A task-oriented environment allows a performer to be judged on their ability rather than, as would happen in an ego-orientated environment, against the ability of other people. Kavussanu (1997) proposed that performers striving for ego goals are most likely to engage in cheating behaviour, play unfairly and be inclined to set out to injure others. A teacher, therefore, could reduce the aggressive tendency of a player by creating a task-orientated environment.

Control of aggression positively promotes the adoption of active and healthy lifestyles. If unchecked, aggressive behaviour can greatly reduce this possibility. Some of the detrimental effects of aggression are described by Silva.

- Silva (1979) proposed that hostile aggression, when demonstrated by an individual, may increase arousal causing reduced concentration resulting in poor performance. Underachievement (as it has been previously seen) can lead to learned helplessness and an inclination to give up.
- Silva's research also indicates that the dysfunctional consequences of aggression extend beyond the immediate performance results, for example aggressive performers are likely to get injured and run a greater risk of being dismissed from the game.
- Performers with aggressive tendencies tend to feel anger and experience less satisfaction after completing activities and have therefore a reduced motive to continue with the activity.

STRETCH AND CHALLENGE

As a coach in a sport that involves physical contact, explain to your team the causes of aggressive behaviour during the game and discuss why you wish to eliminate aggression from team play.

Exam Café

Relax, refresh, result!

Refresh your memory

You should now have knowledge and understanding of:

- personality and its importance in producing effective performance and in following a balanced, active and healthy lifestyle
- attitudes and their influence on performance and lifestyle
- achievement motivation and its effect on performance and on following an active and healthy lifestyle
- attribution theory and the impact of attribution on performance and sustaining a balanced, active and healthy lifestyle
- aggression and its impact upon performance and behaviour.

REVISE AS YOU GO!

1. What is meant by the terms trait, interactionist and social learning perspectives of personality?
2. Identify the characteristics of extroversion, introversion, neuroticism and stability.
3. List the characteristics of Type A and Type B personalities.
4. Identify the drawbacks of personality profiling.
5. Define cognitive, affective and behavioural components of an attitude.
6. Identify the methods that could be used to change an attitude.
7. What is learned helplessness and mastery orientation?
8. Identify and describe the dimensions of Weiner's Attribution model.
9. What is meant by the terms aggression and assertion?
10. Identify the strategies that help to eliminate aggression.

Try to answer these questions yourself. Ask your teacher if you need help.

Get the result!

Examination question

Using psychological theories, explain aggressive behaviour.

Describe three methods a coach might use to eliminate aggressive tendencies of performers and to encourage an active and healthy lifestyle. (6 marks)

Examiner's tips

The question asks for theories. These include Instructional, Social Learning, Frustration Aggression Hypothesis and Aggression-cue Hypothesis. Remember the causes of aggression sometimes known as antecedents are not theories of aggression.

Student answer

Aggression in sport is the deliberate intention to harm or injure an opponent. Aggression is also dysfunctional, for example a punch thrown in a rugby match. The coach must eliminate aggression but should encourage assertion. Assertion is sometimes known as channelled aggression and involves robust play which is both within the rules and aimed at completing the task successfully.

aminer says:

ıile your knowledge correct, the question es not ask for a finition of aggression d assertion. No ırks.

Aggression might be caused if a player feels that the referee has made an unfair decision, such as disallowing a goal in football because of a perceived dubious offside decision. A game between local rivals may be a cause of aggression as there could be a tradition of hostility between the teams. Finally, the nature of the game may stimulate aggression, for example rugby as a contact sport is more likely to trigger conflict than a hockey game.

Examiner says:

Once again your knowledge is accurate but the point has been missed. You write about the causes or antecedents of aggression. The question asks for psychological theories. No marks.

The methods to eliminate aggression include imagery, which focuses on calm states in quiet places, and mental rehearsal, which concerns imagining one's own movements. Positive self-talk and concentrating on repeated words or phrases can lower an inclination to be aggressive. Counting up to ten also gives opportunity to regain composure. Control of somatic arousal through stress management techniques will also prevent aggression from occurring.

aminer says:

od. You mention ɜ ways to eliminate gression. Only three ırks maximum can given.

Improved student answer

The Instinct theory of aggression (Freud) states that a person is born with aggressive tendencies and that aggression is constantly being generated. This innate tendency would explain why a rugby player might strike another in the game situation.

When goal-directed behaviour is blocked, frustration could arise and aggression may be the result. This is predicted by the Frustration–Aggression Hypothesis (Dollard). If the aggressive act brings success and satisfaction, the player will experience a cathartic reaction. A practical example of this theory could be the attacker in football who is continually being tackled. The attacker then elects to foul the defender deliberately.

A stimulus or environmental cue could serve to trigger aggression. This view is presented in Aggression-cue Hypothesis (Berkowitz). The stimulus could be the perception of the ice hockey stick as a weapon, the opposition shirt or seeing a colleague being the recipient of violence. The theories both of Dollard and Berkowitz are said to be interactionist theories.

Examiner says:

Three marks maximum are awarded for the first part of this question. So you need to put three theories in your answer. In this model answer four theories have been included because they are written in the syllabus.

It is best to include practical examples alongside the academic theories.

A fourth theory is Social Learning Theory. Bandura proposed that all behaviour is copied from significant others. For vicarious learning to take place, the role model needs to be similar in age and ability and it is thought that behaviour is more likely to be modelled if the gender is the same. For example, if the champion male tennis player shows hostility towards the umpire, there is a chance it could be copied by a junior player. Aggression is likely to occur if previous aggressive behaviour has been reinforced and if aggression is part of the social and cultural norm of a group.

The methods to eliminate aggression can be addressed under two headings. These headings are cognitive and somatic techniques.

Examiner says:

It is good practice indicate that there are two overarchi techniques to eliminate aggress

Cognitive strategies embrace the process of thought and are designed to lower psychological/cognitive arousal. They include imagery, which focuses on calm states in quiet places, and mental rehearsal, which concerns imagining one's own movements. Positive self-talk and concentrating on repeated words or phrases can lower an inclination to be aggressive. Counting up to ten also gives opportunity to regain composure.

Forgetting or distancing oneself from aggressive cues is a good strategy to prevent aggression, while walking away disengages the player from the situation. Reasoning with oneself that aggression is wrong and that punishment is the likely result is a preventative measure, while rational thinking in general would be advised.

Somatic methods to eliminate aggression refer to physical strategies and these include progressive relaxation techniques and breathing exercises. The use of bio-feedback and any information about the physiological state can help a person to control somatic arousal which may trigger aggression.

aminer says:

ce again a ximum of three rks can be awarded the second part he question. By ering three methods eliminate aggression, ximum marks can secured in this tion.

Emphasis on non-aggressive role models will, furthermore, help to eliminate aggressive behaviour.

Finally, the teacher or coach should create task-orientated goals as opposed to ego-orientated goals. Those who perceive success only as beating others are ego orientated and this pursuit is thought to induce both cheating and aggression. Performers with task orientation are more inclined to enjoy engagement in physical activities and are therefore likely to adopt a healthy lifestyle.

Examiner says:

Reference is made to the pursuit of an active healthy lifestyle.

CHAPTER 9:

Group dynamics of performance

LEARNING OBJECTIVES

By the end of this chapter you should have knowledge and understanding of:

- groups and teams – their impact upon performance and the pursuit of balanced, active and healthy lifestyles
- leadership and the role of a leader in physical activities
- social facilitation and inhibition – the effects of an audience and other participants on performance and lifestyle behaviours.

INTRODUCTION

Groups and teams are of particular interest to the sports psychologist because sport and exercise activities invariably involve people operating collectively. The process of individuals working within a group and the relationships that may exist between several groups is called **group dynamics.**

KEY TERM

Group dynamics

The social processes operating within the group between individual members.

The process of group dynamics is complex and has proved difficult to research. This section, however, aims to set aside those difficulties and focus on two areas.

- Firstly, the ways in which **group cohesion** can be developed.
- Secondly, the influence group dynamics can have on an individual's attitude and motivation when relating to the pursuit of a balanced, healthy and active lifestyle.

It is important to consider the definition of a group. A basketball team, exercise aerobics participants and a class of Physical Education students can be called groups. Conversely, large crowds at football matches and people running independently on adjacent treadmills at a health club do not constitute a 'group'. According to McGrath (1984), **interaction** within the group is the defining factor. In order for interaction to take place, mutual awareness must exist between group members.

KEY TERMS

Group cohesion

The tendency of a group or team to stick together and remain united in the pursuit of its goals and objectives.

Interaction

An action or reaction between two factors or, as it relates to this section, two or more people.

REMEMBER

Interactionist perspectives on the formation of personality and the interactionist view on the expression of aggressive behaviour are discussed in Chapter 8, pages 201 and 202.

> 'Groups are those social aggregates that involve mutual awareness and the potential for interaction.'
> McGrath (1984)

McGrath proposed that as groups must be small enough to allow interdependence, football crowds are too large for mutual awareness to take place. Furthermore, runners operating on treadmills do not interact with one another. Carron and Davies (1998) also highlighted the existence of mutual interdependence as being central to the makeup of a group. They suggested that the following criteria must also apply before sports teams, exercise clubs and classes of Physical Education students can be considered as teams or groups.

Groups should have:

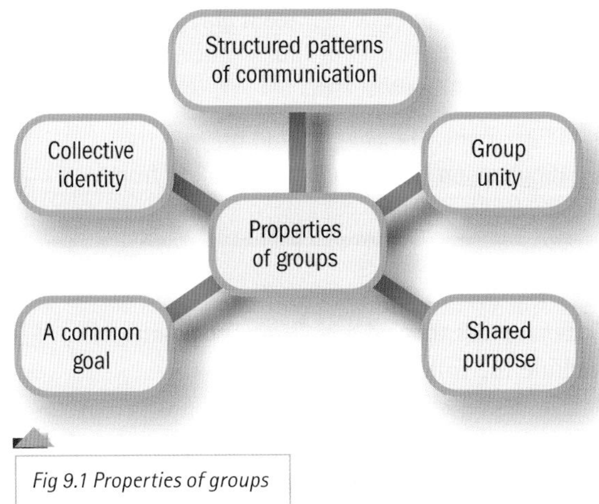

Fig 9.1 Properties of groups

Group performance

STEINER'S MODEL

Actual Productivity = Potential Productivity – losses due to Faulty Processes

(AP = PP – FP)

- Actual productivity is the team performance at a given time during a game or event and refers to the extent of successful interaction.
- Potential productivity is the maximum capability of the group when cohesiveness appears at its strongest.
- Faulty processes mean the factors which can go wrong in team performance. They will impede or even prevent group cohesion and detract from the collective potential of the team.

There are two faulty processes that bring about losses in potential productivity.

1 *Co-ordination losses (the Ringlemann effect)*
Any breakdown in teamwork is regarded as a co-ordination loss and is termed the Ringlemann effect. These losses occur because the operational effectiveness of the group as a unit cannot be sustained for the duration of a match. Even the most carefully planned and rehearsed strategy may fail because of a positional error or because of an ill-timed move.

   Ringlemann stated that problems in team co-ordination are more likely to occur as the team numbers increase. A basketball team comprising only five players is therefore less likely to experience co-ordination problems than a team of fifteen in Rugby Union.

   Research on co-ordination losses was based on studies into tug of war. It was found that a team of eight when operating collectively failed to equal the aggregate weight pulled when each member performed individually.

2 *Motivation losses (social loafing)*
Motivational losses relate to an individual who suffers a decrease in motivation during performance causing the player to withdraw effort and 'coast' through a period of play or even the whole game. This loss of motivation and subsequent relaxation of effort is called social loafing. Social loafing would prevent team co-ordination and inhibit team cohesion.

Fig 9.2 Social loafing and the Ringlemann effect are the major faulty processes that prevent a group becoming a synchronised cohesive unit

Listed below are the negative influences that can cause social loafing and lead to **dysfunctional** behaviour in the context of group dynamics.

- The feeling that others in the team are not trying may cause an individual to make less effort.
- 'Social loafing' will arise if a player feels that their performance is never watched or valued by the coach.
- A player with low self-confidence will develop a strategy of social loafing to protect their self-esteem.
- A player who has suffered a negative experience, possibly in the form of failure, or has been the recipient of negative attribution will tend to 'loaf'.
- A loss of motivation occurs if a task is perceived to be too difficult. This links to 'avoidance behaviour' (see also Chapter 8, pages 209 and 210).

KEY TERM

Dysfunctional

A negative process that inhibits or prevents the completion or continuation of a desired operation.

EXAM TIP

You need to be aware that social loafing is dysfunctional behaviour because it prevents effective teamwork. Notice the link between the causes of social loafing, low self-confidence, negative attribution and avoidance behaviour.

REMEMBER

Low self-confidence, negative attribution and avoidance behaviour are factors that closely relate to learned helplessness. Learned helplessness can be the cause of an individual opting out of sports participation, thus inhibiting the prospect of enjoying an active, healthy and balanced lifestyle.

The elimination of faulty processes and the formation of group cohesion can encourage an individual to adopt an active healthy lifestyle. Spink and Carron (1977) found that in a fitness and exercise setting a person was more likely to persist with an exercise programme if there were high levels of cohesion in the group.

APPLY IT!

Analyse a period of a game situation (preferably played by your school or college).

1 Identify:

   a) situations when group cohesion facilitated good play
   b) circumstances when team play broke down due to the onset of faulty processes
   c) the faulty processes.

2 Discuss how the coach could prevent the Ringlemann effect and social loafing from occurring.

Other factors that adversely affect teamwork include the following:

- injury can disrupt team strategies and break down co-ordination
- a lack of incentive to produce team work will prevent cohesion
- vague individual roles inhibit effective teamwork
- low sum of the players' overall ability makes team play difficult to achieve
- personality can influence team cohesion as people with **low trait confidence** find it difficult to promote group cohesion (Carron, 1994)
- inadequate leadership inhibits teamwork.

KEY TERM

Low trait confidence

The general disposition of low confidence. It tends to be both stable and global.

EXAM TIP

These dysfunctional factors need to be eliminated as they also influence the formation and development of a cohesive group or team.

Factors affecting the formation and development of a cohesive group or team

TASK COHESION AND SOCIAL COHESION

There are two types of cohesion that must be considered. One type applies to sports teams while the other is more relevant to exercise activity groups. The two types of cohesion are:

- task cohesion
- social cohesion.

Although both types of cohesion are important, the nature of the game or activity determines which type of cohesion it is best to form and develop. The correct type of cohesion will help the group to interact efficiently in order to achieve the desired common goal.

- Task cohesion is most important in **interactive sports and activities** such as hockey. Task cohesion relates to the way team members work with each other to complete a task successfully.
- Social cohesion is most important in **co-active sports or activities** like track and field athletics or fitness groups. Social cohesion involves the formation of personal relationships within the group that provide the individual with support and friendship.

Within large groups such as a county netball squad, there is a possibility that **sub-groups** will emerge. Sub-groups impede the formation and development of a cohesive group or team. The coach must therefore assess the dynamics of the group and adopt strategies that will unify the group. These strategies will be looked at on page 230 of this chapter.

KEY TERMS

Interactive sports and activities

Sports or activities such as hockey, netball and rugby in which team members work together and rely on each other.

Co-active sports or activities

Sports or activities such as athletics, equestrian activities and aerobic exercise classes in which individual performance is required.

Sub-groups

Small groups contained within the whole group.

EXAM TIP

An explanation of the strategies that promote teamwork and group cohesion is a popular examination question.

FOUR FACTORS AFFECTING TEAM COHESION

Carron (1993) identified four factors that directly affect team cohesion.

1 *Situational factors*
Situational factors include elements of the specific situation and environment in which the team will operate; for example, the time available, whether the involvement is interactive or co-active, and the tradition of leadership style experienced by the group. The size of the group is also significant as a situational factor because it is more difficult for cohesion to be formed in a large group than it is in one that is small.

2 *Individual factors*
Individual factors refer to the characteristics of the team members. The motivation level and the experience of the individual members are examples of individual factors.

3 *Leadership factors*
Leadership factors involve the style of leadership preferred by the group. As will later be seen,

leadership styles are determined by the task, the position of the leader and the relationship between the leader and group members.

4 *Team factors*
Team factors include collective team goals, good communication and a record of shared success.

FACTORS AFFECTING PARTICIPATION IN A GROUP OR TEAM

In order to promote group or team cohesion, it is important to encourage the participation of individual performers. Based on the factors identified by Carron, several strategies can be implemented to address these issues.

- Allocation of clear roles given to each player can help an individual to feel valued. An awareness of the responsibilities of other team members will ensure the development of mutual understanding between individuals.
- Participation in team-building exercises is good both for task and social cohesion. Spink (1995) proposed that team-building strategies increased cohesiveness and offset the negative effect that large groups have on cohesion.
- An evaluation of each member's performance effectively reduces social loafing.
- The punishment of non-team or non-cohesive players will highlight the importance of group cohesion.
- The selection of team players rather than players who are interested only in their own performance promotes cohesion.
- Development of team goals helps to clarify how team standards encourage effectiveness.
- Rehearsal of set plays during practice facilitates group co-ordination.
- The reinforcement of team success effectively gives team efficiency as the reason or attribution for the achievement of the group.
- Strong leadership will actively encourage group cohesion.

STRETCH AND CHALLENGE

Discuss the factors that prevent group unity and explain the strategies that will promote group cohesion.

GROUP AND TEAM EFFECTS ON BEHAVIOUR

It has been found (Spink and Carron, 1994) that increased levels of group cohesion help an individual to commit to and persist with exercise programmes.

The group can have a positive influence by providing social support and endorsing the value of a performer's contribution. The performer who perceives that their contribution to the team product is valued and unique is likely to experience increased internal motivation. This source of motivation is likely to encourage the adoption of a balanced, active and healthy lifestyle.

REMEMBER

During AS studies on motivation it was stated that those who are intrinsically motivated are more likely to continue participation and be consistent in their efforts.

The desire to conform to the norms and values of a peer group is particularly strong for a young person. If the consensus of the group favours participation in physical activity, there is a good chance that the individual will follow the trend. This desire for confirmation is linked with social learning. If the sporting participation of the group appears attractive and exciting, an individual will be inclined to learn and copy the group behaviour.

In relation to group affinity, Tajfel (social identity theory, 1978) proposed that the norms and values of the group are looked upon positively by an individual if they are a member of that group. If the individual does not belong, however, the same person will adopt a negative perception of the group ethos. This biased perception occurs in order to protect self-esteem, but once having become a member, the individual will conform as part of the team to protect the interests of the group.

Although a phenomenon named 'groupthink' proposed by Janis (1982) stated that by becoming overly strong, group cohesion can stifle individuality and participation, it can be said that overall group membership has a positive influence on the adoption of a balanced, active and healthy lifestyle.

REMEMBER

The peer group is a strong agent in the formation of young people's attitudes; look back at page 205.

Leadership and the role of a leader in physical activities

THE IMPORTANCE OF EFFECTIVE LEADERSHIP

Successful teams have strong leaders and the importance of this role is evident in all categories of sport and exercise activity groups. The performance of a leader is very clear in interactive games and at the head of an exercise group. Although less obvious in co-active situations, the leader's contribution to the effectiveness of a team's performance is also influential.

Leadership may be considered as a behavioural process that influences individuals and groups towards set goals. As such, a leader has the dual function of ensuring player satisfaction while steering the individual or group to success.

As will be seen later in the multi-dimensional model (Chelladurai, 1978), a style of leadership that satisfies the needs of individual performers while achieving the group goal can be a positive influence on lifestyle behaviour.

THE QUALITIES OF A LEADER

An effective leader should have the following qualities:

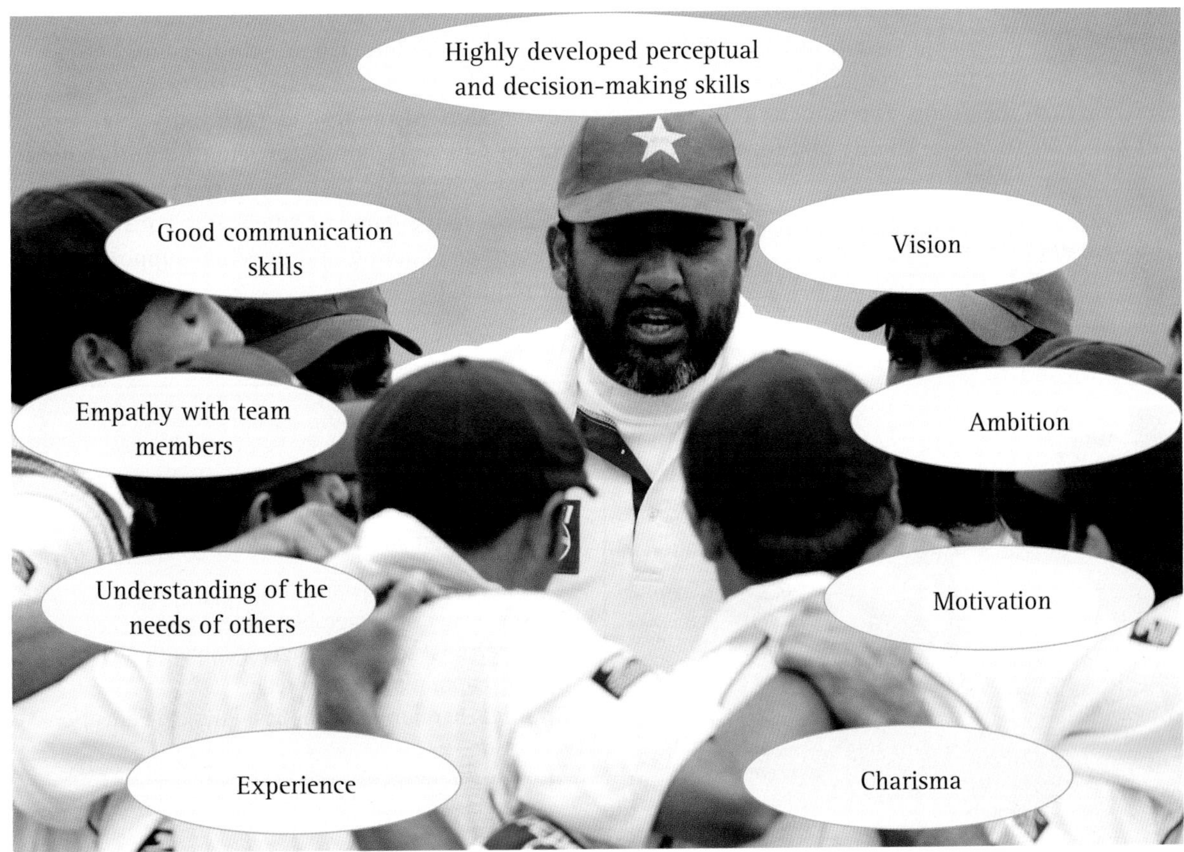

Fig 9.3 The qualities of a leader

REMEMBER

Interactive sports and activities are those in which team members work together and rely on each other, for example hockey. Co-active sports or activities are those in which individual performance is required, such as aerobic exercise classes.

CHARACTERISTICS OF LEADERS

There are three leader characteristics:

1 task-orientated or autocratic leaders
2 social or person-orientated leaders, also referred to as democratic leaders
3 laissez-faire leaders.

THE AUTOCRATIC LEADER

The autocratic or task-orientated leader tends to make all of the decisions and is motivated to complete the task as quickly and effectively as possible. This leadership style is authoritarian and does not take into account the opinions or preferences of the group. The autocratic leader will not delegate responsibility and focuses on group performance and achieving goals. This style would be most effective when quick decisions are needed for large groups of people, for example in interactive games. Furthermore, a task-orientated approach would be required in dangerous, potentially life-threatening situations which are sometimes experienced in outdoor pursuit activities.

Fig 9.4 Autocratic leadership is required in interactive games, but is essential in life-threatening situations

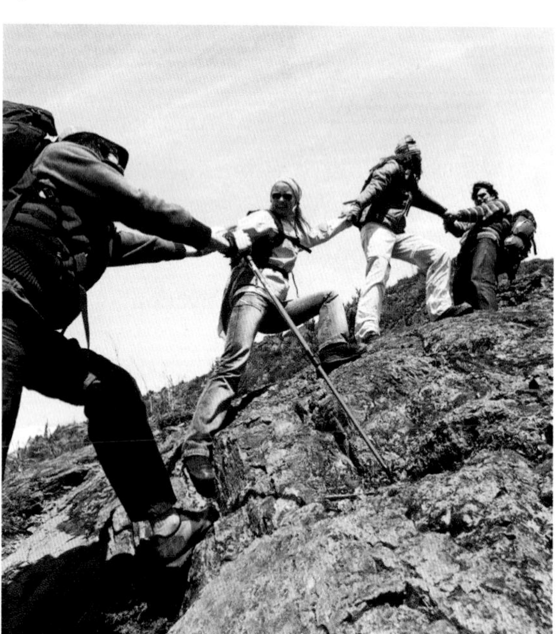

TASK 1

Discuss why an autocratic style of leadership would be most effective in the situation shown in Figure 9.4.

THE DEMOCRATIC LEADER

The democratic leader will share the decisions with the group and is often ready to delegate responsibility. This type of leader believes in consultation and is interested in developing meaningful interpersonal relationships within the team. The belief is that by giving 'ownership' of the task to each individual, the group will work harder, developing unity and a common purpose. This style would be effective in a co-active game or when time constraints are not as exacting and personal support may be required.

APPLY IT!

Consider whether an autocratic or democratic leader characteristic should be adopted in the following examples.

1 The coach of a gymnastics group
2 The leader of an aerobics fitness group
3 A personal trainer when working with a client
4 The captain of a rugby team
5 A teacher during a practical Physical Education lesson.

The characteristic adopted by the leader depends fundamentally upon the 'favourableness' of the situation.

A highly favourable situation	A highly unfavourable situation
Leader's position is strong	Leader's position is weak
Task is simple with clear structure	Task is complex with vague structure
Warm group and leader relations	Hostile group and leader relations

Table 1 Favourableness of a situation

Autocratic or task-orientated leaders are more effective in both the most favourable and the least favourable situations. Democratic or person-orientated leaders are more effective in moderately favourable situations.

EXAM TIP

You need to understand that situation favourableness is a major factor in determining leadership style. You need also to be aware of other factors that influence the leader's approach. Some additional factors are identified in Table 2.

LAISSEZ-FAIRE LEADERSHIP STYLE

In **laissez-faire** leadership, the leader will stand aside and allow the group to make its own independent decisions. This style can happen automatically and will result in a loss of group direction if the leader is inadequate. Lewin (1985) found that when subjected to this style of leadership, group member were inclined to be aggressive toward each other and gave up easily when mistakes occurred.

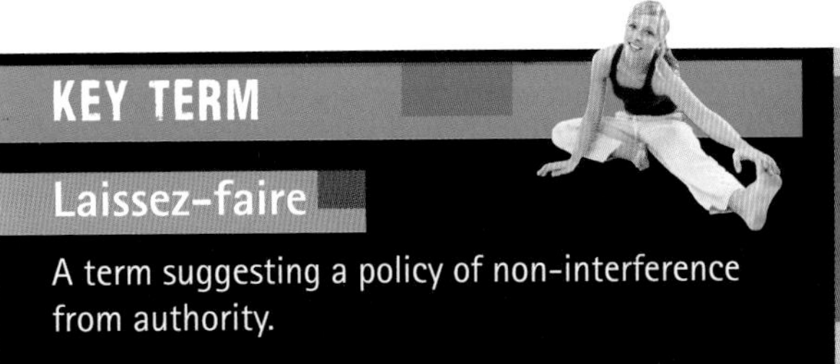

KEY TERM

Laissez-faire

A term suggesting a policy of non-interference from authority.

EMERGENT AND PRESCRIBED LEADERS

The terms 'emergent' and 'prescribed' refer to the background against which a leader is chosen.

- An emergent leader already belongs to the group. Selection to the position of authority can be formal through voting or the role is assumed and the leader is readily accepted by the group.

Autocratic leadership is preferable:	Democratic leadership is preferable:
• when groups are hostile and discipline is needed	• when groups are friendly and relationships are warm
• if groups are large	• if groups are small
• for team players who prefer an instructional approach	• in activities that require interpersonal communication
• in the early or cognitive stage of learning	• when the autonomous stage of learning has been achieved and the performer is expert
• in dangerous situations	• in situations where there is no threat of danger
• when there are time constraints	• when there are no constraints on time
• if the leader's personality is inclined to be authoritarian	• if the leader's personality is inclined to be democratic
• when the leader is male; men prefer an autocratic approach.	• when the leader is female; women prefer a democratic approach.

Table 2 A comparison of democratic and autocratic leadership styles

- A prescribed leader is selected from outside of the group and is an external appointment.

There are advantages and disadvantages for both types of leader selection.

TASK 2

1 Identify an example of an emergent and a prescribed leader from a sporting or physical activity situation with which you are familiar.
2 Give three advantages and three disadvantages of the emergent and the prescribed leader positions.

A critical evaluation of leadership theories

TRAIT APPROACH

Trait theorists believe that leaders are born with the capacity to take charge. Leadership traits are considered to be stable personality dispositions. Such traits may include intelligence, assertiveness and self-confidence. If this is true, a leader should be able to take control of any situation; but in practice, this is highly unlikely.

Tough mindedness and independent thinking are traits that may be helpful in leadership but their importance cannot be proven. Trait theory in general is not a good predictor of behaviour. It is unlikely, therefore, that specific dominant traits alone can facilitate successful leadership.

A significant trait theory is the 'great man theory of leadership', which suggests that the necessary qualities of leadership are inherited by sons (not daughters) whose fathers have been successful in this field. This is not a popular theory. Like early trait personality research, trait research relating to leadership has been inconclusive.

SOCIAL LEARNING THEORY

Social learning theorists propose that all behaviour is learned. Learning comes about through contact with environmental forces. For example, when an aspiring captain judges a situation to have been handled well by an experienced leader, the method will be remembered and copied should a similar situation arise. The process of imitating the successful behaviour of role models is called vicarious reinforcement. It is believed, therefore, that the skills of leadership can be acquired by imitation and developed through experience. The weakness in social learning theory is that it does not take into account the trait perspective. It is unlikely, therefore, that learning alone can facilitate effective leadership.

INTERACTIONIST THEORY

According to this theory, leadership skills emerge because of a combination of inherited abilities and learned skills. Leadership skills are likely to emerge and be acquired when a situation triggers the traits that are of importance to leadership. Gill (2000) indicates that in the context of sport and related physical activity, interactionist theories give a more realistic explanation of behaviour.

REMEMBER

Can you recall the trait, social learning and interactionist views on personality development? (See Chapter 8, pages 197–202.)

THE MULTI-DIMENSIONAL MODEL OF LEADERSHIP

Chelladurai (1978) identified three influences that interact to produce effective leadership (Figure 9.5).

With these influences in mind, Chelladurai proposed that the effectiveness of leadership could be judged upon two outcomes:

1 the degree of success accomplished during a task

Fig 9.5 Chelladurai: three aspects of effective leadership

2 the extent to which the group experienced satisfaction during the process of achieving the goal.

After taking into account all considerations, Chelladurai presented the following multi-dimensional model of leadership (Figure 9.6).

The three influences or antecedents that determine the behaviour adopted by the leader are explained below.

1 Situational characteristics are environmental conditions. Environmental conditions include the following:
   - the type of activity in which the group members are involved, for example interactive or co-active activities
   - the numbers involved in the team
   - the time constraints of the play or overall match
   - considerations about the strengths of the opposition.

2 Leader characteristics include the following:
   - the skill and experience of the leader
   - the personality of the leader, which may well be inclined either towards a person- or a task-orientated style.

3 Group member characteristics. The factors relating to members could involve:
   - age
   - gender
   - motivation
   - competence
   - experience.

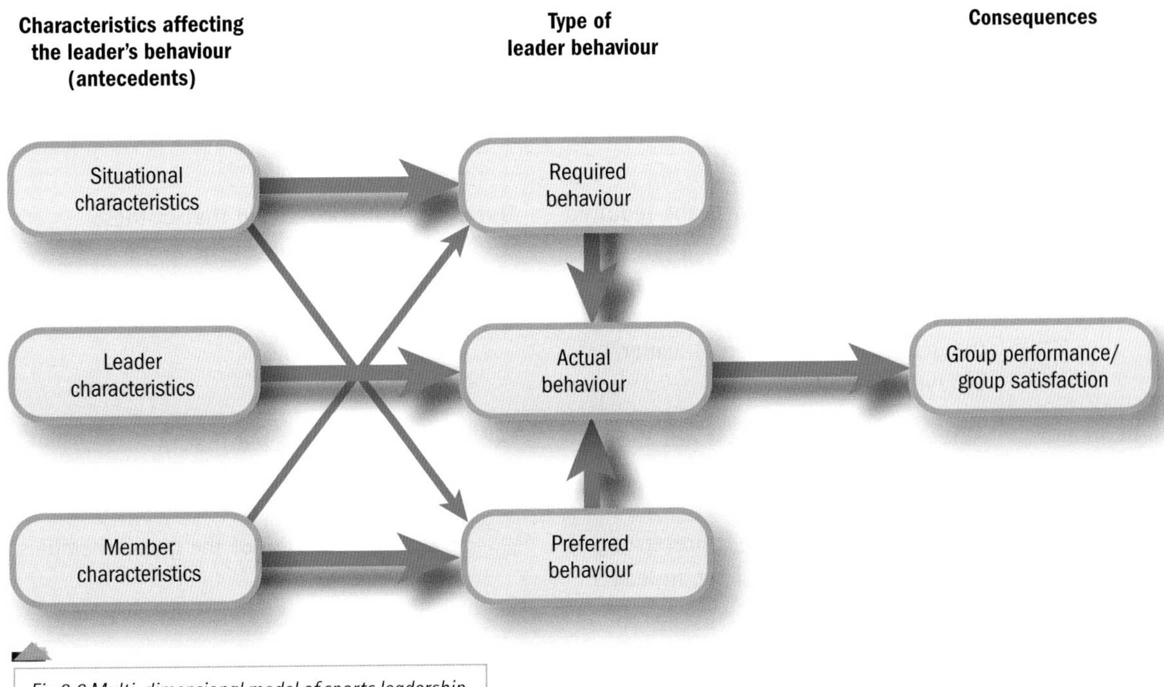

Fig 9.6 Multi-dimensional model of sports leadership

Next, Chelladurai recognised three behaviour types that impact on the leader. These are termed types of leader behaviour as shown in Figure 9.7. Types of leader behaviour are guided by the antecedents.

The key element of the multi-dimensional model is that in order for a leader to achieve a positive outcome, all three aspects of leader behaviour need to agree. An alternative way of describing the agreement or alignment of leader behaviour is to say that the three behaviours need to be **congruent**.

KEY TERM

Congruent

Coincide exactly.

Required behaviour
Required behaviour involves what ought to be done by the leader in certain situations. The leader's behaviour may be dictated by a playing strategy or organisation system.

Actual behaviour
Actual behaviour is what the leader chooses to do as the best course of action in the given situation. Actual behaviour is greatly influenced by the competence of the leader

Preferred behaviour
Preferred behaviour concerns what the group of athletes want the leader to do. The leadership style preferred by the group is usually determined by the member characteristics.

Fig 9.7 Three types of leader behaviour

	Leader behaviour		**Extent of group performance and satisfaction**
Degree of congruence	Actual leader behaviour is the required behaviour to complete the group task successfully and is also the type of leadership that is preferred by the group. Full congruence in leader behaviours exists.	**Outcome**	It is predicted that in these circumstances the group will perform effectively and the satisfaction of the group members will be high.
Degree of congruence	Actual leader behaviour is the required behaviour to complete the group task successfully but is not the type of leadership that is preferred by the group. Incongruence in leader behaviours exists.	**Outcome**	It is predicted that in these circumstances the group will perform effectively but the satisfaction of the group members will be low.
Degree of congruence	Actual leader behaviour is not the required behaviour to complete the group task successfully but is the type of leadership that is preferred by the group. Incongruence in leader behaviours exists.	**Outcome**	It is predicted that in these circumstances the group will perform ineffectively but the satisfaction of the group members will be high.

Table 3 Explanation of Multidimensional Leadership Model

The multi-dimensional model predicts that the degree of congruence between the types of leader behaviour determines one of three possible outcomes.

In order to maximise group effectiveness and satisfaction by bringing together the three types of leader behaviour, Chelladurai proposed five categories of leadership (*Leadership Scale for Sports*, Chelladurai and Saleh, 1980) (Table 4).

Category of leadership	Explanation
Training and instruction behaviour	Improving the performance of athletes through hard training and strenuous conditioning. Instruction will be given on tactics and techniques.
Democratic behaviour	The leader allows group members to become involved in decision making with regard to strategies, practice methods and group goals.
Autocratic behaviour	As seen previously, autocratic behaviour is task-centred and the decisions are made by the leader without group consultation.
Social support behaviour	Concern is displayed by the leader for the welfare of individual group members. This behaviour is characterised by warm relations with individual members.
Rewarding behaviour	Positive feedback rewards good individual and group performance. This behaviour reinforces the value of cohesion.

Table 4 Five categories of leadership (Chelladurai and Saleh, 1980)

Supported by the research of Smoll and Smith (1984), Chelladurai concluded that the satisfaction of young people in particular was promoted by leaders and coaches who demonstrated behaviours reflecting reward, personal development, and training and instruction. This will increase the likelihood of young people adopting a balanced, active and healthy lifestyle.

Fig 9.8 Leaders who support, reward and facilitate learning will, on the evidence of Chelladurai, increase the satisfaction of young people. The adoption of an active, healthy and balanced lifestyle is therefore a stronger possibility

STRETCH AND CHALLENGE

With reference to the multi-dimensional model of leadership, explain the achievement of optimal performance and satisfaction by a group of sports performers. To access case studies from the BBC Sport Academy website, go to www.heinemann.co.uk/hotlinks, enter the express code 6855P and click on the relevant link.

Social facilitation and inhibition

Most sports or physical activities take place in the company of other people, either in the form of spectators or **co-actors**. It is well documented that the presence of other people influences the performance of the individual.

KEY TERM

Co-actors

Fellow performers in the form of opponents, team mates or people in the same exercise group or Physical Education class.

The immediate effect of the presence of an audience is to increase the arousal level of the athlete. An increase in arousal can have either a positive or a negative influence on performance. Many factors determine the effects of arousal on performance.

REMEMBER

The factors that determine the possible influence of arousal on an individual performance are personality, stage of learning, type of skill and level of experience. You might wish to review your AS work on motivation; see Chapter 8 part 1 in *OCR AS PE SB*.

When arousal, stimulated by the presence of an audience, is positive and performance is as a result enhanced, social facilitation is said to have taken place. Conversely, social inhibition is the term given when audience-induced arousal has a negative effect on performance.

TASK 3

Using your knowledge of arousal theories, discuss the circumstances when performance could be facilitated by the presence of others. Discuss also the variables which are likely, in the presence of an audience, to result in social inhibition and thus impinge upon performance and participation in an active lifestyle.

The influence of an audience on performance is well documented. Triplett's application to cyclists in 1898 is thought to be the first example of research in the field of what was to become sports psychology. Much of the current belief relating to audience effects is based around two psychological theories. These theories are:

- drive theory of social facilitation (Zajonc, 1965)
- evaluation apprehension theory (Cottrell, 1968).

DRIVE THEORY OF SOCIAL FACILITATION

In his model of drive theory of social facilitation, Zajonc (1965) recognised different types of audience. These are shown in the model below (Figure 9.9).

Fig 9.9 Zajonc's model of the drive theory of social facilitation

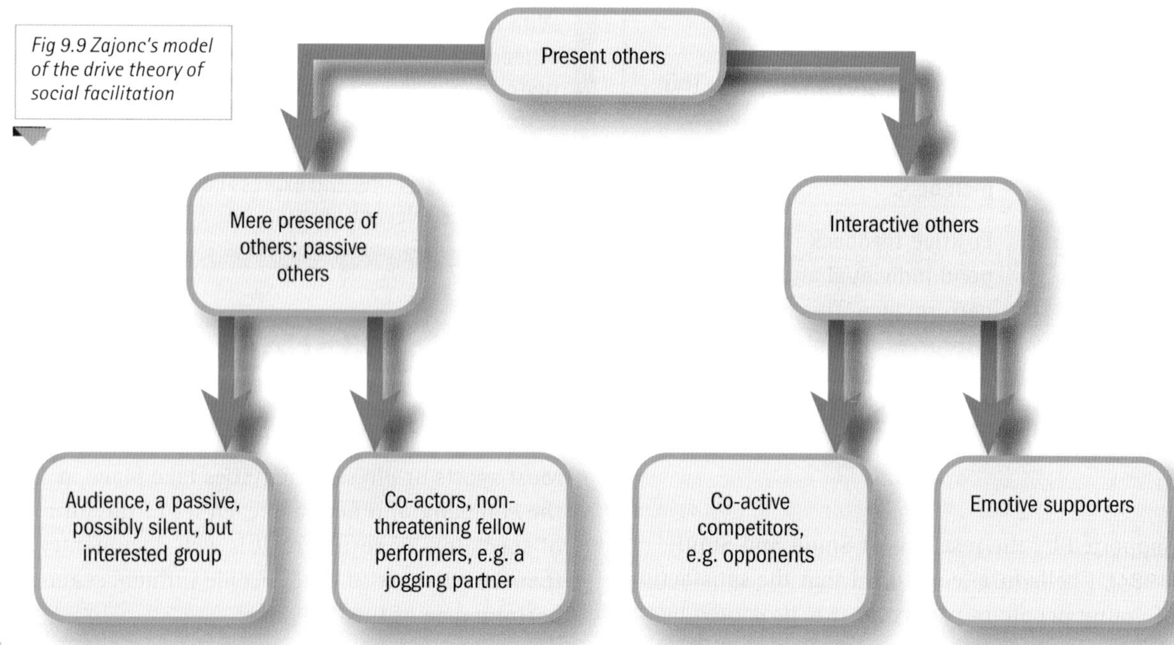

Our interest lies with 'passive others', as Zajonc believed that the 'mere presence' of other people is sufficient to increase the arousal level of the performer. He used drive theory to predict the effect of others on performance.

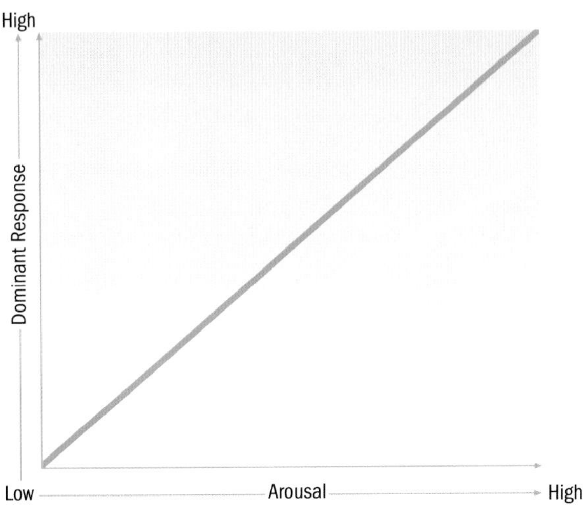

Fig 9.10 Arousal levels in relation to dominant response

Drive theory indicates a relationship between arousal and performance.

- Zajonc proposed that the presence of others in itself is arousing and that arousal enhances the production of **dominant responses** as opposed to subordinate responses.
- Actions that have been already learned are termed 'learned behaviours' and tend to be our dominant responses.

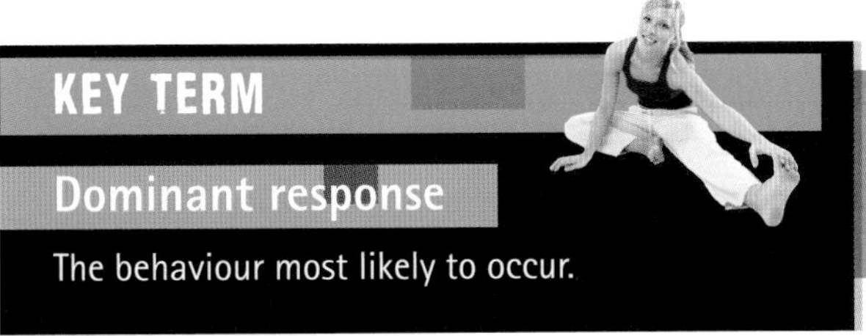

KEY TERM

Dominant response

The behaviour most likely to occur.

High arousal would be beneficial at the expert stage (autonomous phase of learning) because the performer's dominant behaviour would tend towards the correct response. In addition, high arousal facilitates the performance of simple and ballistic skills that are classified as gross.

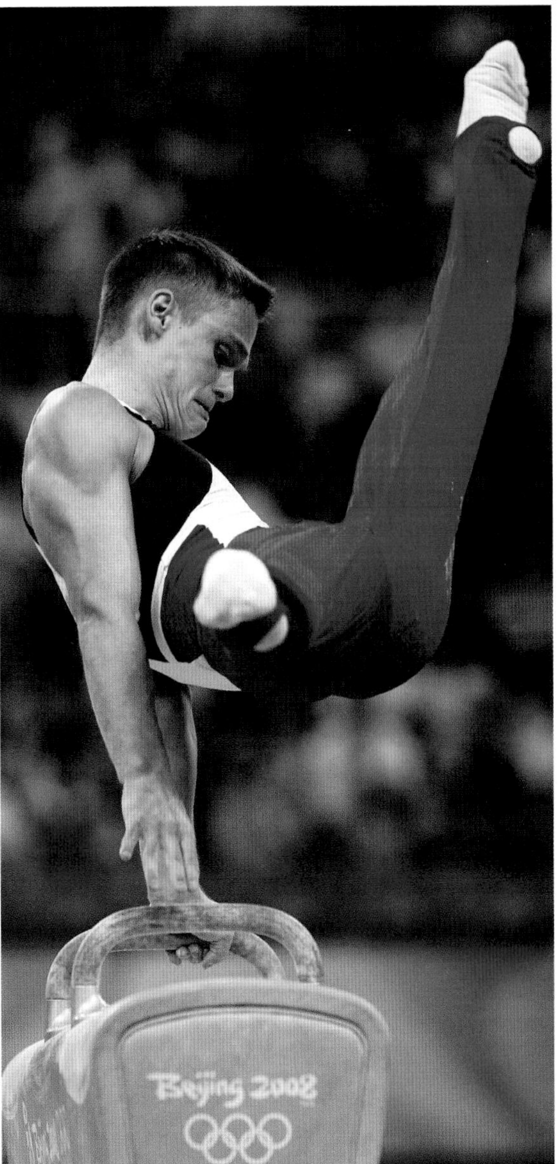

Fig 9.11 J. May (2000) reported that increased arousal impeded the fine motor control required on the pommel horse, but improved the more explosive movement required for the vault

At the novice stage of performance (associative stage of learning), however, the dominant behaviour is likely to be incorrect. High arousal would therefore cause mistakes and thus inhibit performance.

Zajonc's drive theory of social facilitation is supported by the belief that arousal caused by an audience is a natural (innate) reaction.

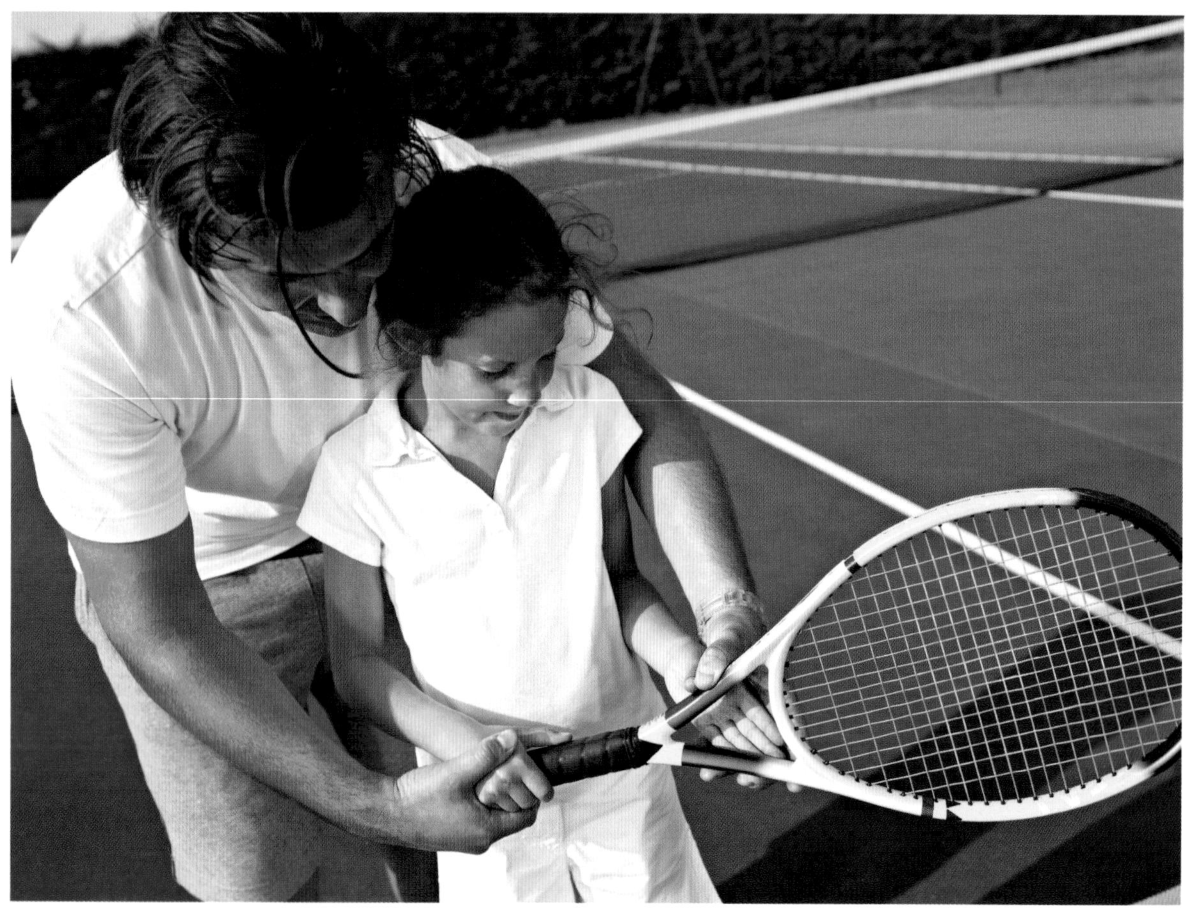

Fig 9.12 The presence of an audience will inhibit the performance of fine motor skills that are still in the process of being learned

Martens (1969) confirmed Zajonc's predictions that the presence of an audience increased arousal and that this impaired the learning of complex skills and facilitated the performance of tasks that had been overlearned (grooved).

A drawback with the drive theory of social facilitation is that Zajonc believed that the presence of the audience and of co-actors had the same effect on sports performance. Landers and McCullage (1976) challenged this assumption. They proposed that sports skills were learned more effectively by an individual when in the presence of co-actors who were also learners but of 'slightly superior ability'. The learning of motor skills therefore can be enhanced by the presence of co-actors while the attention of an audience will inhibit learning. If skill levels can be improved, there is a greater likelihood that sport will become a permanent feature in a person's lifestyle.

EVALUATION APPREHENSION

Cottrell (1968) questioned the belief held by Zajonc that the mere presence of others did in fact raise arousal levels. He proposed that just the 'mere presence' of others was not sufficiently arousing to produce the social facilitation effect. Increases in arousal, according to Cottrell, were only evident when the performer perceived that the audience was assessing or judging a performance. Hence Cottrell's theory was termed 'evaluation apprehension'. It could be the case that the perceived evaluation of the audience inhibits performance. Some athletes may, however, rely upon evaluation to stimulate arousal. Evaluation may therefore have a facilitating effect.

TASK 4

The effects of evaluation apprehension will facilitate or inhibit performance. Discuss the situations in which performance could be enhanced and those when it is likely to deteriorate when the athlete perceives that their skills are being judged.

It is important to be aware of three further theories that relate to the facilitation or the inhibition of performance due to the presence of an audience. These theories must be considered when helping an athlete to cope with audience effects.

THE HOME ADVANTAGE EFFECT

Large supportive home crowds are believed to provide the home team with an advantage and this is known as the home advantage effect. This effect is a very powerful influence and it appears to become stronger as the size of the audience increases (Nevill and Cann, 1998).

PROXIMITY EFFECT

Schwartz (1975) proposed that location of the audience in relation to performance was an important factor in social facilitation. It appears that the performers will experience the effect more intensely if the audience is close. This phenomenon is most evident in indoor sports such as ice hockey and basketball. The proximity of the audience may have either a facilitating or an inhibitory influence. Once again, the outcome is determined not only by the type of skill that is to be performed but also by the personality, stage of learning and level of experience of the athlete.

DISTRACTION – CONFLICT THEORY

More recently, Baron (1986) proposed that the limitations of the performer's attentional capacity can explain the effect of an audience. The models of information-processing indicate that attention can only be given to a limited number of environmental cues. Baron proposed that spectators demand the same amount of attention as would data from the sports situation. This added distraction is yet more competition for attentional space. He concluded that simple tasks requiring little attention are performed best in front of an audience while under similar conditions complex actions would be impaired.

STRATEGIES TO COMBAT THE EFFECTS OF SOCIAL INHIBITION IN PRACTICAL ACTIVITIES

It is important that athletes are able cope with the presence of an audience or large crowd.

- Selective attention would narrow the focus of the performer onto the relevant cues.
- Mental rehearsal and imagery could enhance concentration and help to block out the audience, which can be the source of inhibition.
- The athlete would be advised to engage in positive self-talk to block out negative thoughts that may have been induced by the presence of an audience.
- Practice could be undertaken in the presence of an audience and this would help the athlete to become accustomed to the effects spectators may have on arousal levels.
- The performer should ensure that skills are over-learned and have become grooved to become dominant behaviours. It must be remembered that when arousal increases, dominant responses emerge.
- Confidence-building strategies should be implemented as high self-efficacy will reduce inhibition.
- Positive reinforcement and social support from the coach and team mates will reduce anxiety that may be experienced when performing for an audience.

- Confidence could also be increased by appropriate use of attribution.
- The athlete should be made aware of how concentration is maximised when the ideal level of arousal is achieved.

At the beginning of this chapter, it was said that most sports or physical activities take place in the company of other people, either in the form of spectators or co-actors. With this in mind it is important to prevent the negative effects of social inhibition in order to encourage people to participate. Prevention is achieved by controlling the excessive arousal often experienced when performing for an audience. If control is accomplished, an individual is more likely to feel comfortable in the performance environment and commit to following a balanced, active and healthy lifestyle.

Exam Café

Relax, refresh, result!

Refresh your memory

You should now have knowledge and understanding of:

- groups and teams – their impact upon performance and the pursuit of balanced, active and healthy lifestyles
- leadership and the role of a leader in physical activities
- social facilitation and inhibition – the effects of an audience and other participants on performance and lifestyle behaviours.

REVISE AS YOU GO!

1. What is group cohesion?
2. Outline Steiner's model of group performance.
3. List the factors that prevent the formation of cohesion.
4. Outline the strategies that promote group cohesion.
5. Explain social identity theory (Tajfel, 1978).
6. List the qualities of a good leader.
7. What is an emergent and what is a prescribed leader?
8. Define the terms social facilitation and social inhibition.
9. Explain evaluation apprehension.
10. Identify the factors that combat the effects of social inhibition.

Try to answer these questions yourself. Ask your teacher if you need help.

Get the result!

Examination question

A cohesive group or team can affect an individual's behaviour and the extent to which an individual follows an active and healthy lifestyle.

What is meant by the term social loafing and how would you, as coach, limit the effects of social loafing in order to improve the cohesiveness of your team? (5 marks)

Examiner's tips

This is a very common question and is often completed successfully by exam candidates. The capacity to answer this question is dependent on the understanding of Steiner's model of group cohesion.

Student answer

Social loafing means that a team player is not pulling their weight during a game. It is easier to loaf in games with high numbers in the team like hockey than in a team of five in basketball.

Examiner says:

It is obvious that you understand social loafing but what does 'pulling their weight' mean. This statement is vague.

I would make sure that the team attended lots of social events because then they would get on well with each other and this would reduce social loafing. I would keep statistics of individual performances and point out those who are loafing at the end of the game. I would give prizes to the player who worked hardest during the season, for example player of the season award. I would practice moves in training so that everyone has clear roles and cannot be left out. Finally, I would attribute winning to team cohesiveness.

Examiner says:

Not strictly true. Social cohesion does not guarantee task cohesion.

Examiner says:

Good to include the example.

Examiner says:

Possibly three marks here. Your writing is tedious because every point begins with or contains reference to 'I'.

Improved student answer

Social loafing refers to a loss of personal responsibility and occurs as a result of an individual player losing motivation and withdrawing effort in a team game situation. It would appear that the 'loafing' player is coasting and relying upon the efforts of others.

Examiner says:

A strong definition of social loafing is provided. Technical language is used to good effect.

Social loafing is almost impossible to eliminate completely but its effects can be minimised.

Examiner says:

This statement is true and although it cannot be credited, it gives a base from which the answer can be given.

Players who are less likely to 'loaf' should be preferred in selection and it would be in the best interests of team cohesiveness to select those with the interests of the team at heart. Credit should be given to the individual player and any good play should be positively reinforced. Appropriate goals should be set and emphasised for each individual while individual roles should be clarified. The persistent social loafer could be punished, for example dropped from the team, while team building exercises would encourage social support and friendship groups thus reducing the likelihood of withdrawing effort. Strong leadership in the competitive situation would encourage individual players to sustain effort and do much to develop group cohesion and a team bond. In this context, task as opposed to social cohesion has proved to be more efficient in giving a team a shared purpose. Finally, to limit the effects of social loafing, the coach could practice strategies and rehearse set plays during training, for example a three-player block in volleyball.

Examiner says:

Eight factors are given to reduce social loafing and improve group cohesiveness. Examples are provided. This answer is concise.

CHAPTER 10:

Mental preparation for physical activities

LEARNING OBJECTIVES

By the end of this chapter you should have knowledge and understanding of:

- goal setting as it impacts upon performance and the development and the sustaining of a balanced, active and healthy lifestyle
- self-confidence and its impact on performance and participation in physical activity and in raising self-esteem
- attentional control and its impact upon effective performance
- emotional control and its impact upon performance and in sustaining a balanced, active and healthy lifestyle.

INTRODUCTION

The **perception** formed by an individual of their own ability to succeed during **performance** is the major factor that determines both **participation** and **persistence** in the task and the ultimate achievement of an overall aim. Self-esteem is enhanced by a positive self-perception and in turn this would encourage a person to commit to an active and healthy lifestyle.

KEY TERMS

Perception

A cognitive process that interprets sensory input from the environment.

Performance

The level of competence demonstrated during engagement in activities or tasks.

Participation

Commitment and engagement in a task or activity.

Persistence

To sustain commitment and engagement when difficulties or failures are encountered.

Goal setting

Goal setting can develop positive self-perception and reduce the anxiety that may arise prior to and during performance. The correct use of goal setting can facilitate optimal performance by improving the confidence and increasing the motivation level of the athlete.

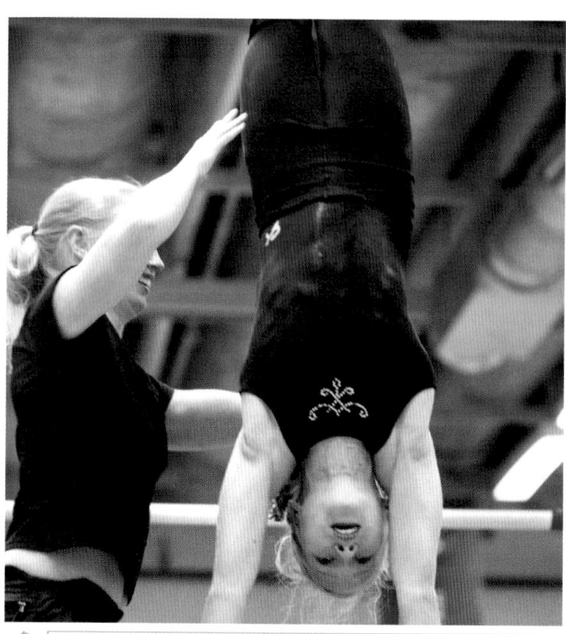

Fig 10.1 Goal setting stimulates participation, encourages persistence and improves performance by raising confidence and increasing motivation

Lock and Latham (1990) suggest that goal setting influences performance in four ways:

1 It directs the attention of the performer onto the required task or strategy.
2 It increases the effort applied by the athlete.
3 It improves persistence when a task becomes difficult or when failure is experienced.
4 The participant becomes increasingly motivated to learn and to apply different approaches to learning in order to complete a task successfully.

Goals are not automatically effective and it can be much easier to set goals than to make them work effectively. As a guide to the correct implementation of goal setting, the application of the SMARTER principle is important (see Table 1).

A critical evaluation of goal types

Goals can be divided into two groups: time-based and activity-based.

TIME-BASED GOALS: 1) LONG-TERM GOALS

A long-term goal is an ultimate aim which may take an extended period of time to complete and achieve. Getting selected by the county rugby squad or changing one's lifestyle by significantly improving health and fitness are examples of long-term goals. Major changes in behaviour, however, cannot be achieved immediately through the pursuit of long-term goals. When set on their own, long-term goals may appear as daunting

Identification of the key letter		Explanation of the key word
S	Specific	Goals should relate directly to the task, for example a netball shooter may adopt a goal to improve the rate of conversion success from 60 per cent to 75 per cent. Specific goals are more effective than non-specific or 'do your best' goals. An example of a non-specific goal would be a shooter in netball trying to improve the rate of conversion with no measurable target.
M	Measurable	Goals should be evaluated and measured against a previous performance or external standard.
A	Accepted	To be effective a goal must be agreed or accepted both by the coach and by the performer.
R	Realistic	Goals should be challenging but attainable. The attainment of a goal which is perceived as challenging develops confidence and motivates the athlete to aim at the next goal.
T	Timed	A time limit should be set to achieve the goal. Consideration must be given, therefore, as to whether the goal is of short, intermediate or long duration.
E	Exciting	Excitement is generated when an accepted goal provides challenge. The stimulation of excitement will offset the possibility of boredom.
R	Recorded	Achievement of or progress toward a target should be written into a log and recorded. (Some coaches use the saying, 'ink it, don't think it.') Recording the attainment of goals can in itself be exciting and motivating.

Table 1 The SMARTER principle

targets to the performer, causing unnecessary increases in anxiety. The implementation of a programme of long-term goals on its own does not improve performance.

2) SHORT-TERM GOALS

Short-term goals are intended to give immediate success and are set initially at the level of the performer's existing capability. Short-term goals are completed in a sequence that becomes progressively more difficult. They form a link between the athlete's initial capability and the long-term goal of achievement. Short-term goals can be useful, therefore, in the attainment of long-term goals. Jarvis (2006) reported that research has found that the most effective goals are short-term.

3) MEDIUM-TERM GOALS

Intermediate or medium-term goals occur during the short-term goal sequence. While they also improve access to long-term goals, intermediate goals endorse the effectiveness of short-term goals and are more significant improvement indicators.

ACTIVITY-BASED GOALS

The three types of activity-based goals are described in the table below. They are known as performance, process and product goals.

A total focus on product goals can create anxiety during competition as the athlete is required to win in order to achieve the goal. Anxiety may cause unnecessary worry about the final outcome, causing the performer to become distracted from the task.

Product goals are also often controlled not by the athlete but by external factors and are therefore another source of anxiety. Winning, for example, is frequently determined by the external factors of task difficulty and luck.

EXAM TIP

Performance goals, process goals and product goals occur frequently in exam questions.

It would appear that the most effective way to improve performance and commitment to participation is to set both performance and process goals. These goals give more control to the participant and are good indicators of an athlete's commitment to training and competition. Performance goals are better than product goals (Cox, 1998).

Goals of all descriptions are more effective in competitive sport when set as formal targets by a coach. To ensure maximum benefit, however, goals that are dictated by the coach must first be negotiated with and agreed by the athlete.

Type of goal	Explanation
Performance goals	Based on judgments made of an individual against their previous performances. An athlete may, for example, strive for a personal best performance. Performance goals are measurable; for example, a batter in cricket will try to improve upon last season's runs average.
Process goals	Concerned with improving techniques to produce a better performance, for example the batter in cricket in an attempt to improve average runs scored may work upon improving footwork during shot execution.
Product goals	Sometimes called outcome goals. Product goals involve defeating other competitors and are concerned therefore with winning outcomes. This type of goal focuses on the end result and is often externally controlled, for example winning a tennis tournament.

Table 2 The three types of activity-based goals

While agreed goals appear to improve competitive performance in sport, it would appear that goals pertaining to participation in exercise and fitness classes are markedly different in formation. Martin (1984) proposed that goals which determine **exercise adherence** should be set by the participant and ought to be flexible rather than fixed; for example, an exercise programme may need to be arranged around a busy work schedule. With this in mind, a participant may feel more comfortable and increasingly inclined to commit to a programme that allows flexibility.

REMEMBER

Attribution theory (see Chapter 8, page 212) identified the locus of causality and stability dimensions. Positive attributions help to improve confidence.

KEY TERM

Exercise adherence

Adopting an exercise regime and persisting with the activities.

APPLY IT!

Set yourself a long-term goal in your sport or exercise activity. Write down short-term goals in order to achieve your ultimate target. Consider the type of goal that you wish to achieve. Apply the SMARTER principle to your targets. Evaluate your chances of success.

It has been seen that goals need to be clearly defined and specific. Targets which are termed as 'do your best' goals are less effective than goals that can be measured objectively. Measurement will give data to the performer about the degree of success and is therefore an important source of information. Measurement will also supply the athlete with essential feedback and provide the coach with information to help set the next short-term goal.

REMEMBER

In your AS studies, it was said that feedback was most effective when accompanied by the setting of a new goal. (See *OCR AS PE SB*, Chapter 7, page 178.)

Goals of 'moderate difficulty' lead to the production of best performance (Kyllo and Landers, 1995). If perceived as too easy, the goal will not sustain the interest of the performer, while a goal of extreme difficulty may cause frustration.

Goals, when set correctly, are actions that give the participant control and empowerment. As a result, according to Bandura (1977), an individual develops a greater sense of '**self-efficacy**'.

Product goals are not always detrimental. While on their own they can inhibit performance, they should not be discounted. It must be remembered that by nature the outcome of many sporting activities require the emergence of an obvious winner. There is a case, therefore, that product goals should be a part of performance preparation. It is recommend that a combination of goal types should be incorporated into preparation and that for every product goal there should be a number of performance and process goals set for the athlete (Filby *et al.*, 1999).

Fig 10.2 Short-term goals must be specific, measurable and link progressively to long-term goals. They must also be negotiated with the participant

EXAM TIP

The SMARTER principle is a popular exam question. You need to be able to identify and explain the SMARTER principle and six types of goals. Goal setting must be applied to the development of an active, healthy and balanced lifestyle.

A critical evaluation of goal types could be a Stretch and Challenge 20-mark question.

REMEMBER

Review the work on achievement motivation in Chapter 8, page 208. The person with high need to achieve (approach behaviour) experiences greatest motivation when there is a 50 per cent chance of success. Under these conditions, the incentive value associated with success is high, thus encouraging commitment to participation, greater persistence and better performance.

Self-confidence and its impact on performance and participation and in raising self-esteem

SELF-CONFIDENCE

The term self-esteem has appeared frequently throughout this Sports Psychology section. Self-esteem refers to a consistent degree of confidence that a person displays across a wide range of situations. Self-confidence describes, therefore, a general disposition which is both stable (relatively unchanging) and global (far-reaching and inclusive).

Self-confidence influences motivation and is therefore a factor that determines the decision to participate in a chosen physical activity. Bandura (1977) proposed that as participants become competent in specific skills they develop a positive self-belief that they can excel in that particular skill. A person who has acquired this positive self-belief is said to have high **self-efficacy**.

KEY TERM

Self-efficacy

Specific self-confidence arising from the perception of a person about their standard of ability in particular activities and situations.

SELF-EFFICACY

Self-efficacy is a specific type of self-confidence and relates to a person's perception of their standard of ability, in particular activities and situations. It tends to be unstable and is therefore changeable.

A rugby player, for example, may have high self-efficacy producing a confident and committed performance for much of the game. The same person, however, may have low self-efficacy in the specific skill of goal kicking and therefore avoid involvement in this area.

According to Bandura, people with high self-efficacy tend to adopt approach behaviour, seek challenges and persevere with tasks. They also tend to attribute success to internal factors that relate directly to themselves, such as ability and effort. These attributions would elevate confidence and increase the expectation of success during the next challenge. Self-efficacy can, therefore, exert a powerful influence on performance by raising the performer's expectation of success.

> 'Once extraordinary performances are shown to be achievable they become commonplace.'
>
> (Bandura, 1977)

REMEMBER

What do you remember about sport-specific motivation and the characteristics of those personalities with a high need to achieve (high Nach)? (See Chapter 8, pages 208–211.)

People with low self-efficacy tend to adopt avoidance behaviour, give up easily and become anxious when tasks become difficult. They also tend to attribute failure to internal factors. In these circumstances, by contrast, internal attributions would reduce expectation of success and induce learned helplessness.

REMEMBER

Attribution retraining was considered as a strategy to promote mastery orientation and as a way to avoid learned helplessness. (See Chapter 8, pages 213–214.)

The level of self-efficacy determines efficacy expectations, which directly influence the choice and commitment an individual makes regarding sporting activities. Most importantly, efficacy expectations can be changed by an input of four types of information. These types of information are the sub-processes in self-efficacy theory.

By applying each of the four sub-processes, the coach can change the negative expectation of those lacking in self-efficacy into positive expectation. This will increase self-efficacy.

SELF-EFFICACY THEORY

1 *Performance accomplishments*
A performer who experiences learned helplessness or a loss of confidence should be reminded of previous successes in the related skill or situation. Reinforcement of past attainments has the most powerful effects upon self-efficacy as it is based on personal mastery experiences.

2 *Vicarious experiences*
This process involves the person who lacks confidence watching others of equal ability perform the problematic skill successfully. The use of a demonstration or a model of the required behaviour reduces worry and develops confidence.

3 *Verbal persuasion*
Verbal persuasion involves convincing the athlete that they have the ability to perform the skill in question. This positive talk or persuasion is an attempt to elevate self-belief and is usually conveyed by the coach. Many successful sports players, however, also reassure themselves through 'positive self-talk' and other cognitive processes relating to stress management.

4 *Control of arousal*
This refers to the evaluation the performer makes of their internal feelings and physiological state. For example, those lacking in self-efficacy may perceive increased heart and respiration rates as symptoms of worry and nervousness and not as indicators of a positive physiological preparation for action.

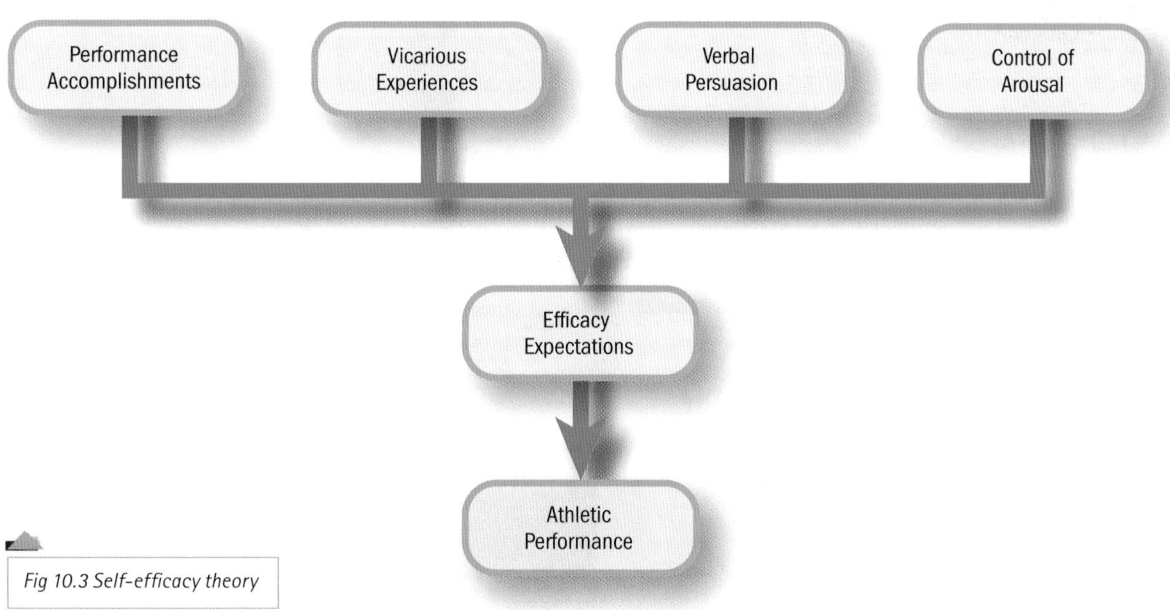

Fig 10.3 Self-efficacy theory

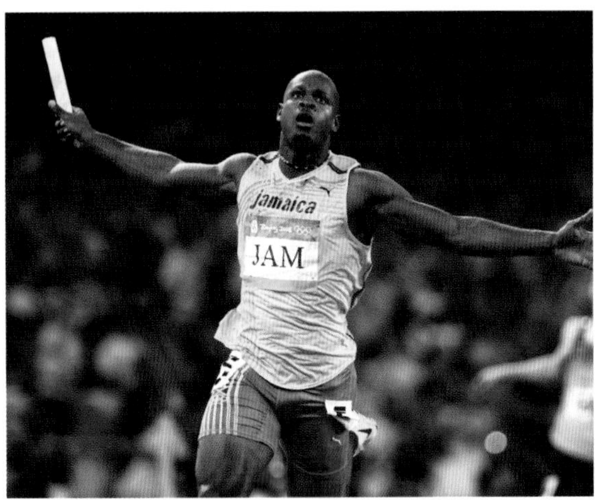

Fig 10.4 The most consistent difference between elite and less successful athletes is that elite athletes possess greater self-confidence (Gould et al., *1997)*

It is established that high self-efficacy is essential at the elite performance standard. It is equally important, however, to the development of an active and healthy lifestyle at a recreational level. While a positive attitude towards exercise does not predict participation (Dishman *et al.*, 1980), it appears that the degree of self-efficacy is the major motivating factor that encourages engagement in fitness activities.

McAuley (1992) stated that if people can develop high self-efficacy expectations in relation to exercise programmes, they are more likely to adopt and persist in healthy lifestyles by taking up physical activities.

REMEMBER

Attitudes can be changed but always remain as uncertain predictors of behaviour. (See Chapter 8, page 214).

Sports confidence theory

Sports confidence theory (Vealey, 1986) measures two factors:

- trait sports confidence (SC trait)
- state sports confidence (SC state).

Trait sports confidence (SC trait) is innate and described as a natural disposition. Like all personality traits it is relatively stable. Trait confidence is different from specific confidence as it relates to a generalised belief of an individual about the extent to which their ability will bring success across a wide range of sports. For this reason trait confidence is also global.

State sports confidence (SC state) can be developed through learning and tends to be unstable and changeable. State confidence relates to an individual's belief about the extent to which their ability will bring success at one particular moment. For this reason, state confidence is also specific to a situation.

State sports confidence directly determines the quality of the skill that is to be performed, for example a putt in golf. The degree of state sports confidence is determined by the interaction of three factors:

1 trait sports confidence
2 the **objective sports situation**
3 the performer's **competitive orientation.**

This interaction is shown in Fig 10.5 below.

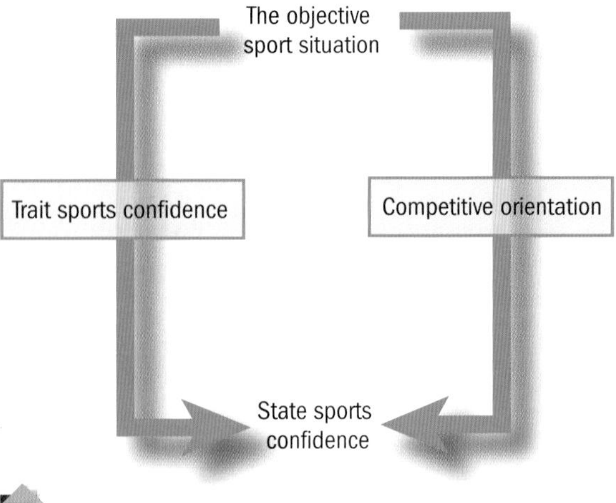

Fig 10.5 Three factors interact to determine state confidence

REMEMBER

Sport-specific confidence (competitiveness) links to Vealey's model of sport confidence.

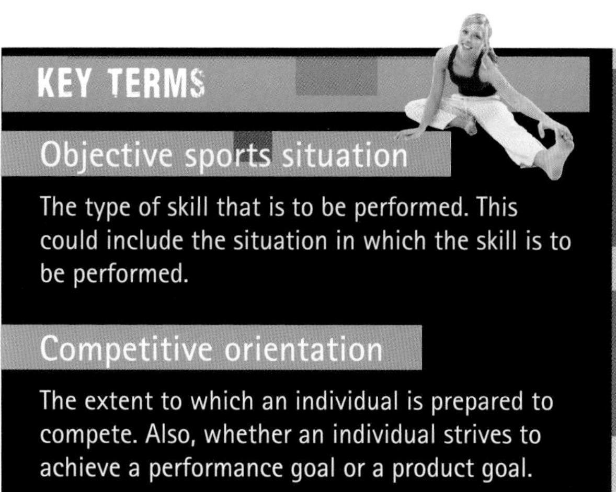

KEY TERMS

Objective sports situation

The type of skill that is to be performed. This could include the situation in which the skill is to be performed.

Competitive orientation

The extent to which an individual is prepared to compete. Also, whether an individual strives to achieve a performance goal or a product goal.

The extent to which the athlete perceives the performance has been successful is termed the subjective outcome and is shown in Fig 10.6. Subjective outcomes produce the following effects:

- An outcome perceived to be good will increase trait sports confidence and competitiveness. State confidence will also increase.
- An outcome perceived as poor will decrease trait sports confidence and competitiveness. State confidence will also decrease.

Most importantly, the variations in the levels of trait sports confidence and competitiveness orientation produce the following effects (Table 3).

A decrease in SC trait and competitiveness will:	An increase in SC trait and competitiveness will:
1 depress SC state	1 elevate SC State
2 reduce self-efficacy	2 increase self-efficacy
3 make the performer feel less confident	3 make the performer feel more confident
4 cause avoidance behaviour.	4 facilitate approach behaviour.

Table 3 Effects of variation in levels of trait sports confidence (SC trait) and competitiveness orientation

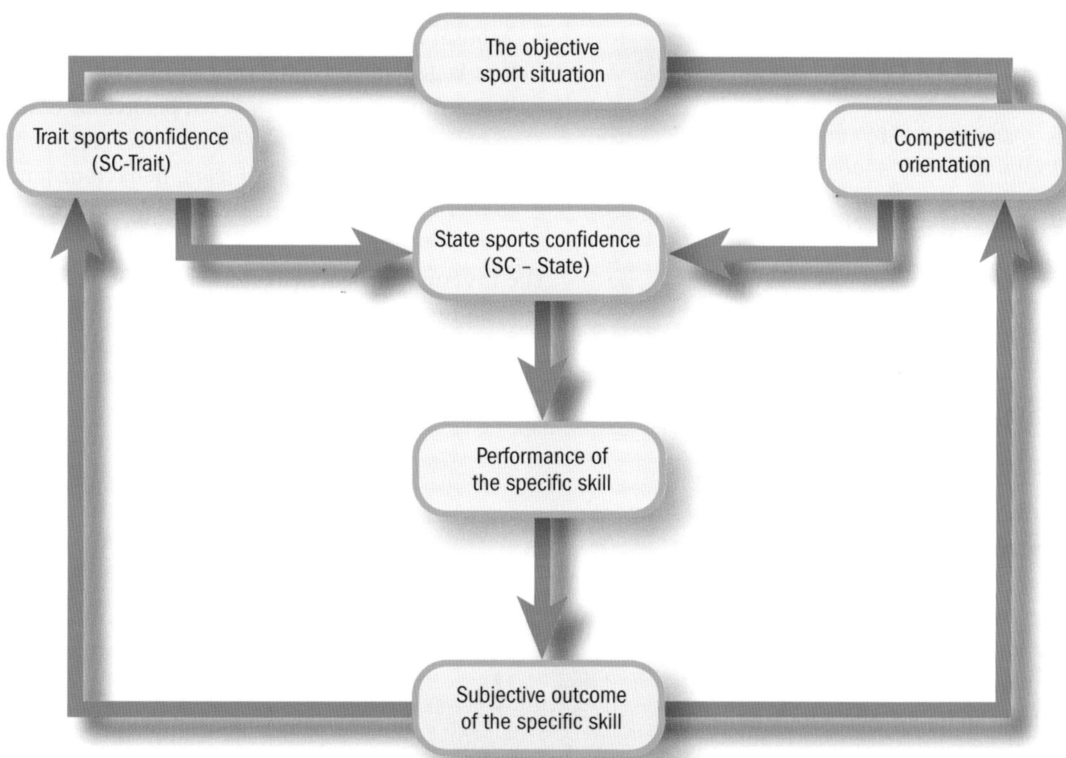

Fig 10.6 Vealey's model of sport confidence shows the formation of state sports confidence and how this type of confidence influences the outcome of a skill

Vealey identified strategies to improve state sport confidence (SC state). They are described below.

1 *Mastery of skill.* This occurs when a skill has been acquired and the performer perceives that progress has been made.
2 *Styling.* Confidence will increase if the athlete can demonstrate a highly-skilled performance to significant others.
3 *Physical and mental preparation* will increase the likelihood of successful performance.
4 *Social reinforcement.* Praise and approval by significant others, particularly in the context of strong team cohesion, will raise confidence.
5 *Effective leadership* promotes confidence in team members.
6 *Environmental comfort.* People who lack self-confidence will be helped if the working conditions are suitable, for example the novice should not be observed when learning a new skill.

Vealey proposed, by way of conclusion, that success in one sport transfers confidence into other sports.

STRETCH AND CHALLENGE

You are the coach of an elite athlete who is returning to training after a long period of injury and rehabilitation. The athlete is lacking in confidence. Discuss the strategies that could be implemented to help the athlete to regain confidence.

Attentional control

Attentional control relates to the extent to which a performer can focus awareness onto the environmental stimuli that are most relevant during an activity. The process of attending selectively to the most important environmental cues involves concentration. The capacity to maintain attentional focus until the skill has been completed indicates the length or span of concentration. Concentration or **selective attention** can be directed by external factors such as **stimulus intensity** and the presence of **warning cues.**

KEY TERMS

Selective attention

The process of focusing onto a specific cue.

Stimulus intensity

The extent to which the stimulus is dominant and distinct when compared to other stimuli.

Warning cue

A stimulus that presents itself prior to the major cue that stimulates a response. The command of 'get set', for example, is a warning cue which precedes the major cue of the gun firing to start a sprint race.

In relation to your studies, the most important determinants of attentional control are cognition and arousal.

- Cognition is the mental processes involved in acquiring knowledge, learning and understanding.
- Arousal is a level of excitement or activation that is generated by the **central nervous system.** When arousal is at a low level, behaviour tends to be lethargic and a person may feel sleepy. When arousal is at a high level, behaviour tends to be frenetic and is often extremely intense.

The Inverted U theory predicts the influence of arousal on the performance of a **motor skill.**

INVERTED U THEORY

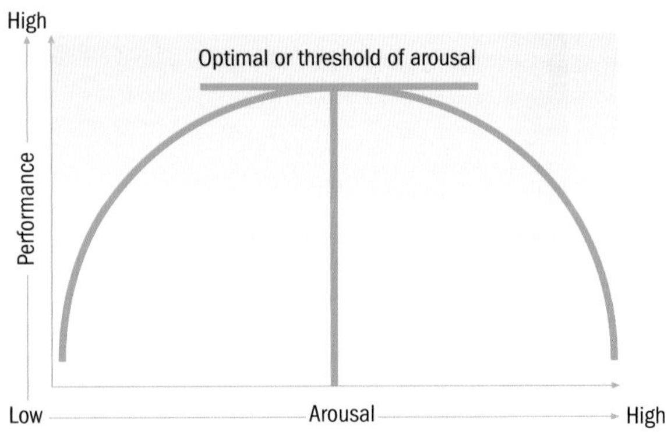

Fig 10.7 Inverted U theory

KEY TERMS

Central nervous system

Comprises the brain and spinal cord. Its main function is information processing.

Motor skill

A learned movement that is deliberately performed in order to achieve a specific aim.

The prediction made by Inverted U theory that arousal level influences performance is straightforward. The reason as to why this is the case is more complex and requires understanding of attentional control and **cue utilisation**.

TASK 1

Using your knowledge of Inverted U theory, discuss the factors that a coach should consider when preparing an athlete for performance.

REMEMBER

Inverted U hypothesis predicts that as arousal increases, so does the quality of performance, up to a critical or optimal point. If arousal continues to increase beyond this threshold, performance will deteriorate. Be aware that as circumstances change, different levels of arousal are required to facilitate performance. (See *OCR AS PE SB*, Chapter 8.1, pages 186–7.)

KEY TERM

Cue utilisation

The process that facilitates maximum attentional control, allowing efficient decision making and effective performance to take place.

CUE UTILISATION HYPOTHESIS

When arousal is low, the perceptual field of the performer widens excessively and access is given to a broad range of often irrelevant environmental cues. To focus selective attention onto the most relevant stimuli is difficult. As a result, the information-processing system is adversely affected, due to an overload of sensory stimuli, and decision making is impeded.

As arousal increases up to the optimal level, the perceptual field will adjust and narrow to the ideal width. Narrowing allows attention to be given to the most important cues only. At this optimal threshold, selective attention is fully operational and the capacity to focus and concentrate is maximised. The capacity to focus selectively is termed cue utilisation.

If arousal increases above the optimal threshold, perceptual focus narrows excessively. Excessive narrowing causes relevant data to be missed and the information-processing system becomes restricted. Effective decision making is therefore impeded. Under these conditions, the performer enters a state of panic. When arousal becomes extremely high, the performer will experience a total disorientation of their senses. This condition is termed hypervigilance.

REMEMBER

Models of information processing and how this process determines the speed and accuracy of decision making were described in *OCR AS PE SB*, Chapter 6.

Although cue utilisation describes how attentional control is maximised, it does not make clear how the performer can adjust the width and direction of attention in response to the varying situations that are encountered in sport. It is necessary, therefore, to look at attention styles as proposed by Nideffer. It is important to understand the link between attention styles and optimum arousal.

STRETCH AND CHALLENGE

Explain the cue utilisation hypothesis, its links to arousal and its effects on performance.

Attention styles

A psychologist named Nideffer presented a model of attention styles. It is based on two dimensions and is shown below.

These dimensions are:

1 width of attention, namely broad and narrow focus
2 direction of attention, namely external and internal focus.

- Broad attention takes in a great deal of environmental information and this includes peripheral cues or stimuli. Broad attention is required in an open skill situation like scanning the defence before passing in basketball.
- A narrow focus is the required concentration on one or a small number of stimuli. This will enable the performer to focus on a specific cue, for example the ball during a tennis serve.
- The broad and narrow dimension is a continuum depicting a gradual change in the amount of information to be processed.

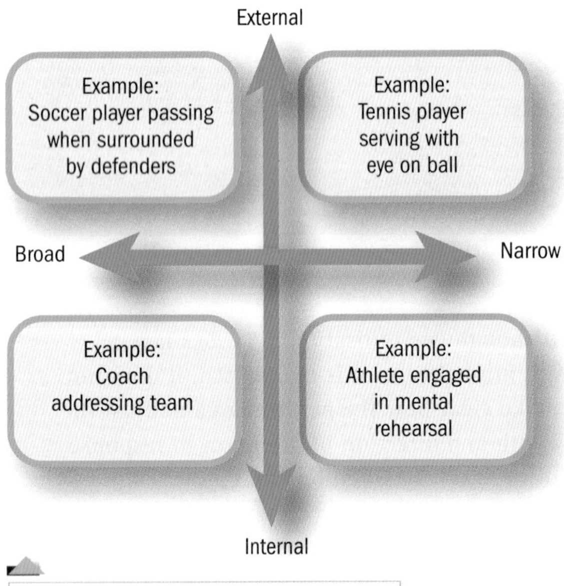

Fig 10.8 Nideffer's model of attention styles

- The external and internal dimensions indicate the direction in which attention is focused. In relation to the performer, an external focus is an outward projection onto an environmental stimulus, for example the narrow focus onto the ball when a performer is making a catch in rounders.
- An internal focus indicates that the performer's attention has been directed inwards and onto the psychological state. A person's psychological state would include thoughts, emotions and the cognitive processes that are involved in decision making.

The model of attentional styles predicts that attention has many effects on individual sport performance. External focus enables the athlete to focus on outside factors such as the position of an opponent in badminton. In addition, this focus can also help as a distraction from physical pain or fatigue such as that experienced in an endurance event like cross-country running. Novice performers tend to use external focus to disassociate from unpleasant physical sensations.

Internal focus, on the other hand, directs attention onto the psychological and physiological condition. Expert performers do not seek distraction from, for example, physical stress. They prefer to direct attention internally as information on the physical state is an important source of feedback. Internal focus also helps the performer to maximise concentration, control anxiety and access the optimal point of arousal.

It is important to understand that optimal performance can only be achieved if the performer has the ability to adopt the attention style that matches the attentional demands of the situation (Nideffer, 1976).

The correct attention style is essential at all times. Should the attention style be too broad when a single cue requires detection, for example focusing on the spinning ball when batting in cricket, information overload would result causing distraction and confusion. Reaction time would also suffer. The correct attention style can help the performer to deal with distractions. For example,

Fig 10.9 Top performers have the ability to change their attention style to match the attentional demands of the situation. This 'shift' of attention is helped by optimal arousal and cue utilisation

a narrow focus is required when a batter plays a forward defence shot in cricket as it is necessary to block out the distraction of close fielders.

Effective attention will serve to prevent negative feelings and enable the performer to make positive attributions during performance, for example the successful vault was executed because the gymnast has high ability levels (an internal, stable and positive attribution).

REMEMBER

Attribution theory (see Chapter 8, page 212) is relevant here. Positive attributions can raise confidence and increase expectation of future success.

A good performer can draw upon the full range of attention styles and this shows a link between attention control and cue utilisation. Optimal arousal and cue utilisation help a performer to change or 'shift' their attention style to match the attentional demands of the situation.

A rugby player, for example, would require broad and external attention before passing in open play, while catching a high ball would require a style which is both narrow and external. If the player is also the captain, a team talk or a tactical decision would be helped by applying an internal and broad attention style. This is because the captain would need to consider many factors relating to the game situation before committing to a decision. Finally, a narrow and internal focus would allow mental rehearsal of a skill prior to the game.

TASK 2

Within your group, set up a practice related to any chosen sport. The nature of practice must cause the performers to use each of the four attention styles. What are the other benefits of the practice that you have undertaken?

Emotional control

You have seen that arousal is a combination of physiological and psychological excitement or activation that determines the intensity of a person's behaviour. The intensity of arousal determines the responsiveness or direction of the individual's behaviour. Activation describes the state of readiness or preparedness that is directly related to the level of arousal and is frequently experienced just prior to performance.

When looking at the Inverted U hypothesis, it is also evident that the optimal point of arousal is associated with the process of cue utilisation, and the increased capacity to 'shift' attentional control makes possible the highest potential performance.

The optimal point of arousal is never the same for any two individuals. Three variables intervene to cause individual variations in the optimal point of arousal.

1 *Personality*
  Extroverts perform best at a high optimal arousal level. An introverted personality type, in contrast, would return full potential at

a low optimal point. Introverts have a very sensitive Reticular Activation System (RAS), which increases the tendency toward anxiety. Extroverts tend to seek the stimulation of the RAS and therefore perform to maximum potential when more highly aroused.

2 *Complexity of task*
Simple tasks such as shot putting tend to be gross, habitual and have a wide margin for error. These skills are best performed when the athlete has a high optimal threshold of arousal. Complex tasks are often more perceptual, manipulative and have less error tolerance. A complex task, for example, which is performed best at a low point of optimal arousal, is spin bowling in cricket.

3 *Level of ability*
The athlete at the expert or autonomous stage of learning would find that high optimal arousal would enhance performance. Those at the cognitive or associative stages, with a greater need to concentrate on basic movements, would maximise the potential to learn and perform if the optimal point of arousal is low.

In Fig 10.10, the unbroken line represents the low optimal arousal level required for one, all, or a combination of the following variables: high task complexity, low ability levels and introverted personality type. The broken line represents the high optimal arousal level required for one, all, or a combination of the following variables: low task complexity, high ability levels and extroverted personality type.

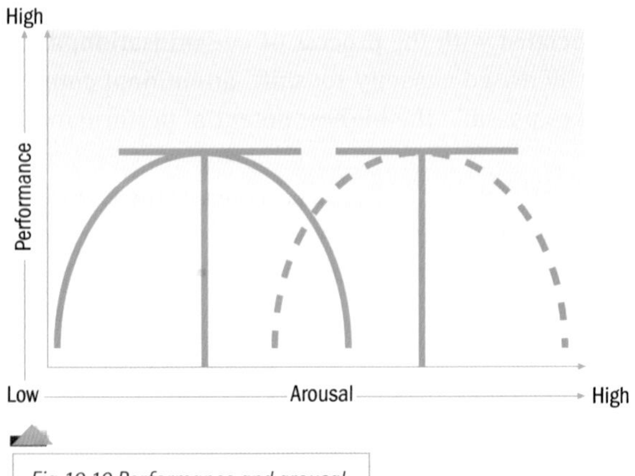

Fig 10.10 Performance and arousal

REMEMBER

The reticular activation system was described as part of the explanation of extroversion and introversion in the section on personality types; see Chapter 8, page 197–200.

ANXIETY AND PERFORMANCE

More recently, the focus has moved away from considering simply the effects of arousal on performance. The relationship between anxiety and sport performance is now considered to have overriding importance. In order to explain the influence of anxiety on performance it is necessary to firstly define and then to outline the varying nature of anxiety.

REMEMBER

Drive theory and Inverted U theory predict the effects of arousal on performance. (See *OCR AS PE SB*, Chapter 8.1, pages 185–7.)

Anxiety is a negative emotional state associated with feelings of worry and nervousness relating to activation or arousal. Confusion arises because it is usual for arousal and anxiety to be discussed together. While arousal is not experienced as either a pleasant or unpleasant sensation, anxiety is considered to be an unpleasant state of high arousal.

There are two forms of anxiety:

1 *Cognitive anxiety* is the thought component of anxiety. It is associated with worry, apprehension and the fear of negative evaluations of performance.

2 *Somatic anxiety* is the physical component and is associated with increases in heart rate and blood pressure. These are the physical symptoms of increased arousal. Somatic anxiety is triggered by cognitive anxiety.

REMEMBER

Catastrophe theory predicts that if high cognitive arousal coincides with a somatic arousal level which has just passed the optimal level, the performance of the individual will drop sharply. (See *OCR AS PE SB*, Chapter 8.1, pages 187–8.)

REMEMBER

The lack of belief experienced by the player taking the penalty is an example of learned helplessness. The performer feels that failure is inevitable and that the outcome cannot be controlled.

In addition to the somatic and cognitive dimension of anxiety, there is a second dimension relating to the stability of anxiety:

- *State anxiety* is a person's immediate condition of anxiety in any one situation. It is usually a temporary emotional response to a situation that is perceived as threatening.
- *Trait anxiety* is a general disposition to perceive certain situations as threatening. Trait anxiety is a part of personality and is relatively stable. Trait anxiety determines the degree of state anxiety that is experienced in any given situation.

STRESS

Stress also requires definition, as this term is often used interchangeably with arousal and anxiety. Stress is the trigger that stimulates increases in arousal and anxiety and typically occurs when a performer meets a demand or challenge of serious consequence with which they feel they cannot cope, for example taking a penalty in football. In this example, taking the penalty is termed a 'stressor' – the source of anxiety and arousal. Conflict, competition and frustration are other examples of stressors in the context of sport.

Long-term stress must be prevented as it will seriously impede a healthy and balanced lifestyle. However, the stimulus of stress in the short term and the subsequent onset of anxiety and arousal can, if controlled, be beneficial to performance in sport. This will be made clear by Hanin's theory of Individual Zone of Optimal Functioning (IZOF) below.

INDIVIDUAL ZONE OF OPTIMAL FUNCTIONING (IZOF)

Hanin (1986) researched specifically on the effect of anxiety on performance. He proposed that there are individual differences in the way people respond to anxiety.

After an examination of the performance of elite athletes, Hanin found that some succeeded when anxiety was low while others achieved success when anxiety was high. Hanin concluded that a general relationship between anxiety and performance did not exist but that each athlete has their own preferred level of anxiety.

As the facilitator of best performance, the preferred level of anxiety is not shown as a point or threshold, as in the Inverted U or Catastrophe theories. Rather, it is presented as band width.

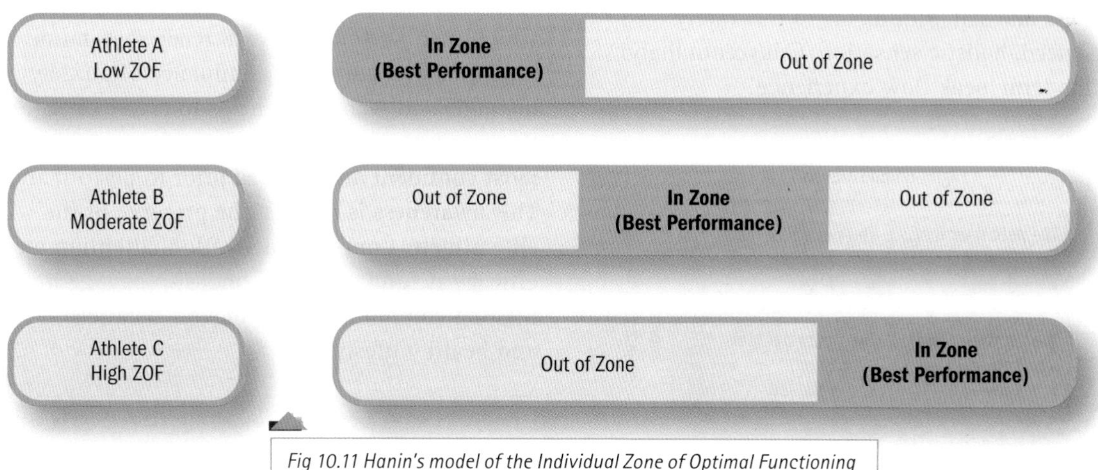

Fig 10.11 Hanin's model of the Individual Zone of Optimal Functioning

In relation to this 'band', the athlete is neither 'psyching up' to nor are they exceeding a threshold of arousal at any point in time. They are simply either within or outside of the zone of anxiety that is their individual preference.

Hanin's model of the Individual Zone of Optimal Functioning is shown in Fig 10.11.

In the example shown in Fig 10.11:

- the success of athlete A is facilitated by a preferred low zone of anxiety
- the success of athlete B is facilitated by a preferred moderate zone of anxiety
- the success of athlete C is facilitated by a preferred high zone of anxiety.

After further developments, Randle and Weinberg (1997) proposed that players in team sports have in general a preference for a lower IZOF than athletes competing in individual events.

STRETCH AND CHALLENGE

Discuss why there are individual differences in the preferred zones of optimal functioning.

PEAK FLOW

Csikszentmihalyi (1990) proposed that quality of skill is achieved when the performer is fully focused and controlled, and is being intrinsically rewarded by the movement performance. In this situation the athlete experiences greatest happiness and self-fulfilment. To this rarely experienced, holistic sensation, Csikszentmihalyi gave the term 'peak flow experience'.

High Somatic Arousal

Low cognitive Anxiety		High cognitive Anxiety
The performer feels: • Excited • Happy		The performer feels: • Anxious • Anger
The performer feels: • Lethargic • Drowsy		The performer feels: • Bored • Fatigued

Low Somatic Arousal

STRETCH AND CHALLENGE

Compare Catastrophe theory (*OCR AS PE*, Chapter 8.1, pages 187–9) with peak flow experience. A comparison can include both similarities and differences.

According to Martens (1992), peak flow experience is most likely to occur when high somatic arousal coincides with low cognitive anxiety.

Other factors can converge to facilitate peak flow experience and these appear to draw most of the Sports Psychology syllabus together. The major factors are outlined in Table 4 (see page 261).

ANXIETY MANAGEMENT TECHNIQUES

There are two types of anxiety management techniques:

1 somatic anxiety management relating to physical processes (see Table 5, page 261)
2 cognitive anxiety management relating to thought processes (see Table 6, page 262).

REMEMBER

Goal setting is a process that when implemented correctly can help to increase specific self-confidence (self-efficacy).

The athlete must be helped to develop self-awareness of the level of arousal or anxiety at which their performance will reach maximum potential. The controlling influence of anxiety management techniques helps to create or recreate the circumstances in which a participant feels most confident and focused prior to performance. This awareness is not just the preserve of the elite athlete. Control of activation, attention and efficacy is fundamental if one is to engage in a lifelong commitment to achieve a balanced, active and healthy lifestyle.

Fig 10.12 Peak flow experience occurs when conditions of high somatic arousal and low cognitive anxiety prevail

Factor facilitating peak flow	Explanation of factor
Anxiety	By controlling cognitive anxiety, the athlete has accessed their preferred zone of optimal functioning.
Concentration	Optimal arousal has been achieved while cognitive anxiety has remained low, allowing cue utilisation to operate.
Attention style	Optimal arousal and controlled anxiety levels help the athlete to match their attention style to the attentional demands of the situation.
Confidence	The athlete has developed trait confidence and high self-efficacy expectations.
Goal setting	The goal or demands of the task are perceived as moderately difficult but attainable. Success will be accompanied by a high incentive value of an intrinsic nature.
Environmental conditions	The athlete perceives the environment to be comfortable. For example, performance is facilitated by the presence of an audience, the coach provides positive feedback and applies attribution positively.
Leadership	Peak flow is more likely to be achieved when an individual is directed to a successful outcome through the process of a preferred leadership style.
Group cohesion	A common goal and good team cohesion help to promote peak flow experience.

Table 4 Factors facilitating peak flow experience

Technique	Description	Critical evaluation of technique
Biofeedback	This technique involves the measurement of physical changes that happen to the body when arousal and anxiety increase. Accurate measurements of changes in heart rate, blood pressure and skin temperature can be taken once it is known that a performer is becoming anxious. Once these changes are being monitored, it is thought that the performer can control the physiological effects of excessive anxiety and adopt a calmer state.	• There is strong evidence that biofeedback is effective in improving performance (Petruzello, 1991). • However, physiological indicators of relaxation are different in each individual, so it is necessary to be aware of variations before the extent of arousal can be assessed. • Biofeedback should not be used without knowing the athlete is over-aroused, as there is no need to reduce the arousal of a person who is already relaxed. • A biofeedback technique takes up time and often requires sophisticated equipment, therefore may not be practical prior to performance.
Progressive Muscular Relaxation (PMR)	This technique, devised by Jacobson in 1929, requires the athlete to increase the tension of the muscles throughout the body and gradually relax each group in turn.	• Many studies have proved that PMR helps relaxation. • It would appear, however, that PMR is only successful when used alongside other relaxation techniques (Cox, 1998). • A major disadvantage with this technique is that it is time-consuming, taking between 30 and 45 minutes to complete.

Table 5 Somatic anxiety management techniques

Technique	Description	Critical evaluation of technique
Imagery	Imagery can be used to help relaxation and focus. It can take two forms: 1 External imagery is when the athlete can picture themselves performing the task successfully. 2 Internal imagery is the mental rehearsal of skills and techniques. It focuses on specific elements of the skill without picturing the whole scene, for example a pass in football can be rehearsed without envisaging other players.	1 External imagery is a very effective technique if the athlete can form the outside picture of performance. However, the athlete must be a skilled and experienced performer if the picture is to be of value. 2 Mental rehearsal is productive because it is thought to stimulate the nervous system and the muscles in a way that replicates the real situation. This kinaesthetic experience can help both learning and confidence. Mental rehearsal can also help to desensitise the performer to the anxiety caused by competitive situations. Mental rehearsal however, is most effective for those at the autonomous stage of learning who can associate the correct kinaesthetic feel of the skill to the correct outcome.
Thought stopping	This technique requires the athlete to refuse to think negatively. Any negative inclination should be stopped and substituted with a positive thought.	Thought stopping may be more effective if a person is inclined to be both confident and extroverted. Individuals with introverted tendencies and those prone to learned helplessness may find difficulty in stopping negative thoughts.
Positive self-talk	Positive self-talk involves the athlete endorsing their own ability or progress by literally talking to him or herself. This is common practice among tennis players and batters facing confidence-threatening situations in cricket.	Speaking aloud commits the athlete to the task and does much to raise confidence. However, positive self-talk is only of value if performers are of a high standard and are experienced.
Rational thinking	It is thought (Martens, 1975) that anxiety grows from an imbalance of perception between ability and situational demands. Rational thinking involves focusing inwardly on the internal and narrow style of attention and evaluating the situation and its possible logical consequences.	Rational thinking works effectively if the athlete has the experience and skill to evaluate a situation realistically. The inexperienced athlete would be unable to make a rational evaluation.

Table 6 Cognitive anxiety techniques

Exam Café

Relax, refresh, result!

Refresh your memory

You should now have knowledge and understanding of:

- goal setting as it impacts upon performance and the development and the sustaining of a balanced, active and healthy lifestyle
- self-confidence and its impact on performance and participation in physical activity and in raising self-esteem
- attentional control and its impact upon effective performance
- emotional control and its impact upon performance and in sustaining a balanced, active and healthy lifestyle.

REVISE AS YOU GO!

1. List the key terms that make up the SMARTER principle.
2. Identify three goals that are determined by time.
3. Explain the meaning of performance, process and product goals.
4. List the four sub-processes of self-efficacy theory.
5. What is competitive orientation?
6. Explain the process of cue utilisation.
7. Draw, label and explain Nideffer's model of attention styles.
8. List the factors that cause the optimal point of arousal to differ.
9. Define the terms arousal, anxiety and stress.
10. List six anxiety management techniques.

Try to answer these questions yourself. Ask your teacher if you need help.

Get the result!

Examination question

Interpret Vealey's model of sports confidence by using examples from sport.

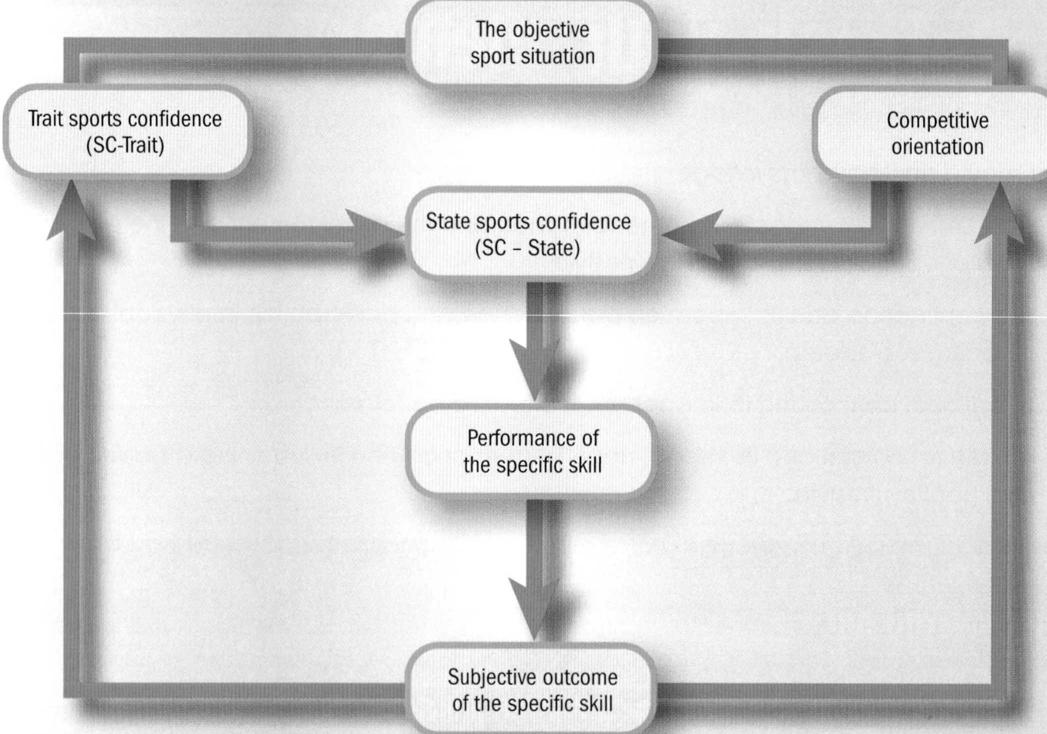

Drawing on your knowledge and understanding of sports psychology, examine the methods you might use to raise the levels of confidence of a sports performer. (20 marks)

Examiner's tips

A Stretch and Challenge question such as the one above draws together a large area of the syllabus. For example, after interpreting Vealey's model, attention must be given to self-efficacy and it is relevant to include goal setting and attribution as methods to raise the levels of confidence of a sports performer.

Student answer

The sports confidence model was presented by Vealey. There are three things that make up the mode. These things are trait confidence, the objective situation and competition orientation. Trait confidence is how confident you feel overall. The objective situation is the situation which can be measured, for example the long jump, and competitive orientation is how competitive you are in all sports.

These factors determine state sport confidence, which is how confident you feel in a specific situation, for example you might feel very confident as a bowler but not as a batter in cricket. State confidence explains the subjective outcome.

If the subjective outcome is good, trait confidence will improve. If trait confidence improves, state confidence will go up.

There is another confidence theory written by Bandura called self-efficacy theory. This just improves confidence in one area, for example serving in tennis. There are four factors to improve your confidence in this theory.

There are other ways to improve confidence. The coach could praise you and set goals for you, for example set a goal to achieve a personal best and then say to you well done. If you are not confident you will develop learned helplessness and give up. You will then not be a physically active person.

Examiner says:

Avoid using the word 'things'. Technical language must be applied.

Examiner says:

The example is not accurate and definitions of the components of Vealy's model are missing.

Examiner says:

The explanation is apparent and the example is good. The word 'you' is not a good expression to use in an examination answer.

Examiner says:

Good to identify the theory and the example is fine, but the components of self-efficacy have not been identified.

Examiner says:

These factors are correct but the expression is poor and technical language is missing. The use of the word 'your' is tedious.

Examiner says:

Good to include technical vocabulary but links have not been made with engaging in physical activity.

Examiner says:

Written communication is well below the standard. Errors, however, are not intrusive.

Improved student answer

The model of sports confidence proposed by Vealey indicates how trait sports confidence (SC trait) can be increased. Trait confidence is the generalised belief held by an individual about the extent to which their ability will bring success across a wide range of sports, for example competence may be shown in aquatic activities and racquet and invasion games. Trait confidence, furthermore, is believed to be global and relatively stable.

Examiner says:

A good start is made by directly addressing the question and the purpose of the model.

Example is given.

Self efficacy theory (Bandura) also proposes to increase confidence. Self-efficacy theory, by way of contrast to Vealey's model, addresses not global confidence but the raising of specific self-confidence. Specific self-confidence relates to the perception of a person about their standard of ability in particular activities and situations. For example, a highly confident rugby player may have considerably less confidence or low self-efficacy in the role of goal kicker. Specific self-confidence is unstable and therefore changeable.

Examiner says:

Good to mention other theories as the question asks for methods to raise confidence levels.

Example is given.

To interpret Vealey's model it is necessary to explain the initial interaction of three components.

Examiner says:

Direct address of question.

Trait sport confidence is thought to be innate and is a reflection of underlying sports potential. The objective sports situation refers to the activity or skill that is to be undertaken, for example a putt stroke in golf. Competitive orientation indicates the level of competitiveness at which the performer will operate. One example of interaction is that a performer with high trait confidence is likely to approach most objective sport situations with a high degree

Examiner says:

Interpretation is now underway with an example. Interaction is also exemplified.

of competitiveness. This disposition is a reflection of a high need to achieve personality in sport specific achievement motivation and is associated with people who are physically active.

[E]xaminer says:
[R]eference to physically [a]ctive life.

The integration of the three factors identified determines the level of state sport confidence (SC state). State confidence describes the confidence with which the athlete will approach the specific sports situation, for example taking a penalty kick in football. State confidence, furthermore, directly influences the behavioural response, which is the competence of skill execution, for example how well the ball is struck and placed during the penalty shot.

Examiner says:
Example included.

As the result of the behavioural response being forthcoming, the performer will make judgements as to the quality and overall success of the action. This judgement is often a personal interpretation and is therefore regarded to be a subjective outcome; for example, an outcome in which the penalty shot first hits the goalpost before entering the net may be attributed to luck by some players and to great ability by others. Those making positive attributions such as ability are likely to be confident high achievers who enjoy the challenges of physical activity.

[E]xaminer says:
[E]xample included.

When judged negatively, a subjective outcome will depress SC state confidence and cause avoidance behaviour. On the other hand, outcomes perceived as good will increase trait sport confidence (SC trait) and promote competitive orientation. In addition, state sport confidence (SC state) will be elevated and there will be an increase in self-efficacy.

Examiner says:
Note the link with attribution, high achievers and physical activity.

As the player becomes more confident, it is likely that they will adopt approach behaviour, for example accepting

[E]xaminer says:
[T]he major proposal of [t]he theory is addressed [h]ere.

Examiner says:

The major proposal of the theory is addressed here.

challenges in difficult situations like taking on the defender in hockey rather than passing the ball backwards to a colleague.

Examiner says:

Achievement motivation is indicated along with an example.

Vealey proposed that success in one sport transfers confidence into other sports. Confidence in a wide range of sports will improve the possibility of lifelong involvement in physical activities.

Examiner says:

Relevance to physically active lifestyles.

The teacher, therefore, must implement strategies to increase the frequency of positive subjective outcomes. This, according to Vealey, can be done by acquiring mastery of the skill, experiencing social reinforcement, undertaking mental and physical preparation and by ensuring the individual is comfortable in the activity environment.

Examiner says:

More strategies to raise confidence.

Self-efficacy theory (Bandura), although focused upon raising specific confidence, also relates to Vealey's sports confidence model. Bandura proposed that four factors promote efficacy expectations.

Examiner says:

Strong explanation of self-efficacy theory.

The recall and endorsement of previous success in sport is a source of greatest encouragement to the athlete. This factor is termed performance accomplishments. Vicarious experience involves the person lacking in confidence observing a competent demonstration. Verbal persuasion involves positive self-talk and reassurance to elevate self-belief. Often an athlete will engage in positive self-talk as a technique to manage high cognitive anxiety, which tends to arise with low confidence and learned helplessness. Finally, it is essential to exercise control of arousal. A performer will tend to evaluate their internal feelings and physiological states. Those lacking in

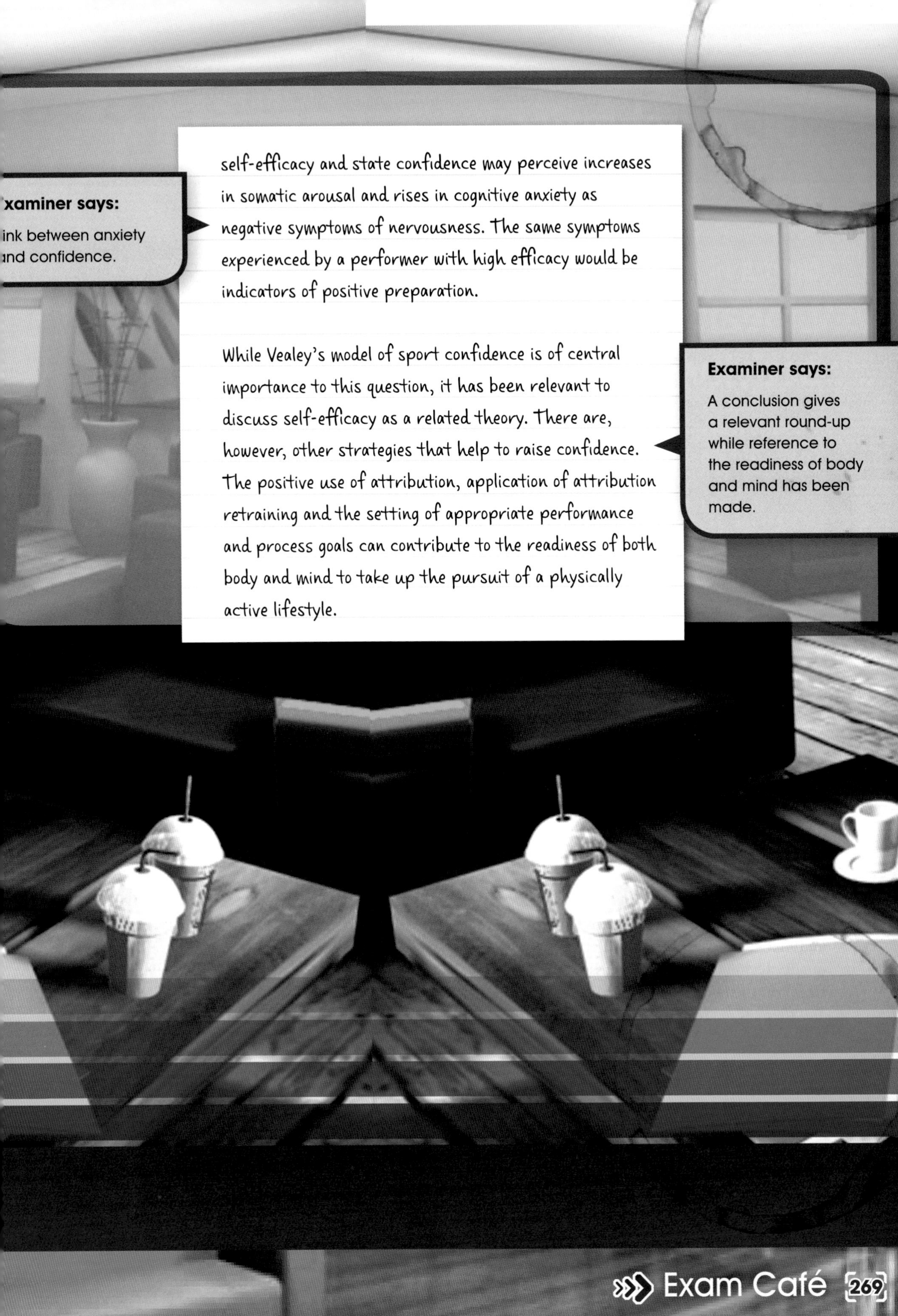

self-efficacy and state confidence may perceive increases in somatic arousal and rises in cognitive anxiety as negative symptoms of nervousness. The same symptoms experienced by a performer with high efficacy would be indicators of positive preparation.

xaminer says:

ink between anxiety
ınd confidence.

While Vealey's model of sport confidence is of central importance to this question, it has been relevant to discuss self-efficacy as a related theory. There are, however, other strategies that help to raise confidence. The positive use of attribution, application of attribution retraining and the setting of appropriate performance and process goals can contribute to the readiness of both body and mind to take up the pursuit of a physically active lifestyle.

Examiner says:

A conclusion gives a relevant round-up while reference to the readiness of body and mind has been made.

Biomechanics

CHAPTER 11:

Linear motion in physical activity

LEARNING OBJECTIVES

By the end of this chapter you should have knowledge and understanding of:

- Newton's three laws of motion
- why there can never be motion without force but there can be force without motion
- what is meant by the terms mass, inertia and momentum, and their relevance to sporting performance
- the quantities used to describe linear motion and their relevance to sporting techniques
- how to distinguish between distance and displacement and between speed and velocity
- how to use equations to make simple calculations for speed, velocity and acceleration
- how to plot and interpret information from distance/time and velocity/time graphs.

INTRODUCTION TO THE SECTION

Biomechanics is often thought of as the science underlying technique; knowledge in this area helps athletes and coaches to develop efficient techniques and correct errors in performance. Most of today's top performers will use biomechanical analysis to improve their technique and take it one step closer to perfection. High quality techniques will place less stress and strain on the body's musculo-skeletal system and thereby reduce the possibility of incurring injury or tissue damage, such as the conditions you learned about last year in your anatomy and physiology course.

There are five chapters in this section on Biomechanics. In the first four chapters, the mechanics of motion will be revisited and the field of biomechanics will be looked at in detail. Some of the concepts involved were introduced to you in Chapter 2 of *OCR AS PE,* so it may be beneficial to review this chapter before reading further. In the final chapter, we will work together to ensure that the knowledge you have built up in working through this section is sufficient to allow you to critically evaluate efficient performance in a range of physical activities.

Before you begin, it is worth pointing out that you do not need to be a mathematical genius to do well in this section of the specification. For the purposes of A-level Physical Education, the study of biomechanics involves very few scientific formulas and no difficult calculations, although definitions remain important. It is hoped that by delving into this section, you will develop an appreciation for biomechanics and use its principles to enhance your own and others' performances – as well as score well in your exam!

INTRODUCTION TO THE CHAPTER

This chapter looks at the mechanical concepts associated with understanding **linear motion.** By this we mean that a body's centre of mass is travelling in a straight or curved line. The first of these concepts is Newton's laws of motion. These three well-known laws explain all the characteristics of motion and are fundamental to fully understanding human movement in sport. The chapter also looks at the important concepts of mass, inertia and momentum and their relevance to sporting techniques. We then go on to explain how the linear motion of a performer can be described in terms of linear measurements, and the quantities of distance, displacement, speed, velocity and acceleration are considered. Analysis of linear motion in this way is useful because many movements in sport happen so quickly that techniques are difficult to analyse by visual observation alone. This is particularly notable in the 100m sprint event. You will learn how to present the data collected in graphical form and how to interpret the shape of such graphs.

KEY TERM

Linear motion

When a body moves in a straight or curved line, with all its parts moving the same distance in the same direction and at the same speed. For example, a performer in the skeleton bobsleigh will travel with linear motion in a straight line when sliding down the straight parts of the track and with linear motion in a curved line when sliding around the bends.

Fig 11.1 Sporting example of linear motion in a straight and curved line

Newton's laws of motion

Newton's laws of motion play an important role in explaining the close relationship between motion and **force.**

KEY TERM

Force

A push or a pull that alters, or tends to alter, the state of motion of a body.

EXAM TIP

For the AS exam, the examiner was happy for you to be able to give different sporting examples for each of Newton's laws. This year, however, the examiner may ask you to state each of the three laws and apply them to one particular sport. It is therefore a good idea to practise this in class.

NEWTON'S FIRST LAW OF MOTION – THE LAW OF INERTIA

> 'A body continues in a state of rest or of uniform velocity unless acted upon by an external force.'
>
> Newton's first law of motion

Newton's first law is often appropriately referred to as the law of **inertia.** In Latin, *inertia* means laziness.

KEY TERM

Inertia

The resistance of a body to change its state of rest or motion. (See also pages 275–276 for more about inertia.)

> 'Everything in the universe is lazy; so lazy that force is necessary to get it on the move, when it then travels in a straight line with constant

speed; so lazy that, once in motion, further force must be applied to slow it down, stop it, speed it up or change its direction.'

A famous biomechanical scientist's explanation of inertia.

As with all of Newton's laws, Newton's first law can be applied to any sporting activity. It explains two fundamental concepts linked with motion and force:

1 It tells us that a stationary body will remain at rest until an external force is applied. For example, for a centre pass in netball, the ball will remain in the centre's hands until she applies a force to the ball to pass it to a team mate.
2 It tells us that a moving body will continue to move with constant **velocity** until made to change its speed and/or direction by an external force. For example, the netball will continue travelling at constant velocity in the direction thrown until caught by another player, when the ball's velocity will decrease. If this player then imparts an external force on the ball, it will travel in a different direction.

KEY TERM

Velocity

The rate of motion in a particular direction (see also page 279).

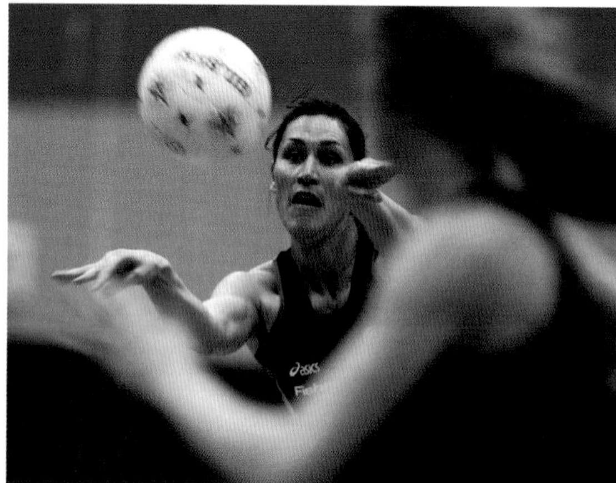

Fig 11.2 Netball players showing an example of Newton's first law of motion

NEWTON'S SECOND LAW OF MOTION – THE LAW OF ACCELERATION

'When a force acts on an object, the rate of change of momentum experienced by the object is proportional to the size of the force and takes place in the direction in which the force acts.'

Newton's second law of motion

Newton's second law is very closely related to Newton's first law. From the first law it is understood that the velocity of a body remains constant until a force acts upon it. Newton's second law explains that any change in velocity will be directly proportional to the amount of force used and will take place in the direction in which the force acts. Again, there are endless examples, but we will stick with netball. A goal shooter who has received the ball in a strong position close to the goal will only need to impart a relatively small amount of force in the direction of the ring. However, a goal shooter who has been forced to the edge of the shooting circle before taking a shot will need to impart a larger amount of force in the direction of the ring as the ball will need a greater change in **momentum** to travel to the goal.

A final concept that comes from Newton's second law is the equation:

Force = mass x acceleration or F = ma

KEY TERMS

Momentum

The quantity of motion possessed by a moving body. Momentum = mass x velocity and is measured in kg m s^{-1}. See also page 276.

Acceleration

The rate of change of velocity.

Fig 11.3 A netball shooter uses Newton's second law of motion to judge the size of force needed to give the correct change in momentum to the ball

REMEMBER

Momentum = mass x velocity. In most sporting examples, to show a force causing a change in momentum, the mass of the body in question does not change. So, a change in momentum is down entirely to a change in velocity.

EXAM TIP

F = ma is the equation you will need to use if you are asked to calculate the size of a force. Remember that the units for force are Newtons (N) and these must be given as well as your answer.

NEWTON'S THIRD LAW OF MOTION – THE LAW OF REACTION

'For every force that is exerted by one body on another, there is an equal and opposite force exerted by the second body on the first.'

Newton's third law of motion

Newton's third law simply states that for every action there is an equal and opposite reaction. It is usual to call one of the forces involved the **action force** and the other the **reaction force.** There are no strict rules that govern which force is which, but for the purpose of sports mechanics, it is presumed that the athlete exerts the action force.

To return to the netball game, Newton's third law can be clearly explained by a player giving a bounce pass to a team mate. The player exerts an action force on the ball in the downward direction. At the same time, the ball exerts a reaction force in the upward direction on the player, felt by a slight increase in pressure on the fingers. The ball then travels down towards the floor and, on contact, the ball exerts a downward action force on the ground that in turn exerts an upward reaction force on the ball and the ball bounces up into the hands of the receiving player.

Newton's third law states that not only does every force have an opposite, but also that this second force is equal in size to the first. Does it not therefore follow that these two forces will cancel each other out and there will be no external force and therefore no movement (Newton's first law)? It is agreed that this is a difficult concept to understand, but it can be explained by the difference in mass of the two bodies concerned: the larger the mass, the smaller the effect of the force and the less the acceleration.

Let's consider the netball bouncing on the court as mentioned above. At the moment of impact, the netball exerts an action force on the court and the court surface exerts a reaction force on the netball. The fact that the ground supports the netball court means it has a colossal mass compared to the mass of the netball. It follows that the reaction force on the ball is great, but the action force on the court is negligible compared to their respective masses.

KEY TERMS

Action force

A force exerted by a performer on another body. For example, the backward and downward action force exerted by a sprinter on the blocks at the start of a race.

Reaction force

An equal and opposite force to the action force exerted by a second body on the first. For example, the forward and upward reaction force exerted by the blocks on the sprinter at the start of a race.

A FINAL THOUGHT ON NEWTON'S LAWS

At this stage, it is important to point out that Newton's first law of motion explains that motion in sport can only be produced when an external force is applied, i.e. there can be no motion without force. However, although this is more difficult to appreciate, it is important to remember that it is possible to have force without motion and this occurs when all opposite forces are balanced. Take, for example, a gymnast performing a handstand on the parallel bars. From our knowledge of Newton's third law, we know that the gymnast exerts a downward action force on the parallel bar that in turn exerts an upward reaction force on the gymnast. These forces are both opposite and equal, meaning there can be no movement and the gymnast remains balanced and still.

TASK 1

1 Copy Table 1 into your file and complete the missing information.

Newton's first law of motion is sometimes called:	
It states that:	
Newton's second law of motion is sometimes called:	
It states that:	
Newton's third law of motion is sometimes called:	
It states that:	

Table 1 Newton's laws

2 Learn each of Newton's laws word for word so that you are able to recite them when asked.

3 Select Newton's first, second or third law and design a poster to display as many sporting applications of this law as you can find. Use pictures or photographs of sporting activities or techniques to help with your explanations. Check that other members of your group are doing different laws so that you have plenty of sporting examples for all three laws.

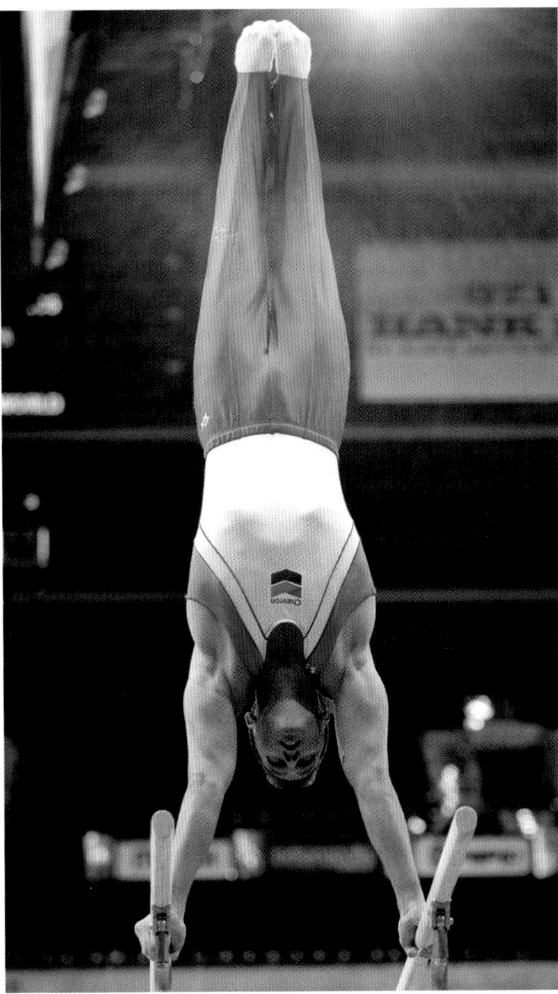

Fig 11.4 A gymnast balancing on the parallel bars demonstrates that there can be force without motion.

APPLY IT!

Choose your two favourite sports and describe as many sporting applications of Newton's three laws as you can for each of the sports you have chosen.

STRETCH AND CHALLENGE

There can be no motion without force but there can be force without motion. Prepare a PowerPoint presentation to explain this statement using Newton's laws of motion, giving plenty of different sporting examples in your answers.

Mass, inertia and momentum

MASS

Mass simply means substance. If a body occupies space, it has mass; the more substance from which it is made, the larger the mass. A large performer in sport, such as a sumo wrestler, may be referred to as 'massive'! Likewise, we can be confident in saying that, in general, a rugby front row forward has a greater mass than a winger.

KEY TERMS

Mass

The amount of matter or substance in a body. An athlete's mass is made from bone, fat, tissue and fluid. Mass is measured in kilograms (kg).

INERTIA

Inertia is the reluctance of a body to change its state of motion. All bodies simply want to continue doing whatever they are doing. They want to remain at rest when still and want to continue moving in the same direction at the same velocity if moving. From Newton's first law of motion, we know that a force is required to change this state of motion. Inertia is directly related to mass, so the bigger the mass, the larger the inertia of a body and the bigger the force must be to change its state of motion. Think about the different weights of bowling balls at a ten-pin bowling alley. It is considerably easier to send a lighter ball towards the skittles than it is a bigger and heavier ball. Similarly, if equal force is applied to a javelin and a shot put, the acceleration of the javelin will be greater. Likewise, once in motion, it requires a larger force to stop a body with greater mass than it does to stop a body of smaller mass. A 100m sprinter will expend greater amounts of energy exploding out of the blocks and building velocity at the start of the race than they will expend in the middle and end segments of the race.

REMEMBER

Inertia is directly related to mass: the greater the mass the greater the inertia and the greater the force needed to get it moving, stop it moving or change its direction.

Consider a rugby prop forward and a rugby winger who are both running at the same speed towards the try line. Although the prop forward would have required a greater force to get him moving in the first instance, once moving he will be very difficult to stop due to his large inertia. It will take a strong and brave tackle to stop him from scoring! The same is true for changing direction. An athlete with a large inertia has to generate a greater force to change direction and it will often take them more time to change direction than a lighter opponent. This is one of the reasons why performers tend to be small and lightweight in sports requiring quick changes of direction such as badminton and squash.

A final thought on inertia is that it is the reason behind having different weight categories in contact sports. For example, in judo it would be very difficult for a lighter competitor with less mass and less inertia to throw a heavier competitor with greater mass and greater inertia.

APPLY IT!

In certain sports a large inertia can be an advantage and in other sports a disadvantage. Discuss this statement with reference to the body build of current sports performers at the top of their game. Are there any exceptions to your findings?

REMEMBER

Inertia resists motion and then persists motion.

MOMENTUM

Momentum is the quantity of motion possessed by a body and is quite simply 'mass on the move'. The amount of momentum possessed by a body depends on its mass and its velocity. If the mass or the velocity of the body increases, the momentum increases and vice versa.

Momentum = mass x velocity
(Mo = mv)

From the above equation for momentum, it follows that a stationary body with zero velocity has no momentum and only bodies that move have momentum. In sports movements there is little opportunity to increase or decrease mass and changes in momentum are entirely due to changes in velocity. For example, a 100m sprinter will have a greater momentum at 70m than at 10m because their velocity is greater (mass has remained unchanged).

Momentum plays a more important role in sports involving collisions or impacts. The result of the impact depends on the momentum of each of the colliding bodies just before impact. The greater the momentum of the body, the more pronounced the effect it has on the other body in its path. A good example here is in rugby: players with a relatively large mass who have the ability to run at a high velocity can generate considerable momentum when at full speed. This makes it very difficult to stop them or slow their forward momentum and they are often able to run through tackles. However, a player with a smaller mass, despite being able to run quickly, can sometimes come off second best when they meet a defender with considerable inertia!

Fig 11.5 Mass, inertia and momentum all come into play in sports involving collisions, such as rugby

TASK 2

1 If you have learned to drive recently, you will know a little about the stopping distances. Use your knowledge of momentum to explain why stopping distances increase with the speed of the car. What would be the impact on stopping distances for a lorry compared to a car?
2 Use your knowledge of inertia to discuss the relevance of the weight of the forward pack at the scrum in a game of rugby.
3 Calculate the momentum of a downhill skier who has a mass of 69kg and is travelling with a velocity of 39m/s.
4 What is the momentum of an athlete whose mass is 65kg and who is running at 8.7m/s?
5 Explain the relevance of momentum to Newton's first and second laws of motion.

EXAM TIP

For any calculation, remember three things:

- always give the equation you are using first
- show all your working
- give the units of measurement.

STRETCH AND CHALLENGE

Mass, inertia and momentum are closely linked. Critically examine the role that each has to play in physical activities, using examples from sport to help explain your conclusions.

Describing linear motion

The following quantities are measurements that are commonly used to describe the linear motion of a body. Their values reveal how far a body moves, how fast it moves and how consistent or inconsistent is its motion.

For the purpose of the specification, you need to be familiar with the following quantities:

- mass (as discussed on page 275)
- distance
- displacement
- speed
- velocity
- acceleration.

EXAM TIP

For each of the quantities listed, you will need to know:

- a simple definition
- a relevant equation where appropriate (remember that any calculation will be very simple!)
- the unit of measurement for the quantity you have calculated.

DISTANCE VERSUS DISPLACEMENT

The measurements of **distance** and **displacement** are used to describe the extent of a body's motion or how far it has travelled.

KEY TERMS

Distance

The path taken in moving from the first position to the second. Distance is measured in metres (m).

Displacement

The shortest straight-line route between two positions in a stated direction. Displacement is measured in metres (m).

Distance is simply the length of the path taken by a body in moving from one position to another and examples from sport are easy to give:

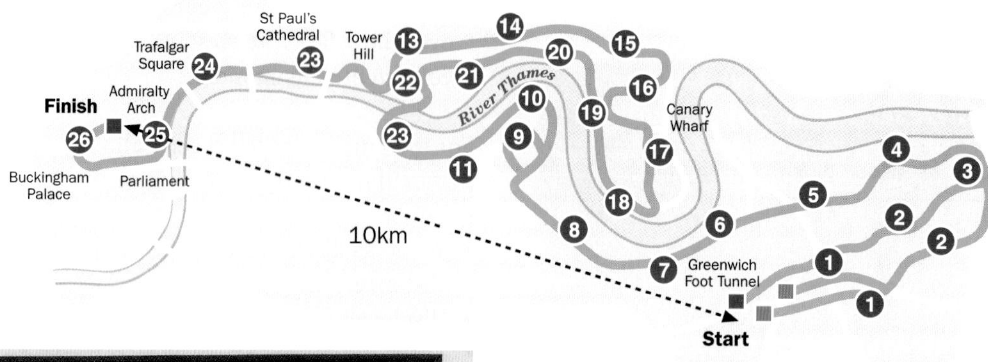

Fig 11.6 In the Flora London Marathon of 2008, Martin Lel ran a distance of 42.2 km and set a new World Record of 2 hours 5 minutes and 15 seconds. This sounds less impressive when we consider it took him over two hours to achieve a displacement of just 10km!

- the distance run by a competitor in the London Marathon is approx 42.2km
- the distance swum by a team in the 4 x 100m Freestyle relay is 400m
- the distance cycled by a female competitor in the Olympic Individual Pursuit event is 3km.

Displacement is a measurement from start to finish 'as the crow flies': the shortest route from the first position to the second.

- The displacement of a competitor in the London Marathon is approx 10km (see Fig 11.6).
- The displacement of a swimming team in the 4 x 100m Freestyle relay in a 50m pool is 0m – the fourth swimmer ends the race at the same point that the first swimmer started it.
- The displacement of a female cyclist in the Individual Pursuit event is 0m – although they cycle a distance of 3km, it is around a 200m track in the velodrome and the start line is also the finish line.

APPLY IT!

Consider field events in athletics. Field judges do not actually measure the distance thrown or jumped but the displacement.

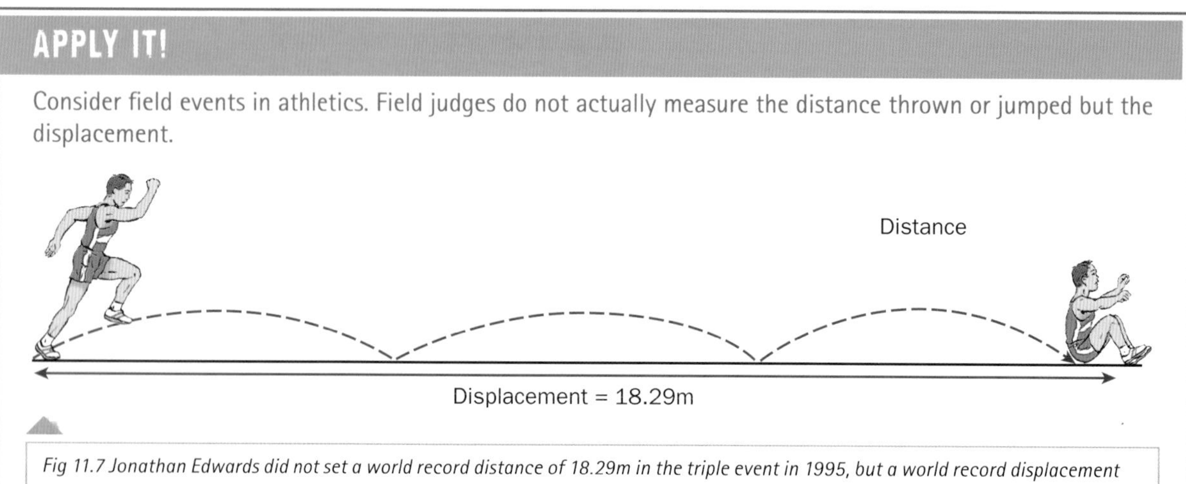

Fig 11.7 Jonathan Edwards did not set a world record distance of 18.29m in the triple event in 1995, but a world record displacement

REMEMBER

When a body moves in a straight line such as the 100m sprint, distance and displacement will have the same value.

SPEED VERSUS VELOCITY

The measurements of **speed** and velocity are used to describe the rate at which a body moves from one position to the next or how fast it is moving.

Speed is the rate of change of distance and its value is calculated by dividing the distance covered in metres by the time taken in seconds.

$$\text{Speed (m/s)} = \frac{\text{distance (m)}}{\text{time taken (s)}}$$

KEY TERM

Speed

A body's movement per unit of time with no reference to direction. Speed is measured in metres per second (m/s).

Velocity is the speed of a body in a given direction, and is the rate of change of displacement. Its value is calculated by dividing the displacement covered in metres by the time taken in seconds.

$$\text{Velocity (m/s)} = \frac{\text{displacement (m)}}{\text{time taken (s)}}$$

Velocity can change when direction changes even though the speed of the body might remain constant.

ACCELERATION

The measurement of acceleration is used to describe the rate at which a body changes its velocity. When velocity is increasing, it is known as positive acceleration and when velocity is decreasing it is known as negative acceleration or **deceleration**. Acceleration is measured in metres per second squared (m/s^2 or ms^{-2}).

v_f = final velocity (m/s)

$$\text{Acceleration (m/s}^2\text{)} = \frac{\text{change in velocity (m/s)}}{\text{time taken (s)}} = \frac{v_f - v_i}{t}$$

Where v_f = final velocity (m/s)
v_i = initial velocity (m/s)
t = time taken (s)

KEY TERM

Deceleration

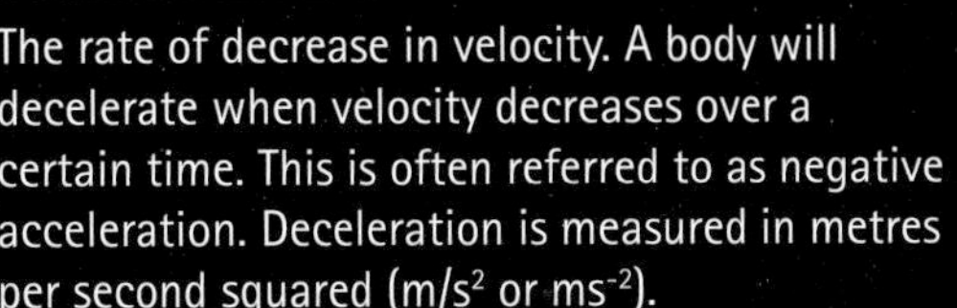

The rate of decrease in velocity. A body will decelerate when velocity decreases over a certain time. This is often referred to as negative acceleration. Deceleration is measured in metres per second squared (m/s^2 or ms^{-2}).

Acceleration is a very important quantity in sport because success in many activities is directly related to an athlete's ability to rapidly increase or decrease their velocity. Consider, for example, a netball player who sprints away quickly to lose their defender and who then needs to stop abruptly on receiving the ball to avoid breaking the footwork rule.

Zero acceleration is where acceleration = 0 m/s^2 and a body is either at rest or moving with constant velocity. According to Newton's first law, the net force on the body is also 0N.

STRETCH AND CHALLENGE

In the 2008 Beijing Olympics, United States swimmer Michael Phelps became the first Olympian in history to win eight gold medals at an individual Olympic games, setting seven world records in the process. Ignoring the two relays, make a list of the times of the six other events he won.

For each event state the following:

- the distance swum
- the displacement swum
- Phelps' average speed during the race
- Phelps' average velocity during the race.

TASK 3

Table 2 gives the split times every 10m for an athlete running the 100m sprint.

Displacement (m)	0	10	20	30	40	50	60	70	80	90	100
Time (s)	0.00	1.86	2.87	3.80	4.66	5.55	6.38	7.21	8.11	8.98	9.83

Table 2 Split times for 100m sprint

1. Calculate the sprinter's velocity at 20m.
2. Calculate the sprinter's acceleration between 0m and 20m.
3. Calculate the sprinter's velocity at 40m.
4. Calculate the sprinter's velocity at 80m.
5. Calculate the sprinter's acceleration between 40m and 80m.

TASK 4

Copy Table 3 onto a sheet of A4 paper and complete the missing information. When you have completed the table, put it into your file as a revision guide for the key terms and quantities you have covered so far in this chapter.

Key term	Definition	Equation (where relevant)	Unit of measurement (where relevant)
Linear motion			
Force			
Mass			
Inertia			
Momentum			
Distance			
Displacement			
Speed			
Velocity			
Acceleration			

Table 3 Definitions, equations and units for terms connected with laws of motion

Graphs of motion

Graphs help us to make sense of motion as they are a useful means of presenting information. By using graphs, changes and patterns in motion can be recognised. Graphs are often used when data is presented very quickly to the naked eye, such as the 100m or 200m sprint events.

There are two types of graph that you need to be familiar with:

- distance/time graphs
- velocity/time graphs, or speed/time graphs.

For the purpose of sports mechanics at A2 level, velocity/time graphs and speed/time graphs can be treated as practically the same. The shape of the curve plotted on these graphs will enable you to know the pattern of motion occurring at a particular moment at time.

EXAM TIP

In a question involving graphs of motion, the examiner is more likely to refer to a velocity/time graph than a speed/time graph.

DISTANCE/TIME GRAPHS

A distance/time graph indicates the distance travelled by an object in a certain time.

KEY TERM

Gradient of graph

The slope of a graph at a particular moment in time.

$$\text{Gradient of graph} = \frac{\text{changes in y axis}}{\text{changes in x axis}}$$

EXAM TIP

For distance/time graphs:

1 Don't forget to:

- plot distance on the y-axis and time on the x-axis
- label the axes and give the units.

Both of the above will get you marks from your examiner!

2 The gradient of a distance/time graph will tell you whether the body is stationary, moving with constant speed, accelerating or decelerating (see Figs 11.7 – 11.10).

Gradient of a distance/time graph

$$\frac{\text{distance}}{\text{time}} = \text{speed}$$

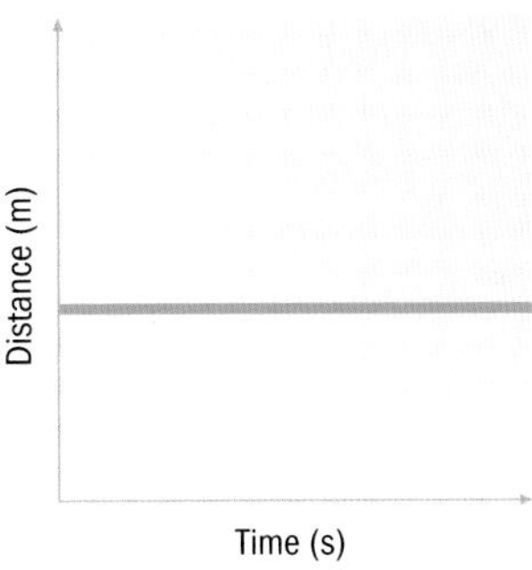

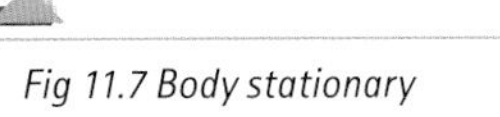

Fig 11.7 Body stationary

The body remains at the same distance over a period of time; it is not moving. For example, a hockey goalkeeper who is stationary before the penalty stroke is struck.

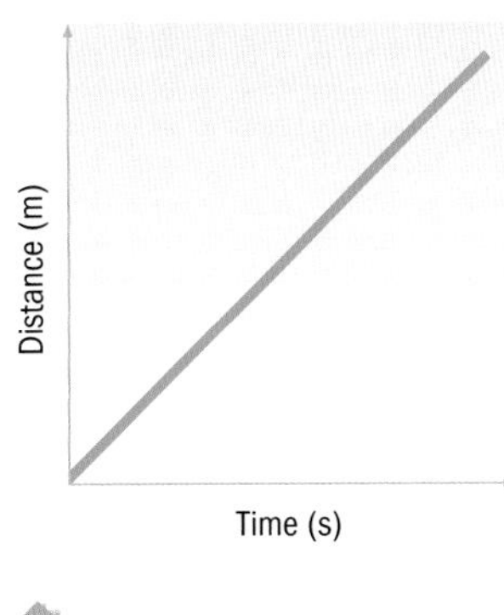

Fig 11.8 Body moving with constant velocity

The body is moving the same amount of distance at a steady rate. The gradient of the graph remains constant, therefore speed remains constant. For example, a middle-distance runner in the intermediate stages of the 1500m race.

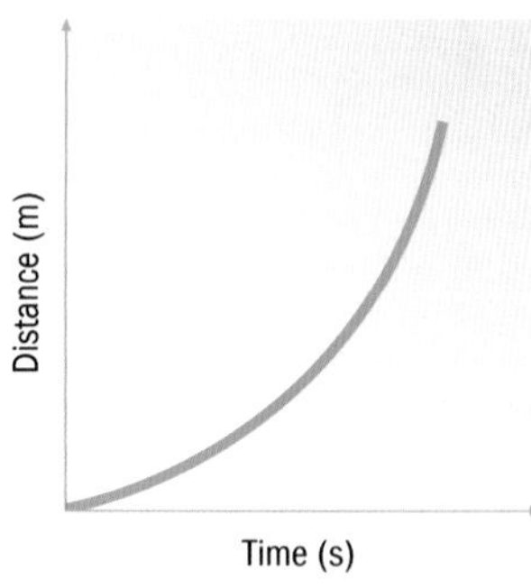

Fig 11.9 Body is accelerating

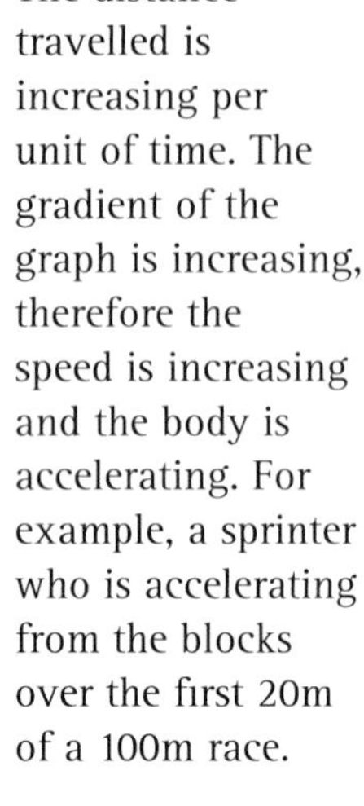

The distance travelled is increasing per unit of time. The gradient of the graph is increasing, therefore the speed is increasing and the body is accelerating. For example, a sprinter who is accelerating from the blocks over the first 20m of a 100m race.

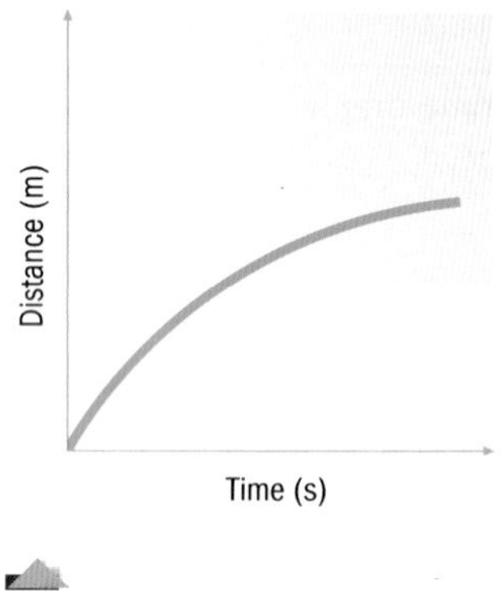

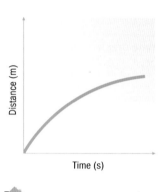

Fig 11.10 Body is decelerating

The distance travelled is decreasing per unit of time. The gradient of the graph is decreasing, therefore the speed is decreasing and the body is decelerating. For example, a downhill skier after the finish line who digs their edges into the softer snow to bring them to a standstill.

REMEMBER

For distance/time graphs:

- horizontal line = no motion (A–B)
- positive curve = acceleration (B–C)
- regular diagonal line = constant speed (C–D)
- negative curve = deceleration (D–E)
- gradient of curve = $\frac{\text{distance}}{\text{time}}$ = speed.

Fig 11.11 A distance/time graph

VELOCITY/TIME GRAPHS

A velocity/time graph indicates the velocity of an object at a certain time.

EXAM TIP

For velocity/time graphs:

1 Don't forget to:

- plot distance on the y-axis and time on the x-axis
- label the axes and give the units.

Both of the above will get you marks from your examiner!

2 The gradient of a velocity/time graph will tell you whether the body is moving with constant velocity, accelerating or decelerating (see Figs 11.12 – 11.14).

Gradient of velocity/time graph

$\frac{\text{change in velocity}}{\text{time}}$ = acceleration/deceleration

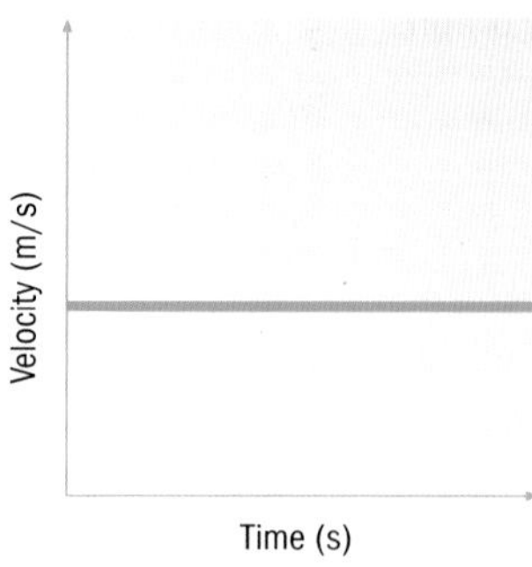

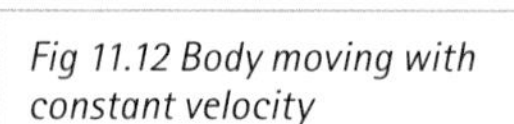

Fig 11.12 Body moving with constant velocity

The body moves with the same velocity during regular time intervals. For example, a golfer walking towards their ball after a drive.

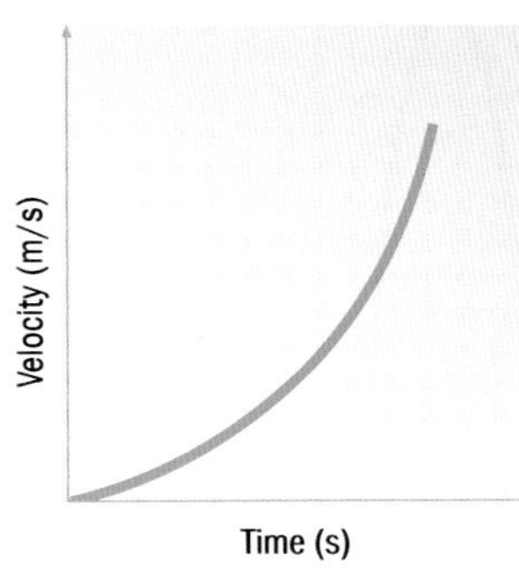

The body is moving with increasing velocity; the gradient of graph increases. For example, a football accelerating from the spot at a penalty kick.

Fig 11.13 Body accelerating

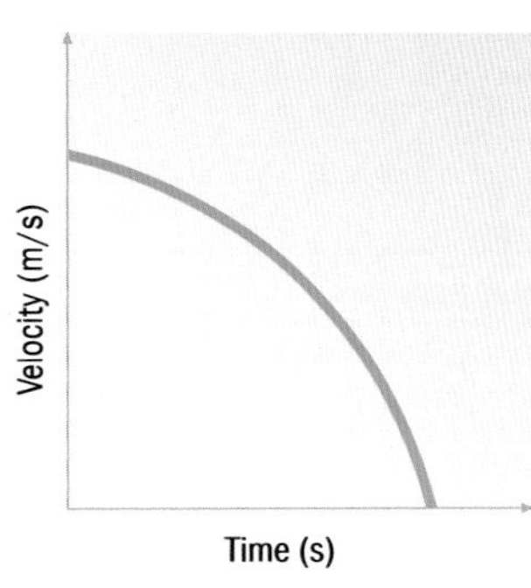

The body is moving with decreasing velocity; the gradient of graph decreases. For example, a cricket ball being caught by a wicket keeper.

Fig 11.14 Body decelerating

TASK 5

For each of the graphs of motion plotted in Fig 11.15 below:

1 state the pattern of motion taking place between the points identified
2 give an example from sport when a curve of this shape might be plotted.

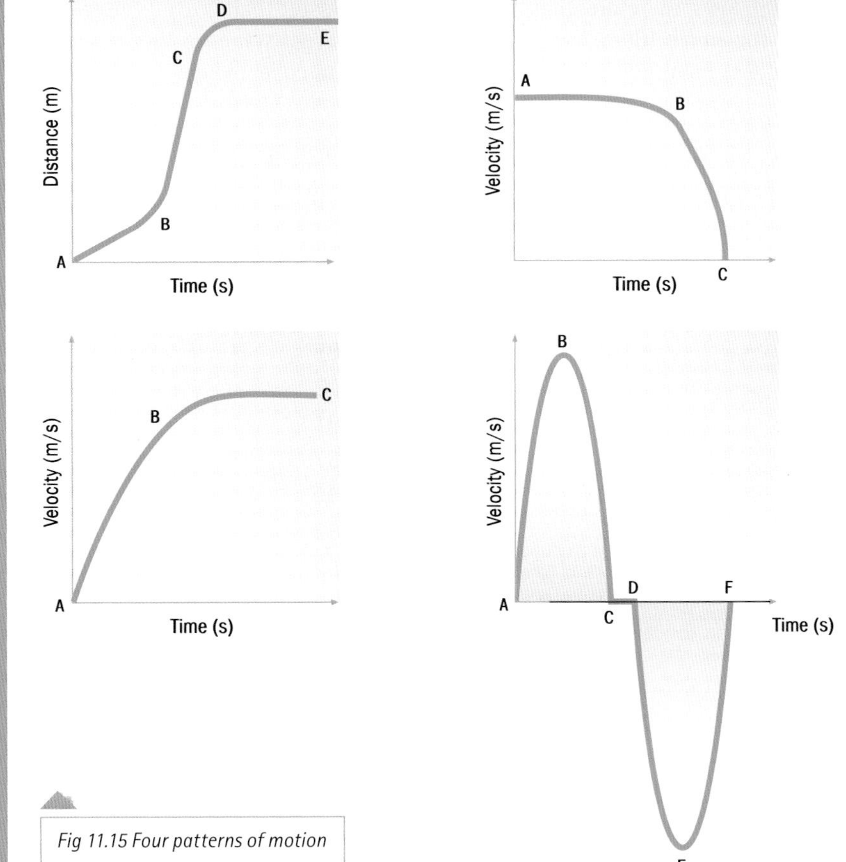

Fig 11.15 Four patterns of motion

REMEMBER

For velocity/time graphs:

- horizontal line = constant velocity (C–D)
- positive curve = acceleration (A–B)
- negative curve = deceleration (B–C)
- a curve or line below the x axis = change in direction
- gradient of curve = $\frac{\text{change in velocity}}{\text{time}}$ = acceleration.

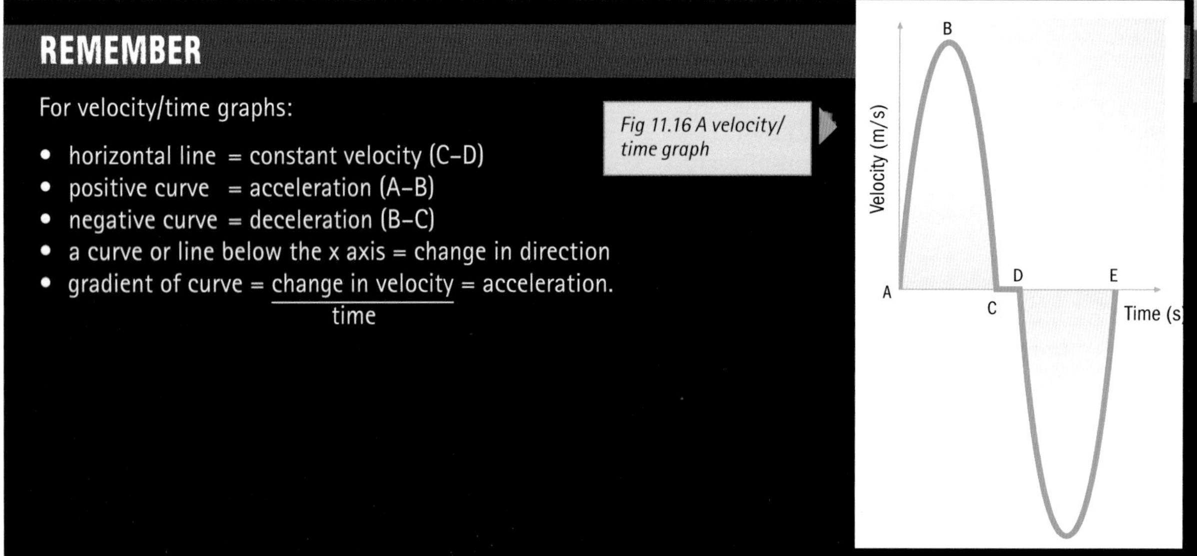

Fig 11.16 A velocity/time graph

APPLY IT!

At the 2008 Beijing Olympics, Usain Bolt became the fastest man on earth. He ran 100m in 9.69 seconds. From this, his average speed can be calculated as approximately 10.3 m/s. However, this is the speed that Bolt averaged over the 100m. At different stages of the race, he would have been running slower than this and at other stages faster.

Immediately after the starting gun fires, Bolt is gaining velocity and running considerably slower than 10.3m/s as he overcomes inertia. It follows, therefore, that he must have run faster than 10.3m/s elsewhere in the race to average this speed over the whole 100m. To know his speed at different stages of the race requires the use of specific video analysis or radar guns and marker points; the data collected can then be analysed using graphs of motion.

Data collected on Bolt's run shows his 10m split times to be those shown in column C of Table 4.

A Time taken (s)	B Displacement (m)	C Time for 10m interval (s)	D Average velocity for this interval (m/s) *
0.00	0	–	0.00
1.85	10	1.85	5.40
2.87	20	1.02	9.80
3.78	30	0.91	10.99
4.65	40	0.87	11.49
5.50	50	0.85	11.76
6.32	60	0.82	12.19
7.14	70	0.82	12.19
7.96	80	0.82	12.19
8.79	90	0.83	12.05
9.69	100	0.90	11.11

Table 4

Using graph paper, plot two graphs:

- a distance/time graph
- a velocity/time graph.

Use each of your graphs to describe the state of motion at various stages of Bolt's run.

ExamCafé

Relax, refresh, result!

Refresh your memory

You should now have knowledge and understanding of:

- Newton's three laws of motion
- why there can never be motion without force but there can be force without motion
- what is meant by the terms mass, inertia and momentum, and their relevance to sporting performance
- the quantities used to describe linear motion and their relevance to sporting techniques
- how to distinguish between distance and displacement and between speed and velocity
- how to use equations to make simple calculations for speed, velocity and acceleration
- how to plot and interpret information from distance/time and velocity/time graphs.

REVISE AS YOU GO!

1. Explain in your own words Newton's first law, making reference to a chosen sport.
2. Explain in your own words Newton's second law, making reference to the sport chosen in question 1.
3. Explain in your own words Newton's third law, making reference to the sport chosen in question 1.
4. Define each of the following terms: mass, inertia, momentum.
5. Explain the benefits of a rugby team having a heavier pack in the scrum.
6. Why does a four-man bobsleigh take longer to stop at the end of its run than a skeleton bobsleigh?
7. State the distance and the displacement travelled in each of the following examples:
   a) a 400m sprint on a 400m track
   b) a 400m sprint on a 200m track
   c) a 100m swim in a 50m pool
   d) a 50m swim in a 25m pool
   e) a 25m swim in a 25m pool.
8. Explain the difference between speed and velocity.
9. Roughly sketch a velocity/time graph for the hockey ball in the following sporting scenario:
   Player A push passes a hockey ball to player B, who traps the ball for a short while and then sends it back to player A, where the ball stops.
10. Explain the shape of the graph you have drawn in question 9.

Try to answer these questions yourself. Ask your teacher if you need help.

Get the result!

Examination question

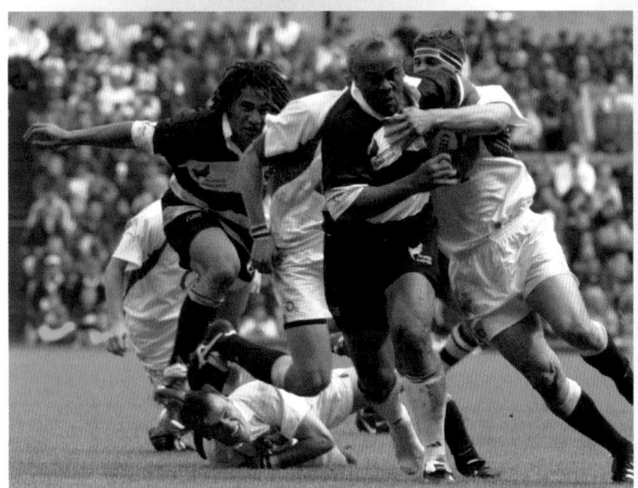

(a) Rugby player
Mass = 122kg

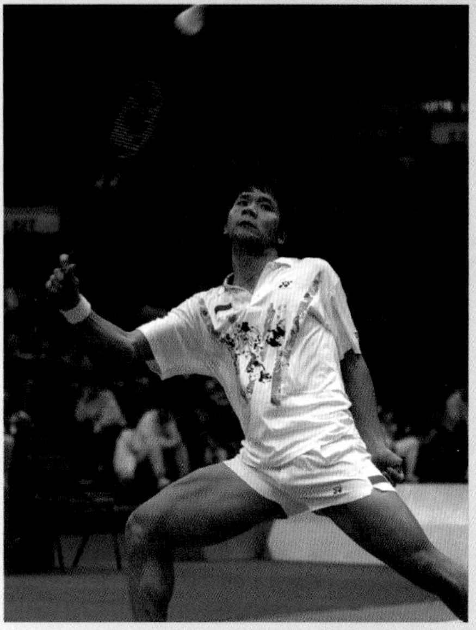

(b) Badminton player
Mass = 72kg

Define the terms mass and inertia and use your knowledge of inertia to explain why the athletes in photographs (a) and (b) above are well suited to their sports. (6 marks)

Examiner's tips

There are two parts to this question, so check the command word for each.

- The first part of the question asks for two simple definitions, so the marks available for this part are likely to be 2 marks: 1 mark for each correct definition. A top grade student would be expected to know their definitions well.
- The other 4 marks will come from the explanation part of the question, so make sure you give sufficient information.

Finally, make certain that your answer is applied to a rugby player and a badminton player.

Student answer

Mass is the weight of a body and inertia is linked to Newton's first law and is the reluctance of a body to change its state of motion. A rugby player has more inertia than a badminton player. This is important because it makes him more difficult to stop moving.

Examiner says:

Your definition of mass is not correct. Weight is a force, whereas mass is simply the size of something. However, your description of inertia is pleasing and I like the way you have applied it to Newton's first law. You have identified that the rugby player has a larger inertia than the badminton player but you have not explained why nor have you linked the inertia of both sportsmen to their respective sports. Your answer therefore lacks the explanation needed to score well in the second part of the question.

Student's improved answer

Mass is the amount of substance in a body. Inertia is the resistance of a body to change its state of motion.

Examiner says:

A straightforward, no-nonsense and accurate start to the answer that will score 2 marks.

Mass and inertia are directly linked. A person with a large mass has a large inertia. In the figure, the rugby player has a larger inertia than the badminton player. A large inertia is useful for a rugby player as it makes it more difficult to get moving, for example in a scrum or a maul. It also makes them more difficult to stop once they are moving, for example in a tackle. A small inertia is useful for a badminton player as they need to be able to move and change direction quickly. The smaller the inertia the less force needed to change their state of motion. So, it is easier for a badminton player to start to move, to stop and to change direction than it is for a rugby player. This is an important part of being able to get to different parts of the court quickly to hit the shuttle. This is as a result of Newton's first law.

Examiner says:

An immediate link made with the specifics of the question.

Examiner says:

Relevant part of the theory identified and immediately applied to the rugby player.

Examiner says:

Accurate application of knowledge of inertia to a badminton player.

Examiner says:

Reference to Newton's first law is impressive. Overall, the candidate has shown a high level of understanding and application of inertia to produce a top-grade answer.

CHAPTER 12:

Force in physical activity

LEARNING OBJECTIVES

By the end of this chapter you should have knowledge and understanding of:

- the definition and measurement of force and the effects of a force on a performer or object
- the concept of net force and balanced and unbalanced forces
- the nature of the vertical forces acting on a sports performer (weight force and reaction force) and an appreciation of the effect they have on the resulting motion of a performer
- the nature of the horizontal forces acting on a sports performer (friction force and air resistance force) and an appreciation of the effect they have on the resulting motion of a performer
- how to sketch simple free body diagrams to identify the type and relative size of the external forces acting on a sports performer at a particular instant in time
- impulse and its relationship to momentum
- how to sketch force/time graphs and appreciate the information that can be gained from them.

INTRODUCTION

At AS level, you learned the effects that a **force** has on a body and applied these to different sporting situations. At A2 level, you will need to take your understanding of force considerably further and look at the specific forces that act on sports performers.

There are two types of force: **internal force** and **external force**. This section is concerned with external forces. Internal forces will be considered in Chapter 14, when you look at lever systems.

This chapter also enables you to draw simple and accurate free body diagrams that describe the motion of a body at a particular moment in time. We conclude this chapter by looking into the important concept of impulse.

KEY TERMS

Force

A push or a pull that alters, or tends to alter, the state of motion of a body. Force is measured in Newtons (N).

Internal force

A force generated by the contraction of skeletal muscle. For example, the force in the biceps brachii during flexion of the elbow caused by concentric contraction.

External force

A force that comes from outside the body, for example weight, reaction, friction, air resistance.

MORE ABOUT FORCE

You already have some fundamental knowledge of force from studying a small amount of mechanics last year in your anatomy and physiology course, and you will also know more than you think from having a working knowledge of Newton's laws of motion.

TASK 1

Remind yourself of what you already know about force by completing the following questions:

1. **Define the term force.**
2. **Identify five effects a force can have on a body and give an example for each effect you have stated. To make this task more challenging, try giving examples from the same sport.**

There are two additional pieces of information about force that need highlighting at this point.

The first being that force can be calculated using an equation derived from Newton's second law:

Force = mass x acceleration
(F = m x a)

EXAM TIP

If you are asked for a calculation in your exam, give the equation you are using, show all your working and don't forget the units of measurement.

The second key point about force is that an arrow on a diagram can represent the force acting on it. However, before drawing this arrow to describe the force, three very important things need to be considered:

1. the point of application of the force – shown by the point at which the arrow begins
2. the direction of the force – shown by the direction of the arrow
3. the size of the force – shown by the length of the arrow. The larger the force, the longer the arrow.

Fig 12.1a Question: From where is the force applied?
Answer: The point of application of the force is at the point of contact of the racquet head with the ball.

Fig 12.1b Question: In what direction is the force applied?
Answer: The force is applied in a forward direction.

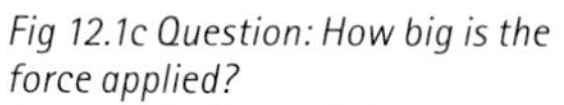

Fig 12.1c Question: How big is the force applied?
Answer: The force of the racquet on a ball at a serve is large, therefore the arrow needs to be quite long.

REMEMBER

All forces must initiate from somewhere on the body. A force cannot initiate from thin air.

EXAM TIP

The force arrow must be accurate in terms of its point of application, its direction and its length to gain marks in an examination question. It is useful to ask yourself three little questions before drawing the force arrow:

- From where is the force applied?
- In what direction is it applied?
- How big is the force applied?

Net force, balanced forces and unbalanced forces

To recap on what we know from Newton's Laws:

1 There can be force without motion, i.e. a force that is not large enough to overcome the inertia of a body will not be able to change its state of motion. For example, when a pack of rugby forwards practise their scrummaging technique against a scrummage machine in a training session, the pack is exerting a force but it is not sufficient to move the machine.

2 There can be no motion without force, i.e. a body will not change its state of motion unless an external force acts on it, and the larger the force the greater the change in this state of motion. For example, the large force caused by the contact of the golf club head on a golf ball at a drive causes the ball to change from being stationary to moving very quickly.

Taking these two mechanical principles a little further leads us to **net force** and the concepts of **balanced** and **unbalanced forces**.

It is useful here to think that the study of motion in sport can be subdivided into **statics** and **dynamics**.

- Statics look at bodies that are in a constant state of motion; that is, bodies that are either at rest or travelling with constant velocity, i.e. bodies that are not accelerating.
- Dynamics is concerned with bodies that are changing their state of motion, i.e. bodies that are accelerating. Remember that acceleration is the rate of change of velocity, and velocity will change when a body speeds up, slows down or changes direction. So, although we may be used to the term accelerating referring to a body that is speeding up, it also covers moving bodies that are slowing down or changing direction. It is important to bear this in mind as you read further.

KEY TERMS

Net force

The overall force acting on a body when all the individual forces have been considered. Net force is also termed resultant force.

Statics

The study of bodies that are in a constant state of motion, i.e. with no acceleration.

Dynamics

The study of bodies that are changing their state of motion, i.e. accelerating.

Balanced forces

When two or more forces acting on a body are equal in size but opposite in direction. The resultant net force is zero.

Unbalanced forces

When force acting in one direction is greater in size than force acting in the opposite direction. The resultant net force is either positive or negative.

BALANCED FORCES

These are present in the study of statics. Forces are balanced when two or more forces acting on a body are equal in size but opposite in direction. Balanced forces can occur in a vertical direction or horizontal direction or both. In all cases the net force is zero. There will be no change to the state of motion of the body: it will remain stationary or moving with constant velocity.

Balanced forces in a vertical direction mean that there is no acceleration in the upward or downward direction. An example of balanced forces in the vertical direction can be seen when a performer carries out a quadriceps stretch as part of their warm-up or cool-down routine. The weight of the performer acts vertically downwards and the reaction force from the ground (from Newton's third law) acts vertically upwards. Both forces are equal in size but opposite in direction – shown in Fig 12.2(a) by both arrows being the same length but pointing in the opposite direction. The net force in the vertical direction is zero.

Balanced forces in the horizontal direction mean that there is no acceleration in the forward, backward or sideways direction (i.e. parallel to the horizon). An example of balanced forces in the horizontal direction can be seen in windsurfing. The force exerted by the strength and body position of the windsurfer is equal and opposite to the force of the wind on the sail. This enables the windsurfer to remain upright. These forces are shown by the arrows in Fig 12.2(b), which are equal in length but opposite in direction. The net force in the horizontal direction is zero.

STRETCH AND CHALLENGE

A body travelling with constant velocity will have balanced forces in both vertical and horizontal directions. Think of two examples from sport where a body is travelling with constant velocity. Make a sketch of this body and draw arrows to represent the forces acting.

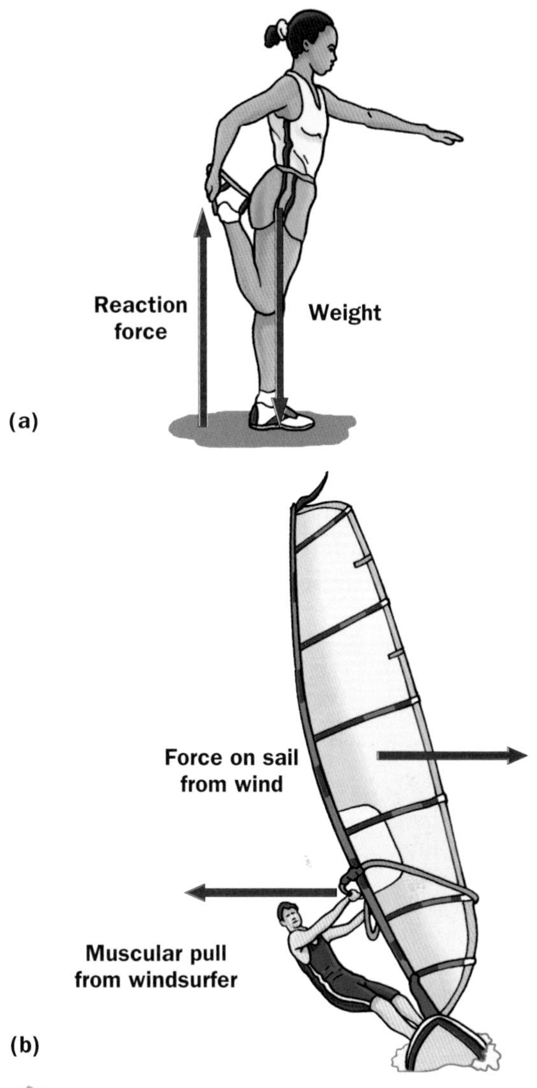

Fig 12.2 Balanced forces in (a) the vertical direction and (b) the horizontal direction. In both cases, forces are equal and opposite in direction; there is no acceleration; the net force is zero; there will be no change to the state of motion of the body

UNBALANCED FORCES

These are present in the study of dynamics. Forces are unbalanced when force acting in one direction on a body is greater in size than force acting in the opposite direction. Unbalanced forces can occur in a vertical direction or horizontal direction or both. In all cases there will be a net force and the body will start to accelerate in the direction of the larger force. There will be a resultant change to the state of motion of the body.

Unbalanced forces in a vertical direction mean that there will be acceleration in the upward or downward direction.

An example of unbalanced forces in the vertical direction can be seen in a vertical jump at takeoff. The upward reaction force is considerably greater than the downward weight force – shown in Fig 12.3(a) by the upward arrow being longer than the downward arrow. This results in a net force in the upward direction and the performer jumps into the air.

Unbalanced forces in the horizontal direction mean that there will be acceleration in the forward, backward or sideways direction (i.e. parallel to the horizon). An example of unbalanced forces in the horizontal direction can be seen in the early stages of the 100m sprint. The forward friction force is considerably greater than the backward air resistance force – shown in Fig 12.3(b) by the forward arrow being longer than the backward arrow. This results in a net force in the same direction of motion and the sprinter accelerates forwards.

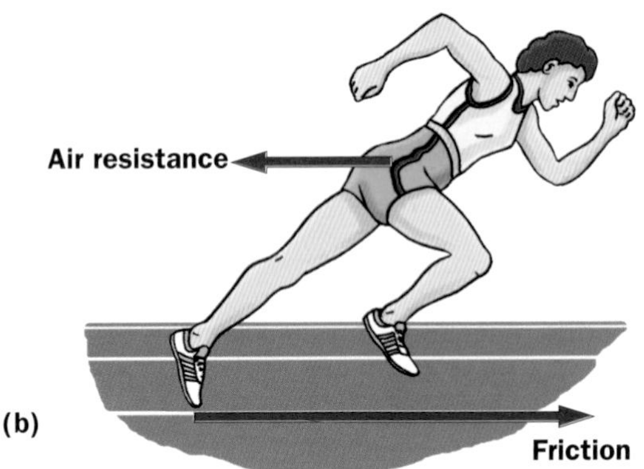

Fig 12.3 Unbalanced forces in (a) the vertical direction and (b) the horizontal direction. In both cases, one force is larger than the other; there is acceleration in the direction of the larger force; there is a net force; there will be a change to the state of motion of the body

STRETCH AND CHALLENGE

A body accelerating forwards and upwards will have unbalanced forces in both the vertical and horizontal directions. Think of two examples from sport where a body is accelerating forwards and upwards. Make a sketch of this body and draw arrows to represent the forces acting.

REMEMBER

- Bodies that are not changing their state of motion are: either stationary or travelling with constant velocity; statics; balanced forces; net force of zero; no acceleration.
- Bodies that are changing their state of motion are: dynamics; unbalanced forces; net force in direction of larger force; acceleration in direction of larger force.

The concept of net force is sometimes a tricky one and you will look at it in more detail in free body diagrams on pages 299.

TASK 2

Using arrows to represent forces, and being careful about their point of application, direction and size, draw the forces acting on the following bodies (Figs 12.4–12.8). To prepare for the next section, label each force with the following:

- downward arrow = weight
- upward arrow = reaction
- forward arrow = friction
- backward arrow = air resistance.

At the bottom of each diagram, make a comment about the net force and whether the forces are balanced or unbalanced.

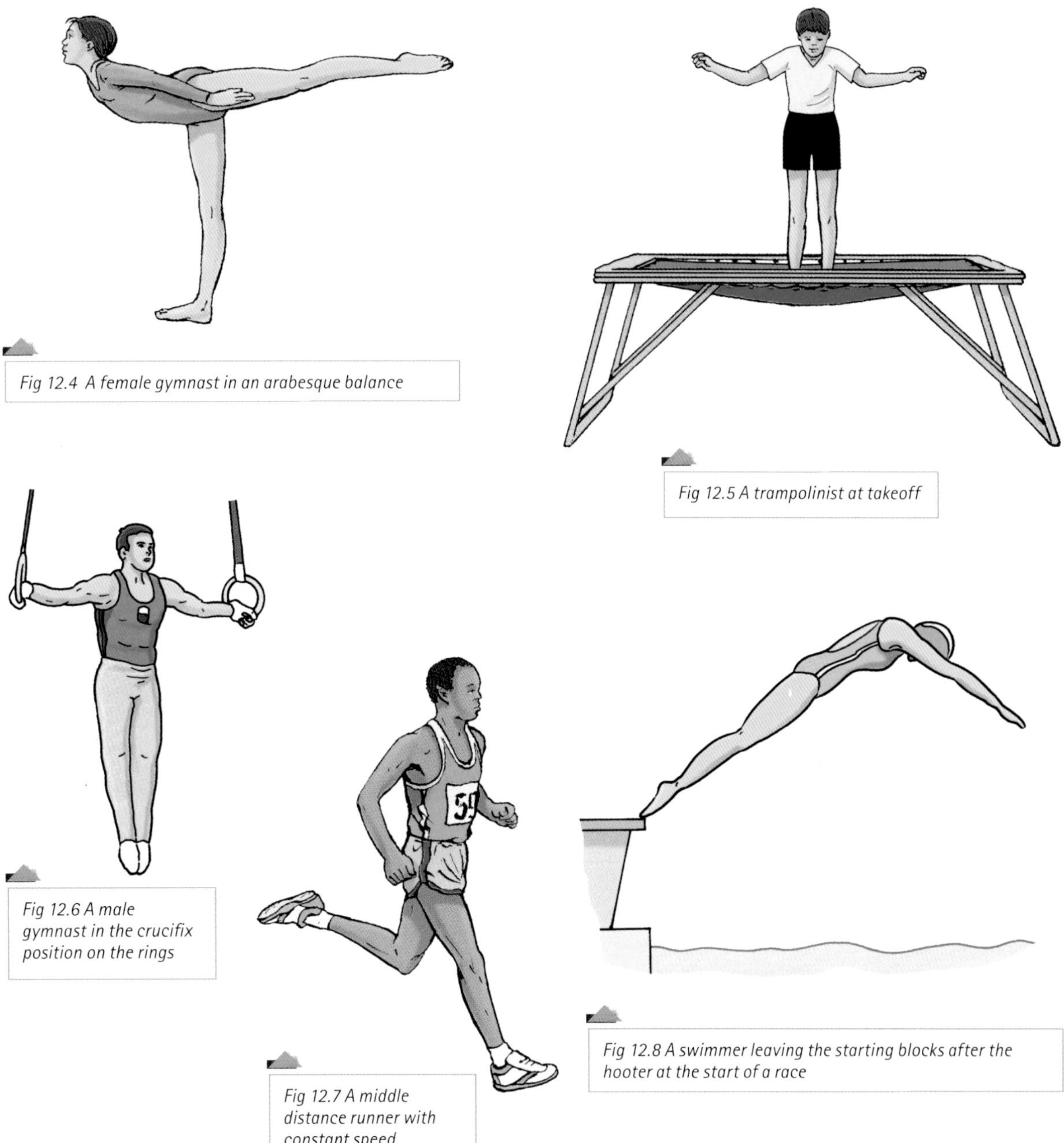

Fig 12.4 A female gymnast in an arabesque balance

Fig 12.5 A trampolinist at takeoff

Fig 12.6 A male gymnast in the crucifix position on the rings

Fig 12.7 A middle distance runner with constant speed

Fig 12.8 A swimmer leaving the starting blocks after the hooter at the start of a race

Types of force acting on a sports performer

The external forces that act on a sports performer on the ground are best divided into vertical forces and horizontal forces.

- Vertical forces are weight and reaction force.
- Horizontal forces are friction and air resistance.

VERTICAL FORCES

WEIGHT

Weight is the **gravitational force** that the Earth exerts on a body and that tends to pull the body towards the centre of the Earth – that is, downwards. The degree of pull between a body and the earth depends on the mass of the body. The greater the mass, the greater the weight force pulling the body downwards. Weight is always acting on all bodies on the Earth's surface (see Fig 12.9).

KEY TERMS

Weight

The force on a body exerted by the Earth's attraction. Weight is measured in Newtons (N).

Gravitational force

The force that attracts a body to the centre of the Earth.

Mass and weight are not the same. The mass of an athlete stays the same, but the weight of the athlete can change depending on their distance from the Earth's core. The further from the Earth's core an athlete stands, the less the Earth's pull on that athlete and the smaller the weight force acting on the athlete. Consider two athletes of equal mass – one performing at the equator and the other performing at the North Pole. Due to the Earth not being perfectly round, the equator is further from the Earth's core than the North Pole, and despite the athletes having the same mass, the athlete at the equator will have less weight to overcome than the athlete at the North Pole.

Fig 12.9 The vertical forces of weight and reaction acting on a tennis player

REMEMBER

Reaction forces will be present at all points of contact. So, a performer in a handstand with two hands on the ground will have two reaction forces. A performer in a sprint start position with both hands and both feet on the ground will have four reaction forces.

APPLY IT!

In the Mexico Olympics of 1968, United States long jumper Bob Beaman set a new world record of 8.90m, beating the previous record by an amazing 55cm. Many reports on this triumph commented on the fact that it was achieved due to the air being thinner at altitude. However, could the weight force acting on Beaman at this distance from the Earth's centre have been less? Could this have been another factor in him achieving this feat?

EXAM TIP

For the tennis player in Fig 12.9, there is no acceleration in the vertical direction. Therefore the forces of weight and reaction are equal and opposite. They are balanced forces, giving a net force of zero. So, the length of the arrow representing weight is equal to the combined length of the arrows representing the reaction force. Be sure to bear this important principle in mind when drawing free body diagrams in your exam. (This is explained further on page 300.)

REACTION FORCE

Reaction forces are a result of Newton's third law of motion. A reaction force will always act whenever two bodies are in contact with each other. For example, consider a tennis player hitting a ball. There will be a reaction force at each point of contact – that is, from each foot in contact with the ground and from the racket in contact with the ball (see Fig 12.9).

HORIZONTAL FORCES

FRICTION FORCE

Friction force occurs when a solid surface of a body moves or tries to move while in contact with the solid surface of another body. For example, it occurs between the soles of a runner's shoes and the running track, and to a lesser extent between the surface of the skis of a downhill skier and the snow. The confusing aspect of friction force is

Fig 12.10 Friction opposes the tendency of one surface to slip or slide over another

that it resists the slipping or sliding motion of the two surfaces. Consider Fig 12.10.

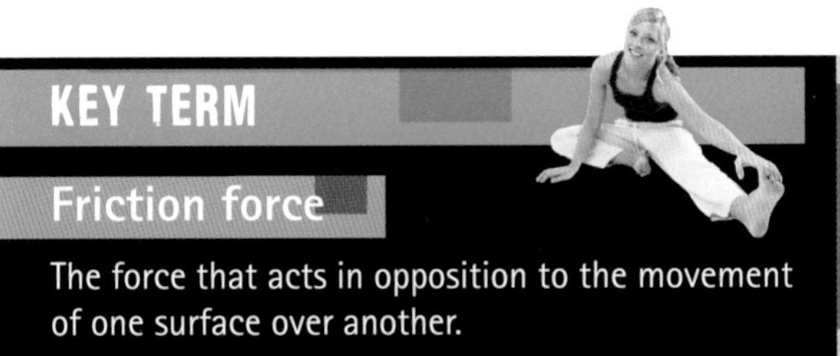

KEY TERM
Friction force
The force that acts in opposition to the movement of one surface over another.

(a) the foot of a runner would tend to slip backwards; friction acts forwards

(b) the skis slide down the hill; friction acts up the hill.

REMEMBER

To decide on the direction of the friction force, first identify the way the surface of the body may slip against the ground. Friction opposes this slipping action and acts in the opposite direction.

MORE ABOUT FRICTION

The amount of friction force an athlete requires varies dramatically from one sport to another. Two of the factors that increase or decrease friction are described below.

1 *The surface characteristics of the two bodies in contact*
To increase friction, one or more of the surfaces needs to be rough. For example, track athletes wear spiked shoes to increase friction with the ground. The spikes stick into the rubbery surface to provide a large friction force that prevents their feet from slipping. This maximises their forward acceleration. Conversely, a downhill skier will want to minimise the friction force because it acts opposite to their direction of motion and will slow their forward acceleration. Downhill ski technicians spend considerable time applying wax to the underside of a racer's skis to decrease the friction between the ski and the snow.

2 *The temperature of the two surfaces in contact*
An increase in temperature will either increase or decrease the friction force depending on the surface characteristics of the bodies in contact. The friction of a ski on snow produces heat that melts a thin layer of snow directly under the ski. This creates a very thin layer of water under the ski upon which the ski glides. The wax applied to a ski, as mentioned above, has water-repellent properties and this is why waxed skis create minimum friction. Conversely, rubber surfaces become sticky when warm. Before a race, superbikes can often be seen on raised stands with their tyres wrapped in covers. These covers are devices that heat the rubber surface of the tyre so that when the race starts, the tyres are at the optimum temperature for holding the road.

TASK 3

1. Think of three examples from sport where an athlete will want to maximise friction. How do they achieve this?
2. Think of three examples from sport where an athlete will want to minimise friction. How do they achieve this?

APPLY IT!

Artificial pitches such as Astroturf create a high level of friction between the surface and the performer's shoe. Sometimes, this friction can be so great that the performer's foot can get stuck in one position causing twisting injuries to the knee or ankle joints.

Friction forces do not only affect sports performers but also the behaviour of balls when bouncing, rolling or sliding over a particular surface. Consider the Grand Slam tennis tournaments where professionals compete on three different court surfaces: hard, grass and clay. Remember that the rougher the surface the greater the effect of friction on the ball when it bounces. Increased friction will slow the ball down after the bounce. The finely mowed grass courts at Wimbledon provide the least friction and the fastest surface. Players who are successful at Wimbledon tend to be powerful servers as the lack of friction on bounce makes their shots very difficult to return. Conversely, the clay courts at Roland Garros in Paris are considerably rougher and provide the most friction on the ball when it bounces. This slows the game down and makes the powerful servers less effective as their opponents have more time to return their shots.

APPLY IT!

Visit the ATP website and look at the current rankings of the top professional male and female tennis players. (To access this site, go to www.heinemann.co.uk/hotlinks, enter the express code 6855P and click on the relevant link.) Carry out some research to identify which of these players is a grass court specialist and which a clay court specialist. Look into their respective successes at Wimbledon compared to the French Open.

Fig 12.11 A change in temperature can increase or decrease friction. Tyre warmers on superbikes will increase friction between the rubber surface of the tyre and the track at the start of the race, giving the rider confidence on the first bend

STRETCH AND CHALLENGE

For the purposes of A-level PE, you have considered friction as a whole. However, there are in fact three types of friction that affect performance in sport. These are static friction, sliding friction and rolling friction. The sport of cycling is a good starting point to research the use of these types of friction in sport. The diversity of events from road racing to BMX to mountain biking to sprint and endurance events in the velodrome means that the design of the tyres is different for each type of bike. Prepare a presentation that explains how the designers of bikes for specific events use their knowledge of friction to optimise performance.

AIR RESISTANCE

Air resistance acts on a body travelling through air. It acts in the opposite direction to the direction of travel of the moving body. For example, in running and cycling events, as the performer sprints forward, air resistance acts backwards. So, air resistance always acts in the opposite direction to the motion of the body. It opposes the acceleration of a body by pushing, pulling or tugging on an athlete.

APPLY IT!

- Consider a time when you may have been on a games field on a windy day and have tried to run into a strong headwind. You may have felt the force of air resistance pushing you back in the opposite direction.
- In athletics, why do you think that the wind speed is given as a positive or negative value next to times for the sprints and distances for the jumps?

There are a number of factors that affect the size of the air resistance force experienced by a body. These are:

1 the velocity of the body
2 the cross-sectional area of the body
3 the shape and surface characteristics of the body.

Each of these factors is discussed in detail on the section on fluid mechanics on page 310.

REMEMBER

The terms air resistance, drag and fluid friction all refer to a force that acts in the direction opposing the motion of a body. Air resistance applies to a body travelling in air only, whereas drag and fluid friction are terms that apply to a body travelling in any fluid environment (that is, a liquid or a gas). The size of the drag force does not only depend on points 1–3 above but also the fluid environment through which the body is travelling. Water has a greater density than air and is harder to push through. An athlete who runs from the beach into the sea, such as at the start of a triathlon, will encounter a greater drag force from the water than the air. Sports performers who try to minimise fluid friction include swimmers and performers travelling quickly through air, such as cyclists, sprinters and skiers. Methods used to reduce the drag forces on these types of performers are discussed on pages 310 and 311.

KEY TERMS

Air resistance

The force acting in the opposite direction to the motion of a body travelling through air.

Drag/fluid friction

The resistance caused by friction in the direction opposite to the motion of a body travelling through a fluid. (Although there is a small difference in these two terms, for the purposes of A-level PE, they can be used synonymously.)

Free body diagrams

Free body diagrams are used to show the forces acting on a body at a particular instant in time. On page 289, you learned that an arrow can be used to represent a force, and the position, direction and length of this arrow must be carefully considered to ensure that each force is represented as accurately as possible.

KEY TERM

Free body diagram

A clearly labelled sketch showing all of the forces acting on a particular object at a particular instant in time.

EXAM TIP

Your examiner will not expect you to be a great artist when sketching a free body diagram. They will expect to see a rough sketch of a stick figure with the force arrows attached, as explained over the next few pages. An example of a free body diagram of a performer running at constant speed is shown in Fig 12.12.

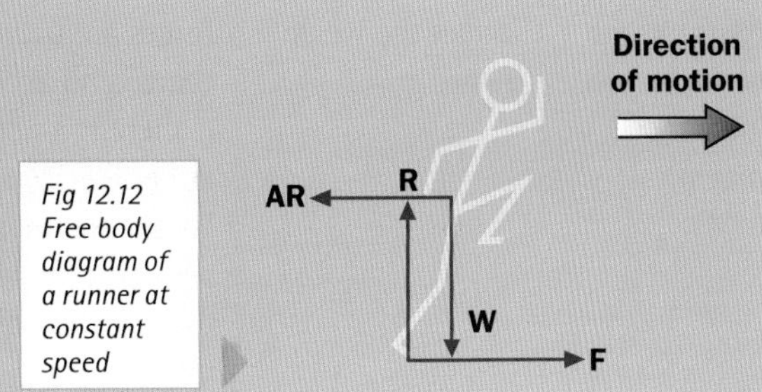

Fig 12.12 Free body diagram of a runner at constant speed

The four forces of weight, reaction, friction and air resistance can be shown on a free body diagram in the form of an arrow. To gain maximum marks in an examination question requires a sketch of a free body diagram and insertion of the arrows to represent the forces in a specific order.

Firstly, consider the vertical forces.

1 Draw on the weight force, as this will always be present.
2 Draw on the reaction force(s) wherever there are two bodies in contact with each other, such as the athlete's foot with the ground or the hockey stick with the ball.
Next, consider the horizontal forces.
3 Draw on the friction force(s) whenever there are two bodies in contact with each other that may have a tendency to slip or slide over each other, such as a swimmer's foot on the starting blocks.
4 Draw on the air resistance force only if the body is moving. Remember that this force will be acting in the opposite direction to motion.

Table 1 summarises how to draw accurate free body diagrams.

KEY TERM

Normal reaction force

The force between two bodies in contact with each other in a direction perpendicular (at 90 degrees) to the surface of contact.

	Vertical Forces		**Horizontal Forces**	
	Weight	**Reaction Force**	**Friction**	**Air Resistance**
Label on arrow	W	R	F	AR
Origin of arrow	Coming from the centre of mass	Coming from the point(s) of contact of two bodies	Coming from the point(s) of contact of two bodies	Coming from the centre of mass
Direction of arrow	Vertically downwards	Perpendicular to the surface of contact – usually vertically upwards (this is the **normal reaction force**)	Opposite to the direction of slip between the two bodies – usually in the same direction as motion	Opposite to the direction of motion of the body
Length of arrow (refer back to page 290 to remind yourself of net force and balanced and unbalanced forces)	Will depend on the mass of the body – the larger the mass, the greater the weight and the longer the weight arrow	As a result of Newton's first and second laws, this will depend on the resulting motion in the vertical direction. If net force = 0, R = W as forces are balanced and there is no acceleration. If there is a net force, either R > W or R < W. Forces are unbalanced and acceleration will occur in the direction of the larger force.	As a result of Newton's first and second laws, this will depend on the resulting motion in the horizontal direction. If net force = 0, F = AR as forces are balanced and there is no acceleration. If there is a net force, either F > AR or F < AR. Forces are unbalanced and acceleration will occur in the direction of the larger force.	

	Vertical Forces		Horizontal Forces
Diagram	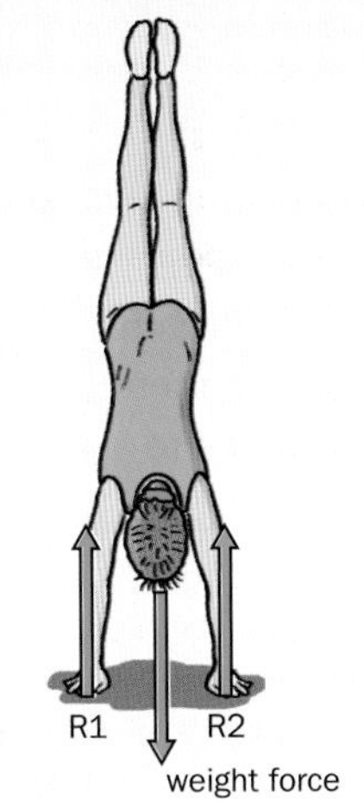 *Fig 12.13 Handstand* Balanced forces, R1 + R2 = W, net force = 0, no acceleration therefore body remains stationary	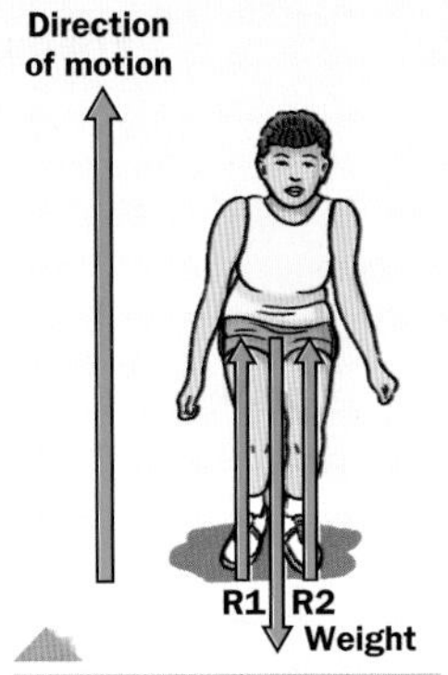 *Fig 12.14 Vertical jump at takeoff* Unbalanced forces, R1 + R2, are greater than W; net force is present – acceleration in the upward direction, to allow the jumper to takeoff 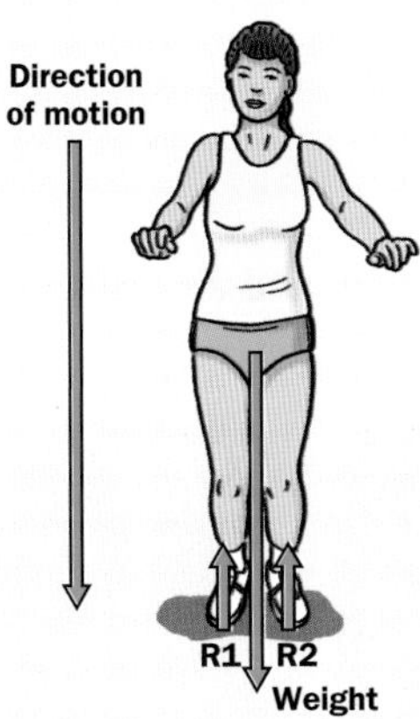 *Fig 12.15 Vertical jump at landing* Unbalanced forces, R1 + R2, are less than W; net force is present – acceleration in the downward direction as the jumper lands.	 *Fig 12.16 Balanced forces* F=AR, net force = 0; no acceleration therefore constant speed  *Fig 12.17 Unbalanced forces* F>AR; net force is present – acceleration in the forward direction, runner's velocity increases 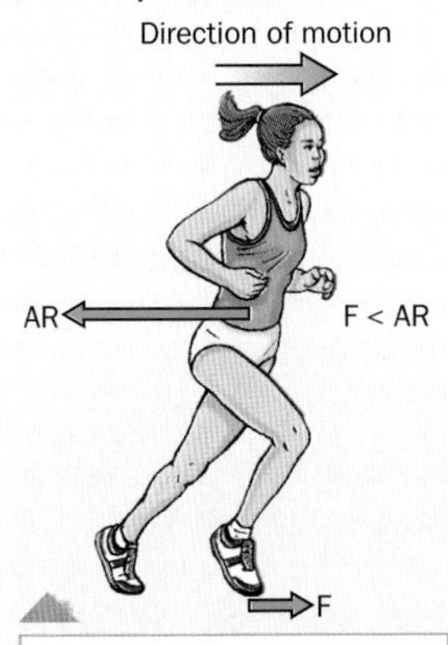 *Fig 12.18 Unbalanced forces* F<AR, net force is present, acceleration in the backward direction, runner's velocity decreases.

	Vertical Forces		Horizontal Forces	
	Weight	Reaction Force	Friction	Air Resistance
Remember	• Draw first • Will always be present • There will only ever be one weight arrow per body	• Draw second • Will only be present if there are two bodies in contact • There could be more than one reaction arrow per body	• Draw third • Will only be present if there are two bodies in contact and there is a tendency to slip or slide over each other • There could be more than one friction arrow per body	• Draw last • Will only be present if there are unbalanced forces, i.e. acceleration • The greater the velocity, the larger the cross-sectional area and the rougher the surface characteristics, the larger the air resistance and the longer the arrow • There will only ever be one air resistance arrow per body

Table 1 The four forces of weight, reaction, friction and air resistance

REMEMBER

In sporting situations where there is more than one point of contact, as shown in the handstand and vertical jump in Table 1, you need to be very careful of the length you make the arrows that represent opposing forces. If net force is zero, opposite forces must balance. So, in the vertical direction, each of the reaction force arrows must be half the length of the weight force arrow (see Fig 12.13). So, the two reaction forces added together will balance out the weight force and, according to Newton's first law, there will be no change in the state of motion of the body – it will remain stationary. The same principle applies in the horizontal direction, when you have two friction forces compared to one air resistance force. For constant speed, the sum of the two friction forces must be equal and opposite to the air resistance.

TASK 4

Find some action pictures from the sports pages of newspapers or the Internet. Stick them onto sheets of plain paper and use them to draw on the forces that are acting. Remember to be very careful in terms of origin, direction and length of arrows, and do not forget to label your arrows clearly. Under each picture identify the relative sizes of the vertical forces and the horizontal forces and link this to Newton's laws by making a comment on the net force, linking it to balanced or unbalanced forces.

EXAM TIPS

Here are four tips for ensuring you score well on a question asking for a free body diagram:

1 Use a stick figure.
2 Draw a direction of motion arrow.
3 Label each of the force arrows correctly.
4 Make a comment about the net force in the vertical direction and the net force in the horizontal direction – even if one of them is zero. This shows the examiner that you fully understand the concept of Newton's laws, net force, and balanced and unbalanced forces.

If you can follow these guidelines, you should score maximum marks every time!

Fig 12.19 shows a model answer to a question where the examiner has asked for a sketch of a free body diagram of a swimmer on the starting blocks at the moment of takeoff.

Fig 12.19 Model answer

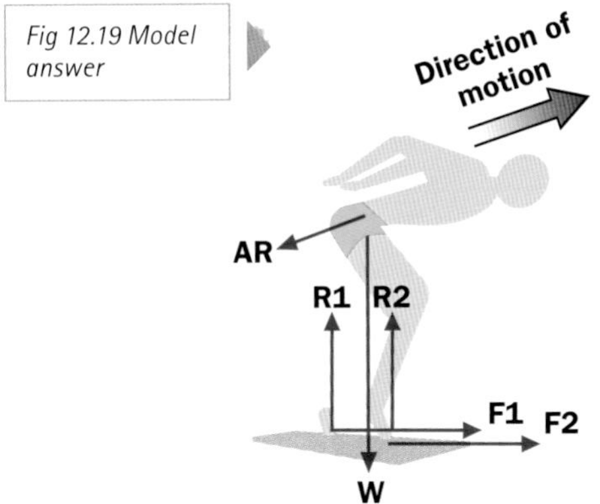

Vertical Forces: R1 + R2 > W; net force is present – acceleration in upward direction

Horizontal forces: F1 + F2 > AR; net force is present – acceleration in forward direction

Impulse

From your study of Newton's laws, you should now be familiar with the fact that force must be exerted to change the state of motion of a body. This force will take a certain amount of time to apply. When performers apply a force over a certain time, we call this **impulse**. It follows, therefore, that to calculate impulse, you multiply the force applied in Newtons (N) by the time for which the force is applied in seconds. Impulse is measured in Newton seconds (Ns).

Impulse = Force x time
I = Ft

KEY TERM

Impulse

The product of force multiplied by the time for which the force acts. Impulse is measured in Newton seconds (Ns).

The relative contributions of the size of the force and the time for which it acts will depend on the type of skill being performed. Some skills require a very large force to be applied over a short period of time, while other techniques require a smaller force to be applied for a longer period of time. Consider the force and time applied to a hockey ball during a hitting action compared to a pushing action.

TASK 5

1 Name two sporting skills that require a large force to be generated over a short period of time.
2 Name two sporting skills that require a smaller force to be applied over a longer period of time.

Athletes can increase impulse in two ways:

1 *By increasing the amount of muscular force they apply.*
The greater the force, the greater the impulse. Consider the force that needs to be generated by a golfer when driving the ball from the tee compared to the force they will need to impart to the ball for a short putt.

Fig 12.20 Sports performers are always trying to increase impulse by (a) applying a very large force over a short period of time or (b) applying a smaller force over a longer time

2 *By increasing the amount of time over which they apply the force.*
The longer the time over which the force is applied, the greater the impulse. Consider the greater time for which the force is applied to a discus during a one-and-three-quarter turn compared to a standing throw.

From Newton's second law we know that an increase in impulse will result in an increase in the rate of change of momentum, causing a larger change in velocity. Athletes are always looking to develop sports techniques to achieve a greater impulse, whether this is to increase momentum or decrease momentum.

TASK 6

1 Elite javelin throwers need to be powerful as well as flexible in their shoulders and back. Use your knowledge of impulse to explain why these two fitness components will enable an elite thrower to impart a greater outgoing velocity to the javelin.
2 Describe one other sporting technique where it is important to optimise impulse and explain how this is achieved.
3 What do you think is the significance of the use of air bubbles in a diving pool during training?

USING IMPULSE TO INCREASE MOMENTUM

In addition to the examples given above to increase impulse, all good high jumpers use a technique to maximise impulse at takeoff. This allows them to generate a greater change in momentum and increase the velocity with which they leave the ground. To achieve this, they lean backwards as they plant their takeoff foot. This allows them to apply a force to the ground over a longer period of time as their body passes over the planted foot. This increased impulse causes a greater upward acceleration to help clear the bar.

USING IMPULSE TO DECREASE MOMENTUM

Knowledge of impulse can also be used to slow down or stop a body safely. There are many sports in which athletes are taught specific techniques so that they extend the time that forces act on their bodies to avoid injury. Consider the significant forces that are imparted to the body of a ski jumper on landing. By flexing at the hip, knee and ankle on contact with the snow, the time during which the forces are applied to the jumper on landing is increased and the impact on the body at this moment in time is significantly decreased. This is the reason why all children are coached always to bend their knees on landing. Similarly, a fielder in cricket who needs to catch a fiercely driven cricket ball will draw their hands backwards at the instant of contact. This increases the time frame over which the force of the ball is applied to their hands, which has two advantages: firstly, it reduces the sting caused by the fast-moving hard cricket ball, and secondly, it prevents the ball bouncing out of the fielder's hands.

APPLY IT!

Performers in sport do not always need to rely on specific techniques to avoid pain or injury in impact situations. Certain equipment used in sport is designed to extend the time over which the force acts on the performer's body. For example, wicket-keeping gloves in cricket, shin pads in hockey and padded helmets used in amateur boxing. Can you think of any other examples?

STRETCH AND CHALLENGE

Sprinting and rowing are continuous skills, but throughout their races, these athletes vary the amount of force and the time for which they apply this force with their muscles. Research some information about variations in stride rate in the 100m sprint and/or stroke rate in a 2000m rowing race. Use your knowledge of inertia and impulse to justify when and why these variations take place.

Fig 12.21 At various stages of a 2000m race, rowers vary the amount of force and the time for which they apply this force with their muscles. Why?

FORCE/TIME GRAPHS TO REPRESENT IMPULSE

Impulse can be represented by the shaded area under a force/time graph. Figure 12.22 shows a force/time graph that can be sketched for a tennis forehand ground stroke.

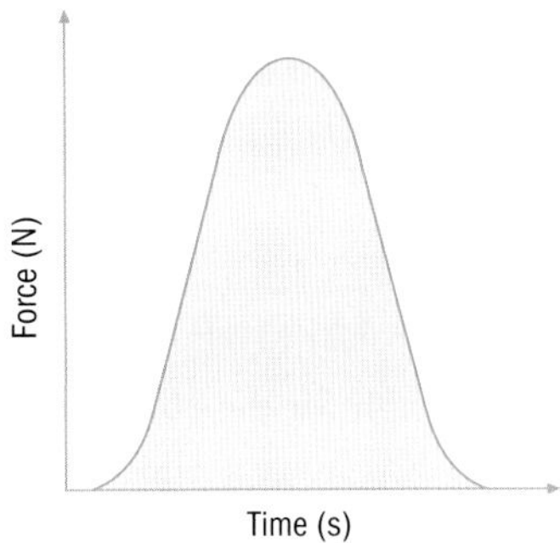

Fig 12.22 A force/time graph for a forehand drive. The shaded area represents impulse

TASK 7

1 Sketch a force/time graph for the following situations:
   a) a hockey ball being hit without follow through
   b) a hockey ball being hit with follow through.
2 Use your knowledge of impulse to discuss the advantages of using a follow through in sporting techniques where a large outgoing velocity is required.

Force/time graphs can also be used to show the impulse applied by a performer on the ground. Two examples that your examiner might ask about are in the takeoff phase of the vertical jump and in the foot plant at different stages of a 100m sprint.

In force/time graphs, a curve below the x-axis shows a negative impulse and a net force in the opposite direction to the resulting motion, and a curve above the x-axis shows a positive impulse and a net force in the same direction to the resulting motion (see Fig 12.23).

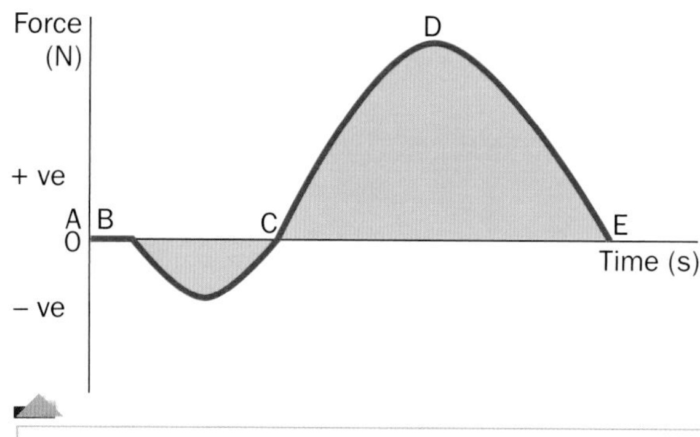

Fig 12.23 Force/time graph for takeoff phase in the vertical jump

EXAM TIP

To explain the shape of force/time graphs, use your knowledge of Newton's laws, net force, and balanced and unbalanced forces.

VERTICAL JUMP TAKEOFF

The force/time graph for the complete takeoff phase in the vertical jump is shown in Figure 12.23 and explained in Table 2. Remember that for a performer executing the vertical jump, there will be two external forces acting on them. These are the vertical forces of weight acting downwards and the reaction force acting upwards.

FOOT PLANT IN SPRINTING

The force/time graphs for the three phases (acceleration, maximum speed and deceleration) of the 100m are shown and explained in Table 3. There is no need for us to go into detail about the technicalities of these forces, so it is sufficient to remember that positive forces are those that act on the sprinter in the direction of the run and negative forces are those that act on the sprinter in the direction opposite to that of the run.

Section of graph	Description	Explanation
A–B: stationary phase	Impulse is 0, therefore net force is 0. Opposing forces are balanced (W = R).	There is no acceleration and jumper remains stationary.
B–C: downward phase	Impulse is negative, therefore net force is negative. Opposing forces are unbalanced with the downward force being larger than the upward (W > R).	There is acceleration in the downward direction, which is considered negative as it is in the opposite direction to the resulting motion. This occurs as the jumper flexes their hips and knees to dip downwards.
C–D: upward phase 1	Impulse is positive, therefore net force is positive. Opposing forces are unbalanced with the upward force being larger than the downward (W < R).	There is acceleration in the upward direction, which is considered positive as it is in the same direction as the resulting motion. This occurs as the jumper applies a large action force on the ground and therefore gains a large reaction force from the ground.
D–E: upward phase 2	Impulse is still positive but reducing in size as the jumper accelerates towards the point where their feet leave the ground (point E).	As the jumper's legs extend further, the action force with which they push against the ground decreases and therefore the reaction force from the ground on the jumper also decreases.

Table 2 Explanation of the force/time graph in Figure 12.23

Force/time graph	Description	Explanation
Acceleration phase/early stage of race Force (N); + ve; 0; – ve; Time (s) Fig 12.24	*First section:* Impulse is negative. The force applied as the foot makes contact with the ground acts opposite to the direction of motion. *Second section:* Impulse is positive. The force applied as the body moves over the supporting foot acts in the same direction as the direction of motion.	*First section:* Forward momentum of sprinter decreases. *Second section:* Forward momentum of sprinter increases. *Overall:* Positive impulse > negative impulse, therefore sprinter achieves a net force in the forward direction. This causes the acceleration seen in the early stages of the race.
Maximum speed/middle stages of race Force (N); + ve; 0; – ve; Time (s) Fig 12.25	*First section:* Impulse is negative. The force applied as the foot makes contact with the ground acts opposite to the direction of motion. *Second section:* Impulse is positive. The force applied as the body moves over the supporting foot acts in the same direction as the direction of motion.	*First section:* Forward momentum of sprinter decreases. *Second section:* Forward momentum of sprinter increases. *Overall:* Positive impulse = negative impulse, therefore the net force acting on the sprinter is zero. There is no acceleration and maximum speed has been reached in the middle section of the race.
Deceleration phase/closing stage of race Force (N); + ve; 0; – ve; Time (s) Fig 12.26	*First section:* Impulse is negative. The force applied as the foot makes contact with the ground acts opposite the direction of motion. *Second section:* Impulse is positive. The force applied as the body moves over the supporting foot acts in the same direction as the direction of motion.	*First section:* Forward momentum of sprinter decreases. *Second section:* Forward momentum of sprinter increases. *Overall:* Negative impulse > positive impulse, therefore sprinter achieves a net force in the direction opposite to the direction of motion. This causes the deceleration seen in the closing stages of the race. This could be due to fatigue, increased air resistance or simply a conscious effort by the sprinter to 'ease up' before the tape.

Table 3 Explanation of the force/time graphs for the three phases of the 100m

APPLY IT!

It has been suggested that elite sprinters minimise negative impulse by pulling through quickly during the initial foot plant. This minimises the time for which negative force acts on their bodies.

STRETCH AND CHALLENGE

Plot a force/time graph to show the impulse achieved by a sprinter while pushing against the starting blocks on hearing the gun fire. Describe and explain your graph.

Exam**Café**

Relax, refresh, result!

You should now have knowledge and understanding of:

- the definition and measurement of force and the effects of a force on a performer or object
- the concept of net force and balanced and unbalanced forces
- the nature of the vertical forces acting on a sports performer (weight force and reaction force) and appreciate the effect they have on the resulting motion of a performer
- the nature of the horizontal forces acting on a sports performer (friction force and air resistance force) and appreciate the effect they have on the resulting motion of a performer
- how to sketch simple free body diagrams to identify the type and relative size of the external forces acting on a sports performer at a particular instant in time
- impulse and its relationship to momentum
- how to sketch force/time graphs and appreciate the information that can be gained from them.

REVISE AS YOU GO!

1. What is meant by the following terms?
   a) Force
   b) Internal force
   c) External force
   d) Net force
   e) Balanced forces
   f) Unbalanced forces
2. Using sporting examples of your choice, describe five effects that a force can have on a body.
3. What are the three all-important considerations to bear in mind when using an arrow to represent force acting on a body at a particular instant in time?
4. Define the following terms:
   a) weight
   b) reaction force
   c) friction
   d) air resistance.

Try to answer these questions yourself. Ask your teacher if you need help.

5. Using examples from a sport of your choice:
   a) give one example of how friction is increased
   b) give one example of how friction is decreased.
6. What is meant by the term drag?
7. Sketch a free body diagram of a sports person of your choice showing all the forces acting on them at a particular moment in time. Make a comment on the net force in the vertical and horizontal directions.
8. Define the term impulse and explain its relationship to changing momentum.
9. Sports performers will look to increase impulse. Describe two ways in which this can be achieved.
10. Graphs a and b are two force/time graphs.

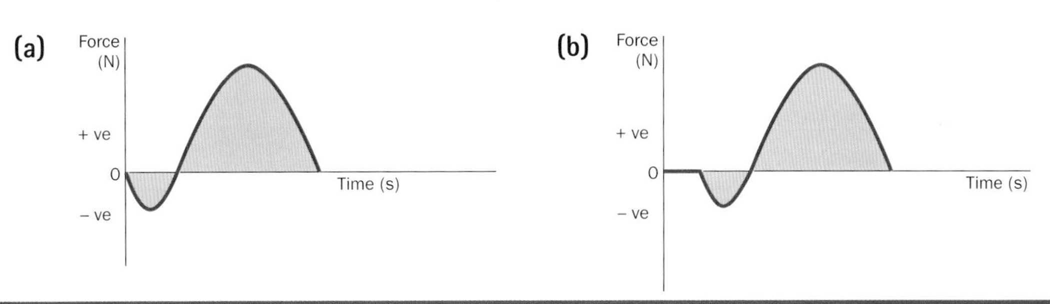

Identify the force/time graph for each of the following:
   i the takeoff phase of a vertical jump
   ii. the foot plant for the acceleration phase of the 100m sprint
   iii. the foot plant for the deceleration phase of the 100m sprint.

Get the result!

Examination question

Sketch a free body diagram to show the forces acting on a sprinter immediately after the start of a 100m race. Comment on the horizontal forces acting on the sprinter and justify their relative sizes in relation to the resulting motion. (5 marks)

Examiner's tips

There are two parts to this question, so check the command word for each. Remember the importance of the origin, length and direction of the arrows used to represent the forces in your sketch of the free body diagram. In your comments for the second part of the answer, to achieve a high grade, make links with Newton's laws and include a remark on net force.

Student's answer

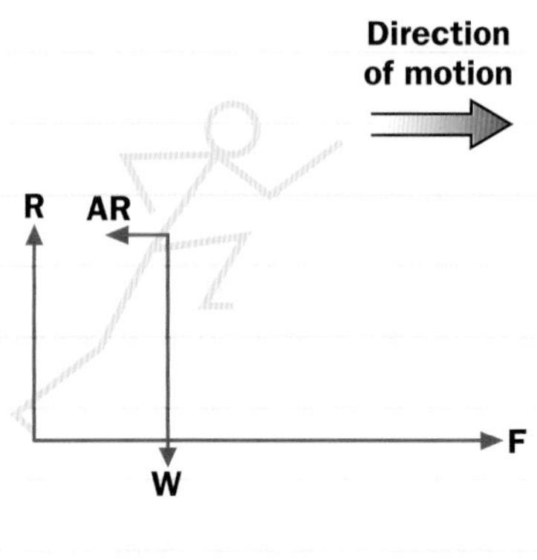

The horizontal forces are friction and air resistance. For a runner that is accelerating the friction force is larger than the air resistance force. This means the runner will accelerate down the track.

Examiner says:

Your answer starts w… an accurate free bo… diagram for a sprint… immediately after th… start of the race. You… confirm that you kno… friction must be larg… than air resistance ir… written response. Ho… you do not justify wh… this is the case by us… Newton's laws or you… understanding of ne… force and unbalanc… forces. Your answer… simply descriptive a… falls short of the dem… of the question.

Student's improved answer

Examiner says:

A clear and simple free body diagram with arrows clearly labelled and accurately representing the four forces of weight, reaction, friction and air resistance. You also included a direction of motion arrow.

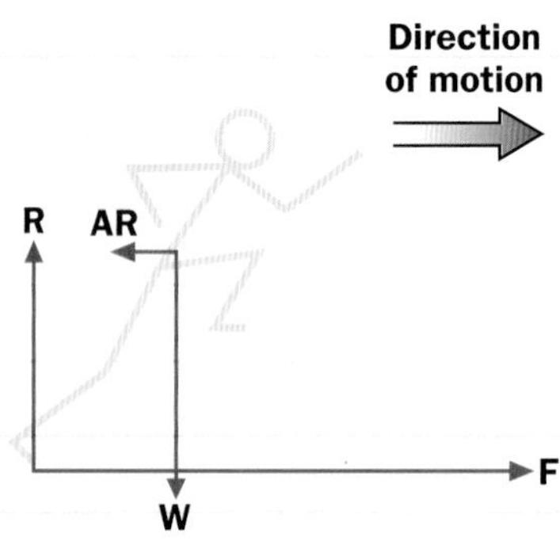

The horizontal forces are friction and air resistance. Friction opposes the tendency of the foot to slip backwards and acts in the same direction as the direction of motion. Air resistance acts in the opposite direction to motion.

Examiner says:

This is a logical way to start your answer by identifying and describing the horizontal forces acting on the sprint…

At the start of the race, the sprinter is accelerating. Therefore, according to Newton's first law, there must be a net force in the forward direction. This is the case because the friction force is greater than the air resistance force. Friction is large because the sprinter will be wearing spikes that dig into the surface of the track. Air resistance is small because, at the start of the race, the sprinter's velocity is relatively low. The horizontal forces are unbalanced and acceleration occurs in the direction of the larger force.

Examiner says:

This is a logical way to start your answer by identifying and describing the horizontal forces acting on the sprinter.

Examiner says:

Already you have shown the quality o… your understanding by mentioning Newton's laws and net force.

Examiner says:

This is good analysi… and proves that yo… know why each for… is the size it is at this instant of time in the race.

As a result of Newton's second law, the greater the friction force the greater the acceleration of the sprinter in the forward direction.

Examiner says:

This concludes a quality answer very well with another reference to Newton's laws.

CHAPTER 13:

Fluid mechanics in physical activity

LEARNING OBJECTIVES

By the end of this chapter you should have knowledge and understanding of:

- the impact of air resistance (drag or fluid friction) on sporting activity and how to apply the concept of reducing drag in certain sports
- how to sketch free body diagrams to identify the forces acting on a projectile in flight and how to use the parallelogram of forces to explain the resultant flight path
- how to explain and apply the Bernoulli principle in a number of different sporting activities
- the three types of spin commonly observed in sporting activities (top spin, back spin and side spin) and their impact on flight path and bounce
- how to sketch detailed diagrams to help explain how the Magnus effect causes spinning projectiles to deviate from their non-spinning flight paths.

INTRODUCTION

A fluid is any liquid or any gas – any substance that can flow. A body that travels through a fluid is slowed down by **drag** forces, or **fluid friction**, so an understanding of **fluid mechanics** allows us to make a judgment on how to increase or decrease the forces acting against a body travelling through the air or in water. Activities that are significantly affected by their fluid environment include swimming, cycling, sprinting and skiing, as well as any sport involving **projectiles**.

KEY TERMS

Drag/fluid friction

The resistance to motion on a body travelling through fluid. The resistance acts opposite to the direction of motion and therefore inhibits velocity.

Fluid mechanics

The study of objects or bodies that travel through a fluid. Fluid mechanics are particularly significant for bodies travelling through water or for those with high velocity travelling through the air, such as projectiles.

Projectile

Human bodies or objects launched into the air that are subject to the forces of weight and air resistance only.

In this chapter we will begin by considering how sport science enables performers to minimise drag and thereby maximise velocity. We will then apply our knowledge of force to different types of projectile that are observed in sporting activities and consider the factors that affect their flight paths. This analysis leads us on to looking at the effect of spin on projectiles in the air and on bouncing when they come back down to the ground.

Air resistance/drag/fluid friction

You will recall from Chapter 12 that a friction force occurs when a solid surface of a body moves while in contact with the solid surface of another body. Fluid friction can therefore be considered as the force that occurs when a solid surface of a body moves while in contact with a fluid surface. This could be the fluid friction caused by a swimmer travelling through water or that caused by a tennis ball travelling through air.

A NOTE ABOUT TERMINOLOGY

You will see from the key terms box above that the terms air resistance, drag and fluid friction basically mean the same thing. For the purposes of this chapter, we will continue to use the term air resistance as this was the force introduced in Chapter 12. It is worth remembering everything we talk about obviously relates to the other two terms as well.

STRETCH AND CHALLENGE

Air resistance will vary depending on the air conditions. When air temperature increases, its density decreases and this reduces air resistance. Likewise, air resistance is smaller at higher altitudes than at sea level due to the air being less dense. While a smaller air resistance force may be an advantage to runners, jumpers and throwers in athletics, it can be a disadvantage to athletes such as badminton players because a shuttle hit with the same force at altitude as at sea level will travel further and therefore is at greater risk of landing out.

Research the effect of reducing or increasing air resistance in badminton.

The three factors that affect the size of the air resistance force acting on a body are:

- the velocity of the body
- the cross-sectional area of the body
- the shape and surface characteristics of the body.

(See also page 313.)

The greater the velocity of a body travelling through a fluid, the greater the air resistance it will encounter. It is for this reason that fast-moving athletes, such as swimmers, sprinters and cyclists, do their utmost to use knowledge of cross-sectional area, shape and surface characteristics to minimise these forces.

The larger the cross-sectional area of a body travelling through a fluid, the greater the air resistance it will encounter. Therefore, athletes such as swimmers, cyclists and downhill skiers make every effort to adopt body positions that minimise their cross-sectional area. This is called **streamlining.** A streamlined shape is like a teardrop or an **aerofoil.**

KEY TERMS

Streamlining

Shaping a body so that it causes the least drag when travelling through a fluid.

Aerofoil

A streamlined shape with a curved upper surface and an under surface that is predominantly flat – like the cross-section of the wing of an aircraft.

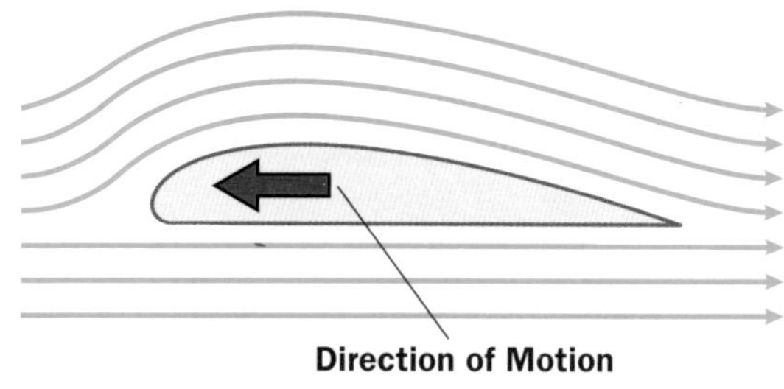

Fig 13.1 A teardrop or aerofoil shape is a streamlined shape that minimises air resistance due to the small cross-sectional area that is at right angles to the direction of fluid flow and the gradual curve into a tapered back, which allows smooth airflow over its surface

The shape and the surface characteristics of the body travelling through a fluid also affect the amount of air resistance. Any lumps or bumps that affect the shape of a body will increase air resistance. Likewise, the rougher the surface that comes into contact with the fluid, the greater the effect of air resistance. The aerofoil shape in Figure 13.1 would reduce air resistance even further if it was covered in a smooth surface.

APPLY IT!

Consider the sport of competitive cycling. Air resistance is reduced to a minimum by:

- making the bike from lightweight metal and modern materials to reduce weight
- having a large disc rear wheel that tilts the frame downwards towards the front and eliminates any air resistance that might be caused by spokes
- adopting a low head position with back parallel to the ground
- wearing a super-smooth one-piece skin-tight suit, skin-tight gloves and shoes without laces
- shaving arms, legs and face
- wearing a smooth-surfaced shaped helmet.

These factors help the cyclist adopt an aerofoil, streamlined shape, which keeps the frontal cross-sectional area to a minimum. All surfaces that come into contact with the air are smooth and slick and some cyclists have even been known to spray their bodies with silicone to reduce drag even further.

Fig 13.2 The aerofoil, streamlined shape of a cyclist

Fig 13.3 The Speedo LZR Racer swimsuit streamlines the body while swimming

APPLY IT!

The Speedo LZR Racer swimsuit caused a stir in the swimming world when it was first introduced. While a large number of swimmers have broken World and Olympic records when wearing this specialist full-body suit, critics of the suit have referred to it as 'technological doping'. Some have gone so far as to suggest that it might have an adverse effect on the body in the long term by causing circulatory disorders due to its excessive tightness that restricts blood flow.

STRETCH AND CHALLENGE

1 Research the technology behind the Speedo LZR Racer swimsuit and explain its advantages to swimmers.
2 Within your class, hold the following debate: 'This house believes that the Speedo LZR Racer swimsuit should not be legal and is a form of technological doping.'

TASK 1

1 Consider the 100m sprint. Give two reasons why air resistance increases during the race. Try to relate your answer to the forward acceleration of the athlete at the start and end of the race.
2 Sprinters and skiers are always trying to minimise the effect of air resistance acting on them, which slows them down. Design a poster that explains the methods employed to reduce drag by a sprinter or skier of your choice. Include a picture or photograph of your chosen athlete.

Projectiles

In sport there are a considerable number of events in which bodies are projected into the air to follow a certain flight path. These bodies can either be an athlete who propels him or herself into the air (such as a high jumper or a long jumper in athletics), or can be an object that an athlete hits, kicks or throws into the air (such as a shot put, a rugby ball or a badminton shuttle). Whenever an athlete breaks contact with the ground or an object is released, it becomes a projectile.

PARABOLAS AND FLIGHT PATHS

Once propelled into the air, two forces act on a projectile: weight and air resistance. As the effect of air resistance increases, the more a projectile will deviate from a true **parabola**.

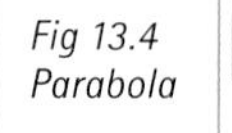

Fig 13.4 Parabola

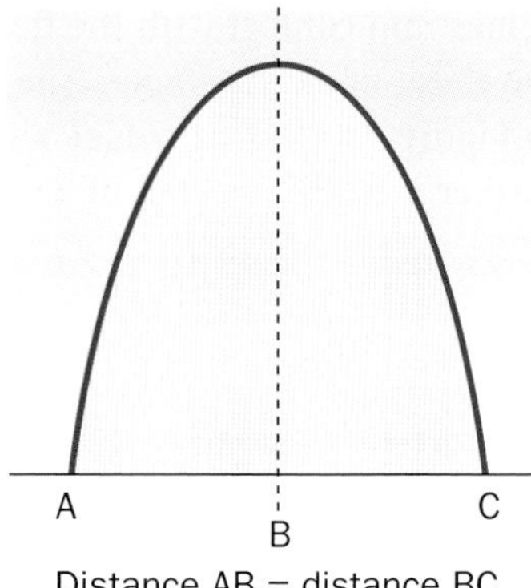

The relative sizes of these forces of weight and air resistance will affect the flight path.

- Projectiles that have a large weight force and small air resistance force, such as a shot put, follow paths close to a true parabola.
- Objects that travel at high velocity that have a large cross-sectional area and a rough outer surface are most affected by air resistance and therefore follow flight paths that deviate from a true parabola. This is the case for golf balls, footballs and badminton shuttles.

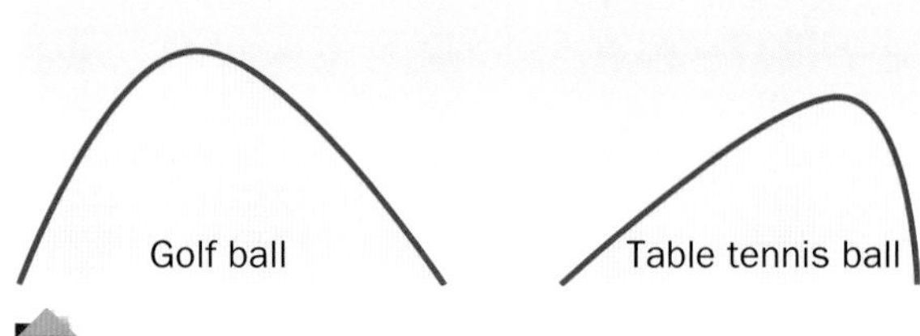

Fig 13.5 Objects with large mass are least affected by air resistance and more likely to follow a parabolic flight path

It is also true that the relative contribution of air resistance compared to weight increases as the mass of an object decreases. Consider a golf ball and a table tennis ball being projected into the air with the same amount of force. The golf ball will follow a flight path closer to a true parabola and will be less affected by air resistance because it is heavier.

KEY TERM

Parabola

A uniform curve that is symmetrical about its highest point.

REMEMBER

Once in flight, the projectile is not in contact with another body so cannot be affected by reaction or friction forces, which rely on two solid bodies to be in contact with one another.

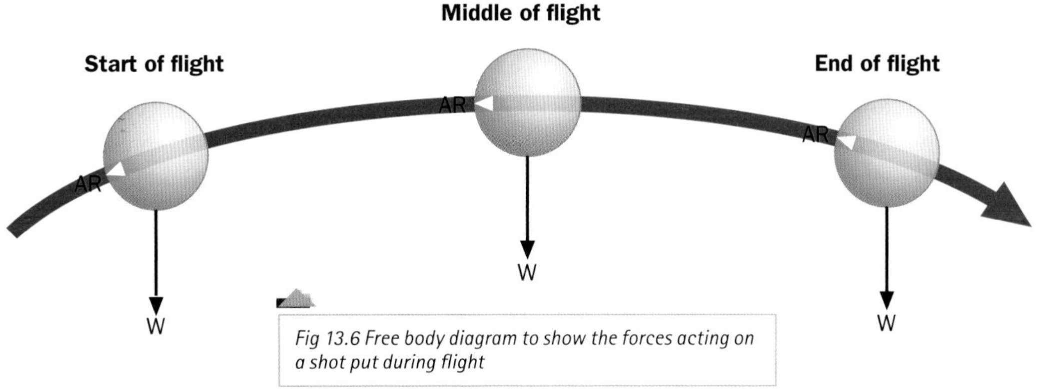

Fig 13.6 Free body diagram to show the forces acting on a shot put during flight

REMEMBER

The only two forces that act on a projectile are weight and air resistance. The effect of air resistance increases with:

- a decrease in the mass of the body
- an increase in the velocity of the body, the cross-sectional area of the body and the roughness of the surface of the body.

FORCES ACTING ON A PROJECTILE DURING FLIGHT

The forces acting on a projectile during flight can be represented using a free body diagram. The importance of the point of application, direction and size of the force arrow used to represent weight and air resistance still holds true. The greater the mass of the projectile, the longer the weight force arrow needs to be. The greater the velocity, the cross-sectional area or the roughness of the surface of the projectile, the longer you must make the air resistance arrow.

To look at the effect of varying contributions of weight compared to air resistance on flight paths, consider two extremes of projectile: the shot put and the badminton shuttle. Looking at the forces acting on the shot put, the weight force will be greater than the air resistance force. The shot put is heavy and has a relatively small cross-sectional area compared to its mass. It also has a reasonably smooth outer surface and is normally projected into the air at a lesser velocity than a badminton shuttle that has been hit by a fast-moving racket. These three factors mean that the air resistance force acting on a shot put is relatively small. A free body diagram for the shot put during flight is shown in Figure 13.6.

On the other hand, the shuttle is very light and has a feathery outer surface that will affect the airflow over it quite considerably. Consider a

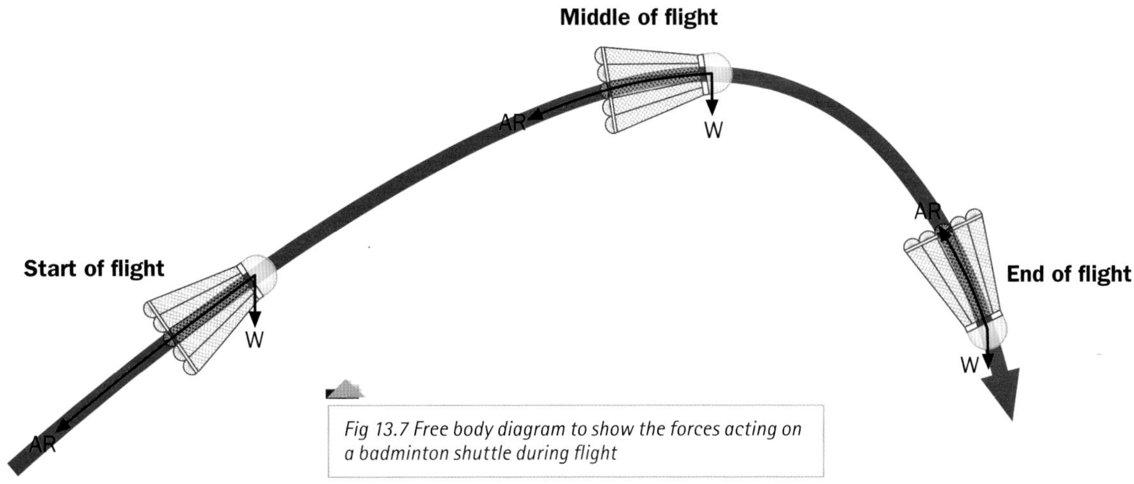

Fig 13.7 Free body diagram to show the forces acting on a badminton shuttle during flight

shuttle that has been projected into the air after a high serve. Its outgoing velocity is very high, as it has been struck with a large force by the head of the racket. For these reasons, it is greatly affected by air resistance at the start of its flight. It is important to remember that the effect of air resistance reduces during flight as the shuttle is slowing down. A free body diagram for the shuttle during flight is shown in Figure 13.7.

PARALLELOGRAM OF FORCES

A single net force can represent the two forces of weight and air resistance that act on a projectile. The direction and length of the net force is determined by sketching a parallelogram of forces. This is a method used to calculate the net force of two different forces (F1 and F2)

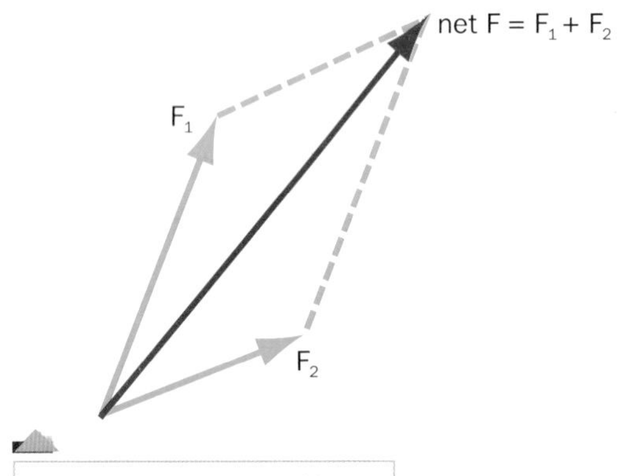

Fig 13.8 A parallelogram of forces

acting together on a body. It is calculated by constructing a parallelogram where the two force arrows are two of the sides. A diagonal arrow from the origin of the two forces to the furthest corner of the parallelogram represents the net force (net F) acting on the body.

REMEMBER

Net force is the overall force acting on a body when all the individual forces have been considered. Net force is also termed resultant force.

A projectile has a weight force acting from the centre of mass going vertically downwards and an air resistance force acting from the centre of mass going in the opposite direction to the direction of motion. To calculate the net force, you construct a parallelogram that uses these force arrows as two of its sides. The force arrow drawn diagonally from the centre of mass to the furthest corner of the parallelogram is the net force acting on the projectile.

Figure 13.9 shows how to find the net force acting on (a) a shot put and (b) a badminton shuttle during the upward phase of their flight paths. It also shows how the position of this net force can be used to explain the flight paths of these two very different projectiles.

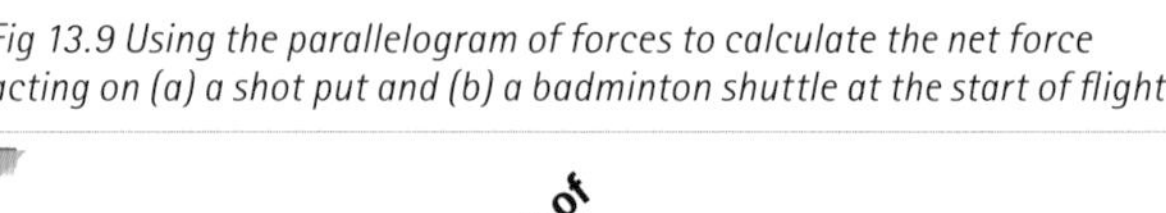

Fig 13.9 Using the parallelogram of forces to calculate the net force acting on (a) a shot put and (b) a badminton shuttle at the start of flight

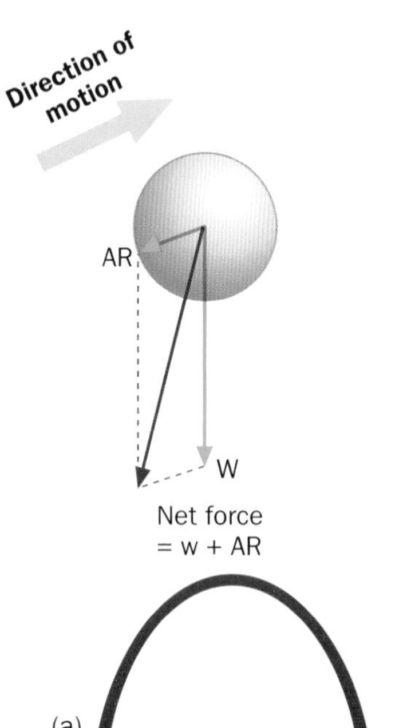

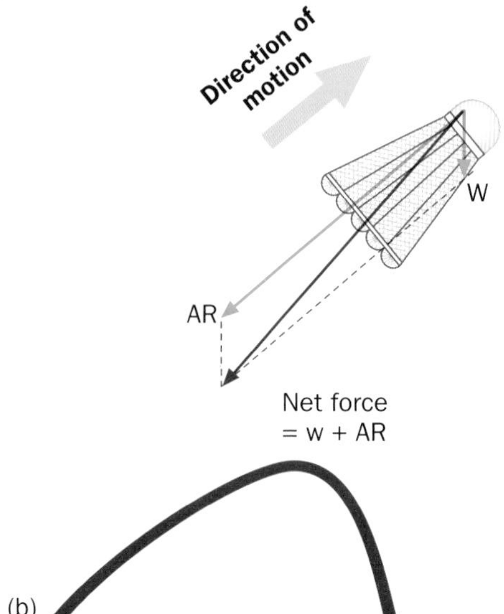

TASK 2

Sketch a free body diagram for each of the projectiles listed below. Construct a parallelogram of forces to show the net force acting on each projectile and explain the type of flight path the projectile will follow. For the purposes of this task, consider the point soon after takeoff for each projectile.

- Long jumper
- Tennis ball
- Football
- Golf ball
- Rugby ball

EXAM TIP

To ensure you score maximum marks on a question that requires you to construct a parallelogram of forces to explain the flight path of a projectile, make sure you do the following:

- include a direction of motion arrow
- start the weight and air resistance arrow from the same point: the centre of mass of the projectile
- think carefully about the relative lengths of these arrows by considering the mass, velocity, cross-sectional area and surface characteristics of the projectile
- make sure the direction of the air resistance arrow is opposite the direction of motion
- construct a parallelogram of forces using the weight and air resistance arrows as two of the sides
- draw in and label the net force that travels diagonally from the centre of mass to the furthest corner of the parallelogram
- use the position of the net force in relation to the position of the weight and air resistance forces to explain the flight path.

LIFT FORCE

If a projectile can gain an upward **lift force** during flight, it will stay in the air for a longer time and achieve a greater horizontal distance. To understand the science behind the creation of a lift force on projectiles, it helps to look at the aerofoil again. If the aerofoil is tilted at a certain angle, called the **angle of attack**, the air that travels over the curved upper surface has to travel further than the air that is deflected underneath the aerofoil's flatter under-surface. Therefore, the air above the aerofoil is travelling at a higher velocity than the air below it.

A Dutch-Swiss mathematician called Daniel Bernoulli discovered that an increase in the velocity of a fluid causes a decrease in pressure. This is known as the **Bernoulli principle.** It shows that:

- where flow is fast, pressure is low
- where flow is slow, pressure is high.

So, there is a lower pressure above the aerofoil and a higher pressure below it and this pressure gradient produces a lift force.

KEY TERMS

Lift force

Force that acts perpendicular to the direction of travel for a body moving through a fluid.

Angle of attack

The angle at which a projectile is tilted from the horizontal. Lift force will increase as the angle of attack is increased up to a certain point (usually around 17 degrees).

Bernoulli principle

States that molecules in a fluid exert less pressure the faster they travel and more pressure the slower they travel.

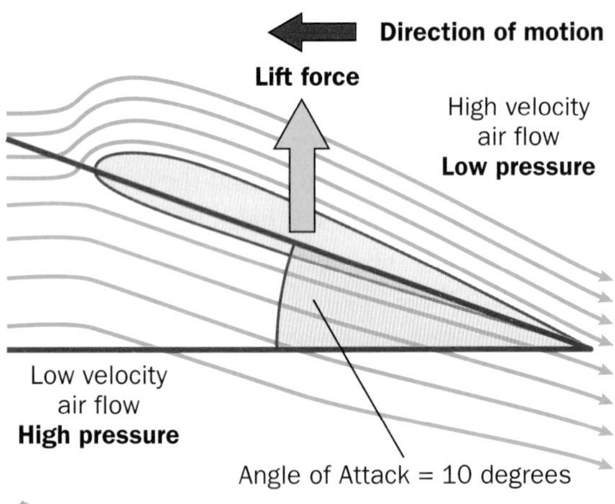

Fig 13.10 The Bernoulli principle working to produce a lift force on an aerofoil travelling at a 10-degree angle of attack

Figure 13.10 shows how the Bernoulli principle works to produce a lift force on an aerofoil at a 10-degree angle of attack.

REMEMBER

Aerofoils are the most efficient shapes found so far that can generate lift while at the same time minimising air resistance.

From your understanding of respiration, you know that all gases will flow from areas of high pressure to areas of low pressure. So, when the Bernoulli principle is applied to a projectile where there is a pressure gradient between the two surfaces, air molecules will be pushed from the area of high pressure to the area of low pressure, generating a force in the direction of the high pressure area.

KEY TERMS

Pronate

To rotate the radio-ulnar joint so the palm faces downwards.

Supinate

To rotate the radio-ulnar joint so the palm faces upwards.

STRETCH AND CHALLENGE

Lift is also generated on an aerofoil travelling at a certain angle of attack due to Newton's Third Law. As the air molecules hit the under surface of the aerofoil, this surface imparts a downwards action force on the air molecules, which in turn impart an equal and opposite upward force on the aerofoil. Therefore Newton's Third Law of Motion and the Bernoulli principle work together to apply a lift force to the aerofoil.

REMEMBER

Newton's Third Law of Motion states: 'For every force that is exerted by one body on another, there is an equal and opposite force exerted by the second body on the first.' (See Chapter 11, page 273.)

UPWARD AND DOWNWARD LIFT FORCE

Strange as it may seem, a lift force does not always work in an upward direction; it also works in a downward direction depending on the angle of attack and the shape of the projectile. Some sports make use of an upward lift force, while other sports rely on a downward lift force.

Discus and javelin throwers make use of an upward lift force. At the point of release, a good discus thrower will present the discus at the correct angle of attack, so that the air that travels over the top of the discus has to travel a further distance than the air that travels underneath. The air above the discus travels faster than the air below. Using the Bernoulli principle, this means that a lower pressure is created above the discus than below it, causing a pressure gradient that produces an upward lift force on the discus. This allows the discus to stay in the air for longer and achieve a greater horizontal distance. This principle is illustrated in Figure 13.11.

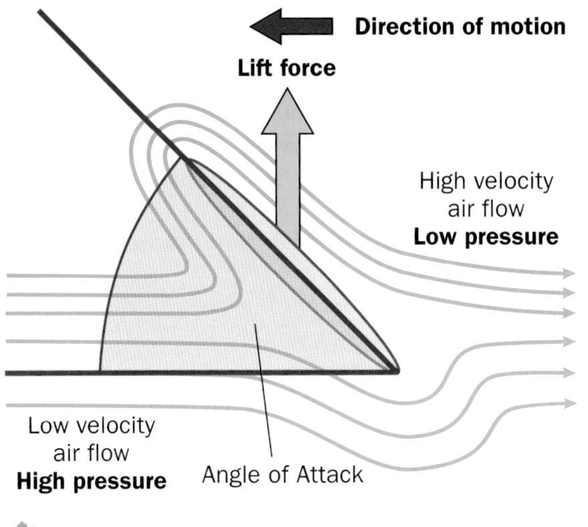

Fig 13.11 The Bernoulli principle working on a discus during flight to produce a lift force

APPLY IT!

Before the current rules that govern the shape, size and weight of a competition javelin were introduced, technicians designed javelins to optimise the lift force acting on them. In 1984 an East German athlete called Uwe Hohn, throwing such a javelin, recorded a massive 104.80m. After this, rules had to be changed as the lives of athletes and spectators at the far end of stadiums would be in danger! The current World Record was set in 1996 by Jan Zelezny and stands at 98.48m, which gives you some idea as to how much further these early javelins could fly. You can see Hohn's and Zelezny's javelin throws by going to www.heinemann.co.uk/hotlinks, entering the express code 6855P and clicking on the relevant links.

Carry out some research on how the design of Hohn's javelin differed from that of Zelezny's.

TASK 3

1 The optimal angle of attack for a discus to create lift is 17 degrees. Explain what would happen to a discus that was travelling at speed through the air at the following angles of attack:
   a) 90 degrees
   b) 120 degrees.
   Draw diagrams to help explain your answers.
2 Sketch a diagram to show the Bernoulli principle working on a javelin during flight. Use the diagram to help explain how a lift force is imparted to the javelin.

TASK 4

Using your knowledge of air resistance and lift force, explain the following techniques employed by ski jumpers:

- they wear tight-fitting smooth bodysuits and helmets
- on the approach slope, they crouch low with their back parallel to the slope
- at take off, they angle their skis upwards.

The sport of motor racing makes use of a downward lift force. Motor racing cars have rear spoilers attached to them that are angled in such a way that the lift force created by the Bernoulli principle acts in a downward direction. This pushes the car into the track, creating a greater frictional force to enable the tyres to stick to the track better, making it safer to turn corners at speeds in excess of 200 km/h (122 mph).

Spin

Imparting spin to a projectile at the point of release requires an **eccentric force**. Spin will affect the flight path of the projectile and the way it bounces on landing. You need to be familiar with three types of spin: topspin, backspin and sidespin.

- Topspin causes a ball to dip during flight and drop to the ground sooner. It will also cause the ball to skim off the surface quickly on bouncing.
- Backspin will keep a ball in flight for longer and, on bouncing, it will be slowed down.
- Sidespin will cause a ball to swerve left or right and, on bouncing, it accelerates even further in the same direction.

KEY TERM

Eccentric force

Force whose line of application passes outside the centre of mass of a body, causing the resulting motion to be angular.

REMEMBER

To generate angular motion you need an eccentric force. So, a tennis player who wishes to impart topspin to their forehand, will brush the racket head around the back and over the top of the ball. This imparts a force that travels outside the centre of mass of the ball and causes it to spin forwards.

It is important to apply knowledge of friction force to help understand the effect of spin in the bounce of a ball. Table 1 explains the effect of the three types of spin on the flight path and bounce of a projectile.

EXAM TIP

The direction in which a ball swerves when sidespin has been imparted depends on whether a right-handed or a left-handed athlete has struck it. To simplify matters, all explanations in this book will refer to a right-handed athlete. It is a good idea for you to do the same in an exam answer and to state this somewhere in your answer.

EXAM TIP

To ensure you score maximum marks when sketching diagrams to show the deviation in flight path caused by spin, be sure that you:

- correctly label your sketch with the type of spin being shown
- state whether the sketch is viewed from the side (for top and back spin) or the top (for side spin)
- use an arrow to indicate the direction of motion
- show the direction of spin of the projectile using an arrow inside the object
- sketch the non-spinning flight path as well as the spinning flight path so that the deviation is obvious
- state the effect of the spin; that is, top spin (dips), back spin (floats), hook (swerves left), slice (swerves right).

See diagrams in Table 1 on the next page.

TASK 5

Describe examples from sports where athletes use the three types of spin to gain an advantage over their opponents.

THE MAGNUS EFFECT

Heinrich Gustav Magnus (1802–70), a German scientist, discovered that spinning balls also generate a lift force. This is called the Magnus effect. The lift force produced as a result of the Magnus effect explains the curved flights of balls that have been struck with spin in a variety of sports.

KEY TERM

Magnus effect

The Magnus effect explains the deviations in flight paths of spinning balls in sport, especially tennis, golf, football, table tennis and cricket.

Table 1 The effect of three types of spin on the flight path and bounce of a projectile

Type of spin	Effect on flight path	Effect on bounce	Examples from sport
Topspin	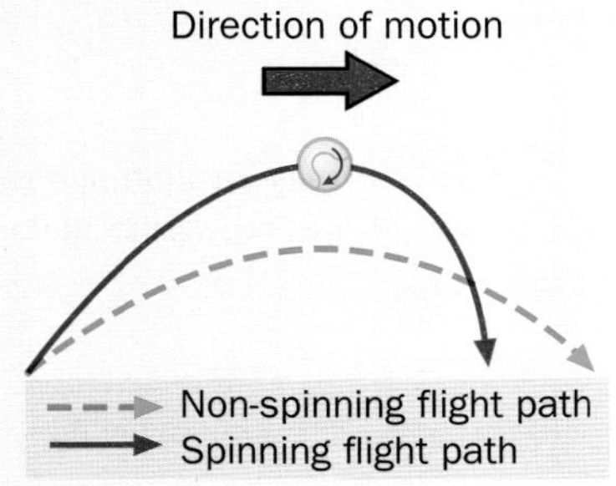 Direction of motion Non-spinning flight path Spinning flight path Fig 13.12a	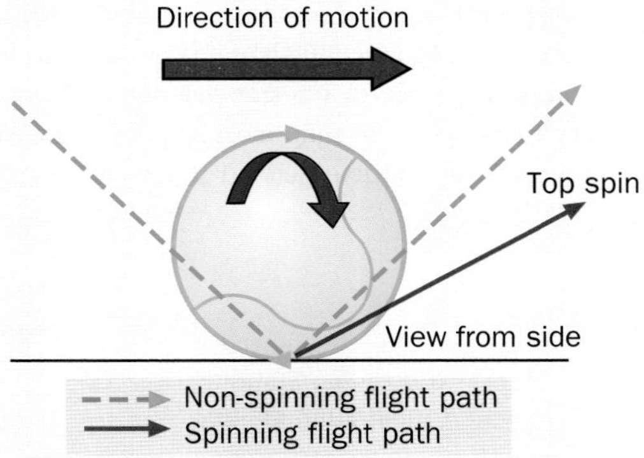 Direction of motion Top spin View from side Non-spinning flight path Spinning flight path Fig 13.12b	Tennis players make full use of the effects of topspin. The fact that it causes the ball to 'dip' means that they can hit the ball very hard while ensuring that it will still drop into the court and not sail beyond the baseline. On bouncing, the ball will then accelerate low into their opponent, giving them less time to play the shot.
	Topspin causes the ball to 'dip' during flight, which reduces the horizontal distance covered.	The bottom surface of the ball that hits the ground on the bounce wants to slide backwards. Friction will oppose this sliding motion and act in a forward direction. Therefore, friction acts in the same direction as the direction of motion, which causes the ball to accelerate off the surface quickly and at a smaller angle to that of a non-spinning ball.	
Backspin	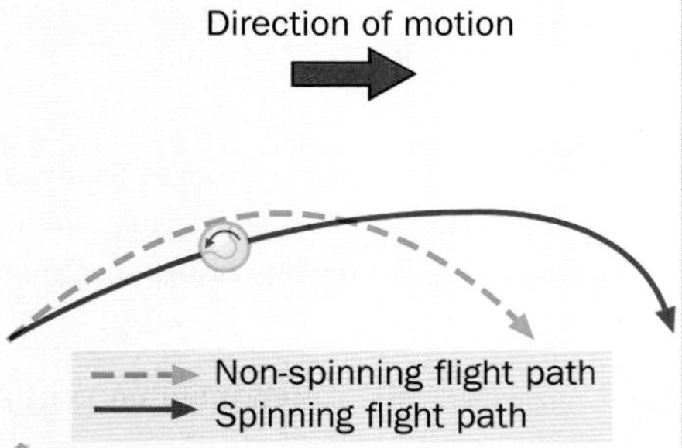 Direction of motion Non-spinning flight path Spinning flight path Fig 13.12c	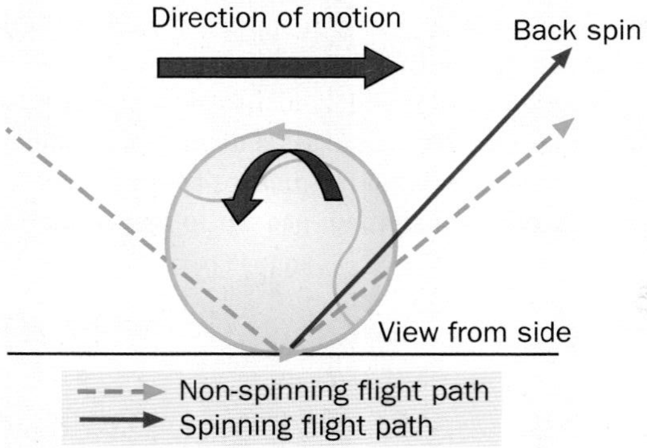 Direction of motion Back spin View from side Non-spinning flight path Spinning flight path Fig 13.12d	In baseline rallies, tennis players often use backspin to play a drop shot. The fact the ball 'floats' means that it will have enough height to clear the net but will decelerate significantly on bouncing. This, coupled with the fact that the bounce will be very upright, makes it difficult for the player's opponent to run from the baseline in time to play the shot before the second bounce.

Table 1 (Contd.)

Type of spin	Effect on flight path	Effect on bounce	Examples from sport
	Backspin causes the ball to 'float' during flight, which increases the horizontal distance covered.	The bottom surface of the ball that hits the ground on the bounce wants to slide forwards. Friction will oppose this sliding motion and act in a backward direction. Therefore, friction acts in the opposite direction to the direction of motion, which causes the ball to decelerate off the surface slowly and at a greater angle to that of a non-spinning ball.	
Sidespin	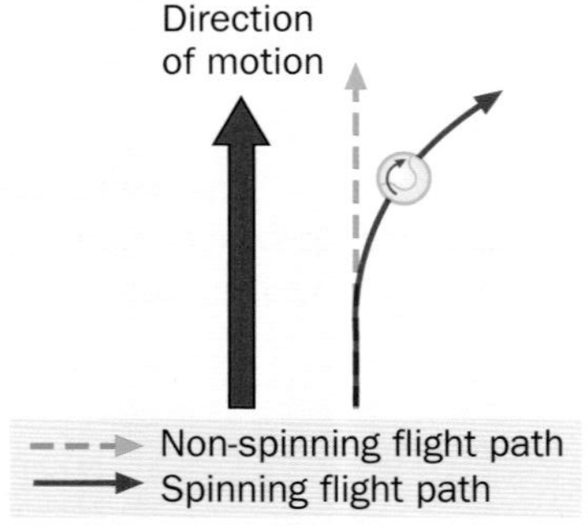 Fig 13.12e	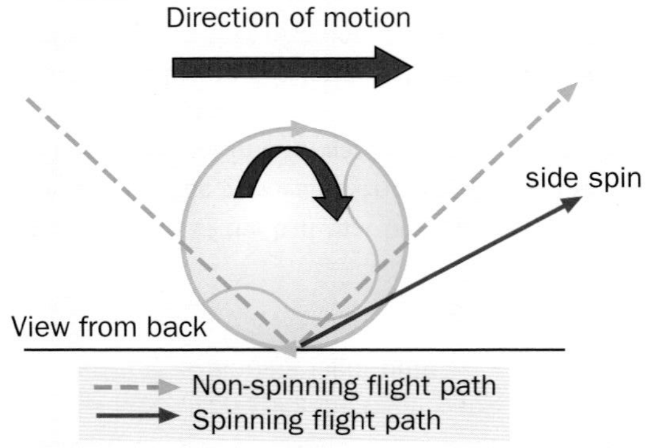 Fig 13.12f	Table tennis players use sidespin to great effect. Not only will it cause the ball to swerve during flight, but on bouncing, the ball will accelerate away from the table, forcing the player's opponent out wide to make a return.
	Sidespin causes the ball to 'swerve' left for hook and right for slice.	The bottom surface of the ball that hits the ground on the bounce wants to slide from right to left. Friction will oppose this sliding motion and acts left to right. Therefore, friction acts in the same direction as the direction of motion, which causes the ball to accelerate even further right from the surface than that of a non-spinning ball.	

Fig 13.13 Footballers make use of the Magnus effect to make a ball swerve around a wall of defenders into the top corner of the goal

The Magnus effect is important in all sports in which athletes want to bend the flight of a ball. The Magnus effect is commonly seen at work in tennis, golf, football, table tennis and cricket. Certain footballers, such as the Portuguese player Cristiano Ronaldo, are internationally renowned for their magical ability to curve free kicks around a wall of defenders and into the top corners of the goal (Fig 13.13).

HOW THE MAGNUS EFFECT WORKS

As a spinning ball moves through the air, its spinning surfaces will affect the airflow around it. As an initial explanation, consider the tennis ball in Figure 13.14 that has been hit with top spin.

To understand Figure 13.14, it is useful to consider the two surfaces of the ball that affect the air flow separately.

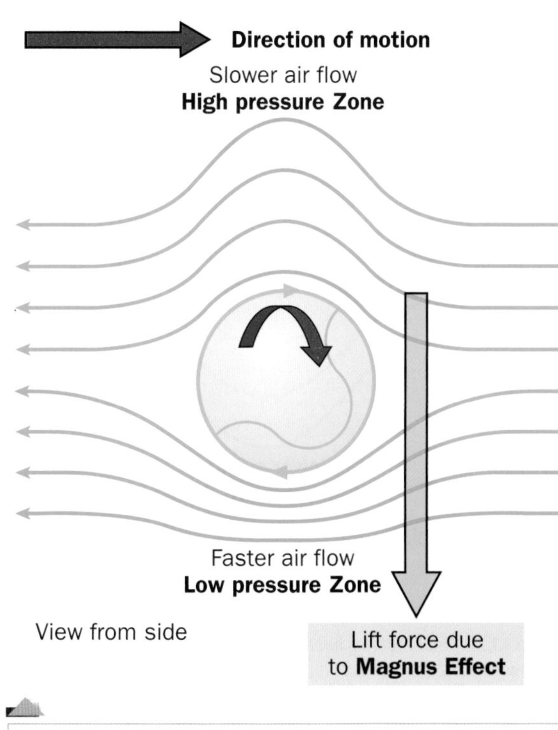

Fig 13.14 A ball that has been struck with topspin has a downward lift force as a result of the Magnus effect

- *The top of the ball:* the surface of the ball is travelling in the opposite direction to airflow. This causes the air to decelerate and, according to the Bernoulli principle, creates a high pressure.
- *The bottom of the ball:* the surface of the ball is travelling in the same direction as the airflow. This causes the air to accelerate and, according to the Bernoulli principle, the faster moving air sets up a lower pressure.
- *Consequence*: having higher pressure on the top surface of the ball and lower on the bottom surface creates a pressure differential. This causes a downward lift force to act on the ball. The ball dips and the distance travelled is decreased from the non-spinning flight path.

- *The top of the ball:* the surface of the ball is travelling in the same direction as the airflow. This causes the air to accelerate and, according to the Bernoulli principle, the faster-moving air sets up a lower pressure.
- *The bottom of the ball:* the surface of the ball is travelling in the opposite direction to airflow. This causes the air to decelerate and, according to the Bernoulli principle, creates a high pressure.
- *Consequence*: Having lower pressure on the top surface of the ball and higher on the bottom surface creates a pressure differential. This causes an upward lift force to act on the ball. The ball floats and the distance travelled is increased from the non-spinning flight path.

The same explanation can be adapted for a ball hit with back spin in Figure 13.15.

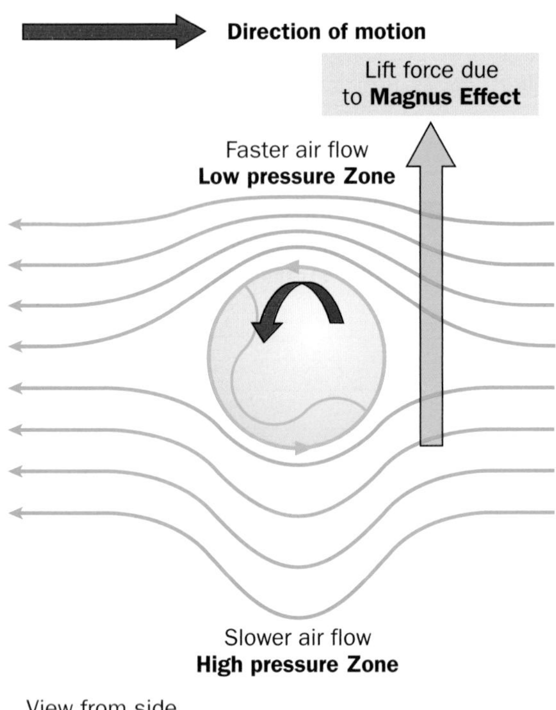

Fig 13.15 A ball that has been struck with backspin has an upward lift force as a result of the Magnus effect

EXAM TIP

To ensure you score maximum marks when sketching and explaining the lift force produced as a result of the Magnus effect on spinning projectiles, follow these eleven stages.

1. Label the type of spin to be sketched (top/back/hook/slice).
2. Identify the best way to view the diagram (side view/top view).
3. Show clearly the direction of motion arrow.
4. Draw the projectile.
5. Insert an arrow inside the projectile to show the direction of spin.
6. Place an arrow on the affected surfaces of the projectile to show their direction of travel (that is, opposite to, or in the same direction as the airflow).
7. Draw in the airflow lines.
8. State where airflow velocity is fast and where airflow velocity is slow.
9. Using your knowledge of the Bernoulli principle, state where pressure is high and where pressure is low.
10. Insert the 'lift force due to Magnus effect' arrow.
11. Explain your diagram by taking each surface in turn and writing the consequence.

TASK 6

Using Figs 13.14 and 13.15 and the explanation for topspin and backspin on the previous page, explain the effect of the Magnus effect on a ball that has been hit with each of the two types of sidespin: hook and slice.

STRETCH AND CHALLENGE

The Magnus effect explains the deviations in flight path for balls where spin has been imparted at the point of release. The explanation behind swing bowling in cricket is a little different. Research the science behind swing bowling in cricket.

Exam Café

Relax, refresh, result!

Refresh your memory

You should now have knowledge and understanding of:

- the impact of air resistance (drag or fluid friction) on sporting activity and how to apply the concept of reducing drag in certain sports
- how to sketch free body diagrams to identify the forces acting on a projectile in flight and how to use the parallelogram of forces to explain the resultant flight path
- how to explain and apply the Bernoulli principle in a number of different sporting activities
- the three types of spin commonly observed in sporting activities (top spin, back spin and side spin) and their impact on flight path and bounce
- how to sketch detailed diagrams to help explain how the Magnus effect causes spinning projectiles to deviate from their non-spinning flight paths.

REVISE AS YOU GO!

1 Define the following terms:
   a) fluid
   b) fluid friction
   c) streamlining
   d) aerofoil
   e) parabola.
2 Using a sport of your choice, give two examples to show how a performer can minimise the 'tugging' effect of air resistance.
3 Draw a free body diagram to show the forces acting on the following projectiles during flight:
   a) a shot put
   b) a badminton shuttle.
4 Use the parallelogram of forces to explain the flight paths of:
   a) a shot put
   b) a badminton shuttle.
5 Briefly describe the Bernoulli principle and explain how it can be applied to the flight of a ski jumper.
6 Describe how a sport makes use of an upward lift force.
7 Describe how a sport makes use of a downward lift force.

Try to answer these questions yourself. Ask your teacher if you need help.

8 Name the type of spin that has been imparted to produce the deviations in flight path in the following examples:
   a) a golf drive where the ball has curved to the right
   b) a table tennis shot where the ball has floated over the net to land deep on the other side of the table.
9 Draw a diagram to explain the effect of a lift force on a ball that has been struck with top spin.
10 Describe the effect of top spin on the bounce of a ball and explain the advantages this might have for a tennis player using this type of spin.

Get the result!

Examination question

Use your knowledge of the Bernoulli principle to explain the flight path of a discus. (6 marks)

Examiner's tips

This is quite a challenging question with an 'explain' command word, so consider your answer carefully and make sure you have given enough information for a 6-mark question. The question is applied and requires you to use the Bernoulli principle to explain the flight path of a discus. Your answer will therefore need to be applied, but there is also scope for a full explanation of the Bernoulli principle here. A diagram may help support your explanation.

Student answer

The flight path of a discus is not a true parabola. This is due to the to a lift force that acts on the discus as it flies through the air. The lift force is caused by the Bernoulli principle.

Examiner says:

The basic requirements of the answer are here. The asymmetric flight path of the discus has been identified and the student has recalled the presence of a lift force, which is essential when discussing the Bernoulli principle. However, there is no detailed explanation and the answer falls below the demands of the question.

Examiner says:

You have done well to immediately apply your answer to the discus and bring in some specialist vocabulary – great start!

Examiner says:

Likewise, you have accurately explained the crucial aspect of the Bernoulli principle.

Examiner says:

This is a great diagram that really shows you have a full and thorough understanding of this part of the specification. An excellent answer – well done!

Improved student answer

If the discus is released with the correct angle of attack, it will follow an asymmetric flight path. At the correct angle of attack, the air molecules that travel over the top of the discus have to travel further than those that travel underneath. This creates a faster air flow over the top of the discus. According to the Bernoulli principle, an increase in the velocity of a fluid causes a decrease in pressure. So, the pressure above the discus is lower than the pressure below it. This causes a pressure differential that creates a lift force in the direction of the low pressure area, i.e. upwards. This causes the discus to 'float' and stay in the air for longer.

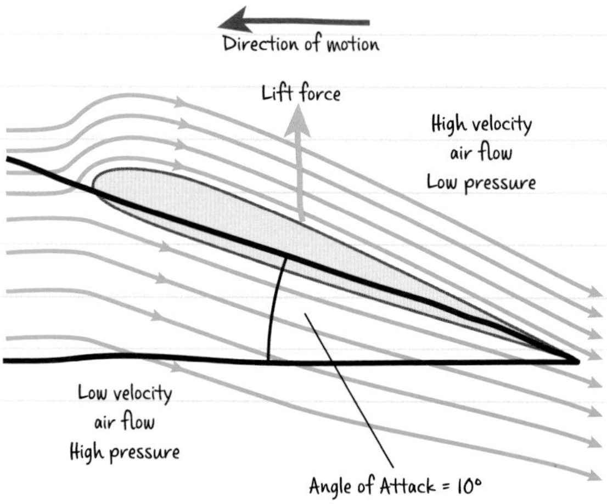

Direction of motion

Lift force

High velocity
air flow
Low pressure

Low velocity
air flow
High pressure

Angle of Attack = 10°

Examiner says:

This is a succinct and accurate description of the air flow around the two surfaces of the discus, which builds the background information needed to explain the Bernoulli principle.

Examiner says:

Reference to a lift force is certainly what is required for any question on the Bernoulli principle, and you have used this to describe the flight path of a discus.

CHAPTER 14:

Stability and angular motion in physical activity

LEARNING OBJECTIVES

By the end of this chapter you should have knowledge and understanding of:

- centre of mass and its relationship to balance, rotation and efficiency of technique
- the three types of lever system in relation to human movement and the advantages and disadvantages of second and third classes of lever system
- how to define and calculate the units of measurement for the moment of a force
- the three major axes of rotation, giving examples of sporting movements that occur around them
- the quantities used to describe angular motion and their relevance to sporting techniques
- what is meant by the terms moment of inertia and angular momentum and their relevance to sporting performance
- the law of conservation of angular momentum and be able to give examples of how athletes use this principle in a number of sporting activities.

INTRODUCTION

In this chapter you will revise centre of mass and its link with the stability of a body as well as look at how the human body uses lever systems to best effect during sporting activities.

This leads on to rotation, and you will build upon your knowledge of **angular motion** that was introduced at AS-level.

KEY TERM

Angular motion

When a body or part of a body moves in a circle or part of circle about a particular point called the axis of rotation.

Most movements in sport involve some form of rotation. Beth Tweddle is an English gymnast who is internationally renowned for her ability to swing and circle around the uneven bars. Similarly, Tom Daly, a young British diver, is a real crowd pleaser as he spins in the air to complete somersaults and twists before stretching

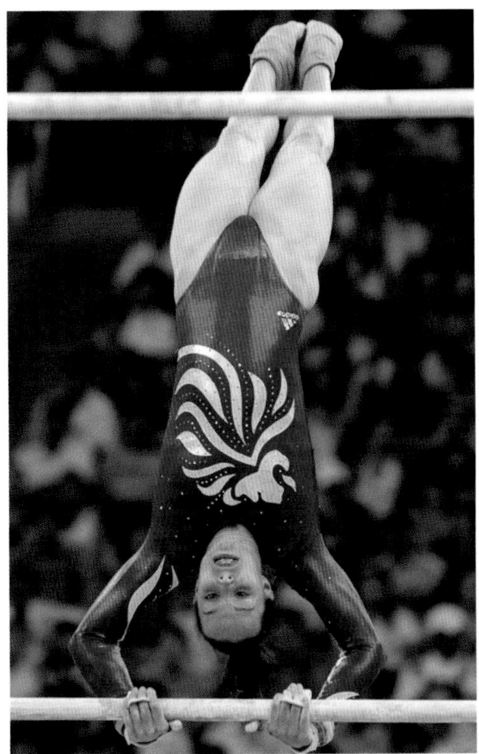

Fig 14.1 Performers in sport apply the principles behind angular motion to somersault, twist, spin, swing, turn or circle

out for an elegant entry into the water. Effective performance in any sporting activity that requires an athlete to somersault, twist, spin, turn, swing or circle will be reliant on an understanding of the principles behind angular motion.

As you read through this chapter, you will be able to see the similarities between the principles governing angular motion and the principles governing linear motion that we looked at in Chapter 11. You will recognise words such as displacement or velocity, but in this section these quantities are preceded by the word 'angular', so you should become accustomed to using the terms 'angular displacement' or 'angular velocity'. The chapter ends with a full explanation of the law of conservation of angular momentum, which shows how performers can use knowledge of angular mechanics to control their rate of spin.

Stability

There are many situations in sport when performers want to assume a very stable position from which they are very difficult to move. Consider the stance taken by a pack of forwards at the scrum in rugby or by a sumo wrestler at the beginning of a competition. Likewise, there are numerous moments in sport when performers want to be able to move easily out of one position into the next. Consider the sprinter posed to explode forwards on the bang of the gun or the gymnast dismounting from the beam. **Stability** therefore depends on how much force is required to disturb a body from its position of **equilibrium**. The more stable a body, the larger the force required to move it. If we compare a sumo wrestler who is balanced on all fours with a gymnast in a handstand position, both performers are in equilibrium but the sumo wrestler is more stable than the gymnast because a larger force is required to move him from his position of equilibrium. Stability is closely linked to **centre of mass**.

KEY TERMS

Stability

The ability of a body to return to equilibrium or its original position after being displaced. A stable body is not easily moved from its position of equilibrium. A less stable body is easily moved from its position of equilibrium.

Equilibrium

A body is in equilibrium when the net force = 0. (See Chapter 12, page 299.)

Centre of mass

The point at which the body is balanced in all directions.

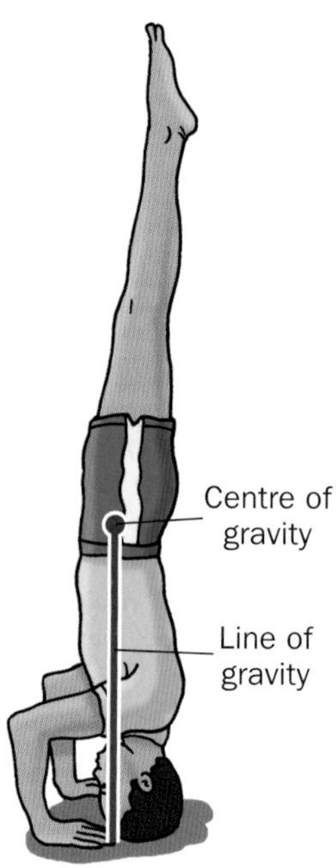

Fig 14.2 This diagram of a gymnast performing a headstand shows the line of gravity, extending from the centre of mass vertically down to the ground, and the base of support – the area on the ground enclosed by the points of contact of the performer's body on the ground

REMEMBER

In the human body the centre of mass is not a fixed point located in a specific part of the body; its location will vary depending on body position and it can even lie at a point outside the actual substance of the body. Refer back to pages 52–54 in *OCR AS PE* to revisit the principles you learned about centre of mass last year. When you have done this, answer the questions in the task overleaf.

TASK 1

1. Explain why the position of the centre of mass is different in males than that of females.
2. Explain how a performer can change the position of their centre of mass. Give some examples from sport of when this happens.
3. Explain how the position of the centre of mass can actually lie outside the substance of the body. Give some examples from sport of when this happens.

APPLY IT!

In 1968, Dick Fosbury was the first to introduce the Fosbury flop technique in the high jump. With the spine and hips being fully extended and the majority of the weight of the body falling below the hips, the high jumper can make their centre of mass pass under the bar while their body clears it. Compare this to the scissors technique, where the high jumper must lift their centre of mass over the bar in order to clear the same height. A jumper using the Fosbury flop technique does not have to lift his centre of mass such a great distance in order to clear the bar and therefore does not require so much force at takeoff. This makes the Fosbury flop a far more efficient technique than the scissors jump.

Fig 14.3 The Fosbury flop technique means the position of the centre of mass moves outside the body and the jumper can clear the bar while their centre of mass passes underneath it

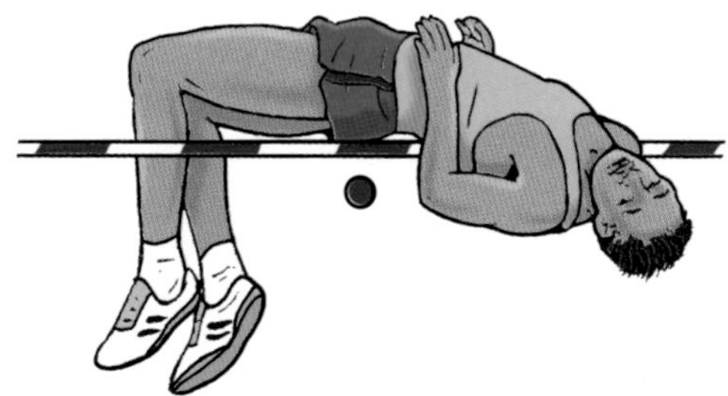

MAXIMISING AND MINIMISING STABILITY

The following mechanical principles increase the stability of a performer. It follows, therefore, that performers need to do the opposite to decrease their stability.

- *Performers increase their stability when they lower their centre of mass.* In combat or impact sports, performers will lower their centre of mass to make it more difficult for their opponents to move them. On landing, ski jumpers lower their centre of mass by flexing at the hip and knee to help them maintain balance.
- *Performers increase their stability when they increase the size of their base of support.* A gymnast on the beam is more stable when she has two feet in contact with the beam rather than just one foot, as this increases the area of her base of support. Likewise, a headstand is a more stable balance than a handstand which, in turn, is more stable than an arabesque.
- *Performers increase their stability when their line of gravity is central to their base of support.* In a sprint start in track athletics, the 'on your marks position' is more stable than the 'set' position. This is because in the first position the line of gravity falls at the centre of the base of support, whereas in the second position it has shifted forwards and lies very close to the hands.
- *Performers increase their stability by increasing their body mass or inertia.* If all the factors listed above are the same for two performers,

the performer with the larger mass will have a greater stability. This is the reason for different weight categories in combat sports and also the extremes of body types that can be observed between certain positions in rugby and other impact sports.

REMEMBER

A performer will be stable as long as their line of gravity falls within the area of their base of support. As soon as the line of gravity falls outside the centre of the base of support, a performer becomes unstable.

APPLY IT!

Performers in sport do not always want to have their line of gravity within their base of support; sometimes it is to their advantage to assume an unstable position. Consider the action of running: each time you lift your back foot and your body travels over your front foot, your line of gravity falls outside your base and you are constantly moving from a stable position to an unstable position. The same is true of games players when they side step, dodge or swerve to trick their opponents. You could say that a moving body is always trying to catch up with its line of gravity.

STRETCH AND CHALLENGE

1 Another method that a performer can use to increase their stability is to extend their base of support in the direction of the oncoming force. Think about the mechanical reasons why this would increase stability and give some examples from sport when performers might use this technique.
2 When cyclists and skiers travel round a bend, they lean into the turn so much that their line of gravity falls outside their base of support. Explain why they do not fall over.

TASK 2

Give an example from sport for each of the factors listed in the Stretch and Challenge box that explains why a performer would want to:

- increase their stability
- decrease their stability.

Lever systems

The use of levers occurs in all sports because a performer's muscles, bones and joints work together as a lever system to produce angular motion. A **lever system** is a simple structure that consists of a rigid object that rotates around a fixed axis when two unequal forces are applied to it.

KEY TERM

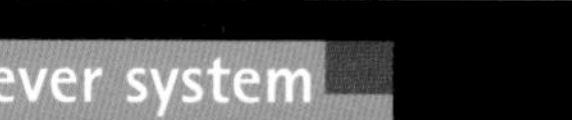

Lever system

A rigid structure, hinged at one point (the fulcrum) and to which two forces (the load and effort) are applied at two other points.

COMPONENTS OF A LEVER SYSTEM

A lever system has three components:

- the **fulcrum** / F = the fixed point
- the **load** / L = the weight to be moved
- the **effort** / E = the source of energy.

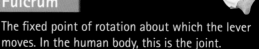

KEY TERMS

Fulcrum

The fixed point of rotation about which the lever moves. In the human body, this is the joint.

Load

The resistance or weight to be moved. In the human body, this is the weight of the body part being moved.

Effort

The force being applied that causes the lever to move. This is the agonist muscle in the human body.

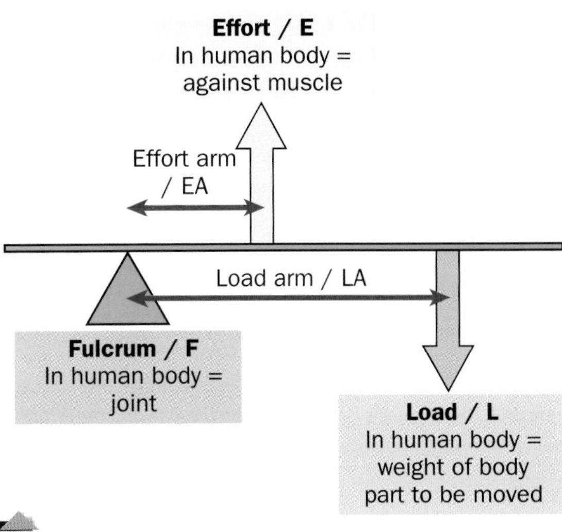

Fig 14.4 The three components of a lever

In the body:

- the joint acts as the fulcrum
- the weight of the body part being moved plus the weight of whatever the performer is trying to move (for example a cricket bat or a shot put) is the load
- the agonist muscle that contracts to cause the movement is the effort.

In addition, every lever system has a load arm and an effort arm:

- **load arm** / LA = the perpendicular distance from the fulcrum to the load
- **effort arm** / EA = the perpendicular distance from the fulcrum to the effort.

KEY TERMS

Load arm

The perpendicular distance of the load from the fulcrum.

Effort arm

The perpendicular distance of the effort from the fulcrum

REMEMBER

In a lever system, the force of the load will attempt to make the lever rotate in one direction, while the force of the effort will attempt to make it rotate in the opposite direction. Due to gravity, the load will always act downwards, so this will help you to decide the direction of the effort arrow. In a first-class lever, the effort acts downwards and in a second- and third-class lever, the effort acts upwards.

TYPES OF LEVER SYSTEM AND THEIR APPLICATION TO HUMAN MOVEMENT

The position of the fulcrum, load and effort in relation to one another determines the type of lever system and the application for which they are best suited. As you will see later in the chapter, this is linked with the length of the load arm in relation to the length of the effort arm.

There are three types of lever system:

- In a first-class lever system, the fulcrum is located between the load and the effort.
- In a second-class lever system, the load is located between the fulcrum and the effort.
- In a third-class lever system, the effort is located between the fulcrum and the load.

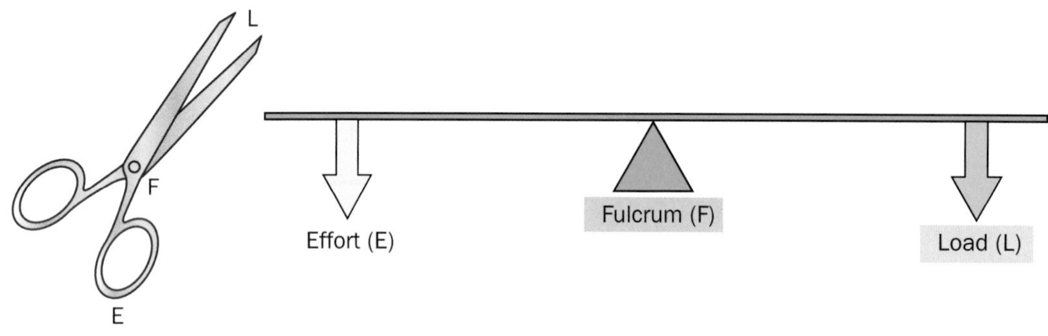

Fig 14.5 The fulcrum is located between the load and the effort, making the scissors an example of a first-class lever system

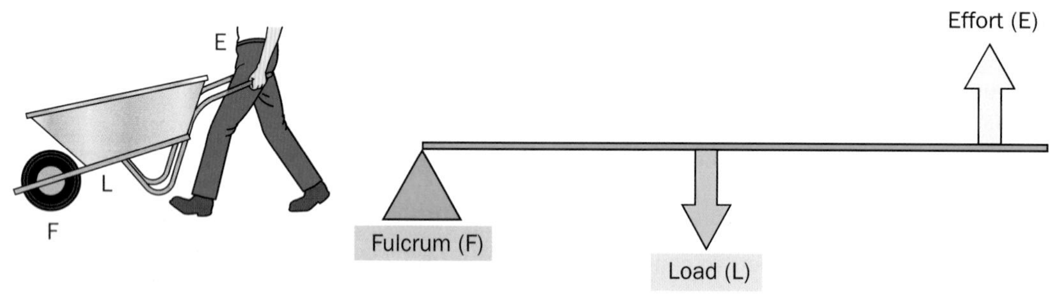

Fig 14.6 The load is located between the fulcrum and the effort, making the wheelbarrow an example of a second-class lever system

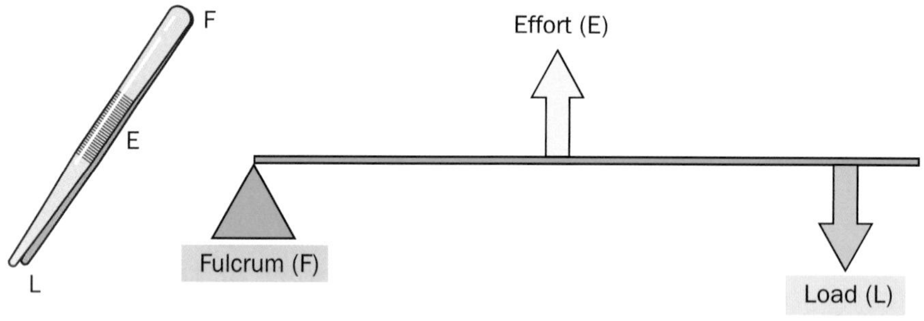

Fig 14.7 The effort is located between the fulcrum and the load, making the tweezers an example of a third-class lever system

Performers in sport use all three types, although the third class of lever system is by far the most common.

FIRST-CLASS LEVER SYSTEM

There are two examples of a first-class lever system that you need to know in the human body. The first is found in extension of the neck (see Fig 14.8 overleaf).

REMEMBER

A handy way to remember how to classify levers is to bear in mind the component of the lever system that sits in the middle of the three components. In a first-class lever, this is the fulcrum; in a second-class lever it is the load; in a third-class lever it is the effort. You could remember this using the following little rhyme:

1 – 2 – 3
F – L – E.

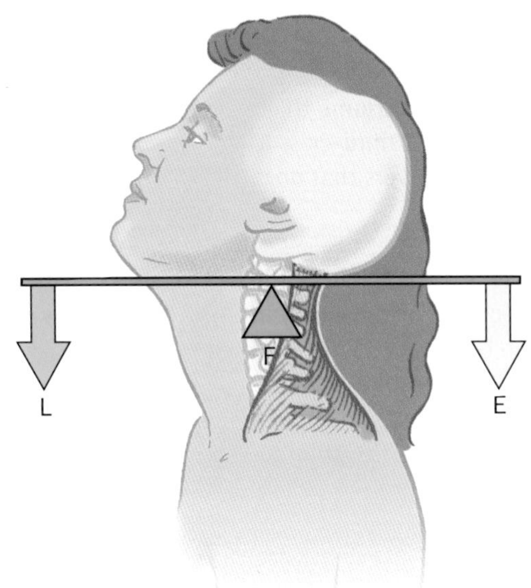

Fig 14.8 Extension of the neck is a first-class lever system

- The fulcrum (F) is the joint between the atlas and the skull.
- The load (L) is the weight of the head being tilted backwards.
- The effort (E) is the force applied by the trapezius muscle as it contracts to pull the head backwards.

The second example is in extension of the elbow during an overarm throw, as shown in Fig 14.9.

- The fulcrum (F) is the elbow joint.
- The load (L) is the weight of the lower arm (plus the weight of any implements or ball that might be in the hand).
- The effort (E) is the force exerted by the triceps brachii as it pulls on the ulna.

Fig 14.9 An overarm throw is another example of a first-class lever system

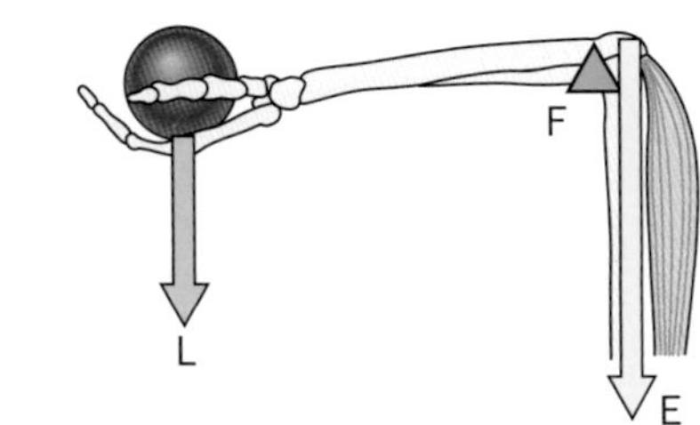

SECOND-CLASS LEVER SYSTEM

There is one example of a second-class lever system that you need to know in the human body. It is found at the ball of the foot on a number of occasions in sport. For example, when a performer pushes against the ground to take off for a jump or pushes against the blocks during a sprint start in the 100m sprint (see Fig 14.10).

- The fulcrum (F) is the joint between the metatarsals and the phalanges.
- The load (L) is the weight of the body being lifted.
- The effort (E) is the force applied by the gastrocnemius muscle as it contracts to pull the calcaneous upwards.

Fig 14.10 Standing on tiptoe gives a second-class level system at the metatarsals/phalanges joint

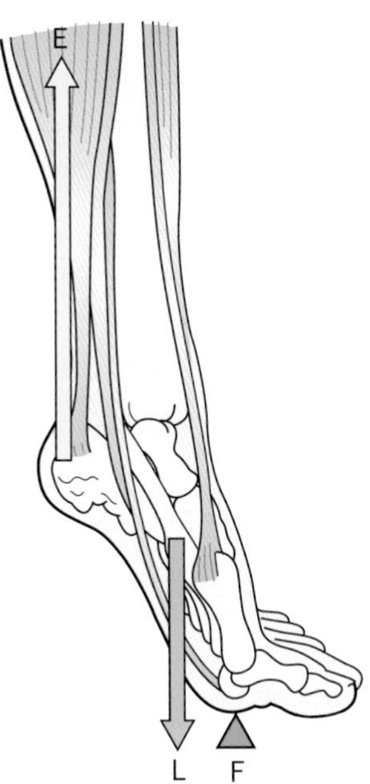

REMEMBER

The second-class lever system is seen at the ball of the foot when a performer is pushing against the ground. For example, pushing off against the ground to take off for a jump or pushing on the blocks during a sprint start in athletics or a racing dive in swimming.

EXAM TIP

For the ball of the foot second-class lever system, it is very important to remember the fulcrum is the joint between the metatarsals and the phalanges, not the ankle joint. This is a very common mistake seen by examiners.

THIRD-CLASS LEVER SYSTEM

There are many examples of third-class lever systems that you need to be aware of in the human body. One straightforward example is found in flexion of the elbow joint (see Fig 14.11).

- The fulcrum (F) is the elbow joint.
- The load (L) is the weight of the lower arm (plus the weight of any implements or balls that might be in the hand).
- The effort (E) is the force applied by the biceps brachii muscle as it contracts to pull the lower arm upwards.

TASK 3

Using a named activity of your choice, give three examples of when you would make use of a third-class lever system.

Fig 14.11 Flexion of the elbow joint is a third-class lever system

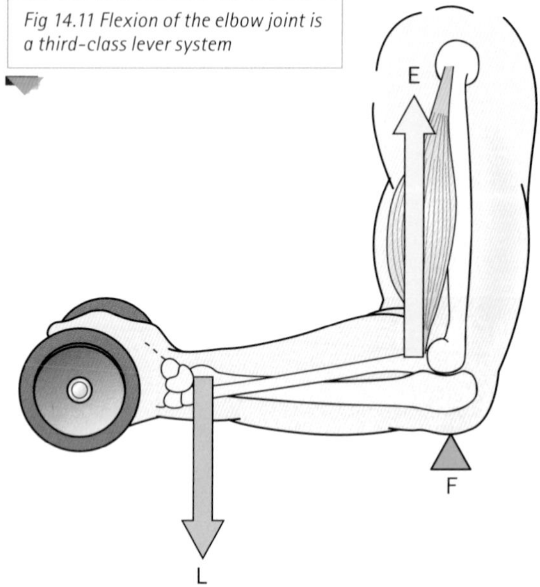

EXAM TIP

You can safely assume that your examiner is asking about a third-class lever if you have a question on levers that does NOT involve the following:

- extension of the neck (first-class lever)
- extension of the elbow in an overarm throw (first-class lever)
- the foot pushing against the ground at takeoff or driving against the ground or starting blocks in running or swimming (second-class lever).

ADVANTAGES AND DISADVANTAGES OF DIFFERENT TYPES OF LEVER SYSTEM

In a second-class lever system, with the load lying between the fulcrum and the effort, the effort arm is greater than the load arm. This means that this lever system enables a performer to apply a relatively small effort to move a large load. This is termed **mechanical advantage**. Second-class lever systems are therefore efficient at moving a heavy load, but only over a small distance and at the expense of speed and range of movement. For example, when jumping, the second-class lever at the ball of the foot will move the weight of the entire body a relatively small distance.

KEY TERMS

Mechanical advantage

This allows a lever system to move a large load with a relatively small effort. It occurs in second-class lever systems where the effort arm is greater than the load arm.

Mechanical disadvantage

This means the effort would need to be considerably bigger than the load in order to move the load. It occurs in a third-class lever system where the load arm is greater than the effort arm.

In a third-class lever system, with the effort lying between the fulcrum and the load, the load arm is greater than the effort arm. This is termed **mechanical disadvantage**. Third-class lever systems enable a performer to accelerate a load through a large range of movement but the performer will struggle to move heavy loads. For example, in the upward phase of the biceps curl, the distance moved by the insertion of the biceps brachii (the effort) need only be small to ensure that the dumbbell (the load) is moved through a far greater range of movement. Also, if you consider that both distances are achieved in the same time, the speed of the load is faster than the speed of the effort.

REMEMBER

- In a second-class lever, EA > LA = mechanical advantage. This allows a large load to be moved over a small distance.
- In a third-class lever, LA > EA = mechanical disadvantage. This allows only a relatively small load to be moved with a high speed of acceleration over a large range of movement.

TASK 4

1 a) Carry out the following sporting techniques and, for the joint identified, work out the position of the fulcrum, load and effort:
- Execution phase of kicking a football – knee joint
- Recovery phase of underarm bowling action in rounders – elbow joint
- Takeoff phase of a vertical jump – metatarsals/phalanges joint
- Execution phase of the serve in tennis – elbow joint.

b) For each sporting technique, sketch a diagram of the lever system identifying all its components. Comment on the type of lever system being used and the advantages of this type of lever system.

Moment of force or torque

The **moment of force**, or **torque**, is the turning effect produced by the force as the lever rotates about the fulcrum. It is calculated using the following equation.

Moment of force = force x perpendicular distance from fulcrum
Moment of force = F x d

Unit of measurement: Newton metres (Nm)

KEY TERM

Moment of force/torque

The effectiveness of a force to produce rotation about an axis. It is the product of the size of the force multiplied by the distance of the force from the fulcrum. It is measured in Newton metres (Nm).

Fig 14.12 The moment of a force is equal to the size of the force multiplied by the perpendicular distance of the force from the fulcrum

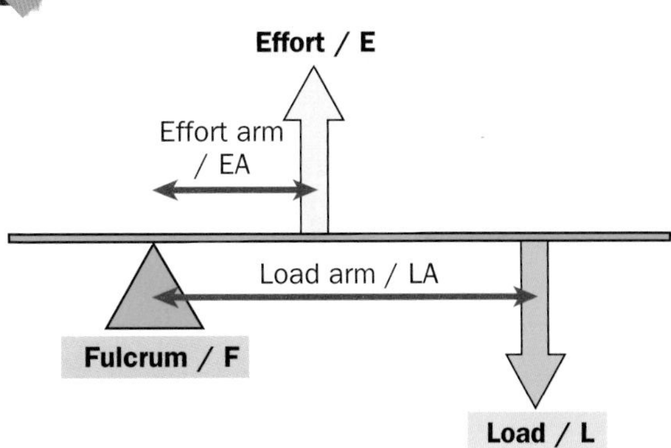

TASK 5

Calculate the moment of the effort (E) as an athlete lifts the dumbbell in the upward phase of a biceps curl. Remember to show all your working and give the units of measurement.

Fig 14.13 The upward phase of a bicep curl

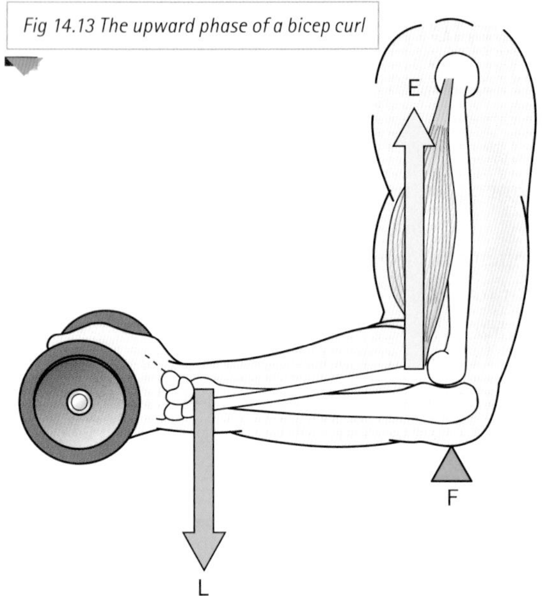

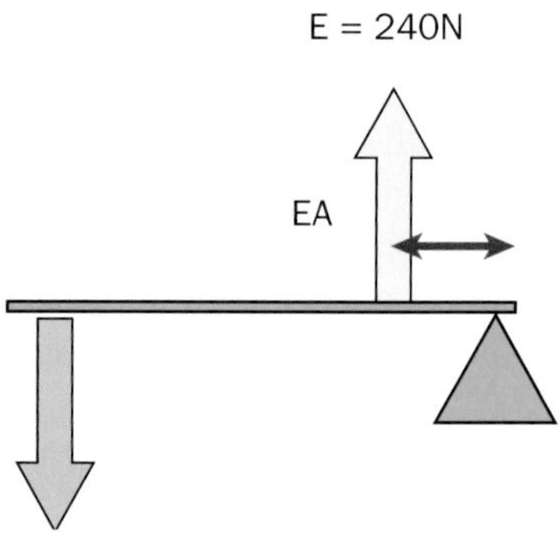

Generating a larger force or increasing the distance of the point of application of the force from the fulcrum can increase the moment of a force. It is common practice in many sport techniques to increase the moment of a force by increasing its distance from the fulcrum. This creates a longer lever that generates a greater acceleration and range of movement as an object is hit.

Fig 14.14 The longer the lever, the greater the range of movement and the outgoing acceleration of the ball

Taking tennis as an example, the presence of a racket in the hand of a player increases the load arm and therefore increases the moment of the force acting on the ball at the point of contact. This causes a greater acceleration of the ball away from the head of the racket. The same principle can be applied in a number of other sports including cricket, hockey, golf, rowing and swimming.

TASK 6

1. Identify three sports where a performer benefits from a long load arm. Explain why this is an advantage.
2. Why do you think that in a set of golf clubs, the driver has a longer shaft than the pitching wedge?

The principle axes of rotation

The angular motion of a body is commonly described with reference to the **principle axis of rotation.** There are three principle axes of

KEY TERMS

Axis of rotation

An imaginary line or point about which the body, or part of the body, rotates. For example, the leg rotates about the hip joint when kicking a football.

Principle axis of rotation

An axis of rotation that is directed through the body's centre of mass. The human body has three principle axes of rotation: the longitudinal axis, the transverse axis and the frontal axis.

rotation, which all pass through the centre of mass (see Fig 14.15):

- The longitudinal axis runs from top to bottom and passes through a performer's centre of mass. A spin in ice skating or a turn in trampolining are examples of rotation about the longitudinal axis.
- The transverse axis runs from left to right and passes through a performer's centre of mass. A somersault is an example of rotation about the transverse axis.
- The frontal axis runs from front to back and passes through a performer's centre of mass. A cartwheel is an example of rotation about the frontal axis.

Fig 14.15 The principle axes of the body pass through the centre of mass

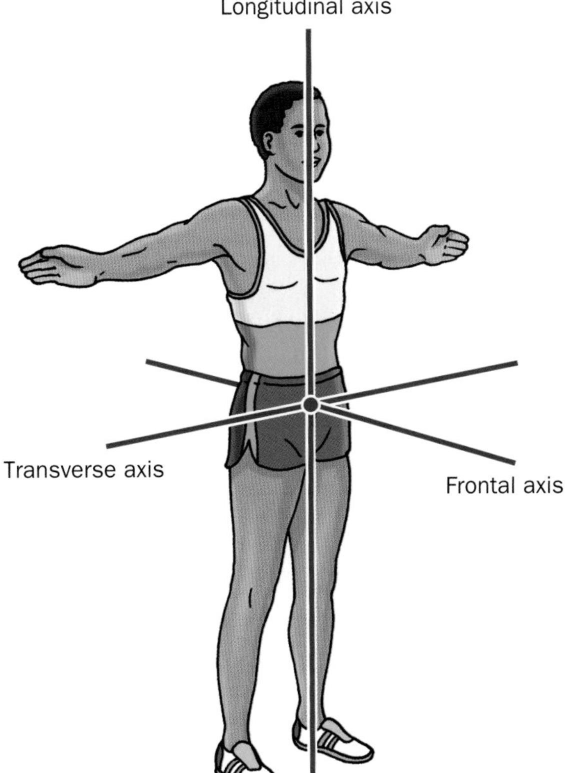

REMEMBER

For rotation or angular motion to occur, an eccentric force must be applied. This is a force whose line of application passes outside the centre of mass of a body, causing the resulting motion to be angular.

EXAM TIP

In a question on angular motion, it is always a very good idea to identify the axis of rotation before going on to answer the rest of the question.

STRETCH AND CHALLENGE

The joint movements that you studied last year in your AS anatomy course can be described according to the axis about which they rotate. This is because bones, joints and muscles act as lever systems which rotate about a fixed point.

Using your knowledge of the axes of rotation, identify the axis about which the following joint movements occur:

- flexion and extension
- horizontal flexion and extension
- abduction and adduction
- rotation
- plantar flexion and dorsiflexion
- lateral flexion
- pronation and supination.

Describing angular motion

The following quantities are measurements that are commonly used to describe the angular motion of a body. Their value tells us how far and how fast a body spins, turns, somersaults or circles.

- Angular distance
- Angular displacement
- Angular speed
- Angular velocity
- Angular acceleration.

EXAM TIP

For the purposes of the specification, you need to be familiar with each of the quantities listed. You will need to know:

- a simple definition
- a relevant equation where appropriate (remember that any calculation will be very simple!)
- the unit of measurement for the quantity you have calculated.

KEY TERM

Radian (rad)

The unit of measurement for angular distance and angular displacement.

REMEMBER

All of the quantities you are required to know to describe angular motion have a linear equivalent. Look back over Chapter 11, pages 277–279, to remind yourself of these; you will see that the angular quantities have exactly the same meaning – it is just that they have the word 'angular' preceding them.

It is also worth pointing out that angular distance and angular displacement are measured in **radians (rad)**. It is not necessary for you to understand this term, simply to appreciate that a radian is the angular equivalent to a metre and simply a way to measure the angle moved by a rotating body.

ANGULAR DISTANCE VERSUS ANGULAR DISPLACEMENT

The measurements of **angular distance** and **angular displacement** are used to describe the extent of a body's angular motion or how far it has rotated.

- Angular distance is the angle through which a body has rotated in moving from one position to another.
- Angular displacement is the smallest angular change between the starting and finishing positions.

KEY TERMS

Angular distance

The angle through which a body has rotated about an axis in moving from the first position to the second. The angle is measured in radians.

Angular displacement

The shortest change in angular position. It is the smallest angle through which a body has rotated about an axis in moving from the first position to the second. The angle is measured in radians.

EXAM TIP

Try to become familiar with using radians to measure angles rather than degrees. They are, in fact, the Standard International Unit for describing angular motion, so you will come across them in exam questions. Be prepared!

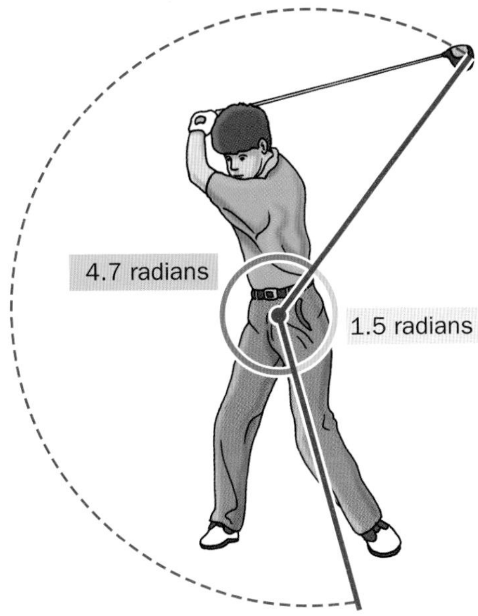

Fig 14.16 A golf drive to show the difference between angular distance and angular displacement

Consider the golfer in Fig 14.16. In rotating from position A to position B, the club head has travelled an angular distance of 4.7 radians but an angular displacement of 1.5 radians.

ANGULAR SPEED VERSUS ANGULAR VELOCITY

The measurements of **angular speed** and **angular velocity** are used to describe the rate at which a body is rotating.

KEY TERMS

Angular speed

The angular distance travelled in a certain time. It is measured in radians per second (rad/s).

Angular velocity

The angular displacement travelled in a certain time. It is measured in radians per second (rad/s).

Angular speed is the rate of change of angular distance and its value is calculated by dividing the angular distance moved in radians by the time taken in seconds.

$$\text{Angular speed (rad/s)} = \frac{\text{angular distance (radians)}}{\text{time taken (seconds)}}$$

Angular velocity is the rate of change of angular displacement and its value is calculated by dividing the angular displacement moved in radians by the time taken in seconds.

$$\text{Angular velocity (rad/s)} = \frac{\text{angular displacement (radians)}}{\text{time taken (seconds)}}$$

EXAM TIP

Angular velocity is more likely to crop up in an exam question than angular speed because it is a more precise description of how fast the body is rotating. This is because angular velocity gives an indication of direction.

TASK 7

1 The legs of a trampolinist performing a seat drop rotate 1.5 radians in 0.6 seconds. Calculate the angular velocity of the trampolinist's legs.
2 When driving the golf ball from the tee, the head of the club rotates 9.2 radians in 0.8 seconds. Calculate the angular velocity of the club head.

REMEMBER

For any calculation, remember the three things you learned in Chapter 11:

- always state the equation you are using
- show all your working
- give the units of measurement.

ANGULAR ACCELERATION

The measurement of **angular acceleration** is used to describe the rate at which a body changes its angular velocity. Its value is calculated by dividing the change in angular velocity in radians per second by the time taken in seconds.

$$\text{Angular acceleration (rad/s}^2\text{)} = \frac{\text{Change in angular velocity (rad/s)}}{\text{Time taken (s)}}$$

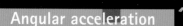

KEY TERM

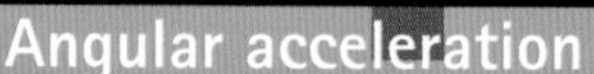

Angular acceleration

The rate of change of angular velocity. It is measured in radians per second squared (rad/s^2).

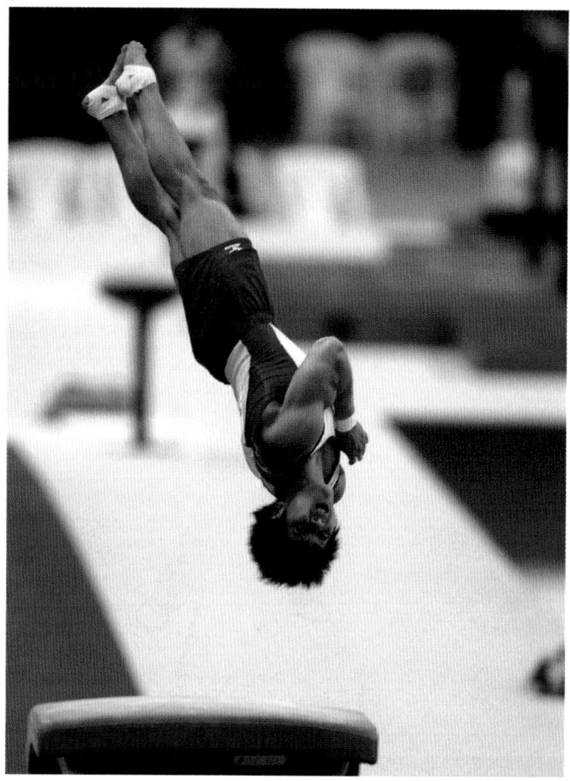

Fig 14.17 The gymnast continues to turn about his axis of rotation with constant angular momentum until acted upon by an external torque as he hits the ground

ANGULAR ANALOGUES OF NEWTON'S LAWS APPLIED TO ROTATING BODIES

In Chapter 11, one of the first concepts we considered was the importance of Newton's laws of motion in governing our understanding of linear motion. The same is true when it comes to angular motion, and a direct analogy can be made between linear and angular motion in this respect. The only difference in Newton's laws when they are applied to rotating bodies is in the terminology used. The concept behind each law remains exactly the same.

ANGULAR ANALOGUE OF NEWTON'S FIRST LAW OF MOTION

> *'A rotating body continues to turn about its axis of rotation with constant angular momentum unless acted upon by an external torque.'*
>
> (Newton's First Law of Motion)

An application of this law can be seen when a gymnast lands from performing a vault (Fig 14.17). In the second flight stage, as they push from the top of the vault to land, the gymnast may be performing a series of somersaults or twists. They will continue to rotate until they land, when the ground exerts an external torque on them to change their state of **angular momentum**.

KEY TERM

Angular momentum

The quantity of angular motion possessed by a rotating body. It is the product of moment of inertia multiplied by angular velocity. It is measured in kgm^2/s. See page 345 for more detail.

The angular analogue of Newton's First Law of Motion is fundamental to a full understanding of angular motion and is discussed in more detail on page 345.

APPLY IT!

What are the two axes of rotation about which the gymnast is turning in Fig 14.17? What is the name of the third axis of rotation?

REMEMBER

A torque is a rotational force.

TASK 8

1 By replacing the linear terminology with the angular equivalent shown in the table below, write out carefully the angular analogues for Newton's Second Law and Newton's Third Law. Then give an example from sport for each of these laws.

Replace this linear term ...	With this angular term ...
body	rotating body
move	rotate about its axis of rotation
velocity	angular velocity
force	torque
momentum	angular momentum

2 Give the angular term for each of the linear terms listed below:
- distance
- displacement
- metre
- angular speed
- angular acceleration.

EXAM TIP

The use of the correct scientific terminology in an exam answer will gain you valuable marks in a levels mark scheme, which will be used to award you 20 marks in the fourth part of your Biomechanics question.

Moment of inertia

Moment of inertia is the linear equivalent of inertia and applies to the tendency of a body to initially resist angular motion and the tendency of a body to want to continue rotating about its axis of rotation once undergoing angular motion. It is an important concept and is relevant in all sporting situations where angular motion occurs.

KEY TERM

Moment of inertia

The resistance of a rotating body to change its state of angular motion. All bodies will initially resist rotation and then, once they are rotating, will want to continue to turn about their axis of rotation.

APPLY IT!

Moment of inertia can be looked upon as angular resistance and angular persistence. Consider when you were younger and enjoyed going on the merry-go-round in the park (Fig 14.18). To get this apparatus spinning, you needed to apply a relatively large force by running alongside the merry-go-round and pushing on the bars. However, once you had achieved this and jumped on, the merry-go-round seemed to spin forever until you dragged your foot along the ground to slow it down. This is another example of the angular analogue of Newton's First Law, where a rotating body (the merry-go-round) will continue to turn about its axis of rotation (the longitudinal axis) until acted on by an external torque (a foot dragging along the ground).

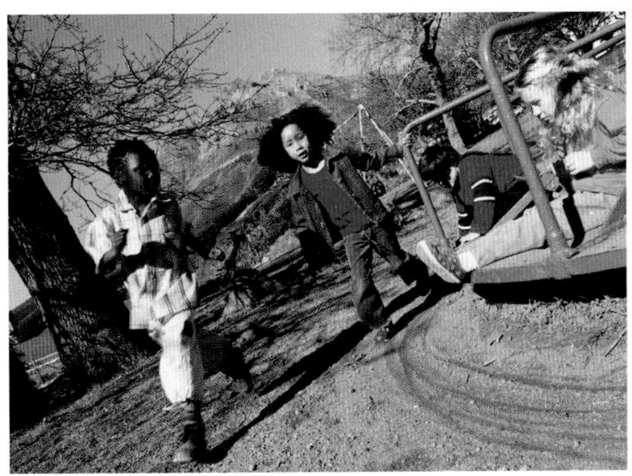

Fig 14.18 A park merry-go-round provides one example of the angular analogue of Newton's First Law

There are two significant factors that determine the size of the moment of inertia of a rotating body:

- the mass of the body
- the distribution of the mass of the body from the axis of rotation.

THE MASS OF THE BODY

The larger the mass, the greater the moment of inertia and the more resistance and persistence the body puts up against angular motion. Conversely, the smaller the mass, the smaller the moment of inertia and the less resistance and persistence to angular motion. For example, a heavy cricket bat is more difficult to swing than a lighter one, as its resistance to angular motion is greater. However, once swinging, the heavier bat is more difficult to control or stop than the lighter bat, as its persistence to angular motion is greater.

THE DISTRIBUTION OF THE MASS OF THE BODY FROM THE AXIS OF ROTATION

The further the distribution of mass from the axis of rotation, the greater the moment of inertia; the closer the distribution of mass to the axis of rotation, the smaller the moment of inertia. For example, a gymnast performs two consecutive somersaults about the transverse axis. For the first somersault the gymnast is in a tucked position and for the second they are in a straight position. The gymnast has a higher moment of inertia when performing the straight somersault because in this position their mass is distributed further from the axis of rotation. In this position, the gymnast has a greater persistence to angular motion, which explains why this is a more difficult somersault than a tucked somersault.

Fig 14.19 The gymnast is rotating about her longitudinal axis. (a) Moment of inertia is high as the distribution of mass is a long way from the axis of rotation. (b) Moment of inertia is low as the distribution of mass is close to the axis of rotation

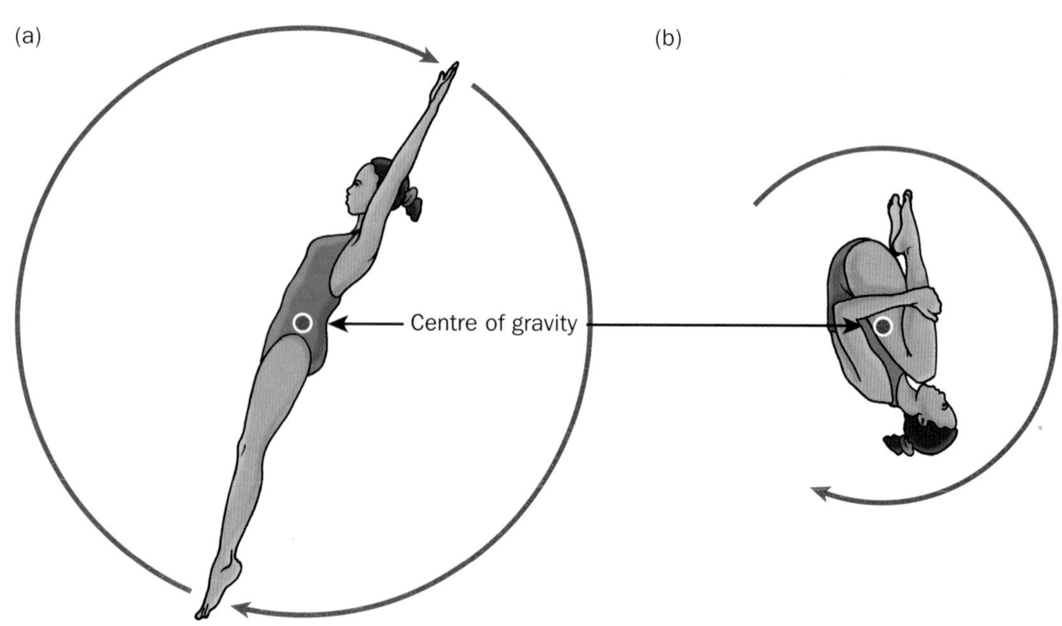

EXAM TIP

Always identify the axis of rotation in the first instance before making a judgment on the body position where moment of inertia is high and the body position where moment of inertia is low. This is important because when an outstretched body (as in Fig 14.19a) rotates about the transverse axis it has a high moment of inertia, but when it rotates about the longitudinal axis it has a low moment of inertia.

INCREASING OR DECREASING MOMENT OF INERTIA

Once a body is rotating, it is possible to increase or decrease its moment of inertia. This is commonly observed in figure skating when a skater begins a spin with their arms stretched out to the side and during the spin brings their arms into their body. The skater is rotating about the longitudinal axis. When they bring their arms into their body the distribution of mass from the axis of rotation is greatly reduced and the moment of inertia becomes significantly smaller. With a small moment of inertia, rotation is easier as there is less resistance to angular motion and the skater can spin faster.

APPLY IT!

When doing somersaults, divers reduce their moment of inertia about the transverse axis by pulling their body into a tight tuck after takeoff. The closer they can pull their body to the axis of rotation, the easier and quicker they can spin. So, a lean diver with a high degree of flexibility will find it easier to rotate than a muscular diver. This is one reason why the elite divers appear to be so thin.

The principle of increasing or decreasing moment of inertia can also be applied to a specific body part rotating about a particular joint. Consider the action of the leg during sprinting where it rotates about the hip joint. The leg is turning about the transverse axis. In the drive phase of the leg action, the sprinter's leg is extended. The mass is distributed away from the hip joint (the axis of rotation) and the leg has a high moment of inertia. During recovery, flexion of the knee brings the mass of the leg closer to the hip joint and reduces moment of inertia. Reducing moment

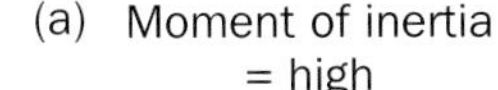

Fig 14.20 When rotating about the longitudinal axis, moment of inertia is decreased by bringing the arms in towards the body. This makes rotation easier and faster

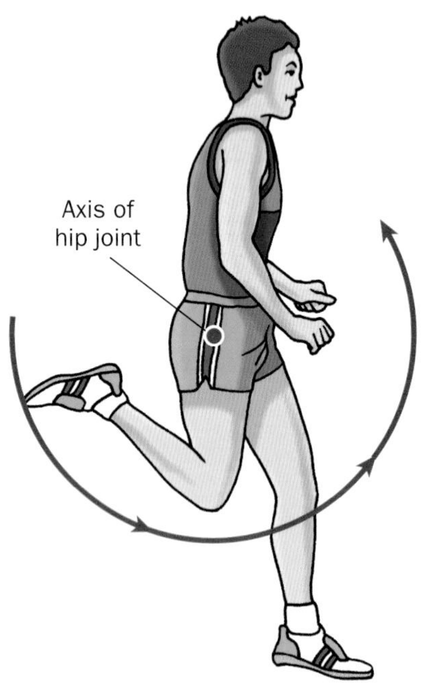

Fig 14.21 The moment of inertia of the sprinter's leg is decreased in the recovery phase, allowing their leg to turn about the hip joint easily and quickly

of inertia makes rotation easier and faster and the sprinter is able to bring the leg through quickly to begin another drive phase. This partly explains why a high knee lift is important to efficient sprinting technique where leg speed is important, but not so vital to middle-distance running techniques.

REMEMBER

Remember that the smaller the moment of inertia, the easier and quicker the rotation. A small moment of inertia has less resistance to angular motion.

STRETCH AND CHALLENGE

Consider the speeds achieved by elite sprinters compared to elite middle distance runners compared to elite race walkers. Use your knowledge of moment of inertia to explain these variations in speed.

TASK 9

1 Explain why a high elbow on a bent arm is an important coaching technique when teaching someone to swim front-crawl.
2 For each of the examples given in Fig 14.22, answer the following three questions.
   a) Around which axis is the performer rotating?
   b) How can the performer decrease their moment of inertia?
   c) What will happen when they decrease their moment of inertia?

Fig 14.22

Angular momentum

Angular momentum refers to the amount of angular motion that a rotating body possesses (see page 340). The amount of angular momentum possessed by a rotating body depends on its moment of inertia and its angular velocity. A high moment of inertia or a large angular velocity will create a large angular momentum.

angular momentum = moment of inertia x angular velocity

In sports involving rotation it is often important for athletes to generate a large angular momentum at takeoff. In high diving, for example, a diver needs to create sufficient angular momentum at the start of the dive to allow them to perform the numerous somersaults and twists that occur later. This is why a diver ensures that their body is extended and spread out at takeoff, giving them a high moment of inertia and a large angular momentum with which to complete the dive.

THE LAW OF CONSERVATION OF ANGULAR MOMENTUM

The angular momentum generated at takeoff is conserved during flight. For example, the angular momentum a diver generates at takeoff remains the same while the diver is in flight. This principle is also evident in a spinning ice skater, despite the fact they are in contact with the ground, because the frictional force between the smooth surface of the blade and the ice is so small that it can be ignored.

KEY TERM

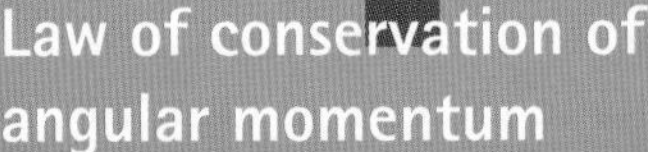

Law of conservation of angular momentum

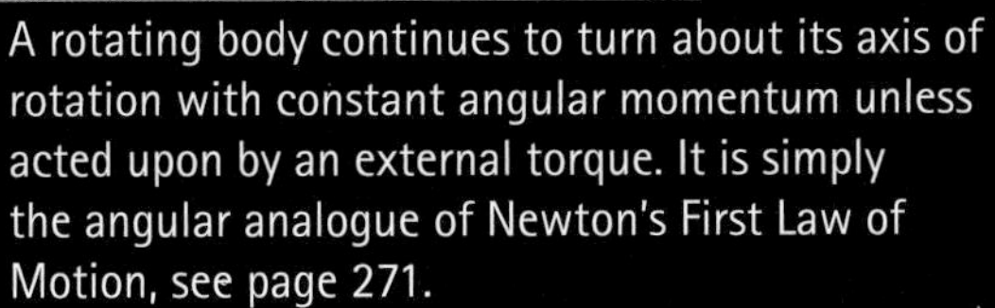

A rotating body continues to turn about its axis of rotation with constant angular momentum unless acted upon by an external torque. It is simply the angular analogue of Newton's First Law of Motion, see page 271.

The **law of conservation of angular momentum** is a result of the angular analogue of Newton's First Law and explains why a decrease in moment of inertia can increase a body's rate of spin or angular velocity.

To be able to apply this law to sporting techniques, we need to remember two important concepts.

- Angular momentum is the moment of inertia multiplied by the angular velocity.
- Once in flight, a performer can manipulate their moment of inertia by changing body position. By bringing their mass closer to the axis of rotation they will decrease their moment of inertia; by spreading their mass further away from the axis of rotation they will increase the moment of inertia.

So, for angular momentum to remain constant:

- decreasing the moment of inertia will cause an increase in angular velocity, so the performer will rotate quicker
- increasing the moment of inertia will cause a decrease in angular velocity, so the performer will rotate slower.

Consider two particular sporting examples where performers take full advantage of the law of conservation of angular momentum: diving and figure skating.

DIVING

Consider the diver in Fig 14.23, who takes off from the 10m platform to complete a one-and-a-half-back somersault about the transverse axis.

EXAM TIP

The relationship between angular momentum, moment of inertia and angular velocity can be seen in a graph like the one shown in Figure 14.23. This is a graph that shows the angular motion of a rotating body and you need to be familiar with it.

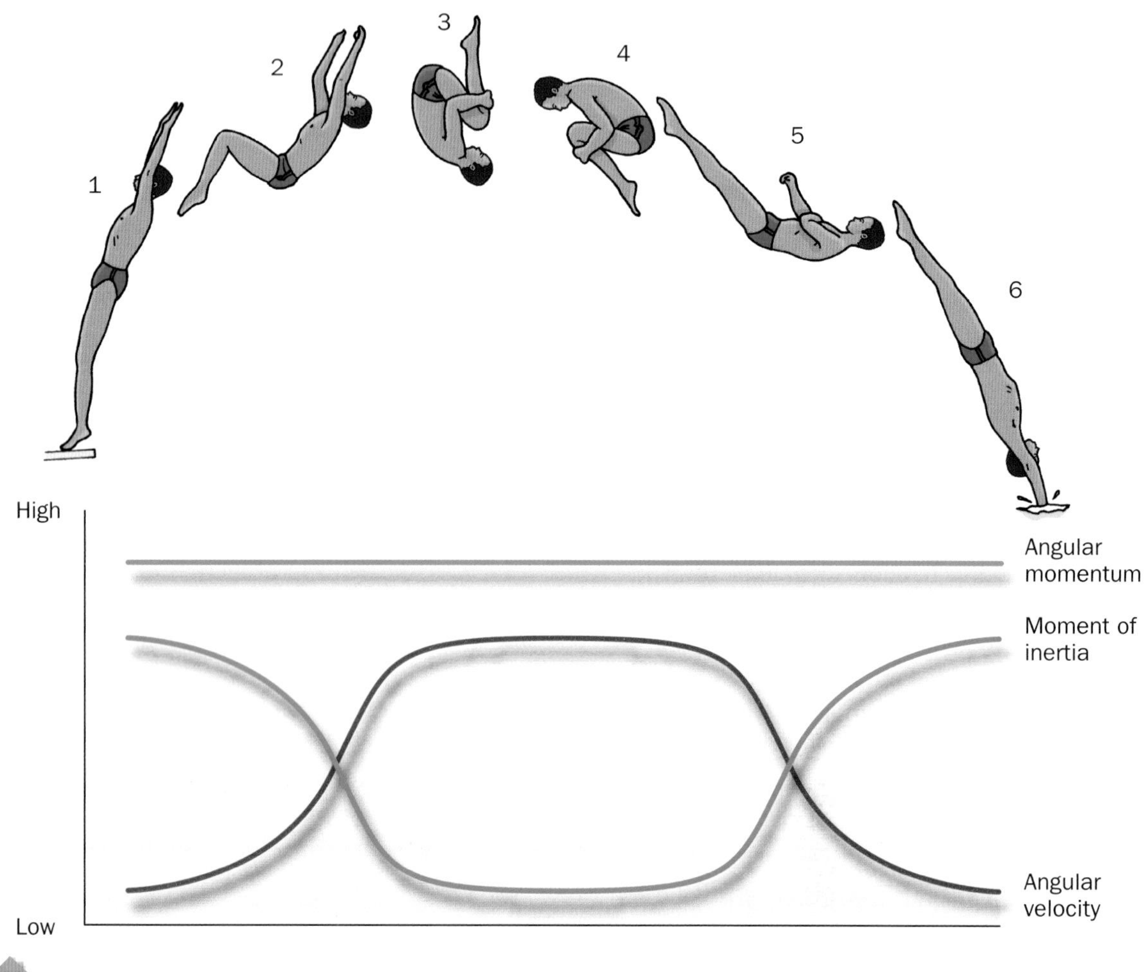

Fig 14.23 A diver makes use of the law of conservation of angular momentum to control his rate of spin about the transverse axis

According to the law of conservation of angular momentum, the amount of angular momentum generated at takeoff stays the same during flight until the diver hits the water on entry. At takeoff, the diver must ensure a large moment of inertia by spreading their body away from the transverse axis. This gives them a large angular momentum to enable them to complete the dive in the small amount of time they have in flight (less than two seconds from the 10m board). In positions 2, 3 and 4 the diver brings their arms, legs and head in towards the axis of rotation, therefore significantly decreasing their moment of inertia. This causes angular velocity to increase and the diver spins quicker during this section of the dive. To control their entry into the water and avoid over-rotation, the diver needs to reduce their rate of spin towards the end of the dive. To do this they spread their body out again, away from the axis of rotation, as shown in positions 5 and 6. This increases their moment of inertia and decreases their angular velocity to ensure a controlled entry into the water.

FIGURE SKATING

Another example of a performer manipulating their moment of inertia to increase or decrease rate of spin occurs when a figure skater performs a multiple spin about the longitudinal axis. During the spin, angular momentum is conserved, even though it could be argued that there is the presence of an external torque with the skate in contact with the ground. In actual fact, this torque can be ignored, as the friction between the tiny blade and the smooth surface of the ice is so small as to be negligible.

At the start of the spin, the skater's body position is with both arms out to the side and one leg extended behind them. This means the distribution of mass is a long way from the longitudinal axis. This gives the skater a large moment of inertia and a large angular momentum at the start of the spin. The skater then pulls both arms and the outer leg inwards and will often cross their arms across their chest and cross their ankles. This greatly decreases their moment of inertia, which in turn considerably increases their angular velocity and the skater spins very quickly. When the skater spreads their arms and legs out again, their moment of inertia increases once again and the rate of spin reduces. (See Fig 14.24.)

Fig 14.24 Spinning skater

APPLY IT!

Working with a partner, help each other explain how a slalom skier uses conservation of angular momentum to their advantage.

STRETCH AND CHALLENGE

Long jumpers rotate forwards at takeoff. This is due to the presence of an eccentric force. The jumper exerts a downward force on the ground with their takeoff foot, and the ground, in turn, exerts an equal and opposite upward reaction force on the jumper. This reaction force passes behind the jumper's centre of mass to initiate a forward rotation.

Explain the methods used by a long jumper during flight to prevent this clockwise rotation. You will need to look at the angular analogue of Newton's Third Law of Motion to help you answer this question.

Exam Café

Relax, refresh, result!

You should now have knowledge and understanding of:

- centre of mass and its relationship to balance, rotation and efficiency of technique
- the three types of lever system in relation to human movement and the advantages and disadvantages of second and third classes of lever system
- how to define and calculate the units of measurement for the moment of a force
- the three major axes of rotation, giving examples of sporting movements that occur around them
- the quantities used to describe angular motion and their relevance to sporting techniques
- what is meant by the terms moment of inertia and angular momentum and their relevance to sporting performance
- the law of conservation of angular momentum and be able to give examples of how athletes use this principle in a number of sporting activities.

REVISE AS YOU GO!

1. Identify a stable position in a sport of your choice and explain the mechanical principles that make it so stable.
2. Identify the components of a lever system and apply them to human movement.
3. Describe and sketch a diagram of the three types of lever system. For each type, give a sporting example of when it is used in the human body.
4. Discuss the advantages and disadvantages of a second-class lever system.
5. Define the moment of a force and state how it can be increased.
6. Name the three principle axes of the body and give a sporting example of a rotation that occurs about each of these axes.
7. Define angular velocity and give the equation and units of measurements for it.
8. State the angular analogue of Newton's First Law of Motion.
9. Explain what is meant by the term moment of inertia.
10. Define angular momentum and explain the law of conservation of angular momentum, giving a sporting example of this concept.

Try to answer these questions yourself. Ask your teacher if you need help.

Get the result!

Examination question

Explain how the spinning ice-skater in Fig 14.24 is able to increase her rate of rotation. (6 marks)

Fig 14.24

Examiner's tips

As always, check the command word first. It is an 'explain' question so make sure that your answer really does this. Remember to always give the axis of rotation, so that you get the correct body position for increasing and decreasing moment of inertia. The question is asking you about a spinning skater so make sure you apply your knowledge of angular motion to this example in your answer. Finally, be careful to give enough information to achieve all six of the marks available.

Student answer

The skater will spin quicker when they bring their arms and legs towards their body. This decreases their moment of inertia and makes them spin faster.

Examiner says:

You have attempted to answer the question and are along the right lines. I like the fact that you have used some specialist vocabulary by realising the question is asking about moment of inertia. However, you have made two critical mistakes. Firstly, you have not identified the axis of rotation and secondly there is no real explanation here.

Improved student answer

The skater is rotating about the longitudinal axis. If we ignore the tiny frictional force between the blade of the skate and the ice, the law of conservation of angular momentum can be applied. This states that once spinning, the skater will rotate with constant angular momentum until acted upon by an external torque. This is the angular analogue of Newton's First Law of Motion. Angular momentum = moment of inertia x angular velocity. Moment of inertia is the resistance of a rotating body to angular motion. It depends on the distribution of the skater's mass from the longitudinal axis. When the skater starts spinning, they want to have a high moment of inertia by having their arms and one leg outstretched away from their body. To decrease their moment of inertia about the longitudinal axis during the spin, the skater must bring both arms and legs in towards the body. In order for angular momentum to remain constant, a decrease in the moment of inertia will cause an increase in angular velocity and the skater will spin quicker.

Examiner says:

The perfect start! You have identified the axis of rotation.

Examiner says:

You have now described the law, applied it to the spinning skater, linked it to Newton's First Law of Motion and given an equation – brilliant!

Examiner says:

You have done well to apply the importance of a performer having a high moment of inertia at the start of rotation – students regularly miss this.

Examiner says:

This ties up your answer well by bringing it back to the law of conservation of angular momentum – tidily and logically done. This is a thorough, accurate and applied answer that would link well to any mark scheme. Superb!

Examiner says:

Well done! Straight away you have identified the mechanical princip that is the route to being able to expla the example given. was important to ge this in early in your answer.

Examiner says:

Moment of inertia is relevant to any rotating body and you have shown a good level of understanding and application of this concept.

Examiner says:

Again, you show a f appreciation for the concept of momen of inertia.

CHAPTER 15:

Critical evaluation of the quality, effectiveness and efficiency of performance

LEARNING OBJECTIVES

By the end of this chapter you should have knowledge and understanding of:

- how to review and judge your level of understanding of the topics covered in Chapters 11–14
- how to apply the knowledge you have gained from Chapters 11–14 to:
  - running activities such as sprinting, endurance running, swerving, side stepping and dodging in team games
  - jumping activities such as long jump, high jump, triple jump, simple jumps in trampolining and gymnastics, jumping in team games, ski jumping
  - throwing activities such as shot put, javelin, discus throwing, passing and shooting in team games
  - hitting/kicking activities such as shots in tennis, badminton, golf, cricket, rounders, free kick or corner kicks in football, conversions in rugby
  - rotating activities such as rotating skills around the principle axes in gymnastics, diving, trampolining, skating, slalom skiing.

INTRODUCTION

It will be good news to hear that there is nothing extra to learn in this chapter. If you have understood and can apply the topics covered in the previous chapters in the Biomechanics section of this book, you have every reason to expect to score well in your biomechanics exam question. This final chapter is simply intended as a review and a way for you to check that you are confident at applying relevant areas of the specification to different types of physical activity.

To make things a little easier, we have arranged the different types of physical activity into five groups:

- running activities
- jumping activities
- throwing activities
- hitting/kicking activities
- rotating activities.

REMEMBER

This critical evaluation does not cover every sport skill that your examiner might ask about. However, by working through the tasks you will notice biomechanical principles that keep reappearing from one type of activity to the next, so whatever skill is being considered, these principles are always present. Get to know them and understand their effect on performance then learn them thoroughly! It will help you considerably with scoring well on the exam paper.

EXAM TIP

In your A2 paper, there will be one question on biomechanics worth 35 marks. This question will be split into four parts. The first three parts will be worth a sum total of 15 marks (averaging 5 marks per part). The fourth part of the question is worth 20 marks. To answer this part effectively you will need to:

- show detailed knowledge from a number of areas of the biomechanics specification
- use accurate and specialist vocabulary in your answer
- link theoretical knowledge to its effect on performance throughout your answer
- use a high quality of written communication that is fluent to read and includes relatively few errors.

It is therefore strongly recommended that you spend sufficient time and thought reading through Chapter 15 and completing the tasks set. If you find this relatively straightforward, you should have little concern about the 20-marks part of the question. Good luck!

Running skills, for example sprinting

NEWTON'S LAWS OF MOTION

First Law: on the starting blocks, the sprinter will remain at rest until an external force acts – in this case it is the upward and forward reaction force from the blocks.

Second Law: the greater the force applied by the sprinter on the blocks and during the first few strides on the track, the greater their acceleration at the start of the race.

Third Law: every time the sprinter pushes backwards on the track with their driving leg, the track exerts an equal and opposite forward force on the athlete.

DESCRIBING LINEAR MOTION/GRAPHS OF MOTION

Data given on distance/displacement and time taken allows calculations to be made on speed, velocity and acceleration and graphs of motion to be plotted. A velocity/time graph for the 100m sprint would look like Fig 15.1.

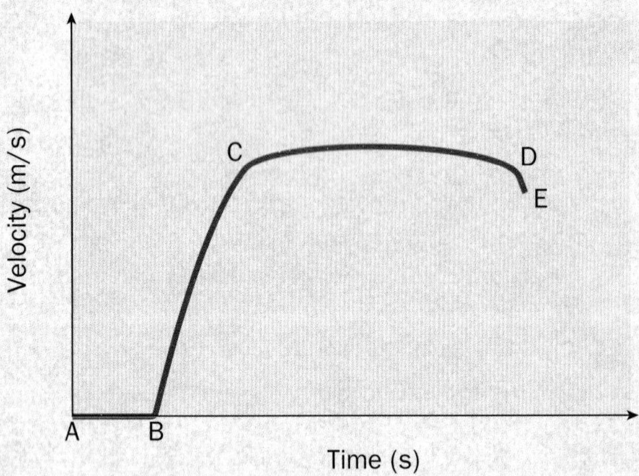

Fig 15.1 Velocity/time graph of motion for sprinting

A–B: sprinter is stationary (on the blocks)
B–C: sprinter is accelerating at the start of the race
C–D: sprinter has reached maximum speed
D–E: sprinter is decelerating as they tire and as air resistance increases towards the end of the race

NET FORCE ACTING ON SPRINTER DURING 100M SPRINT

- During the acceleration phase, net force is positive. Horizontal forces are unbalanced.
- When the sprinter has achieved their maximum speed and is travelling with constant velocity, net force = 0. Horizontal forces are balanced.
- When the sprinter is decelerating slightly at the end of the race, net force is negative. Horizontal forces are unbalanced.

TYPES OF FORCE/FREE BODY DIAGRAM

The following external forces are acting on the sprinter to varying extents throughout the race.

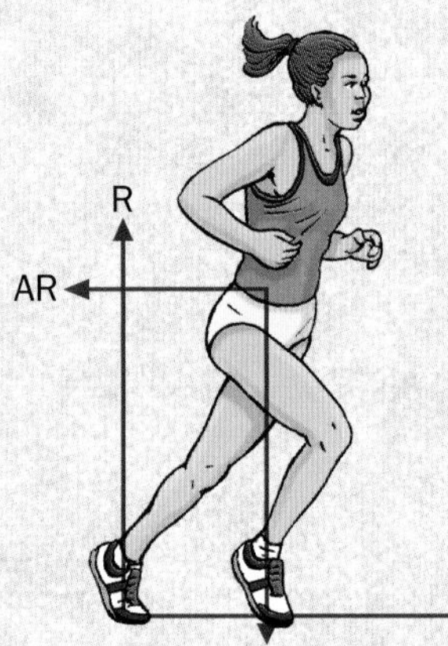

- Weight
- Reaction force
- Friction force
- Air resistance

For example, Fig 15.2 shows a free body diagram to represent the forces acting on a sprinter during the acceleration phase of the sprint.

Fig 15.2 Forces acting on a sprinter during the acceleration phase of the sprint

STABILITY

Stability relates to how much force is needed to disturb a body from its equilibrium. The stability of the sprinter varies with the three stages of the sprint start:

- *'On your marks'*: sprinter is most stable because the centre of mass is low, the area of the base of support is large and the line of gravity is central to the base of support.
- *'Set'*: the sprinter remains stable but is less stable in this position, as although the area of the base of support remains the same, the centre of mass is higher and the line of gravity is closer to the edge of the base of support, having shifted forwards.
- *'Bang'*: the sprinter is unstable. They have lifted their hands so the line of gravity falls outside the area of their base of support. Their centre of mass has been raised further and they have reduced the area of their base of support.

LEVER SYSTEMS

In sprinting, there are two types of lever being used.

- A second class lever is used as the ball of the foot drives from the starting blocks and the ground at the end of each drive phase (Fig 15.3).

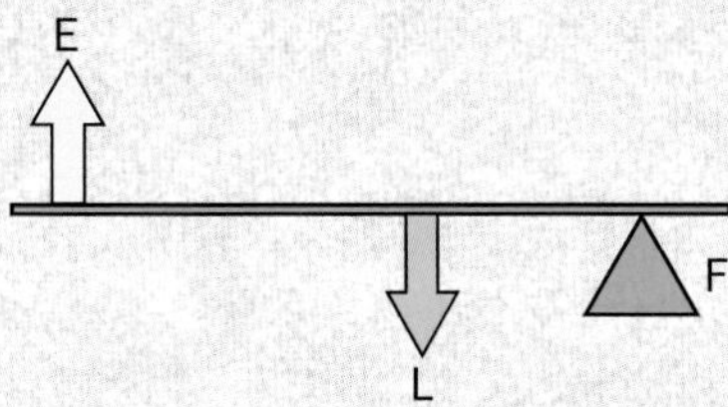

Fig 15.3 Second class lever: load lies between the fulcrum and the effort.

F = joint between the metatarsals and the phalanges
L = weight of the body being moved
E = force exerted by the gastrocnemius muscle as it contracts concentrically to cause plantar flexion of the ankle

- There are a number of third class levers being used but one would be in the flexion of the hip as the leg comes through on recovery (Fig 15.4).

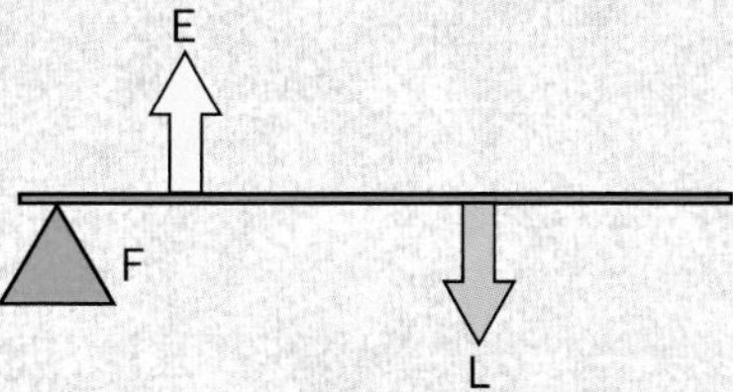

Fig 15.4 Third class lever: effort lies between the fulcrum and the load.

F = hip joint
L = weight of the leg being rotated
E = force exerted by the iliopsoas muscle as it contracts concentrically to cause flexion of the hip

IMPULSE

Impulse = Force x time
I = Ft

During the acceleration phase of the run, a force/time graph to represent the impulse of the sprinter's foot plant would look like Fig 15.5. Here the positive impulse is greater than the negative impulse, resulting in a positive net force in the direction of travel. According to Newton's First Law, this will cause acceleration in the early stages of the race.

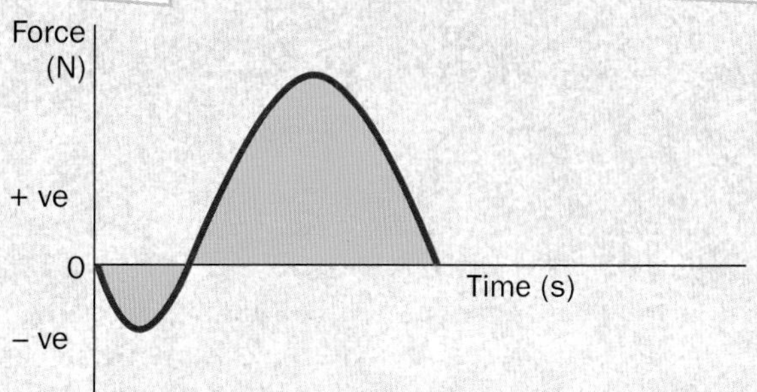

Fig 15.5 Force/time graph to show acceleration phase of a run

AIR RESISTANCE

Air resistance is a hindrance to sprinters as it acts in the opposite direction to their direction of motion and works against them to slow them down. As the sprinter becomes more upright after the start and as their velocity increases, the effect of air resistance becomes greater. Sprinters will try to keep the negative effect of air resistance to a minimum by keeping low for as long as possible after the sprint start and by wearing tightly fitted and specially designed sprinting suits. These reduce the sprinter's cross-sectional area and ensure a smooth outer surface for air molecules to flow past.

MOMENT OF INERTIA

This is the resistance of a rotating body to change its state of angular motion. It depends on the mass of the body and the distribution of the mass from the axis of rotation. In sprinting it can be applied to the leg position during recovery. As the leg rotates around the hip joint it is travelling around the transverse axis. The high knee lift during recovery brings the distribution of the mass of the leg close to the axis of rotation. This gives a small moment of inertia and allows the leg to rotate quickly and easily and enables the sprinter to have a fast leg speed.

TASK 1

Within your class, create similar sheets to show how the biomechanical concepts identified above relate to:

- endurance running
- swerving, side stepping or dodging in team games.

Can you think of any additional biomechanical concepts that could be applied to your examples?

Jumping skills, for example long jump

NEWTON'S LAWS OF MOTION

First Law: the jumper will remain running at optimal speed on the approach run until acted upon by an external force at takeoff. Once the jumper plants their foot on the takeoff board, the board applies an upward reaction force on the jumper, which causes them to change their state of motion.

Second Law: the greater the reaction force generated at takeoff, the greater the upward acceleration achieved by the long jumper.

Third Law: at the point of takeoff, the long jumper exerts a large downward force on the ground, which in turn applies an equal and opposite reaction force on the jumper. This allows the jumper to accelerate upwards at takeoff.

NET FORCE

Net force acting on the long jumper during their approach run is positive as they accelerate from a stationary position at the start of their run to reaching their optimal speed at the moment of takeoff.

Horizontal forces are unbalanced. The force acting in the same direction as motion is larger than the force acting in the opposite direction. In this case, friction is greater than air resistance. A long jumper can maximise friction by wearing spikes and minimise air resistance by wearing a tight-fitting, Lycra bodysuit. They will also start their approach run in a slightly crouched position and gradually become more upright, so as to reduce their cross-sectional area. (For the net force acting on the long jumper during flight, see the Projectiles box below.)

TYPES OF FORCE/FREE BODY DIAGRAM

The following external forces are acting on the long jumper to varying extents throughout the phases of run up, takeoff, flight and landing.

- Weight
- Reaction force
- Friction force
- Air resistance

For example, Fig 15.6 is a free body diagram to represent the forces acting on a long jumper at the moment of takeoff.

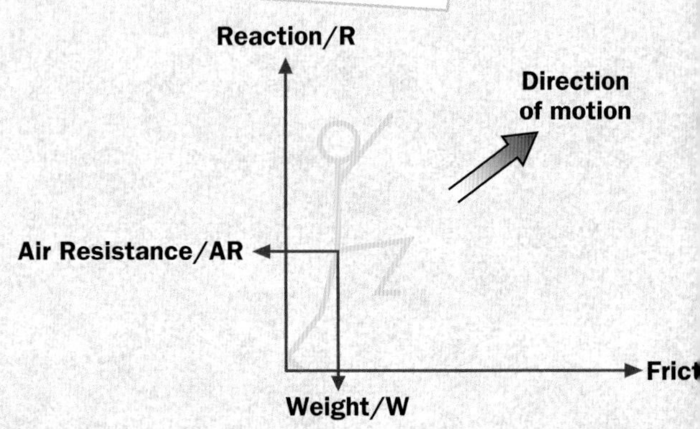

Fig 15.6 Forces acting on a long jumper at the moment of takeoff

- Vertical forces: R > W therefore net force is positive and acceleration occurs in upwards direction.
- Horizontal forces: F > AR therefore net force is positive and acceleration occurs in forward direction.
- Overall, there is a net force in the forward and upward direction allowing the long jumper to take off from the board.

IMPULSE (AT TAKEOFF)

On the penultimate stride, the long jumper will lean backwards slightly and dip into the ground a little more, lowering their centre of mass. This allows the long jumper's takeoff foot to stay in contact with the ground for longer, as it takes more time for their body to overtake the takeoff foot and for the centre of mass to rise to the takeoff height. This means that the time for which the force is applied at takeoff is increased. Using specialist vocabulary, impulse is increased, where Impulse = Force x time. Applying this to Newton's second law means that a greater impulse will result in an increase in the rate of change of momentum and increase the velocity with which the long jumper leaves the ground. This gives the performer a greater upward acceleration and height at takeoff. This can be shown in the following force/time graph (Fig 15.7).

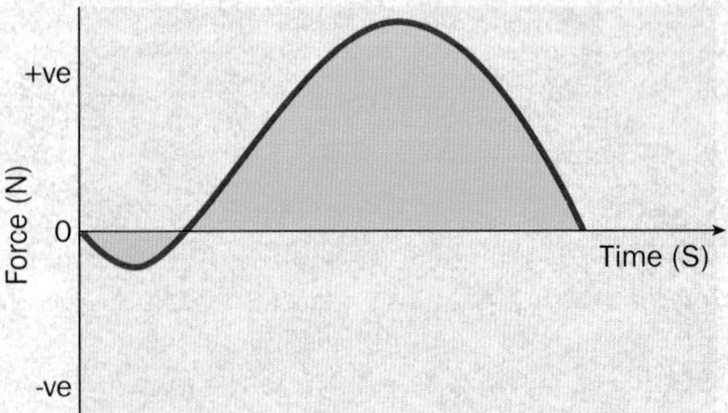

Fig 15.7 A greater impulse gives the performer a greater upward acceleration at takeoff

PROJECTILES

From the moment the long jumper's foot leaves the takeoff board to the moment they land in the sand pit, the long jumper is a projectile. During flight, two forces act on the jumper: weight and air resistance. For a human body that is in flight for a small amount of time, air resistance is negligible compared to weight. Therefore, the centre of mass of the jumper follows a path that is very close to a true parabola; that is, a uniform curve that is symmetrical about its highest point.

A free body diagram of a long jumper in flight is shown in Fig 15.8.

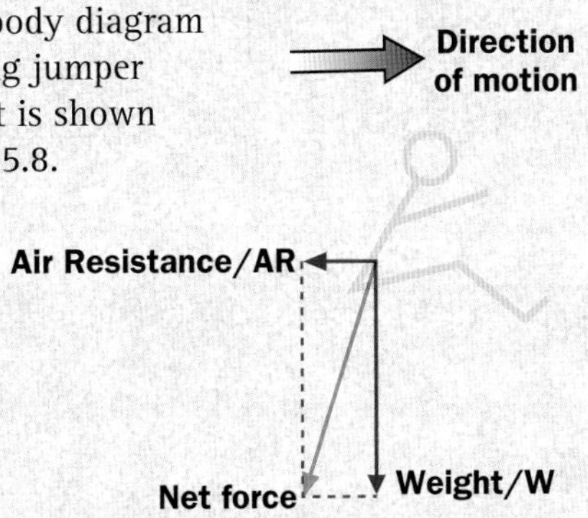

Direction of motion

Air Resistance/AR

Weight/W

Net force

Fig 15.8 Forces acting on a long jumper in flight

If a parallelogram of forces is used to calculate the net force acting on the long jumper during flight, you can see that the net force is in almost the same direction as the weight force. This makes the jumper's centre of mass travel as if under the influence of weight alone, and it therefore follows a flight path that is very close to a true parabola.

CENTRE OF MASS AT TAKEOFF

At takeoff, the reaction force exerted on the jumper by the ground (as a result of Newton's Third Law) passes behind the jumper's centre of mass. This is an eccentric force that generates angular motion. Therefore, during flight there is a tendency for the long jumper to rotate forwards. In order to counteract this rotation, the long jumper uses various techniques during flight, most commonly the 'hang' or the 'hitchkick'.

CENTRE OF MASS DURING FLIGHT

It is worth noting that the body position of the long jumper shown in Fig 15.8 is the position adopted just before landing. In this position, with arms and legs stretched out in front, much of the jumper's mass is in front of their hips. Therefore the centre of mass of the jumper has moved forwards and is in a position that lies outside the substance of their body. This benefits the jumper as, with the centre of mass so far forwards, it minimises the risk of them falling backwards into the pit on landing.

LEVER SYSTEMS

During the approach run, takeoff, flight and landing phases of a long jump, the performer will be using all three lever systems. Arguably, however, the most important of these will be the second class lever system found at the ball of the foot at takeoff. Being a second class lever, the load lies between the fulcrum and the effort, giving a greater effort arm. This gives the lever system mechanical advantage, allowing it to move a heavy load over a small distance. In this case, the second class lever at the foot propels the jumper into the air at takeoff and is shown in Fig 15.9.

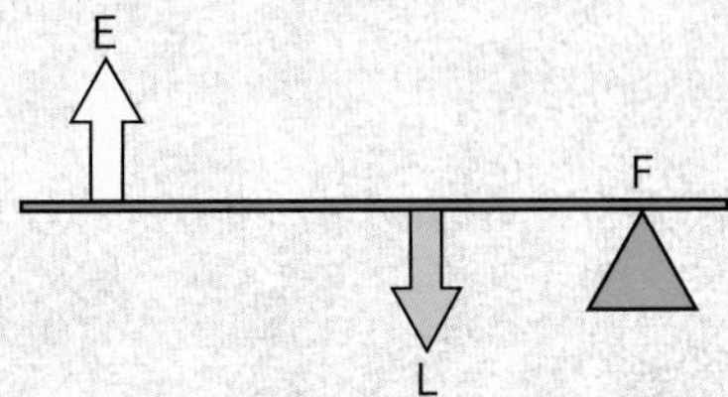

Fig 15.9 Second class lever at the foot at takeoff

F = joint between the metatarsals and the phalanges
L = weight of the body being moved
E = force exerted by the gastrocnemius muscle as it contracts concentrically to cause plantar flexion of the ankle at the point of take off.

TASK 2

Within your class, create similar sheets to show how the biomechanical concepts identified above relate to:

- high jump
- triple jump
- a straight jump on a trampoline or a vertical jump in a team game of your choice
- ski jumping.

Can you think of any additional biomechanical concepts that could be applied to your examples?

Throwing skills, for example javelin

NEWTON'S LAWS OF MOTION

First Law: as a projectile during flight, the javelin will continue to travel with a certain velocity until acted upon by an external force on landing. When the javelin hits the ground on landing, the ground exerts a force on the javelin, which causes it to severely change its state of motion and stop.

Second Law: the greater the force generated by the thrower at the moment of release, the greater the outgoing velocity of the javelin and the javelin will travel in the direction in which this force acts.

Third Law: at the point of landing, the javelin exerts a large force on the ground, which in turn applies an equal and opposite reaction force on the javelin. This causes the javelin to stop.

NET FORCE

Net force acting on the javelin thrower during their approach run is positive as they accelerate from a stationary position until they reach their desired speed at the moment of release.

Horizontal forces are unbalanced. The force acting in the same direction as motion is larger than the force acting in the opposite direction. In this case, friction is greater than air resistance. A javelin thrower can maximise the friction force between their shoes and the ground by wearing spikes.

(For the forces acting on the javelin during flight, see the section on lift force below.)

TYPES OF FORCE/FREE BODY DIAGRAM

The following external forces are acting on the javelin thrower as they accelerate into their run:

- Weight
- Reaction force
- Friction force
- Air resistance

Fig 15.10 Free body diagram of javelin thrower in run up to throwing javelin

The free body diagram at this point would look like Fig 15.10.

IMPULSE

The longer the time for which a force can be applied to the javelin, the greater the impulse given to the javelin. (Impulse = Force x time.) From Newton's second law, a greater impulse will cause a greater rate of change of momentum and the javelin will leave the thrower's hand with a greater outgoing velocity. To maximise the time for which the force is applied to the javelin, the thrower will delay the point of release until the last possible moment by

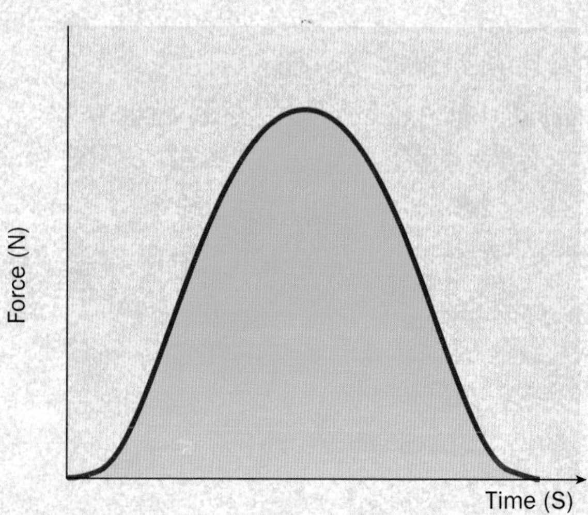

Fig 15.11 Force/time graph to show the impulse given to a javelin by a thrower with good technique at the moment of release

using a follow-through to complete the throw. A force/time graph to show the impulse given to a javelin by a thrower with good technique at the moment of release is shown in Fig 15.11.

AIR RESISTANCE

Air resistance will affect the flight path of a javelin, as it is a fast-moving projectile travelling through air. Three factors affect the size of the air resistance force acting on the javelin: its velocity, its cross-sectional area and its surface characteristics. Given the correct angle of release and the smooth nature of the surface of the javelin, it is only the first of these three that is really of any consequence. However, if thrown at the correct angle of release, the javelin acts like an aerofoil during flight and this is better explained in the section on lift force below.

PROJECTILES

The javelin is a projectile from the moment it leaves the thrower's hand to the moment it lands in the grass landing segment. During flight, three forces act on the javelin: weight, air resistance and lift.

LIFT FORCE

At the correct angle of attack, the javelin will gain an upward lift force during flight (Fig 15.12).

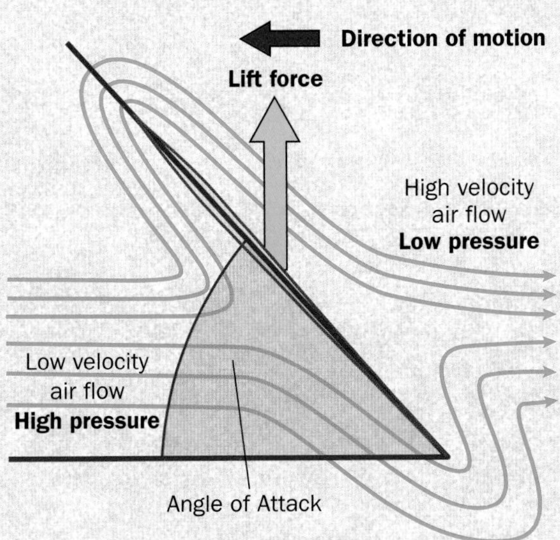

Fig 15.12 Lift force acting on a javelin during flight

The air that travels over the top of the javelin has to travel a further distance than the air that travels underneath it. The air above the javelin travels faster than the air below. Using the Bernoulli principle, this means that a lower pressure is created above the javelin than below it, causing a pressure gradient that produces an upward lift force on the javelin. This allows the javelin to stay in the air for longer and record a greater horizontal distance.

LEVER SYSTEMS

During the preparation, execution and recovery phases of a javelin throw, the performer will be using all three lever systems. At the elbow joint, during the overarm throwing action used to release the javelin, there is a first class lever system acting, which looks like Fig 15.13.

Fig 15.13 First class lever system at the elbow joint during point of release of javelin

F = elbow joint
L = weight of the lower arm plus the javelin
E = force exerted by the triceps brachii muscle as it contracts concentrically to cause extension of the elbow at the point of release.

TASK 3

Within your class, create similar sheets to show how the biomechanical concepts identified above relate to:

- shot put
- discus
- throwing, passing or shooting in a team game of your choice

Can you think of any additional biomechanical concepts that could be applied to your examples?

Hitting skills, for example topspin serve in tennis

NEWTON'S LAWS OF MOTION

First Law: during the ball toss, the ball will move straight up and straight down unless an external force acts upon it. In this case, it is the force of the racket head that makes contact at the highest point, causing the ball to change direction and accelerate towards the net.

Second Law: the greater the force generated by the racket head on the ball at the point of contact, the greater the outgoing velocity of the ball and the ball will travel in the direction in which this force acts.

Third Law: at the point of contact that is the top of the ball toss, the racket head exerts a force on the ball, which in turn applies an equal and opposite reaction force on the racket head. This can be seen by a slight distortion of the strings of the racket at the point of contact.

STABILITY

As the tennis player stands behind the baseline and prepares to serve, they are in a stable position. Their feet are shoulder-width apart, giving them a comfortable base of support with their centre of mass and line of gravity over the centre of their base of support. As they throw the ball into the air, their body weight transfers to their front foot, moving their line of gravity closer to the edge of the base of support. This makes them less stable. Then, as they throw their racket arm at the ball and make contact in front of the body, their line of gravity falls outside their base of support, making them unstable.

NET FORCE

The net force acting on the tennis player when they are at their most stable is zero, i.e. as the server stands behind the baseline preparing to start the serving action. The net vertical force is zero and the net horizontal force is zero. This means the player is in a state of equilibrium and will remain in that position until acted on by an external force that is larger than the body's inertia, which will change its state of motion.

TYPES OF FORCE/FREE BODY DIAGRAM

The forces acting on the server in the position described in the net force section above are equal and opposite. The free body diagram at this point would look like Fig 15.14.

Vertical forces: R1 + R2 = W
Net vertical force = 0
Horizontal forces: F1 = F2
Net horizontal force = 0

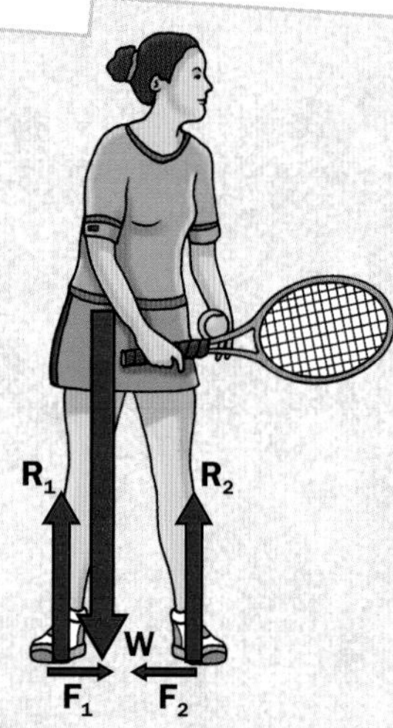

Fig 15.14 Free body diagram to show tennis player in a stable position before serve.

LEVER SYSTEMS

During the preparation, execution and recovery phases of the serve, the tennis player will be using all three lever systems. Arguably, however, the most of important of these is the third class lever system found at the shoulder joint during extension. Being a third class lever system, the effort lies between the fulcrum and the load, giving a greater load arm. Although this gives the lever system mechanical disadvantage, meaning it would struggle to move a heavy load, it enables the tennis player to accelerate the racket head through a large range of motion. This gives a greater outgoing velocity to the ball at the point of impact and allows the top tennis players of today to serve at speeds in excess of 100 mph (160 km/h). The third class lever at the shoulder is shown in Fig 15.15.

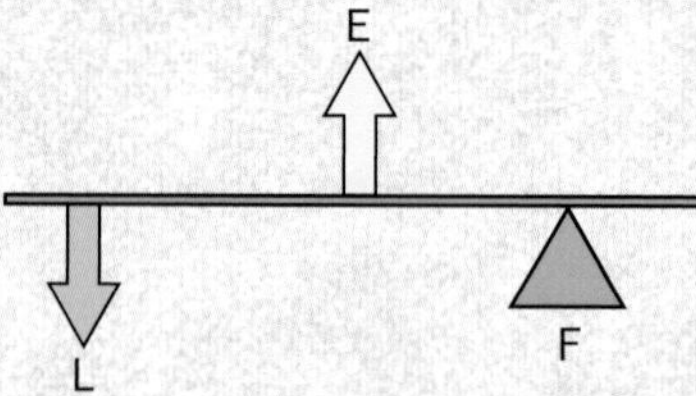

Fig 15.15 Third class lever at the shoulder of a tennis player during serve

F = shoulder joint
L = weight of the arm plus tennis racket
E = force exerted by the posterior deltoid muscle as it contracts concentrically to cause extension of the shoulder

IMPULSE

The longer the time for which a force can be applied to the ball from the racket head, the greater the impulse given to the ball. (Impulse = Force x time.) From Newton's Second Law, a greater impulse will cause a greater rate of change of momentum and

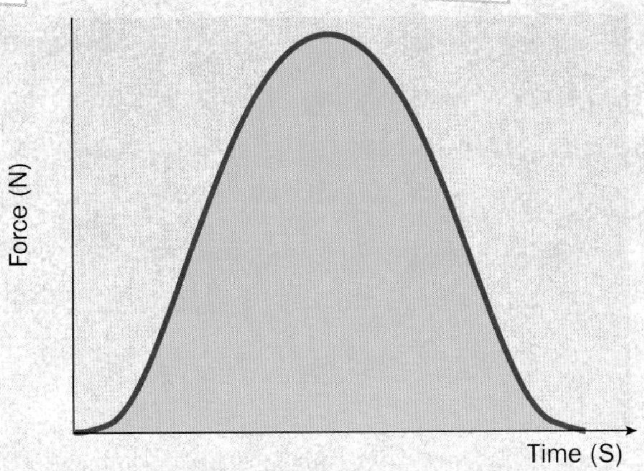

Fig 15.16 Force/time graph to show impulse given to a tennis ball by a player with good technique

the ball will leave the racket with a greater outgoing velocity. To maximise the time for which the force is applied to the ball, the tennis player will brush round the side of the ball and use a follow through. A force/time graph to show the impulse given to the tennis ball by a player with good technique is shown in Fig 15.16.

AIR RESISTANCE

Air resistance will affect the flight path of a tennis ball hit with topspin, as it is a fast-moving projectile travelling through air. Three factors affect the size of the air resistance force acting on the ball: its velocity, its cross-sectional area and its surface characteristics. The fact that the outer surface of a tennis ball is rough means that it is more affected by air resistance than a ball of a similar shape and size with a smooth outer surface. However, the fact that the ball is spinning as it travels through the air means that air resistance has a very particular affect on its flight path; see the section on spin below.

PROJECTILES

The spinning tennis ball is a projectile from the moment it leaves the racket to the moment it bounces on the court surface. During flight, three forces act on the spinning ball: weight, air resistance and lift.

SPIN

In order to impart topspin to the ball, the tennis player exerts an eccentric force at the point of impact. This force travels outside the tennis ball's centre of mass and will affect the flight path and behaviour of the ball on landing. Topspin causes the ball to dip during flight and drop to the ground sooner. This allows the player to hit the ball very hard during the service action but still ensure that the ball lands within the service court on the other side of the net. The flight path of a tennis ball hit with topspin is shown in Fig 15.17.

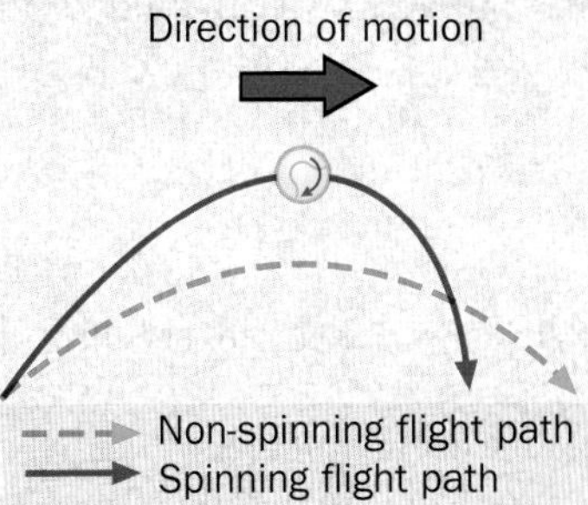

Fig 15.17 The flight path of a tennis ball hit with topspin

Topspin also causes the ball to skim the surface quickly on bouncing and accelerate towards the player's opponent, giving them less time to make an effective return of serve. The effect of bounce on a ball hit with topspin is shown in Fig 13.12b on page 319.

The bottom surface of the ball that hits the ground on the bounce wants to slide backwards. Friction will oppose this sliding motion and act in a forward direction. Therefore, friction acts in the same direction as the direction of motion, which causes the ball to accelerate off the surface quickly and at a smaller angle to that of the non-spinning ball.

LIFT FORCE

A ball hit with topspin will generate a lift force. This is called the Magnus effect and explains the fact that a spinning ball will deviate from its original flight path (see Fig 13.14 on page 321). As the tennis ball hit with topspin moves through the air, its spinning surfaces affect the air flow around it.

The top surface of the ball is travelling in the opposite direction to airflow. This causes the air over the top of the ball to decelerate and, according to the Bernoulli principle, creates high pressure. The bottom surface of the ball is travelling in the same direction as airflow. This causes the air to accelerate and, according to the Bernoulli principle, creates low pressure. This forms a pressure differential between the upper and lower surfaces of the ball, which causes a downward lift force. This is what makes the ball dip.

Rotating skills, for example diving (10-metre platform)

STABILITY

At takeoff, as the diver mentally prepares for their dive, they are in equilibrium but they are not very stable. This is because although their line of gravity falls within their base of support, it would not take much force to disturb the diver from this position and become unstable. Divers usually take one of two positions at takeoff – they either stand upright on tip toes with arms raised above their head (Fig 15.18) or they assume a handstand position (Fig 15.19).

In both positions, the diver has a relatively small degree of stability as their centre of mass is raised and their base of support is small. Therefore, when they are ready to begin their dive, they only need to generate a small amount of force to make them unstable and enable them to start their rotations.

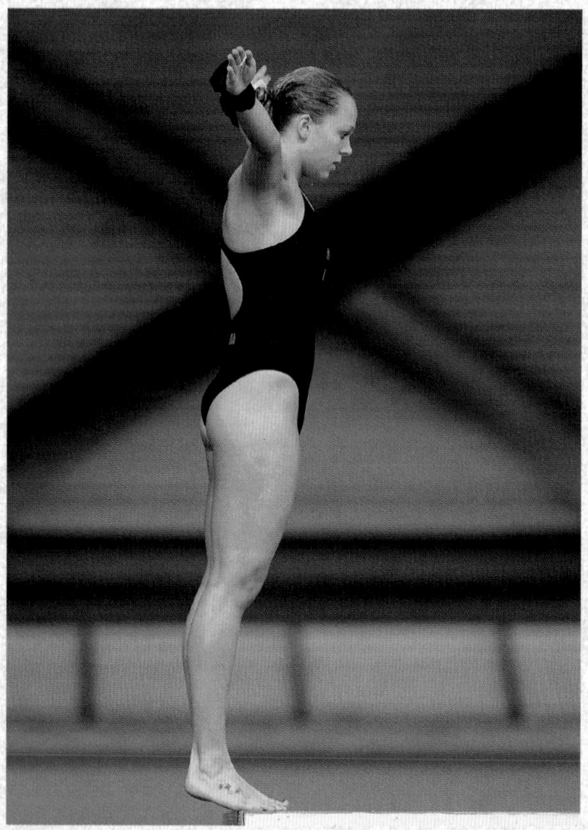

Fig 15.18 Standing position for takeoff

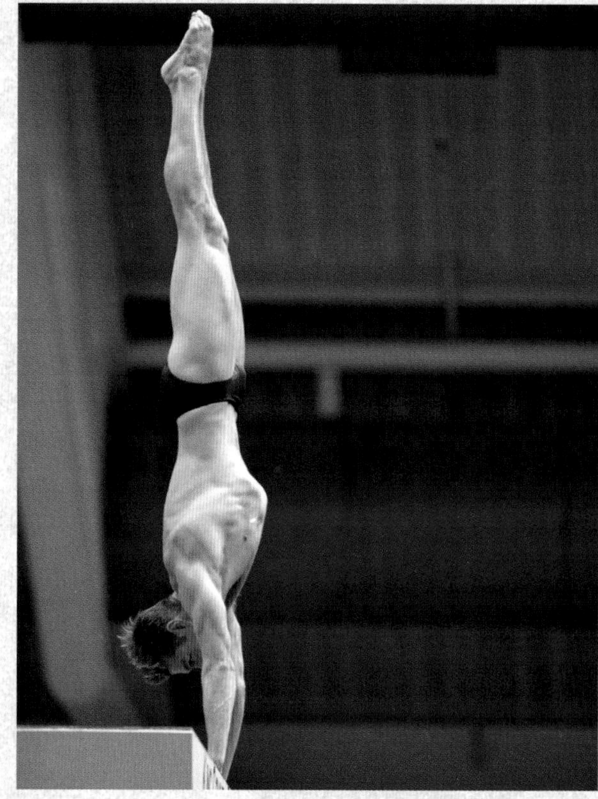

Fig 15.19 Handstand position for takeoff

LEVER SYSTEMS

During the takeoff for the dive, the diver who is standing upright will rely on the second class lever at the ball of the foot. Here, the load lies between the fulcrum and the effort giving a greater effort arm. This gives the lever system mechanical advantage allowing it to move a heavy load over a small distance. In this case, the second class lever at the foot propels the diver into the air at takeoff; it is shown in Fig 15.20.

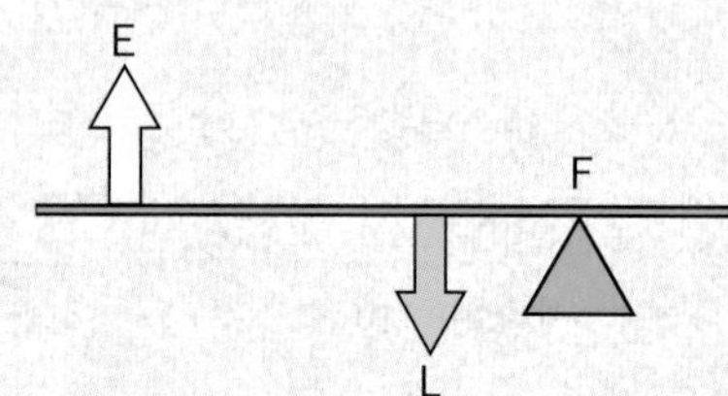

Fig 15.20 Second class lever at the foot which propels diver into air at takeoff

F = joint between the metatarsals and the phalanges
L = weight of the body being moved
E = force exerted by the gastrocnemius muscle as it contracts concentrically to cause plantar flexion of the ankle at the point of takeoff

ROTATION

To generate rotation at takeoff, an eccentric force acts upon the diver. As the diver topples over the board, they then push with their feet to generate a reaction force from the board that travels outside the diver's centre of mass. This produces a moment of force or torque, which causes the diver to rotate. (Moment of force = force x perpendicular distance of force from fulcrum.) During the flight phase of a 10-metre platform dive, the diver will perform a number of somersaults and twists. When they are somersaulting, they are rotating about their transverse axis and when they are twisting they are rotating about their longitudinal axis.

DESCRIBING ANGULAR MOTION

Angular distance, angular displacement, angular speed, angular velocity and angular acceleration are measurements that can be used to describe the angular motion of the diver. The larger their values, the greater the quantity of angular motion possessed by the diver. For example, a diver will have a higher angular velocity in a tucked somersault dive than a piked somersault dive. The reasons for this are explained in section on moment of inertia and angular momentum below.

MOMENT OF INERTIA

The moment of inertia of the diver is the resistance of the diver's body to change its state of angular motion. It can be thought of as angular resistance and angular persistence. The moment of inertia of the diver will depend on their mass and the distribution of their mass from the axis of rotation. The closer the diver can pull their body into the axis of rotation, the smaller their moment of inertia. When somersaulting about the transverse axis, the diver can minimise their moment of inertia by tucking their body in tight. This reduces their moment of inertia and makes rotation easier in a tucked position, compared to a pike position, compared to a straight body position. When twisting about the longitudinal axis, the diver can minimise their moment of inertia by bringing their arms and legs in close to their central axis. This reduces their moment of inertia and makes rotation easier. This is because a small moment of inertia has less resistance to angular motion.

ANGULAR MOMENTUM

Angular momentum refers to the amount of angular motion possessed by the diver as they rotate during flight. It depends on their moment of inertia and their angular velocity. (Angular momentum = moment of inertia x angular velocity.) The law of conservation of angular momentum, states that a rotating body continues to turn about its axis of rotation with constant angular momentum unless acted upon by an external torque. This is the angular analogue of Newton's First Law and basically means that the angular momentum the diver generates at takeoff will be conserved until they enter the water.

For a two-and-a-half inward back somersault, a diver will use the principle of the law of conservation of angular momentum in the following way.

- At takeoff the diver will create a high angular momentum by keeping their body extended with their distribution of mass a large distance from the transverse axis. This gives the diver a high moment of inertia.
- In order to complete the back somersault in the time before they hit the water, the diver must reduce their moment of inertia considerably to ensure that angular velocity is increased. The diver does this by bringing their arms and legs into a very tight tuck. This reduces their distribution of mass from the transverse axis and, for angular momentum to be conserved, increases their angular velocity.
- The diver will open out again once the dive has been completed to increase their moment of inertia and slow their angular velocity to allow a controlled entry into the water.

TASK 4

Within your class, create similar sheets to show how the biomechanical concepts identified above relate to:

- other types of rotation in diving, gymnastics or trampolining
- a spinning ice skater or an ice skater that jumps to perform a full turn
- a slalom skier.

Can you think of any additional biomechanical concepts that could be applied to your examples?

Exam Café

Relax, refresh, result!

Refresh your memory

You should now have the knowledge and understanding of:

- how to review and judge your level of understanding of the topics covered in Chapters 11–14
- how to apply the knowledge you have gained from Chapters 11–14 to:
  - running activities such as sprinting, endurance running, swerving, side stepping and dodging in team games
  - jumping activities such as long jump, high jump, triple jump, simple jumps in trampolining and gymnastics, jumping in team games, ski jumping
  - throwing activities such as shot put, javelin, discus throwing, passing and shooting in team games
  - hitting/kicking activities such as shots in tennis, badminton, golf, cricket, rounders, free kick or corner kicks in football, conversions in rugby
  - rotating activities such as rotating skills around the principle axes in gymnastics, diving, trampolining, skating, slalom skiing.

Get the result!

Examination question

Figure 15.21 shows the forces acting on a sprinter as they accelerate towards maximum speed in the first 60–70m of a 100m race.

Identify the forces A–D and evaluate how the sprinter can maximise their acceleration during this phase of the race.

(6 marks)

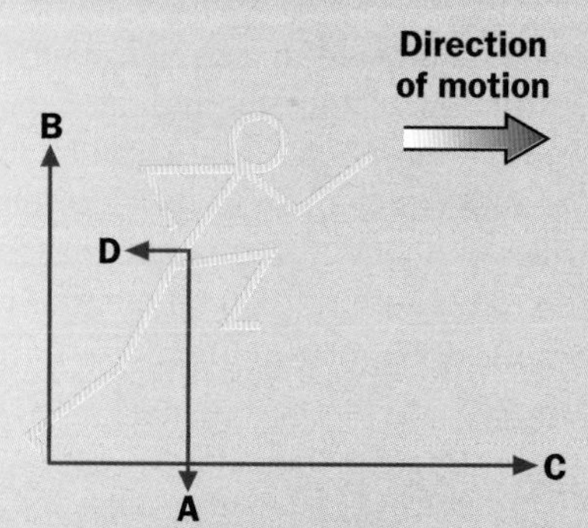

Fig 15.22

Examiner's tips

This question has two parts. The first part is a straightforward identify section, whereas the second part is more demanding with a command word of 'evaluate'. This means that some thought needs to go into your answer as you are required to bring together your knowledge of biomechanics to explain how the sprinter can generate a large acceleration. It follows that there will be a greater mark allocation given to the 'evaluate' section. You should therefore aim to presume a 1 : 5 split to play safe, so make sure you give enough information to achieve all six of the marks available.

Examiner says:

Quite good. Everything you have written is correct and you have shown me that you have a good understanding of force, particularly friction. You have also explained why wearing spikes will increase friction. However, you have not fully answered the question, which asks how the sprinter can maximise acceleration, and you have only told me how they can maximise friction. There are other biomechanical concepts that need to be explained to ensure you score full marks.

Student answer

A = weight

B = reaction

C = friction

D = air resistance

The sprinter can maximise force C, friction, by wearing running spikes. The spikes stick into the rubbery surface of the track. This gives a large friction force and prevents any backward slipping of the sprinter's feet on the track.

Improved student answer

A = weight

B = reaction

C = friction

D = air resistance

To maximise their acceleration, the sprinter needs to make the forward friction force as large as possible and the backward air resistance force as small as possible. This will give the sprinter a greater net force in the same direction of motion, which according to Newton's First Law will cause a change to their state of motion. Newton's Second Law states that the larger this net force, the greater the acceleration of the sprinter. To increase the friction force, the sprinter could wear spikes, which will apply a greater pressure on the track and prevent any backward slipping motion of the feet. They can also apply a large force with their leg that pushes backwards on the track. According to Newton's Third Law the track will then apply an equal and opposite reaction forced in the forward direction. To keep the air resistance force small, the sprinter should try to keep their body position low and wear tight-fitting clothing with a smooth outer surface. This will reduce their cross-sectional area and keep the effect of air resistance low.

Examiner says:

Well done – these are the correct forces.

Examiner says:

This is a great start to the second part of the question as it shows you have a full appreciation of what is being asked of you. The fact that you have used the specialist term of 'net force' is most impressive.

Examiner says:

You have done well to bring in Newton's laws as these will always be relevant and you can't go far wrong by applying them in your answer. You have described and explained Newton's first and second laws accurately and in detail.

Examiner says:

Here you show a full application of the forward force of friction acting on the sprinter and explain how it can be optimised on the track.

Examiner says:

And here's your application of Newton's third law, to complete the set – well done!

Examiner says:

This last section certainly sets you apart from many and will ensure you achieve a high grade as you link the importance of a small air resistance force with the importance of a large friction force to maximise acceleration. You show a good understanding of air resistance and the factors that affect it.

As a whole, this is a well-constructed answer that flows logically to show that you have good appreciation of efficient sprinting technique. There is scope to expand your answer further by mentioning impulse and showing an understanding of its relationship to the foot plant during the acceleration phase of the race. However, you have already covered enough points for a top mark. This is a super answer that is accurate and well explained – well done!

CHAPTER 16:

Energy

LEARNING OBJECTIVES

By the end of this chapter you should have knowledge and understanding of:

- how to define energy, work and power
- the role of ATP; the breakdown and re-synthesis of ATP; coupled reactions and exothermic and endothermic reactions
- the three energy systems: ATP/PC; alactic; the lactic acid and aerobic system
- the contribution of each energy system in relation to the duration/intensity of exercise
- the predominant energy system used related to type of exercise
- the inter-changing between thresholds during an activity, for example the onset of blood lactate accumulation (OBLA), and the effect of level of fitness, availability of oxygen and food fuels, and enzyme control on energy system used
- how the body returns to its pre-exercise state: the oxygen debt/excess post-exercise oxygen consumption (EPOC); the alactacid and lactacid debt components; replenishment of myoglobin stores and fuel stores and the removal of carbon dioxide
- the implications of the recovery process for planning physical activity sessions.

Energy concepts

Before looking at energy definitions, it is useful to understand where energy begins and ends. There are many forms of energy but you are required to understand just three forms. These are better learned if you follow the original source of all energy: light from the sun. Plants convert light energy into stored **chemical energy**, which humans then obtain by their consumption of those plants or of the animals that eat plants. People store this energy as carbohydrates, fats or proteins – chemical compounds composed of carbon, hydrogen and oxygen bonds storing energy. We do not directly use energy from these chemical stores for muscular work but further store this chemical energy in the form of a high energy compound called **adenosine triphosphate (ATP)** within our muscles. Energy stored within the compound ATP is termed **potential energy** and it is readily available as an energy source for the muscles to contract. The energy used to make the muscles contract is termed **kinetic energy**. Fig 16.1 shows the conversion of energy from light to chemical to potential and finally to kinetic energy in the form of muscular contractions.

KEY TERMS

Energy stored within the bonds of chemical compounds (within molecules).

Adenosine triphosphate (ATP)

Chemical energy stored as a high energy compound in the body. It is the only immediately usable source of energy in the human body.

Potential energy

'Stored' energy which is ready to be used when required.

Kinetic energy

Energy in the form of muscle contraction/joint movement.

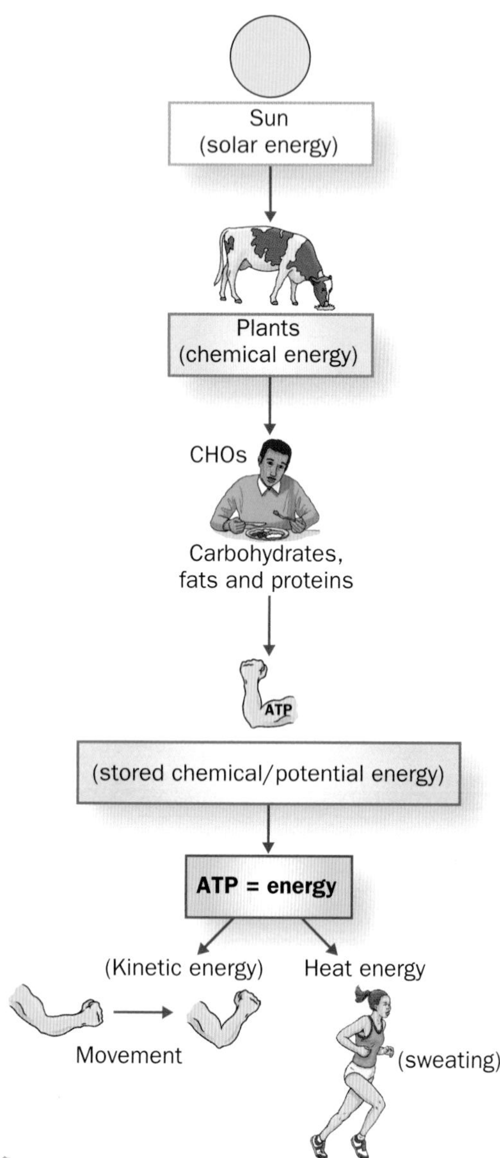

Fig 16.1 Energy conversion from light to kinetic energy

ENERGY

Energy is the ability to perform work or put mass into motion. When applied more directly, energy refers to the ability of the muscles to contract (kinetic energy) and apply force that may limit or increase performance in physical activity.

Energy is usually measured in joules (J), which is the unit to describe the force 1 Newton (equivalent to 1 kilogram) acting through a distance of 1 metre. Energy is also measured in calories, where 1 calorie is equal to 4.18 joules.

WORK

Work is done when a force is applied to a body to move it over a certain distance. It is expressed as follows:

Work = **force** (N) x distance moved (m)

The units of measurement for work are joules (j).

KEY TERM

Force

A pull or push that alters, or tends to alter, the state of motion of a body. It is measured in Newtons (N).

APPLY IT!

Remember that 1 Joule = 1 Newton (1 Newton acting through a distance of 1 metre). Hence, to move a 100-metre sprinter weighing 75 kg a distance of 1 metre requires a force of 750 N, and therefore to move the sprinter 2 metres requires a force of 1500 N.

STRETCH AND CHALLENGE

'The body's maximum efficiency of converting food into motion is about 27 per cent. Hence the body is actually not very efficient at converting chemical energy into kinetic energy.'

1 What do you think happens to the remaining percentage of energy?
2 Discuss the statement above in relation to the efficiency of the human body.

TASK 1

Calculate the work to move a sprinter weighing 85 kg a distance of 4 metres.

TASK 2

Rank the 100-metre sprinters listed in Table 1 from the most powerful (1) to the least powerful (4).

Table 1

Athlete weight (kg)	100m time (seconds)	Power (W)	Rank
75	12		
70	11		
85	12		
80	12		

POWER

Power is the rate at which work can be done, i.e. work divided by time. Hence power is force multiplied by distance divided by the time taken.

$$\text{Power} = \frac{\text{work}}{\text{time}} = \frac{\text{force (N) x distance (m)}}{\text{time (seconds)}}$$

The units of measurement for power are watts (W).

In simple terms, force multiplied by distance represents pure strength, but when divided by time it represents speed.

APPLY IT!

If a 100-metre sprinter weighing 75 kg moves 1 metre in 4 seconds, power would be calculated as follows:

$$\text{Power} = \frac{\text{force (N) x distance (m)}}{\text{time (seconds)}}$$
$$= \frac{750\ \text{N}}{4\ \text{s}}$$
$$= 187.5\ \text{W}$$

APPLY IT!

A body builder will typically have a greater leg muscle mass than a 100-metre sprinter and therefore a greater maximal strength. However, a body builder will fatigue quickly whereas the sprinter can apply the force quicker and repeatedly to resist fatigue for longer.

Adenosine triphosphate (ATP)

As you saw on page 366, energy from ATP that is stored within muscles provides the kinetic energy for muscles to apply force to participate in physical activity. Fig 16.2 shows that the **compound** ATP is made up of one complex element, adenosine, and three simple phosphate (P) elements held together by high energy bonds. When the **enzyme ATPase** breaks the bond between the last two phosphates, this releases the store of potential energy for muscular contractions. This is termed

Fig 16.2 ATP structure and high energy bonds

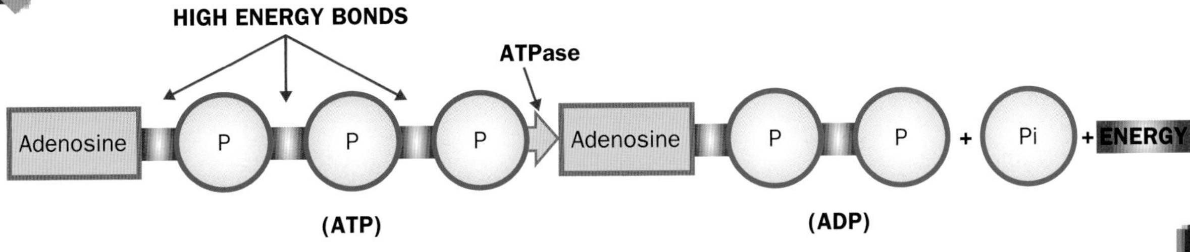

an **exothermic** reaction as it releases energy and in doing so it leaves behind a compound termed adenosine diphosphate (ADP). Although this is more complex, it is easier to think of ADP as having lost its high energy bond between the last two phosphates.

KEY TERMS

Compound

A mixture of elements.

Enzymes

Protein molecules that act as catalysts for the body's chemical reactions. The enzyme name typically ends with the suffix *-ase*.

ATPase

The enzyme that helps break down ATP to release energy.

Exothermic

A chemical reaction that releases energy as it progresses.

Fig 16.2 highlights that the major role of ATP is to act as a potential energy store to supply the energy for muscle contractions (kinetic energy). But why is it so important? ATP is the *only* usable source of energy that the body/muscles can utilise for work. Hence no ATP means no energy for work and thus muscle fatigue.

ATP is a simple compound which can be quickly broken down and is stored exactly where it is needed within the muscles. However, there is a major problem in that the body only has limited stores of ATP – enough to supply energy for approximately 2–3 seconds of muscular work. So, how can athletes exercise for long periods if the only usable source of energy runs out after 2–3 seconds?

ATP RESYNTHESIS

Since ATP is the only usable source of energy for work, it is clear that the body needs to rebuild ATP as quickly as it uses it. This is achieved by a process called ATP resynthesis, by which the breakdown of ATP into ADP becomes a reversible reaction.

The simplest way to understand how ATP resynthesis works is to think of what was removed from ATP to form ADP. You will remember that energy from the last two P bonds was removed and used for muscular work. Therefore, to re-synthesise ADP back into ATP, additional energy is needed to rebuild the bond between the two phosphates. This reversible reaction requires energy and is therefore termed an **endothermic** reaction.

KEY TERMS

Endothermic

A chemical reaction that requires energy to be added for it to progress.

Coupled reactions

When the products from one reaction, such as energy, are then used in another reaction.

There is, however, one major problem: where does the energy to resynthesise ADP back into ATP come from? The body has three energy systems: ATP/PC, lactic acid and aerobic, which have the same function. Via **coupled reactions**, these supply energy to re-synthesise ADP back into ATP. As you will see, these three energy systems do not work in isolation but work together to provide a constant supply of energy to resynthesise ATP. You will also see that the relative contribution of energy supplied from each energy system is primarily dependent upon the duration and intensity of exercise.

EXAM TIP

When answering energy system questions, always ask 'where has the energy come from?' If it is not ATP then it cannot be used for muscular work; it is more likely to be energy that has been released to resynthesise ADP back into ATP as part of a coupled reaction.

KEY TERMS

Anaerobic

A reaction that can occur without the presence of oxygen.

Sarcoplasm

Fluid-like gelatine that fills the spaces within the muscle cells and is a store of glycogen, fat, proteins, enzymes and myoglobin.

The ATP/PC (Alactic) system

The ATP/PC energy system provides energy, via coupled reactions, to resynthesise ADP back into ATP. PC (phospho-creatine) is another high-energy phosphate compound which stores potential energy. When ATP levels fall and ADP levels increase, this stimulates the release of the enzyme creatine kinase, which breaks down the PC bond releasing energy (exothermic reaction). This energy cannot be used for muscular work but is coupled to the resynthesis of ADP back into ATP. Fig 16.3 below shows this coupled reaction, where the energy released from PC is used to resynthesise ADP back into ATP in an endothermic reaction.

Although the ATP/PC system can work aerobically, it does not require oxygen so is termed **anaerobic** and takes place in the **sarcoplasm** of muscle cells. As a simple compound located exactly where it is required, PC is quickly broken down. However, with limited stores and with just one PC resynthesising only one ATP, it can only supply energy to resynthesise ATP for 3 to 10 seconds during an all-out maximal sprint.

Fig 16.3 Break down of PC coupled to the resynthesis of ATP.

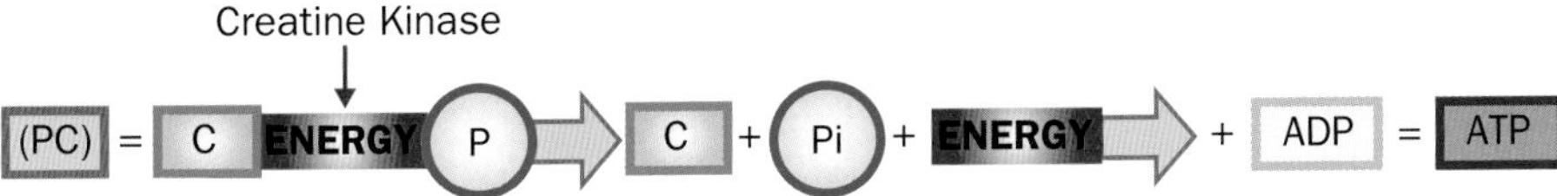

Fig 16.4 is a graphical representation of how PC is broken down in order to maintain the body's supply of ATP during a sprint. There are no fatiguing by-products, creatine and Pi remain in the muscle cell until, during recovery, they are resynthesised back into PC via energy from the aerobic system.

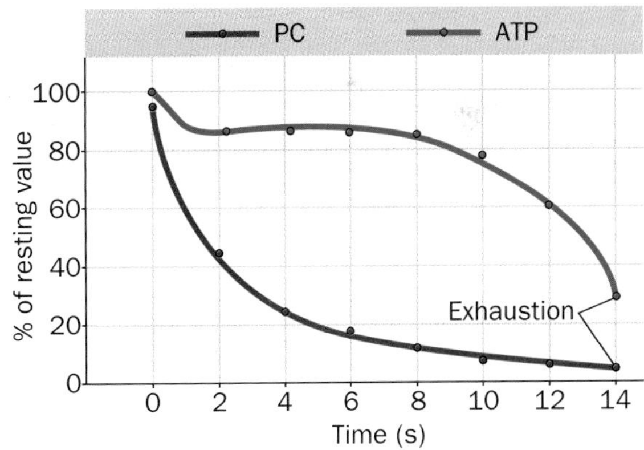

Fig 16.4 Breakdown of PC coupled to ATP resynthesis during sprinting (Source: J. Wilmore and D. Costill, Physiology of Sport and Exercise, *2nd edition, 1998)*

APPLY IT!

The ATP/PC system is the predominant energy system used when requiring high intensity, very short duration moments or events, for example the 100-metre sprint, long/triple jump and team games requiring explosive jumping to head, catch or dive for a ball.

REMEMBER

The energy from the breakdown of PC is not used for muscular work but to resynthesise ADP back into ATP in a coupled reaction.

TASK 3

The advantages and disadvantages in Table 2 also provide the answers to explain when and why the ATP/PC system is used. For each of the advantages and disadvantages listed, identify whether they explain either when or why the ATP/PC system will be used.

TRAINING ADAPTATIONS

Anaerobic training, which overloads the ATP/PC system, increases the body's muscle stores of ATP and PC. This delays the **threshold** between the ATP/PC and the lactic acid system and thus increases the potential duration of high intensity exercise for up to 1–2 seconds.

KEY TERM

Threshold

The point when one energy system stops being the predominant energy provider for the resynthesis of ATP.

EXAM TIP

Don't be misled by questions which ask you to explain when and why the energy systems are used. Simply answer which of the advantages/disadvantages are applied to when or why as highlighted in Tasks 3, 4 and 5.

Lactic acid system

The lactic acid (LA) energy system breaks down the fuel glucose to provide energy, via coupled reactions, to resynthesise ADP back into ATP. Glucose ($C_6H_{12}O_6$) is supplied directly from the digestion of carbohydrates or from glycogen – the stored form of carbohydrate located in the muscles and liver and readily available as an energy fuel. The decrease in PC stores activates the enzyme glycogen phosphorylase to break down glycogen into glucose, which is then further broken down in a series of reactions called glycolysis. Like the ATP/PC system, the LA system takes place in the muscle cell sarcoplasm and does not require oxygen so is termed **anaerobic glycolysis**.

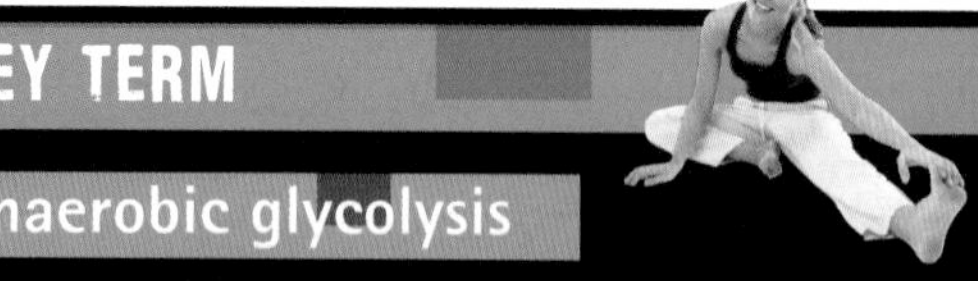

KEY TERM

Anaerobic glycolysis

The partial incomplete breakdown of glucose into pyruvic acid.

Table 2 Advantages and disadvantages of the ATP/PC system

Advantages	Disadvantages
• Does not require oxygen • PC stored in muscle cell as readily available energy source • Simple/small compound so very quick reaction/resynthesis of ATP • Automatically stimulated by a decrease in ATP and increase in ADP • Provides energy for explosive high-intensity exercise/movements • No fatiguing by-products • PC can itself be quickly resynthesised so recovery time quick	• Only small amounts of ATP and PC stored in muscle cells • 1 PC resynthesises 1 ATP • Only provides energy to resynthesise ATP for up to about 8–10 seconds

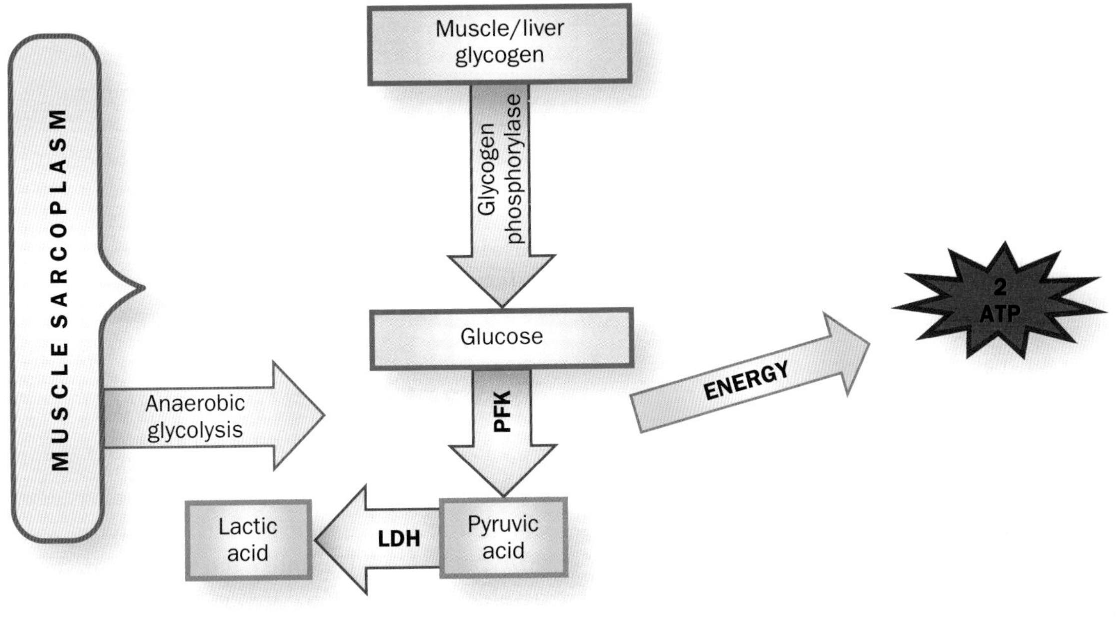

Fig 16.5 Anaerobic glycolysis – the breakdown of glycogen into glucose and ATP

During glycolysis, the enzyme phosphofructokinase (PFK) initiates the partial breakdown of glucose into pyruvic acid (pyruvate $C_3H_4O_3$), but in the absence of sufficient oxygen, pyruvic acid is further broken down into lactic acid by the enzyme lactate dehydrogenase (LDH). Fig 16.5 summarises how the breakdown of one mole of glucose is coupled to the resynthesis of two moles of ATP.

Although more complex and therefore slower than the reactions of the ATP/PC system, the LA system is still a relatively quick process as it is not dependent upon oxygen. Furthermore, glycogen is readily available as an energy fuel in the muscles.

The LA system provides energy to resynthesise ATP during the first 2–3 minutes of high-intensity short-duration anaerobic activity. If exercise is flat out to exhaustion, the LA system may only last for up to 30 seconds, but if the intensity is lowered then duration may prolong for up to a few minutes of anaerobic activity. The main limitation of the LA system is due to the onset of blood **lactate** accumulation (OBLA). As **lactic acid** ($C_3H_6O_3$) accumulates it decreases the pH (higher acidity) within the muscle cells, which inhibits the enzymes involved in glycolysis and thus prevents the breakdown of glucose and induces muscle fatigue.

KEY TERM

Lactate/lactic acid

Anaerobic glycolysis produces lactic acid ($C_3H_6O_3$), but it is quickly converted into a substrate salt called lactate which is easier to disperse via the blood stream. Although different compounds, the terms 'lactate' and 'lactic acid' are often used interchangeably.

REMEMBER

The energy released from glycogen/glucose via anaerobic glycolysis is not used for muscular work but to resynthesise ADP back into ATP in a coupled reaction.

APPLY IT!

The LA system is the predominant energy system for the 400-metre sprint and for midfield team games players when they have a high number of repeated high-intensity sprints without any time to recover.

TRAINING ADAPTATIONS

Repeated bouts of anaerobic training which overload the LA system increase the body's tolerance to lactic acid and its buffering capacity against high levels of lactic acid. Similarly, they increase the body's stores of glycogen. This has the effect of delaying the OBLA and prolonging the lactic acid system threshold by delaying fatigue. This allows athletes to work at higher intensities for longer periods, which is invaluable in events such as the 400-metre sprint/hurdles and 50–100m events in swimming. It also allows team games players to carry out a higher percentage of repeated sprints before muscle fatigue occurs.

REMEMBER

Don't be misled by questions which ask you to explain when and why the energy systems are used. Simply answer which of the advantages/disadvantages are applied to when or why as highlighted in Tasks 3, 4 and 5.

TASK 4

For each of the advantages and disadvantages listed in Table 3, identify whether they can explain when or why the LA system will be used.

APPLY IT!

The ATP/PC and LA systems are the predominant energy systems used during the first few minutes of high-intensity low-duration exercise. However, they are unable to provide all the energy required beyond this time and they are both reliant on the aerobic energy system to help them recover during and after exercise.

The aerobic energy system

The aerobic or 'oxidative' system breaks down glycogen, glucose and fats to provide energy, via coupled reactions, which is used to resynthesise ADP back into ATP. Unlike the LA system, the aerobic system uses oxygen to completely break down one mole of glucose into H_2O and CO_2 in three complex stages:

- Stage 1: Aerobic glycolysis
- Stage 2: Kreb's cycle
- Stage 3: Electron transport chain (ETC)

STAGE 1: AEROBIC GLYCOLYSIS

Aerobic glycolysis is the same process as anaerobic glycolysis except that the presence of oxygen inhibits the accumulation of lactic acid by diverting pyruvic acid further into the aerobic system. Pyruvic acid combines with coenzyme A to form Acetyl CoA. This is a complex series of reactions which is easier learned diagrammatically in stages using Fig 16.6 and translating (+) into 'combines with' and (=) into 'to form'.

Table 3 Advantages and disadvantages of the LA system

Advantages	Disadvantages
• Large glycogen store in muscle/liver is readily available as a potential energy source • Resynthesises two molecules of ATP – more than the PC system • Requires fewer reactions than the aerobic system so provides a quicker supply of energy • Glycogen phosphorylase and PFK enzyme activation due to a decrease in PC • Provides energy for high-intensity exercise lasting between 10 and 180 seconds • Can work aerobically and anaerobically	• Not as quick as ATP/PC system • Produces lactic acid, which is a fatiguing by-product • Reduces pH (increased acidity) which inhibits enzyme action • Stimulates pain receptors • Net effect is muscle fatigue and pain

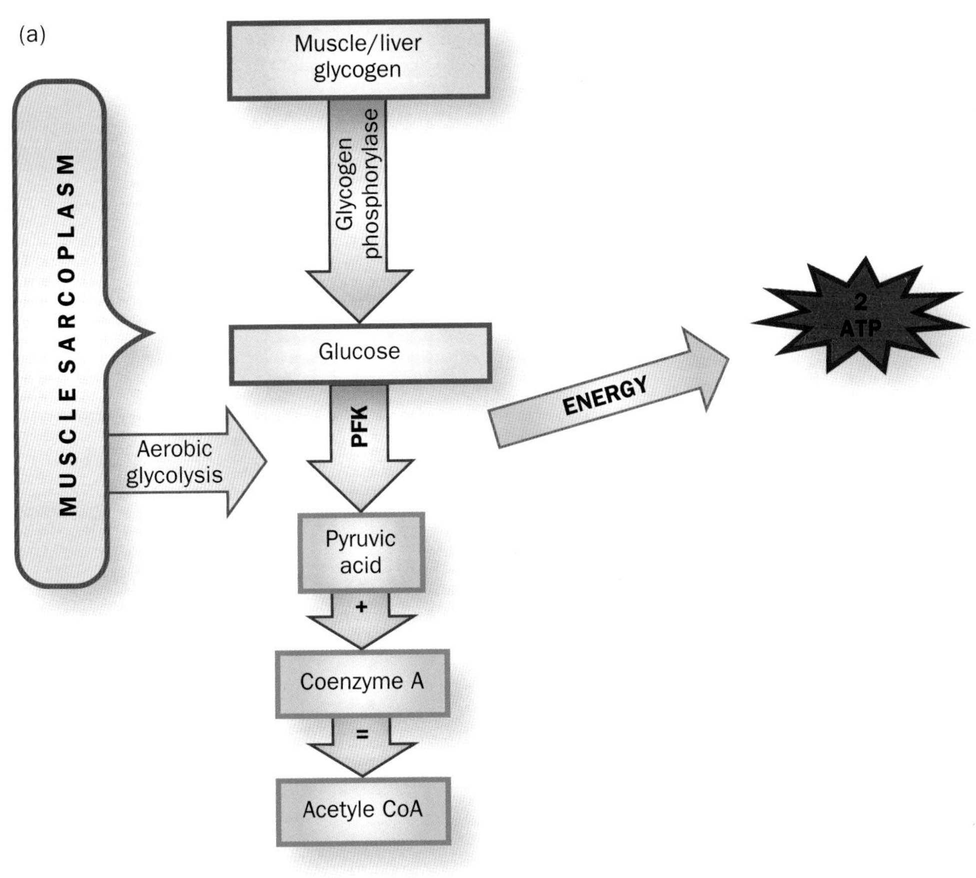

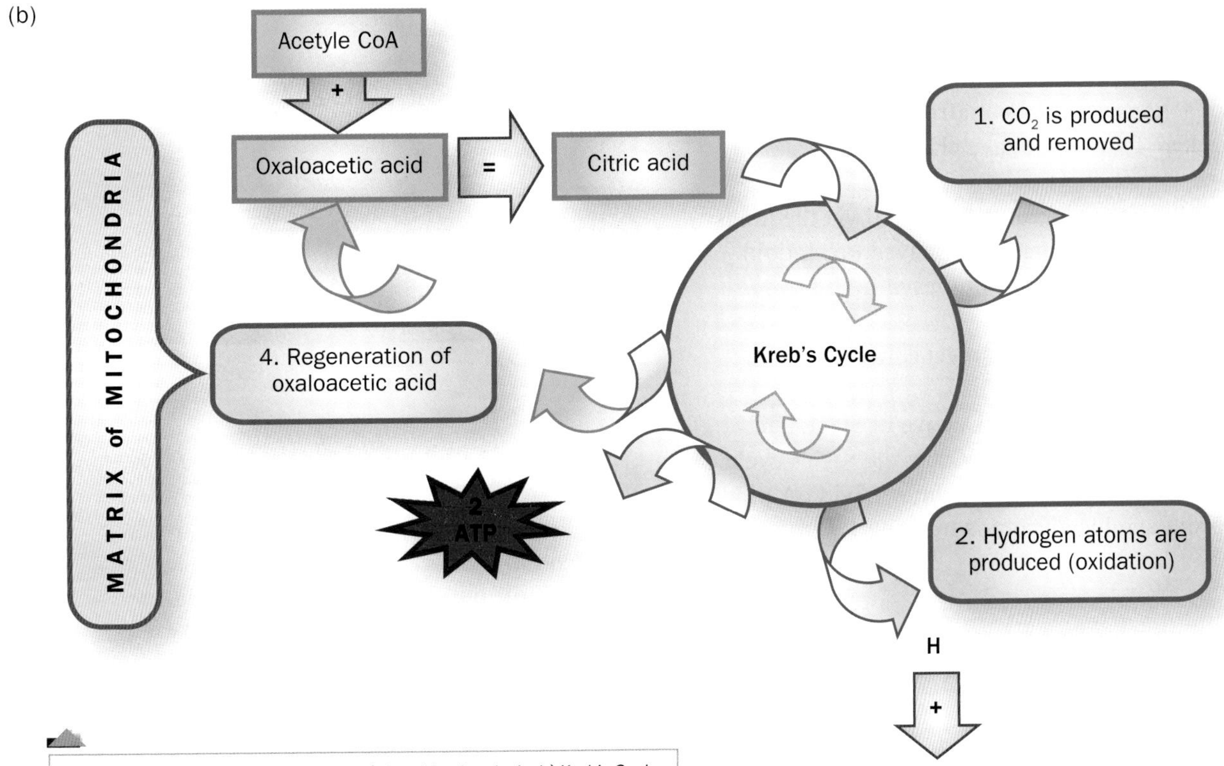

Fig 16.6 The aerobic energy system: a) Aerobic glycolysis; b) Kreb's Cycle

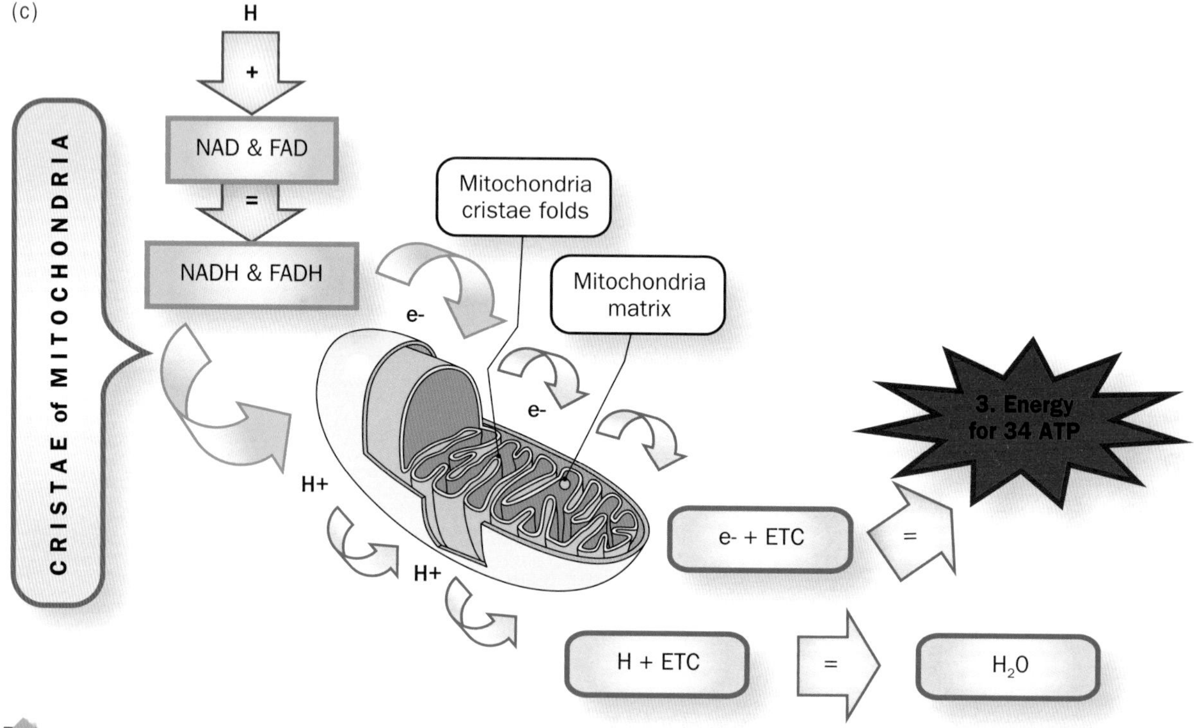

Fig 16.6 c) Electron transport chain (ETC)

STAGE 2: KREB'S CYCLE

The Acetyl CoA from Stage 1 combines with oxaloacetic acid to form citric acid. This is then further broken down in a series of complex reactions within the **matrix** of **mitochondria**, where four events take place:

1 CO_2 is produced and removed via the lungs
2 hydrogen atoms are removed (oxidation)
3 energy is produced to resynthesise two molecules of ATP
4 oxaloacetic acid is regenerated.

Follow the four events above in Stage 2 of Figure 16.6b to identify how the Kreb's cycle can continue to break down the Acetlyl CoA produced from aerobic glycolysis in Stage 1.

KEY TERMS

Matrix

Intracellular fluid within the mitochondria where oxidation takes place.

Mitochondria

Small sub-unit (membrane) sites of a muscle cell where aerobic respiration takes place.

EXAM TIP

You should never write in an answer that aerobic glycolysis is the same as anaerobic glycolysis. You must write out the process again but add the changes that occur in the presence of oxygen.

STAGE 3: ELECTRON TRANSPORT CHAIN (ETC)

In Stage 3 the hydrogen atoms combine with the coenzymes NAD and FAD to form NADH and FADH, and are carried down the electron transport chain (ETC) where hydrogen is split into H^+ and e^-. This takes place within the **cristae** folds of the mitochondria, where three important events take place:

1 the hydrogen electron (e^-) splits from the hydrogen atom and passes down the ETC
2 this provides sufficient energy to resynthesise 34 ATP
3 the hydrogen ion (H^+) combines with oxygen to form H_2O (water).

KEY TERM

Cristae

Internal membrane/compartments/fold-like structures within mitochondria.

Follow the three events above in Stage 3 of Figure 16.6c to identify how the ETC completes the full breakdown of glucose by converting hydrogen into H_2O and providing energy to resynthesise 34 ATP.

The total energy produced via the aerobic system is therefore 38 ATP:

- 2 ATP from aerobic glycolysis
- 2 ATP from the Kreb's cycle
- 34 ATP from the ETC.

This is summarised by an equation that represents aerobic respiration:

$$C_6H_{12}O_6 + 6O_2 = 6CO_2 + 6H_2O + \text{energy (for the resynthesis of 38 ATP)}$$

(glucose) + (oxygen) = (carbon dioxide) + (water) + energy

Although seemingly complex, this equation is simply showing that glucose ($C_6H_{12}O_6$) is completely broken down by oxygen ($6O_2$) in the aerobic system into carbon dioxide ($6CO_2$) and water ($6H_2O$) to release sufficient energy to resynthesise 38 ATP.

EXAM TIP

If the equation for aerobic respiration is too daunting, just remember to describe the process without the complex equation.

Table 4 The advantages and disadvantages of the aerobic system

Advantages	Disadvantages
• Large potential glycogen and FFA stores available as an efficient energy fuel	• Slower rate of ATP resynthesis compared with LA system due to points 2–4 below
• Efficient ATP resynthesis when good O_2 supply guarantees breakdown of FFAs	• Requires more O_2 supply (15 per cent more for FFAs)
• Large ATP resynthesis: 38 ATP from one molecule of glucose compared to 2 ATP from LA system and 1 from ATP/PC	• More complex series of reactions
• Provides energy for low/moderate-intensity high-duration exercise (3 minutes to 1 hour)	• Cannot resynthesise ATP at the start of exercise due to initial delay of O_2 from the cardiovascular system
• No fatiguing by-products; CO_2 and H_2O easily removed	• Limited energy for ATP during high-intensity short-duration work

FATS

Triglycerides (fats) are broken down by enzymes termed lipases into free fatty acids (FFA) and glycerol and used as an energy fuel within the aerobic system. Although very complex, FFAs are simply broken down into Acetyl CoA, which enters and is broken down by the Kreb's cycle and the ETC in a process termed beta-oxidation.

FFAs produce more Acetyl CoA and consequently produce far greater energy than the breakdown of glycogen/glucose. However, FFAs require approximately 15 per cent more oxygen than that required to break down glucose, and for this reason glycogen/glucose is the preferred energy fuel during moderate or high-intensity activity.

REMEMBER

The energy from the breakdown of glycogen/glucose/fats in the aerobic system is not used for muscular work but to resynthesise ADP back into ATP in a coupled reaction.

TASK 5

The advantages and disadvantages also provide answers to explain when and why the aerobic system is used. For each of the advantages and disadvantages listed in Table 4, identify whether they explain when or why the aerobic system will be used.

APPLY IT!

The aerobic system is the primary energy system for ATP resynthesis during low/moderate-intensity, high-duration activity lasting from 3 minutes to several hours, for example team sports such as hockey and football and long distance cycling, swimming and marathon events. The aerobic system is also active during recovery and stoppages, even during anaerobic activity when it helps to restore ATP and PC stores.

TRAINING EFFECTS

Specific 'aerobic' training causes a number of beneficial adaptations which help to improve the aerobic energy system's efficiency to resynthesise ATP:

- increased storage of muscle and liver glycogen
- increased mobilisation of aerobic enzymes
- earlier use of FFAs as a fuel source thereby helping to conserve glycogen stores.

The net effect of the above adaptations is that they increase/prolong the aerobic threshold thereby increasing the potential intensity of performance. This delays muscle fatigue by increasing the intensity at which the onset of blood lactate accumulation is reached and by maximising its efficiency to remove lactate during periods of recovery.

Energy continuum

The energy continuum shows how the energy systems interact to provide energy for the resynthesis of ATP. It also highlights the predominance/percentage of each of the three energy systems related to the duration and intensity of the activity.

Each physical activity or sport an athlete participates in requires a different percentage of energy from each energy system, as they rarely work in isolation. Some activities/sports are mainly aerobic while others are anaerobic, but most use a combination of all three energy systems. Fig 16.7 shows a standard graph to represent the energy continuum in context of exercise duration. Fig 16.8 summarises how exercise intensity among other factors may affect which energy system is used. You will be required to explain how all the factors numbered in Fig 16.9 affect the energy system used.

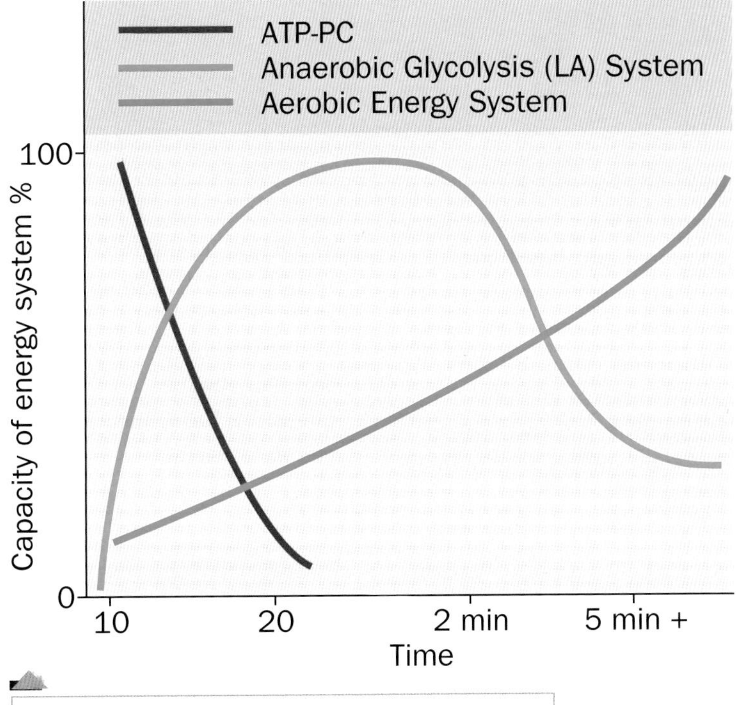

Fig 16.7 Energy system interaction linked to exercise duration

1. Exercise Intensity & Duration

2. Energy System THRESHOLD

LA System
Aerobic System
ATP
ATP-PC
Energy System thresholds
Anaerobic work
Aerobic work

Predominant E system/s

Overall performance / work rate

0.1 s 1/3 s 10 s 2/3 min 45+ min

Time (sec/min)

3. O_2 transport / supply

4. Food / Fuel available

5. Enzyme activation levels

6. Fitness level

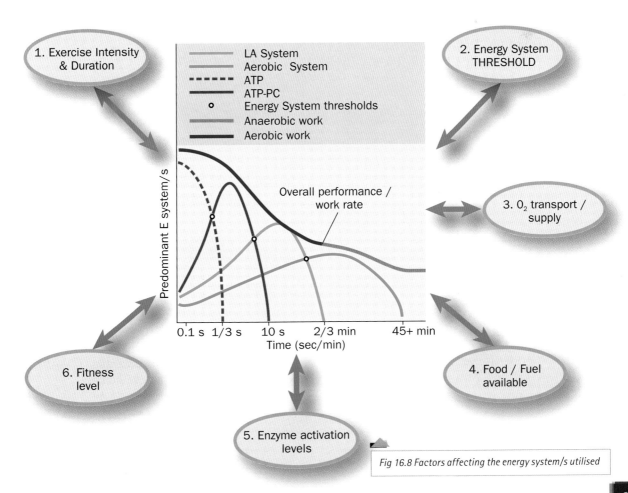

Fig 16.8 Factors affecting the energy system/s utilised

Factors affecting the energy systems used

INTENSITY AND DURATION OF EXERCISE

Figs 16.7 and 16.8 show that it is a combination of both exercise intensity and duration that determines the predominant energy system/s being used. When the exercise intensity is anaerobic (high intensity, short duration) then the ATP/PC and LA systems will be the predominant systems, whereas if the intensity is aerobic (medium/low intensity, long duration) the aerobic system will be predominant.

When exercise intensity reaches a point that the aerobic energy system cannot supply energy quick enough, it has to use the lactic acid system to continue to provide energy for the resynthesis of ATP. You will remember that the LA system produces lactic acid as a by-product. During higher intensity exercise, lactate production will start to accumulate above resting levels and this is termed the 'lactate threshold'. When blood lactate levels reach 4 mmol/L, the exercise intensity is referred to as 'the onset of blood lactate accumulation' (OBLA; see Fig 16.9). This 4 mmol/L is an arbitrary standard value for when OBLA is reached and in essence represents a point where the production of lactate exceeds the speed of its removal. OBLA will continue to increase if this exercise intensity is maintained or increased and will eventually cause muscle fatigue. Fig 16.10 shows that after training the intensity level for lactate threshold is increased and this subsequently delays the point that OBLA is reached and therefore increases the potential duration/threshold of the lactic acid energy system.

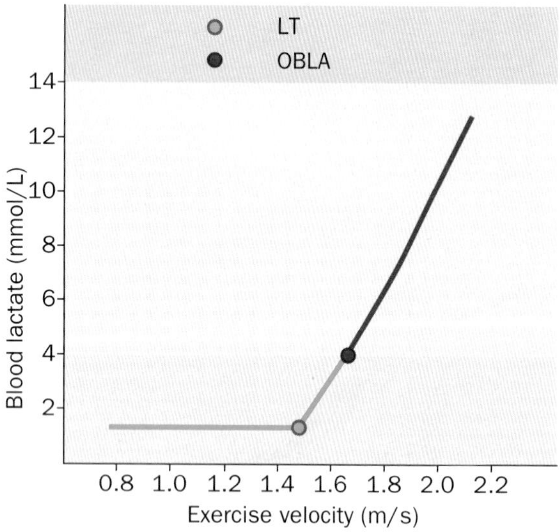

Fig 16.9 The link between lactate threshold and OBLA

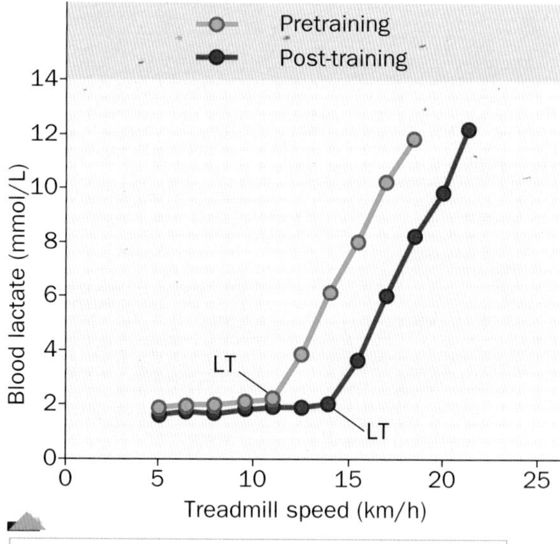

Fig 16.10 The effect of training on the lactate threshold

APPLY IT!

- A sprint athlete may have the potential to sprint at a higher/the same intensity for a longer duration before OBLA induces muscle fatigue.
- An endurance athlete can exercise just below the lactate threshold/OBLA at a higher pre-training intensity without inducing muscle fatigue.

TASK 6

1 Make a copy of Table 5, including the headings as shown.

Table 5

Activity	Percentage ATP/PC	Percentage Anaerobic	Percentage LA	Percentage Aerobic
100m	70	90	20	10

2 Provide approximate percentages in columns 3 and 5 for the following activities/sports in respect of how much they are predominantly aerobic or anaerobic:

- triple jump
- marathon
- basketball
- 1500m
- badminton
- hockey
- netball
- golf
- gymnastics
- rowing
- skiing
- football
- swimming
- tennis
- rugby
- volleyball
- your own sport if not included.

3 Now split the anaerobic percentage between the ATP/PC and LA systems in columns 2 and 4.

4 Discuss why there may be varying percentage differences between you and your peers.

ENERGY SYSTEM THRESHOLDS

A threshold represents the point at which one energy system is taken over by another as the predominant energy system to provide the energy to resynthesise ATP. It shows the potential duration that each energy system can act as the predominant system and is summarised in Table 6.

It is important to note that the energy system threshold alters in response to a combination of both intensity and duration of exercise and will not always follow the route of ATP/PC, LA and then aerobic systems as depicted in Fig 16.7. For example, a cyclist cycling at a low intensity will be using the aerobic system as the predominant energy system, but upon reaching a steep hill for a couple of miles will exceed the intensity threshold of the aerobic system and the lactic acid system will take over as the predominant system. Similarly, a 200m sprinter may be running at an

Table 6 Energy system thresholds

Performance duration	Energy system/s involved (predominant system in *italics*)	Practical example
Less than 10 seconds	*ATP/PC*	Triple jump/100m sprint
10–90 seconds	ATP/PC *LA*	200–400m sprint 100m swim
90 seconds to 3 minutes	*LA* Aerobic	Boxing (3 minute rounds) 800m /1500m
3+ minutes	*Aerobic system*	Low-impact aerobics class Marathon

intensity of about 85 per cent of their maximal, whereas a 400m sprinter may be at 65 per cent and the 800m runner below this again. This shows that although all these events are predominantly LA/anaerobic (high intensity, short duration) events, by changing the intensity the duration before the threshold of the LA system is reached can be altered. Similarly, during team games a performer will be continually switching between all three energy systems and will not be limited to the times in Table 6, which assume that exercise continues to use the same energy system until it is completely exhausted. The ATP/PC system in particular demonstrates this as Table 6 suggests it can last for up to 10 seconds of flat-out sprint activity. However, during a team game the aerobic system is continually resynthesising ATP/PC during periods of recovery. This allows it to repeatedly be used intermittently during the game as the predominant system when explosive/short sprint-type movements are performed.

EXAM TIP

A common mistake is to think a threshold is when an energy system 'stops' providing energy to resynthesise ATP. If you do use the term 'stop', it is best to word your response as 'stops being the predominant energy system'.

OXYGEN AVAILABILITY

As long as there is a sufficient supply of oxygen, the aerobic system can provide the energy to resynthesise ATP. If oxygen supply falls below that demanded for the exercise, then the aerobic system threshold is met and the LA system will begin to breakdown glucose anaerobically to resynthesise ATP. The availability of oxygen is dependent upon the efficiency of the respiratory and cardiovascular systems to supply oxygen to the working muscles and ultimately determines the efficiency and therefore threshold of the aerobic system to resynthesise ATP. Oxygen supply also affects which food fuels can be broken down to resynthesise ATP.

FUEL AVAILABILITY

As long as the body has sufficient stores of PC it is able to use the ATP/PC system for very high-intensity short-duration activity/movements. PC stores are limited but are available at the start and after recovery during exercise. If exercise intensity starts too high, then PC stores will quickly deplete and continued high-intensity explosive activity cannot be sustained. PC stores can be conserved by pacing and by resynthesising PC stores during periods of recovery using spare energy from the aerobic system.

Glycogen is the major fuel for the first 20 minutes of exercise, initially because oxygen supplies are limited as it takes 2–3 minutes for the cardiovascular systems to supply sufficient oxygen. Similarly, glycogen is readily available in the muscles, requires less oxygen and therefore is quicker/easier to break down than free fatty acids (FFAs), to allow a higher aerobic intensity of activity. After about 20–45 minutes there is greater breakdown of fats alongside glycogen as the energy fuel. Although FFAs are a more efficient fuel than glycogen, they require about 15 per cent more oxygen to break them down and will result in the athlete having to work at lower intensities. The greater the liver/muscle glycogen stores, then the longer the performer can work aerobically at a higher intensity.

When glycogen stores become almost fully depleted, after about two hours, FFAs have to be used for aerobic energy production, and unless exercise intensity is reduced it can bring on the sudden onset of fatigue which many athletes refer to as 'hitting the wall'. Similarly, once the onset of blood lactate accumulation (OBLA) is reached the body has insufficient oxygen available to burn FFAs and therefore has to break down glycogen 'anaerobically' to continue resynthesising ATP. Generally it can be said that high-intensity short-duration activity will break down glycogen as the energy fuel, for example a team game player will use glycogen when sprinting. Low-intensity long-duration aerobic activity will break down FFAs and glycogen as energy fuel, for example in a team game a player will use FFAs to last the full duration of the game.

Table 7 Factors affecting enzyme activation for the energy systems

Activating factor	Releases controlling enzyme/s	Activating energy system
Increase in ADP; decrease in ATP	Creatine Kinase	PC
Decrease in PC	PFK	LA system
Increase in adrenalin; decrease in insulin	PFK	Aerobic system

ENZYME ACTIVATION LEVEL

You will remember that enzymes are catalysts that activate the many reactions that help break down PC, glycogen, glucose and FFAs to provide the energy to resynthesise ATP. Hence, without enzymes there would be no reactions and therefore no energy for ATP resynthesis. Table 7 summarises the factors that activate the enzymes for each of the energy systems.

FITNESS LEVEL

Generally, the more aerobically fit the performer, the more efficient their respiratory and cardiovascular systems are to take in, transport and use oxygen to break down glycogen and FFAs aerobically to resynthesise ATP. Aerobic athletes have also shown that they can start to use FFAs earlier during sub-maximal exercise and therefore conserve glycogen stores. The net effect is that the aerobic threshold in terms of intensity and duration can be increased as the lactate threshold/OBLA would be delayed. A typical untrained athlete would reach OBLA at approx 50/56 per cent of their **VO_2 max**, whereas an aerobic-trained athlete wouldn't reach OBLA until about 85/90 per cent of their VO_2 max.

In the same way, an anaerobic-trained athlete will increase their ATP/PC, glycogen stores, anaerobic enzymes and tolerance to lactic acid, which would increase the threshold of both the ATP/PC and LA systems.

KEY TERM

VO_2 max

Maximum oxygen consumption attainable during maximal work.

APPLY IT!

A marathon runner uses glycogen/glucose as the primary energy fuel for the first 20–30 minutes of exercise. After about 45 minutes, glycogen stores begin to deplete and there is a greater mix of glycogen and FFA fuels as exercise continues. FFAs can only be broken down aerobically and require 15 per cent more oxygen. This places greater demands on the cardiovascular system to deliver sufficient oxygen quickly enough to sustain exercise intensity. As glycogen depletion increases, more FFAs have to be used. If the exercise intensity is to be maintained there will be insufficient oxygen supply to break down FFAs and the LA system would be used to break down the remaining glycogen stores. As a consequence this will bring about the onset of blood lactate accumulation (OBLA) and thus eventually muscle fatigue. The athlete would have the choice to reduce their exercise intensity to match their body's capacity to supply oxygen and continue using the aerobic system to break down the FFAs. After about two hours, glycogen stores are almost fully depleted and the runner will most likely 'hit the wall' and has two options: slow down to a pace where the available oxygen supply can break down FFAs aerobically, or risk muscle fatigue and failure to complete the race. This stresses the importance of conserving, maintaining or increasing the body's most important energy fuel – glycogen.

On pages 488–491 we will be looking in more detail at the use of nutritional ergogenic aids before, during and after exercise in an attempt to overcome this problem of glycogen depletion.

TASK 7

Evaluation and planning for the improvement of performance.

1 Record two minutes of your A2 practical activity. If you are a continuous performer record the start, middle and finish of your event.
2 Now watch back the recording but identify when each of the energy systems is the predominant system being used.
3 Write a commentary on the two-minute clip, linking your descriptions of the actions taking place to the predominant energy systems you identified in question 2.
4 Show your clip to a peer/other person while providing an oral commentary.
5 Explain why each of the actions in the first two minutes of your A2 practical activity used the energy systems you linked them to in question 3 above. Use the factors affecting the energy system to guide you.
6 Repeat your oral commentary but now include your explanations from the previous question.

EXAM TIP

The oral commentaries in Task 7 are excellent preparation for your oral evaluation and appreciation talk which is part of your coursework in A2. Keep the recorded clip as you will need it for later tasks practising commentary work. So if you start to collate them you will have the major part of this coursework already prepared.

Recovery process

Before introducing what the recovery process is all about, it will be beneficial for you to have completed Task 8 below for you to acknowledge why an understanding of the processes involved are important for your own participation in physical activity and pursuing a healthy and active lifestyle.

TASK 8

Ensure all performers carry out the same, appropriate warm-up prior to completing the investigation.

In a group of six, working in pairs with one performing and one timing/recording, complete the following investigation:

- Each performer carries out three maximal sprint repetitions, with each sprint consisting of a 10 x 10-metre shuttle sprint (about the length of a badminton court; there and back counts as two).
- The timer records the total time and the recovery times for each of the three shuttle sprints as identified below:
  - Performer 1 is allowed 10 seconds recovery between each 10 x 10-metre shuttle sprint

– Performer 2 is allowed 30 seconds recovery between each 10 x 10-metre shuttle sprint
– Performer 3 is allowed 180 seconds recovery between each 10 x 10-metre shuttle sprint.

Record your results in Table 8 below. Show the + or – time, as compared with the performer's first shuttle time, for the second and third shuttles, and add these together for a total + or – time in the final column.

Table 8

Performer	First 10 shuttles	Second 10 shuttles	Third 10 shuttles	Total + / - sprint times from first shuttle
1.		(+/-)	(+/-)	
2.		(+/-)	(+/-)	
3.		(+/-)	(+/-)	

Compare/discuss your results in relation to the rest/relief interval and each subject's performance and answer the following questions.

1 What happened to the performance of each subject?
2 Do any of the relief intervals allow sufficient time for a full recovery?
3 If you were trying to improve your subject's muscular endurance, which recovery time would you choose? Explain your answer.
4 If you were trying to improve your subject's speed, which recovery time would you choose? Explain your answer.
5 List three opportunities within a team game of your choice where you can allow time for recovery.
6 How would knowledge of the recovery process be beneficial to you as a performer or a coach?

The task investigation above highlighted that the recovery process is concerned with the events occurring in the body primarily *after* a performer has completed exercise. But when and why is it important for a performer/coach to have an understanding of the recovery process? It is important to maintain a performer's readiness to perform:

- during exercise, to allow the performer to maintain performance, for example repeated sprints during a team game
- after exercise, to speed up their recovery in time for their next performance, for example the same or next day.

REMEMBER

Remember the processes involved in the energy systems when considering the events taking place in the recovery process.

Task 9 identifies that the recovery process involves both the removal of the by-products produced during exercise and the replenishment of the fuels used up during exercise. We will identify the products that are removed and those that are replenished now as we look at the recovery process in more detail.

The main aim of the recovery process is to restore the body to its pre-exercise state; in other words, to return it to how it was before a performer started exercise.

TASK 9

An exhaustive bout of exercise like that completed in Task 8 causes many changes within muscle cells, for example an increase in lactic acid. Create a table using the following headings:

1. Changing factor	2. Increase/decrease	3. Action to reverse change

1 Make a list in the 'Changing factor' column of any additional internal changes that you think will take place (refer to the energy systems for some pointers to help you).
2 Indicate in the 'Increase/decrease' column if the change increases or decreases during exercise.
3 Indicate in the 'Action to reverse change' column what is required to reverse the changes you have identified.

At AS-level you saw that the body does not immediately return to resting levels after exercise, but that respiration and heart rate remain elevated during recovery. This is the key process of recovery known as **excess post-exercise oxygen consumption** (EPOC; formerly termed the oxygen debt). This excess oxygen consumption, above that of a resting level during recovery, explains why respiration remains elevated after exercise to restore the body to its pre-exercise state. Figure 16.11 shows that EPOC is thought to consist of two stages, an initial rapid recovery stage, termed alactacid debt, and a slower recovery stage termed lactacid debt.

KEY TERMS

Excess post-exercise oxygen consumption (EPOC)

The excess oxygen consumption, above that at a resting level, during recovery, to restore the body to its pre-exercise state.

Alactacid

The 'a' before lactacid signifies it is without lactic acid.

Fig 16.11 EPOC showing alactacid and lactacid stages of recovery process

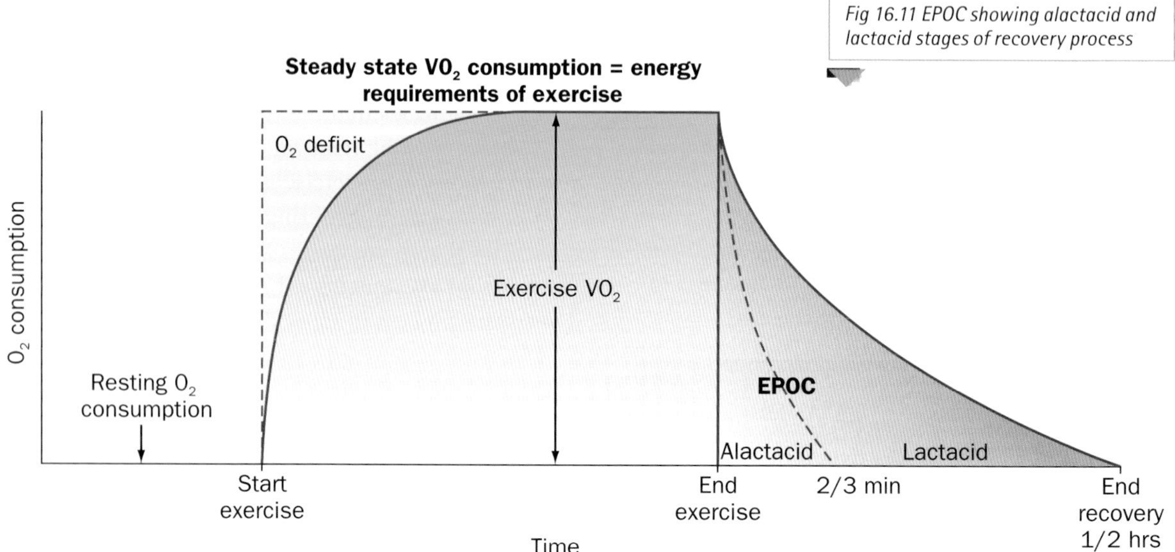

ALACTACID DEBT (RAPID RECOVERY STAGE)

The alactacid stage is also termed the restoration of phosphogen stores, as the elevated respiration primarily helps resynthesise the muscles' store of ATP and PC. It also helps replenish the muscle stores of **myoglobin** and haemoglobin.

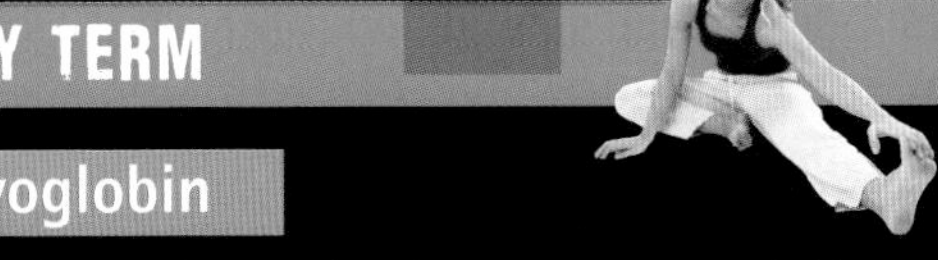

KEY TERM

Myoglobin

Red pigment in muscles that stores oxygen before passing it on to mitochondria for aerobic respiration.

The alactacid stage requires approximately 3–4 litres of oxygen and takes about three minutes to fully restore ATP/PC stores. However, approximately 50 per cent are restored within about 30 seconds and about 75 per cent in 60 seconds.

LACTACID DEBT (SLOW RECOVERY STAGE)

The lactacid stage is a slower process primarily responsible for the removal/re-conversion of lactic acid/lactate. Early research findings suggested that lactic acid is converted into either:

- pyruvic acid, to enter the Kreb's cycle and to be used as a metabolic fuel
- glycogen/glucose
- protein.

However, it is now thought that a significant percentage of EPOC is to support the elevated metabolic functions taking place after exercise, namely:

- high body temperatures remain for several hours after vigorous exercise
- hormones, such as adrenalin, remain in the blood stimulating metabolism
- cardiac output remains high helping to reduce temperature.

The lactacid stage requires approximately 5–8 litres of oxygen and can remove lactic acid from between 1 and 24 hours after exercise depending upon the exercise intensity and the levels of lactic acid that have to be removed.

Fig 16.12 shows how the intensity of exercise can affect the rapid and slow stages of EPOC; a few points are worth noting. First, excess post-exercise oxygen consumption will always be present irrespective of exercise intensity. The oxygen deficit (shortage of oxygen supply during exercise) and EPOC are both lower during aerobic

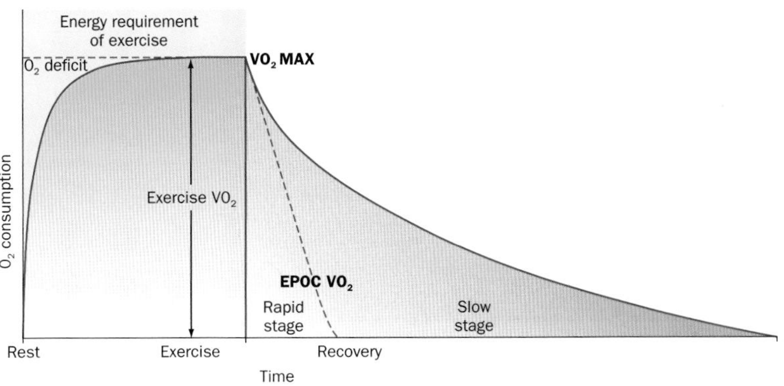

Fig 16.12 EPOC during a) aerobic and b) anaerobic activity (Source: adapted from D. Mcardle, Exercise Physiology, *p.136)*

activity than during anaerobic activity. Aerobic exercise shows a steady state where the oxygen supply (VO_2) meets the requirements of the exercise and therefore has a smaller EPOC, having only a small oxygen deficit and not producing high levels of lactic acid that require removal. Anaerobic exercise shows that a steady state of aerobic work cannot be maintained so the oxygen supply is lower than the exercise requirements. This increases the oxygen deficit and OBLA, producing high levels of lactic acid requiring removal and, consequently, a higher EPOC as it takes longer for oxygen consumption to return to pre-exercise levels.

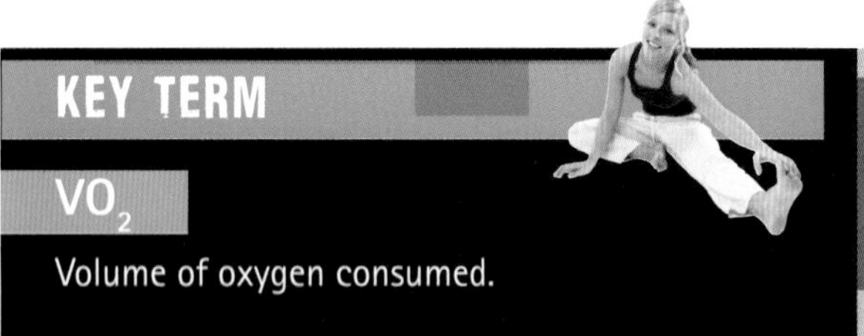

KEY TERM

VO_2

Volume of oxygen consumed.

CO_2 REMOVAL

Increased levels of CO_2, formed as a by-product of respiration during exercise, are carried by a combination of blood plasma within red blood cells as **carbonic acid** (H_2CO_3) and **carbaminohaemoglobin** ($HbCO_2$) to the lungs where it is expired. The high metabolic functions after exercise along with chemoreceptor stimulation of the cardiac and respiratory control centres ensure respiration and heart rate remain elevated to help aid the removal of CO_2.

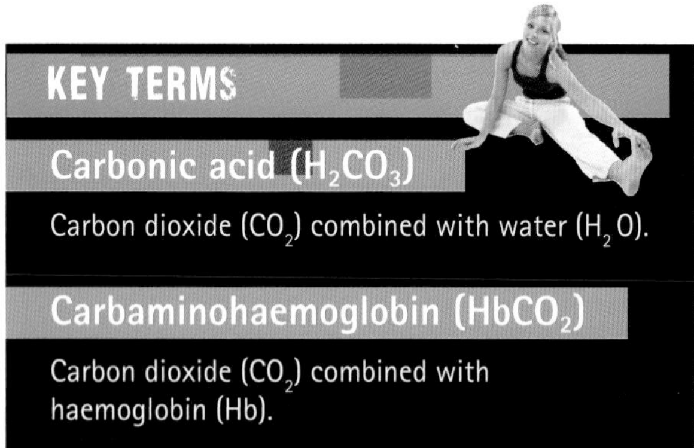

KEY TERMS

Carbonic acid (H_2CO_3)

Carbon dioxide (CO_2) combined with water (H_2O).

Carbaminohaemoglobin ($HbCO_2$)

Carbon dioxide (CO_2) combined with haemoglobin (Hb).

GLYCOGEN REPLENISHMENT

The body's store of muscle and liver glycogen can quickly deplete, and this is a major factor in muscle fatigue. Fig 16.13 shows that a large percentage of glycogen can be replaced up to 10–12 hours after exercise, but complete recovery can take up to two days in more prolonged endurance exercise. It has been shown that fast twitch muscle fibres can replenish glycogen stores quicker than slow twitch fibres. Fig 16.13 also shows that glycogen restoration can be almost completely recovered if a high carbohydrate diet is consumed, especially when eaten within the first two hours of recovery. Nutrition is considered in more depth in Chapter 19, but many athletes now replenish glycogen stores by consuming carbohydrate-rich drinks, which are thought to be quicker to break down and more easily ingested than large bowls of pasta immediately after exercise.

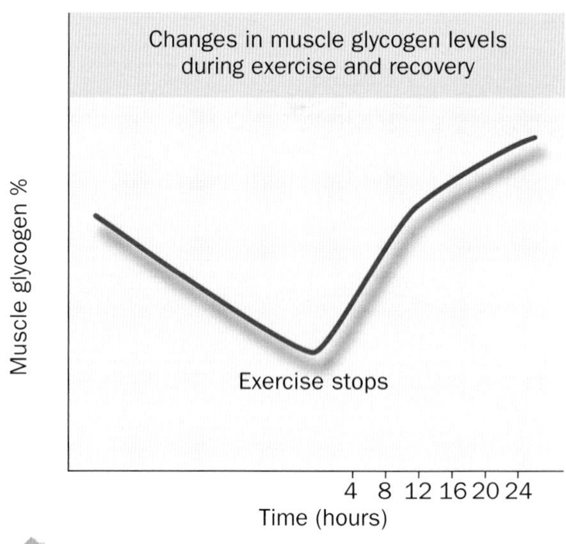

Fig 16.13 Energy depletion and restoration

IMPLICATIONS OF THE RECOVERY PROCESS FOR PLANNING PHYSICAL ACTIVITY SESSIONS

An understanding of the recovery process provides some guidelines for planning training sessions in respect of optimising both the work

Table 9 Total exercise, average O_2 uptake and blood lactate levels during continuous and work-relief training (Source: adapted from D. McArdle, *Exercise Physiology*, page 139)

Work–relief ratio (same intensity/speed)	Total running distance (m)	Average O_2 uptake (L/min)	Blood lactate level (mg 100 ml blood)
4 minute continuous to exhaustion	1422	5.6	150.0
10 seconds work 5 seconds relief (20 minutes work in 30-minute session)	7294	5.1	44.0
15 seconds work 30 seconds relief (10 minutes work in a 30-minute session)	3642	3.6	13.66

intensity and recovery intervals. This is commonly referred to as the work–relief ratio, using a training method termed **interval training**.

KEY TERM

Interval training

A form of training incorporating periods of work interspersed with periods of recovery.

Table 9 above shows that a performer training at the same intensity, using work–relief ratios (rows 2 and 3) can train, for a longer distance, at a lower average **VO_2 max** and with a lower blood lactate level compared with continuous work, which causes exhaustion after only 4–5 minutes (row 1). Hence, work–relief interval training is more efficient as it increases the quality/intensity of training within a training session and consequently improves energy system adaptations. Similarly, by altering the work–relief intervals, the training can target specific energy systems appropriate to the performer.

KEY TERM

VO_2 max

Maximum volume of oxygen that can be consumed during maximal work.

- For training aimed at improving speed, using the ATP/PC system, the work ratio may be less than 10 seconds and the relief ratio is typically longer (ratio 1 : 3) to allow time for the ATP and PC stores to fully recover (2–3 minutes).
- Training aimed at improving the body's tolerance to lactate to improve speed endurance using the lactic acid system, could either keep the work ratio less than 10 seconds but decrease the duration of the relief ratio (ratio 1 : 2 – i.e. 30 seconds relief only allows 50 per cent ATP/PC restoration) and/or increase the duration of the work ratio, which both increases lactate production and overloads the lactic acid system.
- For training aimed at improving a performer's VO_2 max using the aerobic system, the work–relief ratio is normally longer in duration and intensity, just below the anaerobic threshold. The relief ratio is typically shorter (ratio 1 : 1), which helps reduce the OBLA and delay muscle fatigue and therefore prolong the aerobic system adaptations.

APPLY IT!

Some elite marathon runners and cross-country skiers can perform at up to 90 per cent VO_2 max without significant lactic acid production (OBLA).

GENERAL RECOVERY TRAINING APPLICATIONS

- Complete a warm-up prior to training to increase respiration rate/O_2 supply before exercise starts and thereby reduce the oxygen deficit.
- During anaerobic work, where lactic acid accumulates, an active recovery after training elevates respiration which helps speed up lactic acid removal (see Fig 16.14).
- A moderate intensity seems optimal for the active recovery but this can vary; for example, 35–45 per cent VO_2 max for cycling and 55–60 per cent VO_2 max for running.
- However, during steady state aerobic exercise, where little lactic acid is produced, a more passive recovery has been shown to speed up recovery more than an active recovery. In this case an active recovery actually elevates metabolism and delays recovery.
- Anaerobic speed/lactate tolerance training will both help to increase ATP and PC muscle stores.
- Use all available opportunities, breaks and time-outs, etc., to allow the restoration of ATP, PC and oxygen myoglobin stores during training/performance.
- Use tactics or pacing to control/alter intensity to meet the training objectives.
- Aerobic training will help improve oxygen supply during and after recovery from exercise.
- A mix of anaerobic and aerobic training will help delay the ATP/PC and lactic acid thresholds.
- Use heart rate as an indicator of exercise intensity, OBLA threshold and recovery state, as heart rate mirrors respiratory recovery.

TASK 10

Evaluation and planning for the improvement of performance

1. Locate the two-minute clip you used in Task 7 for your energy systems commentary. Read through your commentary while watching the clip again.
2. Now watch the recording but this time identify when the alactacid and lactacid stages of EPOC are taking place. This should include both during and after if applicable.
3. Write a commentary on the two-minute clip, linking your identification of when the recovery EPOC is taking place to the actual events taking place, for example myoglobin stores are starting to be replenished.
4. Show your clip to a peer/other person while providing your oral commentary.
5. Repeat your oral commentary but this time explain the link between the different energy systems used and the different stages of EPOC, including glycogen restoration. For example, how the ATP/PC system is linked to alactacid immediately recovery starts between or after activity.

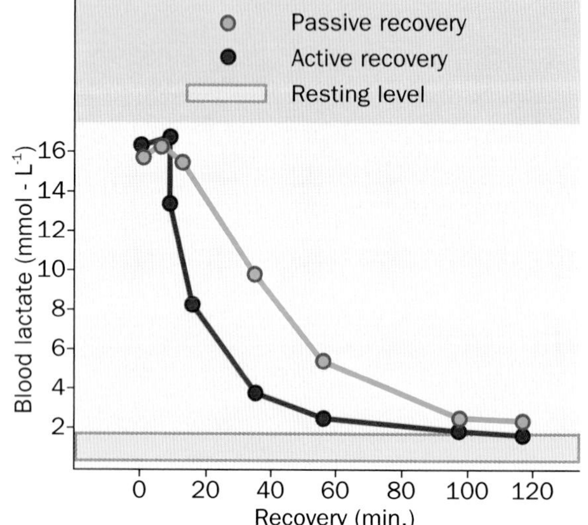

Fig 16.14 The effects of active recovery on lactic acid removal

STRETCH AND CHALLENGE

Investigation into 'exercise-to-rest' interval training.

1 Work in groups of three, two performing and one recording. Performers 1 and 2 take turns to complete as many press-ups as they can in one continuous performance time. This is timed and counted (choose any appropriate method, for example bent-knee press-ups) to establish a base-level value.
2 Allow at least 5 minutes between task 1 and task 3 and 4.
3 Performer 1 adds twenty to their press-up base-level value total and then divides the total into 10-second work intervals, each followed by a 20-second relief interval.
4 Performer 2 divides their total base-level work time into 10-second work intervals and completes as many press-ups as they can in each 10-second work interval each followed by a 20 second relief interval.
5 For each performer, add up the total time on work and the number of press-ups completed.
6 Compare this with the work time and number of press-ups completed in task 1.
7 Discuss and compare the performers' results.
8 What other types of performance could 'exercise-to-rest' interval training be applied to?

Example: Base-level value = 60 press-ups in 120 seconds. Add 20 = 80 press-ups; 8 press-ups in 10 seconds repeated 10 times. 80 press-ups completed in a total work time of 100 seconds compared with 60 press-ups in 120 seconds.

Exam**Café**

Relax, refresh, result!

You should now have knowledge and understanding of:

- how to define energy, work and power
- the role of ATP; the breakdown and re-synthesis of ATP; coupled reactions and exothermic and endothermic reactions
- the three energy systems: ATP/PC; alactic; the lactic acid and aerobic system
- the contribution of each energy system in relation to the duration/intensity of exercise
- the predominant energy system used related to type of exercise
- the inter-changing between thresholds during an activity, for example the onset of blood lactate accumulation (OBLA), and the effect of level of fitness, availability of oxygen and food fuels, and enzyme control on energy system used
- how the body returns to its pre-exercise state: the oxygen debt/excess post-exercise oxygen consumption (EPOC); the alactacid and lactacid debt components; replenishment of myoglobin stores and fuel stores and the removal of carbon dioxide
- the implications of the recovery process for planning physical activity sessions.

REVISE AS YOU GO!

1. Define energy, work and power, giving the correct units for each.
2. What is ATP and why is it so important?
3. Briefly describe the processes involved in the three energy systems.
4. Explain the energy continuum and provide practical examples to show how the intensity and duration of exercise determine which energy system is predominant.
5. Define and explain the term OBLA.
6. Outline three factors which can affect which energy system is used.
7. Define oxygen debt/EPOC and explain the purpose of the recovery process.
8. Identify and outline the two components of oxygen debt/EPOC.
9. Describe how the store of oxygen myoglobin and glycogen are replenished and CO_2 removed after exercise.
10. How would knowledge of recovery process help a coach to plan a training session?

Try to answer these questions yourself. Ask your teacher if you need help.

Get the result!

Examination question

Using examples from a game situation, explain when and why your performer uses each of the three energy systems. (6 marks)

Examiner's tips

There are three parts to this question, each having two sub-parts, which may distract you from identifying the main command words.

- The three parts are the three energy systems, each of which has two sub-parts requiring you to apply the command words 'when' and 'why'.
- The command words for all three parts are 'using examples' and 'explain', so it is important that you do both for all three parts to the question.
- Although not always, it is generally wise when questions ask for examples to assume the marking scheme will limit the maximum mark available if no examples are provided.
- Check the number of marks available (6 marks) and work out how many may be awarded for each part of the question. Three energy systems and six marks should point you towards two marks each, but don't forget that each system has to include when and why to cover all parts of the question (as long as examples are provided).
- A quick plan would ensure you cover all parts of this question; for example:

Explain	When	Why	Example
ATP/PC			
Lactic acid			
Aerobic			

Student answer

During a hockey game, the three energy systems all work together to provide energy to resynthesise ATP in coupled reactions in what is known as the energy continuum.

The ATP system is used when the goalkeeper dives explosively to save a low shot, whereas the lactic acid system is used for

Examiner comment

Although accurate the information you have supplied here is irrelevant in regard to the question.

longer but less intense anaerobic sprints repeated for more than 10 seconds – this is the ATP/PC system. The aerobic energy system is used for exercise lasting more than 2-3 minutes. It allows the midfield player to last the duration of the full game including all the aerobic jogging and non-anaerobic sprinting-type work.

Examiner commen

Although not concise you have accurately identified when the three energy systems are used with a mixture of descriptions, time frames and good practical examples from hockey. Use of the terms 'intensity' and 'duration' would have helped clarify your answer.

The ATP system is used at the very start of exercise because there is insufficient oxygen available as it can work anaerobically and PC is stored where we need it in the muscles. The lactic acid system is used because the player has run out of ATP/PC and needs continued sprints as it can also work anaerobically, breaking down glucose via anaerobic glycolysis. The aerobic system is used during the jogging because there is lots of oxygen available and glucose and fats can be used in aerobic glycolysis. This provides lots of energy but only when running at a lower intensity than the lactic acid and ATP/PC systems.

Examiner comment

You have split your answer into all the when and why. Try to anticipate the mark scheme and mirror your answer.

Examiner comment

You have shown a good understanding of why each energy system is used and applied your understanding to clear examples.

Examiner commen

Excellent use of the word 'because' throughout which is a great way of ensuring you do explain 'why' the energy systems are used.

All three energy systems interact to allow the player to jog, run, sprint and recover throughout the hockey game and continually change throughout the game, the goalkeeper would predominantly use the ATP/PC system and the midfielder use a greater percentage of the aerobic system.

Examiner commen

This information is all irrelevant to the question.

Examiner comment

Although maximum marks would be awarded, you have a tendency to answer with all the information you know and not be as concise as you could be for a six-mark question. For example, you wrote an irrelevant start and finish, and applied examples twice for when and why rather than together. Providing the same example to explain when and why for each energy system mirrors the mark scheme and would help you to answer in a more concise manner and save you time.

CHAPTER 17:

Application of the principles of training

LEARNING OBJECTIVES

By the end of this chapter you should have knowledge and understanding of:

- how to apply the principles of training: moderation, reversibility, specificity, variance, overload and progression
- how to apply knowledge of the principles of training to periodisation
- how to define periodisation and macro, meso and micro cycles
- how to plan a personal health and fitness programme that will promote sustained involvement in a balanced, active and healthy lifestyle; the plan should include the principles of training.

INTRODUCTION

In Chapter 18 we will be studying in depth the health components of physical fitness – aerobic capacity, strength, body composition and flexibility – with regard to how they benefit and promote sustained involvement in a balanced, active and healthy lifestyle. This will require you to plan a personal health and fitness programme for each of these health components using the training methods that will be covered in detail later. It is widely accepted that effective training follows several basic guidelines that should be applied to all forms of training; these are known as the 'principles of training'. It is therefore more sensible to gain an understanding of these principles before studying the health components of fitness, so that you can apply these principles when planning health and fitness programmes.

EXAM TIP

The principles of training are easier to recall if you can visualise 'Mrs Vopp' who is 'Testing' the 'WC' (toilet). This will help you recall the principles of training including some additional principles normally included on exam marking schemes. Hence:

- 'Mrs' = moderation, reversibility, specificity
- 'Vopp' = variation, overload, progression and periodisation
- 'Testing' = select an appropriate test for the fitness component
- 'WC' (toilet) = warm up and cool down.

Application of the principles of training

MODERATION

An easy way to remember the principle of moderation linked to a healthy lifestyle is to think of the advice on alcohol consumption: 'a little in moderation is OK but too much is bad for you'.

Fig 17.1 Moderation: a balance between too much or too little training load to achieve adaptation

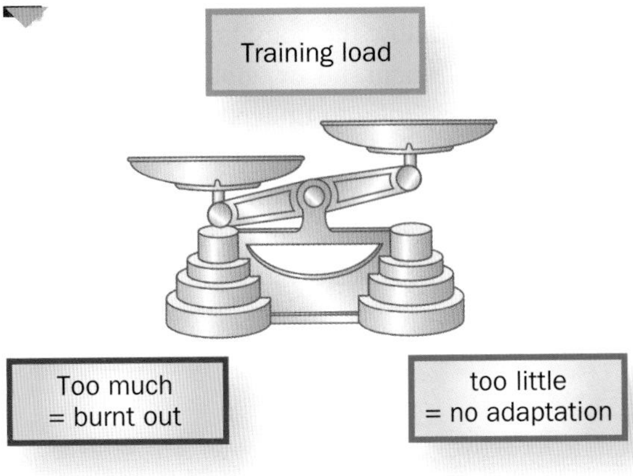

If too much training or exercise (overload) is undertaken too quickly, the likely result will be a mixture of overuse injuries, especially to joints and musculo-skeletal tissues, and physical and mental fatigue (burn out). Equally however, if too little overload (exercise) is undertaken, very few adaptations to training will be achieved at all.

TASK 1

Discuss the following questions.

1 You now understand the importance of training in moderation, but how do you know if the training programme you plan will be too little or too much to ensure adaptations take place without injury or burn out?
2 What are the implications of moderation on setting fitness targets/goals?

APPLY IT!

Lifting weights that are too light will not cause the body to adapt and improve the performer's strength, whereas lifting very heavy weights when you first start training will cause injuries to the joints/muscles.

Reversibility

Having identified that training (**overload**) in moderation will allow the body to adapt and become more efficient, for example via improved strength, it is also vital to understand that the opposite occurs in a period of inactivity. Hence the adaptations to training are reversed if the training is reduced or stops. This is best remembered by the phrase 'Fitness – if you don't use it you lose it'.

One of the most significant adaptations to be reversed in response to inactivity is known as **atrophy**. This is a decrease in the size of muscle cells and takes place after approximately 48 hours. It is estimated that if you stop training the fitness/adaptations gained will be reversed in a third of the time it took to gain them. It is also important to understand that fast fitness gains/adaptations are quicker to reverse than those gained over a long period, and that aerobic adaptations reverse quicker than anaerobic adaptations.

KEY TERMS

Overload

When the body is made to work harder than it normally does, in order to cause adaptation.

Atrophy

Decrease in the size of muscle cells.

APPLY IT!

During periods of injury, holidays or illness, if you stop training your adaptations will reverse and upon resuming training you will need to start again at a lower level than when you stopped training.

TASK 2

1 If you train for a charity 10-kilometre fun run for a period of three months, how long will it take for your fitness adaptations to be reversed?
2 It takes approximately 48 hours before the start of muscle atrophy. How can you ensure that this does not take place in your weekly training programme?

SPECIFICITY

The key to understanding specificity is to make the link between training, adaptations and the sport/activity. In other words, specific training elicits specific adaptations critical for a specific sport/activity. In simple terms this is saying the choice of training must reflect the demands of the sport/activity. For example, lifting heavy weights in the multi-gym is better suited to an Olympic weight lifter than a marathon runner.

Specificity is applied in two ways:

1 *The individual* – each performer has a different rate of adaptation in response to different types of training, primarily due to genetic variations.
2 *The sport/activity* – the predominant energy system/s, the major fitness components, movement patterns, muscle fibre type and muscles/joints used for that particular sport/activity.

APPLY IT!

Long distance cyclists will undertake predominantly aerobic/endurance training on a bike and concentrate on their lower body leg muscles. A 50-metre swimmer will undertake predominantly anaerobic training in the pool and concentrate on whole-body exercises for their legs, arms and core (trunk) areas.

TASK 3

1 What is the problem when applying specificity to a team game? How could you overcome this problem?
2 How would you ensure that specificity was applied to a training programme for your own practical coursework activity?

VARIANCE

Do you already know what type of training, exercises, equipment, practices, etc., you will be undertaking before you actually turn up for training? How does this make you feel prior to training?

Hopefully your training is varied, so that the experience is always fresh. If your training is continually repeated, this can lead to boredom and a lack of interest or motivation to continue. Variety also helps prevent repetitive strain/overuse injuries, such as osteoarthritis, stress fractures and shin splints, which are common with performers such as ballet dancers.

Variety is the spice of life and this is just as true for training. When there are so many different methods of training, equipment, practices and exercises available, there are no excuses for training to lack variety.

APPLY IT!

Movement patterns specific to swimming don't always have to be done in the water – they can be repeated within resistance training using free weights, multi-gym, body weights, circuit training exercises and using rope/pulley resistance machines.

Fig 17.2 Variance in training is important to prevent boredom and lack of motivation

When we looked at moderation we identified that adaptations take place in the region between where the training is too low or too high; this area is termed the 'training or adaptation zone'.

KEY TERM

Training/adaptation zone

An area of intensity where adaptations occur in response to training/overload, i.e. when training occurs in moderation and is at neither too high nor too low an intensity.

TASK 4

1 List any repetitive strain injuries that are common to your own coursework activity.
2 Can you explain why your activity does/does not have any repetitive strain injuries?
3 How can you prevent these from occurring when planning a training programme?

OVERLOAD

The training/adaptation zone (see Fig 17.3) is an area of 'overload' where the body is working harder than its normal capacity and therefore adapting to the training.

Overload is achieved by adjusting/increasing FITT:

- *Frequency* – how often you train, for example weekly (micro-, meso- and macro-cycles)
- *Intensity* – how hard you train, for example faster, heavier, less recovery, etc.
- *Time* – (duration) how long you train for, for example a 30-minute or 60-minute session
- *Type* – aerobic or anaerobic training as covered within specificity.

PROGRESSION

As the body adapts to the training overload, its fitness capacity will increase to this level of overload. In this instance, the body will remain at this fitness level if the training remains the same. To ensure the body's fitness capacity increases further, the overload (training) needs to be gradually increased to keep the body adapting.

Fig 17.3 Two variations of adaptation/training zone diagrams

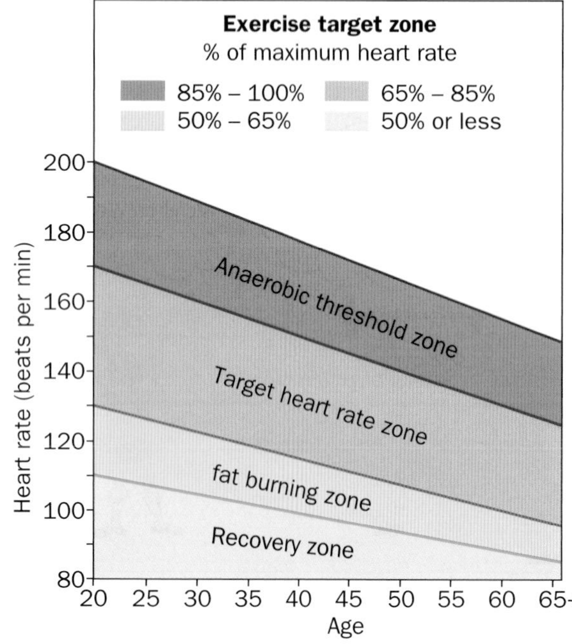

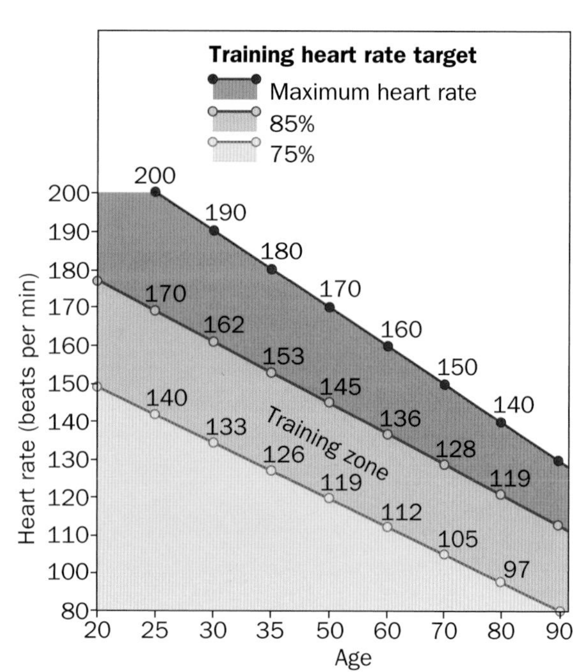

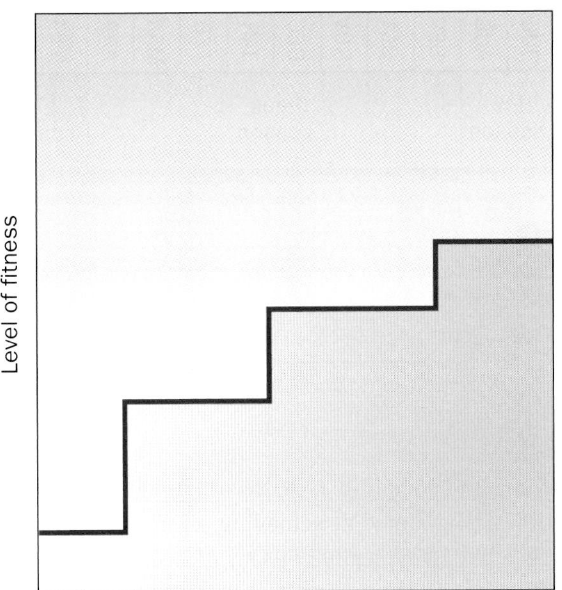

Fig 17.4 Progressive overload

The link between overload and adaptations is termed progressive overload. This highlights the importance of interspersing overload with periods of recovery to allow the body time to adapt. Fig 17.4 shows that the fitness adaptations are greater earlier in training and slow down as training increases. A point of diminishing return may eventually be reached where any further progression of training overload may bring about little or no adaptations and could lead to burn out.

STRETCH AND CHALLENGE

A simple method of calculating an athlete's training overload/intensity is Borg's scale, a 'rating of perceived exertion' (RPE) which uses either a 10 or 15 rating scale.

Calculate the RPE of your next training/competitive performance using Borg's scale (easily available from an Internet search or from your teacher).

Periodisation

Periodisation is the organised division of training into a number of specific blocks, periods or phases. The main objective of periodisation is to ensure athletes progressively develop to reach a skill/physiological peak at the correct time for an ultimate sporting target. This target could be a competition event, for example the Olympic

TASK 5

1 Look at Table 1 below. Complete the Week 1 column to show your present weekly training overload for your coursework practical activity.
2 Now complete the Week 3 and Week 6 columns to show how you may increase the overload to achieve progressive overload.
3 How many changes to FITT did you make between Weeks 1 and 3 and Weeks 3 and 6?
4 What may happen if your progression is too fast?
5 What may happen if progression is too slow?
6 How will you know when it is time to increase/decrease the overload?

Table1

	Week 1	Week 3	Week 6
Frequency			
Intensity			
Time			
Type			

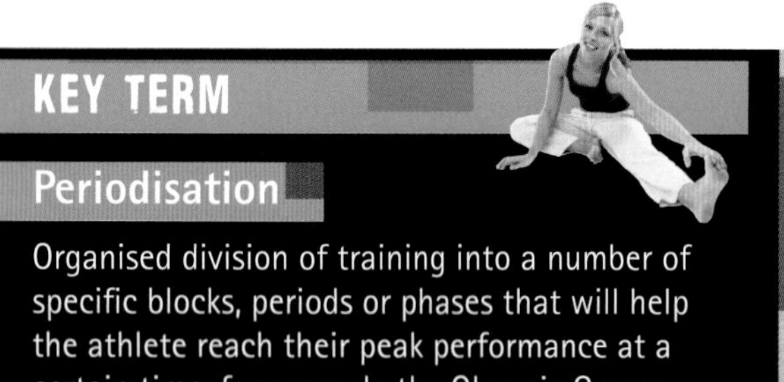

KEY TERM

Periodisation

Organised division of training into a number of specific blocks, periods or phases that will help the athlete reach their peak performance at a certain time, for example the Olympic Games.

JUL	AUG	SEP	OCT	NOV	DEC	JAN	FEB	MAR	ARP	MAY	JUN
Pre season		Peak season								Off season	

Fig 17.5 Example of a simple periodised training year for Rugby Union

Games or World Championships, or to improve the athlete's general fitness level in order to sustain a healthy and active lifestyle.

In its simplest form, periodisation divides the training year into three phases: pre-season, competition season and transition (off)-season (see Fig 17.5), with each phase having its own specific aims. As training has developed periodisation has become much more complex, but in simple terms you need to apply three basic structures when planning a training programme: macro-cycles, meso-cycles and micro-cycles.

MACRO-CYCLE

A **macro-cycle** (Fig 17.6a) is a longer-term plan of training aimed at achieving a long-term goal/ objective. It typically consists of a single-year block of training; for example, ensuring peak physical condition for the competition season with one year's training being very much like the next. However, athletes such as those competing in the Olympics or World Championships may have macro-cycles lasting as long as four

Fig 17.6 The divisions within periodisation: (i) macro-cycle; (ii) simple meso-cycle; (iii) typical meso-cycles; (iv) micro-cycles; (v) units (four including game)

Training year

a)

Macro-cycle

b)

Pre-season Meso-cycle 1	*Competition* Meso-cycle 2	*Off season* Meso-cycle 3

c) and d)

M1.1	M1.2	M1.3	M2.1	M2.2	M3.1	M3.2
2 weeks	4 weeks	1 week	27 weeks	5 weeks	4 weeks	9 weeks

e)

Monday	*Tuesday*	*Wednesday*	*Thursday*	*Friday*	*Saturday*	*Sunday*
Skill training	Rest	High-intensity training	Rest	Low-intensity aerobic run	Game	Rest

Key: M1 = Meso-cycle 1

KEY TERMS

Macro-cycle

Long-term plan/goal of training, typically lasting at least a year.

Mega-cycle

A macro-cycle which may last several years.

Meso-cycle

Medium-term plan/goal of training, typically lasting between 4 and 16 weeks (1–4 months).

years; these are sometimes termed **mega-cycles**. Similarly, a one-year period could have two macro-cycles, each with a separate goal/objective. Irrespective of the length and number, macro-cycles are made up of a number of meso-cycles.

MESO-CYCLE

A **meso-cycle** is an intermediate block of training aimed at achieving a particular medium-term goal/objective, for example to increase strength, power or endurance. It typically lasts between 4 and 16 weeks. In it simplest form, a macro-cycle could consist of three meso-cycles, namely pre-season, competition and off-season (or transition) training. However, when the training is planned in greater detail, each of these three meso-cycles can be further divided to form an even greater number of shorter intermediate-term goals. Fig 17.6 b) and c) show how the three, pre-season, competition and off-season meso-cycles can be further divided into seven meso-cycles.

The basic structure of these seven expanded meso-cycles is outlined under the preseason, competition and off-season headings below. In contrast, Fig 17.7 shows a typical two-season training year characteristic of a swimmer or track athlete who may have two major 'peaks', for example a swimmer's short- and long-course season or an indoor and outdoor athletic season.

PRE-SEASON

- *Meso-cycle 1.1/Basic fitness phase* – this part of the training cycle is characterised by the development of a basic/general all-round fitness.

Fig 17.7 A two-season periodised training year for a swimmer

Short course: Macro-cycle 1, Sept–March (Club/district/regional championships)					Long course: Macro-cycle 2, April–Aug (Regional/national championships)				
M1	M2	M3	M4	M5	M6	M7	M8	M9	M10
10 weeks	10 weeks	7 weeks	2 weeks	1 week	4 weeks	8 weeks	5 weeks	2 weeks	2 weeks
General endurance training 1	Specific endurance training 1	Competition 1 preparation	Comp 1 (2 x) Taper + event	Rest/recovery	General endurance 2	Specific endurance 2	Competition 2 preparation	Comp 2 (2 x) Taper + event	Off-season recovery

- *Meso-cycle 1.2/Specific event phase* – characterised by training that will progressively increase in intensity and focus on the fitness components important for the individual/event, for example develop/change the speed, appropriate energy system, techniques and skills ready for competition.
- *Meso-cycle 1.3/Pre-competition phase* – as competition season approaches, the focus is to integrate all the aspects above. The total training load/volume is normally reduced, but any remaining high-intensity training will attempt to mirror that of the actual event while allowing longer recovery intervals. Practice games or trials are normally incorporated prior to the actual competition phase.

COMPETITION SEASON

- *Meso-cycle 2.1/Maintenance phase* – here the aim is to maintain fitness levels between competitions and remain injury-free. Training continues but is reduced, with periods of lower intensity, adequate rest days and an appropriate diet. The focus lies with competition-specific preparation, for example strategy/team play/technique, but there should be no significant technical changes (unless unavoidable).
- *Meso-cycle 2.2/Monitoring and recovery phase* – at this stage it is important to monitor closely for signs of overtraining/burn out, and taper down training intensity and increase recovery if necessary as the tail end of the season approaches.

TRANSITION/OFF-SEASON

- *Meso-cycle 3.1/Rest/recovery phase 1* – this stage consists typically of an initial period of rest or low-level active recovery and any remedial treatment for injuries, etc.

- *Meso-cycle 3.2* – A gradual build-up of low-level training/activity or cross-training to help start preparing the body for the start of pre-season training; for example, swimmers should get out of the water and footballers could get on the golf course.

Meso-cycles 3.1 and 3.2 are typically between 2 and 4 weeks' long; however, the longer the competition season, the greater the rest/recovery phase that may be required.

The length and number of meso-cycles is dependent upon the activity and the individual. Fig 17.7 shows that a swimmer or track athlete may have a two-season sport (two competition events in a season) in contrast to a one-season sport like football, which has a 7–8-month competition season. There are also all-season sports like road running.

MICRO-CYCLE

A **micro-cycle** is simply a number of training sessions which form a recurrent **unit**. Although they can last up to three weeks, a micro-cycle is typically one week of training aimed at achieving a short-term objective/goal.

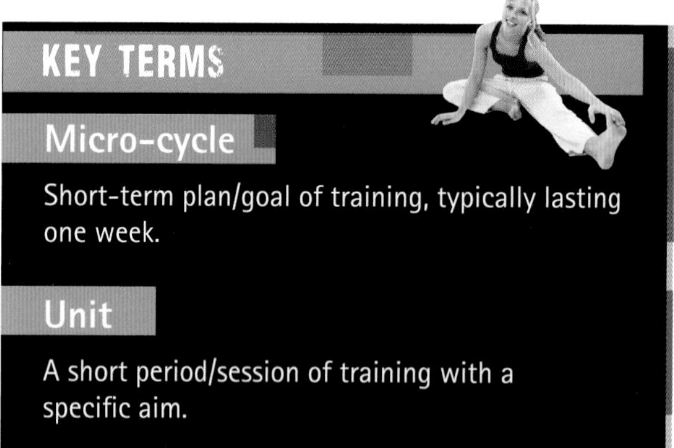

KEY TERMS

Micro-cycle

Short-term plan/goal of training, typically lasting one week.

Unit

A short period/session of training with a specific aim.

APPLY IT!

If your training consists of a hard day, an easy day and a rest day followed by the same hard-easy-rest pattern, then this represents your micro-cycle.

The term 'unit' is also used in periodisation and can refer to each individual training session or different parts of an individual session. For example, an athlete training three times a week would have a micro-cycle consisting of three units. Alternatively, one session of training with two aims – flexibility and strength training – may require a session made up of two units.

TASK 6

1 List the typical schedule of training sessions, including games and rest days, that you undertake until you get to a point where you start repeating the same recurrent unit over again.
2 Have you a weekly or longer micro-cycle? How many units do you have in your micro-cycle?

STRETCH AND CHALLENGE

1 Research and compare the 'undulating' and 'double' periodisation models.
2 Explain which of the two models is most appropriate to your coursework practical activity.

A useful source to support this activity is found by going to www.heinemann.co.uk/hotlinks, entering the express code 6855P and clicking on the relevant link.

Information can also be found on www.pponline.co.uk.

BENEFITS OF PERIODISATION

Aside from the main aim of ensuring an athlete reaches a peak performance at the correct time for their sporting target, periodisation ensures that many of the principles of training are applied when planning a training programme:

- *Moderation/reversibility* – helps prevent overtraining by ensuring adequate recovery but at the same time not allowing time for fitness/skills to decrease.
- *Specificity* – each block is designed to prepare a specific performance component, for example sprint-start training can be focused on the needs of the individual performer/sport-specific.
- *Variance* – training is split into smaller units to maintain motivation, avoid boredom and overtraining, and allow recovery.
- *Overload* – enables the performer to manipulate training intensity, volume, frequency and rest.
- *Progression/testing* – monitoring/testing helps guide the performer when the training overload may require:
  - stepping up to increase adaptations
  - decreasing to spot/prevent overtraining and burn out
  - the tapering down of training intensity and an increase in recovery time.
- *Warm up/cool down* – each unit of training should incorporate a warm up and cool down.
- *Flexible*:
  - focuses training and the setting of short-term, long-term and time-phased goals
  - a double periodisation model allows the performer to peak twice for a number of competitions, for example the qualifying round and the actual championship (this approach is not recommended for endurance sports)
  - an undulating periodisation model allows the long-season team to perform to best maintain fitness and prevent too much overload/burn out.

TASK 7

1 Divide up your own activity into a periodisation programme of training.

TASK 8

Evaluating and planning for the improvement of performance

1 Rehearse your periodised plan and give a detailed oral description/explanation to a peer performing the same practical activity.
2 Ask your peer to provide feedback on your oral description.
3 Identify and explain the benefits of a planned periodised training programme and where/how the principles of training may be incorporated.

4 Repeat your oral commentary but this time state the benefits of using periodisation and when/how the principles of training are applied.

STRETCH AND CHALLENGE

Research and discuss the development of long-term athletic development (LTAD) using information at www.sportscoachuk.org. Evaluate which principles of training have a strong association/link with LTAD.

Testing

The principles of moderation and progression linked to overload highlight the need for testing. Testing will enable the athlete/coach to monitor whether the training load is correct:

- at the start of training, to ensure the overload is not too high/low
- during training, to assess when it may need increasing to ensure further adaptations or even decreasing to prevent burn out.

The physical fitness tests you are required to describe and apply when planning a health or fitness training programme are shown in Fig 17.8. They demonstrate the need to match an athlete's capacities (test results) with that of the requirements demanded of their activity before any training programme is planned.

STRETCH AND CHALLENGE

Look at Fig 17.8.

1 What type of activity/performer do you think the red line (requirement) is representative of?
2 What does the performer's capacity profile (blue line) indicate that they should be including when planning their own training programme?
3 What is the ideal capacity rating profile in relation to the requirement profile?
4 What advice might you suggest to the performer in light of their capacity tests?

Fig 17.8 Health fitness component matched to fitness tests

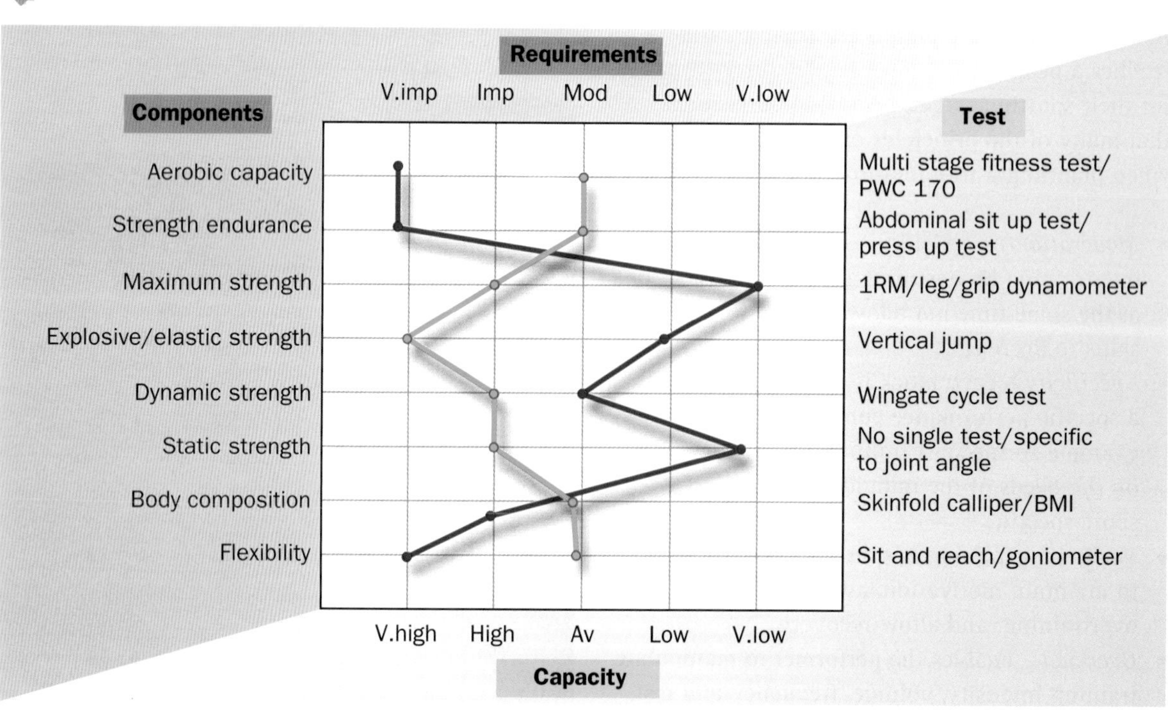

TASK 9

Working in a group with other students who are performing the same practical coursework activity as you, complete steps 1–5 below. Your teacher may provide you with a blank copy of the grid shown in Fig 17.8.

1 Look ahead at Chapter 18 to gain an understanding of each fitness component and discuss their application to your activity (see pages 408; 425–430; 445; 459–60).
2 Now identify the requirement rating of each fitness component in relation to your activity using Fig 17.8. Mark each requirement rating with a cross (X) on the grid.
3 Draw a linked line to show the requirement rating profile for your activity.

You may wish to complete steps 4 and 5 below later, when you study each of the health fitness components separately.

4 Identify the test protocols (description) in Chapter 18 for each fitness component identified in point 1.
5 Carry out the test for each fitness component. Mark the grid with a cross (X) where the capacity rating intersects with each fitness component (use a different colour). Draw a linked line to show your capacity rating profile.

You may need to decide on your own capacity ratings after the whole group test results are completed, or you may use those provided in Chapter 18. Alternatively, ask your teacher for average capacity ratings.

Warm up

A warm up should precede any activity or training as it helps prepare the body physically and mentally for the exercise to follow. Furthermore, linked to the principle of moderation, it is unwise to jump into physical activity too quickly.

A warm up should consist of three phases:

1 *Pulse-raising activities*: aerobic sub-maximal exercise to increase muscle temperature/elasticity and cardiac output (Q), heart rate (HR) and minute ventilation (VE), in order to redistribute blood from organs to muscles (vascular shunt).

2 *Mobility* – controlled joint movements should rehearse activity movement patterns to help mobilise and lubricate joint structures.

3 *Stretching* – active muscles used in the training exercise should be stretched.

REMEMBER

The benefits of a warm up on skeletal muscle tissue and the cardiovascular system were covered in *OCR AS PE*, pages 34–35 and 88–89.

REMEMBER

Minute ventilation (VE) is the volume of air inspired/expired in one minute.

The benefits of a warm up include the following:

- It prepares the cardio-respiratory and musculo-skeletal systems for more intense exercise.
- It increases:
  - muscle temperature thereby increasing oxygen dissociation, nerve impulse conduction and contraction, thereby improving muscle force, speed and reactions
  - enzyme activity required for cellular respiration

  - release of synovial fluid, lubricating joint structures
  - elasticity of muscle/connective tissues
  - redistribution of blood flow (Q) from organs to muscles (vascular shunt).
- It reduces:
  - risk of injury
  - early onset of anaerobic work, build-up of lactic acid and early fatigue.

Cool down

It is recommended that an active cool down should follow any activity/training as it helps speed up the recovery process to a pre-exercise state. A cool down should consist of two phases:

- pulse lowering activities – moderate/low-intensity aerobic activity
- stretching of active muscles.

REMEMBER

The benefits of a cool down on skeletal muscle tissue and the cardiovascular system were covered in detail in *OCR AS PE*, pages 34–35 and page 89.

The benefits of a cool down include:

- maintains venous return (VR), stoke volume (SV), cardiac output (Q), minute ventilation (VE) and blood pressure
- gradually reduces muscle temperature
- stretching returns muscles to their pre-exercise length
- reduces the risk of injury and DOMS
- flushes capillaries with oxygenated blood
- speeds up removal of lactic acid
- prevents blood pooling.

TASK 10

Plan a warm up and cool down for a training session specific to your practical coursework activity.

Exam Café

Relax, refresh, result!

Refresh your memory

You should now have knowledge and understanding of:

- how to apply the principles of training: moderation, reversibility, specificity, variance, overload and progression
- how to apply knowledge of the principles of training to periodisation
- how to define periodisation and macro, meso and micro cycles
- how to plan a personal health and fitness programme that will promote sustained involvement in a balanced, active and healthy lifestyle; the plan should include the principles of training.

REVISE AS YOU GO!

1. Outline the phrase which will help you recall the principles of training.
2. Apply the principle of moderation in respect of a performer returning to training after three weeks out of competition due to injury.
3. Apply the principle of reversibility in the guidance you would provide an athlete requesting information on how they should plan their training sessions throughout the week.
4. How would knowledge of the principle of variance help maintain a performer's motivation towards continued participation in physical activity?
5. Outline the phrase which will help you recall the principles of overload.
6. What is the link between the principles of overload and progression?
7. Use a practical example to help explain each of the six principles of training.
8. Define periodisation.
9. Outline the three components typical of a periodised training year.
10. Outline three benefits of using periodisation.

Try to answer these questions yourself. Ask your teacher if you need help.

Get the result!

Examination question

Periodisation is a training principle that splits training into specific blocks. Explain how a performer might use periodisation to structure their training programme for one year. (6 marks)

Examiner's tips

- It is important that you identify, from the question leader, that it directs candidates towards specific blocks: the three main cycles of periodisation – macro-, meso- and micro-cycles.
- Similarly, the question leader directs you to a one-year training programme which should be linked to the off-season, pre-season and competition season as another avenue to access marks.
- The command word is 'explain', so it is important that you apply this to all three cycles/seasons of the question.
- This is an open-ended question requiring you to choose a performer of your choice and therefore it is wise to assume the marking scheme may limit the maximum mark available, if no examples are provided.
- Check the number of marks available (6 marks) and work out how many may be awarded for each part of the question. Three blocks/season parts and six marks should point you towards two marks each.
- A quick plan, outlined in the table below, would ensure you cover all parts of this question.

Explain	Macro-training or off-season	Meso-training or pre-season	Micro-training or competition season
1.			
2.			

Student answer

The division of training into a number of specific blocks is done to ensure athletes progress to reach a physiological peak at the correct time for a sporting target or long-term goal. A swimmer may have a long-term full-season goal to qualify for the national finals. This would be their macro-cycle and would

Examiner comment

Excellent opener which clearly defines periodisation.

include building their physical and skill-related fitness to be at their peak for this time.

The mid-term goal may be to reach and qualify for the regional finals to access their long-term goal and termed the meso-cycle. This may be three or four months of training aimed specifically at improving strength/lactate tolerance to help achieve this goal.

The smallest cycle, the micro-cycle, is a short-term goal which could be a number of weeks aimed at improving a specific skill weakness. It could consist of specific drills aimed at improving the efficiency of this skill weakness.

Each training session is termed a unit and it could be that one session a week could be devoted to the skill work above while the remaining units may be aimed at improving physical fitness.

A more simplistic method of periodisation is splitting the training year into pre-season, competition season and off-season, but this is typically used by team game players whose seasons are more or less the same year upon year.

Examiner comment

Immediate application to a specific performer helps ensure explanations are also likely to be more specific.

High-quality explanation and application show good understanding and ensures all marks accessed.

Examiner comment

Good use of applied timescale to help explain.

Examiner comment

Again, good timescale and application of different examples specific to the performer.

Examiner comment

Stretch and challenge answer showing an excellent level of depth of understanding to a specific training session.

Examiner comment

An excellent answer, well thought through and concise with specific and varying examples. This is an exemplary extended essay-style answer which is first-rate preparation and representative of the style required for the 20-mark question.

CHAPTER 18.1:

Health components of physical fitness: Aerobic capacity

LEARNING OBJECTIVES

By the end of this chapter you should have knowledge and understanding of:

- how to define aerobic capacity and explain how a performer's VO_2 max is affected by individual physiological make-up, training, age and sex
- how to describe and apply methods of evaluating aerobic capacity; how to assess your own VO_2 max, comparing your result to the aerobic demands of your chosen activities
- the different types of training used to develop aerobic capacity
- the use of target heart rates as an intensity guide
- the energy system and the food/chemical fuels used during aerobic work
- the physiological adaptations that take place after prolonged periods of aerobic physical activity
- how to plan a programme of aerobic training based on your own assessment of your aerobic capacity and the requirements of your activity.

INTRODUCTION

Chapter 18 is split into four parts looking at the four health components of physical fitness and identifying the health benefits of a sustained balanced, active and healthy lifestyle. The four parts consist of:

- Part 1: Aerobic capacity
- Part 2: Strength
- Part 3: Flexibility
- Part 4: Body composition.

Aerobic capacity

Aerobic capacity is defined as the ability to take in, transport and use oxygen to sustain prolonged periods of aerobic/sub-maximal work. This definition shows that aerobic capacity is dependent upon the efficiency of the systems studied in AS anatomy and physiology, namely:

- pulmonary ventilation and external respiration (take in O_2)
- internal transport via the heart, blood and blood vessels (transport O_2)
- muscle cells to use O_2 for energy production (use O_2).

VO_2 max

Aerobic capacity is closely associated with VO_2 max and the two terms are often used interchangeably, but there is a distinct difference. VO_2 max is defined as the highest rate of oxygen consumption attainable during maximal/exhaustive work.

STRETCH AND CHALLENGE

Compare the definitions of aerobic capacity and VO_2 max.

1. Discuss why an endurance athlete with a lower VO_2 max may well beat another competitor with a higher VO_2 max.
2. What are the main similarities and differences between the two definitions?

An ability to work at a high percentage of VO_2 max (below anaerobic threshold) is thought to be one of the best indicators of aerobic endurance.

Table 1 Typical values for VO_2 max across a variety of activities

Activity/sport	Male VO_2 max average (ml/kg/min)	Female VO_2 max average (ml/kg/min)
Non-athlete	45–54	36–44
Track athletes	60–85	50–75
Swimming	50–70	40–60
Football	42–64	–
Rugby	55–60	–
Volleyball	50–60	40–56
Cycling	62–74	47–57
Rowing	60–72	58–65
Cross-country skiing	65–94	60–75
Gymnastics	52–58	36–50

This is why many aerobic athletes have this ability as a main training objective within their periodised training programme. Table 1 shows typical values for VO_2 max across a variety of activities.

APPLY IT!

The American Tour De France cyclist Lance Armstrong had a VO_2 max of 85 ml/kg/min.

STRETCH AND CHALLENGE

Although a high VO_2 max is typical of aerobic athletes, the ability to work at a high percentage of VO_2 max, hence a higher anaerobic threshold/OBLA, is a better indicator of aerobic performance than is VO_2 max itself. Sedentary individuals' anaerobic threshold is typically about 50/60 per cent of VO_2 max, whereas elite aerobic athletes may work above 85 per cent of VO_2 max.

EXAM TIP

You will find it easier to remember the VO_2 max definition by simply putting the 'max' before the term 'VO_2' to remind you that it is the maximum volume of oxygen and link it to 'consumed during max work'.

Factors affecting VO_2 max

You will be required to name and explain the factors which affect VO_2 max to enable you to plan a training programme aimed at improving aerobic capacity. The following headings list the factors you are required to know.

INDIVIDUAL PHYSIOLOGICAL MAKE-UP

We have already identified that aerobic capacity is dependent upon the efficiency of four body systems, which similarly affect an athlete's VO_2 max – namely:

- respiratory system to consume O_2
- heart to transport O_2
- vascular system to transport O_2
- muscle cells to use O_2.

Although we can primarily link an efficient respiratory system to an increase in VO_2 max, it is the additional contribution of the heart, circulatory system and muscle efficiency that collectively allows an athlete to increase their aerobic capacity. Just as importantly, the higher the VO_2 max, the greater potential the athlete has to work at a higher level of their VO_2 max, just below the anaerobic threshold, thereby increasing their work intensity and delaying fatigue.

HEREDITY/GENETICS

Heredity/genetics can account for as much as half the variation in VO_2 max, for example whether an athlete has a higher percentage of Type I and Type IIa (FOG) oxidative fibres. Similarly, an athlete's individual response to training varies because of genetic variation, and therefore their individual level of adaptation may affect how much their VO_2 max may increase.

However, heredity only indicates an individual's potential to have a high VO_2 max; it is ultimately the aerobic training they undertake that helps them achieve their full potential.

TRAINING

Specificity of training ensures that a programme of aerobic training will increase VO_2 max due to the long-term adaptations to aerobic training, and links directly to an athlete's individual response to training (see Fig 18.1.1). Although an individual's response varies, a maximum level of aerobic conditioning can be reached within approximately 8 to 19 months of heavy endurance-based training. The more specific the aerobic training to the sport performed and the athlete's needs, the greater the potential improvement in that sport.

KEY TERM

Specificity

Specific training elicits specific training adaptations (see page 395).

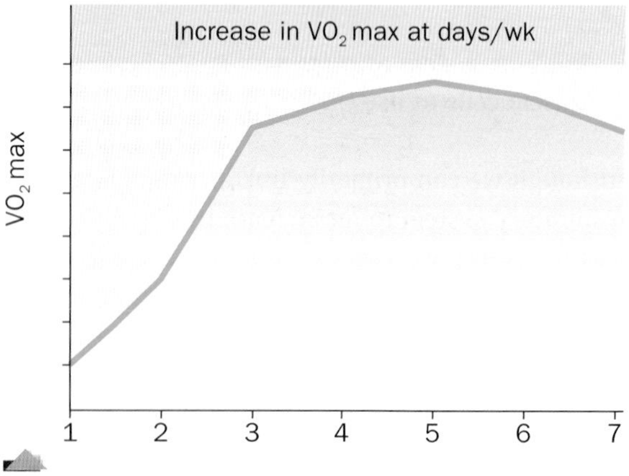

Increase in VO_2 max at days/wk

VO_2 max

1 2 3 4 5 6 7

Fig 18.1.1 VO_2 max response to number of days training per week

APPLY IT!

A sedentary performer may only be able to use 3–4 litres of oxygen per minute (L/min) compared with an elite distance runner who can use up to 6–7 L/min.

EXAM TIP

Ensure you specify 'aerobic training' when naming factors affecting VO_2 max and do not simply refer to 'training'.

TASK 1

Analyse the graph in Fig 18.1.1.

1 What conclusions can you make about the frequency of training and VO_2 max?
2 What principle of training is not met when training 6–7 days a week?
3 What is the likely cause of your conclusions to the previous question?

APPLY IT!

Elite aerobic athletes undertake high levels of training at approximately 85 per cent plus of their VO_2 max, whereas non-athletes work at lower levels of training at approximately 65 per cent VO_2 max.

AGE

The limitation in oxygen transport to the muscles and a decreased **a-VO_2 diff** are the main causes of a reduced VO_2 max. It is thought that VO_2 max decreases approximately 1 per cent per year

Table 2 Changes in VO_2 max among active men (adapted from J. Wilmore and D. Costill, *Physiology of Sport and Exercise*, 2nd edition, 1998)

Age (years)	VO_2 max (ml/kg/min)	Percentage change from 25 years
25	47.7	–
35	43.1	-9.6
45	39.5	-17.2
52	38.4	-19.5
63	34.4	-27.7
75	25.5	-46.5

due to a decrease in the efficiency of the body systems (see Table 2). The age at which VO_2 max starts to decrease will of course vary due to the level of adaptation/training and the individual's response to training, but it is thought to have two main causes:

- *Cardiovascular* – maximum heart rate (HR), cardiac output (Q), stoke volume (SV) and blood circulation to muscle tissues decrease due to a decreased left ventricular contractility/elasticity.
- *Respiratory* – lung volumes, for example max VE (minute ventilation), decrease linearly after maturation, again due to a decrease in elasticity of lung tissues and thoracic cavity walls.

APPLY IT!

Although VO_2 max decreases with age, this is partly due to decreased activity levels. Table 2 may therefore be misleading in that continued aerobic training with elderly performers will maintain/slow down any decline in VO_2 max. High-level aerobic training has an even greater slowing down effect on the rate of VO_2 max decline up to around 50 years of age, but still decreases after this point. This highlights the importance of sustaining involvement in physical activity to prolong and promote a balanced, active and healthy lifestyle late into adulthood.

KEY TERM

a-VO_2 diff

The difference between the percentage of oxygen (O_2) in the blood consumed and the percentage of oxygen exhaled. An increased a-VO_2 diff reflects a greater percentage of oxygen used and therefore a decrease in the percentage of oxygen exhaled, and vice versa.

REMEMBER

Minute ventilation is the volume of air inspired/expired in one minute.

GENDER

VO_2 max values for women are generally 20–25 per cent lower than those for men; the female average equals 60–70 ml/kg/min while for males it is 70–75 ml/kg/min. However, women are disadvantaged by having a greater percentage of body fat, since this decreases VO_2 max when measured per kilogram of body mass. A woman's lower VO_2 max is primarily due to their smaller body size:

- a smaller lung volume decreases external respiration and oxygen intake
- a smaller heart increases resting heart rates, lowering stoke volume (SV) and cardiac output (Q) at maximal rates of work
- lower blood/haemoglobin levels decrease oxygen transport and blood flow.

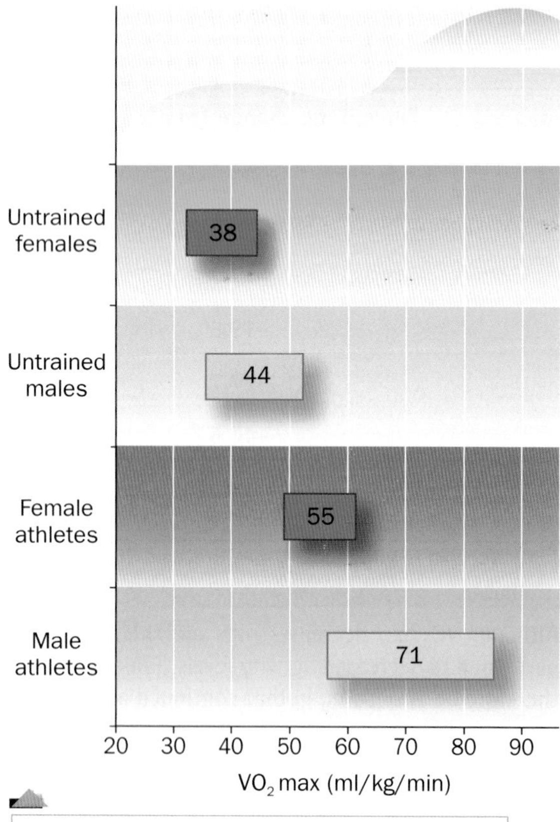

Fig 18.1.2 Variation in VO_2 max with gender and training

Table 2 and Fig 18.1.2 shows the gender differences across different activities and highlights that the difference is much less (10–15 per cent) in highly trained aerobic-type activities.

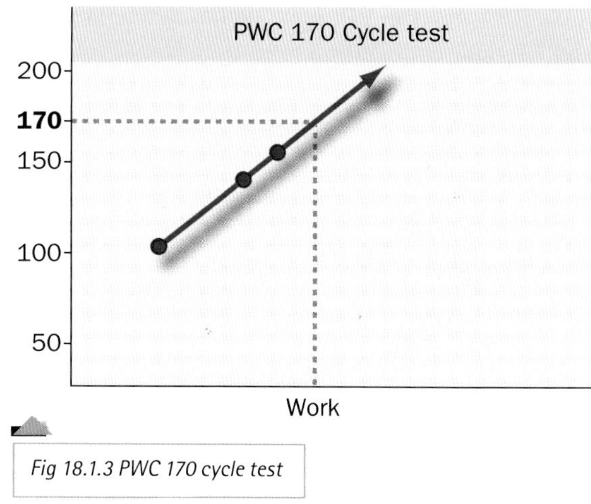

Fig 18.1.3 PWC 170 cycle test

PHYSICAL WORKING CAPACITY TEST (PWC 170)

The PWC 170 test is a sub-maximal test on a cycle ergometer. The performer cycles at three progressive low-to-moderate work intensities (100–115 bpm, 115–130 bpm and 130–145 bpm) and their HR values are recorded. As HR increases linearly with work intensity, a line can be drawn through these points on a graph, which can be extended to predict the intensity level that they would be working at when their HR reaches 170 bpm. This figure is chosen as an approximate anaerobic, close to maximal, level of work based on the assumption that VO_2 max is closely linked to maximal HR (see Fig 18.1.3).

Measurement

Remember that monitoring or testing is an essential tool to ensure that progressive overload and moderation of training are matched to the requirements of the activity and individual capacities of the performer. There are many tests for aerobic capacity/VO_2 max, which vary both in reliability and validity, but in most cases it is their practicality which is the most important factor, allowing the performer to regularly re-test to monitor their progress.

The two tests you are required to know are both 'indirect' tests which estimate/predict a VO_2 max value based on their test results, in contrast to the more accurate direct tests.

MULTI-STAGE FITNESS TEST (MSFT)

The MSFT is a progressive and maximal 20-metre shuttle run test, with the 20-metre distance timed by a bleep which progressively becomes shorter until the athlete cannot keep up or drops out. This provides a level and shuttle number score which is then compared with standardised tables to estimate/predict a VO_2 max value for males and females.

STRETCH AND CHALLENGE

Evaluate the advantages and disadvantages of the MSFT and the PWC 170 tests. Include the suitability of these tests for different levels of performer or the general population in your response.

TASK 2

1 With staff supervision, ensuring that the test protocol and guidelines are strictly followed, complete the MSFT and record your level and shuttle number. (Note: maximal testing is not always appropriate and care should always be taken to screen participants before any fitness testing. A Physical Activity Readiness Questionnaire (PARQ) should be completed by each student before they take part in a fitness test. They should be fully informed of the test protocol and that they can stop the test at any time. Parental permission for students less than 18 years old is advised.)

2 Translate your level/shuttle result into a predicted VO_2 max value using tables provided by your teacher or entering them into Excel spreadsheets available via an Internet search (go to www.heinemann.co.uk/hotlinks, enter the express code 6855P and click on the relevant link to access some relevant sites).

3 Evaluate your VO_2 max value against the capacity score in Fig 18.1.4.

4 Go back to Task 9 in Chapter 17 (page 403) and compare your capacity rating (score) to your initial assessment of the aerobic requirement of your chosen activity.

5 Compare and discuss your results with your peers.

Fig 18.1.4 VO_2 max norms and capacity ratings as a percentage of population

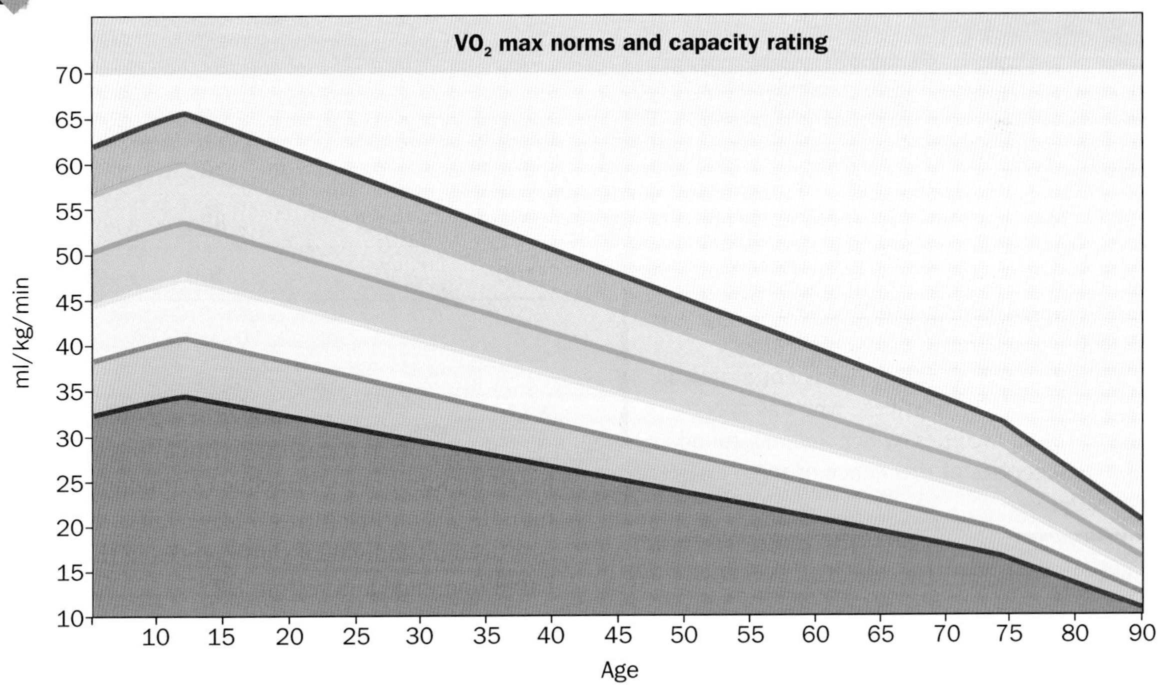

CAPACITY RATING	% OF POPULATION
EXCELLENT	3
VERY GOOD	8
GOOD	22
AVERAGE	34
FAIR	22
POOR	8
VERY POOR	3

Fig 18.1.5 Direct VO_2 max testing

APPLY IT!

The most valid and accurate direct measurement of VO_2 max is made using expensive, highly complex gas analysis equipment (see Fig 18.1.5). This measures and compares the amount of oxygen inspired and expired as work intensity is progressively increased, either on a raised treadmill or cycle ergometer, until a near exhaustion state is reached. This is not practical unless you are an elite athlete who has access to such testing facilities, which are only found at national centres of excellence or sports universities.

Aerobic training

To enable you to plan a programme of training to develop aerobic capacity, you will be required to describe four types of training: continuous running, repetition running, fartlek and interval training. Irrespective of the type of training being used, and having established the importance of progressive overload and the need to monitor training adaptations, it is essential that you measure the intensity of training to ensure the performer is training within the 'training zone'. VO_2 max would be an accurate measure of training intensity, although it is not the most practical measure while training, and for this reason target heart rates are more often used as an intensity guide for training.

The two training zone graphs shown in Chapter 17 (Fig 17.3, page 396) show that HR needs to be within a percentage of maximum HR to cause any adaptations to occur. Furthermore, any given HR percentage can be equated to an approximate VO_2 max percentage (see Table 3).

Table 3 Approximate VO_2 max percentages

Percentage of maximum heart rate (HR)	Percentage of VO_2 max
50	28
60	42
70	56
80	70
90	83
100	100

A simple formula to calculate the appropriate HR percentage, often termed the critical threshold and based on Karvonen's Principle (220 minus age = max HR), is outlined below. Note that it does takes into account individual's differences in that it is based upon age and resting HR.

Critical Threshold = Resting HR + % (max HR – resting HR)

For example, for 60% HR for a 17-year-old with a resting HR of 72:

CT= 72 + (0.60 x 131) 79 = 151 (203 - 72 = 131) = (max HR – resting HR)

The required HR percentage will vary depending upon the specific adaptations sought by the performer, with general health at the lower end and just below the anaerobic threshold at the top end of the critical threshold (training zone). The American College of Sports Medicine (ACSM) suggests an HR percentage above 55 per cent max for at least 20–30 minutes three times a week to encourage less fit, sedentary performers for general health benefits. However, most guidelines suggest an HR percentage above 65 per cent max is required, although the higher the HR percentage the greater the aerobic adaptations will take place in response to training.

TASK 3

1 Calculate your own critical threshold using the equation on page 414.
2 Calculate your own 'healthy lifestyle' 55% HR max.
3 Calculate your individual HRs specific to the general training objectives shown in Table 4.
4 What percentage HR do you think your training should incorporate to cause the specific adaptations for your own practical activity?
5 Compare and discuss your results with your peers.

AEROBIC TRAINING METHODS

Aerobic training involves whole-body activities like running, cycling, rowing and swimming, and is aimed at overloading the cardio-vascular/ respiratory systems to increase aerobic capacity/ VO_2 max.

Overload is achieved by applying the principle of FITT (see also Chapter 17, page 39). We will now apply the FITT principle specifically to aerobic capacity.

- F= Frequency, for example a minimum of 3–5 times a week for a minimum of 12 weeks
- I = Intensity, measured using HR per cent (as identified in Task 3) within the critical threshold/training zone
- T= Time/duration, for example a minimum of 3–5 minutes to 40+ minutes (elite)
- T= Type: overloading the aerobic energy systems

CONTINUOUS TRAINING

Continuous training involves steady state sub-maximal work (running, cycling, swimming, rowing) for prolonged periods (20–30 minutes plus). This type of training is more suited to long distance/endurance athletes, when the oxygen demands of the training are met by the supply from the cardio-vascular systems. The HR should be above the critical threshold (minimum 55 per cent max), but as already highlighted this may increase depending upon the specific training objectives (see

Table 4 Per cent max HR applied to training objectives

Training zones (per cent)	Heart rate (HR)	Training objectives
60		Fat burning /re-energise glycogen stores
70		Develop oxygen transportation systems
80		Improve lactic acid threshold
85		Lactic threshold
90+		Speed

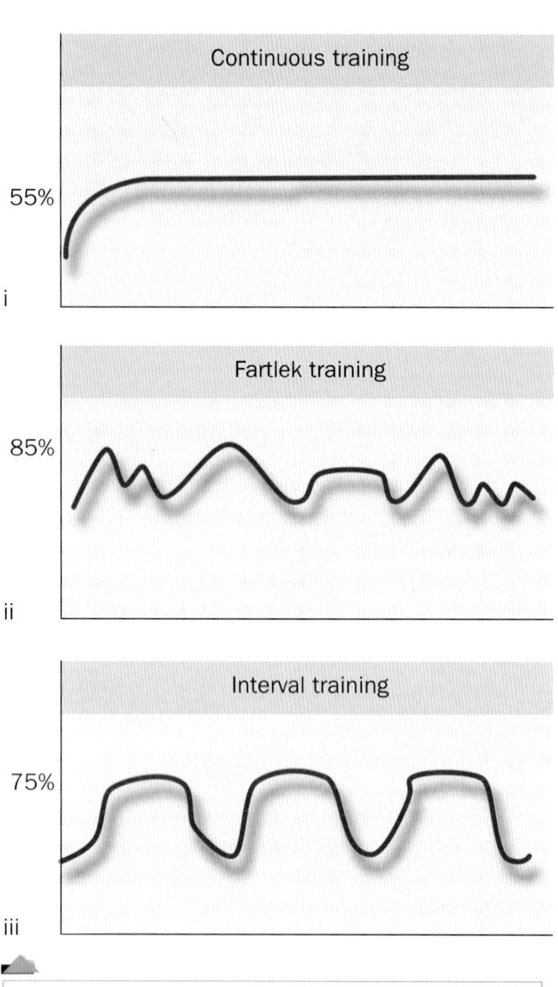

Fig 18.1.6 Heart rate percentage response to aerobic training methods

Fig 18.1.6i). Continuous training is often used as early pre-season training to develop a general level of aerobic endurance before more intense training is introduced.

FARTLEK TRAINING

Fartlek (speed play) training is continuous steady state training interspersed with varied higher intensity work periods and slow recovery periods. It is really a mixture of continuous and interval training that adds variation of higher intensity work, typically being a mixture of sprints, terrain (hills, sand or grass) or any exercises that intersperse the steady state work. The HR will remain above the critical threshold and within the training zone to ensure training adaptations occur and will overload both the aerobic and anaerobic energy systems (see Fig 18.1.6ii).

Fartlek training can be formally or informally organised specifically towards the activity, and for this reason it is ideal for games players whose matches are never exactly the same intensity, to improve their VO_2 max and recovery process. For example, two 45-minute training sessions (halves) with a mix of continuous running interspersed with sprints and skill drills with a 15-minute drinks break (half time) would be specific to football. Individual players may also complete different types, lengths and intensity of sprint/skill work specific to their position; for example, midfield players could have shorter but more frequent sprints with less recovery while forwards could have longer, less frequent sprints with longer recovery.

TASK 4

1 Design a fartlek session for your main practical activity, ensuring it reflects the principle of specificity.
2 Complete this session and monitor your HR during what you feel are low, moderate and high intensity periods. Evaluate whether your HR is above your critical threshold and which training objectives your HR reflects within your training zone from the table you completed in Task 3.

INTERVAL TRAINING (REPETITION RUNNING)

Interval training consists of periods of work interspersed with periods or recovery (relief) and can be easily modified for specific training needs by adjusting any of the four components that an interval session contains.

1 *Interval duration* – or distance (for example, 3–4 minutes or 1000 metres).
2 *Interval intensity* – HR per cent/hill work, etc.
3 *Recovery/relief duration* – increase or decrease in recovery time and whether it is active or passive.
4 *Number of work–relief intervals* – for example, 2 x 2000m and 800m recovery or 4 x 1000m and 400m recovery.

Interval training sessions are often described using a ratio to express the 'work-relief'; for example, a typical aerobic ratio of 2 : 1 would describe the work interval as being double the recovery; a ratio of 1 : 1 describes the work interval being the same as the relief.

- The work ratio for aerobic training is typically higher and lower for the relief, with a lower number of work-relief intervals. Recall that the principal aim is to increase aerobic capacity – the ability to sustain prolonged periods of aerobic/sub-maximal work – and therefore full recovery is not required (see Fig 18.1.6iii).
- In contrast, for anaerobic interval training the work ratio is typically lower and the relief higher to allow a fuller recovery (1 : 3+), and therefore there is an increase in the number of work–relief intervals.

The main advantage of interval training is that it improves the quality/intensity of training by allowing the performer to recover so that each work interval is higher intensity than if they performed continuous training.

It is important to consider progressive overload when using interval training and not adjust too many of the four training parameters at the same time, for example increasing intensity at the same time as decreasing the recovery. Table 5 summarises the interval training guidelines for both aerobic and anaerobic athletes.

Repetition running is interval training under another name but is more suited to distance runners who have very formalised training programmes. A 5000m runner may, for example, split the event into five 1000-metre aerobic work intervals with a shorter relief period, to allow the performer to increase their intensity of running speed, which would falter without any relief. Over a period of time they would aim to reduce their recovery/relief until a point when they can run the whole 5000m without any relief.

TASK 5

1 Plan an interval training session aimed at improving your aerobic capacity for your own activity. Ensure you use all four components of an interval training session.
2 If you are an anaerobic performer, plan an interval session aimed to improve general health as part of a healthy lifestyle (which, interestingly, all anaerobic athletes should be undertaking to improve their recovery process as well as good health).
3 Imagine you have completed this session once a week, along with other aerobic training, for a period of 4 weeks and that your body has adapted to this overload. Identify how you would add progressive overload using each of the four components of your interval session if you were planning the session for week 5 (even though you would only be likely to change one or two of these components at once).

Table 5 Summary of interval training guidelines for aerobic and anaerobic athletes

Interval training	Aerobic athlete	Anaerobic athlete
Interval duration	3–5+ minutes (longer)	0–90 seconds (shorter)
Interval intensity	Low/moderate = 50–75% VO_2/hr max	High/sprint = 70–95% VO_2/hr max
Interval relief	1 : 1 / 1.1 : 2 – active jog/walk/run	1–90 seconds / 1 : 2±1 : 2
Ratio of work–relief	1 set of 3–5 repetitions	2–6 sets of 1–10 repetitions
Frequency	3–5 sessions weekly	3–6 sessions weekly
Specificity	Aerobic energy system	ATP/PC/LA energy system

Energy system and food fuels during aerobic work

Although ATP (adenosine triphosphate) and PC (phospho-creatine) are the immediate fuels for any aerobic exercise, we will be looking specifically at those that provide energy to resynthesise ATP during aerobic work. Irrespective of the type of aerobic training used, the energy to resynthesise ATP during aerobic work is supplied from the aerobic system. This will involve all three stages of the aerobic system as described on pages 372–376 of Chapter 16, namely:

- aerobic glycolysis
- Kreb's cycle
- electron transport chain (ETC).

Aerobic work is fuelled from glycogen/glucose and free fatty acids (FFAs), but this varies depending upon the duration and intensity of the aerobic training and the availability of glycogen and FFAs. A summary of the fuels used during aerobic work is listed below; this is outlined in more detail in Chapter 16, page 380.

- Glygogen/glucose is the major fuel for the first 20–40 minutes of exercise.
- During mild to more severe muscular effort, the body relies mostly on glycogen/glucose for fuel.
- After about 20–45 minutes there is greater breakdown of fats alongside glycogen as the energy fuel.
- As the duration of exercise increases, after about 20–45 minutes glycogen stores start to deplete and there is a greater mix of glycogen and fats to fuel aerobic work.
- Fat provides substantial energy during prolonged, low-intensity activity, for example fell walking.
- When glycogen stores become almost fully depleted after about two hours, FFAs have to be used for aerobic energy production.
- If exercise intensity is too high then the onset of blood lactate accumulation (OBLA) is reached and glycogen has to be broken down 'anaerobically' to continue resynthesising ATP.

TASK 6

The popular activity of aerobics/step has long being used predominantly by women to help reduce weight loss (fat). Let's look at this activity in more detail and apply our knowledge of food fuels to evaluate its effectiveness in decreasing body weight.

A typical aerobics/step class consists of a 5–10-minute warm-up, 30–40 minutes of cardio-vascular work followed by 10–15 minutes of body weight exercises and a 5-minute cool down.

1. Analyse when and which major food fuels are being used to provide energy to resynthesise ATP during the aerobics/step class.
2. Does this activity help towards weight loss?
3. What might you change in relation to this training session to rectify any of your conclusions to Question 2?
4. What other benefits are gained by this type of aerobic training?

AEROBIC ADAPTATIONS

We have already identified that aerobic training will overload the aerobic systems and increase their efficiency to take in, transport and use oxygen for prolonged periods of aerobic sum-maximal activity. However, you are required to explain in more detail the specific physiological adaptations that take place in respect of the four anatomy and physiology areas you studied in your AS course. The specific adaptations to the four systems of the body in response to aerobic training are summarised in Table 6. Table 6 highlights that it is the adaptation of the cardio-vascular/respiratory systems along with muscle/metabolism adaptations which collectively improve both the health benefits for an active lifestyle and improved aerobic performance.

Table 6 Summary of adaptations to aerobic training

Adaptations	Resultant increase/decrease	Net effect
RESPIRATORY SYSTEM		
Respiratory muscles become stronger	Increase in: • efficiency of mechanics of breathing • maximum exercise lung volumes (f x TV = VE) • maximal breathing rate • respiratory fatigue resistance • maximum VE due to increased f x TV. Decrease in: • sub-max breathing rate.	Increased VO_2 max
Increase in alveoli surface area	Increase in: • external respiration/diffusion • a-VO_2 diff (less O_2 exhaled = more used).	
CARDIO-VASCULAR SYSTEM: HEART		
Hypertrophy (increase in myocardium size/ thickness/volume)	Increase in: • volume EDV (filling capacity) • ventricular stretch and recoil • force of ventricular contraction (emptying) • stroke volume (SV) • HR recovery after exercise. Decrease in: • ESV (volume after contraction) • Resting and sub-maximal HR (<60 = bradycardia).	• Increased blood flow • Increased maximal cardiac output (Q) • Increased O_2 transport
VASCULAR SYSTEM		
Increased elasticity of arterial walls to vasodilate/constrict	Increase in: • vascular shunt efficiency, to redistribute Q from organs to active muscles • BP regulation • exercise systole BP leading to improved blood/ O_2 supply. Decrease in: • resting systole/diastole BP.	• Increased circulatory efficiency • Improved O_2/CO_2 transport
Increased number of red blood cells/ haemoglobin volume Increased plasma volume	Increase in: • gaseous exchange/O_2 transport • venous return (VR) • stroke volume (SV) and cardiac output (Q). Decrease in: • viscosity during exercise, despite increased water loss (to sweat).	
Increased capillarisation (density) of alveoli and Type I muscle fibre tissues	Increase in: • surface area • a-VO_2 diff • time for diffusion • removal of CO_2/lactic acid during OBLA. Decrease in: • distance of diffusion • velocity of increased blood flow.	

Table 6 (Contd.)

Adaptations	Resultant increase/decrease	Net effect
MUSCULAR SYSTEM		
Increased Type I and IIa hypertrophy/ efficiency (due to increase in size/strength)	Increase in: • strength and reducing fatigue • skill efficiency. Decrease in: • energy costs.	Increased maximal capacity of muscle fibres to generate ATP aerobically
Increased muscle capillarisation	Increase in O_2/CO_2 transport/diffusion of exercise.	
Increased Type IIa fibre ability to work aerobically	Increase in: • fibre type percentage working aerobically • ability to use fuel and O_2. Decrease in: • OBLA.	
Increased myoglobin stores	Increase in O_2 storage and transport to mitochondria.	
Increased aerobic enzymes	Improved: • reliance on metabolism of fat instead of glycogen • aerobic metabolism of glycogen.	
Increased speed/ ability to use fats earlier	• Conserves glycogen stores • Increases amount of ATP from fats	
Increased number of mitochondria	Improved utilisation of O_2/fat for aerobic metabolism	
Increased muscle glycogen/fat stores	Increase in energy fuels to resynthesise ATP	
CONNECTIVE TISSUE		
Increased strength of muscle tendons	–	• Increased strength of musculo-skeletal lever system to endure prolonged activity • Less risk of injury • Reduced rate of ageing
Greater thickness/ strength of ligaments	–	
Increased thickness/ compression of cartilage	–	
Increased calcium content/ strength of bones	–	
Reduced body fat composition	Decrease in dead weight leading to an increase in efficiency (Power to weight ratio)	

Table 6 (Contd.)

Adaptations	Resultant increase/decrease	Net effect
HEALTH LIFESTYLE AREAS		
Combined effects	• Increase in the lactate threshold • Delay of OBLA	
Overall net effect: Increase in VO_2 max	Increase in: • intensity of aerobic performance • duration of aerobic performance • skill/work efficiency.	
Aerobic metabolism	Increase in: • muscles' ability to use fuels/O_2 • ability of body to mobilise/supply fuels and O_2 to working muscles. Dependent upon individual fitness at start, but 20–30% improvement possible with sedentary inactive.	• Increase in maximum rate of aerobic work/ endurance. • Decrease in lactate production.

EXAM TIP

It may be useful to review your AS anatomy and physiology notes to help refresh your knowledge and understanding of how these structures adapt in response to aerobic training.

REMEMBER

- EDV stands for 'end-diastolic volume' – before contraction, this refers to the volume of blood in the ventricle at the end of the relaxation/filling phase.
- ESV stands for 'end-systolic volume' – after contraction, this refers to the volume of blood remaining in the ventricles at the end of the contraction phase.

See also *OCR AS PE*, page 66.

Aerobic summary

All athletes and non-athletes can benefit by improving their aerobic endurance. For sedentary individuals, cardio-vascular endurance should be the primary focus of training for health and fitness. Although relatively small aerobic adaptations may occur, sedentary individuals performing regular activity may gain a marked improvement in endurance which will help them sustain a healthy and active lifestyle. A sedentary training programme should be energetic but realistic, permitting individuals to sustain activity for about 20–30 minutes to allow sufficient training effects. However, for some individuals 20–30 minutes may not be attainable. It is important to understand that even minimum training effects are seen if activity elevates heart rate to 130–140 bpm for 10 minutes on three days a week to achieve a training effect. In contrast, athletes will use the FITT principle to ensure their aerobic training lies higher within the training zone to increase the level of aerobic adaptations, so that their aerobic capacity matches the specific requirements of their activity.

APPLY IT!

Increasing the aerobic capacity of golfers will help them decrease fatigue which in turn allows them to maintain their concentration for longer.

TASK 7

Evaluating and planning for the improvement of performance.

1 Plan a programme of aerobic training for a sedentary performer to increase their ability to sustain an active and healthy lifestyle.
2 Rehearse your training plan and orally describe/explain it in detail to a peer who will provide feedback.

Exam Café

Relax, refresh, result!

Refresh your memory

You should now have knowledge and understanding of:

- how to define aerobic capacity and explain how a performer's VO_2 max is affected by individual physiological make-up, training, age and sex
- how to describe and apply methods of evaluating aerobic capacity; how to assess your own VO_2 max, comparing your result to the aerobic demands of your chosen activities
- the different types of training used to develop aerobic capacity
- the use of target heart rates as an intensity guide
- the energy system and the food/chemical fuels used during aerobic work
- the physiological adaptations that take place after prolonged periods of aerobic physical activity
- how to plan a programme of aerobic training based on your own assessment of your aerobic capacity and the requirements of your activity.

REVISE AS YOU GO!

1. Define aerobic capacity and VO_2 max.
2. What are typical values for VO_2 max for a healthy 18–20-year-old?
3. Describe the PWC 170 test.
4. List the factors that could limit VO_2 max.
5. What is the training zone and what alternative terms are used to describe it?
6. How can an athlete measure if they are working within their training zone?
7. List the training methods that can increase VO_2 max.
8. Describe briefly interval training as a method of improving VO_2 max.
9. Outline the vascular adaptations that occur after an extended period of aerobic training.
10. What training guidelines would you suggest for a sedentary person who is motivated to improve and achieve a healthier lifestyle?

Try to answer these questions yourself. Ask your teacher if you need help.

Get the result!

Examination question

Making reference to the physiological adaptations that occur in the cardiovascular and respiratory systems, explain why a trained performer can work at a higher intensity before reaching their VO_2 max. (6 marks)

Examiner's tips

- It is important to clarify that there are three topic areas which need addressing for this question; cardio (heart), vascular and respiratory systems.
- Similarly, it is important to identify that 'VO_2 max' is directing you to aerobic capacity physical adaptations and not anaerobic or neural adaptations.
- The main command word 'explain why' is easily identifiable, but its link to the adaptation of the three topic areas is essentially the link you should have made.
- Check the number of marks available (6 marks) and work out how many may be awarded for each part of the question. Three topic areas and six marks should point you towards two marks for each topic area, but don't forget that each area has to include an adaptation and an explanation to cover all parts of the question.
- Linked questions like this one often restrict the mark scheme if both parts are not visited, for example adaptations are described but without an explanation of how this increases work intensity prior to VO_2 max.
- A quick plan like the one below would ensure you visit all parts of this question.

Area	Adaptation	Explanation of increase in work intensity
Heart		
Vascular		
Respiratory		

Student answer

The physiological adaptations that increase VO_2 max occur in response to an extended period of aerobic training.

Examiner comment

Good introduction focusing on the main context of the question.

The cardiovascular system consists of the heart and vascular system, blood vessels and blood. The heart myocardium

Examiner comment

Clear distinction of the two cardiovascular systems ensuring both topic areas are visited.

increases in size, termed hypertrophy, and is able to contract with more force increasing both stroke volume and cardiac output. *Bradycardia*, a resting HR below 60, is a second adaptation of the heart which due to the increased SV does not have to beat as often for the same cardiac output and similarly this allows a greater maximum potential cardiac output and hence potential work intensity.

Examiner comment

Good use of specialist scientific vocabulary and each adaptation immediately linked to an explanation of how this increases work intensity.

Examiner comment

Good reference back to the question ensures you are still on task and not drifting from the focus of the question.

Vascular adaptations primarily consist of an increase in capillarisation of the heart, skeletal muscles and respiratory structures (alveoli) which increases the gaseous exchange of O_2 and CO_2 in the muscles and alveoli of the lungs. Additional blood volume increases the red blood cells and therefore blood haemoglobin levels, increasing the transportation of O_2 to the working muscles, again increasing the intensity of work achievable.

Examiner comment

Again, good use of scientific language.

Examiner comment

Again, reference back to the question with the adaptation immediately linked to an explanation of how this increases work intensity.

Respiratory adaptations primarily consist of increased alveoli cross surface area, which along with the increased alveloli capillarisation increases gaseous exchange in the lungs at the end of external respiration. The respiratory muscles themselves become stronger and more efficient, which both delays respiratory fatigue and increases the pulmonary ventilation volumes, thereby increasing the amount of air/O_2 inhaled and available for gaseous exchange.

Examiner comment

Again, concise use of scientific language with reference back to the question with the adaptation immediately linked to an explanation of how this increases work intensity.

The net effect of all these adaptations is an increase in the ability to take in and transport O_2 to the working muscles, which allows them to work at a higher intensity before reaching their VO_2 max.

Examiner comment

Good summary linking back to the question focus.

Examiner comment

This was an excellent answer showing a high level of understanding along with excellent scientific language. The answer was concise and directly answered the question linking the adaptations immediately to an explanation of how they increased work intensity/VO_2 max. If you can visualise the likely marking scheme it makes great sense to mirror this with your answer, this eases and simplifies the marking process for your examiner.

CHAPTER 18.2:

Health components of physical fitness: Strength

LEARNING OBJECTIVES

By the end of this chapter you should have knowledge and understanding of:

- how to define types of strength
- factors that affect strength
- how to describe and apply methods of evaluating each type of strength
- how to describe and evaluate different types of training used to develop strength – use of multi-gym, weights, plyometrics and circuit/interval training
- the energy system and the food/chemical fuels used during each type of strength training
- the physiological adaptations that take place after prolonged periods of physical activity
- how to plan a programme of strength training based on the assessment of an individual's strength and the strength requirements of a chosen activity.

Types of strength

Strength is a generic term that describes the application of a force against a resistance. However, when applying the principle of specificity to plan a training programme, you need to consider the different types of strength that are important for sustaining and improving participation in physical activity and maintaining a healthy lifestyle. The five different types of strength and the respective methods of evaluating them, which you are required to know, are outlined below.

MAXIMUM STRENGTH

Maximum strength is the maximum force the neuromuscular system can exert in a single voluntary muscle contraction. When applied, it represents the maximal weight an individual can lift just once – 1 RM (repetition maximum).

KEY TERM

Maximum strength

The maximum force the neuromuscular system can exert in a single voluntary muscle contraction.

1 RM

The maximal weight an individual can lift just once.

TASK 1

1. Under staff supervision and with safe and effective technique, establish your 1 RM for a given exercise (decided by a member of staff). Ensure you have a minimum of two minutes' recovery before attempting any subsequent lift at a heavier weight.
2. Describe the movement of your final 1 RM in terms of speed and Borg's 10-point scale of rate of perceived exertion (RPE).

REMEMBER

Borg's scale, a rating of perceived exertion (RPE), is a simple method of calculating an athlete's training overload/intensity. It uses either a 10 or 15 rating scale and is easily available from an Internet search.

Few sports actually depend solely on maximum strength. Although weightlifters are normally associated with having high levels of maximum strength, their actual events require them to apply force explosively. A 1 RM is normally at a resistance so strong that it is lifted very slowly at some point in the lift, as the muscular force applied is more/less efficient at different joint angles during a lift. Some of the events in the world's strongest man competition more closely reflect a true 1 RM than traditional sporting activities. For a more sedentary individual aiming for a healthy lifestyle, maximal strength training may carry more health risks than any benefits gained.

LEG DYNAMOMETER

1 Subject should stand with both feet on base.
2 Adjust chain to accommodate test protocol. Perform the test. Subject should lift in a gradual vertical motion.
3 The pointer on the dial indicates the force exerted. Each test should consist of three trial measurements. The result is the average.

Fig 18.2.1 Leg dynamometer

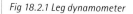

MEASURING MAXIMUM STRENGTH

We have already established that the measurement for maximal strength is the 1 RM. Similar to static strength (see page 427), it is specific to different parts/joints and muscles. Consequently the leg press and bench press exercises would represent maximum strength tests for the lower limbs and upper body (shoulders) respectively. The most widely used tests are the hand/grip and leg dynamometer tests, as there is a high correlation between handgrip/leg strength and overall body strength.

GRIP DYNAMOMETER

Dial is set to zero and performer holds grip with straight arm above their head. As they bring the arm down to their side they apply maximal grip strength, which is recorded on the dial for the best of three attempts.

Fig 18.2.2 Grip dynamometer

Table 1: Normative tables for maximum leg and grip strength

Leg	Poor	Fair	Average	Good	Excellent
Male	<137	137–159	160–213	214–240	>241
Female	<49	49–65	66–113	114–135	>136
Grip	**Poor**	**Fair**	**Average**	**Good**	**Excellent**
Male	<39	<39–44	45–50	51–55	>56+
Female	<19	19–24	25–30	31–35	>36+

STATIC STRENGTH

Static strength is the force exerted by the neuromuscular system while the muscle length remains constant/static; for example, holding a weight steady in the same position. This type of strength is the same as that which in AS level we termed an isometric muscle contraction, when a force is applied but there is no change in the muscle length.

KEY TERM

Static strength

The force exerted by the neuromuscular system while the muscle length remains constant.

TASK 2

Ensure the elbows are kept still by the side during the bicep curl exercise.

1 Lift and hold still a moderate/heavy weight during a bicep curl at an angle of 55 degrees. Time how long this can be held for.
2 Repeat 1 above but hold the same weight at 90 degrees.
3 Repeat 1 and 2 but keep increasing the weight until you reach the maximum weight you can hold at each of the joint angles.
4 Which was the most efficient joint angle for applying force?
5 Compare and discuss your results.

MEASURING STATIC STRENGTH

Task 2 shows that there is no single or generic test for static strength since strength varies and is specific to any given joint angle. Similarly, Task 2 highlights that maximum static strength is measured at specific joint angles that approximate the most favourable angle for a given muscle group. For example, free weight arm curl strength

Fig 18.2.3 Strength relative to joint angles

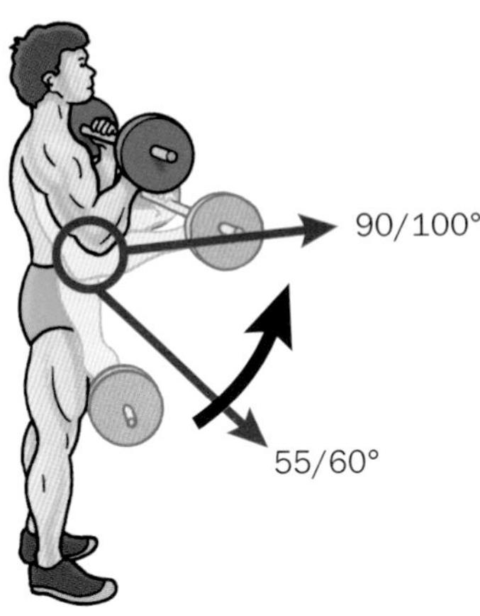

is greatest at around 90–100 degrees and weakest at around 55–60 degrees (see Fig 18.2.3). Athletes therefore need to assess when and at what angles their activity requires them to exert a static force or isometric contraction, and include specific strength training exercises for the appropriate muscles acting around that joint(s).

APPLY IT!

A gymnast on the rings holding a crucifix position (anaerobic static strength) or a pistol shooter holding their arm up (aerobic static strength) are good examples of different intensities of static strength. Thus a gymnast would need strength training that involved them holding their body weight out in the crucifix position.

EXPLOSIVE/ELASTIC STRENGTH

Explosive/elastic strength is the ability to expand a maximal amount of energy in one or a series of strong, sudden high-intensity movements or apply a successive and equal force rapidly. Elastic strength is very similar to

KEY TERM

Explosive/elastic strength

The ability to expand a maximal amount of energy in one or a series of strong, sudden high-intensity movements or apply a successive and equal force rapidly.

power but it predominantly uses the ATP/PC system. This is because although it is anaerobic, it represents movements of a higher intensity but of shorter duration than dynamic strength, which predominantly uses the LA system.

Explosive strength takes advantage of the stretch reflex in that eccentrically lengthening a muscle prior to it concentrically contracting (shortening) takes advantage of the recoil effect from the elastic properties of muscle, which adds force to the concentric muscle contraction.

APPLY IT!

The triple jump is an excellent example of a sequential series of high intensity movements that reflects explosive strength similar to those in most throwing, sprinting and jumping activities.

MEASURING EXPLOSIVE/ELASTIC STRENGTH

There are various explosive strength tests, mostly associated with the lower body. The vertical jump test or broad jump is the most widely used explosive strength test (see Task 3).

Fig 18.2.4 Vertical jump test

TASK 3

Complete the vertical jump test. If you do not have access to a vertical jump board, follow the instructions below.

Chalk the end of your fingertips and stand facing a wall with your arms above your head and fingertips stretched upwards and feet against the wall. Mark the position of your highest fingertip on the wall. Standing side onto the wall and from a static position, you can bend and swing your arms (M1), jump as high as you can and mark the wall above your original standing height (M2). Measure the difference between your initial and highest jump height in cm.

1 Compare your results with the rest of your group and against the norm table provided (Table 2) to rate your vertical jump height.
2 What factors may affect any differences in results across your group?

DYNAMIC STRENGTH

Dynamic strength is the ability of the neuromuscular system to overcome a resistance with a high speed of contraction. It is more often referred to as 'anaerobic capacity' and in this respect predominantly uses the lactic acid system of energy production. Dynamic strength is the functional application of strength (force x distance) and speed (divided by time) which represents 'power' as covered in Chapter 16 (see page 367).

Table 2: Vertical jump test – national norms for 16–19-year-olds (www.brianmac.demon.co.uk/eval.htm)

Gender	Excellent	Above average	Average	Below average	Poor
Male	>65cm	50–65 cm	40–49 cm	30–39 cm	<30cm
Female	>58cm	47–58 cm	36–46 cm	26–35 cm	<26cm

KEY TERM

Dynamic strength

The ability of the neuromuscular system to overcome a resistance with a high speed of contraction.

REMEMBER

In Chapter 16 you found that if two individuals can lift the same weight, but one can lift it faster, that person is generating more power.

APPLY IT!

Power is a key component of throwing, sprinting and jumping, which are used in all the major invasion/team games and racquet, aquatic and athletic events.

MEASURING DYNAMIC STRENGTH

The most accepted test for dynamic strength is the Wingate Cycle Test, performed while seated on a cycle ergometer. After a warm-up period (HR 150 bpm), the athlete pedals as fast as possible without any resistance and within 3 seconds a fixed resistance, calculated according to body weight, is applied to the flywheel. The athlete then pedals 'all out' for 30 seconds. The flywheel revolutions are recorded in 5-second intervals to produce a graph of power against time, which can be compared against norms for specific activities or used to measure improvements to training. The highest power output, observed during the first 5 seconds of the test, represents the 'peak anaerobic power' output and reflects the capacity of the immediate ATP/PC energy system. The lowest power in the last 5 seconds is compared to peak power to provide the rate of decline/fatigue. This represents the anaerobic capacity, the combined ability of both the ATP/PC and lactic acid system to produce energy, and this is shown as the average power output during the whole test.

This test is obviously advantageous and specific to cycling and not running events, although there are comparable running-type tests (RAST). You could also use the vertical jump test as a test of leg power, although it is more reflective of elastic than dynamic strength.

STRETCH AND CHALLENGE

1 Visit the closest university with exercise science facilities that can provide a full Wingate Cycle Test at a reduced fee. This will provide you with a print out of your results which will clearly show your initial peak anaerobic power curve, representing your ATP/PC system, and followed by a lower but steadily declining power curve that reflects your lactic acid system.
2 Research the Running-based Anaerobic Sprint Test (RAST) developed at the University of Wolverhampton to test an athlete's anaerobic capacity. (To access some useful sources, go to www.heinemann.co.uk/hotlinks, enter the express code 6855P and click on the relevant links.)
3 What are the advantages of the RAST test over the Wingate Cycle Test?

STRENGTH ENDURANCE

Strength endurance is the ability of a muscle to sustain or withstand repeated muscle contractions or a single static action. This highlights the close association of strength endurance with aerobic capacity, in that strength endurance is the ability of the muscles to 'use' the oxygen taken in and transported to the muscle cells. It is also important to differentiate between whole-body endurance and local muscular endurance; the

KEY TERM

Strength endurance

The ability of a muscle to sustain or withstand repeated muscle contractions or a single static action.

latter is a specific area/muscle group that can sustain repeated muscle contractions. Strength endurance is essential in prolonged sub-maximal-type exercise that requires a high percentage of slow twitch oxidative fibres and which is dependent upon the aerobic energy system.

MEASURING STRENGTH ENDURANCE

There are localised tests for differing muscle groups of the body, but all are evaluated by the number of repetitions performed at a given percentage of your 1 RM. The push-up test would be a suitable test of arm and shoulder endurance.

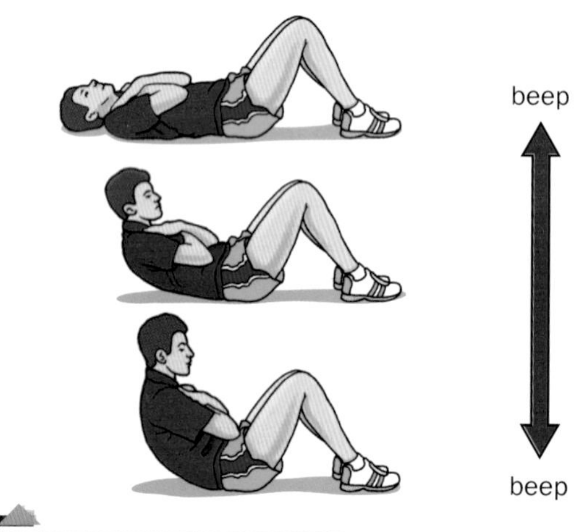

Fig 18.2.5 Abdominal sit-up test

However, the most widely used test is the former NCF abdominal sit-up test, where the performer, with arms crossed and held against the chest, sits up and down in time to a series of bleeps. The bleeps progressively get faster and faster until the performer drops out and the stage/number is compared against a normative table for males and females to achieve a rating.

TASK 4

1 Complete the NCF abdominal sit-up test and compare your results with the normative values (Table 3).
2 Did you find that any other muscles other than the abdominals were worked or brought on DOMS after the test?
3 What does this imply about the test in that it is named the abdominal sit-up test?

APPLY IT!

A canoeist would have specific local strength endurance in their arms/upper body compared to their legs.

Table 3 Normative values for the NCF abdominal sit-up test (Source: Brian Mac)

Stage	Number of sit-ups (Cumulative)	Standard male	Standard female
1	20	Poor	Poor
2	42	Poor	Fair
3	64	Fair	Fair
4	89	Fair	Good
5	116	Good	Good
6	146	Good	Very Good
7	180	Excellent	Excellent
8	217	Excellent	Excellent

SUMMARY

Although five types of strength are covered in the specification, you can see that three types of strength are most widely applied to physical activity and a healthy lifestyle. Elastic and dynamic strength represent anaerobic strength whereas strength endurance represents aerobic strength. Although maximum and static strength are important in specific activities/movements, maximum strength directly correlates with good elastic/dynamic strength, and similarly static strength is important for specific movements in activities like the rings in gymnastics.

Factors affecting strength

You will have already compared and started to question why there were differences in results across your group/peers when you completed the tests for the different types of strength. You will need to show that you understand the factors that affect strength, which are summarised below.

1 *Muscle composition:*
The greater the:
a) percentage of fast twitch muscle fibres
b) cross-sectional area of muscle
c) muscle size,
the greater the potential force that can be generated or applied.

2 *Gender:*
There is little gender difference in strength between males and females, except that female strength is generally lower than males because:
- females generally have less muscle mass, cross-sectional area and muscle size
- they have less testosterone than males.

3 *Age:*
- Female peak strength is reached between the age of 16 and 25 years; for males it occurs around 18–30 years.
- Greatest gains are made between the age of 20 and 30 years for both males and females, when testosterone levels peak.
- Strength generally decreases with increasing age due to a decrease in testosterone leading to less muscle mass and a less efficient neuro-muscular system.

4 *Physical inactivity:*
Atrophy (decrease in muscle size) starts after approximately 48 hours of inactivity and induces the loss of muscle strength already gained from training (reversibility).

5 *Strength training:*
Appropriate/specific strength training increases strength/hypertrophy while preventing atrophy.

6 *The weakest point in the range of motion:*
This is specific to the relative angle of a given joint.

APPLY IT!

Well-trained distance runners may have 80 per cent slow twitch fibres in their leg muscles, whereas by contrast sprinters may have up to 75 per cent fast twitch fibres. Middle distance runners and typical team game players often have a more equal distribution of fibre types.

REMEMBER

Refer to *OCR AS PE*, pages 32–34, for a full description of muscle fibre types.

TASK 5

1 Measure the circumference of the muscles used in Task 1.
2 Compare the circumference with the results of the 1 RM in Task 1.
3 Analyse the results from the class and give reasons for individual differences.

Strength training methods

The strength training methods you are required to describe and evaluate to develop strength are:

- the multi-gym
- free weights
- circuit and interval training
- plyometrics.

All these strength training methods achieve the same aim in that they all require the performer to apply a force against a resistance, which creates the overload to initiate the performance/ health adaptations.

STRENGTH TRAINING TERMINOLOGY

Strength training uses specific terminology, primarily repetition, sets and resistance, which you will be expected to understand and apply when providing guidelines to improve strength.

- Repetitions are the number of times an exercise is repeated, for example 10 repetitions.
- The specified number of repetitions along with a rest period then forms an individual set; for example, a performer lifting a weight ten times equates to ten repetitions which once completed forms a single set.
- The weight lifted is termed the resistance. A strength training programme is normally expressed as sets multiplied by repetitions at a given resistance (normally in kilograms); for example, 3 x 10 x 50 kg equals three sets of ten repetitions of a 50-kg weight.
- You also need to understand and apply the term repetition max (RM); remember that 1 RM represents the maximum resistance you can lift just once and therefore a 10 RM represents the maximum resistance you can lift just 10 times.

GENERIC STRENGTH TRAINING GUIDELINES

General strength training guidelines are easier to understand by placing the different types of strength across a continuum linked to general guidelines for repetitions and resistance along with other guidelines which are summarised below.

- Resistance/load needs to be at least 50 per cent of the maximum capacity for a given muscle/ group, while evidence suggests that loads in excess of 80 per cent increase the risk of muscle damage.
- Fig 18.2.6 shows that maximum strength training generally uses low repetitions and higher resistance, whereas endurance strength uses high repetitions and low resistance.
- Similarly, Fig 18.2.7 shows that in relation to the development of power the resistance is moderate, thus allowing higher repetitions so that a higher speed of movement can be achieved.
- Moderation: general strength conditioning needs to be established before focusing on specific muscle groups to prevent overtraining.
- Exercise large muscle groups before smaller muscle groups – this prevents the smaller muscles from being fatigued before they act as stabilisers to support larger muscle groups. For example, the small wrist muscles stabilise the wrist when lifting a standing bicep curl bar.
- Use periodisation of training to prevent overtraining by varying the volume and intensity of training.
- Allow appropriate recovery between individual exercises and exercise sessions.
- Specificity: training with slow joint movements will increase strength only at slow speeds, whereas faster movements will increase strength at both fast and slow speeds.

Fig 18.2.6 A comparison of repetition/resistance guidelines for endurance and maximum strength

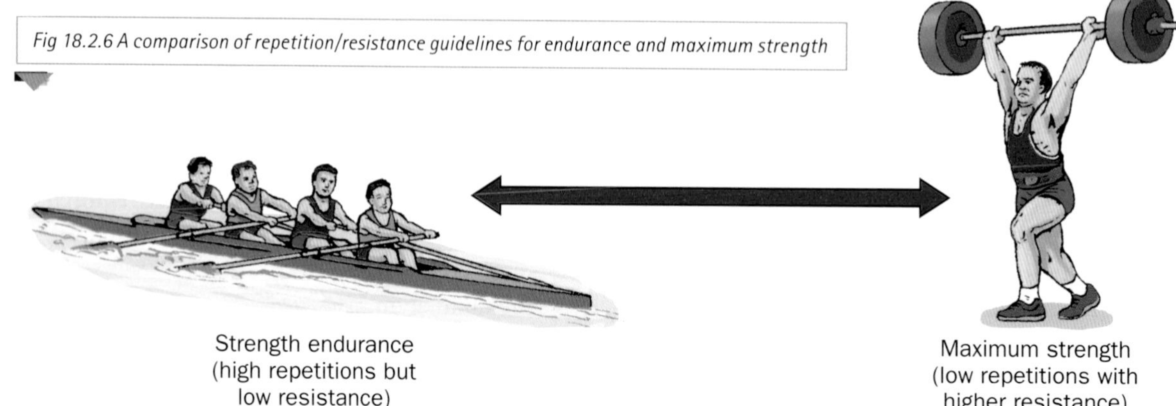

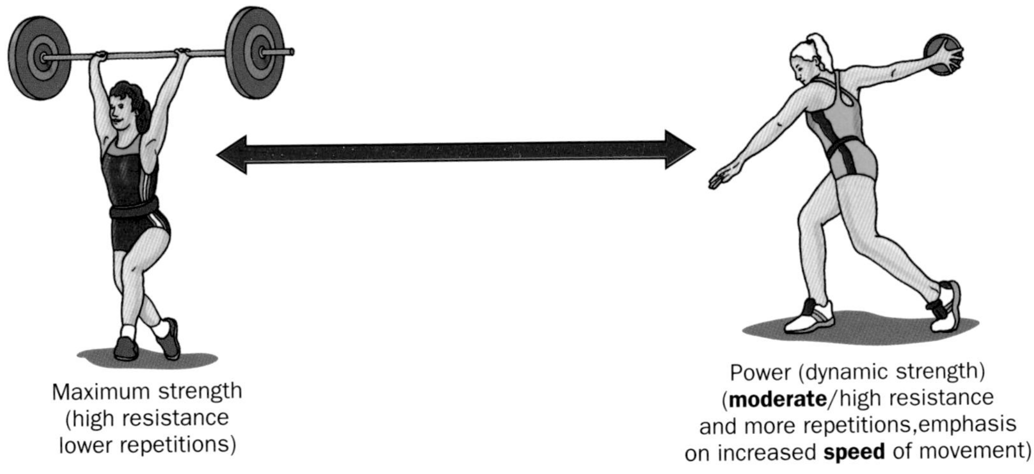

Fig 18.2.7 A comparison of repetition/resistance guidelines for maximum and dynamic (power) strength

- Use progressive overload using the repetition, set and resistance guidelines.

It is important to understand that different sources will provide different recommended guidelines for developing the respective types of strength. However, they will follow a similar pattern to those listed on page 432, which is summarised in Table 4.

REMEMBER

Interval training guidelines were summarised in Table 5 in Chapter 18.1, page 417.

Table 4 Summary of circuit and resistance strength training guidelines for aerobic and anaerobic athletes

Circuit training	Aerobic athlete	Anaerobic athlete
Interval duration	3–5+ minutes/20 minutes (longer)	0–90 seconds (shorter)
Interval intensity	Low/moderate = 50–70%/<speed	High = 70–85%/>speed
Interval relief	Lower: 1 : 1 /jog/walk/jog	Higher: 90 seconds to 3 minutes/1 : 3+
Ratio of work–relief	3–4 circuits; more reps/stations	3–5 circuits of fewer reps/stations
Frequency	3–5 sessions weekly	3–7 sessions weekly (48 hours between sessions if same muscle group)
Specificity	Aerobic energy system	ATP/PC/LA energy system
Resistance training	**Aerobic athlete**	**Anaerobic athlete**
Duration (repetitions)	More reps – 10+ (20+ common)	Fewer reps – 1–10
Intensity (weight)	Low/moderate = 50–70% of 1 RM	High = 70–95% of 1 RM/>speed
Relief/recovery	Lower 1 : 2 (30–60 seconds)	Higher/full 1 : 3+ (2–5 minutes)
Number of work–relief (sets)	Fewer: 3–5 sets of 10+ reps	More: 3–6 sets of 1–10 reps
Frequency	3–5 per week	3–7 sessions weekly (48 hours between sessions if same muscle group)
Specificity	Aerobic system	ATP/PC/LA system (>speed of motion)

TASK 6

Complete the strength needs analysis (Table 5) below for your coursework activity by writing a response to questions a–f. The completed table could be used to help you design a specific programme of strength training.

Fig 18.2.8 Multi-gym is a flexible strength training method

MULTI-GYM

A multi-gym is a series of specialised exercise machines that incorporate a range of resistance exercises with adjustable weight stacks. Each exercise machine or station targets specific groups of muscles by providing a resistance against which the performer has to apply a force. A multi-gym is safe and good for general strength development; however, it is not always specific to joint/movement patterns as they occur in actual sporting activities. The repetitions, sets and resistance can be easily adjusted to suit the specific strength requirements of an activity and therefore it is a flexible strength training method.

FREE WEIGHTS

Free weights are non-mechanical weights that are free standing and which therefore offer improved specificity for joint movement patterns. They are therefore good for general/specific strength development. Free weights also require the less active muscle groups to work isometrically as fixators, which helps improve balance and co-ordination more specific to actual performance

Table 5 Strength needs analysis

Question	Response
a) What type(s) of strength does your activity require?	
b) What muscle(s) need to be trained?	
c) What energy system should be stressed?	
d) What is the major type of muscle contraction(s) used?	
e) What type of speed and movement patterns does your activity include?	
f) What general repetition and resistance guidelines are appropriate for your activity?	

movements. Again, repetitions, sets and resistance can be easily adjusted to suit the specific strength requirements. However, free weights are not as safe as a multi-gym and often require a 'spotter' (second person assisting) when lifting a heavy resistance. Free weights are therefore not recommended for the less experienced individual aiming at improving their general strength development for a healthy lifestyle.

There are too many and far too complex variations of resistance training (simple set; pyramid systems), using both the multi-gym and free weights to describe in detail. Many of these are worth using, but they can be badly applied and actually cause an imbalance of strength development across the body. For this reason, in terms of an active and healthy lifestyle, there is one method worth highlighting that is more likely to ensure a well-balanced strength development promoting good posture and body alignment for everyday health. This method is termed a '**super set**' and consists of working pairs of antagonistic muscle groups without any rest between each set; for example, the biceps curl and the triceps press or the quadriceps and the hamstrings (see Fig 18.2.9). In addition to balancing the strength development of opposing muscle groups, a super set also ensure more work within a given session which better maintains heart rate and promotes aerobic/cardiovascular adaptations in addition to strength adaptations.

KEY TERM

Super set

Resistance training which works pairs of antagonistic muscle groups without any rest between each set.

APPLY IT!

A super set will help prevent the poor posture that arises from too many repetitions of abdominal resistance exercises at too high a resistance in order to develop a 'six-pack' and forgetting to exercise the lower back/erector spinae group which leads to a premature forward flexion/curvature of the back as the erector spinae become lengthened and weaker.

PLYOMETRIC TRAINING

Plyometric training incorporates jumps, bounds and hop-type exercises and is linked to the development of power: explosive, elastic and dynamic strength. Plyometrics is based upon knowledge of the **stretch reflex** to recruit more **motor units** to increase force production. Upon

KEY TERMS

Stretch reflex

A protective reflex mechanism when a muscle(s) will concentrically contract (shorten) in response to being overstretched, especially in response to a high speed of muscle stretch.

Motor unit

A motor neurone (nerve transmitter from brain to muscle) and the muscle fibres it innervates (contracts).

Fig 18.2.9 A super set: two sets of 10 reps for both exercises/muscle groups above would be completed twice following the order of the arrows and without any rest period between the two exercises

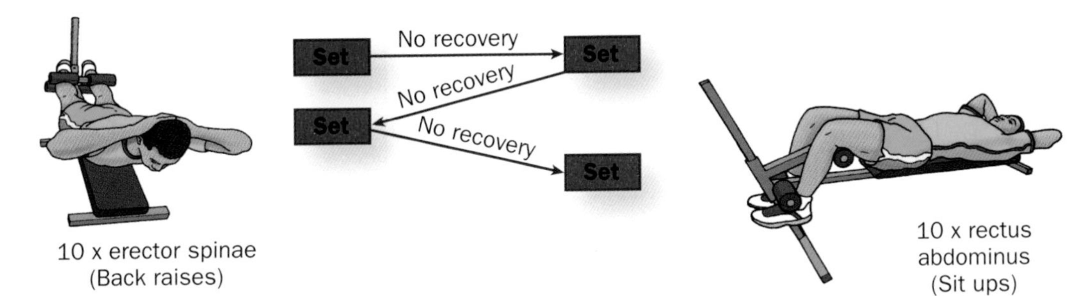

Fig 18.2.10 Plyometric techniques

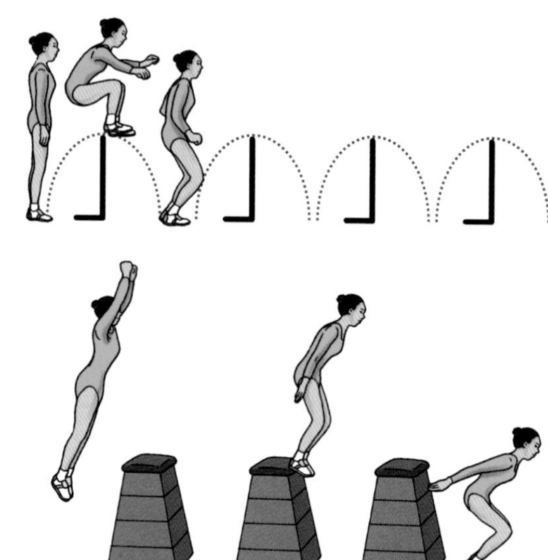

landing after a jump, the quadriceps is quickly and eccentrically lengthened which initiates the stretch reflex, a powerful elastic recoil reaction to prevent injury. If a concentric (voluntary) contraction immediately follows, the recoil force from the stretch reflex is added to the concentric force and this increases the overall force/strength produced.

Plyometric training involves placing an eccentric stretch on a muscle to initiate the stretch reflex; this recruits increased motor units/muscle fibres, which preloads the elastic/contractile properties of muscle fibres to increase the force of contraction. Fig 18.2.10 shows that most plyometric exercises are associated with the lower (leg) muscles, but they can also be applied to all skeletal muscles.

Plyometrics is at the top of a strength training pyramid. It carries increased risk of injury and delayed onset of muscular soreness (DOMS), which primarily results from eccentric muscle contractions causing structural damage within muscle tissues. For this reason, good pre-strength is essential before undertaking plyometric training; it should not be undertaken by more sedentary individuals who are just starting training and only looking to achieve good general strength. Moderation, progressive overload and warm-up/cool-down are also essential to help reduce the effect of injury and DOMS.

TASK 7

1 Complete and measure the vertical jump (leg power) test under the three conditions below.
   i. Bend the legs but hold for 10 seconds and then jump (no second bend/bounce before jumping).
   ii. Flex/bend the legs prior to jumping.
   iii. Jump from a bench and then jump.
2 Share your group results in Table 6 below.
3 What happened to jump height from 1 to 3?
4 Can you explain the results?

Table 6 Group results for Task 7

Name																		
1																		
2																		
3																		

CIRCUIT/INTERVAL TRAINING

This strength training method uses a series of exercises termed stations that form one complete circuit (see Fig 18.2.11) which can be repeated a set number of times. The performer's body weight often acts as the resistance, but a circuit could be completed using a multi-gym. The stations are normally ordered to alternate muscles/groups to allow them time to recover. However, if the aim is to increase the lactate tolerance of a muscle/group, the same station/exercise can be repeated one or more times before moving on to the next station; this is termed 'stage training'.

Circuit training is very similar to interval training as there is a natural 'relief' between stations and circuits, and for this reason the energy system and type of strength developed can be altered by adjusting the same parameters identified with interval training in Chapter 18.1 (see page 417).

- *Work/interval intensity* – number of circuits completed (3–6); number of stations (10–15); number of repetitions (11–20+)
- *Work/interval duration* – length of the work interval
- *Relief/interval duration* – recovery time (0–30 seconds)
- *Number of work/relief intervals*

TASK 8

1 Design a circuit specific to your coursework activity using your body weight as the resistance.
2 Compare your circuit with one of your peers and discuss any differences.

STRETCH AND CHALLENGE

The use of ankle weights, pulleys and parachutes are some modern methods of strength training.

Investigate the effectiveness of these training methods/aids to increase strength.

Fig 18.2.11 *Circuit training can be easily adapted for skill training, with fitness exercise stations replaced or combined with technical drills specific to an activity*

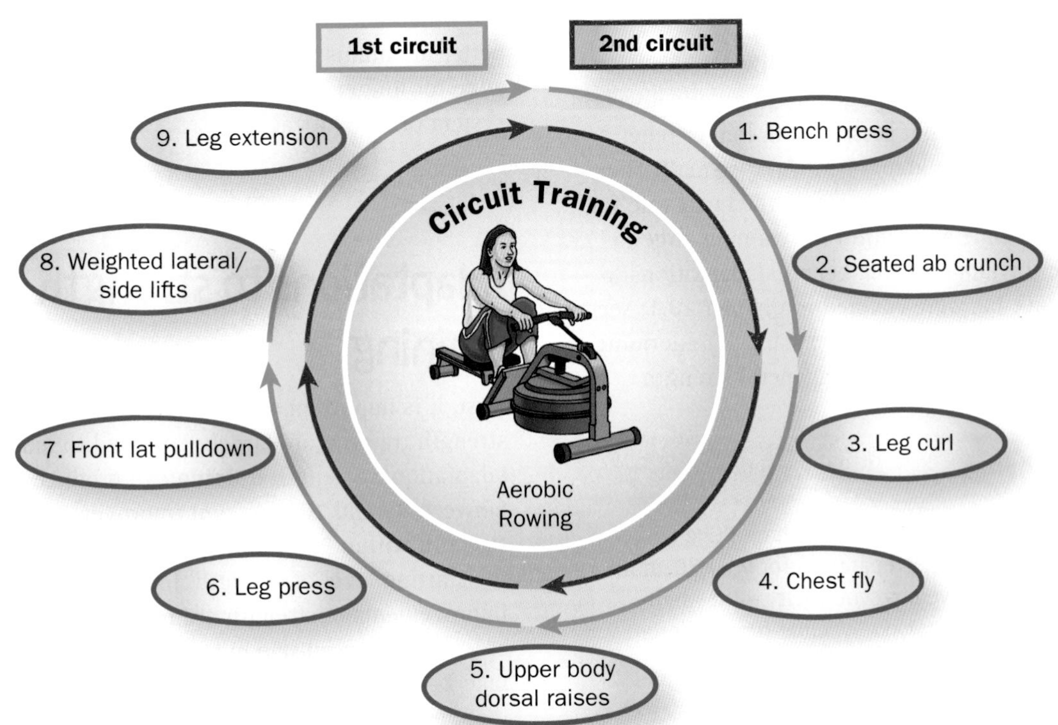

Fig 18.2.12 Energy systems linked to strength

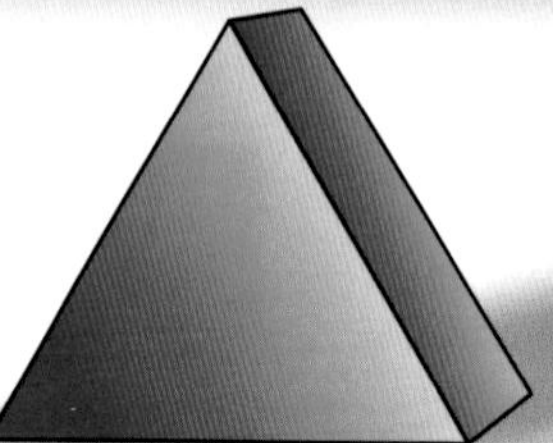

The energy system and food fuels

A simple way to link energy systems to the different types of strength is to create a pyramid with the three most applicable types of strength and their respective energy systems and food/fuels at each corner (see Fig 18.2.12).

REMEMBER

Have a look back at Chapter 16, pages 375–379, for more information on energy systems and food fuels.

However, in terms of a healthy lifestyle it is important to acknowledge that in a typical weight training/free weight session with longer relief periods, the total amount of work is small. Thus the work does not always raise the heart rate for sufficient time and within the training zone to enable the more aerobic benefits/adaptations to take place (as were covered in Chapter 18.1; see pages 418–421). This is not meant to undermine the importance of effective general strength development in terms of good body posture/alignment. It also reinforces the use of a super set, which does not allow any relief and therefore better maintains heart rate within the training zone for longer than a simple set or pyramid system of weight training.

EXAM TIP

Attempting the following Stretch and Challenge activity is excellent preparation for your 20-mark question as it develops synopticity – the ability to evaluate and apply knowledge from different areas of the physiological specification.

STRETCH AND CHALLENGE

Sketch Fig 18.2.12 on a blank page and add the following to the respective three corners:

1 the three different processes of 'recovery' (think outside the box!)
2 the three different types of fibre (you may place more than one type at some corners)
3 any other areas of the physiological specification that you could place in any of the three corners.

Adaptations to strength training

First, it is important to note that the effects of strength training are largely confined to muscle adaptations. Strength training can produce between 25 and 100 per cent improvement in strength within 3–6 months, depending upon the starting level of strength. Interestingly, early improvements in strength are reported without any increase in muscle hypertrophy, which can take 2–3 weeks to adapt. So how can we explain these early strength gains?

TASK 9

Read the following article.

'Angela Cavallo, a 5 foot 8 large-framed 50-year-old mother in Lawrenceville, Georgia, watched as her then-teenage son's 1964 Chevy Impalacar, which was jacked up in the driveway, fell off the jack pinning him under the car. Hollering to the neighbour kid to get help, Angela grabbed the side of the car with both hands and pulled up with all her strength as two neighbours reinserted the jack and dragged the boy out. At a guess she kept the car propped up for five minutes but figures she couldn't have picked the car up under normal circumstances, attributing her feat to adrenaline; however, a doctor says an adrenaline rush wouldn't last five minutes and suggests what we're seeing here wasn't so much superhuman strength as endurance in the face of otherwise overwhelming pain.'

(Associated Press, 1982)

1 Can you provide any explanations to account for such common accounts of superhuman strength?
2 Look at Fig 18.2.13. Discuss why early strength gains are reported before any physical (hypertrophy) adaptations have occurred?

Fig 18.2.13 clearly shows that strength improvements are a result of both neural and physiological adaptations; also, that short-term early strength gains are primarily due to neural adaptations and long-term gains are largely due to hypertrophy (physiological) changes. The neural and physiological adaptations leading to greater force production/strength are summarised in Table 7.

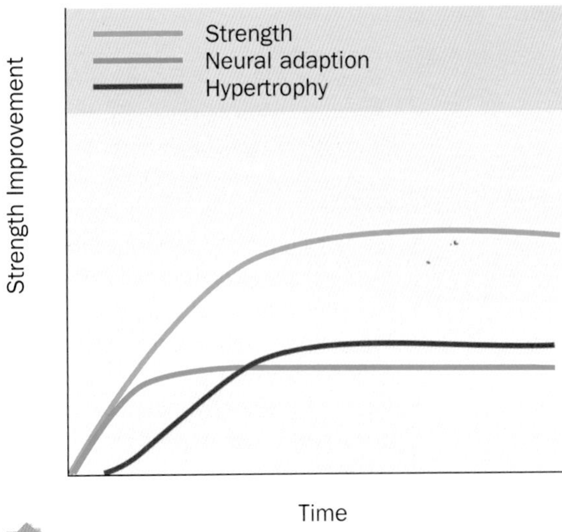

Fig 18.2.13 Strength improvements as a result of neural and physiological adaptations

EXAM TIP

You will be expected to explain both the neural and physiological adaptations that take place in response to prolonged periods of physical activity/training.

Table 7 Neural and physiological adaptations leading to greater force production/strength

Neural adaptations:	
• Increased recruitment of additional fast twitch muscle fibres • Increased recruitment of motor units • Improved co-ordination and simultaneous stimulation of motor units • Reduction in proprioreceptor/antagonist muscle inhibition allowing the antagonist to stretch further and the agonist to contract with more force	
Physiological adaptations:	
Skeletal muscle	• Hypertrophy – increase in muscle size (predominantly in fast twitch fibres) and/or hyperplasia – increase in muscle fibre number • Increased number/size of contractile protein (width of actin/myosin filaments) • Increased actin/myosin cross-bridges

Table 7 (Contd.)

Metabolic	• Increase in ATP, PC and glycogen stores • Increased buffering capacity/tolerance of fast twitch fibres to work with high levels of lactic acid • Increase efficiency to remove lactic acid • Increased glycolytic enzyme actions: glycogen phosphorylase and PFK • Net effect: increased anaerobic threshold/capacity and recovery of ATP/PC/LA system • Increased intensity/duration of performance and delaying of OBLA/fatigue
Other adaptations:	
• Increased strength of connective tissues – tendons, ligaments and bones (increased calcium production), which helps offset early symptoms of osteoporosis. • Social/psychological: an increased hypertrophic body is often seen as attractive and therefore desirable and may increase an individual's self-esteem and social standing in both sporting and lifestyle contexts.	

STRETCH AND CHALLENGE

1 Research the process of hyperplasia.
2 Why is research data inconclusive?
3 Two additional short-term responses to strength training are acute muscle soreness and DOMS. Research the differences and similarities between these two short-term responses. Include the causes, symptoms, effect on performance and how they may be reduced.

APPLY IT!

The muscular system adapts much quicker than the skeletal system. As a consequence, if too much heavy resistance training is undertaken by younger individuals whose skeletal system (growth plates) has not fully developed, the stronger muscles can actually force the skeletal system to deform from its natural alignment. A good example is 'bow' legs in football with those that play/train excessively at a young age.

CARDIOVASCULAR ADAPTATIONS

There are also cardiovascular adaptations associated with pure strength training which need to be considered in relation to a healthy lifestyle; these are:

- hypertrophy of the heart
- increased blood pressure
- slight increase in capillary density
- decreased volume of the left ventricle.

The adaptations demonstrate the effects of pure strength training as undertaken by weightlifters and bodybuilders, who lift low repetitions but many sets of very heavy weights very slowly, involving a large percentage of isometric contractions.

- Powerful muscle contractions obstruct arteries passing through active muscles increasing blood pressure and making it harder for the heart to force stroke volume (SV) out.
- This causes the heart to hypertrophy. Heart walls become thicker and stronger and the ventricles can sometimes become smaller in volume to help pump blood against high arterial blood pressure during isometric contractions.
- Larger heart muscle fibres also increase the distance/speed for O_2/CO_2 diffusion, which may limit metabolic functioning and although inconclusive may increase the risk of coronary heart disease.
- Increasing muscle mass (hypertrophy) has to be carried and without any increase in mitochondria it may even decrease aerobic strength endurance.
- Undertaking both strength and endurance training together may hinder strength adaptations.

APPLY IT!

The ventricular volume of heavy weight lifters can be similar/smaller than sedentary people, although the mass of the cardiac muscle is significantly greater.

REMEMBER

Isometric resistance training should be avoided by individuals with moderate to high blood pressure (hypertension).

ENDURANCE STRENGTH ADAPTATIONS

Compared with anaerobic strength training, strength endurance training has little effect on muscle tissue adaptations, except for an increased muscle mitochondria and capillary density. In general, strength endurance training increases the metabolic rate by increasing aerobic capacity via the improved efficiency of the cardiovascular/respiratory systems as seen in Chapter 18.1, pages 418–421.

Strength training and a healthy lifestyle

It should now be apparent that there are many mixed/conflicting messages with respect to strength training that need clarifying, especially with regard to a healthy lifestyle.

HEALTH OR PERFORMANCE?

First, it is important to recognise that most of the negative effects of strength training are felt in pure maximum strength training undertaken by weightlifters and bodybuilders who lift low repetitions but many sets of very heavy weights very slowly, involving a large percentage of isometric contractions. Power athletes who reduce the resistance to allow them to emphasise the speed of movement do not undergo this large isometric effect. However, the fact that some evidence suggests strength and endurance training together may hinder strength (power) development conflicts with the view that increased cardio-vascular adaptations will allow anaerobic athletes to increase their recovery and removal of the by-products of anaerobic respiration.

In terms of a healthy lifestyle, there is no question that good strength has a major role to play in sustaining and improving participation in physical activity and maintaining a healthy lifestyle. The World Health Organisation (WHO) and the American College of Sports Medicine (ACSM) recommend strength training alongside cardiovascular training to help enhance and maintain muscular strength and bone health. More specifically, the ACSM recommend 8 to 10 strength-training exercises of 8 to 12 repetitions of each exercise twice a week. An increased muscle mass will increase energy expenditure, which may help achieve a more healthy body composition (reduced fat mass). Hence, with appropriate resistance, both children and the elderly alongside athletes can benefit from strength training.

TASK 10

Go back to Task 6 on page 434 and Task 9 in Chapter 17 (page 403) where you identified your own assessment of strength and the strength requirements of your coursework activity.

- Pair up with someone who has the opposite type of strength requirements to your own, for example anaerobic versus aerobic.
- Separately, use the knowledge covered in this section to plan a programme of training based on your assessment of your own strength and the requirements of your activity.
- Compare your training programmes and highlight the similarities and differences between the more aerobic and anaerobic programmes.

STRETCH AND CHALLENGE

Following on from Task 10 above, complete points 1–3:

1. List the principles of training you have included in your planned programme of training.
2. Which principles did you miss out? Why did you not include them in your programme? How might you ensure you do not miss them out in the future?
3. Which principles of training did you simply define and which did you apply?

Exam Café

Relax, refresh, result!

Refresh your memory

You should now have knowledge and understanding of:

- how to define types of strength
- factors that affect strength
- how to describe and apply methods of evaluating each type of strength
- how to describe and evaluate different types of training used to develop strength – use of multi-gym, weights, plyometrics and circuit/interval training
- the energy system and the food/chemical fuels used during each type of strength training
- the physiological adaptations that take place after prolonged periods of physical activity
- how to plan a programme of strength training based on the assessment of an individual's strength and the strength requirements of a chosen activity.

REVISE AS YOU GO!

1. List the five types of strength.
2. Name a test to measure each of the five types of strength.
3. Identify and explain three factors that affect strength.
4. Describe a typical circuit training plan.
5. Identify three physiological adaptations that occur after a period of strength training.
6. Account for any initial increases in strength before any physical adaptations take place.
7. Identify three neural adaptations that occur after a period of strength training.
8. Which method of resistance training makes the best use of time and can help ensure good muscle balance is achieved?
9. Name and explain the theory that plyometric training is based upon.
10. Evaluate the principle of moderation in respect of a sedentary participant who initially undertakes plyometric training to improve their strength as a means to achieving a healthier and active lifestyle.

Try to answer these questions yourself. Ask your teacher if you need help.

Get the result!

Examination question

Identify and define the type of strength most relevant to a 100-metre sprinter. Design a weight training programme to improve this type of strength. (6 marks)

Examiner's tips

This is a clear two-part question which should immediately allow you to divide the six available marks into a two-mark and a four-mark answer.

- The command words in the first part, 'identify and define', represent two straightforward recall responses. However, despite its simplicity, if you did identify the wrong type of strength you would lose the two-marks part and restrict your access to the four marks in part two.
- The command word 'design' is asking you to apply your knowledge of the principle of training to your knowledge of what should be incorporated within a weight training programme.
- Although the question does not ask for an example, part one has named a 100-metre sprinter and this should be applied throughout your answer to ensure you stay focused on the question.
- A quick plan for part two would ensure you cover all parts of the question:

Principles of training (MRSVOPP)	Sets	Reps	Recovery

Student answer

The most relevant type of strength would be explosive/elastic strength, although dynamic strength does also contribute towards the latter part of the race. Explosive strength is the ability of the neuromuscular system to expend a maximal amount of energy/force in one or a series of strong sudden high intensity movements/contractions.

The principle of training should be incorporated when designing any training programme.

Examiner comment

Excellent, concise start to the first part of the question, immediately identifying and then defining the correct type of strength.

Examiner comment

Good understanding that the command word 'design' requires the application of the principles of training to a weight training programme.

Specificity implies that the main energy system trained should be the ATP/PC and similarly the major muscle groups of a sprinter (legs) should be targeted.

Examiner comment

Named principle with two excellent examples of its application to the 100-metre sprinter.

Overload using the FITT principle implies that for the sprinter they should train at least three but up to five times a week. Intensity (the resistance/weight to be lifted) should be about 80 per cent of their 1 RM. Three to six sets of about 8-10 repetitions should be lifted. Recovery between sets should allow for a greater/full recovery (2-3 minutes for full alactacid/ATP/PC recovery), so they can emphasise the speed of movement as they are trying to improve speed/power.

Examiner comment

Good use of FITT to ensure full coverage of the principle of overload and linked to the sprinter.

Examiner comment

Excellent and concise application of frequency, intensity, sets/reps and recovery

Examiner comment

Excellent Stretch and Challenge response linking the 2–3 minute recovery period to the alactic recovery process and application to speed/power.

By altering one or a combination of sets, frequency, reps, resistance and recovery during the training programme, progressive overload can be maintained throughout the training programme, but not all at once as this would be too much overload at once and may cause burn out or injury.

Examiner comment

Moderation not named but linked well to progressive overload.

Examiner comment

This is a top-grade response, beginning with a concise response to the question. The candidate shows an excellent understanding of 'design' as a command word, with links to the principles of training specific to the 100-metre sprinter. Effective use of scientific language throughout and the link of the 2–3 minute recovery between sets to the alactacid recovery indicates to the examiner that this is a high-level answer.

CHAPTER 18.3:

Health components of physical fitness: Flexibility

LEARNING OBJECTIVES

By the end of this chapter you should have knowledge and understanding of:

- how to define flexibility
- factors that affect flexibility
- how to describe and apply methods of evaluating flexibility
- different types of training used to develop flexibility
- the physiological adaptations that take place after prolonged periods of physical activity
- how to plan a programme of flexibility training based on self-assessment of flexibility and the flexibility requirements of your activity.

Defining flexibility

Flexibility is the range of motion around a joint (for example the shoulder) or a series of joints (for example the vertebrae).

- Flexibility is joint-specific; thus someone flexible at the shoulder may have poor flexibility in the vertebrae.
- Flexibility is sport-specific: for example, a rugby player requires less flexibility but more strength and stability in the shoulder joint than a gymnast, who requires very good strength, stability and flexibility.
- Flexibility has two components: static flexibility and dynamic flexibility.

KEY TERMS

Flexibility

The range of motion (RoM) around a joint or a series of joints.

Static flexibility

The range of motion (RoM) without taking into account the speed of movement.

Dynamic flexibility

The range of motion (RoM) taking into account the speed of movement and reflecting the joint's resistance to movement.

Static flexibility is the range of motion (RoM) without taking into account speed of movement. It is the maximum RoM a muscle or connective tissues will allow with an external force, for example holding the hamstring stretch at the end of its RoM in Figure 18.3.1a.

Dynamic flexibility is the range of motion which takes into account the speed of movement and reflects the joints' (muscle/connective tissues) resistance to movement; for example, the straddle jump in Fig 18.3.1b.

Although not ensuring it, static flexibility is a prerequisite to dynamic flexibility. For example, good static adductor/hamstring flexibility (Fig 18.3.1a) forms the basis for achieving good dynamic flexibility (Fig 18.3.1b). In respect of the principle of specificity, static flexibility is important to those performers who hold static balances, such as dancers and gymnasts during floor routines, whereas dynamic flexibility is important in high-velocity movement sports like sprinting, throwing and, again, gymnastics. It is also important to differentiate between flexibility

Fig 18.3.1a Static flexibility

Fig 18.3.1b Dynamic flexibility

and **stretching**; flexibility being the range of movement (RoM) and stretching being the training method used to increase flexibility.

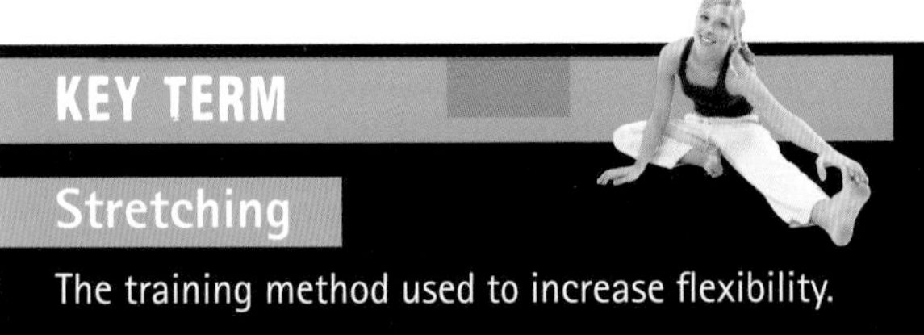

KEY TERM

Stretching

The training method used to increase flexibility.

TASK 1

Identify examples of when static and dynamic flexibility occur in the performance of your coursework activity.

APPLY IT!

Football and netball players require good hip flexion/abduction but furthermore need to produce this RoM at high speeds when stretching to tackle or landing under control.

The importance of flexibility

Flexibility is probably the most undervalued and neglected health fitness component and yet is critical for sports participation or to promote a healthy lifestyle. If you don't stretch it is only a matter of time before some body tissue will break down leading to injury. Most trainers agree that flexibility training should form an integral part of training, but what are the proposed benefits of increased flexibility?

The benefits of flexibility training include:

- reduced risk of injury (prevention)
- improved posture, alignment and ergonomics
- reduction of delayed onset of muscular soreness (DOMS)
- performance enhancement:
  - flexible muscles perform better than tight muscles
  - improves range of motion at joints
  - increased range of motion for applying force (power)
  - improved economy of movement (strength endurance/aerobic capacity)
  - improved motor performance/skills.

Factors affecting flexibility

Having established why flexibility is important, you are required to understand what factors may limit flexibility so that you can account for these when planning a flexibility training programme. The factors affecting flexibility are summarised in Table 1 below.

KEY TERM

Muscle spindles

Proprioreceptors within muscles which send information on the length and rate of change of muscles to the central nervous system (CNS).

TASK 2

1 Sit on a chair with your upper back slumped (poor posture).
2 Maintain this posture and lift both your arms above your head.
3 Straighten yourself up with back straight (good posture) and lift both arms above your head.
4 Repeat part 2 but maintain your finish position (slumped). Now attempt to move other parts of your body to enable you to raise your hands fully above your head as in part 3.
5 Discuss your results.
6 What does this task highlight in respect of joint flexibility?

Table 1 Factors affecting flexibility

Factor	How it affects flexibility
Type of joint	A ball and socket joint innately has a full RoM; a pivot joint only allows rotation; a hinge joint only allows flexion or extension
Joint shape	The arrangement, shape and alignment of the joints' articulating surfaces/bones dictate RoM, for example the shoulder joint has increased RoM having a shallow joint cavity compared with the hip's deeper cavity which limits RoM but increases stability
Length/elasticity of connective tissues	In and around muscles and joints: the tendons, ligaments, epi/peri/endo-mysium of muscle, fascia and joint capsule all limit RoM
Muscle length/elasticity	The muscle spindles activation point before it initiates the stretch reflex (when a muscle is rapidly stretched) prevents further RoM
Gender	Generally females are more flexible than males
Age	Flexibility is greater in children and decreases as a person ages due to decrease in elasticity of muscle and connective tissues
Elasticity	The suppleness of skin and adipose tissue
Temperature	Elasticity of muscles and connective tissues is increased as temperature increases by 1–2 degrees Celsius, hence a warm-up should be performed
Muscle mass	Excess muscle mass around a joint restricts joint RoM
Nerves	Nerves pass through the joints; as joints are taken through a full RoM, nerves become stretched or compressed and trigger a stretch reflex within the muscles, increasing their resistance to stretch
Hypermobility	Inherited (double-jointed) or trained factors increasing RoM but can lead to joint instability and increase the risk of injury
Flexibility training	Stretching within a training programme may maintain/increase RoM

REMEMBER

Look back at Chapter 1 of *OCR AS PE*, pages 7–11, for a reminder of synovial joint structure and its affect on joint RoM.

STRETCH AND CHALLENGE

Task 2 highlights what Shirley Sahrmann, an American physiotherapist, terms 'relative flexibility'. She suggests the body will move through the point of least resistance to achieve a particular RoM. Part 1 and 2 showed that a slumped posture prevented the thoracic (upper back) from extending, which is necessary for full elevation of the arms. If this continues for long enough then the body will look elsewhere to use another area of relative flexibility to achieve the same RoM. Part 4 should have highlighted that the lower back or elevation of the shoulder itself were the alternative points of least resistance, which would eventually lead to the breakdown of these joints due to the excessive movements required (for example lower lumbar back pain).

Can you think of a popular strengthening exercise, commonly performed in excess for the main purpose of body image and which is likely to cause the thoracic vertebrae to move into flexion as highlighted in Task 2?

Measuring flexibility

As already highlighted, flexibility is joint-specific so there is no one single test to measure flexibility. Specific tests for specific joints are used; the one most widely known and used is the sit and reach test, which is used primarily to measure flexibility of the hip and lower back and which is outlined below.

PROCEDURE FOR SIT AND REACH TEST

Note: subjects should have performed an adequate warm-up before conducting the sit and reach test.

Using a sit and reach box (32 cm in height, 75 cm long and 45 cm wide, the first 25 cm of which extends over the front edge of the box towards the subject), with shoes removed, the subject places their feet against the box with legs straight and knees locked. The subject reaches forward and over the box, pushing a straight object (ruler) as far as possible along the scale on the box with extended fingertips. The subject should hold the final position steady for 2–3 seconds and the score is recorded.

TASK 3

1. Working in a small group, each member should complete the sit and reach test.
2. Record your individual group's scores into a table.
3. Compare and discuss your results.
4. Critically evaluate the use of the sit and reach test to evaluate flexibility.

GONIOMETRY

The most valid, accurate and recognised measure of flexibility is goniometry, which uses a double-armed goniometer (angle ruler) to measure the number of degrees from a neutral starting

Fig 18.3.2 Measuring RoM using a goniometer

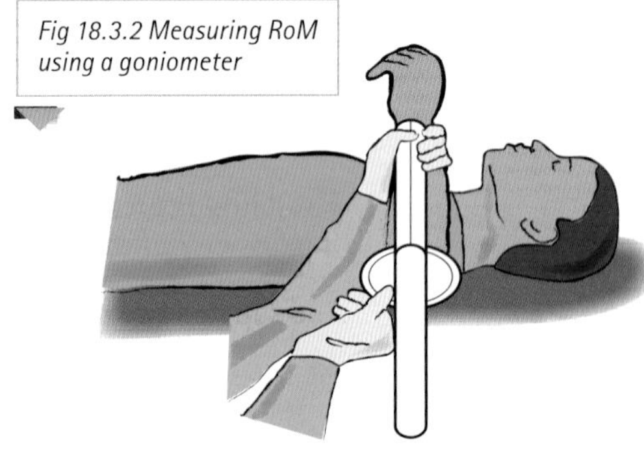

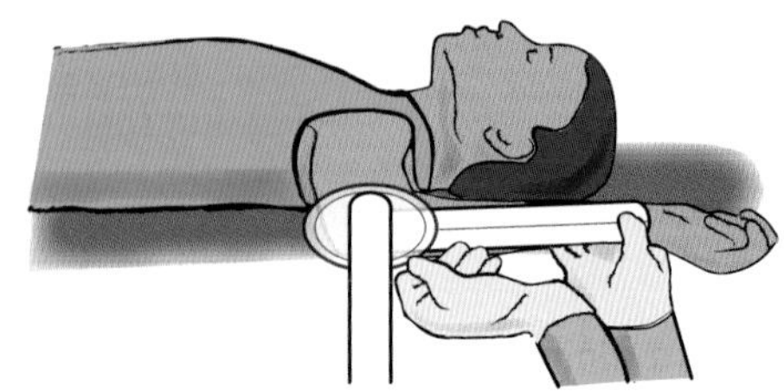

position to the position at the end of a full RoM at specific joints. Task 4 is a simplified introduction to the use of goniometers to measure flexibility at selected joints.

PROCEDURE FOR MEASURING SPECIFIED JOINTS USING A GONIOMETER

Note: If you do not have access to a goniometer, use a 180-degree angle ruler or a 360-degree protractor when measuring the RoM at the joints outlined below.

Place the centre of the angle ruler or goniometer over the joint being measured and have the subject move the limb into the desired RoM until they reach or feel the first point of resistance to this movement. Move the arm of the angle ruler to match the angle of the limb moved and read off the angle measure in the centre of the ruler.

- *Hip flexion*: lay flat on your back, keeping your left leg straight and flat on the ground. Move the opposite leg as close as possible to your chest while flexing the knee.
- *Hip extension*: Lay flat on your front, keeping your left leg straight and flat on the ground. Lift the opposite leg, keeping it straight up as high as possible off the ground.
- *Hip abduction*: Lay flat on your back keeping the left leg straight and flat on the ground. Move the opposite leg as far away to the right as you can.

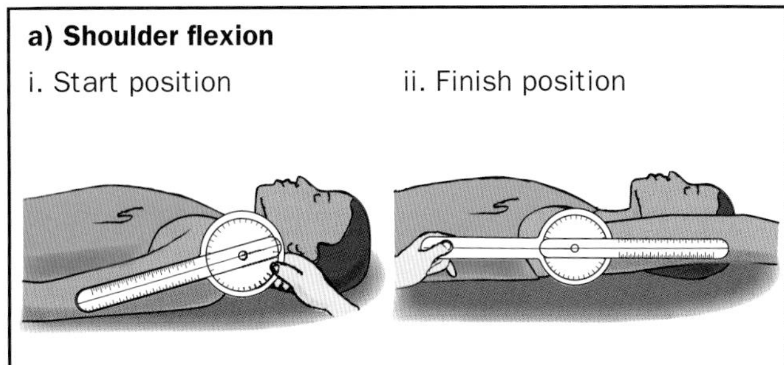

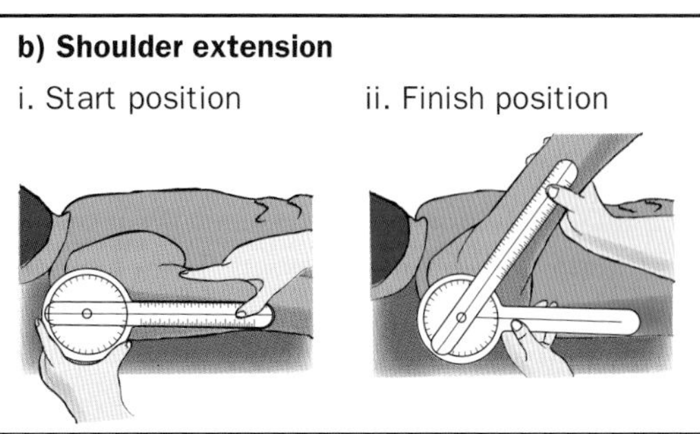

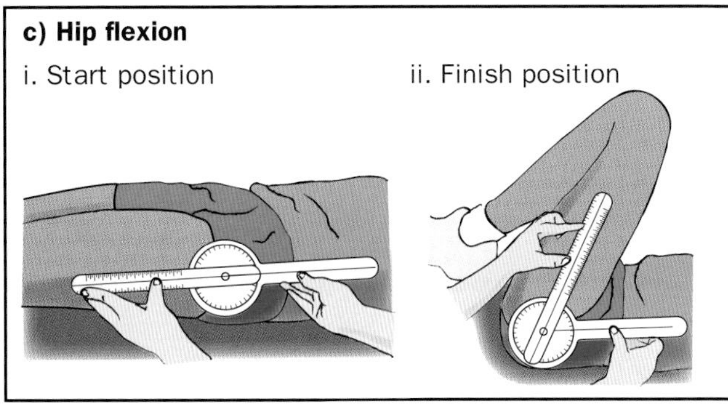

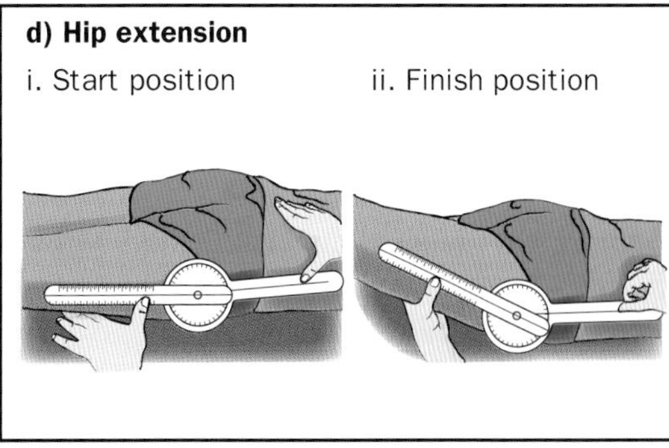

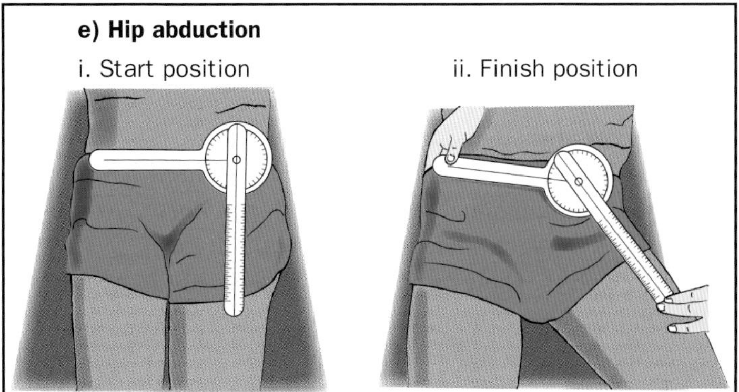

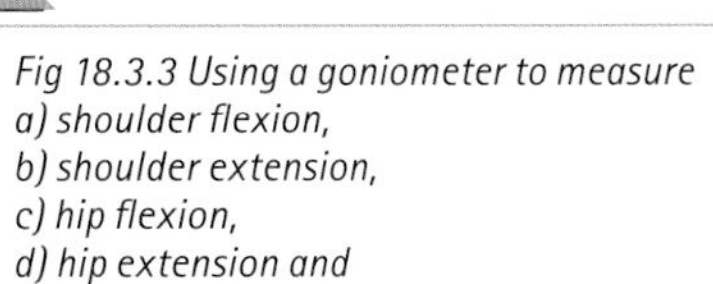

Fig 18.3.3 Using a goniometer to measure a) shoulder flexion, b) shoulder extension, c) hip flexion, d) hip extension and e) hip abduction

TASK 4

1 Working in a small group, complete the measurements for the joint movements shown in Figure 18.3.3 in Table 2 below.
2 Compare and discuss your group's findings.
3 Are any of the factors affecting flexibility evident when comparing your group's results? (You may need to indicate what the individual's main activity is and if they include stretching within their regular training.)
4 Repeat the hip flexion measurement but this time have the opposite leg bent with the foot flat on the ground and note what difference this makes to the degree of RoM.
5 Repeat the hip flexion measurement but keep the leg being measured straight at the knee and note what difference this makes to the degree of RoM.

Table 2

Name	Shoulder flexion	Shoulder extension	Hip flexion	Hip extension	Hip abduction

- *Shoulder flexion and extension*: With the arm straight and in line with your body (0 degrees neutral) lift it as high as you can forwards (flexion) and backwards (extension).

KEY TERMS

Maintenance stretching

Stretching as part of a warm up and cool down; it helps to maintain an individual's RoM but does not increase it.

Developmental stretching

Whole or part training sessions (a minimum of 10–15 minutes) devoted solely to stretching, which increases an individual's RoM.

Flexibility training

We have already identified that flexibility training is widely incorporated as an integral part of preparation for physical activity with the primary role being injury prevention and improved performance. Flexibility is either maintained or improved by stretching and it is important to clarify the misconception that stretching as part of a warm up and cool down (typically too short) will represent true flexibility training. Stretching as part of a warm up and cool down is termed **maintenance stretching** which, as it states, helps to maintain an individual's current RoM, and does not, as often thought, increase RoM. Flexibility training involves whole or part training sessions (a minimum of 10–15 minutes) devoted solely to stretching. This is termed **developmental stretching** as it helps to develop RoM.

You are required to know four different types of stretching (training) that are used to develop flexibility in order that you can apply them when designing flexibility training programmes. Irrespective of the type of stretching undertaken, the aim is to stretch the muscle/connective tissues around a joint just beyond the end point of resistance (RoM) or in some cases further through its extreme point of resistance to cause long-term adaptations in the length of these tissues. In order to stimulate sufficient overload for these tissues to adapt and lengthen, the general guidelines use the FITT principle as outlined next:

- *F= Frequency*, for example 2 to 4 times a week depending upon the requirements of the individual's activity and initial flexibility level of the performer
- *I = Intensity*, varying from a mild tension (no pain) stretch to a stretch through the extreme point of resistance, depending upon the method being used
- *T= Time*/duration, for example hold each stretch for a minimum of 10 and maximum of 30+ seconds and repeat 3 to 6 times depending upon the number and type of stretching being performed and the flexibility level of the performer
- *T= Type*: (static, dynamic, ballistic or PNF stretching).

Specificity is also crucial; it requires the performer to identify the requirements of their activities against their joints' RoM and to consider:

- which joints require their RoM increasing or possibly maintaining or decreasing
- the body position and velocity or speed at which these joint(s) are moved through
- the most appropriate type of stretching from those outlined below.

Similarly, having identified that temperature increases RoM, stretching should always be preceded by a warm up or should take place after a training session when the body temperature is warm.

REMEMBER

A warm up increases core body temperature which increases RoM and reduces the risk of injuries due to the increased elasticity of muscles, tendons and ligaments (see *OCR AS PE*, page 34).

STATIC STRETCHING

Static stretching is subdivided into static active and static passive stretches.

- Static active stretches are unassisted, with the performer actively completing a voluntary static contraction of an agonist muscle to

Fig 18.3.4 Static stretches

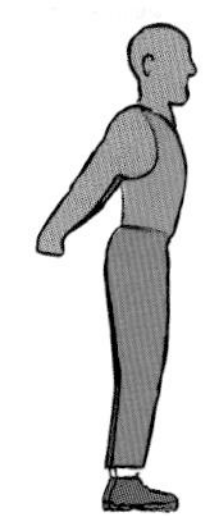

Chest
(Pectoralis major)

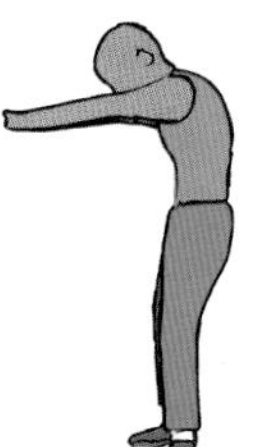

Upper back
(Trapezius)

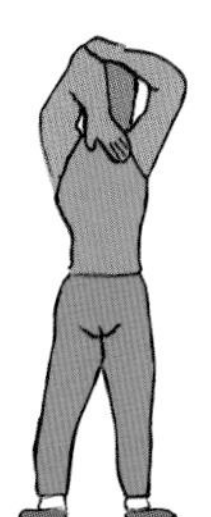

Back of
upper arms
(Triceps)

Calf
(Gastroc nemius)

Back of thighs
(Hamstrings)

Lower back
(External obliques)

Back of thighs
(Hamstrings)

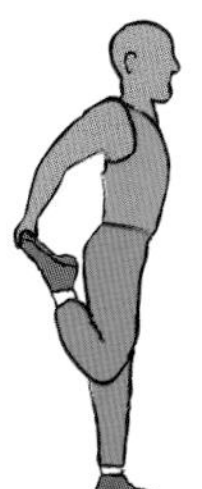

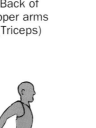

Front of
thighs
(Quadriceps)

Inner thighs
(Adductors)

create the force to stretch the antagonist muscle just beyond its end point of resistance, while held still, to increase the RoM at a joint.
- Static passive stretches are assisted by an external force, for example gravity, apparatus or a partner, to help move the joint just beyond its end point of resistance to stretch the muscle/connective tissues.

Static stretching has long been thought to be the safest method and, despite being the slowest, the most effective form of stretching to increase the length of muscle/connective tissues. However, current research findings do question these long-held views, primarily on the grounds that static stretching fails to prepare the joints for the more dynamic and powerful RoM that are involved in the actual activity to be performed.

BALLISTIC STRETCHING

Ballistic stretching involves the use of momentum to move a joint forcibly through to its extreme end of range or point of resistance. It involves fast, swinging, active or bouncing movements to complete the joint's full RoM. Ballistic stretching has long been thought of as the least effective method of stretching as it fails to allow adequate time for the tissues to adapt to the stretch and creates muscle tension, making it more difficult to stretch connective tissues. It also carries a greater risk of muscle soreness/injury. Ballistic stretching is thought to produce limited long-term adaptations for increasing muscle length and primarily has been promoted and used by performers whose activities involve similar, fast, dynamic and active RoM of joints. Ballistic stretching should only be performed by athletes who already have a good range of flexibility in the muscle/connective tissues being stretched.

DYNAMIC STRETCHING

Dynamic stretching, in simple terms, is a more controlled version of ballistic stretching. It has evolved as a result of the growing research suggesting static stretching impairs the subsequent performance of speed, power and

Fig 18.3.5 Ballistic/dynamic stretches

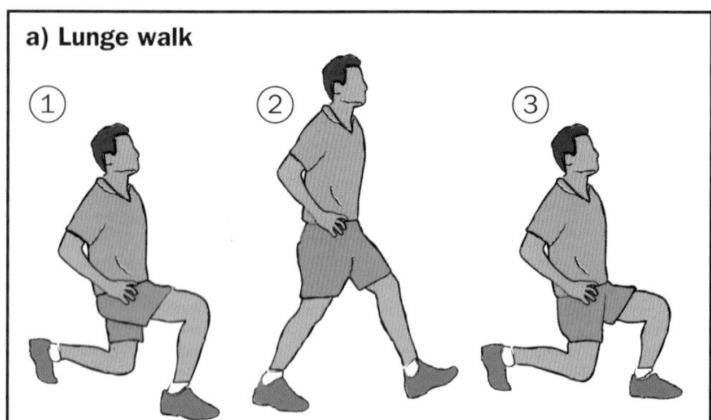

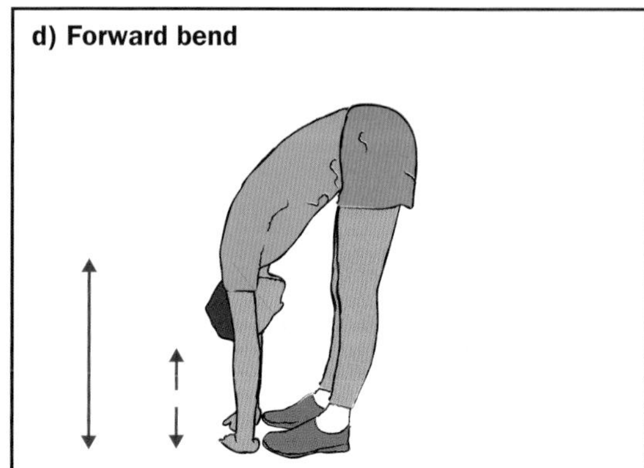

strength work. Dynamic stretching involves taking the muscles through a joint's full RoM, with muscle tension but with the entry and exit under more control and therefore not the extreme end point of resistance as with ballistic stretching.

Dynamic stretching can be performed actively or passively as with static stretching, and evidence suggests that it better develops a more optimum level of 'dynamic' flexibility essential for all activities. As with ballistic stretching, dynamic stretching should only be performed by athletes who already have a good range of flexibility in the muscle/connective tissues being stretched.

STRETCH AND CHALLENGE

1 Research and discuss the relative benefits of the progressive velocity flexibility programme (PVFP) recommended by Zachazewski in 1990. (Recommended source: *Peak Performance Sports Injury Bulletin*, March 2008, No 77); information can be found on www.pponline.co.uk/subs/get/flexireport.pdf

2 What connections does PVFP have to static, ballistic and dynamic stretching?

PROPRIORECEPTIVE NEUROMUSCULAR FACILITATION (PNF)

Until the recent arguments in favour of dynamic stretching, PNF was thought the most effective, and also the most complex, type of stretching. PNF has many variations, all of which attempt to inhibit the stretch reflex mechanism to increase flexibility.

In Chapter 18.2 (page 435–6) you saw how plyometrics aims to induce the stretch reflex prior to a concentric contraction to increase force production. PNF actually seeks to inhibit this stretch reflex to allow a greater stretch of the muscle/connective tissues. Muscles contain muscle spindles which, when a muscle is stretched, stimulate the central nervous system via the spinal cord to activate the stretch reflex. The muscle contracts in a protective mechanism to prevent the muscle from being overstretched and this is what PNF attempts to stop occurring.

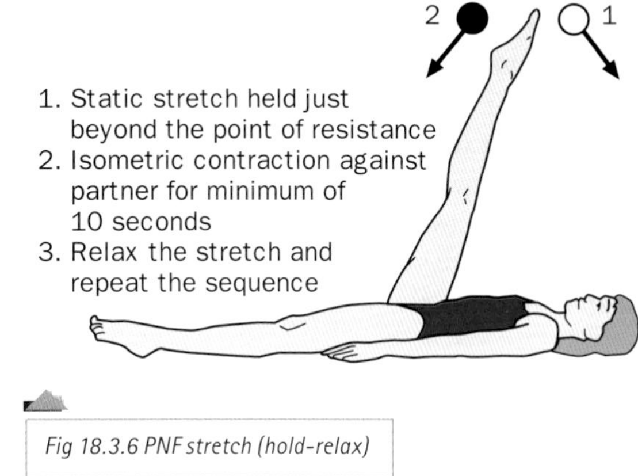

2
1
1. Static stretch held just beyond the point of resistance
2. Isometric contraction against partner for minimum of 10 seconds
3. Relax the stretch and repeat the sequence

Fig 18.3.6 PNF stretch (hold-relax)

The 'contract-relax' is a simple variation of PNF techniques which, when renamed 'static-contract-relax', consists of three clear stages which are easier to remember (see Figure 18.3.6).

1 *Static*: muscle stretch just beyond point of resistance.
2 *Contract*: isometric muscle contraction held for a minimum of 10 seconds.
3 *Relax*: muscle relaxed and sequence repeated at least three times.

The isometric contraction inhibits the stretch reflex allowing the muscle to be stretched further in each consecutive PNF stretch. Most PNF techniques require the assistance of a partner to resist the movement of the performer as they isometrically contract the stretched muscle. Although PNF is a more complex technique, requiring more time to learn and to tolerate the greater discomfort and therefore risks, most research has shown PNF to produce quicker and equal or better flexibility gains than traditional static stretching.

TASK 5

Prepare a presentation to explain to the rest of the group the science behind PNF training.

SUMMARY

Research and guidance for flexibility training is not as clear as most athletes would like, but it is important to understand that there is no single right or wrong way to stretch and that all methods of stretching have some merits. The following points attempt to summarise the current research guidelines:

- Dynamic stretching may be more appropriate for a warm up than static stretches to increase subsequent speed, power and strength work.
- Static/PNF stretches may be more appropriate at the end of a session to help muscle relaxation using:
  - maintenance stretches to return muscles to their pre-exercise length
  - developmental stretches to increase RoM (increased FITT).
- Limit static/PNF stretching to less than 20 seconds to prevent loss of subsequent speed, power and strength work.
- Greater static/PNF stretching is more appropriate in muscles/connective tissues around joints with poor RoM.
- Evidence suggests that if you do not have time to warm up properly, it is arguably better not to stretch at all than attempt to stretch a cold muscle!

TASK 6

As a coach taking on two new 400m hurdlers, outline a flexibility training plan for the two following athletes:

- Athlete A: a district hurdler who has moved clubs/area and has no limiting flexibility issues.
- Athlete B: a powerful ex-rugby winger with good potential and interest in the hurdle event with a history of recurring hamstring injuries.

Flexibility training adaptations and benefits

The adaptations to stretching are linked directly to an increase in the elasticity of muscle and connective tissues, which limit the RoM around a joint. These adaptations and their associated benefits are summarised below:

- increased elasticity/length of muscle/connective tissues
- increased resting length of muscle/connective tissues
- muscle spindles adapt to the increased length reducing the stimulus to the stretch reflex
- increased RoM at a joint before the stretch reflex is initiated
- increased potential for static and dynamic flexibility (RoM)
- increased distance and efficiency for muscles to create force and acceleration
- increased RoM reduces potential for injury to muscle/connective tissues during dynamic sports movements.

EXAM TIP

Exam questions often refer to the benefits of flexibility training – think of benefits and adaptations as the same thing and you will not misinterpret this type of question.

APPLY IT!

Increased RoM at the hip joint will allow a runner to increase their stride length. A golfer with increased RoM at the hips, shoulder and vertebrae will be able to take the club further back parallel to the target on the backswing. This will create a greater distance for the club head to travel and to apply force on the downswing, thereby increasing club head speed and force at impact, thus increasing the speed/distance the ball travels.

TASK 7

In groups, list examples from within your sports activities that will benefit from an increased RoM.

TASK 8

Evaluating and planning for the improvement of performance

1 Refer back to Tasks 3 and 4 and Task 9 in Chapter 17 (page 403) and recall your flexibility requirements and own rating – do you now still agree with your initial requirement rating?
2 Plan a programme of flexibility training based on your own assessment of flexibility and the flexibility requirements of your activity.
3 Apply the principles of training as appropriate within your planned programme.
4 Rehearse your training plan and orally describe or explain it in detail to a peer who will provide feedback.

Conclusion

All athletes and non-athletes can benefit by improving their flexibility, but the difficult question is what is good flexibility when it is both joint and sport-specific? Rugby players' shoulder joints are a good example of this. The shallow socket makes this ball and socket joint prone to dislocation during impact; this is why players try to increase strength and muscle mass around the joint to decrease RoM but increase stability. This emphasises the need for athletes to assess the type of flexibility and the joints which may require greater flexibility for their chosen activities. A hurdler, for example, will require even greater range of motion for dynamic flexion and abduction at the hip than a typical team games player would. A sedentary individual, as a minimum, would need to assess their work and active lifestyles and ensure their flexibility is sufficient to prevent injuries during their daily activities.

What is known is that the body has a tendency to allow certain muscles/connective tissues to tighten or shorten, and this can affect body posture and may lengthen or weaken the antagonistic muscles. Consequently this may alter an individual's neutral body alignment. Muscles/connective tissues affected include:

- the hamstrings
- rectus femoris
- tensor fascia lata
- piriformis adductors
- gastrocnemius and quadratus luborum
- pectoralis major
- trapezius.

Those listed very often cause postural musculoskeletal pain, the most common being the lower (lumbar) and upper (cervical) regions of the spine. The key, and difficulty, is to balance strength training with flexibility training in order to meet the performer's combined activity requirements. What seems clear is that flexibility, specific to the activity and joints, is critical for sports participation or to promote a healthy lifestyle. Remember: if you don't stretch to maintain your specific flexibility requirements, it is only a matter of time before some body tissue will break down leading to injury.

ExamCafé

Relax, refresh, result!

Refresh your memory

You should now have knowledge and understanding of:

- how to define flexibility
- factors that affect flexibility
- how to describe and apply methods of evaluating flexibility
- different types of training used to develop flexibility
- the physiological adaptations that take place after prolonged periods of physical activity
- how to plan a programme of flexibility training based on a self-assessment of flexibility and the flexibility requirements of your activity.

REVISE AS YOU GO!

1 Define static and dynamic flexibility.
2 Why is flexibility an important health component of physical fitness?
3 Explain three factors that can affect flexibility.
4 Explain why flexibility is so specific.
5 What is the most accurate method of measuring flexibility?
6 How do we increase flexibility?
7 Outline the general FITT (overload) guidelines for stretching.
8 What is the main difference between ballistic and dynamic stretching?
9 Explain why PNF allows muscle to stretch further.
10 Identify two benefits of an extended period of flexibility training.

Try to answer these questions yourself. Ask your teacher if you need help.

Get the result!

Examination question

Describe *two* types of stretching that could be used to develop flexibility.

Explain the physiological changes to skeletal muscle and connective tissue after flexibility training. (6 marks)

Examiner's tips

This is a clear two-part question. It is essential that you follow the directive in italics and describe two types of stretching.

- The command word for part one is 'describe'. The question therefore does not require you to explain and complicate your response.
- Part two implies you understand that flexibility (joint range of motion) improves after flexibility training. Your response should attempt to follow the command word 'explain' and use the term 'because'.
- It is important to identify that part two is asking for the structural adaptations only and not asking you to apply the adaptations as to how they may affect performance.
- Check the number of marks available (6 marks) and work out how many may be awarded for each part of the question. Two descriptions should point you towards two marks each, and thus two marks will be awarded for the adaptations to skeletal muscle/connective tissues.
- A quick plan would ensure you cover all parts of this question:

Type of stretching	Description
A	
B	

Student answer

Two contrasting methods of stretching are static and ballistic stretching.

Static stretching involves a performer (static active) or partner (static passive) moving their joint/antagonist muscle to a position just beyond its end point of resistance, whereas ballistic stretching uses momentum to take a joint/antagonistic muscle through its full/extreme range of movement or end point of resistance. In static stretching the stretch is held for at least 6 seconds but normally 10+ seconds, whereas a ballistic stretch is not held at all as the stretch reflex mechanism is initiated and the stretch/movement is immediately repeated with a bouncing-type action.

Examiner comment

You successfully chose to compare your descriptions. This is impressive as it is a more difficult response.

Examiner comment

Good clarification of static active and static passive stretching.

Examiner comment

Concise and excellent use of technical language and depth of understanding exemplified here.

Examiner comment

Good description and clarification of stretch duration, and excellent higher level understanding of the stretch reflex involvement in ballistic stretching.

Examiner comment

Good clarification that you understand what the question requires.

The increase in joint range of motion is primarily due to an increase in the length and elasticity of the muscle and connective tissues around a joint, and this is because the muscles spindles within a muscle, proprio-receptors, get used to this increased length before they initiate the stretch reflex which allows a greater range of motion.

Examiner comment

Excellent use of the words 'due to' and 'because', which is a great way of ensuring you explain the physiological changes Again, great use of technical language.

Examiner comment

Not required for the question but summarises the question well anyway.

Static stretching is a safer and more effective method than ballistic stretching.

Examiner comment

A top-grade response, starting with a concise identification of two types of stretching. Although not required, this candidate successfully compared the two methods and ensured that all descriptions were clear and concise. There is also excellent use and understanding of technical language specific to stretching.

CHAPTER 18.4:

Health components of physical fitness: Body composition

LEARNING OBJECTIVES

By the end of this chapter you should have knowledge and understanding of:

- what is meant by body composition
- different methods of assessing body composition
- how to calculate a person's body mass index (BMI)
- basal metabolic rate (BMR) and the different energy requirements of different physical activities
- how to estimate your daily calorific requirements based on your BMR and average additional energy consumption
- how to evaluate critically your own diet and calorie consumption
- the health implications of being overweight or obese and how this impacts on involvement in physical activity.

INTRODUCTION

Before we look at body composition, it is important that you don't mix up body size and build (somatotype) with body composition. Body size refers to a performer's height and weight, whereas build refers to their relative muscularity, height or fatness of their frame/shape. Standard ideal weight charts based on height estimate the recommended weight for individuals, as shown in Table 1 on page 460.

Body composition refers to the chemical make-up of the body and is split into two components: **fat mass** and **lean body mass** (fat-free mass). Fat mass refers to the percentage of body weight that is stored as fat (within adipose tissue). Lean body mass is the weight of the rest of the body, i.e. all the body's non-fat tissues including bone, muscle, organs and connective tissues. Fig 18.4.1 shows that two individuals may have the same weight but their body composition and shape can vary significantly, whereas Fig 18.4.4 (page 462) shows how fat mass and lean body mass make up the total body mass (weight).

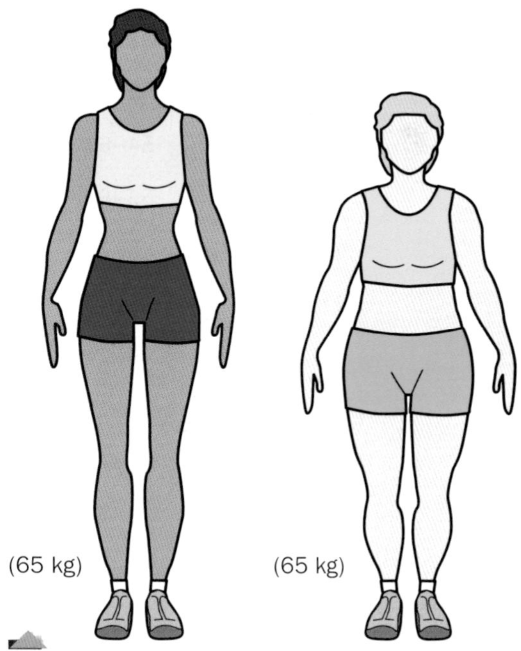

Fig 18.4.1 Height and weight do not always reflect body composition

KEY TERM

Fat mass

Percentage of body weight that is stored as fat (adipose tissue).

The average male has 12–18 per cent body fat, while the average female has 22–28 per cent. Typical values for elite athletes are 6–12 per cent for men and 12–20 per cent for women. Table 2 on page 461 shows typical body fat percentage for a variety of sports.

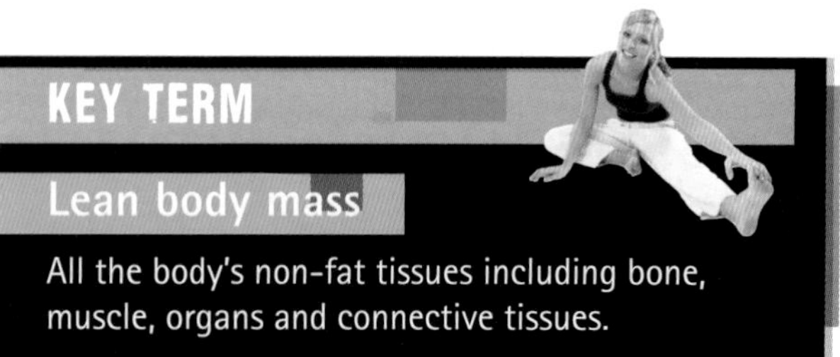

Lean body mass

All the body's non-fat tissues including bone, muscle, organs and connective tissues.

Table 1 Ideal weight based on height for male and females (adapted from www.brianmac.co.uk)

Height		Men		Women	
Feet and inches	Metres	kg	lbs	kg	lbs
4' 7"	1.40	-	-	40–53	88–116
4' 9"	1.45	-	-	42–54	92–119
4' 11"	1.50	-	-	43–55	94–121
4' 11½"	1.52	-	-	44–56	97–123
5' ½"	1.54	-	-	44–57	97–125
5' 1"	1.56	-	-	45–58	99–128
5' 2"	1.58	51–64	112–141	46–59	101–130
5' 2½"	1.60	52–65	114–143	48–61	105–134
5' 3½"	1.62	53–66	116–145	49–62	108–136
5' 4½"	1.64	54–67	119–147	50–64	110–141
5' 5"	1.66	55–69	121–152	51–65	112–143
5' 6"	1.68	56–71	123–156	52–66	114–145
5' 6½"	1.70	58–73	127–161	53–67	117–147
5' 7½"	1.72	59–74	130–163	55–69	121–152
5' 8½"	1.74	60–75	132–165	56–70	123–154
5' 9"	1.76	62–77	136–169	58–72	128–158
5' 10"	1.78	64–79	141–174	59–74	130–163
5' 10½"	1.80	65–80	143–176	-	-
5' 11½"	1.82	66–82	145–180	-	-
6' 0"	1.84	67–84	147–185	-	-
6' 1"	1.86	69–86	152–189	-	-
6' 2"	1.88	71–88	156–194	-	-
6' 2½"	1.90	73–90	161–198	-	-
6' 3½"	1.92	75–93	165–205	-	-

Table 1 provides a guide to a healthy weight range for an individual's height and gender. The table does not take into consideration age or frame size. A person with a petite physique ought to aim for an ideal weight at the lower end of the range. A person of the same height but with a larger frame could quite satisfactorily weigh in at the top of the range.

Table 2 Percentage body fat for male/female athletes in a variety of sports

Sport	Male	Female
Baseball	12–15%	12–18%
Basketball	6–12%	20–27%
Cycling	5–15%	15–20%
Field Hockey	8–15%	12–18%
Rowing	6–14%	12–18%
Swimming	9–12%	14–24%
Track – Runners	8–10%	12–20%
Track – Jumpers	7–12%	10–18%
Track – Throwers	14–20%	20–28%
Triathlon	5–12%	10–15%
Volleyball	11–14%	16–15%

TASK 1

1. Identify your ideal weight based on your height in Table 1.
2. Identify your ideal weight based on your height using the ideal body weight calculator available at www.heinemann.co.uk/hotlinks (enter the express code 6855P and click on the relevant link).
3. Are you at, below or above your ideal weight?
4. Discuss your differences in relation to body size and build.
5. What are the problems with using ideal weight tables?

APPLY IT!

It may be important for a basketball player to be tall, but if their percentage of body fat is too high they will not be able to move their total body weight at the speed and agility required to perform to their optimum in the full game. Similarly, the traditional high body fat mass of sumo wrestlers has changed significantly over the last 10 years, to that of a more muscular lean body mass, as the sport has become faster requiring more power and speed.

Fig 18.4.2 The traditional high body fat mass of sumo wrestlers (left) has been replaced with a more muscular lean body mass (right)

The ideal size for an athlete depends on the sport or event and sometimes the position they play in their sport (consider the various body sizes in a basketball, netball or rugby team). Although body size and build are important for athletes, their body composition is of greater concern. Standard ideal weight charts based on height do not provide accurate estimates of what athletes should weigh, as they do not account for body composition. Additional weight is not normally a concern if it is lean muscle mass (muscle mass weighs three times more than fat per unit of volume), which can actually contribute towards performance. Body composition tends to concentrate more on the percentage of fat tissue than lean body mass, and in most sports the athlete will try to keep levels of body fat to a minimum, as generally performance is increased the lower the percentage of body fat.

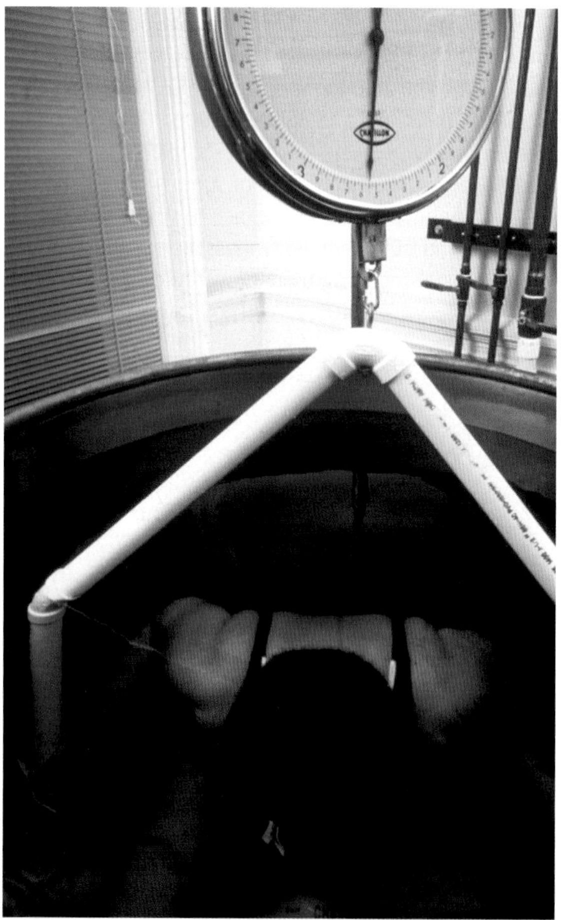

Fig 18.4.3 Hydrostatic weighing

TASK 2

Can you think of any sports for which an increased body fat percentage is preferable?

Before identifying the importance and application of body composition, you need to know the different methods by which it is assessed. This will enable you to understand what percentages of fat mass are classified as normal, overweight, obese and typical of different sports performers.

Body composition assessment

HYDROSTATIC WEIGHING

The most commonly used and accepted measure of body composition is hydrostatic weighing, where the athlete is weighed while totally immersed in a water tank. The difference between the athlete's scale weight and underwater weight is the athlete's fat mass percentage (the density of the water and trapped air in the lungs are normally taken into account). Fat is less dense and floats in water so the more fat the individual has the greater the difference between the dry and wet weights. Although accepted as practically the most accurate measure of body fat composition, hydrostatic weighing is not readily available to

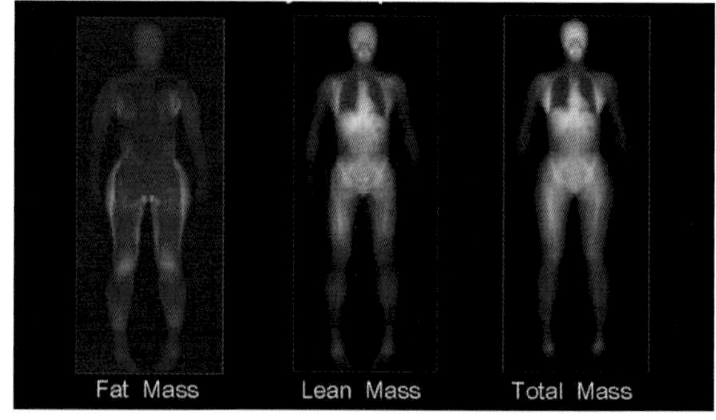

Fig 18.4.4 Dual-energy X-ray absorptiometry showing how fat and lean mass total whole body mass

most. Furthermore, it only estimates the density of fat-free mass, which varies according to gender, age and race.

TASK 3

1. For a simplistic body girth assessment of body composition, go to www.heinemann.co.uk/hotlinks, enter the express code 6855P and click on the relevant link.
2. Complete the body girth measurements at the respective sites and enter your results into the calculator to estimate your body fat percentage.
3. Compare and discuss your results.

KEY TERM

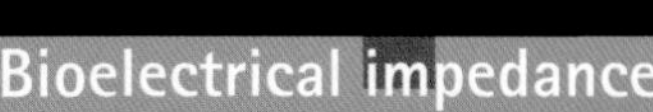

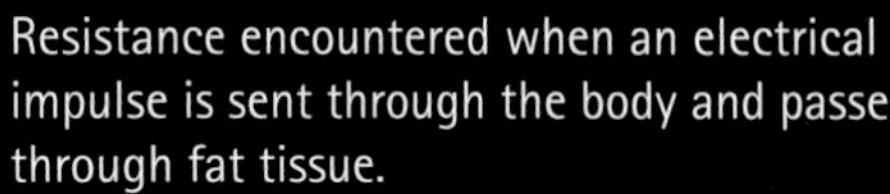

Bioelectrical impedance

Resistance encountered when an electrical impulse is sent through the body and passes through fat tissue.

BIOELECTRICAL IMPEDANCE SPECTROSCOPY (BIS)

Body fat scales use the Bioelectrical Impedance Analysis (BIA) technique. This method measures body composition by sending a low, safe electrical current through the body. This current passes freely through the fluids contained in muscle tissue, but encounters resistance when it passes through fat tissue; this is termed **bioelectrical impedance**. When set against a person's height and weight, the scales can then compute their body fat percentage.

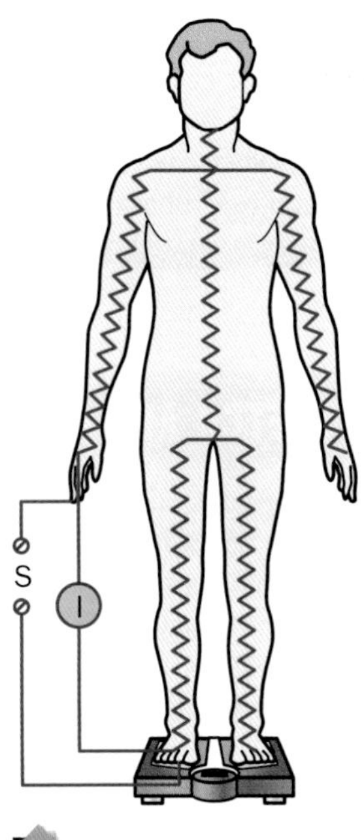

Fig 18.4.5 Body fat scales use the BIA technique

Although this method is reasonably accurate, it is not so practical. Since BIA relies on the fluid levels of fat-free mass, such as muscle tissue, it is affected by the level of hydration of the performer. Similarly, it uses average populations to determine body fat per cent and these may be less appropriate for elite athletes who carry more lean muscle tissue. Hence an individual's eating habits (alcohol, caffeine, etc.), the amount of exercise performed, the time of day, etc., cause variations in a person's weight and levels of hydration and therefore affect accurate readings of body composition.

SKINFOLD MEASURES: SKINFOLD CALLIPERS

Skinfold callipers are the most widely used method of assessing body composition due to them being accessible, cheap and more practical for use by performers and coaches. Skinfold callipers measure in millimetres the level of subcutaneous fat below the skin from selected sites on the body (see Fig 18.4.6a–d), and the sum of these skinfolds is used (in an equation) to estimate body fat percentage. Various skinfold tests are available which measure different sites on the body, but the four most common sites are the triceps, biceps, subscapular and suprailiac. More detailed tests use up to six sites, some of which are gender specific since body fat is stored and distributed differently between males and females. Multiple skinfold fat measurements provide a good estimate of body composition. Despite its ease of use, testers need to be properly trained and specific sites on the body measured to ensure accuracy.

Table 3 Four common sites for measurement of skinfold fat thickness using skinfold callipers: a) triceps; b) subscapula; c) biceps; d) suprailiac

Site	Method	
Triceps	Take a vertical skinfold parallel to upper arm, halfway between the shoulder and the elbow.	Fig 18.4.6a
Subscapula	Take a diagonal skinfold across the back, just below the shoulder blade.	Fig 18.4.6b
Biceps	Take a vertical skinfold halfway between the elbow and top of the shoulder on the front of the upper arm.	Fig 18.4.6c
Suprailiac	Take a diagonal skinfold along the line of the iliac crest, just above the hip bone.	Fig 18.4.6d

TASK 4

1 Take your body fat measures in millimetres for the four sites in Fig 18.4.6a–d.
2 Calculate your estimated body fat percentage by entering your total body fat measure in millimetres into the calculator provided on www.heinemann.co.uk/hotlinks (enter the express code 6855P and click on the relevant link).

STRETCH AND CHALLENGE

1 Find out about the Yuhasz skinfold technique by going to www.heinemann.co.uk/hotlinks, entering the express code 6855P and clicking on the relevant link.
2 Complete the skinfold measurements and enter your results, including age and gender, into the Yuhasz calculator.
3 Compare and account for any differences between the results you obtained for Task 4 and the Yuhasz results.

STRETCH AND CHALLENGE

Owen Anderson, writing in *Peak Performance* (March 2003, No.178), reviewed a new method of body composition measurement called the 'Bod Pod' which claims to eliminate the inaccuracies of skinfold equations and requires little knowledge or expertise for its use.

Research the use of the 'Bod Pod' and summarise its effectiveness as an alternative to the body composition assessment methods already covered. To read Owen Anderson's original article, go to www.heinemann.co.uk/hotlinks, enter the express code 6855P and click on the relevant link.

Body Mass Index (BMI)

Now that you have an understanding of the different methods of assessing body composition, you can now compare these with another method which is presently being used by the government to measure weight and obesity – **body mass index** (BMI). But why is BMI used to measure weight and obesity when it does not actually measure body composition in respect of fat mass and lean body mass percentage?

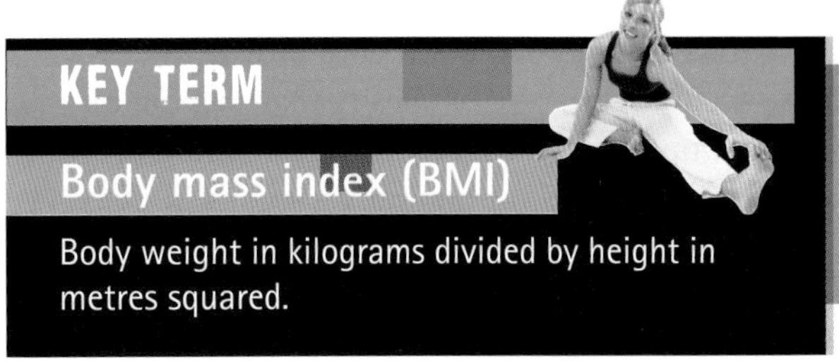

Body weight in kilograms divided by height in metres squared.

Body mass index (BMI) is a measure of an adult's weight in relation to their height, or more specifically their weight in kilograms divided by their height in metres squared. The normal acceptable range for adult BMI varies between organisations and countries, but 20.1–25.0 for men and 18.5–23.8 for women are norm values.

Table 4 simplistically explains what your BMI is indicative of. BMI does *not* directly measure

Table 4 BMI values and meaning (Source: adapted from www.nhs.uk)

BMI	What does your BMI score mean?
Below 18.5	You are underweight for your height; this is a health risk and too low for optimal health.
18.5–24.9	Well done for being in the ideal weight-for-height range. But remember that it's still important to eat a healthy diet if you want to stay in that range, and to ensure that your body has all the nutrients it needs.
25.0–29.9	Your weight is just above the ideal range. That's fine if you're a keen athlete with plenty of body muscle, but if this isn't the reason for your higher BMI, your health is beginning to suffer from the extra stored fat and you are at greater risk of weight-related health problems. Check your diet and make small changes to prevent more weight gain, and to help lose the extra weight.
30.0–34.9	This is a wake-up call: change your diet now. You are at a much higher risk of developing ill-health due to your weight. You're ten times more likely to get diabetes, and your weight is increasing your risk of arthritis, heart disease and some cancers. Your weight means you have a shorter life expectancy, and weight-related health concerns will reduce your quality of life. Remember, even a 5–10 per cent weight loss will have a major benefit on your health. So what are you waiting for?
35.0+	It's likely that you already know that your weight is seriously affecting your health. You're at raised risk of heart disease, stroke and premature death. In addition to making lifestyle changes, you should discuss your weight issues with your GP or district nurse, as you may need the additional support of a health professional. A BMI of 39+ indicates that you are very obese.
Lose weight	If your BMI has revealed that you're overweight, then it's time to take action. Even a modest weight loss will reap fantastic health benefits. Losing 5–10 kg (11–22 lb) improves back and joint pain, lowers your risk of developing diabetes, reduces breathlessness and improves your sleep quality, helping you to feel fitter and more energised throughout the day. Losing 10 per cent of your weight lowers blood pressure, improves blood sugar control and lowers total cholesterol. And don't forget the positive outlook you'll get when you successfully lose weight and take control of your diet and lifestyle.

percentage of body fat, but it does provide a more accurate measure of obesity than relying on weight alone. It offers a very simple measure of 'fatness' that allows for natural variations in body shape and enables an individual to check whether they are at risk of weight-related health problems for a particular height.

Despite BMI not directly measuring fat mass, it is related/correlated to body composition and gives a better estimate of obesity than standard height/weight tables, such as Table 1. Although BMI is a useful guide for most of the adult population, it doesn't work for everyone. It is not suitable for young children, pregnant women, older people, athletes and those with a higher than average muscle mass. Heavier muscles can push the BMI measurement over the normal range, so heavily muscled rugby players and body builders will have 'obese' BMIs, even though their body fat percentage may be within and even below those recommended for good health. Despite its failings, in recent years the BMI has become the medical standard used to measure weight and obesity. As you will see later, BMI is presently used as part of the government's objectives to slow down the trend of increasing obesity rates within the UK.

Fig 18.4.7 Heavier muscles can push the BMI measurement over the normal range

TASK 5

Calculate the BMI of the All Black rugby player Jonah Lomu, who had a weight of 124 kg and a height of 1.96 m aged 19 years. Discuss your findings.

APPLY IT!

BMI calculation for a 90 kg athlete who is 1.75 m tall:

Height squared = 1.75 x 1.75 m = 3.06 m^2

Weight divided by height squared: $\frac{90 \text{ kg}}{3.06 \text{ m}^2} = 29.4$ BMI

A BMI of 29 is overweight/borderline obese

TASK 6

1. Calculate your own BMI using the equation above.
2. Now go to www.heinemann.co.uk/hotlinks, enter the express code 6855P and click on the relevant link. Add your height and weight figures into the two online BMI calculators and obtain your BMI reading from each.
3. Identify your BMI from Table 5.
4. Compare your BMI values against the information in Table 4.
5. What are the advantages and disadvantages of using BMI?

Why is body composition important?

Now that you have identified what body composition is and how it can be measured, you need to identify the health implications of being overweight or obese and how this impacts on involvement/performance in physical activity.

Table 5 BMI assessment scale (Source: Heart Screen Inc.)

BMI	Height (inches)																		
Weight (lbs)	58	59	60	61	62	63	64	65	66	67	68	69	70	71	72	73	74	75	76
100	21	20	20	19	18	18	17	17	16	16	15	15	14	14	14	13	13	13	12
105	22	21	21	20	19	19	18	18	17	16	16	16	15	15	14	14	14	13	13
110	23	22	22	21	20	20	19	18	18	17	17	16	16	15	15	15	14	14	13
115	24	23	23	22	21	20	20	19	19	18	18	17	17	16	16	15	15	14	14
120	25	24	23	23	22	21	21	20	19	19	18	18	17	17	16	16	15	15	15
125	26	25	24	24	23	22	22	21	20	20	19	18	18	17	17	17	16	16	15
130	27	26	25	25	24	23	22	22	21	20	20	19	19	18	18	17	17	16	16
135	28	27	26	26	25	24	23	23	22	21	21	20	19	19	18	18	17	17	16
140	29	28	27	27	26	25	24	23	23	22	21	21	20	20	19	19	18	18	17
145	30	29	28	27	27	26	25	24	23	23	22	21	21	20	20	19	19	18	18
150	31	30	29	28	27	27	26	25	24	24	23	22	22	21	20	20	19	19	18
155	32	31	30	29	28	28	27	26	25	24	24	23	22	22	21	20	20	19	19
160	34	32	31	30	29	28	28	27	26	25	24	24	23	22	22	21	21	20	20
165	35	33	32	31	30	29	28	28	27	26	25	24	24	23	22	22	21	21	20
170	36	34	33	32	31	30	29	28	27	27	26	25	24	24	23	22	22	21	21
175	37	35	34	33	32	31	30	29	28	27	27	26	25	24	24	23	23	22	21
180	38	36	35	34	33	32	31	30	29	28	27	27	26	25	24	24	23	23	22
185	39	37	36	35	34	33	32	31	30	29	28	27	27	26	25	24	24	23	23
190	40	38	37	36	35	34	33	32	31	30	29	28	27	27	26	25	24	24	23
195	41	39	38	37	36	35	34	33	32	31	30	29	28	27	27	26	25	24	24
200	42	40	39	38	37	36	34	33	32	31	30	30	29	28	27	26	26	25	24
205	43	41	40	39	38	36	35	34	33	32	31	30	29	29	28	27	26	26	25
210	44	43	41	40	38	37	36	35	34	33	32	31	30	29	29	28	27	26	26
215	45	44	42	41	39	38	37	36	35	34	33	32	31	30	29	28	28	27	26
220	46	45	43	42	40	39	38	37	36	35	34	33	32	31	30	29	28	28	27
225	47	46	44	43	41	40	39	38	36	35	34	33	32	31	31	30	29	28	27
230	48	47	45	44	42	41	40	38	37	36	35	34	33	32	31	30	30	29	28
235	49	48	46	44	43	42	40	39	38	37	36	35	34	33	32	31	30	29	29
240	50	49	47	45	44	43	41	40	39	38	37	36	35	34	33	32	31	30	29
245	51	50	48	46	45	43	42	41	40	38	37	36	35	34	33	32	32	31	30
250	52	51	49	47	46	44	43	42	40	39	38	37	36	35	34	33	32	31	30
255	53	52	50	48	47	45	44	43	41	40	39	38	37	36	35	34	33	32	31
260	54	53	51	49	48	46	45	43	42	41	40	38	37	36	35	34	33	33	32
265	56	54	52	50	49	47	46	44	43	42	40	39	38	37	36	35	34	33	32
270	57	55	53	51	49	48	46	45	44	42	41	40	39	38	37	36	35	34	33
275	58	56	54	52	50	49	–	–	–	–	–	–	–	–	–	–	–	–	–

(NB: 1 stone = 14 lbs; 1 foot = 12 inches)

First, let's clarify what being overweight and obese means and how this links to energy expenditure and energy intake.

OVERWEIGHT AND OBESITY

Overweight and **obesity** occur as a result of an imbalance between energy intake (food consumption) and energy expenditure (work/physical activity). If energy intake exceeds expenditure then energy is stored as fat (adipose tissue). Therefore to lose weight, energy expenditure must exceed intake.

To fully understand how to influence the balance between energy expenditure and energy intake, you need knowledge of basal metabolic rate (BMR), energy measurement (METS) and calorific intake.

KEY TERMS

Overweight

Body weight exceeding the normal standard weight based on height/frame size (Table 1 page 460), or having a BMI between 25.0 and 29.9.

Obesity

Having a very high amount of body fat (20–25 per cent men and 30–35 per cent women) in relation to lean body mass, or having a BMI over 30.

Fig 18.4.8 Neutral energy balance = constant weight

TASK 7

Sketch a set of scales similar to those in Fig 18.4.8 to show the following relationships between energy intake and expenditure:

1 Positive = weight gain
2 Negative = weight loss

Energy Expenditure

BASAL METABOLIC RATE (BMR)

Metabolic rate is the body's rate of energy expenditure, and therefore **basal metabolic rate** is the lowest rate of energy expenditure needed to sustain the body's essential physiological functions while at rest (after 8 hours of sleep and 12 hours of fasting). The term 'resting metabolic rate' (RMR) is more often used in order to avoid the need to measure sleep and is the term used in this section.

KEY TERMS

Metabolic rate

The body's rate of energy expenditure.

Basal metabolic rate

The lowest rate of energy expenditure needed to sustain the body's essential physiological functions while at rest (after 8 hours of sleep and 12 hours of fasting).

When calculating the body's total daily energy expenditure, the RMR accounts for about 60–75 per cent, physical activity contributes 20–30 per cent, and the energy used in the process of eating, digesting, absorbing and using food, referred to as the **thermic effect**, accounts for the remainder (see Fig 18.4.9). To calculate these three components of your total energy expenditure you need to be able to calculate each aspect shown in Fig 18.4.9.

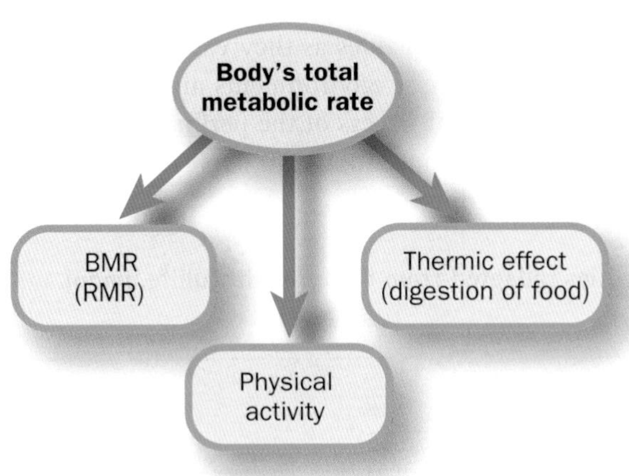

Fig 18.4.9 Body's total energy expenditure

KEY TERMS

Thermic effect

The energy used in the process of eating, digesting, absorbing and using food.

Calorie (cal)/ Kilocalorie (kcal)

The amount of heat energy needed to increase the temperature of one kilogram of water by 1 degree Celsius – exactly 1000 small calories, or about 4.184 kilo Joules (kJ). Calorie (cal) and Kilocalorie (kcal/Kcal) are the same and are used interchangeably.

Numerous equations offer a simple and quick way to calculate your RMR in terms of **calories** per day/hour, an example of which is shown below:

- *For adult males* – Multiply the body weight by 10, add double the body weight to this value (i.e. for a 150 lb male, 150 x 10 + 300 = 1,800 cal/day and ÷ 24 = 75 Calories/hr)
- *For adult females* – Multiply the body weight by 10, add the body weight to this value (i.e. for a 150 lb female, 150 x 10 +150 = 1,650 cal/day and ÷ 24 = 69 Calories/hr)

This figure represents the amount of calories you need to consume to sustain your body's energy requirements at rest (RMR).

TASK 8

Calculate your own RMR using the formula above.

Now you have established how to calculate the energy expenditure of your resting metabolic rate, you need to know how to calculate the additional energy expenditure for any physical activity you undertake. One of the most practical methods for calculating the energy expenditure of physical activity is the **Metabolic Equivalent Task (METs)** method.

KEY TERM

Metabolic Equivalent Task (METs)

The ratio of a performer's working metabolic rate relative to their resting metabolic rate.

METABOLIC EQUIVALENT TASK (METS)

METs use oxygen consumption per unit of body weight per minute (ml O_2/kg/min) to estimate exercise intensity, as oxygen consumption is directly proportional to the energy expenditure during activity.

At rest your body uses approximately 3.5 ml O_2 per kilogram of body weight per minute (3.5 ml/kg/min) and this equates to 0.0175 kcal/kg/min. Hence, 3.5 ml/kg/min or 0.0175 kcal/kg/min equals 1 MET and equates to your resting VO_2. This reflects the resting metabolic rate (RMR), i.e. the energy cost of sitting quietly. Hence, METs reflect the ratio of a performer's working metabolic rate relative to their resting metabolic rate, so two METs indicates the energy expended is twice that at rest, three METs reflects triple the resting energy expenditure, etc.

REMEMBER

VO_2 is the volume of oxygen consumed.

Tables 6 and 7 list the energy cost of specific activities using METs values and show that a person's calorific consumption (energy expenditure) can typically be three to six times higher during moderate activity and six times higher when being vigorously active. METs tables vary from one source to another and are only approximate values as they vary between individuals, exercise environments and the changing level of fitness of the performer. They are sometimes thought to overestimate energy expenditure.

Table 6 METs/hr expended on home and occupational activities (adapted from http://healthfullife.umdnj.edu/archives/METsTbl.htm)

METs	Activity/occupation
1.3	Standing
1.5	Reading, talking on telephone
1.8	Sitting in class, studying, note-taking
2.0	Walking on job, at 2 mph (in office or lab area), easy casual
2.0	Light gardening
2.0	Light office work, light use of hand tools (watch repair or micro-assembly, light assembly/repair); standing, light work (bartending, store clerk, assembling, filing)
2.5	Walking downstairs
2.5	Cooking, light housekeeping, shopping
2.5	Somewhat heavier gardening
2.5	Brisk walking: pushing stroller with child, walking dog
3.0	Standing, light/moderate work (assemble/repair heavy parts, welding, auto repair, pack boxes for moving, etc.), patient care (as in nursing); driving heavy tractor, bus, truck
3.0	Washing car or windows, mopping, moderately vigorous playing with children, sweeping outside house, vacuuming, picking fruit or vegetables, scrubbing floors
3.5	Walking on job, 3 mph (one mile every twenty minutes), in office, moderate speed, not carrying anything, or carrying only light articles
4.0	Raking lawn, planting shrubs, weeding garden, heavy yard work or gardening activities
4.0	Masonry, painting, paper hanging, moderately heavy lifting, moderately heavy farm work
5.0	Walking downstairs or standing, carrying objects about 25–49 lb (11–22 kg)
5.0	Digging, spading, vigorous gardening, using heavy power tools; general gardening, mowing lawn (hand mower)
5.0	Painting, carpentry, cleaning gutters, laying carpet, other vigorous activities
5.0	Chopping wood
6.0	Using heavy tools (not power) such as shovel, pick, spade; driving heavy machinery, forestry
6.5	Walking downstairs or standing, carrying objects about 50–74 lb (22.6–33.6 kg)
6.5	Loading and unloading truck (standing); moving heavy objects; heavy farming work
7.5	Walking downstairs or standing, carrying objects about 75–99 lb (34–45 kg)
8.0	Heavy farming

Table 7 Approximate METs per hour values for activities (adapted from http://healthfullife.umdnj.edu/archives/METsTbl.htm)

Activity	METS	Activity	METS
Sitting/lying quietly	1.0	Hiking (hilly)	6.5
Walking (less than 3.2 km/hr level surface)	2.0	Aerobic dance, high impact	7.0
Bowling	2.5	Badminton, competitive	7.0
Yoga/stretching	2.5	Backpacking	7.0
Cycling (50 watts, light effort)	3.0	Dancing (vigorous)	7.0
Golf (electric trolley)	3.0	Skating (ice/roller)	7.0
Resistance training (light/)moderate)	3.0	Rowing machine (100 watts, moderate effort)	7.0
Volleyball (recreational)	3.0	Stationary cycling (150 watts, moderate effort)	7.0
Walking (4 km/hr)	3.0	Swimming laps (freestyle, slow, moderate or light effort)	7.0
Horse riding	3.5	Basketball game	8.0
Rowing machine (50 watts, light)	3.5	Circuit training, including some aerobic stations, with minimal rest	8.0
Walking (5.6 km/hr, level surface)	3.8	Football	8.0
Cricket	4.0	Hockey	8.0
Dancing (moderate/fast)	4.0	Outdoor cycling (12–13.9 mph; 19.3–22.4 km/hr)	8.0
Water aerobics, water calisthenics	4.0	Singles tennis, squash, racquet-ball	8.0
Badminton (social singles and doubles)	4.5	Skiing downhill	8.0
Calisthenics	4.5	Running (12 min/mile)	8.5
Golf (carrying/walking)	4.5	Squash	8.5
Table tennis	4.5	Basketball	9.0
Aerobic dance, low impact	5.0	Running (5.2 mph; 3.2 km/hr; 11.5-minute mile)	9.0
Doubles tennis	5.0	Skiing cross-country (vigorous)	9.0
Gymnastics	5.5	Running (6 mph; 9.7 km/hr; 10-minute mile)	10.0
Aerobic dancing	6.0	Swimming laps, freestyle, fast, vigorous effort	10.0
Basketball, non-game	6.0	Stationary cycling, 200 watts, vigorous effort	10.5
Outdoor cycling (16.1–19.2 km/hr)	6.0	Running (6.7 mph; 10.8 km/hr; 9-minute mile)	11.0
Resistance training vigorous	6.0	Rowing machine, 200 watts, very vigorous effort	12.0
Slow jogging	6.0	Running (7.5 mph; 12.1 km/hr; 8-minute mile)	12.5
Swimming (recreational, light)	6.0	Outdoor cycling, more than 20 mph (32.2 km/hr)	16.0
Walking (7.2 km/hr, level surface)	6.3		

APPLY IT!

Cross-country skiing with a METs value of 8.0 means that you would be using eight times the energy expenditure/kilocalories used compared with when sitting at rest (RMR).

TASK 9

To gain the most basic, rough estimate of your daily calorific requirements, choose the appropriate equation from below, based on your activity level.

1 For sedentary people: weight (lbs) x 14 = estimated cal/day.
2 For moderately active people: weight (lbs) x 17 = estimated cal/day.
3 For active people: weight (lbs) x 20 = estimated cal/day.

Note: sedentary is defined as little or no aerobic sessions per week; moderately active is defined as 3–4 aerobic sessions per week; active is defined as 5–7 aerobic sessions per week.

With your RMR and the METs value for your particular activity/daily activity, it is possible to estimate the number of calories you use while participating in physical activity. A quick and simple way to translate this into calories is to multiply your RMR by the activity's METs value. For example:

A 150 lb female footballer undertaking a 60-minute football game (8.0 METs) will use 550 calories:

$150 \times 10 + 150 \div 24 \times 8.0 = 550$

The above calculation provides an approximate figure for estimating the caloric energy expenditure. By stating that 0.0175k cal/kg/min is equal to 3.5 ml/kg/min, you can use a more accurate calculation of the energy expenditure into kilocalories (kcal) for physical activity using METs. The following example uses the same performer as above, a 150 lb female footballer undertaking a 60-minute football game (MET 8.0).

150 lb = 68.1 kg (1 lb = 0.454 kg)
8 METs x 0.0175 = 0.14 kcal/kg/min (1 MET = 0.0175 kcal/kg/min)
0.14 x 68.1 = 9.534 kcal/min
9.534 x 60 = 572.04 kcal (full duration of the activity)

An alternative equation, using the same figures and which brings the same results, is shown below.

Total calories burned = (METs x 3.5 x your weight in kg) ÷ 200 x duration in minutes
= 8.0 x 3.5 x 68.1
= 1906.8 ÷ 200
= 9.534 kcal/min x 60 minutes
= 572.04 kcal/hour

TASK 10

Calculate the energy expenditure for a performer weighing 75 kg who performs 25 minutes of recreational swimming with a METs value of 6.0.

TASK 11

Using the MET values in Tables 6 and 7 use your own weight in kg to calculate your DAILY energy expenditure into kcal for physical activity in one typical 24-hour day. To do this use the equation:

MET value x 0.0175 x weight in kg x minutes exercised

(recall that one MET equates to 0.0175cal/kg/min).

a) Add this daily physical activity energy expenditure value to your RMR value from Task 8.
b) What does this figure represent?
c) How might this be beneficial to you in terms of maintaining balanced energy intake and energy expenditure?

STRETCH AND CHALLENGE

1 Using the MET values in Tables 6 and 7, use your own weight in kg to calculate your WEEKLY energy expenditure into kcal for physical activity in one typical week by using the equation: MET value x 0.0175 x weight in kg x minutes exercised (recall that one MET equates to 0.0175kcal/kg/min):
   - Walking to college: ½ hour at a 4 km/hr pace: = 1.5 METs for 5 days = 1.5 METs x 150 min.
   - Playing hockey for 1 hour moderately vigorously = 8 METs x 60 min.
   - 1 hour vigorous gardening work = 4 METs x 60 min.
   - 3 x ½ hour light housekeeping, shopping = 2.5 METs x 90 min.
   - Weekly total = 7.5 + 8 + 4 + 7.5 = 27 METs

2 Add this physical activity energy expenditure figure to your RMR figure from Task 8.

3 How might this be beneficial to you in terms of maintaining balanced energy intake and energy expenditure?

For elite athletes who are training heavily, calculations of energy expenditure are used to indicate their required nutritional intake in terms of calories in order that energy intake equals energy expenditure. This prevents the danger of athletes not having sufficient energy to fuel the activity demands. Similarly, the kcal/min value can be used to calculate how many minutes of exercise (depending upon its METs value) an athlete should undertake in order to ensure they are using equal calories for expenditure as they are for energy intake. If energy intake outweighs expenditure, then it will be stored as fat body mass and lead to overweight/obesity-related health problems.

STRETCH AND CHALLENGE

The thermic effect of food (TEF) refers to the increase in energy expenditure required to digest food. This is beyond the specification requirements for A2, but there is a simple equation to determine its value. Once you have calculated your daily intake in kilocalories (see Task 12 on page 475), use the equation below and add this figure along with your RMR and physical activity energy expenditure figures to enable you to estimate your total energy expenditure.

TEF = total kcals consumed x 10%
For example: 3000 kcals consumed/day x 0.10 = 300 kcals expended for TEF

Energy intake

Energy intake is food consumed, or dietary intake. You need to be able to evaluate critically your own diet and calorie consumption. Recommended daily calorie intake varies from person to person, but there are guidelines for calorie requirements you can use as a starting point.

The UK Department of Health Estimated Average Requirements (EAR) give a daily calorie intake of 1940 calories per day for women and 2550 for men, but this can vary greatly depending on lifestyle, age, height, weight, activity and body composition. A balanced diet should contain:

- approximately 10–15 per cent protein
- no more than 30 per cent fat
- 55–60 per cent carbohydrate (CHO)
- include foods from what is termed the '5 a day' main nutrient food groups, as shown in Fig 18.4.11, to ensure vital vitamins, minerals, water and roughage are included.

Fig 18.4.10 Components of a balanced diet

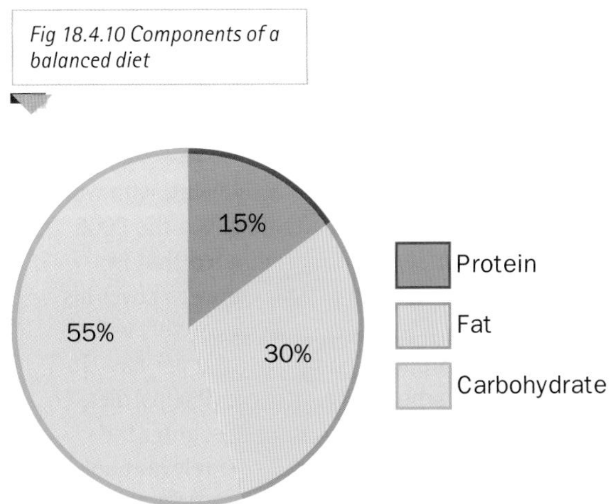

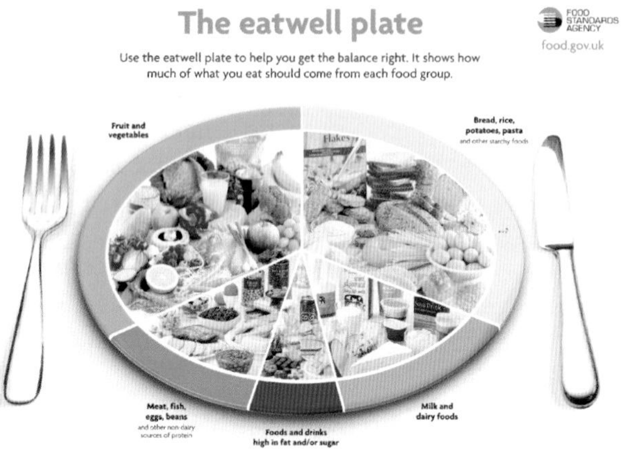

The eatwell plate

Use the eatwell plate to help you get the balance right. It shows how much of what you eat should come from each food group.

Fruit and vegetables

Bread, rice, potatoes, pasta and other starchy foods

Meat, fish, eggs, beans and other non-dairy sources of protein

Foods and drinks high in fat and/or sugar

Milk and dairy foods

Fig 18.4.11 The eatwell plate is a government food guide showing the proportion and types of foods that make up a healthy balanced diet

The '5 a day' food groups shown in Fig 18.4.11 are:

- bread, cereal (including breakfast cereals) and potatoes (starchy foods)
- fruit (including fresh fruit juice) and vegetables
- meat and fish
- milk and dairy foods
- fats and sugar.

It is important to understand that a performer participating in a high volume of training, especially endurance training, is likely to require an increased percentage (an additional 10–15 per cent) of carbohydrate intake in what's commonly referred to as an athlete's diet. Athletes undertaking large amounts of physical activity (high energy expenditure) will often consume up to 5000 to 6000 kcal a day to refuel the kcal required to maintain their activity/recovery levels.

APPLY IT!

Newspapers reporting on Michael Phelps, who won eight Olympic swimming gold medals in the 2008 Beijing Olympics, typically exaggerated that he was consuming over 10,000 kcal a day to cover his energy expenditure demands. However, this would more likely be around 5000–6000 kcal per day. (To read an online article about Michael Phelps' diet, go to www.heinemann.co.uk/hotlinks, enter the express code 6855P and click on the relevant link.)

CALORIE COUNTING

There is not sufficient space to outline all the calorific values of your dietary intake in this book. A more practical and accurate calculation can be found by using a number of free calorie counter tools accessible via the Internet, some of which are included in Task 13.

Task 12 uses calculations that base their estimate of RMR energy expenditure on 1.3 calories being required per hour per kg of weight, and estimate physical activity energy expenditure as 8.5 calories per hour of activity per kg of weight. For example, a male performer weighing 75 kg would have a RMR of 2340 calories a day (75 x 1.3 x 24) and with 90 minutes of physical activity would have an energy expenditure of 956 calories a day (75 x 8.5 x 1.5). This would therefore produce a total daily energy expenditure of 3296 calories a day. This figure provides an indication of what the performer should be consuming in terms of energy intake, depending on whether their target is to achieve a negative, positive or neutral energy balance (see Fig 18.4.8 on page 468). More specifically, we can now apply our recommended percentages for a balanced diet to this total energy expenditure figure to calculate that in the example above:

- 1813 (55 per cent of 3296) calories need to come from CHOs
- 989 (30 per cent of 3296) calories need to come from fats
- 494 (15 per cent of 3296) calories from proteins from across the '5 a day' food sources.

However, these three food sources provide different energy yield in calories per gram: CHOs and protein provide 4 calories per gram while fats provide 9 calories per gram. Therefore, the performer would require a dietary consumption of:

- (1813 ÷ 4 =) 453 grams CHOs
- (989 ÷ 9 =) 110 grams fat
- (494 ÷ 4 =) 124 grams protein.

As you are now probably aware, calorie counting is not a simple task. This is why most elite athletes have a nutritionist to calculate what and how much they should be consuming.

TASK 12

1 Using the daily calorie counter available at www.heinemann.co.uk/hotlinks (enter the express code 6855P and click on the relevant link), estimate your daily calorie intake requirements.
2 Compare this with your total daily energy expenditure calculated in Task 11.
3 Subjectively evaluate your *actual* daily dietary/calorie intake compared with that suggested from the calculator in respect of carbohydrates, fats and proteins and in relation to the '5 a day' food groups. (Note: the calculator uses a recommendation of 57 per cent CHO, 30 per cent fats and 13 per cent protein, so the figures will vary slightly from the 55/30/15 division in the text earlier.)
4 How might you alter your dietary intake now that you have a more accurate idea of your energy intake requirements?

STRETCH AND CHALLENGE

A more accurate but time consuming way of measuring your energy intake is by counting the actual calorific value of the food/drink you consume.

1 Go to www.heinemann.co.uk/hotlinks, enter the express code 6855P and click on the relevant link to access a website which lists calorific values for a selection of popular brands and basics foods.
2 Calculate the calorific intake of one average day and compare this with your estimate in Task 12.
3 Alternatively, if you would like to know the calorie and nutrition content of foods not included in this calorie counter, go to www.heinemann.co.uk/hotlinks, enter the express code 6855P and click on the relevant link to access a comprehensive and accurate food database free for 24 hours.

HEALTH IMPLICATIONS OF BEING OVERWEIGHT/OBESE

Now that you have an understanding of energy expenditure and energy intake, you need to be more aware of the health implications of having a positive energy balance, where energy intake is greater than energy expenditure which leads to weight gain and an individual becoming overweight or obese.

Before you identify the negative health effects of increased fat/body weight, it is important to establish that fat is not always bad. In Chapter 16 (page 376) you saw that fat is an essential energy fuel for endurance activity, but in addition it has a role as insulation against the cold and protection of vital organs. However, if you recall from your AS study on coronary heart disease (see *OCR AS PE*, pages 94–95), too much fat composition/obesity is one of the risk factors, alongside smoking, which is linked to a rise in coronary heart disease.

In health terms, although obesity is not a disease, it is recognised as a health hazard. Too much fat is associated with:

- an increased risk of diabetes
- an increased risk of cancers
- long-term stress on the cardio-vascular systems leading to coronary heart disease, angina, varicose veins, deep vein thrombosis, increased blood lipids, atherosclerosis (disease of arteries), high blood pressure, stroke, poor temperature regulation, low fatigue resistance, renal/gall bladder disease, respiratory problems, lethargy and surgical operations at much higher risk
- overload of joints, especially lower body joints, which adversely impacts on body posture and alignment and consequently leads to musculo-skeletal pain/injuries like lower back pain typical of lower lumbar lordosis of the spine
- psychological harm due to the associated stigma, ridicule, staring, bullying, etc.
- under performance in both physical and mental work, such as education.

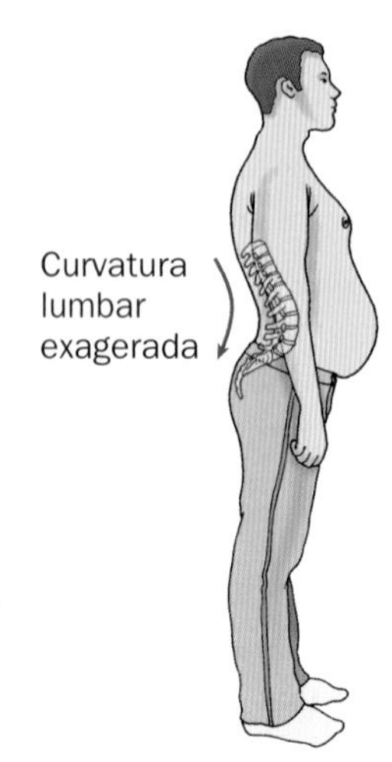

Fig 18.4.12 Lordosis of the vertebrae – an excessive inward curve (extension) of the lower lumbar vertebrae – is a condition associated with obesity

So why should we be so concerned about obesity? Below is a compilation of facts and estimated trends from government and international bodies related to obesity which makes startling reading.

- There has been an alarming increase in obesity over the last 10 years in the UK. Most adults in the UK are already overweight. Modern living ensures every generation is heavier than the last – known as 'passive obesity'. This is linked to a sedentary lifestyle.
- A European Commission league table shows that Britons are among the heaviest people in Europe, with the average person being overweight (an average BMI of 25.5).
- Obesity increases with age and about 76 per cent of men and 68 per cent of women aged 55–64 years are overweight or obese; this figure has roughly doubled since the mid-1980s. Almost two-thirds of adults (62 per cent) and a third of children (30 per cent) are either overweight or obese.
- By 2050, 60 per cent of men and 50 per cent of women could be clinically obese. Research warns that a third of British adults and a fifth of children will be obese by 2010 if trends continue. The Government Office for Science's Foresight programme suggests that, without action, these figures will rise to almost nine in ten adults and two-thirds of children by 2050.
- Rates of obesity are rising in children (see Fig 18.4.13). Fewer than 5 per cent of children walk/cycle to school, compared with 80 per cent twenty years ago. Schools are blamed for adding to the problem by selling off playing fields, having no proper sports halls and doing too little to offer healthy lunches. There is a strong indication that approximately 80 per cent of obese children will become obese adults.
- Obesity-related illnesses put pressure on families, the NHS and society more broadly. Without action, the cost to society is forecast to reach £50 billion per year by 2050.
- Obesity causes 18 million sick days a year, with an estimated £1–2 billion annual cost to the NHS and £2–3 billion cost to the wider economy through lost productivity.
- Reijo Kemppinen, Head of the European Commission in the UK, summarised the situation well when he said 'Obesity is one of the major issues affecting this generation and both men and women and all races and age groups seem to be affected by the growing tendency to become obese.'

The above points paint a bleak picture of the looming threat that being overweight and obese has on the health of the population of the UK, and you will need to consider what the government is doing about it.

Figures 18.4.13, 18.4.14 and 18.4.15 graphically summarise the prevalence of obesity and estimated numbers for adults and children.

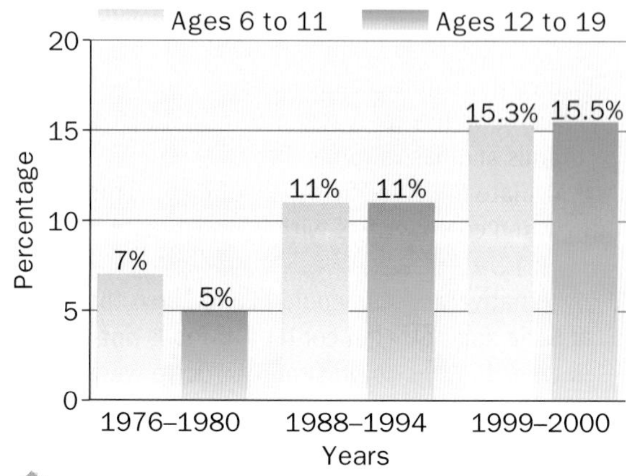

Fig 18.4.13 Increasing trend of childhood obesity, 1976–2000 (Source: How Stuff Works, 2007)

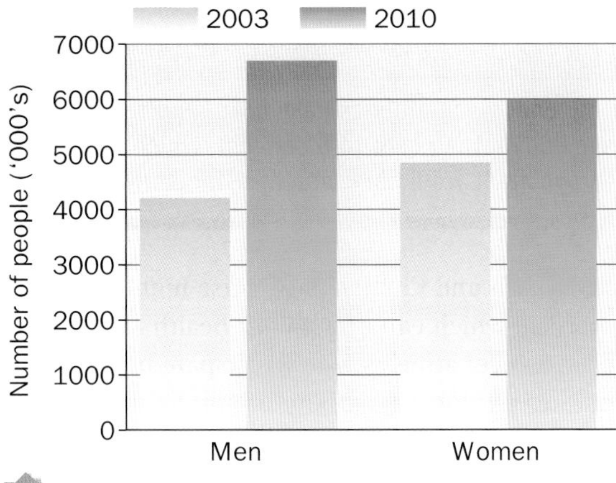

Fig 18.4.14 Estimated number of adults overweight and obese, 2003 and 2010, by gender (Source: Department of Health)

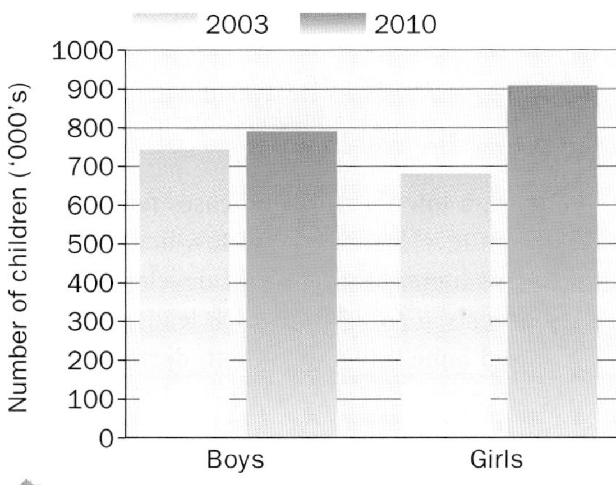

Fig 18.4.15 Estimated number of children overweight and obese, 2003 and 2010, by gender (Source: Department of Health)

STRETCH AND CHALLENGE

The statistics related to obesity were collated from the following sources, which you can refer to and research for a more detailed analysis:

- *The Mail Online*, 'Overweight Britons are among the fattest in Europe', 14 November 2006
- UK Obesity Statistics
- Department of Health, The National Child Measurement Programme: Guidance for PCTs (2008–09 school year)
- Healthy Weight, Healthy Lives 2006 Health Survey for England

TASK 13

Consider the following government statement, made in October 2007 when announcing its new ambition to combat obesity: 'to be the first major country to reverse the rising tide of obesity and overweight in the population by ensuring that everyone is able to maintain a healthy weight. Our initial focus will be on children; by 2020, we aim to reduce the proportion of overweight and obese children to 2000 levels.'

1. What schemes or projects are you aware of that are attempting to achieve this government ambition?
2. How does the government's ambition impact on involvement and performance in physical activity?
3. What advice would you give to the government, based on your knowledge from this chapter, in order for it to achieve its ambition?

PERFORMANCE IMPLICATIONS OF BODY WEIGHT

A main characteristic of successful performers is a low body fat content (above that required for good health).

Athletes generally carry less body fat due to their increased physical activity levels (energy expenditure and metabolic functioning), which over time has chipped away at their fat stores. However, this does not necessarily mean that an athlete will have a low overall body mass/weight, as heavily muscular athletes will have a high body mass alongside a low fat mass. Anaerobic/sprinter-type athletes tend to have a heavier body mass with more musculature of the upper and lower body and a low fat mass, while endurance athletes have a lower body mass with smaller muscles but with a very low body fat (see Figs 18.4.16 and 18.4.17).

A low fat mass is more significant in endurance performers as any weight not directly linked to maintaining metabolism and muscular performance has to be carried for longer, wasting energy that could be used for increasing the intensity or prolonging their performance.

Increased weight from muscle mass is fine if it adds power/force specific to the improvement of the activity of the performer.

Note: In the above categorisations, we are only describing the power-to-weight ratio potential and not looking at skill, which can make up for optimum power-to-weight ratio.

APPLY IT!

Fat mass reduces the power-to-weight ratio (Newton's Second Law: acceleration is inversely proportional to mass of the object) and may impair an athlete's optimum performance.

STRETCH AND CHALLENGE

Discuss the following statement: 'Is there an ideal body weight/body composition?'

APPLY IT!

Some endurance athletes have been reported to have body fat per cent of 6 per cent, which for an average adult would be classed as unhealthy!

The Stretch and Challenge exercise highlights one issue which can affect both health and performance: athletes who participate in high volumes of physical activity are prone to the opposite effect of obesity and can end up with too little body fat.

- Body fat less than 5 per cent in men and 10–15 per cent in women is thought to affect the immune system, thereby increasing the risk of illness. This is typical in elite endurance athletes, resulting in impaired training and performance.
- Female athletes are at further increased risk of irregular menstrual cycles below 18 per cent body fat.
- Similarly, a low fat mass decreases female oestrogen levels. Alongside a low body mass, this increases the risk of developing osteoporosis, a condition which leads to decreased bone mineral content, decreased bone strength and increased risk of bone fracture, causing problems later in life for post-menopausal women.

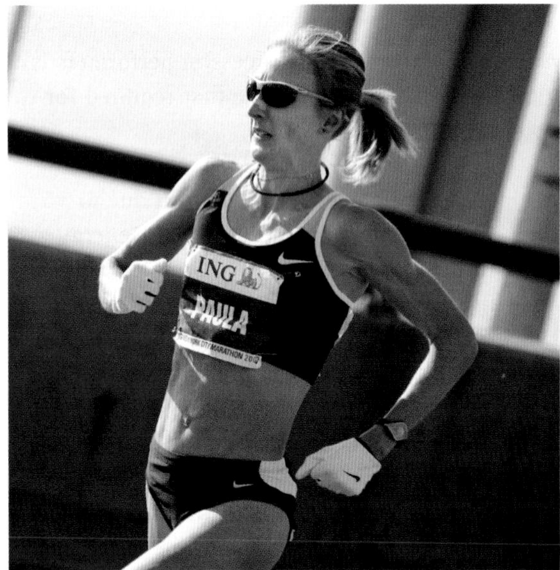

Fig 18.4.16 Paula Radcliffe is a distance athlete with lower body mass and smaller lean body mass

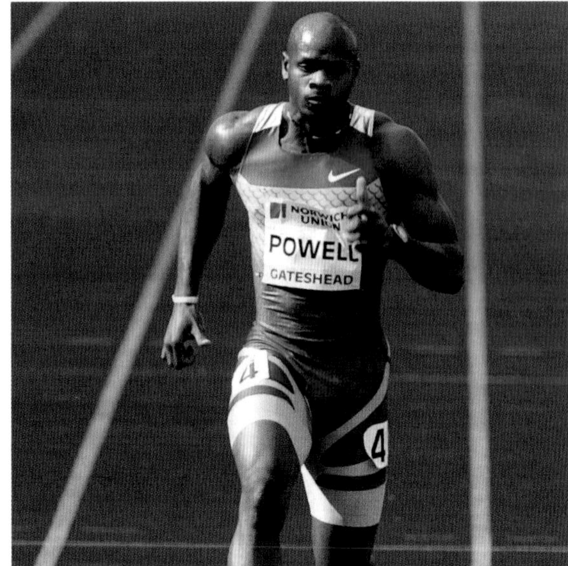

Fig 18.4.17 Asafa Powell is a power athlete (200m sprinter) with a greater body mass and greater lean muscle mass

REMEMBER

Osteoporosis was described in *OCR AS PE*, pages 36–7.

IMPLICATIONS FOR INVOLVEMENT

For overweight and obese individuals, involvement in physical activity has both physical and psychological health implications. You have already covered all the negative health effects, but consider that such individuals participating in any weight-bearing physical activity will have:

- increased energy expenditure cost, load bearing of joints and risk of injury
- decreased joint mobility/flexibility, economy of movement and fatigue resistance.

It is therefore not surprising that many people who are overweight/obese do not regard physical activity positively. Add to this the psychological impact of how they may be perceived by themselves and by others due to the associated stigma of being overweight, it is understandable that many overweight/obese people may not wish to be seen or involved in an athletic environment, semi-clothed, flushed, sweating and out of breath.

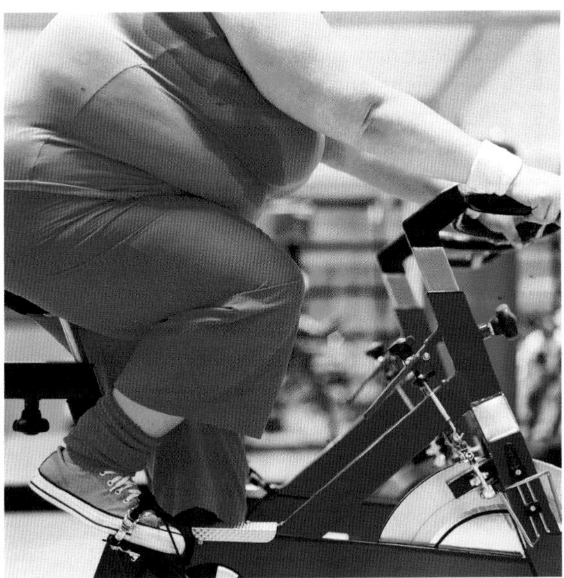

Fig 18.4.18 Many people who are overweight/obese do not regard physical activity positively

APPLY IT!

As a Physical Education student, you are less likely to have avoided physical activity for reasons linked to obesity, but think back to a situation when you were aware of an overweight/obese person exercising and think seriously about what your reaction was. Did you try helping or offer support? Did you stare, ridicule or laugh? Were you apathetic and did neither? What would you do now?

Now that you have established the effects of being overweight and obese on health, performance and involvement in physical activity, you need to look back and consider the effect that participation in physical activity may have on body composition and more specifically fat mass.

Effects of physical activity on body composition

We have already identified that inactivity is a major contributor towards obesity, so clearly engagement in physical activity will help reduce obesity.

Physical activity increases energy expenditure; remember that energy expenditure primarily consists of activity expenditure and RMR:

- By increasing physical activity the number of calories burned also increases.
- In addition to the calories burned during physical activity, a significant calorie expenditure is incurred post-exercise (see Chapter 16, page 386) and this increases the metabolic rate for several hours and up to 24 hours after prolonged exhaustive exercise.
- Exercise minimises the loss of lean body tissue (muscle mass) which burns more calories than fat mass.
- Exercise can increase lean body tissue (muscle mass) thereby burning even more calories.
- Exercise increases the mobilisation/use of fat as an energy fuel.

- All the above factors in turn have the effect of increasing the bodies RMR, so more calories are being burned when the body is at rest.
- Also, there is some support to suggest that exercise may suppress appetite so that calorific intake better balances energy intake (this may help decrease energy intake, i.e. prevent overeating).

In summary, physical activity helps create a negative energy balance by speeding up weight loss and ensuring a greater percentage of the lost weight is fat and not lean muscle mass.

STRETCH AND CHALLENGE

In 2005, the government asked Foresight, the UK Government's science-based futures think tank, to carry out a review of how we can respond sustainably to the prevalence of obesity in the UK over the next 40 years. Foresight reported its findings in 'Tackling Obesities: Future Choices' in October 2007, of which the main findings are listed below.

- The obesity 'epidemic' cannot be prevented by individual action alone and demands a societal approach.
- Tackling obesity requires far greater change than anything tried so far, and at multiple levels: personal, family, community and national.
- Preventing obesity is a societal challenge, similar to climate change. It requires partnership between government, science, business and civil society.
- Exercise is crucial as part of the wider process of tackling obesity.

Do you agree with these findings based on the concerns about obesity covered earlier in this chapter?

You now will have developed a wide range of knowledge based on the study of body composition and its application to both health and participation in physical activity, and no doubt appreciate that this is a complex area of study. You should now be able to evaluate and implement for yourself and advise others on the basic guidelines in relation to body composition for both health and performance.

STRETCH AND CHALLENGE

In Task 14 you saw that the UK government's 2020 'ambition' for obesity was initially to focus on reducing the proportion of overweight and obese children to 2000 levels by 2020. Earlier strategies have now been updated and expanded into 'Healthy Weight, Healthy Lives', a cross-government obesity strategy for England published in January 2008, which is wide-ranging and sends a clear signal to local areas by including the following:

- the Department of Health (DH), which is responsible for the overall obesity policy
- the Department for Children, Schools and Families (DCSF), responsible for tackling childhood obesity
- making obesity a national priority within the NHS Operating Framework (Vital Signs) and the Child Health Public Service Agreement (PSA)
- all Primary Care Trusts (PCTs) are required to implement the National Child Measurement Programme (NCMP) and develop plans to tackle child obesity and to agree them with their Health Authorities.

1. Investigate and summarise the PCT's role in implementing the NCMP.
2. What are your thoughts as to its effects on tackling obesity?
3. What are your views on the fact that it is non-statutory guidance and that parents/ children can opt out?
4. Guidance now suggests only using the term 'overweight' and not 'obese'. What are your thoughts on this?

EXAM TIP

The following body composition summary is purposely not bulleted to help you learn to write in essay style in continuous prose, as required for your extended 20-mark questions which require you to 'critically evaluate'.

Summary

It is clear that being overweight and obesity are increasing, and that poor diet and physical inactivity are having a substantial effect on health and involvement in physical activity and a healthy lifestyle, both in childhood and in later life. Child obesity is one of the most serious challenges and is linked to a number of poor outcomes (physical, social and psychological), requiring action to prevent the current upward trend.

Although height, weight and BMI are not a true or accurate measure of body composition and have many failings, they are regarded by the UK government as an excellent tool for tracking and analysing trends in childhood obesity. In this regard, height, weight and BMI measurements provide enormous potential in supporting the government's strategy to help people lose weight and live healthy lives. This explains the use of BMI by the Primary Care Trusts (PCTs) in primary schools to implement the National Child Measurement Programme (NCMP). Skinfold measurements are more practical to use and, even in the hands of a non-expert, as long as the same protocols are used, they can provide ongoing monitoring of an individual's body composition fat level and allow them to plan more accurately their training and dietary intake. With too little/much fat/weight being detrimental to performance, any changes throughout a season can be picked up and indicate if dietary/activity changes are required.

In attempting to help reduce obesity and decrease fat mass/weight, we need to look at the link between energy expenditure and energy intake. Inactivity is a major cause of obesity; fat mass does tend to decrease as the volume of training increases and exercise is possibly as important as overeating and is therefore an essential part of any weight reduction programme. Decreasing your dietary intake alone may decrease fat mass but is also likely to decrease your lean body mass and RMR, whereas with exercise both are maintained or even increased. Although body fat levels may adversely affect performance, reducing fat mass does not guarantee improved performance. By simply increasing the energy expenditure of training and decreasing energy intake by restricting your diet, you are more likely to decrease performance due to a lack of energy fuels.

The balance between energy expenditure and intake shows that exercise alone, like dietary intake, is not a practical prescription for losing weight. Exercise increases RMR so we can expect it to lead to weight loss, but it is not that simple. Energy expenditure during exercise is dependent upon the intensity of the activity and also on body weight, as more body weight requires more energy to move it. In practice, overweight individuals are not capable of carrying out the sufficient intensity of activity required and, due to their lack of fitness, any exercise would initially use carbohydrates as a fuel and not fats. Similarly, the normal advice to undertake low-intensity exercise to use more fats may be well-founded, but obese individuals are unlikely to have the time available or be able to endure the duration required to have any real effect.

Ageing is a further problem as the body's rate of burning calories naturally decreases, partly due to a decrease in muscle mass and increase in fat mass. Fat mass is less metabolically active in terms of calorie burning, and at the same time the diet tends to remain the same and over time fat mass continues to increase. Add a more sedentary and inactive lifestyle to ageing and this increases the imbalance between energy intake and expenditure even further. Regular physical activity helps reverse this imbalance by increasing/maintaining energy expenditure and RMR, and so when you are not exercising you are likely to be burning more calories – even while you are asleep.

It is important to appreciate that weight loss should not always be the main focus as research shows that, after regular activity, fat loss is often replaced by an equal amount of or increase in lean muscle mass with overall body mass remaining unchanged or even increased. This can be viewed as good weight and, over the long term, this is more beneficial as muscle burns more calories than fat. This highlights the importance of including even the simplest of strength resistance training programmes two to three times a week to help increase lean muscle mass to improve body composition. This is an important point for people to understand, especially women or those with the primary purpose of losing weight; that a change in body composition and not just weight loss is a desirable goal whether it is for health or performance.

With regard to the use of exercise to increase energy expenditure, the question to ask is: at what intensity should you exercise? Too low an intensity of activity and it takes too long a duration to complete; too high an intensity and it increases carbohydrate and not fat use. Research has often suggested that to lose body fat and improve body composition, performers should exercise at lower intensities; this is thought to increase fat use in preference to carbohydrates. This optimum point for burning body fat has been termed either fat zone, fat burning zone or fatmax (see Fig 18.4.19).

Owen Anderson, reviewing this area of work in *Peak Performance*, summarised that the most efficient way to decrease body fat mass is to create a negative energy balance, where energy expenditure is above that of energy intake, for an extended period of time. Applying the principle of overload by increasing exercise intensity, duration or frequency or a combination of these, would be more beneficial than trying to keep within any variation of the so-called 'fat burning zones'.

As many yo-yo dieters have found, weight lost quickly, usually returns just as quickly. It is much more effective to retain or increase your lean muscle by maintaining your glycogen stores, your water stores (hydration) and by undertaking sufficient exercise to ensure a negative energy balance. This should result in a slower, but more lasting weight loss, as the deficit in calories is more likely to come from fat stores.

The main concept to grasp is that muscles are the key element as they increase calorific expenditure, both during activity and at rest by increasing RMR, which together over time have the effect of decreasing body fat. Any weight gain due to physical activity is good weight (lean body mass) and, coupled with a reduction in food intake, exercise speeds

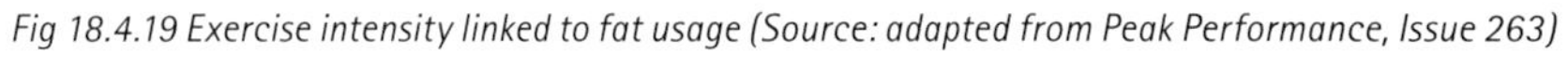
Fig 18.4.19 Exercise intensity linked to fat usage (Source: adapted from Peak Performance, Issue 263)

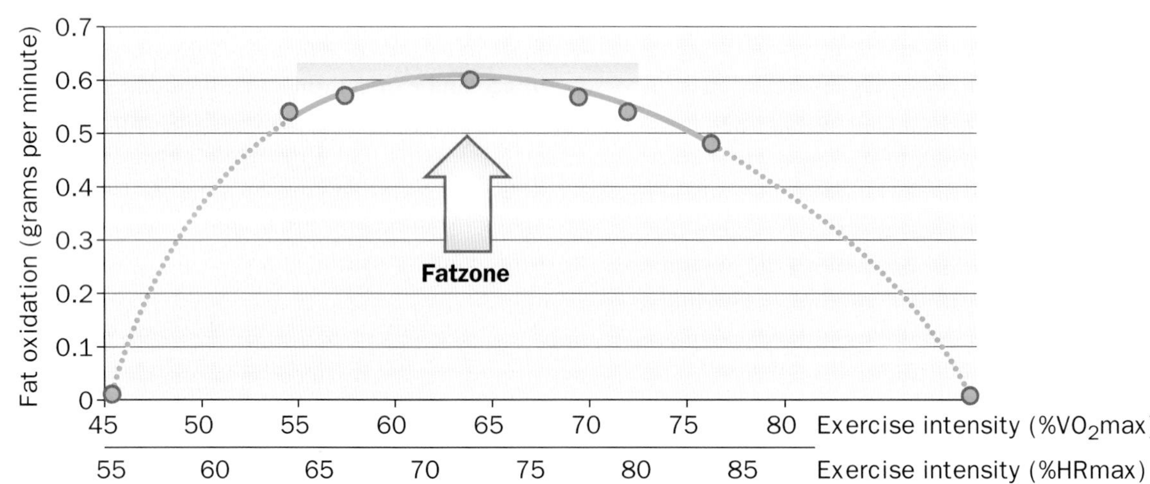

up weight loss and ensures that more of the lost weight is fat than muscle. A last word of warning: the bad news is that any change is not permanent, and can easily be reversed if old habits are revisited. As we age, RMR continues to slow down, and although ageing is one thing that cannot be stopped, we can slow its effects down by maintaining a balanced diet and regular involvement in physical activity to maintain a healthy lifestyle and better quality of life.

TASK 14

1 Investigate the terms 'fat zone', 'fat burning zone' or 'fatmax'. (To access a useful website, go to www.heinemann.co.uk/hotlinks, enter the express code 6855P and click on the relevant link.)
2 What variations of exercise intensity are suggested to increase the use of fat for energy expenditure?

Exam Café

Relax, refresh, result!

Refresh your memory

You should now have knowledge and understanding of:

- what is meant by body composition
- different methods of assessing body composition
- how to calculate a person's body mass index (BMI)
- basal metabolic rate (BMR) and the different energy requirements of different physical activities
- how to estimate your daily calorific requirements based on your BMR and average additional energy consumption
- how to evaluate critically your own diet and calorie consumption
- the health implications of being overweight or obese and how this impacts on involvement in physical activity.

REVISE AS YOU GO!

1. Define body composition.
2. Provide typical body fat percentages for the average male and female.
3. Identify the different methods of assessing body composition.
4. Define BMI and comment on its validity as a measurement of body composition.
5. Differentiate between being overweight and obese.
6. Explain the concept of energy balance in respect of energy expenditure and energy intake.
7. Define BMR/RMR and explain the use of METS to help calculate the energy requirements of different physical activities.
8. Outline the contents of a balanced diet and identify how a so-called athlete's diet may vary from a balanced diet.
9. Identify five negative health implications of being overweight and obese.
10. How does being overweight/obese impact on involvement in physical activity? And conversely, how does involvement in physical activity affect overweight and obesity?

Try to answer these questions yourself. Ask your teacher if you need help.

Get the result!

Examination question

The UK government's 2007 ambition on obesity is 'to be the first major country to reverse the rising tide of obesity and overweight in the population by ensuring that everyone is able to maintain a healthy weight.'

Explain the health implications of obesity and the role that increased participation in physical activity may have on helping to maintain a healthy weight. (6 marks)

Examiner's tips

The question leader directs candidates towards the negative effects of increasing obesity and the positive aim of reducing and then maintaining a healthy weight, which mirrors the marking scheme.

- There are two clear parts to this question: negative effects of obesity and how activity can positively reduce and then maintain a healthy weight.
- The command word is 'explain' so it is important that you explain both parts to the question.
- Check the number of marks available (6 marks) and work out how many marks may be awarded for each part of the question. Two parts and six marks should point you towards three marks each, but you should anticipate that the mark scheme will require you to visit both parts to achieve maximum marks.
- A quick plan would ensure you cover all parts of this question:

	Explain	Explain	Explain
Negative effects of obesity			
Activity to reduce weight			

Examiner comment

Direct and immediate response to the question.

Examiner comment

Good use of 'because' to explain.

Student answer

Obesity is a major health risk in the UK.

Obesity increases coronary heart disease because it increases the risk of high blood pressure/hypertension and atherosclerosis, which can lead to angina or heart attack and ultimately death.

Examiner comment

Accurate and specific use of technical language written in a concise format. However, this answer lacks breadth as all responses are cardiovascular health implications; this will only access 2 of the 6 marks available.

Obesity also decreases performance as any fat weight is weight that needs to be carried and therefore wastes energy expenditure.

Examiner comment

Not relevant as it is not a health implication, although it is good evidence of application to performance.

Examiner comment

Good introduction showing you understand the link between exercise, obesity and a healthy weight.

Increased participation in physical activity helps to reduce obesity and therefore helps maintain a healthy weight.

Physical activity helps to create a neutral or negative energy balance by increasing energy expenditure.

Examiner comment

Good concise use of specific technical language.

Examiner comment

Again, good use of specific technical language.

Regular physical activity similarly has the effect of increasing the resting metabolic rate, which again increases energy expenditure during rest.

Resistance training can also increase muscle mass, which again increases energy expenditure as it burns more energy than fat mass.

Examiner comment

Excellent specific link to resistance training to increasing muscle mass and linked to expenditure.

Examiner comment

Although not on the mark scheme, this is a good conclusion to an excellent answer.

Exercise also encourages individuals to live a healthier lifestyle and thereby eat healthier and stop smoking, which are other risk factors of developing CHD.

Examiner comment

An excellent answer; although only the cardio-vascular health implications were covered in part one of the question. Excellent detail and use of technical language, and the role of activity was concisely and accurately outlined.

CHAPTER 19:

Performance enhancement

LEARNING OBJECTIVES

By the end of this chapter you should have knowledge and understanding of:

- the positive and negative effects of each type of aid, together with the type of performer who would benefit from its use
- the legal status of each type of aid
- how to evaluate critically the use of ergogenic aids in order to be able to make informed decisions about their use
- the following aids to perfomance:
  - dietary manipulation, pre/post-competition meals/supplements and food/fluid intake during exercise
  - use of creatine supplements; human growth hormone; gene doping; blood doping and recombinant erythropoietin (Rh EPO)
  - use of cooling aids to reduce core temperature and aid recovery
  - use of training aids to increase resistance, for example pulleys and parachutes
  - the effects of alcohol, caffeine and anabolic steroids.

INTRODUCTION

Performance enhancement aids, commonly referred to as ergogenic aids, is a generic term to describe anything that enhances performance. If you wear specific footwear for your activity to improve grip or wear a Speedo LZR swimsuit (see Chapter 13, page 311), you are making use of performance enhancement aids, which we will refer to as ergogenic aids as we go on. These examples clearly highlight that the vast majority of ergogenic aids are in fact legal to use, although you might make the mistake of thinking negatively and of 'drug cheats' when hearing the term. Ergogenic aids are not a new phenomenon and they have been around a long time: the ancient Greeks took 'magic mushrooms' (hallucinogens), and in the early years of the Tour de France cyclists consumed a cocktail of substances, containing among other substances alcohol and speed (amphetamine).

With the advent of technology, the practice and use of ergogenic aids has increased to such an extent that the International Olympic Committee (IOC) and World Anti-Doping Agency (WADA) has now produced a list of ergogenic aids that are banned and those that have restrictions. Similarly, national and international governing bodies of sport have produced their own codes of practice and lists of banned ergogenic aids, although these vary from one country or governing body to another. Despite these banned lists, as recent times have shown, the practice of using banned ergogenic aids has not stopped and in many cases pharmaceutical technology has allowed the so-called cheats to remain a step ahead of the testing procedures. The period has seen the rise of new substances including 'masking' drugs, which hide the use of the banned substances. It is also important to note that the IOC/WADA banned

EXAM TIP

Make sure you are familiar with the first three learning objectives, as these tell you what you need to know about all the aids covered within the specification. The following plan (Table 1) summarises what you are required to know.

Table 1

Aid	Negative effects	Positive effects	Performer benefitting	Legal status	Critically evaluate its use

list and restrictions change and alter as more information is gained. This chapter includes a description and outline of each of the performance enhancement aids you are required to know about for your exam.

TASK 1

Identify the policies and procedures of your own governing body of sport regarding the use of ergogenic aids.

Dietary manipulation

PRE-COMPETITION

Carbohydrate (CHO) loading is a dietary strategy aimed at increasing the body's glycogen stores prior to an event to improve performance time. Various practices exist but the basic outline uses a 10-day method which consists of doing high intensity exercise seven days before an event to deplete muscle glycogen stores. From this point, a diet high in fats and proteins is consumed for around three days to fully deprive the muscle of CHOs on a reduced or tapered training load. This increases the activity of glycogen-synthase, an enzyme which facilitates the breakdown of glycogen. Next, three to four days prior to the event, a diet high in CHOs and fluid and low in fat/proteins is consumed on a low training load. This loads the muscles with glycogen which, due to the increase in glycogen-synthase, increases glycogen storage. More recent research suggests athletes should taper off training as they begin to increase CHO intake.

TASK 2

Sherman's and Astrand's glycogen loading models are two alternative methods of CHO loading. Research and discuss the difference between these models.

Fig 19.1 Foods high in carbohydrate include pasta, rice, bread and potatoes

COMPETITION DAY

A high CHO intake three days before an event ensures enough glycogen stores for competition. Furthermore, a CHO-rich meal 2–4 hours before an event tops up liver glycogen stores just prior to the actual event, to ensure adequate glycogen levels in the liver. High volumes of food and fibre-type foods should not be consumed in the days leading up to and just before competition as these can cause gastro (digestive) problems. Similarly, athletes should avoid eating CHOs an hour before exercise, as this may cause rebound hypoglycemia, which may actually decrease muscle glucose stores and bring on the earlier onset of muscle fatigue. Interestingly, the consumption of a chocolate energy bar five minutes before activity does not cause this reaction and can benefit the performer as an energy fuel during the activity.

TASK 3

Research the concept of 'reactive hypoglycemia' in the context of glycogen supplies. How can you avoid reactive hypoglycemia?

DURING EXERCISE

It is recommended that performers consume frequent but small amounts of food or drink high in CHO during activity of 45 or more minutes' duration to replenish the vital glycogen stores and help delay fatigue. Hence, anyone participating in any activity lasting longer than 45 minutes, from football, rugby, hockey to long distance events such as a marathon, will benefit. However, there is less need to consume CHO during exercise if the activity is less than 45 minutes' duration as the body's stores of glycogen are likely to be sufficient for energy provision.

CHOs consumed vary from the traditional banana, often consumed by tennis players, to soluble glucose tablets, gels and sports jelly beans, but the preferred option is normally via CHO drinks (which we will look at in more detail below).

In summary, the advice for pre- and during activity carbohydrate consumption is that activities over 1 hour duration can be enhanced when CHOs are consumed:

- 2–4 hours before exercise
- just prior (5 minutes) to exercise starting
- at frequent intervals during the activity.

FLUID INTAKE DURING EXERCISE

Fig 19.2 shows the change in hydration (water content) from resting to exercise conditions.

Fig 19.2 Water gain/loss from resting to exercise conditions

Water loss during exercise

Decreasing body water → Decreasing plasma volume → Decreasing stroke volume / Increasing heart rate → Circulatory distress and postural hypotension

Water gain at rest
Fluid intake (60%)
+
Food intake (30%)
+
Metabolic water production (10%)

Water loss at rest
Insensible water loss from skin and respiration (30%)
Sweat loss(5%)
+
Urine (60%)
+
Fecal loss (5%)

Rehydration and recovery = Fluid intake

The body's thirst mechanism does not match the hydration state, so if you feel thirsty you have in fact left hydration a little too late, and for this reason it is best to consume more fluid than your thirst dictates.

Water intake during prolonged exercise reduces the risk of dehydration and optimises performance. It is important to understand that water is just as important as fuel stores, as dehydration leading to an increase in temperature has a detrimental effect on performance, with heat exhaustion being the worst possible outcome (Fig 19.3). Performers are therefore faced with balancing the needs of hydration using 'water' and glycogen restoration during exercise.

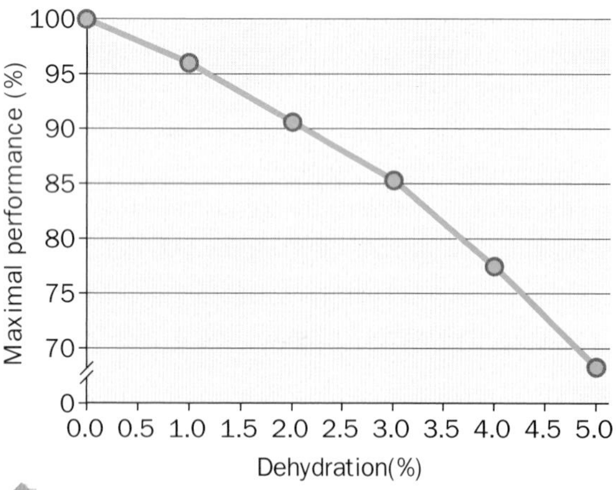

Fig 19.3 The effect of dehydration on performance

Although the specification focuses on fluid intake during performance, it seems common sense that a performer should ensure they are already well hydrated prior to activity to help alleviate many of the issues that arise during performance.

REMEMBER

Remember that most of the energy from the body's metabolic reactions is given off as heat. During exercise, the heat released increases and the body responds by sweating to control body temperature. This increases water loss and unless the performer rehydrates, this will result in dehydration and ultimately raise body temperature, which decreases performance.

APPLY IT!

When you last purchased a sport drink were you aware that there are three different types of sports drinks, each designed to be used at different times and for different purposes? The three different forms of fluid intake produced by the sports drink industry are summarised below; have you being using the right drink for the right purpose and at the right time?

TYPES OF SPORTS DRINKS

- *Hypotonic* drinks have lower levels of glucose (approx 4 per cent glucose) than the blood (5–7 per cent glucose). They are vital during prolonged exercise, when fluid replenishment is primary. Drinking 4–8 g of CHO per 100ml solution every 10–15 minutes reduces the risk of dehydration and provides a partial energy supplement.
- *Isotonic* drinks promote fluid hydration and replenishment of glucose during endurance events of more than 1 hour, having equal levels of glucose as the blood (5–7 per cent glucose).
- *Hypertonic* drinks are suitable as a recovery drink post-activity, having higher levels of glucose (19 per cent). Do not use these during activity because they increase dehydration, since water is needed to help dilute CHO as it is converted into glycogen/glucose.

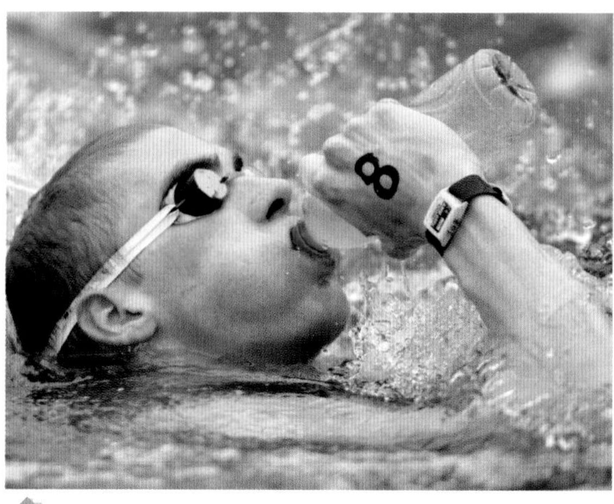

Fig 19.4 When a tri-athlete performs in hot and humid conditions, hydration has to be a primary concern

Note that fluid is absorbed best when it is dilute (plain water) and not combined with glucose, even when at the same concentration as blood (isotonic). Hence, if hydration is your primary concern then simple plain water is all you need and you can save yourself some money too! In addition, considering increased water is utilised in the process of converting CHOs to glycogen, in the process of CHO loading it is essential that additional water is consumed to maintain a hydrated state. Similarly, when activity is performed in particularly hot and humid conditions hydration has to be a primary concern alongside glycogen restoration.

APPLY IT!

To the surprise of many, it is often water-based performers that suffer from dehydration! This is because they tend to be less aware of their temperature and how much they are sweating, and therefore neglect to rehydrate.

APPLY IT!

Make your own isotonic sports drink – one part unsweetened fruit juice and two parts water and a pinch of salt. Ensure you drink glucose drinks through a straw; you may well keep your body healthy and hydrated for years of activity but your teeth and gums will not be thanking you!

POST COMPETITION

The body seems to be highly receptive to breaking down and converting CHOs to glycogen/glucose within the first two hours of recovery thus speeding up the body's glycogen recovery. Recent research has also found that the addition of protein to CHO consumed during the first hours post-exercise may stimulate glycogen recovery rates in performers involved in several consecutive bouts of high-intensity activity over a period of days. Similarly, some research states that there is a 45-minute window of opportunity for optimal refuelling after activity. This means taking a meal or liquid supplement high in CHOs and proteins in approximately a 4 : 1 ratio that includes 10–20 per cent of your total daily calorie intake. Carbohydrate stores used up during short duration exercise can be replenished in a few hours but recovery times vary depending on the intensity and duration of exercise. Long duration activity, where stores are highly depleted, will take longer to recover – sometimes days. Performers more often use hypertonic drinks high in CHO content in preference to large bowls of pasta and rice, which they struggle to ingest after exhaustive bouts of exercise.

REMEMBER

Recall that fluid intake is just as essential when consuming CHOs post-competition to maintain a hydrated state.

Other aids to performance

CREATINE SUPPLEMENTS

Creatine is made up of **amino acids** and is found in some animal foods and naturally in the liver/kidneys. It is stored in small amounts in the muscles as creatine phosphate (PC) and used to resynthesise ATP. Creatine supplements, mostly in tablet form, are taken as part of a performer's diet and aim to increase the performer's PC levels and therefore their ATP/PC system efficiency. Creatine is readily available from the high street and Internet, often with miraculous claims as to what it can achieve, but the long-term effects have yet to be studied as it is still a relatively new form of ergogenic aid. Creatine is currently legal despite much research showing that it can increase performance. Some research suggests that unless high volume intensity training is undertaken alongside creatine supplements they will cause an increase in body mass/non-lean mass which is not desirable for any activity.

KEY TERM

The basic building blocks of proteins.

HUMAN GROWTH HORMONE (HGH)

Human growth hormones (HGH) are produced naturally in the pituitary gland and exist to allow the human body to grow and develop. Synthetically produced, HGH is used by some athletes as a substitute or to complement the use of **anabolic steroids** due to its role in:

- stimulating bone, cartilage and muscle growth
- increasing blood glucose levels
- increasing lipases for the breakdown of free fatty acids (FFAs)
- decreasing overall body fat
- stimulation of protein synthesis in skeletal muscle to enhance healing after musculo-skeletal injuries.

KEY TERMS

Human growth hormones (HGH)

Hormone produced naturally in the body to aid growth and development. HGH can also be made synthetically for use in sport. Its use in sport is illegal.

Anabolic steroids

Synthetic derivatives of the naturally produced hormone testosterone which promotes bone maturation and development of muscle mass. Their use in sport is illegal.

HGH is produced in greater supply in the body during youth and adolescence, but is still supplied through adulthood to a lesser degree as it is needed to assist some metabolic processes. Diet, sleep and, more interestingly, exercise (especially above the lactate threshold) all affect HGH, and simply by following a healthy lifestyle with plenty of exercise and lots of sleep a person can increase the secretion of HGH that they produce naturally.

Although much research is inconclusive, especially regarding the ability of HGH to increase muscle mass and strength, it is thought that optimising secretion of natural HGH is beneficial to sportsmen and women, carrying none of the many risks associated with hormone abuse including joint pain, arthritis, abnormal heart/liver growth, muscle weakness, increased blood fats, glucose intolerance, diabetes, impotence, hypertension and, of course, the consequences of breaking the law! However, growth hormones are undetectable after one day of abstinence and therefore the temptation of the potential improvements is often too high for some athletes to ignore.

APPLY IT!

Body builders are thought to use high doses of HGH as it promotes an increase in fat-free weight, a decrease in fat mass, proposed muscle growth and strength, and aids recovery/repair from training/injuries.

GENE DOPING

The abundance of easily disguisable pharmaceuticals is joined by the latest and most controversial competitive weapon: genetic engineering (DNA). Gene doping is too complex for the scope of this text to examine in any real detail and is frightening in terms of its possible effects on elite competitive sport. There already exists a Human Gene Map for Performance and Health-Related Fitness Phenotypes which is updated every year and published in the journal *Medicine and Science in Sports and Exercise* (see Table 2). This lists the genes which, in different combinations, could hypothetically produce a so-called 'genetically engineered super athlete' for different sporting disciplines, such as aerobic endurance or anaerobic power. Genetic Technologies, a biotech company based in Australia, has developed a DNA test which it claims can identify whether a child has the genetic make-up to excel in either sprint and power sports or endurance sports!

Detailed knowledge of a sports person's 'genetic expression' would be extremely useful for predicting their trainability and thus the specificity of training regimens. The only thing keeping athletes from using

Table 2 The effects of exemplar genes and how performers benefit from them

Gene	Effects	Performers benefiting
ACE-II	Improves efficiency of mitochondria Normally 70 per cent of the fuel energy given off as heat (ACE-II diverts percentage heat energy into making extra ATP)	Extra ATP has been shown to improve aerobic endurance
IGF-1	Increase in enzyme activation for increasing the uptake of amino acids to increase muscle growth/regeneration and strength	Strength/power activities/ performers

genetic manipulation at present is a problem of control, in that you can't shut the gene production off when you want to. Although there is as yet a notable lack of information about how to sequence the genes required for humans, this will inevitably come in time.

> '*Genetic manipulation is there to treat people who have ailments, not there to treat a healthy person but there is a very grey and debatable line separating "health restoration" and "performance enhancement" and considering the health dimension of genetic enhancement, it is arguably a more acceptable method of performance enhancement than drugs.*'
>
> (The IOC President)

Although WADA/IOC have banned all gene doping, if genes are introduced into the tissue, for example a muscle, and not via a drug, it would be virtually undetectable by any current doping control technology and would in fact necessitate DNA testing to be developed. Even with DNA testing, how would we know if the performer inherited it or used gene doping to acquire it when there are already individuals with naturally high levels of some of these so-called sport genes?

APPLY IT!

Craig Sharp, Professor of Sports Science at Brunel University, has suggested that genetic engineering is a Pandora's box with profound implications for sport – some beneficial to sports medicine (gene therapy), some helping the sports scientist and coach (gene profiling), some opening a door to cheating (gene doping). Do the 15-second 200m sprint or the 3-minute mile beckon? Will they be legitimate? Will we be able to tell?

STRETCH AND CHALLENGE

Discuss the following two ideas:

1 If the IOC sanctions genetic engineering, it will be the end of sports as we know it and result in a spectacle of unbelievable performances.
2 From a purely competitive standpoint, if the IOC sanctions genetic engineering then sport might be more exciting, pushing the edge of human capability, testing the limits of speed and endurance well beyond those that science currently accepts.

BLOOD DOPING

Blood doping refers to any means by which a person's total volume of red blood cells is increased. The method consists of the removal (transfusion) and storage of blood from a performer's body about 4–6 weeks before an event. The body then compensates for this blood loss by replenishing its red blood cells to restore its haemoglobin levels. Then, just before the event, the blood that was previously removed is reinfused into the performer therefore increasing their overall red blood cell/haemoglobin volume. An increase in red blood cells/haemoglobin aids in the transportation of O_2 available to the muscles during exercise.

KEY TERM

Blood doping

Any means by which a person's total volume of red blood cells is increased.

RECOMBINANT ERYTHROPOIETIN (RH EPO)

The hormone **erythropoietin (EPO)** is found naturally in the body, secreted by the kidneys. A small amount circulates in the blood to regulate/increase red blood cell production to maintain it at a basal rate. **Rh EPO** is an artificial synthetic copy of erythropoietin which is injected and produces the same results as blood doping in that it increases the production of red blood cells/haemoglobin levels and raises O_2 transport. Testing procedures can now detect high levels of red blood cells/haemoglobin levels, but the use of intravenous fluids to dilute blood prior to testing has seen WADA add these intravenous fluids to the banned list. This has seemingly reduced the use of Rh EPO but has meant that many performers switch back to blood doping where the problem remains in establishing any normative levels for red blood cells/haemoglobin.

KEY TERMS

Erythropoietin (EPO)

Naturally occurring hormone which increases the body's ability to manufacture red blood cells.

Rh EPO

An artificial synthetic copy of erythropoietin.

Recent tests have also shown that Rh EPO is still being used by athletes competing at the highest level and now by those in strength and power sports. However, some athletes have naturally high concentrations, so unless all athletes' normative values are tested early in their careers and used as baseline values to measure against, there is little to be done to prevent this except the suspension of performers with high levels of red blood cells/haemoglobin.

APPLY IT!

Endurance cyclists are common users of Rh EPO.

TASK 4

Altitude training has similar effects to blood doping and Rh EPO and yet is not a banned form of ergogenic aid to enhance performance.

Discuss the argument that blood doping and Rh EPO should be made legal, especially as no recognised way of fully testing for them is currently available and it is difficult to establish any norms for what red blood cells/haemoglobin levels should be.

Cooling aids

Cooling aids are used primarily prior to the activity to reduce core body temperature in a bid to improve performance, or after the activity in a bid to improve the recovery process. There are numerous cooling aids available but the main methods include cold air exposure, water

Fig 19.5 A cooling vest is a practical aid to cooling down

immersion/ice baths, fan cooling, cold water spraying, body/head cooling jacket/vest, cold therapy packs/wraps or simply packing ice into damp towels. Cold air exposure or water immersion have been the predominant methods used but are not practical for most performers, whereas cooling jackets/vests are highly practical, made from wet suit material and designed to be packed with ice.

PRE-COOLING

Pre-cooling, ideally using a cooling jacket or ice-packed damp towels, aims to reduce skin temperature and consequently core body temperature. It should last for between 8 and 30 minutes during warm-ups and/or the intervals between warm-ups and start of performance; temperature guidelines vary between 5 to 16 degrees Celsius. Research suggests that pre-cooling is advisable before prolonged exercise in hot temperatures, with evidence that it helps to sustain intensity and speed, reducing thermal strain, allowing for different pacing strategies and an increase in exercise intensity towards the end of the performance. Performance has also been shown to improve in lower ambient temperatures, suggesting that body cooling has a real role to play in improving performances in all conditions. However, metabolic and cardio-vascular responses, a reduced heart rate and inaccurate perceived exertion, can be affected during the initial 15 minutes of exercise after pre-cooling, so it is advisable to use pacing otherwise performers may be working above their target zones. In such circumstances, cooling the body by too great a degree will not only hamper performance but also pose a health risk.

POST-COOLING

Modern cooling treatments used to treat injuries as part of recovery, termed cryotherapy, may be used in different ways on both acute and chronic injuries. Much research has been carried out on the effects of cooling on damaged soft tissues, and although the benefits are now widely accepted there are varying opinions as to how long the application should be to gain maximum benefit.

The application of ice in the treatment of injuries to soft tissues to reduce swelling and blood leaking into the tissues is not a new method of treatment and has long been part of the principle of RICE when it is assisted by compression, elevation and rest.

APPLY IT!

RICE should be the immediate response when you suffer a soft tissue injury, but how many of you have the equipment (Fig 19.6) and knowledge to carry out the instructions below?

- *Ice* – apply up to a maximum of 10 minutes as soon after the injury as possible and repeat every 2 hours during the first two days after injury. Do not apply ice directly to the skin.
- *Compression* – after ice, apply a compression bandage/wrap to help minimise the swelling to the tissues (see Fig 19.6).
- *Elevation* – raise the injured part to limit blood flow and prevent use of muscles in the injured part.
- *Rest* – rest the injured part as much as possible to allow the healing of damaged tissues.

ICE WRAPS/PACKETS

Ice wraps and packets which simply require squeezing are now widely available and should be in any performer's kit bag. They are used as part

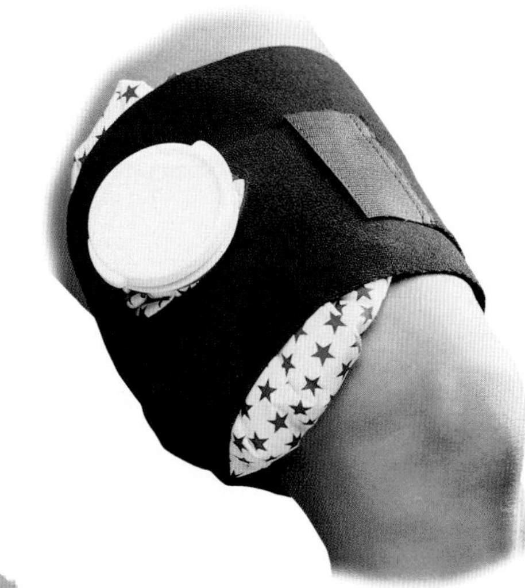

Fig 19.6 Cold therapy wraps help to minimise tissue swelling following injury

of RICE (outlined on page 495) to help provide immediate treatment and speed recovery from any soft tissue injuries.

ICE BATHS

Ice/cold baths have primarily been used for their pain-relieving properties in the treatment of injuries. However, more recently the belief is that:

- blood vessels constrict and blood is drained away from the muscles that have been working (removing lactic acid)
- once out of the bath the capillaries dilate and 'new' blood flows back to the muscles, bringing with it oxygen that will help the functioning of the cells.

This process is thought to improve muscle function, reduce muscle damage and decrease soreness associated with DOMS, which supports the use of ice/cold baths as not just injury/pain treatment but as an ongoing method of injury prevention and exercise recovery.

Fig 19.7 Ice baths can be used in injury/pain treatment and as an ongoing method of injury prevention and exercise recovery

Ice baths are popular in contact sports like rugby and football and with endurance athletes; the England rugby squad and Paula Radcliffe are good examples of the type of athlete who uses this method. For contact sports whole-body ice baths can be considered and for sports that predominantly stress the legs, such as football, field hockey and running, immersion of the lower limbs is only needed. The process consists of the performer immersing their body parts, which they should keep moving to prevent a barrier of warm water forming around their limbs, at a temperature ranging from 5–16 degrees Celsius for 7 to 10 minutes (shorter for just pain relief). Initially start with 1-minute sessions and progress to a maximum of 10 minutes over a period of 10 weeks.

There are, however, various concerns with the use of ice baths:

- different individuals have different sensitivity to ice – some find the ice/cold immediately painful
- if used on the chest region the cold may cause muscle reaction, bringing about angina pain from constriction of coronary arteries
- check skin sensitivity/touch before applying ice – it may indicate nerve impingement and ice will hide or complicate the problem
- do not use with high blood pressure as vasoconstriction will increase blood vessel pressure
- there is decreased efficiency with vasoconstriction (particularly affecting older people)
- the ice burns if placed directly onto skin and can cause tissue/vascular impairment if held on the skin for too long (10 plus minutes).

TASK 5

Research the alternative 'contrast ice baths' method where a performer will alternate between hot and cold showers/ baths. What are the strengths and weaknesses of this method?

Resistance aids

PULLEYS

Pulleys provide another form of resistance to apply a force against to develop strength, in the same way as body weight in circuit training and weights on the multi-gym. However, the main advantage of pulleys is that they better meet the principle of specificity in that they can match more closely the actual movement pattern that is used in the performance activity. A cheaper alternative to pulleys are elasticated resistance bands, however these do not replicate the smoothness of movement that pulleys offer.

Swimmers, in particular, benefit from pulley resistance/ergometer-type machines that allow them to be laid flat and replicate the specific movement patterns of the various strokes against a resistance during the propulsion phase of the arm action (see Fig 19.8).

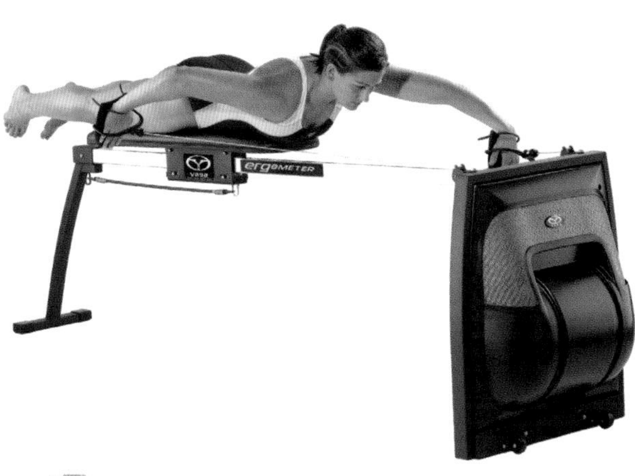

Fig 19.8 Swimmers can particularly benefit from pulley resistance machines

PARACHUTES

As with pulleys, parachutes (chutes) increase the resistance to apply a force against while maintaining the specificity of movement. They are used predominantly in sprint-type running activities. In this regard, chute use is a better form of resistance training than, for example, lifting a weight with the leg muscles while the body is in a standing or sitting position. However, parachutes do make you run with a slower arm and leg action which is not specific to sprinting.

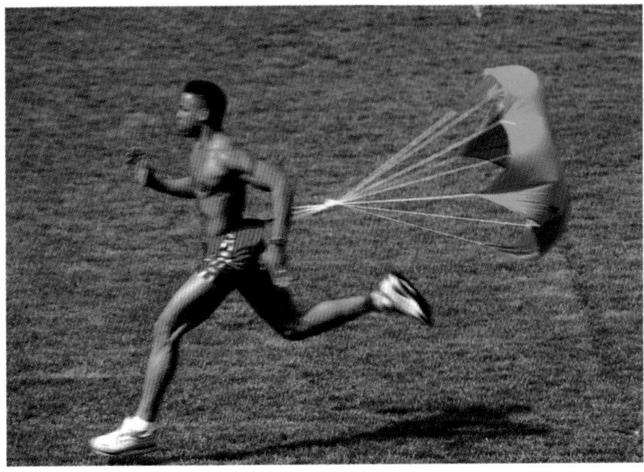

Fig 19.9 The use of parachutes by sprinters can provide fun and variety from routine training

Although there is no solid evidence that the use of speed chutes will improve sprint performances compared to conventional training, it seems that as long as the overall quality of training is kept high, and speed-chutes are not used in excess, they can provide fun and variety from routine training.

Ankle and wrist weights are two other forms of resistance aids which are comparable with chutes.

Other performance enhancement aids to consider

ALCOHOL

Alcohol has no real benefits to sports performance, although it does act as a CHO source of energy and its temporary psychological effects are calming, anxiety reduction and confidence building. In the long-term, alcohol is primarily a depressant and research shows that alcohol decreases both motor skill and physiological performance.

CAFFEINE

Caffeine is widely available and consumed in tea, coffee, cocoa, most soft drinks, many foods and within many medications. Caffeine stimulates the central nervous system (CNS) and acts like a weak amphetamine (stimulant) which increases alertness, concentration and reaction time. It produces increased breakdown of FFAs, increases energy levels and lowers perception of effort. Some performers are known to ingest caffeine tablets prior to exercise to act as a stimulant to kick-start an increase in the breakdown of FFAs (to save their important glycogen stores). Although not banned, the IOC do have a limit beyond which performers should not consume caffeine which equates to around 7–8 strong cups of coffee. Caffeine also acts as a diuretic, increasing urine production and can increase dehydration and therefore heat regulation.

ANABOLIC STEROIDS

Anabolic steroids are synthetic derivatives of the naturally produced hormone testosterone, which promotes bone maturation and development of muscle mass. They are also thought to aid in the repair of muscle tissues and recovery after exercise. (Anabolic refers to the ability of this compound to increase muscle mass or other tissue in the body.) They are easily accessible to purchase over the Internet in various forms: tablets, capsules, a solution for injection and a cream or gel to rub into the skin. The anabolic (building) effect is dependent upon the amount of dosage. It is used for medical reasons for rehabilitation and muscle wastage diseases, and they are a common drug used by body builders and weight lifters.

ANALGESICS/ANTI-INFLAMMATORY AGENTS

Analgesics, from simple over-the-counter non-steroidal aspirin and ibuprofen to the banned form of steroidal **cortisone** injections (unless accompanied by a medical note) act to relieve pain and act as anti-inflammatory agents to relieve swelling are often taken in combination after soft tissue injuries to relieve pain/inflammation.

Analgesics and anti-inflammatory agents are often used prior to competition to mask pain in order to allow performers to participate, even though without them they would be unable to tolerate the pain to perform. Their use in such conditions means they are likely to cause further and more severe injuries.

KEY TERMS

Analgesic

Any medicine that relieves pain.

Cortisone

Steroid hormone produced in the adrenal gland; it can also be reproduced synthetically.

APPLY IT!

Footballers commonly use cortisone injections to mask pain.

MASKING AGENTS

Masking agents all have the same aim: to prevent the identification of another agent, normally a banned illegal one. For this reason, if they are detected they are classified as a positive test in the same way as the substance they would be hiding would have done. Diuretics are a common masking agent that increase urine production, helping athletes to flush steroids from their system.

TASK 6

Evaluating and planning for the improvement of performance: Critical evaluation.

1 Refer back to Task 1 on page 488, where you identified your national and international governing body's guidance/policies on the use of performance enhancement ergogenic aids.
2 Identify and explain which performance enhancement methods (legal or illegal) identified in this chapter could be beneficial to your own activity.
3 Now explain which of the methods you personally would choose to use as performance enhancing aids in your own activity. Explain why you chose them.

ExamCafé

Relax, refresh, result!

Refresh your memory

You should now have knowledge and understanding of:

- the positive and negative effects of each type of aid, together with the type of performer who would benefit from its use
- the legal status of each type of aid
- how to evaluate critically the use of ergogenic aids in order to be able to make informed decisions about their use
- the following aids to perfomance:
  - dietary manipulation, pre/post-competition meals/supplements and food/fluid intake during exercise
  - use of creatine supplements; human growth hormone; gene doping; blood doping and recombinant erythropoietin (Rh EPO)
  - use of cooling aids to reduce core temperature and aid recovery
  - use of training aids to increase resistance, for example pulleys and parachutes
  - the effects of alcohol, caffeine and anabolic steroids.

REVISE AS YOU GO!

1. What are performance enhancement aids?
2. Name a dietary strategy that would benefit an endurance-type athlete.
3. Why is fluid hydration so important?
4. What is the theory behind the use of cooling aids as a recovery aid?
5. Identify four illegal performance aids.
6. Identify three illegal aids that would benefit an anaerobic/explosive athlete.
7. Why are sporting authorities/scientists so concerned about gene doping?
8. What type of athlete would benefit from the use of Rh EPO?
9. What are the possible side effects of using anabolic steroids/human growth hormone?
10. What is the theory behind the use of pulleys and parachutes as performance enhancement aids?

Try to answer these questions yourself. Ask your teacher if you need help.

Get the result!

Examination question

Carbohydrate loading and creatine supplementation are two types of nutritional ergogenic aid.

Discuss the effects of using both these aids referring to the following:

- the type of performer benefiting
- the performance-enhancing qualities
- the associated side effects. (6 marks)

Examiner's tips

- The question leader directs you to two named nutritional performance enhancement aids.
- It is important you identify that the question is NOT asking for a description of CHO loading and creatine supplementation. The command word 'Discuss' highlights that this is a higher weighted question requiring more than simple recall knowledge and understanding. It is essential that you discuss both performance aids as requested in the question.
- This is a two-part question, each with three sub-parts to include in your discussions.
- It is easy to miss but important for you to identify that this question is asking for two practical examples when it asks for the type of performer benefiting.
- Check the number of marks available (6 marks) and work out how many may be awarded for each part of the question. Two performance aids and three areas to discuss should point you towards three marks each.
- A quick plan would ensure you cover all parts of this question:

Discuss	Performer benefiting	Performance effects	Side effects
CHO loading			
Creatine supplements			

Student answer

Carbohydrate loading is a dietary strategy that involves reducing your CHO intake approximately seven days prior to an event while training to reduce your CHO stores and then reducing your training while you intake lots of CHOs one to two days before your competition.

Examiner comment

This introduction is a description of CHO loading and although it shows good knowledge it is irrelevant in regard to the question.

Examiner comment

Good, specific example of an athlete benefiting.

Long-distance endurance/aerobic athletes like a Tour de France cyclist would use this technique as it increases their store of carbohydrate prior to their event. This will delay fatigue and increase the duration they can perform using CHO rather than fats. The side effects are the athlete feeling weak and demotivated while they are starved of CHOs and don't feel like training at all.

Examiner comment

Increased CHO store a good example of performance enhancement but 'glycogen stores' would be more accurate terminology.

Examiner comment

Good link to delaying fatigue but a weak link to increasing endurance capacity. Good example of a negative side affect of CHO loading.

Creatine supplements are used by anaerobic sprint-type athletes like the 200m sprinter. Creatine supplements increase the stores of PC which increases the speed of their recovery and allows them to train harder and more often.

Examiner comment

Good specific example of the type of performer benefitting.

Examiner comment

Good identification of increased recovery time as a performance-enhancement quality but a somewhat weaker link to 'training harder/longer', which lacks the use of more specific technical language.

Creatine has not been used for too long so the long-term side effects may not be known but weight gain and liver problems are thought to be at risk.

Examiner comment

Good awareness of the unknown long-term effects of creatine and an indication of the more likely side effects.

Both of these aids are legal to use.

Examiner comment

Not relevant to the question.

Examiner comment

Despite wavering from the question with some irrelevant information, the answer still visited all parts of the question. There is good application with specific examples for both performance-enhancing aids. The response varied in its quality and use of specific technical language but still fulfilled the requirements of the question. As preparation for the 20-mark 'd' question this would require a more concise and higher level of use/quality of technical language alongside its excellent application with specific examples.

CHAPTER 20:

Improvement of effective performance and the critical evaluation of practical activities in PE

LEARNING OBJECTIVES

By the end of this chapter you should have knowledge and understanding of:

- which practical activity you can choose to be assessed in
- the roles you can choose to be assessed in
- how you will be assessed in each of these roles
- the terms 'standardisation' and 'moderation'
- how you can improve your performance, coaching or officiating.

Introduction to the practical assessment of your course

Advanced level PE has as its central aim the linking of theory to practical and practical to theory. This enables you to gain not only knowledge of theoretical concepts but also an understanding and appreciation of them. You can also apply these concepts to your practical performances in order to improve your standards. Advanced-level PE recognises that students should be able to capitalise on their practical talents by being assessed in practical activities, with these assessments contributing to the examination grade.

In your AS PE studies you would have been informed of the opportunities for assessment in practical activities, so you should be aware of the activities available. This chapter will identify ways in which you can improve the marks you are awarded when you are assessed. Linked to the activity you are assessed in will be the Evaluation and Appreciation of Performance, in which you are required to observe a fellow student, comment on the **strengths** and **weaknesses** of his or her performance, then create an action plan to improve that performance.

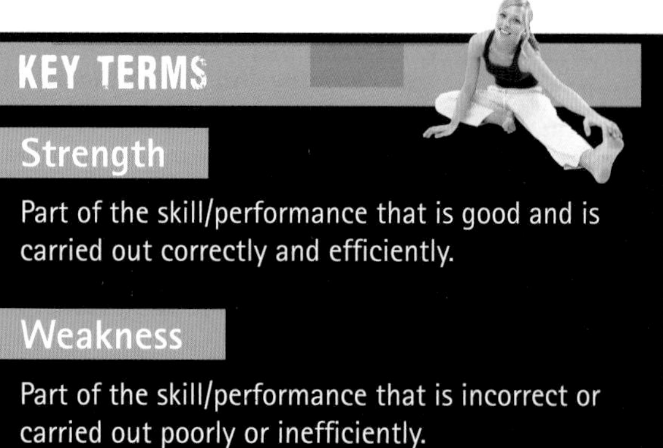

KEY TERMS

Strength

Part of the skill/performance that is good and is carried out correctly and efficiently.

Weakness

Part of the skill/performance that is incorrect or carried out poorly or inefficiently.

Performing your practical activities should help you to understand your theoretical work, while the Evaluation and Appreciation of Performance will help you in your synoptic assessment, for which you will be asked to apply to practical activities theory from the different concepts you have studied. As was indicated in your AS PE studies, you will find useful information in this chapter, but to improve both your practical performance and your Evaluation and Appreciation of Performance there is no substitute for actual practice.

This chapter looks at the practical activities, while Chapter 21 looks at the Evaluation and Appreciation of Performance component.

Your practical performance, knowledge and understanding will be assessed by your performance in one practical activity as a performer, coach/ leader or official together with your spoken comments on a fellow student's performance. In the practical performance component you will be assessed out of 40 marks and in the evaluation and appreciation of performance component you will be assessed out of 20 marks, which enables you to score a maximum of 60 marks. This amounts to 30 per cent of your A2 marks.

MODULE CONTENT

The activities are grouped together into eleven categories, as shown in Table 1. You must choose one activity, which must be one of the two you were assessed in during your AS studies. You can, however, be assessed in a different role, i.e. you can be assessed officiating in the activity at AS but performing it or coaching it at A2. If you decide to change the role from that which you were assessed in at AS level, you should ensure that you can score more marks in it than you would if you did not change.

Examples of the activities that you can be assessed in are given in Table 1, but the full list of activities in which your centre may allow you to take part and be assessed can be found on the OCR website. To access this site, go to www. heinemann.co.uk/hotlinks, enter the express code 6855P and click on the relevant link.

ASSESSMENT

You can be assessed in either:

1 Performing an activity and Evaluation and Planning for the improvement of performance OR
2 Coaching/leading an activity and Evaluation and Planning for the improvement of performance OR
3 Officiating an activity and Evaluation and Planning for the improvement of performance.

Your teacher will assess you throughout your practical activity course. This will enable your teachers to accurately assess you, rather than having just one assessment session towards the end of the course (when you may have an 'off' day). This will ensure that if you are injured they have some marks on which to base their assessment.

The final assessed marks have to be sent to the exam board by the specified date. If your practical activities are done in modular blocks, you will probably be assessed at the end of the module,

Table 1 Activities and their categories

Activity category	Example activities
1 Athletic activities	Track and field athletics
2 Combat activities	Judo
3 Dance activities	Contemporary dance
4 Invasion game activities	Association Football Basketball Field hockey Gaelic football Hurling Netball Rugby League Rugby Union
5 Net/wall game activities	Badminton Squash Tennis Volleyball
6 Striking/fielding game activities	Cricket
7 Target games activities	Golf
8 Gymnastic activities	Gymnastics Trampolining
9 Outdoor and adventurous activities	Canoeing Mountain walking Sailing Skiing
10 Swimming activities	Competitive swimming
11 Safe and effective exercise activities	Circuit training

whenever that is. For some 'summer' activities, this may be very early in your course. You may have to be videoed doing your practical activity.

STANDARDISATION

The teachers in your centre will consult with each other to check that different activities assessed by different teachers or coaches in your centre are all at the same standard.

Standardisation is particularly important for many activities that cannot be done in your centre and are sometimes taught by coaches who are based at clubs. In cases such as these, the Physical Education teacher responsible for A-level will liaise with the coach to ensure that he or she is aware of what you need to do in your activity. This teacher will assess you with the help and advice of the coach.

MODERATION

Sometime between Easter and late May, some students in your centre will be chosen to perform their practical activities alongside students from other centres in your area at a moderation. A moderator from the exam board will look at all these students' performances to check they have been assessed correctly and that marks awarded by the different centres are all at the same level. The moderator knows the correct levels and standards of performance and ensures that all candidates have been treated fairly.

Moderation is part of the examination process so if the moderator asks you to attend the moderation you must do so.

1. Performing an activity

CONTENT OF THE PRACTICAL ACTIVITIES

The OCR specification indicates that the focus of your activities will be on the 'the selection, application and improved performance of skills in an open environment'. These skills will be performed in the situation in which the activity normally takes place. The 'normal' situation will allow you to:

- select the correct skill for a particular situation; for example, choose the correct stroke when batting in cricket
- repeat skills consistently; for example, get the skill right each time you perform it
- adapt skills where and when required; for example, adjust your pass in netball to avoid the opponent marking you from intercepting it
- show your tactical/strategic or choreographic/compositional awareness; for example, putting simple agilities you can perform well in your gymnastics routine rather than complex ones in which you may not do well
- show your knowledge of the activity's rules, regulations and code of practice
- perform to the best of your ability
- demonstrate the principles of fair play and sportsmanship; for example, accepting the officials' decisions without question; not using gamesmanship
- perform all of the above when under pressure.

The 'normal' situation in which the activity takes part is obviously not the same for all the activities. Examples of the 'normal' situation are shown in Table 2.

These 'formal' situations allow you to display the range of skills you have developed while also encouraging you to adapt them to meet the demands made on you. Because it is the 'normal' open environment, tactics/strategies or choreographic/compositional ideas will play a much bigger part than in the conditioned competitive situations you experienced at AS level. For instance, in mountain walking you will need to camp for two nights, which will necessitate you being much more aware of your nutritional needs and camping skills.

If you are to be successful in this open environment, then you will need to have perfected your skills with lots of practice so that they come to you automatically. This will enable you to concentrate on your tactics and strategies.

Table 2

Activity category	Examples of the 'normal' situation
1 Athletic activities	Sprinting – sprint starts, sprint action, finishes together with a timed sprint
2 Combat activities	Judo – formal contest
3 Dance activities	Contemporary dance – choreograph and perform a solo dance routine lasting four minutes containing jumps, leaps, balances, rolls and turns
4 Invasion game activities	Association Football (soccer) – full game
5 Net/wall game activities	Tennis – full game
6 Striking/fielding game activities	Cricket – full game in which you will be assessed in fielding and either batting or bowling
7 Target games activities	Golf – full round
8 Gymnastic activities	Trampolining – a compulsory ten-contact sequence and a voluntary ten-contact sequence
9 Outdoor and adventurous activities	Mountain walking – a three-day expedition with 21 hours of walking covering at least 48 km (30 miles)
10 Swimming activities	Competitive swimming – racing starts, stroke technique in short race, racing finish together with a timed swim
11 Safe and effective exercise activities	Circuit training – three-month exercise programme designed to improve two from: strength, stamina, suppleness, speed

TASK 1

Find out what the 'normal' open situations are for the activity in which you will be assessed.

WHAT ARE THE ASSESSMENT CRITERIA?

There are several key areas that your teacher will be looking at:

- how good your skills are, and the accuracy, control and fluency with which you perform them
- your use of advanced skills when appropriate, and their accuracy, control and fluency
- your understanding and use of strategies and tactics
- your overall standard of performance
- your level of physical endeavour, sportsmanship and flair
- your level of understanding and application of the rules, regulations and code of practice of the activity.

Your teacher will use these criteria to put you into one of five bands: 33–40; 25–32; 17–24; 9–16; 0–8, before he or she finally decides the exact mark to give you out of 40. Your teacher may also use the representative level at which you perform your activity to check that you are in the correct band.

Your teacher will do this assessment over a period of time but might have one final assessment session to finalise your mark.

WHAT WILL I BE REQUIRED TO DO FOR MY ASSESSMENT?

How you will be assessed and what the focus of the assessment will be has been identified for each practical activity. Formal situations are used for your assessment and the list that follows shows the focus of assessment for each specific activity or the focus for all activities in a category where this is more appropriate.

Fig 20.1 Practical activities being performed

- *Track and field athletics*: one event from one of the following areas – track, jumps, throws.
- *Contemporary dance*: jumps, leaps, balances, rolls and turns.
- *Invasion games*: techniques, tactical awareness, understanding and application of rules/ regulations, behaviour.
- *Golf*: club selection and distance; stroke action and target accuracy.
- *Gymnastics*: Vaults and an agility sequence containing three rolls, three jumps, three balances and three agilities together with at least two linking movements.
- *Trampolining*: a compulsory ten-contact sequence and a voluntary ten-contact sequence which must contain a jump, a drop and two somersaults.
- *Mountain walking*: use and interpretation of maps and their symbols, navigation using map and compass, hill-walking skills, organisation and use of equipment, application of safety principles, conservation practices and respect for others, wild camping.
- *Competitive swimming*: one stroke from front crawl, backstroke, breaststroke, butterfly.

These can be found in more detail in the 'Teacher Support – Coursework Guidance' booklet, which can be found on the OCR website (to access this site, go to www.heinemann.co.uk/hotlinks, enter the express code 6855P and click on the relevant link).

Details of the focus for all activities can also be found on this website.

TASK 2

Access the OCR website and identify the assessment focus for your assessed activity. (To access this site, go to www. heinemann.co.uk/hotlinks, enter the express code 6855P and click on the relevant link.)

HOW CAN I IMPROVE MY PRACTICAL ACTIVITY PERFORMANCES?

You should now be aware of how and when you will be assessed as well as the focus for your assessment. This knowledge and understanding should help you plan how to use your time to improve your performances in your practical activities and thereby increase the marks you are awarded.

As you are carrying on with one of the activities in which you were assessed in your AS PE studies, you will be aware of some of your strengths and weaknesses. The first thing you should do is to evaluate your performance in your activity, identify your strengths and weaknesses then create action plans aimed at improving your performances.

Specific information in relation to improving performance in your activities can be found in coaching books, usually published by the governing or organising body. A good source of information for books of this type is given on the Coachwise website; to access this site, go to www. heinemann.co.uk/hotlinks, enter the express code 6855P and click on the relevant link.

When you are looking to evaluate your performance with a view to creating action plans, you should bear in mind the following questions.

- How consistent are you in using your skills accurately, with control and fluency?
- Do you have advanced skills, and can you use them appropriately and successfully?
- How well do you understand and apply strategies/tactics or choreographic/ compositional ideas?
- How much effort and commitment do you put into your activity?
- Do you always display good sportsmanship, playing by the rules of the activity?
- In your activity do you try to be creative and use your initiative?
- Are your levels of physical fitness appropriate for the activity?
- Do you understand and apply the rules, regulations and conventions of the activity?

TASK 3

1 Find the websites of the governing or organising body of your activity and see which coaching manuals are available to help you develop your skills. Alternatively you could access the Coachwise website (to access this site, go to www.heinemann.co.uk/hotlinks, enter the express code 6855P and click on the relevant link).
2 Check in the library of your school or centre to see if these coaching manuals are there for you to use.

PHYSICAL FITNESS

Your knowledge of this aspect of your activity should be improving now through your studies in Exercise Physiology, where you will be gaining an understanding of how training affects you. As you will be taking part in the 'normal' situation in which the activity is performed, your level of physical fitness will be very important. You should use a standardised test for each of the four main components of physical fitness to identify your level and, if you work on it, any improvement you make. You should look at strength, speed, stamina and suppleness together with any other fitness components which are important in your activity.

Fig 20.2 Objective tests can be used to measure fitness

Through your study of Exercise Physiology, you will be able to be more specific about the aspects that are important to you and how to go about improving them. However, you should also seek advice from your teacher and coach. If you can improve your fitness, it will help your all-round performance and also help to improve the mark you get for 'physical endeavour'.

EXAM TIP

Improving your fitness to the top levels indicated by the standardised tests will help you access the top band marks as it will improve your performance.

TASK 4

1 For your activity, consult your teacher or coach, together with the coaching manuals, to establish the important components of physical fitness.
2 Identify and describe a standard test for each of the fitness components important to your activity and use it to test yourself.
3 Construct a training programme designed to improve your physical fitness for your activity.

MENTAL FITNESS

You should make sure that you know the appropriate tactics and strategies, particularly in a team game, and can remember them. Remember also that reaction time is improved by practise so you can work on improving this. You should also try to become accustomed to the competitive/performing situation so that you are not affected by it, and your performance does not deteriorate. In the normal competitive/performing situation you should always be aware of the important information/cues to focus on so that you can ignore the unimportant ones.

REMEMBER

Look back at the section on selective attention in *OCR AS PE*, Chapter 6, page 159.

IMPROVING THE QUALITY AND RANGE OF YOUR SKILLS

If you are following the same activity at A2 that you were assessed performing in at AS, you will have already looked at the level of your skills. If you feel there is still room for improving them and even learning new ones then:

- consult your teacher or coach and the coaching manuals to identify drills or practices that you can use
- consult the coaching manuals to identify the coaching points on which you need to focus
- remember that you will be assessed using these skills in the 'normal' activity situation; your aim therefore should be performing them in that situation
- listen to feedback given by your teacher or coach; this will help you to improve
- refer back to practices you did in your AS studies.

You should also refer to OCR's coursework guidance booklet, which identifies the movement phases through which the skills will be analysed for assessment purposes. These phases may also help you in improving and extending your range of skills. Some examples of these movement phases are identified in Table 3.

You should use these phases to judge how your skills compare to the technical model.

For example if you are a breast stroke swimmer you will judge how your:

- body position compares to the technical model in terms of where your head is and where your body is in the water in the different parts of the stroke
- arm action compares to the technical model i.e. extension of arms, position of hands, use of wrists, initiation of the pull, shape of pull, recovery
- leg action compares to the technical model i.e. shape of kick, position of thighs, position of feet, leg drive, recovery
- breathing i.e. every stroke, when inspiration and expiration take place
- overall efficiency i.e. correct sequence of arm action and leg action, correct body position and breathing technique.

If you are a netball player you will judge how your chest pass compares to the technical model by using the coaching points of the following phases:

- preparation – how you hold the ball, where your feet are, where your body weight is, position of your arms
- execution – extension of arms, use of wrist and fingers, transfer of body weight, direction and flight of ball
- recovery – how ready you are for the next part of play, balance, ready position
- result – is the pass successful, does it have the correct direction, flight and weight.

TASK 5

For your practical activity, identify the movement phases that are used to analyse the activity and its skills.

EXAM TIP

You should try to improve your range of advanced skills together with their accuracy and consistency. This will help you access the higher band marks.

In order to improve both your skills and your performance in general, it is important that you receive, listen and respond to feedback that is given by teachers and coaches.

STRATEGIES/TACTICS AND CHOREOGRAPHIC/COMPOSITIONAL IDEAS

As you are now being assessed in the 'normal' situation in which the activity occurs, strategies and tactics will play a much bigger part in your performance and assessment. While you can only gain experience of strategies/tactics or choreographic/compositional ideas by taking part in the activity, you can improve your knowledge of this aspect by referring to the coaching manuals. You will need to gain experience by taking part in the activity regularly and you will need to adopt a strategy to enable you to achieve this. It may be that you can gain this within your school or college, but you may also wish to increase or widen your experience by joining a club in the local community. If this is the case, you should ensure that the coach or organiser is made aware of what you need to do to improve your assessment.

Table 3 Examples of movement phases used for assessment purposes

Area	Movement phases	
Track and field athletics	Track events:	Posture Leg action Arm action Head carriage Overall efficiency
	Jumping events:	Approach Take off Flight Landing Overall efficiency
	Throwing events:	Initial stance, grip and preparation Travel and trunk position Throwing action Release Overall efficiency
Games	Preparation Execution Recovery Result Overall efficiency	
Competitive swimming	Arm action Leg action Body position Breathing Overall efficiency	

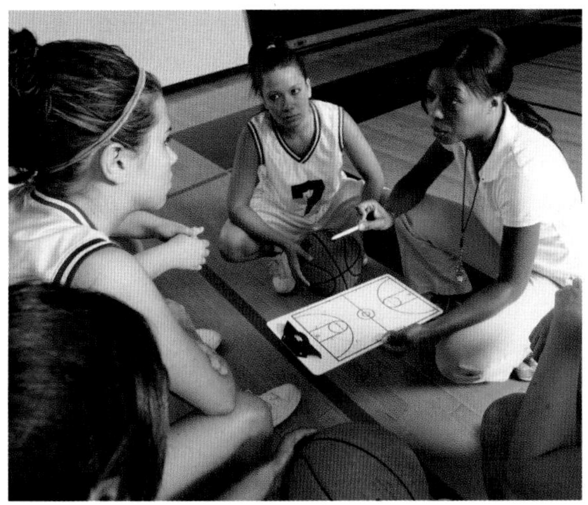

Fig 20.3 Listen and respond to feedback given by your coach.

EXAM TIP

If you improve your knowledge, understanding and application of strategies/tactics or choreographic/compositional ideas then this will not only improve the marks you get for your performance assessment but it will also improve your mark in your Evaluation and Appreciation of Performance assessment.

2. Coaching/leading an activity

You can be assessed in either of the two activities which you were assessed in at AS. You do not have to have been assessed coaching/leading this activity at AS; you may have been assessed performing or officiating this activity at AS.

The OCR specification indicates that the focus of your assessment will be on:

- the performance of basic and advanced skills
- the selection and application of skills and strategies
- understanding of rules/regulation/conventions
- technical knowledge.

The specification indicates that the focus of your assessment of your coaching/leading is on a range of applied and acquired skills, abilities and qualities. These skills will be assessed while you lead safe, purposeful and enjoyable activities. A suitable arena for these activities could be with secondary school pupils or youth groups.

You will coach/lead in a situation which allows you to:

- coach/lead safe, purposeful and enjoyable sessions
- demonstrate basic and advanced skills and strategies
- demonstrate competence in organisational skills in planning and delivering sessions
- demonstrate knowledge and understanding of health and safety procedures
- implement risk assessments
- demonstrate knowledge and understanding of the fitness and health benefits of the activity
- evaluate sessions and plan for improvement
- demonstrate an awareness of child protection issues
- operate the principle of inclusion.

You may, within your centre, undertake the British Sports Trust Higher Sports Leader's Award; the successful completion of this award may allow you to develop many of the skills on which your assessment will be based. Alternatively you could undertake a Governing Body coaching award, which would also develop many of the skills you need.

As with your performance you will need to practise your coaching/leading if you are to improve and you will also need someone to observe you and give you feedback on your performances. There may be opportunities for practice created by your centre but you may have to seek opportunities with local clubs or with your local sports development officer. It is important that you practise your coaching as you will need to develop your ability to motivate, be confident, control and be responsible for groups.

WHAT ARE THE ASSESSMENT CRITERIA?

The focus of your assessments will be on your:

- ability to apply coaching/leading skills in delivering sessions
- organisational and planning skills
- use of a range of coaching/leading strategies
- overall performance in coaching/leading
- awareness of health and safety
- implementation of risk assessments
- awareness of child protection
- awareness of the fitness and health benefits of the activity
- organisational skills in planning and delivering sessions
- knowledge of the rules/regulations of the activity
- evaluative skills.

Your teacher will use these assessment criteria to put you into one of five bands (33–40; 25–32; 17–24; 9–16; 0–8) before they finally decide the exact mark you will be given out of 40. Your teacher will assess you over a period of time but might watch you do a final coaching/leading session to finalise your mark.

In order to produce evidence for your assessment you will have to keep a comprehensive log which contains the following detailed information:

- a record of your coaching/leading activities over a six-month period
- a scheme of work for 10 hours of coaching in which the participants and activities show progression
- evaluations of your sessions
- a video record of you coaching/leading for at least 40 minutes
- health and safety issues relating to the activity and your sessions together with risk assessments undertaken
- details of your first aid qualification
- child protection procedures relevant to the activity

- the health and fitness benefits of the activity for both participants and coaches/leaders
- if you have undertaken either the Higher Sports Leader's Award or a Governing Body coaching qualification, evidence that you have completed it.

You will need to complete this log as you carry out your coaching, particularly in keeping the record of your coaching sessions and their evaluations. You should not leave completion of your log until close to the final date for the submission of assessments.

TASK 6

1. Access the OCR website and look at the assessment criteria descriptors. (To access this site, go to www.heinemann.co.uk/hotlinks, enter the express code 6855P and click on the relevant link.)
2. Ask your teacher/coach or local sports development officer for details of British Sports Trust Higher Sports Leaders Award or Governing Body coaching awards in the activities you are interested in.

REMEMBER

Ensure that your log book contains all the information required and that the information is detailed and presented appropriately.

HOW CAN I IMPROVE MY COACHING/LEADING?

You should now be aware of how and when you will be assessed as well as the focus for your assessment. This understanding will help you plan how you should use your time to practise and improve your coaching/leading and thereby improve the marks you are awarded.

You should observe and evaluate the sessions you are taught as part of your A-level Physical Education course and any additional coaching/leading courses you may undertake. This will allow you to see how other coaches operate and pick up ideas, preferably the ones that work and that you enjoy! If there are any practices that other coaches use which you don't enjoy, you can decide not to use them or determine how you would improve them so you could use them.

It is useful if you identify the skills you need to develop and organise them into groups, these being:

- planning/organisation
- delivery
- evaluative
- technical knowledge.

PLANNING AND ORGANISATIONAL SKILLS

These mainly concern things that you will do before your sessions. They usually ensure that your sessions are safe, enjoyable and successful. Knowing that you have planned and organised your sessions gives you confidence and allows you to concentrate on actually delivering the session and motivating the participants. Planning properly enables the sessions to run smoothly and although the participants might not be aware of all the time you have spent planning, they will appreciate being involved in a purposeful, safe and enjoyable session.

SCHEME OF WORK

Remember that for your assessment you will have to produce a scheme of work for 10 hours of coaching/leading. A scheme of work is a general, overall plan which will identify what you hope to achieve together with the skills you intend to get participants to learn. It will also outline what you plan to do in each of the sessions.

A scheme of work has to be flexible, as in some of your sessions things might not go according to plan, the participants might find the skills you are introducing easier or harder than you thought and you may have to spend more or less time on them than you had planned. However, the scheme of work is important as it outlines what you plan to do, the practices you will use, the facilities and equipment you will use, etc.

Your planning and organisation should include:

- *facilities* – suitability, availability, booking, cost, safety, accessibility, rules of usage
- *equipment* – availability, suitability, quality, quantity, storage, access, maintenance, distribution in sessions
- *participants* – numbers, age, gender, ability, experience
- *health and safety* – risk assessments, first aid availability, emergency procedures
- *child protection procedures* – how you are going to put them into practice
- *objectives* – both long-term and short-term
- *scheme of work* – length, aims, objectives
- *individual session plans*
- *risk assessments.*

REMEMBER

Remember the following well-known sayings:

- failure to plan is planning to fail
- the 6P principal: Proper Preparation Prevents Pathetically Poor Performance.

CHILD PROTECTION

Most Governing bodies have their own policies on child protection, although they will be very similar and deal with safeguarding the welfare of young participants in activities. Child protection procedures focus on:

- ensuring that coaches understand what the term child abuse means
- ensuring good practice in the coaching of young participants
- providing a safe environment for young people
- giving the knowledge and understanding to be able to recognise abuse while also providing a system to deal sympathetically with issues and concerns.

TASK 7

Find out about child protection procedures from organisations such as Sports Coach UK, the governing body of the activity you are focusing on, your local sports development officer and the National Society for the Prevention of Cruelty to Children (NSPCC).

EXAM TIP

You need to ensure that you produce a detailed plan for your sessions. Ensure that you have the plan with you in your session.

When you deliver your sessions you will need to have prepared a detailed plan to follow. You will probably be given a session plan outline by your teachers or, if you undertake one of the courses already mentioned in Task 6, by your course tutor. The sort of information you will need on your session plans will be:

- number of participants, age, gender, experience, ability
- equipment required
- length of session
- objectives of session
- warm-up activities and their organisation
- activities with their coaching points, detailed practices and organisation
- cool down
- risk assessment.

RISK ASSESSMENT

Risk assessment is an important part of your role. It involves the careful, systematic examination of the environment in which an activity takes place, including objects used for that activity, to consider whether there might be anything that could potentially cause harm to people. Risk assessment requires that you identify possible

hazards and **risks** which may occur. Once you have identified possible hazards and risks you then need to think about the precautions that are required to minimise the risks and how to implement them. For example, a possible hazard from playing a cricket match outside for several hours during a hot summer's day is sunstroke; to minimise the risk of sunstroke occurring you would need to ensure that players wore sun hats and sun block and frequently drank fluids.

KEY TERMS

Risk assessment

A risk assessment is a careful, systematic examination of things that in your coaching/leading or officiating could harm people so that you can judge whether risks are suitably controlled or whether more should be done to control them.

Hazard

Any thing or situation that has the potential to cause harm if uncontrolled.

Risk

The chance (likelihood) that somebody will be harmed by the hazard.

In your coaching/leading or officiating, a risk assessment will enable you to judge whether risks are suitably controlled or whether more should be done to control them. In your sessions you should focus on the following:

- venue
- playing surface
- jewellery
- equipment being used (condition) including clothing and footwear
- equipment around the area
- injury.

You will need to check these before each session and have procedures in place to minimise the risks, for example ensuring that participants remove jewellery.

TASK 8

Carry out a risk assessment for a coaching session and complete the appropriate documentation.

DELIVERY

When focusing on your delivery you should think about:

- your appearance, which should be clean, neat, tidy and set an example
- your 'presence' and personality
- giving clear simple instructions
- giving good clear, correct demonstrations
- how you are going to control the group, for example with a whistle
- encouraging, motivating and praising participants
- being enthusiastic and positive
- variation in the tone of your voice
- building a positive relationship with the participants
- treating all participants equally and fairly
- including all participants
- timekeeping.

Fig 20.4 Your appearance should be smart

REMEMBER

Remember when delivering your sessions that you should follow the plan you have devised. However, a good coach is adaptable and you may need to adjust your plan if things do not go quite as you had intended.

Don't forget in the planning of your sessions to ensure that participants have plenty of time to practise the skills you are intending them to learn. You should remember the saying 'Practice makes perfect.' Learners remember by:

- 3 per cent explanation
- 7 per cent demonstration
- 90 per cent practice.

EXAM TIP

Ensure that you have planned your sessions in detail and you have the plan with you. This will give you the confidence to deliver the session with enthusiasm which will provide motivation for the participants ensuring that they enjoy themselves and are successful.

EVALUATION

During and after your session you will need to apply your evaluative skills. These skills enable you to decide what is good about a performance and what is weak and needs to be improved. In your session you will have demonstrated and explained to the participants what it is you want them to do. You will then watch them when they do their practices and identify the good things they do which you will praise them for. If they get something wrong you will have to single these mistakes out and give them practices to enable these points to be corrected. You may do this individually or, if you find that a lot of people in the group have the same fault, you will stop the group and get them all to focus on it. You also need to allow time for the participants to evaluate their own performance.

Another major focus for your evaluative skills will be your **evaluation** of your own performance. Again you will identify what you did well, what was not so good and how you need to change things so that you do better next time. It is important that you do this post-session evaluation as soon as possible after your session, so that things are fresh in your mind. Your teacher, coach or fellow students may also evaluate your session and give you feedback. These evaluations are sometimes referred to as 'reflection.'

KEY TERM

Evaluation

Looking at a performance and identifying what is good about it and what its weaknesses are.

TECHNICAL KNOWLEDGE

Another area of skills that you need to concentrate on is your technical knowledge of the activity you coach/lead. You will need to know the correct technical models for the skills of the activity, the phases they break down into, the coaching points together with the progressive practices to develop them. You can learn these from the sessions you participate in as part of your A-level Physical Education course or you can find them in the coaching manuals which most governing bodies produce. It also improves your credibility with the participants if you can demonstrate the skills that you are coaching, so you will need to practise these skills to ensure that you can demonstrate them correctly.

TASK 9

Consult your teacher/coach and the relevant coaching manuals to identify the skills which you will need to know the coaching points for and be able to give good demonstrations of.

EXAM TIP

Ensure that you know the coaching points and progressive practices of the skills of your activity and are able to do effective demonstrations of them all.

Watching other coaches/leaders is also a good way of improving your own coaching/leading skills. You can observe how they approach situations and see the practices they use for different skills. You can then use the good parts of these sessions and make sure that you do not make the mistakes that you see them make!

TACTICS/COMPOSITIONAL IDEAS

You need to have knowledge of the tactics/strategies or choreographical/compositional ideas of your activity. These will be covered in coaching manuals. You will be able to develop your appreciation and understanding of these aspects by watching performances of the activity as well as observing other coaches. These aspects become more important as the performers you are coaching become more proficient in their skills and are able to focus their attention on these aspects.

STRETCH AND CHALLENGE

Spend time developing your knowledge and appreciation of strategies/tactics or choreographic/compositional ideas in your activity.

TASK 10

Identify the basic strategies and tactics which are used in your activity and explain how you would coach them.

3. Officiating an activity

You can be assessed in either of the two activities you have been assessed in at AS. You do not have to have been assessed officiating this activity at AS; you may have been assessed performing it or coaching/leading it at AS.

The OCR specification indicates that the focus of your assessment will be on:

- the performance of basic and advanced skills
- the selection and application of skills and strategies
- understanding of rules/regulation/conventions
- technical knowledge.

The specification indicates that the focus of your assessment is on a range of applied and acquired skills, abilities and qualities. These skills will be assessed while you officiate safe, purposeful and enjoyable activities. Suitable opportunities for such activities would be working with secondary school pupils or local youth groups.

You will officiate in a situation which allows you to:

- officiate safe, purposeful and enjoyable sessions
- demonstrate basic and advanced skills and strategies
- demonstrate competence in decision-making skills relating to the application of rules/regulations/conventions
- demonstrate knowledge and understanding of health and safety procedures
- implement risk assessments
- demonstrate knowledge and understanding of the fitness and health benefits of the activity
- evaluate sessions and plan for improvement
- demonstrate an awareness of child protection issues.

You may, within your centre, undertake a Governing Body officiating award; the successful completion of this course will allow you to develop many of the skills on which your assessment will be based.

You will need to practise your officiating if you are to improve and you will need someone to observe you to give you feedback as to what you have done well and areas you need to improve on. While there may be opportunities for practice in your centre, you may have to seek opportunities for practice in your local clubs or through your local sports development officer.

The focus of your assessment will be on your:

- ability to apply your officiating skills in sessions
- organisational and planning skills
- use of a range of officiating strategies
- overall performance in officiating
- awareness of health and safety
- implementation of risk assessments
- awareness of child protection procedures
- knowledge of the rules and regulations/ conventions of the activity
- evaluative skills
- awareness of the fitness and health benefits of the activity.

Your teacher will use these assessment criteria to put you into one of five bands (33–40; 25–32; 17–24; 9–16; 0–8) before they finally decide the exact mark you will be given out of 40. Your teacher will assess you over a period of time but might watch you do a final officiating session to finalise your mark.

You will need to keep a detailed log which contains evidence for your assessment. The log needs the following detailed information:

- a record of your officiating over a six-month period
- four evaluations by qualified assessors of sessions officiated
- risk assessments undertaken
- a video record of 40 minutes of you officiating
- information relating to the health and safety issues of your activity
- information relating to child protection procedures in the activity
- the fitness and health benefits both from participating and officiating in the activity.

You should complete your log as you officiate rather than leaving it until your final assessment. It is far easier to put together information relating to your officiating sessions as you do them than to wait until your log is due to be assessed by your teacher.

EXAM TIP

Put your evidence log together as you do your officiating sessions rather than leaving it to the submission date. Make sure it has all the detail required.

TASK 11

Ask your teacher/coach or local sports development officer for details of governing body officiating awards in the activities you are interested in.

HOW CAN I IMPROVE MY OFFICIATING SKILLS?

You should now be aware of how and when you will be assessed as well as the focus of your assessment. This understanding will help you plan how you should use your time to practise and improve your officiating and therefore increase the marks you get in your assessment.

As well as practising your skills and strategies by officiating, it is useful to observe and evaluate others officiating. You can pick up ideas on how to deal with situations and different approaches to interacting with participants, for example. Sometimes when you are observing others you also find out approaches and ways you should not use!

It is useful if you identify the skills you need to develop and organise them into groups, these being:

- planning and organisation
- officiating
- evaluative
- technical knowledge.

You need to complete your planning and organisation prior to your officiating sessions in order that you will be able to officiate successfully. In your planning and organising for your officiating you need to create habits; you should develop routines that you go through prior to officiating. The areas you will be looking at are as follows:

- ensuring that you know the type of participants you will be officiating, i.e. age, gender, ability
- ensuring that you are aware of the nature of the competition and any rules, regulations specific to that competition
- being aware of the venue and how long it will take you to get there
- timings – what time the session starts and the time you will need beforehand to carry out your health and safety checks, risk assessments and consider any child protection issues
- equipment – checks on your own officiating equipment, for example watch, whistle, flags, notebook, pen, together with any personal clothing that you will need
- fitness – maintaining your own physical and mental fitness with appropriate training.

Many of the areas above will be the same for each session that you officiate, but you must still ensure that you go through the process to ensure that you are prepared for the session.

When you actually officiate, your planning and organisation will pay dividends. You will have ensured that you arrive with ample time to carry out your health and safety and child protection checks where appropriate. Most officials will also take the opportunity to introduce themselves and talk to the participants before the session and this takes time.

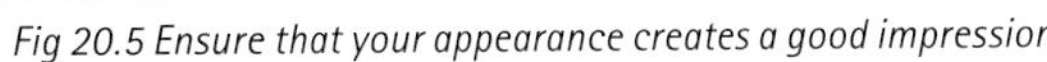

Fig 20.5 Ensure that your appearance creates a good impression

If you are officiating in an activity which also involves other officials, then you will obviously have to meet them and discuss your strategies. You also need to ensure that you have ample time to change into any special clothing that is required and that your appearance creates a good impression with the participants.

CHILD PROTECTION

Refer to page 512 of this chapter for information on child protection.

RISK ASSESSMENT

Refer to pages 512–3 of this chapter for information on risk assessment.

OFFICIATING

Once the session starts you will need to ensure that in your officiating you are:

- decisive – you make considered decisions and communicate those decisions to the participants
- fair to all participants in your application of the rules
- in control – you are firm in your decisions and communicate with the participants.

You should also be aware of:

- communication – you need to ensure that your decisions are understood by the participants and that they understand how you will convey your decisions, for example via whistle, flags, signals
- positioning – you should, if the activity requires it, ensure that you are able to keep up with play and position yourself so that you are able to make good decisions
- team work – in activities where you work with other officials you will need to ensure that you communicate with them and listen to their opinions.

EVALUATIVE SKILLS

Once you have officiated your session you should evaluate your performance. You will need to identify what you did well, what was not so good and how you need to change things so that you do better next time. It is important that you do this post-session evaluation as soon as possible after your session, so that things are fresh in your mind. Your teacher, assessor or fellow students may also evaluate your session and give you feedback. It is also important to realise in your evaluation and other people's evaluations that very few officials or indeed participants and coaches/leaders get everything right all the time. What you are doing in your evaluation is identifying areas where you can improve and make yourself a better official as well as praising yourself for the things you did well. In your evaluation you should cover your preparation and planning for the session, your officiating skills and strategies, your knowledge of the rules and regulations and your fitness.

EXAM TIP

Get an up-to-date copy of your activity's rules and regulations from the governing body.

TECHNICAL KNOWLEDGE

The fourth category of skills you need to look at concerns your technical knowledge and your fitness.

It is essential that an official in any activity has a good, up-to-date knowledge of the rules, regulations and conventions of that activity. You must ensure that you study and know the current rules and how to apply them. Most governing bodies publish their rules and regulations and it is crucial that you get an up-to-date copy of these for your activity.

In activities which require you to be physically fit it is obviously essential that you ensure that you reach a required fitness level and maintain it. Some activities actually carry out fitness tests on their officials! It does not do your credibility any good if you are unable to keep up with play or last the whole of the activity.

EXAM TIP

Ensure that you know and understand all the rules/regulations/conventions of the activity and can apply them accurately, decisively and consistently.

Watching other officials, particularly experienced ones, is a good way to improve your own officiating. You can observe how they apply the rules, communicate with participants and position themselves to see whether they do it differently from you. Remember, however, that every person is different, so another person's approach to officiating may not necessarily work for you.

ExamCafé

Relax, refresh, result!

Refresh your memory

You should now have knowledge and understanding of:

- which practical activity you can choose to be assessed in
- the roles you can choose to be assessed in
- how you will be assessed in each of these roles
- the terms 'standardisation' and 'moderation'
- how you can improve your performance, coaching or officiating.

REVISE AS YOU GO!

1 Identify the activity and role you are going to be assessed in.

Performance:

2 What is the performance situation in which you will be assessed in your activity?
3 Identify the movement phases that are used to assess your activity.
4 Identify the coaching points for the skills in your activity.
5 Identify progressive practices for each of the important skills in your activity.
6 What are the important aspects of physical fitness for your activity?
7 Describe the major strategies in your activity.

Coaching/leading:

8 Identify the aspects which your log book will need to contain.
9 What aspects does your planning and organisation need to cover?
10 What is a risk assessment?
11 What should your coaching/leading sessions be?
12 What are the health and fitness benefits of your activity?

Officiating:

13 Identify the aspects which your log book will need to contain.
14 What aspects does your planning and organisation need to cover?
15 What are the health and fitness benefits of your activity?
16 What is a risk assessment?

Try to answer these questions yourself. Ask your teacher if you need help.

CHAPTER 21:

Evaluation and appreciation of performance

LEARNING OBJECTIVES

By the end of this chapter you should have knowledge and understanding of:

- the evaluation, appreciation and improvement of performance aspect of your assessment
- how to structure your oral response
- how to successfully complete your oral response
- how you will be assessed
- how you can improve your evaluation and appreciation of performance.

INTRODUCTION

In your AS PE studies you had to complete an oral response based on your evaluation of a fellow student's performance in one of your practical activities. At A2 you have to do a similar piece of work when you will be asked to comment on one of your fellow student's performances in the activity in which you have been assessed. The focus will be a fellow student's performance of the activity even if you have been assessed on coaching/leading or officiating.

This element of your practical assessment is part of your synoptic assessment and represents 10 per cent of your A2 mark. In your response you are expected to apply theoretical concepts to the performance you are observing.

What do I have to do in my Evaluation and Appreciation of Performance?

You will observe a fellow student's performance in the activity in which you have been assessed. You will then:

- evaluate the performance, identifying and describing the strengths and weaknesses
- select a major weakness and create an action plan to rectify/improve it
- apply theory from the physiological, psychological and socio-cultural areas you have studied to justify/support your evaluative comments and your action plan.

EXAM TIP

When you carry out your evaluation and appreciation of performance, use a clipboard and paper in order to make notes on what you observe.

HOW DO I DO THIS?

You will do this by talking to your teacher.

EVALUATION

You have already experienced the process of evaluation when you identified the strengths and weaknesses of a performance in your oral response at AS. This time you are going to carry out the same process but also apply theory. You are going to identify what is:

- good about the performance – the strengths
- poor about the performance – the weaknesses.

As you did in your AS response, you must focus on the following areas:

- skills
- tactics/strategies/compositional ideas
- fitness.

To help you do this you may refer to the phases that are used to analyse the activity and its skills (see OCR's Teacher Support – Coursework Guidance booklet).

REMEMBER

In your evaluation you will have to discuss the strengths and weaknesses of skills, tactics/strategies or compositional ideas and fitness.

ACTION PLANNING

Initially, you have to select one of the major weaknesses identified in your evaluation to be the focus of your action plan. This should be one that you think is important to improve first. Having selected the focus, your action plan should have the following:

- a clear realistic goal – improving the major weakness you have identified
- a timescale
- a method for achieving the goal – detailed coaching points and detailed practices.

APPLY THEORY

This involves using theoretical concepts to support and justify your evaluation and action plan. This should include concepts from the three main theory areas:

- anatomical and physiological aspects
- psychological aspects
- socio-cultural aspects.

You now have a clear structure or plan of what it is that you have to do. This can be identified as follows.

1 Accurately identify and describe the major strengths of the performance.
2 Accurately identify and describe the major weaknesses of the performance.
3 Prioritise the weaknesses and select a major weakness to focus on.
4 Construct a viable action plan to remedy this major weakness.
5 Apply theory from physiological, psychological, socio-cultural aspects to support and justify the evaluation and action plan.

TASK 1

Write out your check sheet for your evaluation and appreciation of performance oral response. It should have the five points identified above. You should use this check sheet when you start to practise your observation and oral response.

How can I improve my Evaluation and Appreciation of Performance?

Like your practical performance, this aspect of your assessment is a skill and to improve it you need to practise it and receive feedback. Like other skills, it can be broken down into parts for you to practise.

ANALYTICAL PHASES

It is helpful to know the movement phases that are used to analyse the activity. These can be found in OCR's Teacher Support – Coursework Guidance booklet, which can be found on the OCR website (to access this site, go to www.heinemann.co.uk/hotlinks, enter the express code 6855P and click on the relevant link).

Earlier in this chapter it was suggested that in order to improve your performance it would be helpful for you to make yourself aware of these phases. Some examples of these phases are given in Chapter 20, page 508 If you know these phases and their coaching points for the skills of your activity they will help you to identify what is good about the performance and what aspects are poor.

IDENTIFICATION AND DESCRIPTION OF STRENGTHS

You should start by splitting the activity into the analytical movement phases and identifying strengths in each of these phases. You must focus on the following three aspects:

- skills
- tactics and strategies/compositional ideas
- fitness.

You are going to talk about the positive aspects of the performance.

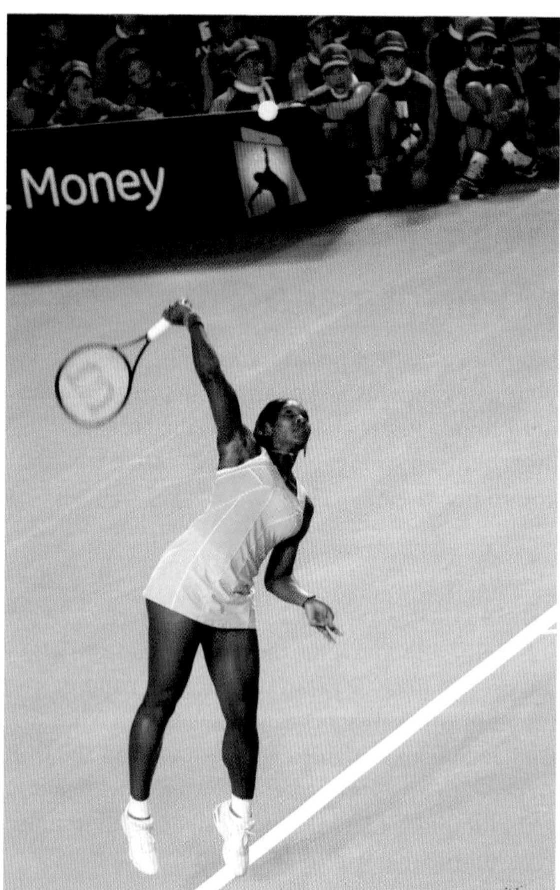

Fig 21.1 Compare the performance you are observing to the technical model

1 Skills

These skills will be being performed under pressure. It is important that you are aware of the 'technical' models to which you are comparing the performance you are observing; they can be found in the relevant governing or organising body coaching manuals. Knowledge of how the skill should be performed enables you to judge how good it is and to justify your evaluation by identifying why it is good. You will also use this knowledge when you are identifying weaknesses and constructing your action plan. You will have to describe the coaching points you are going to give to the performer in your action plan; these will come from the technical model.

In Chapter 20 when you were focussing on improving your performance you will have compared technical models to your own performance by using analytical phases.

Fig 21.1 shows a technical model of the execution phase of a tennis serve. You would use this model and its coaching points to compare it to the tennis serve you are observing. This will enable you to judge what the strengths of the serve are (the coaching points that are correct) and what the weaknesses are (the coaching points that are incorrect).

To do this you will break the serve down into the following phases:

- preparation
- execution
- results
- recovery
- overall efficiency.

In the execution phase, for example, the coaching points would relate to what the racket does, where and how the ball is struck, how the body weight is transferred, flight of the ball.

EXAM TIP

Make sure that you know the coaching points of the technical models of the skills of your activity.

TASK 2

Compile a list of the skills of your activity together with the coaching points of their technical models.

2 Tactics and strategies/compositional ideas

As performers gain a greater grasp of the skills within the activity, they are able to devote more attention to the tactics and strategies involved. They show an increased perceptual awareness accompanied by an increased capacity for decision making. The majority of these increased capacities will be devoted to the performer attempting to influence the outcome of the activity through their use of tactics and strategies. Sometimes this will be shown through better teamwork.

You will need to have a good understanding of the major tactics and strategies used in the activity to be able to evaluate the performer you are observing. This understanding will be gained from your own involvement in the activity but should be further improved by watching others perform your activity as well as reading the appropriate coaching manuals and talking to coaches. You will be comparing the performer you are looking at to what you know they should be doing. This will enable you to identify what they are doing correctly. If they are part of a team, you will probably want to comment on the team's effective use of strategies as well as the individual's contribution.

Tactics may include the formations that teams adopt and an individual player's role in that formation, how players defend, i.e. man-to-man marking, zonal marking. It could also include how a player copes with their own weakness, e.g. in football, not being able to use their weaker foot or how they adapt their play to focus on opponents' weaknesses, such as being weak in the air.

In net/wall games it may be about the player utilising their strengths and manoeuvring their opponent to pressurise weaknesses. For example, if the opponent is not quick, pushing them to the back of the court and then playing a drop shot close to the net.

TASK 3

Refer to a manual from a governing/organising body and your teacher/coach to find out about tactics and strategies/compositional ideas.

3 Fitness

In your AS oral response, you were asked to evaluate the components of physical fitness important to the activity on which you were focusing. Your evaluation can now be further developed by your studies in Exercise Physiology. You should apply this knowledge to your activity which should enable you to identify and evaluate accurately the components of physical fitness appropriate to the performance you are observing. You should evaluate the fitness of the performer you are observing under the following headings as appropriate:

a) physical fitness
- strength/power
- stamina
- suppleness/flexibility
- speed

b) skill-related fitness
- agility
- coordination
- balance
- timing.

There may be other aspects of fitness which are appropriate to your activity and you should discuss these.

You will be focusing on the aspects of fitness you know are important in the activity to assess whether or not the performer you are observing has good levels in these areas. Some of the areas suggested above will be more relevant in some activities than others and you will need to adapt them to suit the activity you are observing. Not only will you comment on the fitness aspects for which the performer has good levels, but also on his or her application of these strengths to their performance.

TASK 4

Make a list of the fitness components which are important in your activity.

EXAM TIP

In your response make sure that you use the correct technical terms that you have learned during your course.

TASK 5

If you have not already done so, access the Coursework Guidance booklet and identify the movement phases for the activity on which you will focus for your evaluation and appreciation of performance.

IDENTIFICATION AND DESCRIPTION OF WEAKNESSES

You should start again by splitting the activity into the analytical movement phases and identifying weaknesses in each of these phases.

This aspect will follow the same structure as the identification of strengths. You are identifying major weaknesses and those for which you can construct a viable action plan. You do not want to be too negative by identifying every small weakness, particularly those that do not significantly affect the performance.

You must also place the weaknesses you identify in a rank order to show which you consider to be the most important for you to rectify. The areas to focus on should be the same as those looked at when identifying strengths: skills; tactics and strategies/compositional ideas; fitness.

1 Skills

You will need to focus on the skills which, when under pressure, the performer either executes poorly or chooses not to use at all. You will be able to identify those performed poorly by comparing them to the correct technical models and the coaching points as well as the level of success. When under pressure some performers will be very inconsistent in some aspects of their skill production. This means they will be successful on one occasion and unsuccessful the next time. When under pressure do they choose not to perform advanced skills indicating they are unsure or lack confidence in them?

2 Tactics and strategies/compositional ideas

These will vary a great deal from activity to activity. They will focus on attempting to outwit the opposition or the environment, and in team activities they will also include teamwork. In individual activities, tactics and strategies will be different, particularly in those activities which are not games-based. They might involve the order in which skills are placed in a sequence to ensure that the skills are performed successfully. In a group activity this could involve capitalising on each individual's strengths.

Again, you will be comparing what your performer does against what you know to be good tactics and strategies for that situation. This will

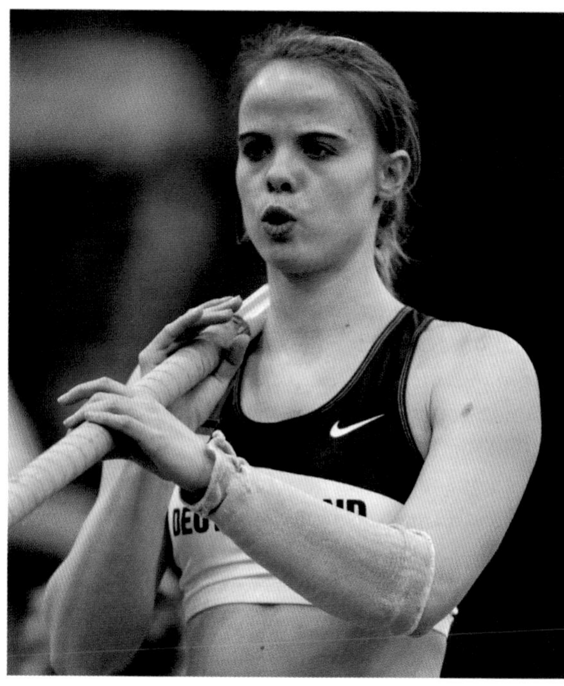

Fig 21.2 A skill being performed under pressure

enable you to identify where he or she is going wrong. This may be focused on the individual you are observing or the team in general. Do not use the same skill as that in Fig 21.2.

3 Fitness

Using the areas of fitness you have determined are important for the activity, you will identify those areas in which, in your opinion, the performer has weaknesses or in which you consider he or she could perform better by having increased levels of fitness. You should also remember that you will only be observing the performer for approximately ten minutes and therefore you may find it difficult to identify weaknesses in some aspects of fitness.

It should have become apparent to you by now that in identifying strengths and weaknesses you are using the same information to determine both aspects. You should, however, ensure that you identify the strengths before the weaknesses, as it is easy to overlook them!

EXAM TIP

Ensure that you cover skills, tactics and strategies/choreographic and compositional ideas in both strengths and weaknesses, not only identifying them but explaining why they are strong or weak.

CONSTRUCT A VIABLE ACTION PLAN TO IMPROVE A MAJOR WEAKNESS

This is where you will select one of the major weaknesses you have identified and create a plan to remedy it, thereby improving the performance as a whole. You will remember from your AS evaluation and planning for improvement in oral response that your **action plan** had to include the following aspects:

- clear, achievable, realistic goal or goals
- timescale
- method for achieving the goals – detailed coaching points and detailed practices.

These must be covered in detail in your action plan.

KEY TERM

Action plan

Contains a clear realistic goal, a timescale and a detailed method of how you are going to achieve the goal.

CLEAR, REALISTIC GOALS

The goals you set will be to remedy a major fault you have identified and thereby improve the performance. All you have to do is select one of the major faults you have identified and which you think is important to be rectified first. You may, in addition, identify more specific goals; for example, to achieve a 75 per cent success rate for first serves in tennis if you have identified a major fault as being the first serve.

EXAM TIP

Ensure that you identify a clear, realistic goal in your action plan.

When choosing the fault you should ensure you are able to suggest ways in which you will be able to remedy it; that is, to construct an action plan. Sometimes it is easier to focus on weaknesses within a skill or fitness area, as these are easier for creating action plans.

It is important to remember that your action plan must relate to the person you have observed and must be intended to help improve one of the major faults you have observed in their performance. It is important, therefore, that you have knowledge of the coaching points of the range of skills of your activity as well as the **progressive practices** to develop them. This will also apply to any fitness aspects which you identify as needing attention. You will need to know fitness regimes to improve the fitness aspects which are important in your activity.

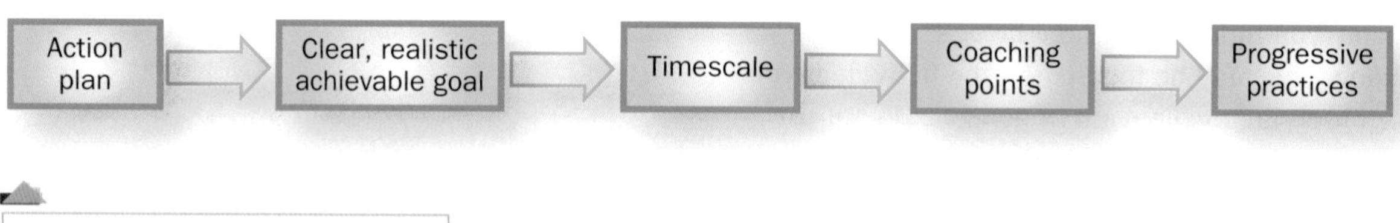

Fig 21.3 Components of your action plan

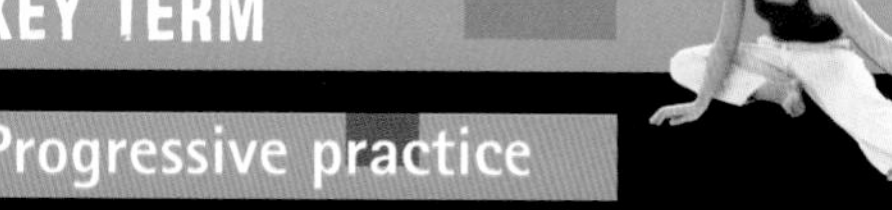

KEY TERM

Progressive practice

A practice that starts with a skill in its simplest, closed situation and goes through a series of stages to practice the same skill in its natural, open situation.

EXAM TIP

Ensure that you know the coaching points and progressive practices for the skills of your activity as well as fitness regimes for developing the aspects of fitness important in your activity.

TIMESCALE

You need to identify how long your action plan is designed to take, how often the practices or training will be and so on. Different action plans will have different timescales. Those designed to develop aspects of fitness will usually be over a longer period than those to develop skills.

You should give an indication of the overall length of the action plan – that is, the number of weeks or months together with the frequency of the sessions (for example, number of times a week). You might also include the length of each of the sessions.

METHOD FOR ACHIEVING THE GOALS

Here you will outline the practices and drills you will suggest that the performer does to remedy the weakness. This should be done in detail, identifying the coaching points for the skills you wish to be improved as well as each of the practices you will use. Remember that, as in your AS oral response, the practices you identify should show progression going from simple to complex and closed to open. You should, however, be realistic, starting the practices at a level that is appropriate to the performer you are observing.

You should demonstrate your knowledge of training by identifying exactly the aspects of fitness you are going to focus on together with their relevance and application in the activity. You should describe in detail the fitness regimes you would prescribe to improve these aspects of fitness. You might also include details of tests you would apply to see if they have improved.

REMEMBER

Your action plan needs to cover detailed coaching points, detailed progressive practices and a detailed timescale.

APPLICATION OF THEORETICAL KNOWLEDGE

You are also required to explain or justify your evaluative comments and your action plan by applying theory from the physiological, psychological and socio-cultural subject areas. This is not as difficult as it first appears, but needs to be practised. You should identify theory areas from each of the three subject areas which you can apply to your activity. Start off with a small list and see how you can apply these to your activity. You could begin with the following.

Physiological:

- What are the important joints and their movements involved in the activity/skill?
- What are the major muscles/important muscle groups involved?
- What are the physical fitness requirements of the activity?

Psychological

- Classification of the skills involved – is the activity gross/fine, closed/open and so on?
- Identification of the underpinning abilities – which abilities are important to the activity/skill?
- Information-processing demands – is there a lot of interpretation of information and are there decisions to be made?

Socio-cultural

- What is the performer's position on the performance pyramid; what level is the performer at?
- Is there local support for the activity from the governing or organising body? What facilities or opportunities are there for those involved in the activity?
- What is the role of the media in the activity – is there good coverage of the activity? Are there role models to relate to?

You should write these down and use your list to remind you when you practise. Once you are able to apply these theory areas to your activity, you should add to the list, gradually building up the theory you are able to apply to support your observations. You should be able to identify other theory areas from your course notes. By doing this you will build up your 'bank' of theory areas you know how to apply.

When you are being assessed in your Evaluation and Appreciation of Performance, you may not be able to apply all the theory areas you have learned and practised in the performance you are observing, as they may not be relevant to that particular performance. You are not expected to apply all the theory you have learned. You should aim at applying three or four concepts from each of the three theory areas, but remember that they must be relevant to the performance you have observed.

EXAM TIP

In the socio-cultural area you may be able to use information from your AS oral response in relation to opportunities for participation and progression in the activity. Obviously it must be the same activity as you are observing at A2!

Some students will apply their theory as they go through their plan; that is, they will apply theory to the strengths and weaknesses they identify and when they introduce their action plan. Others will wait until they have reached the end of their observations and then apply theory to support what they have said. You should try both methods and see which works best for you.

EXAM TIP

You may, when you are assessed, want to use your clip board and blank paper to write down your list of theory topics that you will try to apply to the performance you observe.

TASK 6

Create a list of two or three theoretical concepts that you can apply to support your observations. Add these to your check sheet, identifying the outline structure of your response.

You should refer to OCR's Teacher Support – Coursework Guidance booklet for examples of other theory areas that are suggested as being relevant to apply to your observations. They are only suggestions and you should not think that you will be able or required to apply them all!

PRACTISING YOUR EVALUATION AND PLANNING FOR IMPROVEMENT

You should practise your Evaluation and Appreciation of Performance as many times as you can. Like any skill, you should break it down to its simplest form, practice this, then move on to practice the next stage until you have mastered the complete skill. At each stage you should add that stage on to those you have already mastered.

The following stages would be appropriate for you to practise.

- Identifying the strengths in each of the movement phases.
- Identifying the weaknesses in each of the movement phases.
- Identifying a major weakness and creating a viable action plan to remedy it and improve the performance.
- Applying two to three concepts from each of the three theoretical areas.
- Increasing the number of concepts applied.

It may be that you can practise by looking at a video of the activity you are focusing on and you can record your response on tape, so that you can listen to it and evaluate it yourself.

WHAT WILL HAPPEN WHEN I AM ASSESSED?

Your teacher will ask you to watch one of your fellow students performing the activity. They will ask you to focus on particular aspects of the performance or particular performers. You will observe a performance you have not seen before. After you have watched the performance for some time, your teacher will ask you to comment on it. When you have started your response, you may well be able to look at the performance again to refresh your memory.

When you have observed the performance, the teacher will say something like, 'You have just observed the effective performance of Alex. Describe the strengths and weaknesses of the performance and create an action plan to improve a major weakness of the performance. You should apply your knowledge from physiology, psychology and socio-cultural areas to support your comments and action plan.'

The teacher will expect you to go through the stages already identified (as follows).

1 Identify and describe the strengths of the performance.
2 Identify and describe the weaknesses of the performance.
3 Prioritise the weaknesses and select the major weakness.
4 Create a viable action plan on which you:
   a) have clear, realistic, achievable goals
   b) identify a timescale
   c) identify the detailed coaching points you will use
   d) identify the detailed practices you will use.
5 Apply theory to support your observations from:
   a) physiological areas
   b) psychological areas
   c) socio-cultural areas.

EXAM TIP

When you first start your evaluation and appreciation assessment, write down on your clipboard and paper the five stages of your response so that you are reminded of what you have to talk about.

If you get stuck or miss out a stage, the teacher will probably ask questions to help direct you. These questions should be the type that will guide you to think about a particular stage or area, rather than needing a specific answer. Examples of these questions could include the following.

- What were the good elements of the performance you have just seen?
- What are the causes of the faults/weaknesses?
- If you were Alex's coach, what would you do in order to improve one of the major weaknesses which you have identified?

Remember, this is your opportunity to tell your teacher how much you know and understand by applying it to the performance you observe. Ideally, once your teacher has asked you the starting question you should be able to keep talking about what you have seen until he or she wants you to stop!

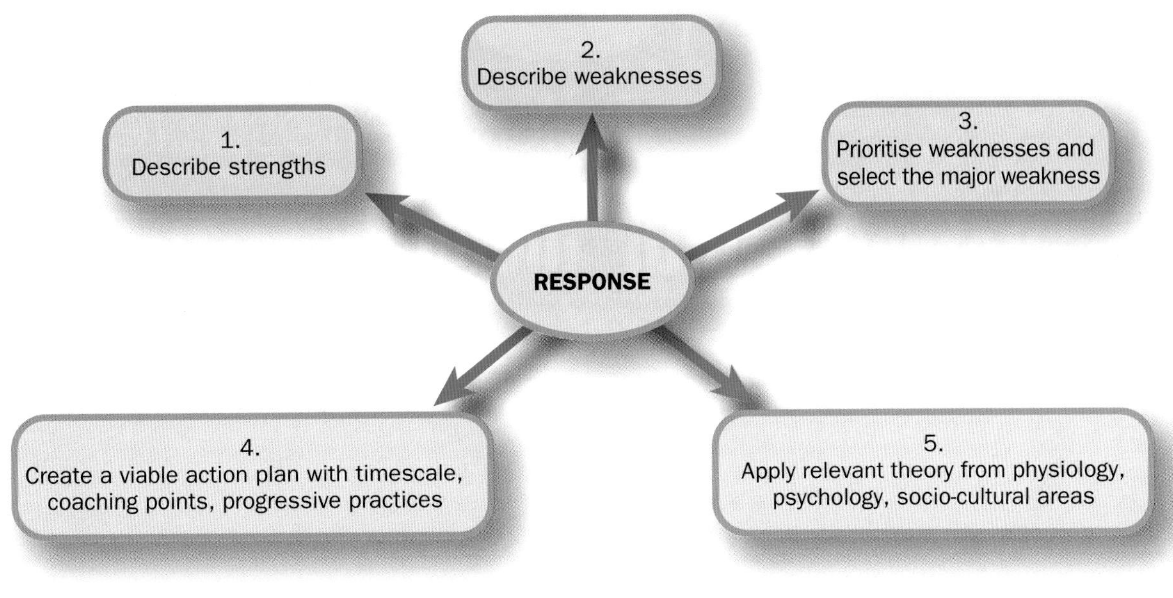

Fig 21.4 Structure of evaluation, appreciation and the improvement of performance response.

REMEMBER

Take your time. Don't start to talk before you have had sufficient opportunity to observe the performance. Also remember to make notes and refer to them. You might forget to talk about some of the points you have seen.

ASSESSMENT CRITERIA

Your teacher will be using the following criteria to assess you:

- accuracy of the description of the major strengths in relation to the skills, tactics/compositional ideas and fitness of the performance
- accuracy of the description of the major weaknesses in relation to the skills, tactics/compositional ideas and fitness of the performance
- accuracy of the prioritising of the areas of the performance which need improvement
- creating a viable action plan which contains all the detailed coaching points, a range of detailed progressive practices together with a timescale
- justification of the evaluative comments and the action plan with the appropriate application of a range of relevant physiological, psychological and socio-cultural knowledge and concepts.

Your teacher will use these criteria to put you into one of four bands: 16–20, 11–15, 6–10, 0–5. They will then give you a definite mark out of 20 within the band.

EXAM TIP

Try to apply theory throughout your response, i.e. apply theory to help explain why aspects of the performance are strong or weak, and to justify why you are using certain types of practice for particular skills, etc.

ExamCafé

Relax, refresh, result!

Refresh your memory

REVISE AS YOU GO!

You should now have knowledge and understanding of:

- the evaluation, appreciation and improvement of performance aspect of your assessment
- how to structure your oral response
- how to successfully complete your response
- how you will be assessed
- how you can improve your evaluation and appreciation of performance.

1. Name the activity you have selected on which to do your evaluation, appreciation and the improvement of performance oral response.
2. Write out the five stages you will go through when you do your evaluation and

Try to answer these questions yourself. Ask your teacher if you need help.

Index

Page numbers in **bold** type refer to key terms